TRILLION YEAR SPREE

The History of Science Fiction

BOOKS BY BRIAN W. ALDISS

Trillion Year Spree 1986

Seasons in Flight 1986

Helliconia Winter 1985

Helliconia Summer 1983

Helliconia Spring 1982

An Island Called Moreau 1981

Life in the West 1980

A Rude Awakening 1978

Enemies of the System 1978

Last Orders 1977

The Malacia Tapestry 1977

The Eighty-Minute Hour 1974

Frankenstein Unbound 1973

The Billion Year Spree 1973

A Soldier Erect 1971

The Hand-Reared Boy 1970

Barefoot in the Head 1970

Report on Probability A 1969

Cryptozoic 1968

The Dark Light Years 1964

Greybeard 1964

Long Afternoon of Earth 1962

Galaxies Like Grains of Sand 1960

Starship 1959

No Time Like Tomorrow 1959

TRILLION YEAR SPREE

The History of Science Fiction

by

BRIAN W. ALDISS

with

DAVID WINGROVE

"Without the aid of the imagination all the pleasures
of the senses must sink into grossness"
—— MARY WOLLSTONECRAFT,
*Letters Written During a Short Residence
in Sweden, Norway and Denmark*

NEW YORK   ATHENEUM   1986

Library of Congress Cataloging-in-Publication Data

Aldiss, Brian Wilson, ——
    Trillion year spree.

    Reprint. Originally published: Billion year spree.
London: Weidenfeld and Nicholson, 1973.
    Bibliography: p.
    Includes index.
    1. Science fiction, English—History and criticism.
2. Science fiction, American—History and criticism.
I. Wingrove, David. II. Title.
PR830.S35A38   1986   823'.0876'09   86-47682
ISBN 0-689-11839-2

The authors of this book
dedicate it with respect and
affection to two men also
concerned with the history and
histories of science fiction:
Sam Lundwall and
Marshall Tymn

Contents

Introduction   13

PART ONE: OUT OF THE GOTHIC

I.   On the Origin of Species: Mary Shelley   25

II.   Something Monomaniacal: Edgar Allan Poe   53

III.   Honourable Ancestors: Good Places and Other Places   69

IV.   The Gas-Enlightened Race: Victorian Visions   89

V.   The Great General in Dreamland: H. G. Wells   117

VI.   The Flight from Urban Culture: Wells's Coevals   135

VII.   From Barsoom to Beyond the Borderlands: Swords, Sorceries and Zitidars   155

VIII.   In the Clutches of the Zeitgeist: Mainly the Thirties   175

IX.   The Future on a Chipped Plate: The Worlds of John W. Campbell's *Astounding*   207

PART TWO: INTO THE BIG TIME

X.   After the Impossible Happened: The Fifties   233

XI.   The Dawn of the Day of the Dumpbin: Cinemas, Computers, Colleges and Canticles   271

XII.   The Day of the Life-Style: Into the Sixties   285

XIII.   The Men in Their High Castles: Dick and Other Visionaries   309

XIV.   The Stars My Detestation: Sailing the Seventies   339

XV.   How to Be a Dinosaur: Seven Survivors   383

XVI.   The Future Now   407

Notes   445

Bibliography   489

Index   491

List of Illustrations

following page 160

Miniature of Mary Shelley by Reginald Easton (*Bodleian Library*)

An Experiment on a Bird in the Air Pump by Joseph Wright (*National Gallery, London*)

The tombstone of Jules Verne, from *Amazing Stories*

H. G. Wells on the set of *Things to Come*

Edgar Rice Burroughs (*Edgar Rice Burroughs Inc*)

Cover of Edward S. Ellis's *The Huge Hunter*

European proto-SF magazines: *Der Orchideengarten* and *Hugin*

Hugo Gernsback hearing through his teeth

Frank R. Paul and *Amazing Stories*

Hubert Rogers and *Astounding Science Fiction*

Portrait of John W. Campbell by Kelly Freas

Olaf Stapledon (*courtesy of Agnes Z. Stapledon*)

following page 352

John Schoenherr *Analog* cover illustrating *Dune*

Alex Schomburg cover for *Fantastic*

Robert A. Heinlein, L. Sprague de Camp and Isaac Asimov during World War II (*US Navy*)

Arthur C. Clarke (*Fred Clarke*)

Frederik Pohl (*Wolfgang Jeschke*)

Philip K. Dick

New Worlds in 1968, cover design by Charles Platt and Christopher Finch

Forrest J. Ackerman, Harry Harrison and Brian Aldiss at an SF symposium in Rio de Janeiro (*Cine-Foto Real*)

Michael Moorcock (*Grafton Publishing*)

J. G. Ballard (*Fay Godwin*)

A scene from *Solaris*

A scene from *Star Wars*

A cover for an SF convention booklet

William Gibson

Greg Bear

SF authors at NASA HQ in Houston (*Rosemary Herbert*)

Text illustrations

page 11   A German depiction of Daedalus and Icarus, 1493

page 23   A French illustration of an electrical flying machine, dating
from 1775

page 231 Drawing by Alah Hunter

TRILLION YEAR SPREE

The History of Science Fiction

A German interpretation of the Greek myth of Daedalus and Icarus. This first depiction of men flying appeared in F. Riederer's *Spiegel der Wahren Rhetorick*, published in Freiburg in Breisgau, 1493.

Introduction

Someday my father would stop writing science fiction, and write something a whole lot of people wanted to read instead.

—Kurt Vonnegut: *Galápagos*

You are standing on a vast flat plain. Something appears on the horizon and moves rapidly towards you. It is a shaly hillside on which a cave is evident, its mouth fortified. It whirls by.

Something else is approaching. A series of objects moves towards you. A village on stilts wading into a lake. A small brown city with mud walls. A pyramid, encrusted with bronze. A ziggurat. Immense fortifications from the Aztec culture. The palisades of ancient Zimbabwe. The intricate temples of the East, Angkor Wat, Borabadur. Chinese mausoleums.

The monstrous structures loom up and pass, throwing their shadows briefly over the plain. Monuments to life, to death, to conquest. And to piety—the Gothic cathedrals of Europe drift past.

Tombs, towers, universities.

Something else, moving with great noise and gasps of smoke. Nearer and nearer it comes, at first labouring, a cumbersome shape with a high smoke stack. Refining itself as it approaches, writhing through metal metamorphoses. Now it is sleek and streamlined, rushing forth on metal rails, its carriages trailing snake-like behind it. As it hurtles by, there is a hint in its mutating shape of the rocket ships which lie in its future.

Why is this machine different from all the other shapes, as it roars out of the industrial revolution towards us?

Because it has the power to move itself. Because it is the first thing on land ever to move faster than a cheetah, a stag, a galloping horse.

Because it brings us into a world of timetables, where we have to conform to a thing's convenience, not it to ours. Because the timetables induce us to look ahead to the material world stretching like the endless plain before us.

Because it emerges from the eighteenth century vibrating with technological change.

Science fiction is one of the major literary success areas of the second half of the twentieth century. It is now largely—in emphasis and in fact—an American art form, coinciding with a time of great technological evolution and with the rise of the USA to super-power status.

The origins and inspirations for science fiction lie outside the United States, though within the period of the Industrial Revolution. As we might expect. Only in an epoch when a power source more reliable than ocean currents or the wind, faster than the horse, has been developed, can we expect to find a literature that will concern itself with problems of power, either literal or metaphorical. Such problems lie at the heart of SF, the fiction of a technological age.

Nowadays, everyone knows of SF and thinks he or she knows what it is. Not everyone reads, not everyone approves. But every age gets the art it deserves.

Good SF does not necessarily traffic in reality; but it makes reality clearer to us.

This is the story of science fiction, told from its humble beginnings right up to the present day. It is a wonderful and fascinating story, even to those who are not necessarily aficionados. When Cinderella finally makes it to the ball, everyone is pleased. (Except those Ugly Sisters.)

But what is science fiction? Read on.

This book has grown out of *Billion Year Spree*, which was published in 1973. Since then, science fiction has gone forth and multiplied to a remarkable extent. What was once virtually a secret movement has become part of the cultural wallpaper. This new book chronicles and makes sense of that dramatic growth, while discussing the milestones along the way.

Anyone even remotely connected with the science fiction field knows that great advances are taking place. But are such alterations tokens of a wider general acceptance or of a dismal decline in standards? Indecision, an awareness of crisis, is in the air. We hope to clarify the situation, whether or not all our arguments are found immediately acceptable.

All discussion of science fiction involves generalization. The time has never existed when "science fiction" was a homogeneous commodity—regurgitated, it might be, by some vast alien mass mind. True, attempts have been made from various points of the literary compass to impose uniformity—by Michel Butor, by John W. Campbell, by fandom. Most writers evade such stereotypes. Yet still the trade mark "science fiction" carries much weight with friends and foes alike.

At any time, there are only individuals working under a common banner, though some individuals are more individual than others. Some would like to get out from under the banner. Others would like to get further in. Many march with overweening pride under the banner.

Those who subscribe most ardently to a set of common derived conventions will produce the most clearly defined generic fiction. Those who are most independent will produce work which—obviously enough—pays least heed to the restrictions of formula and will transcend it.

To defy or meet expectations? Both are well-recognized literary ploys.

The difficulty—the infinitude of SF—lies in the obdurate fact that it is both formulaic and something more than a genre. It is a mode which easily falls back into genre.[1] The model is flexible, changing with the times. New designs are forever produced. SF can be conventional and innovative at one and the same time.

The science fiction field flourishes best when both kinds of writer, the iconoclast and the iconolater, exist in tension, one set distrusting the other. But there is rarely close agreement even between members of the same set. Some writers do not feel themselves to be members of either set, and reject categorization.

This point requires stressing at a time when some publishers have set up clearly defined SF lines. Others publish only SF. The perils of such monoculture are twofold: generic (generally action) SF will get published while less flamboyant work is rejected; and a boom-or-bust situation, an unpleasant symptom of SF publishing, will be perpetuated.

SF cannot exist without divergent opinions. The material with which it deals is itself controversial. Shall we increase technology until the whole surface of the planet is covered by concrete and steel? Is all religion an aberration? Is war inevitable? Will artificial intelligence take over our governance, and is that desirable? Do we need to conquer space? How would utopia come about? What of our immortal souls?

Of course, the ability to generalize is a vital instrument of reason. Without the ability to deal in generalities, we should have no laws. If this book did not trade in generalities, we should have no book. We talk of the Thirties, for instance, as if those years had a unique flavour, like raspberries or mangoes. We all know this was not the case. It still remains convenient to point to "the Thirties" or "the Sixties", sure of a general understanding.

There is an argument which says that SF has no history, and that the story in this book is another generalization, and a false one. That E. E. Smith has no place in a book with Lucian of Samosata, or A. E. van Vogt with Jonathan Swift. That no evolution such as is described ever took place. That the pulp magazines are entirely irrelevant to the writings of Aldous Huxley or George Orwell.

This argument, put forward by the Disintegrators, is ingenious—too ingenious. It is an argument which pays attention to the aims of the writer. A history of science fiction, however, must pay attention to the interests of the reader. And to the reader of science fiction, Thomas More's *Utopia* is as interesting as Burroughs's Barsoom, or *1984* as *2010*. C. S. Lewis is as rewarding as Robert Heinlein. In this volume, we are entirely on the side of the reader. Definite generic interplays exist.

One generalization we shall be unable to abolish. That is the generalization which says that all science fiction is rubbish. Generalization-22.

Generalization-22 is not solely the creation of the hostile outside world. It has been fostered in part by the SF world, who have insisted for several generations that its kind of reading is Different. And not just Different but Better. Such defensive boasting is counter-productive. The illogic is apparent: this latest dismal SF novel by X (once so brilliant when we were young) is not better than Y, the new Argentinian novelist's first book. But maybe, just maybe, the next brilliant SF novel by Z may be even better than Y's second novel. Literary judgement has to deal with individual cases, not with a cattle market.

The sooner this truth is acknowledged within the SF field, the sooner we shall convert the heathen and make Generalization-22 obsolete. One of the unreasonable hopes of this book is that it may convert the odd heathen here and there. The heathen always have their own viewpoint.

For many, science fiction has become an environment. It contains all they wish from life. Yet an SF story or novel consists of words, like any other kind of book. And generally a recognizable form of words—a particular kind of narrative guarantees much of SF's interest. Yet the form, which is an inheritance of the Gothic, is often ignored. The Gothic was a type of romance developed in the late eighteenth century, relying on suspense and mystery and containing a number—a limited number—of startling props. A word more about that.

The rise of industrialization fostered the growth of large manufacturing towns and the spread of cities. People were obliged to live among strangers to make their living. Church bells were replaced by the more exacting railway timetable.

The effects of these unprecedented changes—cumulating in our day in an *umwelt* of continual change—was far-reaching. The human psyche was not immune to them.

The fiction that evolved to accommodate this situation—a middle class fiction, somewhere between romance and realism, as it was between science and myth—was the Gothic fantasy. Backward-looking and nostalgic at first, it developed rapidly during the nineteenth century to confront more closely the conditions which nurtured it.[2] The archetypal figures of cruel father and seducing monk were transformed into those of scientist and alien.

Designed as pure entertainment, as "escapism", the Gothic proved to have remarkable strengths when it traded on current fears, hopes, and obsessions. It could venture where the solid realistic social novel could not go. Although the social novel is seen as the dominant literary form of the nineteenth century, its doppelganger, the Gothic, kept in silent step with it, from *Frankenstein* at the century's beginning to *Dracula* at its end. Indeed, the archetypal figures who emerged from those novels are now familiar all over the world; Oliver Twist, Madame Bovary, and Anna Karenina enjoy a more tenuous existence beyond their respective volumes than do Frankenstein and Count Dracula.

Such a thing as pure genre does not exist. The Gothic is by no means homogeneous. It can incorporate and reinforce itself by the qualities of Romance and of a partial Realism. Quest novels, which enjoy such popularity in the nineteen-eighties, are clearly a blend of Gothic fantasy and veins of story-telling far more ancient. But impurity, adaptation, invention, even imitation, are of the essence of story-telling. Listeners and readers require novelty; they also require the touchstone of familiarity.

One strong Gothic theme is that of descent from a "natural world" to inferno or incarceration, where the protagonist goes, willingly or otherwise, in search of a secret, an identity, or a relationship. This volume embraces many stories with such motifs, from famous exercises such as Jules Verne's adventures at the centre of the earth to Frankenstein's descent into charnel houses, Dracula's descent to his earth-coffins, or the journey to Trantor, in effect a total underground planet, to the metaphysical search for his father undertaken by the less-known hero of *Land Under England*.

This reluctant protagonist developed from the distressed maidens of Mrs Radcliffe into modern figures. The vital role emerged, via the refinements of Poe, Wilkie Collins, and Conan Doyle, into the modern detective or private eye. Along the way, the role divided, to become also the scientist, the inventor, the space-traveller.

The need to find a secret, an identity, a relationship, accompanied the questing traveller to other worlds or futures. Industrialization had assisted many sciences, including geology and astronomy. A new comprehension of the dynamism of the natural world (once regarded as a static stage for a theological drama) was incorporated in Charles Darwin's theory of evolution, one of the great gloomy interventions of the nineteenth century which still colours our intellectual discourse. Evolution provided an essential viewpoint powering the new sub-species of Gothic, science fiction. Here, it seemed, was a key to the most puzzling, most impressive question of identity of all—the identity of mankind. A mere brute in clothes, a degenerate ape, a culmination of eon-long processes, a godling?

And evolution also provided a clue in that dark search for a relationship. In the struggle for survival, who are our friends? Is the alien always to be feared? Should we not regard ourselves as some kind of alien? Shall we become Utopians and live in peace?

Many questions to be dramatized, treated deeply or frivolously. Along with the changed questions went elements practically unchanged since Ann Radcliffe's day: the climate, the effects of the light, the desolate scenery. No longer in fifteenth century Italy, perhaps . . . but on a planet just as remote from us. In that remoteness lies another marked feature of science fiction, alienation. Both the Industrial Revolution and evolution have brought a marked sense of isolation to humanity in general: isolation from one another—and from Nature, so often seen in science fiction as an enemy to be conquered, as if we were no longer ourselves a part of the natural world.

Trillion Year Spree is a very much revised, altered, and enlarged version of the 1970s book. It includes and attempts to digest all that has been happening in the science fiction field over the last two decades.

What has not altered in that time are my convictions. True, I have changed my opinions of this or that; how could it be otherwise? But my basic convictions have merely strengthened over the intervening years. I refer to certain ideas which, tentatively proposed before, roused anger, shock, vituperation, threats of violence, and occasional acceptance, in my readers.

Of course I understand that bosoms can scarcely be expected to remain tranquil in companies where SF is supported, is idolized, is a way of life. Any deviation from an established order of ritual must be challenged. Equally, one must stand by one's beliefs.

Foremost among these beliefs is a certainty about the origins of SF. Of course, it is in a way a Stone Age truth to say that SF began with Mary Shelley's *Frankenstein* (1818). The more we know, the less certain we can be about origins; the date of the Renaissance becomes less clear decade by decade as research goes on.

Nevertheless, bearing in mind that no genre is pure, *Frankenstein* is more than a merely convenient place at which to begin the story. Behind it lie other traditions like broken skeletons, classical myth, a continent full of *Märchen* tales. But Mary Shelley's novel betokens an inescapably new perception of mankind's capabilities, as is argued in Chapter One. Moreover, *Frankenstein* is marvellously good and inexhaustible in its interest. Not a negligible point.

Were there women writers before Mary Shelley? Research into this subject is carried out in all the world's universities. One name at least emerges, that of the lively Margaret Cavendish, impoverished Duchess of Newcastle, whose *The Description of a New World, called The Blazing World* was published in 1666. The absence of Margaret Cavendish and Mary Shelley from standard literary histories reminds us that science fiction is not the only thing against which learned men have harboured baseless prejudices.

Before I wrote, almost no one paid any attention to that old pre-Victorian novel of Mary Shelley's. Having seen travesties of the theme on film and television, they believed they knew what they did not. The situation has remarkably improved since then. (After writing the history, I wrote a novel, *Frankenstein Unbound*, designed to draw attention to its great original.)

Like all discoveries, this one was prompted by more than circumstantial evidence. It was born of a wish to refute certain nonsensical claims previously put forward, which did a mode of writing I much enjoyed no honour.

My belief in SF has not diminished over the intervening years, and remains strong at a time when true science fiction appears under threat, swamped by an avalanche of imitations and wish-fantasies in the United States and, in England, the virtual disappearance of young science fiction writers, thanks to the chill climate of discouragement which there prevails.

For all its tragic flaws, its absurd pretensions, its monstrous freights of nonsense, the platonic ideal of science fiction remains alive, as the literature most suited to our progressing and doom-threatened century, the literature most free to take aboard new perspectives, new manifestations of the *zeitgeist*.

Critics expected the Gothic to go away. It never has. Born pseudonymously from the mind of Horace Walpole, fourth Earl of Orford, it proved to have all the adaptability of a living species. Critics expected SF to go away. It never has. It is the urban literature and will, we hope, exist as long as there are cities, in whatever form.

Both the thesis that *Frankenstein* marked a beginning and that SF was a Gothic offshoot were so unacceptable that *Billion Year Spree* scarcely received any reviews in those journals in which its appearance should have been instantly greeted; indeed, had it not been for the vigilant intervention of my old friend and ally, Harry Harrison, those reviews would have been even sparser.

It is hard to recognize now the confusion that existed then. Before my book appeared, there was no accepted idea of when SF began. Some critics claimed it all started in a semi-juvenile pulp magazine in the twenties, others that Homer wrote science fiction. Ludicrously enough, these were often the same critics. Yet to have no understanding of this matter is to have no understanding of the function and nature of SF.

The new synthesis I developed was embodied in my definition of science fiction, contained in Chapter One. Of course that definition has been challenged, and rightly. Of course I have wanted to improve it. And rightly. And I have done so by one word.

The definition defines both function and mode, which together comprise SF's nature. The pretensions of the first part of the definition are defused by the limitations of the second. The Gothic is, after all, a mode of entertainment, generally ranked below what we may call for convenience the modern novel.

My definition is the only one to link content and form, which are inseparable.

Here perhaps I should add parenthetically that neither I nor my collaborator, David Wingrove, have any aversion to the modern novel; we do not adopt the philistine stance of so many commentators, in praising SF at the expense of the modern novel, with which we are tolerably familiar.

We take SF seriously, and would be crazy not to; but we do not forget that it is in the main a commercial genre, and treated as such even by some of its most honoured practitioners. Our title acknowledges as much. A trillion years is no laughing matter; a spree is.

Part of the problem of seeing SF in true perspective lies in the difficulty of judgement attendant on the early SF magazines, notably Hugo Gernsback's. Most of the opprobrium first visited on *Billion Year Spree* centred round my comments on Gernsback and his magazines. Yet no convincing argument was put forward to make me retract what I said. One has merely to consult the texts.

Those readers who enjoyed such magazines as *Amazing Stories* and *Wonder Stories* in their youth—often their extreme youth—naturally retain fond memories of those pages and those days. Nostalgia, however, provides no sound basis for literary judgement. The covers of those old magazines retain a weird specialized attraction; but the reading matter between the covers is, almost without exception, unutterably poor. This situation did not improve until about 1938 and a small miracle.

If we do not perceive this, if we believe that these pathetic tales, in which the namby-pamby has intercourse with the sensational, represent some kind of a Golden Age, then we can have no engagement with contemporary SF, at least in its higher reaches. Appreciation is not omnivorous.

It is an old-fashioned idea, yet not entirely false, that we read to develop our understanding and aesthetic appreciation. That is part of our pleasure. Reading, like the taking of lovers, rarely begins in exalted taste. Cultivation is important. If we remain loyal to the reading of our childhood, it is a false loyalty, a puppy-love. Uncle Hugo has his place in sub-literature, perhaps an honoured place. But we must set his works aside with a sigh, to see clearly how greatly SF has evolved and sophisticated itself since then.

As much needs saying, though it is obvious enough. A lot rests on that obvious truth, for what follows from it provides the whole *raison d'être* of this volume. Our chronicle has a thesis, never insisted upon: that the best SF being written today is an improvement on the crude SF of the early magazines; that it has acquired many skills and graces, possibly at the expense of new ideas; that we are now in a Modern Period of SF, the birth of which may be dated roughly from the first publication of *Dune* in 1963–4, which period actually exhibits many of the same traits as does the modern novel, in terms of amplification and sophistication at the expense of innovation; that there remains much to be admired, as well as much to be deplored; that recent achievements are real, and to be praised. Our perspective is a positive and forward-looking one, as we hope will be acknowledged.

An argument has been advanced recently which says that it is impossible to write a history of science fiction. That SF consists merely of the worst. That such writers as Gore Vidal in *Messiah*, or Olaf Stapledon in *Last and First Men*, or Doris Lessing in her *Canopus in Argus* series, knew nothing of the continuity of science fiction, of its traditions, or of its rules (which means in fact a few prescriptions laid down by a small clique of, in the main, non-writers); and in consequence cannot be said to be a part of science fiction at all.

This is a fallacy. If we can imagine that a playwright like Eugene O'Neill, or a poet like Thomas Hardy, or a novelist like Gabriel García Márquez, knew nothing of the history of the drama, poetry, or the novel, the fact would in no way lessen the contributions those writers made to their chosen medium, or to the influence they had on those who followed them.

There is no such entity as science fiction. We have only the work of many men and women which, for convenience, we can group together under the label "science fiction". Many dislike that label; many glory in it.

Throughout the book, as previously, we allow only the abbreviation "SF". That down-market appellation "sci-fi", sometimes heard on the lips of the would-be trendy in the media and elsewhere, is purposely avoided. We bow to the fact that much of what passes for science fiction these days is nearer fantasy. SF can, after all, be imagined to stand for science fantasy, as it can for speculative fiction (for those who are attached to that term).

Billion Year Spree concluded with a prediction concerning the future rise of SF-as-study and an SF academia. The prediction has been fulfilled beyond my expectations. There was then almost no body of SF scholarship; nor was there more than the smallest student body. Now SF is a recognized discipline in universities and colleges across the United States. Such associations exist as the

SFRA, the Science Fiction Research Association, which was amiable and perceptive enough to bestow on me a Pilgrim Award, mainly for the earlier edition of this book, and the IAFA, the International Association for the Fantastic in the Arts—which has kindly presented me with its first Distinguished Scholarship Award—to which two societies the most eminent SF scholars belong.

Following this development, publishers have sprung up who publish nothing but SF criticism. Not all criticism is of the first rank, as is to be anticipated of such a youthful discipline, but we may have every expectation that it will improve, strengthening its present rather remote relationship with real English and becoming more adventurous in its subject matter. Journals like *Fantasy Review* do much to raise the quality of discussion.

Trillion Year Spree is devised for the enjoyment of the reader, that reader whom Dr Johnson and Virginia Woolf rejoiced to call "the common reader"; nor has anything changed in that respect. But we move with the times. More rigour has now been shown. The book is designed to serve in schools where SF is on the curriculum. It provides, as no other volume does, a synoptic grasp of the whole field, with as much neutrality and freedom from favouritism or prejudice as its authors can contrive between them.

Yet it remains, in some aspects, a personal book. I have excluded all discussion in the text of my own writing, whether fact or fiction; yet the book is imbued—or so I hope—with the intuitions gained from many years as a writer of science fiction (and not only science fiction). My hope is that it may prove of some value to my fellow writers, so hostile to it first time round, and to beginner writers.

Perhaps I have not always shown what some may regard as proper reverence. I am too familiar with it for that: my first SF story was written when I was eight.

Nor are these aspirations mine alone. The extensive work and research involved in the compilation of this book would never have been undertaken, let alone completed, without the assistance of my staunch ally, David Wingrove. Indeed, more than assistance. Perfect collaboration.

Appreciation is not omnivorous. I felt I could not bring the same fresh eye to the books, films, and events of the startling last fifteen years as I did to previous ones. A more eager and energetic—a younger—presence was required.

David and I met many years ago. As a fan, he surveyed me first through field-glasses from a neighbouring property, the way one spots rare old birds of a migratory nature. There has been nothing migratory about our friendship since, which dates from the moment he set down his field-glasses and came up our drive. *Billion Year Spree* was one of the first SF books he read, so he makes a particularly appropriate partner in the enterprise.

I played a minor part in two of David's critical works, *The Science Fiction Source Book*, and *The SF Film Source Book*, as well as forming the main dish in the Brian Griffin and David Wingrove *Apertures: A Study of the Writings of Brian W. Aldiss*. It has been a pleasure to work with him in collaboration. His enthusiasm and cheerfulness have never failed.

Our opinions are not always identical. If they were, it would be useless for us to work together. Many of the judgements are his, not mine. For a lot of readers, David will have written the more interesting part of the book. We have modified but rarely altered each other's opinions. We have rewritten each other's texts to such an extent that it is now hard to determine who exactly said what.

A word to critics who dislike science fiction. The over-productivity of science fiction writers is a byword. There is a lot of it about, and it is popular. For some, that is enough to condemn it without further enquiry. The question upon which all literary criticism runs on the rocks is this: if it is good, can it be popular; if it is popular, can it be good?[3]

We take the reasonable point of view that science fiction gives pleasure to many people; our task is to compare the varying degrees of pleasure. We find SF (some of it) immensely readable and enriching.

Conversations with many friends have greatly helped in forming critical opinions. Especial thanks must go to Michael Collings, Patrick Edington and Charles N. Brown. Also to Dr Robert Collins of Florida Atlantic University, whose influence has been greater—and more benign—than he probably realizes. The title, *Billion Year Spree*, was first mentioned in print in 1964. Much has happened since then. Friends change, publishers change, the world changes. But I am happy to acknowledge now, as I did then, the help of my wife Margaret as we sailed these endless seas of paper. She it was who aided us through successive drafts, and poured the whole enterprise through the word-processor into its present form.

Woodlands   BRIAN W. ALDISS
Boars Hill
Oxford
July 1986

Part One

OUT OF THE GOTHIC

This wonderful electrical flying machine was depicted in a French work, *Le philosophe sans prétention, ou l'homme rare*, by Louis Guillaume de la Follie, published in Paris in 1775. It shows that interest in practical applications of electricity was alive some while before Mary Shelley wrote.

CHAPTER I

On the Origin of Species:
Mary Shelley

The mirrors of the gigantic shadows which futurity casts upon
the present . . .
—Percy Bysshe Shelley: *The Defence of Poetry*

"The stars shone at intervals, as the clouds passed from over them; the dark
pines rose before me, and every here and there a broken tree lay on the ground; it
was a scene of wonderful solemnity, and stirred strange thoughts within me."
Thus Victor Frankenstein, after an encounter with the creature he has created
out of dismembered corpses, while he tries to decide whether or not to build it a
mate.

The shattered scenery, the sense of desolation, the speaker's dilemma—
ghastly but hardly the sort of quandary one regularly meets—are all characteristic of a broad range of science fiction. As for Victor's strange thoughts, science
fiction is a veritable forest of them.

That forest has reached such proportions that a new formal exploration is
necessary. The present authors hope to drive a new motorway through the heart
of the forest. Without marking every tree, we will provide a contour map of the
whole science fiction landscape.

To emerge from the undergrowth of our metaphor, this volume investigates
the considerable corpus of writing which, with other media, has come to be
regarded as science fiction in order to illuminate what is obscure, and to increase
the enjoyment of what is already enjoyable.

In this first chapter, we attend to three matters. We look at the dream world of
the Gothic novel, from which science fiction springs; we identify the author
whose work marks her out as the first science fiction writer; and we investigate
the brilliant context—literary, scientific, and social—from which she drew life
and inspiration.

As a preliminary, we need a definition of science fiction.

Many definitions have been hammered out. Most of them fail because they
have regard only to content, not form. The following may sound slightly
pretentious for a genre that has its strong fun side, but we can modify it as we go
along.

*Science fiction is the search for a definition of mankind and his status in the universe
which will stand in our advanced but confused state of knowledge (science), and is
characteristically cast in the Gothic or post-Gothic mode.*

The final word of our definition is chosen with deliberation. Science fiction is one mode of writing among several. It is often tamed to generic writing and generic expectations for commercial reasons. A wider potential remains.

There's a corollary to our definition. The more power above the ordinary that the protagonist enjoys, the closer the fiction will approach to hard-core science fiction. Conversely, the more ordinary and fallible the protagonist, the further from hard-core. It is often impossible to separate science fiction from science fantasy, or either from fantasy, since both modes are part of fantasy in a general sense. Nevertheless, one admires the boldness of Miriam Allen deFord's dictum, "Science fiction deals with improbable possibilities, fantasy with plausible impossibilities" (in her Foreword to *Elsewhere, Elsewhen, Elsehow*).

My shorter definition of SF may also be mentioned, since it has found its way into a modern dictionary of quotations. This is—*Hubris clobbered by nemesis*. By which count, ordinary fiction would be hubris clobbered by mimesis.

One etymological dictionary offers such definitions of fantasy as "mental apprehension", "delusive imagination", and "baseless supposition"—terms which serve well enough to describe certain types of science fiction. H. G. Wells pointed to a similarity between the two genres when he said of his early stories, "Hitherto, except in exploration fantasies, the fantastic element was brought in by magic. Frankenstein even, used some jiggery-pokery magic to animate his artificial monster.* There was trouble about the thing's soul. But by the end of last century it had become difficult to squeeze even a momentary belief out of magic any longer. It occurred to me that instead of the usual interview with the devil or a magician, an ingenious use of scientific patter might with advantage be substituted . . . I simply brought the fetish stuff up to date, and made it as near actual theory as possible."[1]

Thus science assimilates fantasy. Fantasy is almost as avid in assimilating science; in 1705, Daniel Defoe wrote *The Consolidator: or, Memoirs of Sundry Transactions from the World in the Moon*, featuring a machine that would convey a man to the Moon, which was inspired by popular expositions of Newton's celestial mechanics. In its wider sense, fantasy clearly embraces all science fiction. But fantasy in a narrower sense, as opposed to science fiction, generally implies a fiction leaning more towards myth or the mythopoeic than towards an assumed realism. (The distinction is clear if we compare Ray Bradbury's Mars with the painstakingly delineated Mars of Rex Gordon's *No Man Friday* or Frederik Pohl's *Man Plus*; Bradbury's Mars stands as an analogy, Gordon's as a Defoe-like essay in definition and Pohl's as a projection of ongoing NASA activity).

We must understand that the science fiction search for that "definition of mankind" is often playful. And what the definition does not do is determine whether the end product is good, bad, sheer nonsense, or holy writ (as Heinlein's *Stranger in a Strange Land* was taken as holy writ). Definitions are to assist, not overpower, thinking.

*This is not the case at all; Wells's memory was at fault.

The definition takes for granted that the most tried and true way of indicating man's status is to show him confronted by crisis, whether of his own making (overpopulation), or of science's (new destructive virus), or of nature's (another Ice Age). And that there are forms of fiction which may appear to fulfil the definition but nevertheless are not science fiction—generally because they are ur-science fiction (existing before the genre was originated), from Dante's great imaginary worlds of *Inferno, Purgatorio,* and *Paradiso* onwards—or because they transcend the Gothic format, as do *Moby-Dick,* Thomas Hardy's novels, John Cowper Powys's *A Glastonbury Romance,* the plays of Samuel Beckett, Thomas Pynchon's writings, and so forth.

If this all sounds somewhat all-embracing, nevertheless this volume errs on the side of exclusiveness. Our preference is for that elusive creature, "real SF", which has set itself apart from other modes of literature by embracing technological imagery, and by perceiving its characters as statistics.

Having fought the good fight to define SF, we have to admit defeat in distinguishing between SF and fantasy. Fantasy's eel-like versatility as a descriptive term is well-known. Other critics have had the same problem: "We often find ourselves wondering if we can really distinguish between, say, science fiction and Fantasy"[2] remarks one scholar.

This book, however, makes it clear that we can recognize SF fairly easily, although it is rarely found in a pure isolated state. Just like oxygen.

It so happens that the most ancient forms of literature are often recognizably kin to science fiction; voyages of discovery, mythical adventures, fantastic beasts, and symbolic happenings are part of a grand tradition in storytelling which the realistic novel of society has only recently rejected. Thus, the *Epic of Gilgamesh,* with the world destroyed by flood, the Hindu mythology, the *Odyssey, Beowulf,* the Bible—and practically everything down to *Mickey Mouse Weekly*— have been claimed at one time or another by science fiction fans with colonialist ambitions.

The phrase in my definition about "advanced knowledge" takes care of that bit of grandiose aspiration. Science fiction is NOW, not Then.

Nevertheless, Milton's *Paradise Lost,* Book II, with Satan crossing that "vast vacuity" between his world and ours, looks suspiciously like the pure quill.

Frontiers are by tradition ill-defined. Happily, it is no difficult matter to identify the first true example of the genre.

Only in the late 1920s was the term "science fiction" used as a kind of generic trade mark. It was regarded as an improvement on the more ludicrous term "scientifiction". The mode itself was already in being, although this went unacknowledged for a time. The term was first applied to crudely constructed stories appearing in various American pulp magazines, of which *Amazing Stories* (1926 onwards) was the earliest. For more substantial British exercises in the same fields—many of an earlier date—the term "scientific romance" was sometimes used.

This somewhat parvenu feeling about science fiction has led its adherents to claim for it, in contradictory fashion, both amazing newness and incredible antiquity. Early potted histories of the genre liked to indulge their readers by cantering briskly back through Greek legends of flying gods like Hermes and satirical voyages to Moon and Sun undertaken by Lucian of Samosata in the second century AD.[3] Although science fiction can no more be said to have "begun" with Lucian than space flight "began" in Leonardo da Vinci's notebooks, this tired old litany is still chanted in various sequestered parts of the globe.[4]

On the long struggle upwards from Lucian to the celebrated date of 1926, the historians scoop in Thomas More, Rabelais, Cyrano de Bergerac, Jonathan Swift, and a whole clutch of eighteenth-century bishops. One of the more learned anthologists, in a Croatian science fiction anthology, enlists Dante and Shakespeare to the ranks[5], while the first chapter of Genesis has also been claimed, perhaps with more justification.

Trawls for illustrious ancestors are understandable, in critics as in impoverished families. But they lead to error, the first error being the error of spurious continuity—of perceiving a connection or influence where none exists. Forgetting that writers write with the flux of life going on about them, scholars rake through their books and pass over in a couple of pages the thirteen long centuries that lie between Lucian and Ariosto.[6]

The second error to which this ancestor search has led is the interpretation of science fiction as mainly a series of imaginary voyages to the Moon and other planets.

Interplanetary flight forms a noteworthy element in science fiction. In the nineteen-fifties, when space fever was high, it formed a major element. The rocketship became SF's trade mark, and SF became "space fiction". All rocketeers were science fiction readers, it is safe to say, in Germany as in the USA. The development and refinement of scientific imagining from Kepler on towards technological reality is a thrilling story in itself. This story has been documented by Marjorie Hope Nicolson.[7]

But the subject matter of SF is richly complex. It encompasses more than simply interplanetary flight. Fortunately, it is not necessary to leave this planet to qualify as a science fiction writer. It is not necessary, either, to write specifically about technological developments. The imagery of technology and science is often employed for symbolic ends. All depends on the inclination of the individual author.

Science fiction is also diverse. Previous Lucian-to-Verne approaches to its diversity fail to grasp both its response to the world beyond the study window and to its sense of Inwardness. Such mechanistic approaches became out of date with the entry of talented women writers into the field, exploiting in several cases the social aspects of SF.

As with all the arts, science fiction is more concerned than ever before with its own nature. The intention of this volume is not to banish science fiction's illustrious ancestors, who are as essential to it as cathedrals to a study of architecture, but to rescue them from a perspectiveless gloom.

The greatest successes of science fiction are those which deal with man in relation to his changing surroundings and abilities: what might loosely be called *environmental fiction*. With this in mind, we hope to show that the basic impulse of science fiction is as much evolutionary as technological. While thinking in these terms, it will be appropriate to regard Lucian and the other pilgrim fathers as relations of science fiction writers, just as we regard the great apes as relations of man, to be allowed all due respect for primogeniture.

The evolutionary revolution and the Industrial Revolution occurred in the same period of time.

The quickening tempo of manufacture becomes more noticeable in Great Britain in the second half of the eighteenth century, at a time when populations were beginning to increase rapidly. This traditional incentive to industrial advance was coupled with the roster of inventions with which we are familiar from school: Hargreaves's spinning jenny, Cartwright's power loom, Watt's steam engine, and so on.

Industry was not alone in undergoing transformation. The American Declaration of Independence in 1776 and the French Declaration of the Rights of Man in 1789 were documents in man's revision of his attitude to his own kind. It is no coincidence that the abolition of slavery was a burning issue at this time. Or that Western man now began to alter his attitude towards his God.

It is from this changeable cultural climate that science fiction emerged—with a discreetly blasphemous nature it still retains, or did in its lean and hungry days before the seventies.

Speculations on evolution and natural selection were current at the end of the eighteenth century. The ancient Greeks had held enlightened views on these matters, Thales believing that all life originated in water, and Anaximenes that it came into being spontaneously from the primaeval slime. Later, in Christian Europe, the Bible defeated any such ideas, and a literal interpretation of Genesis generally held sway.

The debate on whether species were fixed or mutable was a long one. It gained force in the eighteenth century following the impact of Pacific exploration. The world of the South Seas—the first region of the globe to be opened up scientifically—provided new stimulus to old questions of how our planet, its animals, and its humans, had come about.

In the last decade of the century there appeared a remarkable fore-shadowing of the theory of evolution, its arguments properly buttressed, its references up to date. Its author was Darwin—not Charles Darwin of the *Beagle*, but his grandfather, Erasmus Darwin. Erasmus Darwin (1731–1802) was a doctor by profession, a contemporary of Diderot and the Cyclopaedists, fired by their ideas. He was a witty and forceful talker with an enquiring mind. He leads us to Mary Shelley.

Many inventions stand to Erasmus Darwin's credit, such as new types of carriages and coal carts, a speaking machine, a mechanical ferry, rotary pumps, and horizontal windmills. He also seems to have invented—or at least proposed—a rocket motor powered by hydrogen and oxygen. His rough sketch shows the two gases stored in separate compartments and fed into a cylindrical combustion chamber with exit nozzle at one end—a good approximation of the workings of a modern rocket, and formulated long before the ideas of the Russian rocket pioneer Tsiolkovsky were set to paper. The best discussion of this most interesting man and his inventions is by Desmond King-Hele.[8]

Darwin was a member of a distinguished group of men living and working in the English Midlands, which were then in the forefront of the world's manufacturing life. In 1776, Matthew Boulton took Dr Johnson and Boswell on a tour of his famous Soho iron works, and said to Johnson (as quoted in Boswell's *Life of Johnson*), "I sell here, Sir, what all the world desires to have— POWER." As well as industry, literary and scientific societies prospered. A melancholy thought two centuries on, when the manufacturing life of this part of the world, where the Industrial Revolution grew up, now lies in ruins.

During this time, Erasmus Darwin had his portrait painted by Joseph Wright of Derby, whose paintings of scientific experiments are among the first of their kind. Of these, Wright's *An Experiment on a Bird in the Air Pump* is the most dramatic. Its group of figures is illuminated by the lamp on the experimenter's table. All is darkness round about them. Most of the group look on in rapt attention. A young girl weeps at the fate of the bird in its glass prison, struggling as the oxygen is exhausted. Behind the drama, the moon shines in at a casement.

Wright painted other scenes of industry, but *An Experiment* lingers in the mind. It is a testimony to the interest people then took in scientific experiment. Out of this exciting and inspiring intellectual environment was to come *Frankenstein*. One cannot help but wonder if Mary Shelley knew Wright's painting; it seems probable, since Wright's name was linked with that of Samuel Taylor Coleridge, a friend of Mary's father. Wright died in August 1797, the month and year in which Mary Shelley was born.[9]

The division between the arts and sciences had not then grown wide. Among his other capacities, Erasmus Darwin was a copious—and famous—versifier. In his long poems he laid out his findings on evolution and influenced the great poets of his day. His is the case of a once-gigantic, now-vanished reputation. Coleridge referred to him as "the first *literary* character of Europe, and the most original-minded man". By his grandson's day he was quite forgotten.

Erasmus's mighty work *Zoonomia* was published in two volumes in 1794 and 1796. It explains the system of sexual selection, with emphasis on primaeval promiscuity, the search for food, and the need for protection in living things, and how these factors, inter-weaving with natural habitats, control the diversity of life in all its changing forms. Evolutionary processes need time as well as space for their stage management. Erasmus emphasises the great age of the Earth. In this he contradicts the then-accepted view, established by Bishop James Ussher in the seventeenth century, that God performed the act of creation in the year 4004 BC, probably about tea-time—although the Scot, James

Hutton, had declared in 1785, thrillingly, that the geological record revealed "no vestige of a beginning, no prospect of an end".

The philosophical movements of the nineteenth century which were tinged with Darwinism tended towards pessimism; philosophical men like Tennyson were all too aware of "Nature red in tooth and claw". Erasmus, in his heroic couplets, took a more serene view—an eighteenth-century view, one might say: equable, even Parnassian. It is easy to imagine that this century would have withstood the shock of evolutionary theory better than its successor.

> Shout round the globe, how Reproduction strives
> With vanquish'd Death—and Happiness survives;
> How Life increasing peoples every clime,
> And young renascent Nature conquers Time.

These lines come from the last canto of *The Temple of Nature*, posthumously published in 1803. Of course they strike us as slightly daft.★ Erasmus concentrated on summing the whole course of evolution so far, from the almost invisible life of the seas to mankind and man's civilizations. In this poem of four cantos and some two thousand lines, he speaks of the way in which a mammal foetus relives the previous stage of evolution and of the survival of the fittest, as well as prophesying with remarkable accuracy many features of modern life— gigantic skyscraper cities, piped water, the age of the automobile, overpopulation, and fleets of nuclear submarines:

> Bid raised in air the ponderous structure stand,
> Or pour obedient rivers through the land;
> With crowds unnumbered crowd the living streets,
> Or people oceans with the triumphant fleets.

As we can see, Erasmus Darwin qualifies as a part-time science fiction writer! More securely than anyone before him, he has a grasp of future possibility.

His thrusts at church and state aroused his opponents and Darwin's voice was effectively silenced. Parodies of his verse in George Canning's *Anti-Jacobin*, entitled *The Loves of the Triangles*, mocked Darwin's ideas, laughing at his bold imaginative strokes. That electricity could ever have widespread practical application, that mankind could have evolved from lowly life forms, that the hills could be older than the Bible claimed—those were sorts of madnesses which set readers of the *Anti-Jacobin* tittering. Canning recognized the subversive element in Darwin's thought and effectively brought low his reputation as a poet.

As for his reputation as scientific innovator—that also was overshadowed.

★ Erasmus is deft as well as daft, for instance in this couplet describing the marine organisms whose structures go to form chalk deposits:

> Age after age expands the peopled plain,
> The tenants perish but their cells remain.

Once the famous grandson appeared luminous on the scene, eclipse was total. The reinstatement of this remarkable man (like the reinstatement of Mary Shelley) is recent.[10] King-Hele lists seventy-five subjects in which he was a pioneer.

One modern science fiction writer at least is interested in Erasmus Darwin. Charles Sheffield's *Erasmus Magister* (1982) paints a genial portrait of him as a kind of predecessor of Sherlock Holmes.

Most remarkably, Erasmus speculated on the origins of the universe. Before the eighteenth century closed, he framed the earliest intimations we have of the Big Bang hypothesis: "It may be objected, that if the stars had been projected from a Chaos by explosions, that they must have returned again into it from the known laws of gravitation; this however would not happen, if the whole of Chaos, like grains of gunpowder, was exploded at the same time, and dispersed through infinite space at once, or in quick succession, in every possible direction."

This in a footnote to Erasmus's *The Economy of Vegetation* (1791).[11] Before its long eclipse, Erasmus Darwin's thought illuminated those poets whose response to nature was closest to his own—the Romantics. Wordsworth and Coleridge owe him much; Shelley's debt is considerable, going far beyond echoes of similar lines. Shelley was a poet of science, a rebel, an atheist, an ardent lover of freedom and the west wind. No wonder he admired Erasmus, in whom also these qualities were strong.

As we shall see, there is another direction in which Darwin's influence on science fiction is both powerful and immediate.

We should recall here two novels published contemporaneously with the first volume of Erasmus Darwin's *Zoonomia*. William Godwin's *Caleb Williams* (regarded as the first psychological pursuit story), and Mrs Radcliffe's *The Mysteries of Udolpho* (regarded as the high point of Gothic) were both published in the year 1794.

Although Godwin and Erasmus never met, they had friends and sympathies in common, and were pilloried together as atheistical writers, most notably in the *Anti-Jacobin*. Godwin was a novelist and liberal philosopher whose reputation stood high among the poets and writers of his time. He married Mary Wollstonecraft, another contributor to the debate of the age, especially in her *Vindication of the Rights of Woman* (1772).

William Hazlitt reported that Coleridge "did not rate Godwin very high (this was caprice or prejudice, real or affected), but he had a great idea of Mrs Wollstonecraft's powers of conversation". So had the Swiss painter Henry Fuseli, who fell in love with her. After various misfortunes, Mary Wollstonecraft married Godwin and bore him a daughter, Mary.

This Mary grew up to write *Frankenstein* when still in her teens. Her novel is unique. But behind every unique work stand the predecessors to which it owes a cultural debt. In the case of *Frankenstein* we need to look at the Gothic fashion from which it emerged.

Edmund Burke's essay on *The Sublime and the Beautiful* appeared in 1756. It became an arbiter of taste for many decades. Its influence lingers today. Burke distinguished between beauty, which is founded on pleasure and is placid, and the sublime, which inspires awe and terror and, with pain as its basis, disturbs the emotions. He speaks of "delightful horror, which is the most genuine effect and truest test of the sublime". If the perception reads strangely now, a welter of splatter movies has dulled our taste buds.

Art, as usual, copied art. The Ossianic poems were the first to fulfil Burke's specifications.* They were counterfeits by an ingenious Scot, James Macpherson, and immediately branded as counterfeit by Horace Walpole among others; but their enormous Celtic ghosts, giants, cliffs, storms, and buckets of blood thrilled many writers and artists, among them Fuseli, as well as much of the literate population of Europe.

The Ossian poems made their appearance from 1760 to 1763. In 1765 *The Castle of Otranto* was published pseudonymously. So popular was it that the author, Horace Walpole, admitted his identity in a preface to the second edition.

The Castle of Otranto is established as the earliest Gothic novel. One commentator claims that the whole Gothic revival began with a dream.[12] On a June night in 1764, Walpole had a nightmare in which he saw a gigantic hand clad in armour, gripping the bannister of a great staircase. When he woke, he began writing his novel.[13]

Walpole was an antiquarian. His most lively monument is not *Otranto* but Strawberry Hill, his residence, his own conception, built in Gothic style, which is to say, in imitation of a medieval style. His dream was influenced by the *Prisons* of Piranesi[14]—another artist, like Wright or Stubbs, still in vogue today.

If *The Castle of Otranto* owes something to Piranesi, *Vathek* has more of Tiepolo in it. This single and singular novel by the eccentric William Beckford is full of magic and wit. Published in 1786, it nods to both Samuel Johnson's *Rasselas* and the *Arabian Nights*. Beckford's version of Strawberry Hill was the architecturally daring Fonthill Abbey (too daring—the tower collapsed after some years and the building was demolished).

Beckford wrote *Vathek* in French. Byron told Beckford's daughter, the Duchess of Hamilton, that *Vathek* was his gospel, and that he always carried a copy of the book with him. With its Faust-like theme, in which the calif Vathek sells himself to the powers of evil in exchange for the treasures of the pre-Adamite sultans, it had a natural appeal to what might be called the Byronic side of Byron. While *Vathek* is a much more enjoyable novel than Walpole's, both have exerted wide fascination—Beckford's not least on Oscar Wilde, whose *Picture of Dorian Gray* uses a similar theme and nods to Burke's dictum on the sublime.

The late eighteenth century was a time of botanical renaissance, brought about by the classification of plants by the Swede Linnaeus and, more especially,

---

*Perhaps the first painting to meet Burke's definition is George Stubbs's *White Horse Frightened by a Lion* (1770), a masterpiece containing beauty and sublimity. Stubbs was a capable scientist as well as a masterly animal painter.

by the voyages to the South Seas of Sir Joseph Banks and Captain Cook (killed in Hawaii in 1779). Cook carried back to Europe not only fantastic landscapes and images, from the ice world of the Antarctic to the gigantic heads of Easter Island, but a treasury of plants: three thousand species, one thousand of them unknown to botany. The world was alive with news of itself.

These influences show in Erasmus Darwin's poems. In *The Loves of the Plants* (with its Fuseli decoration engraved by William Blake), he makes reference to the Antarctic and tells how

> Slow o'er the printed snows with silent walk
> Huge shaggy forms across the twilight stalk

a couplet which has left its imprint in that very Gothic poem, Coleridge's *Rime of the Ancient Mariner*, when the accursed ship is driven to the Southern Pole:

> And through the drifts the snowy clifts
> Did send a dismal sheen:
> Nor shapes of men nor beasts we ken—
> The ice was all between.

Today, Darwin's method of expressing exact technical detail in heroic couplets and describing the sex life of plants in human terms appears odd. We hardly expect Bentham and Hooker to talk like Pope's *Rape of the Lock*. The loss is ours. Before Victorian times, art and science had not come to the division that SF tries to bridge.

By the beginning of the nineteenth century, the Gothic craze was abating. It had produced its best-remembered work, including Matthew "Monk" Lewis's *The Monk*, a novel overloaded with licentious monks, romantic robbers, ghosts, and a bleeding nun, as well as episodes of murder, torture, homosexuality, matricide, and incest. Even Lord Byron was shocked. Ann Radcliffe's two most famous novels, *The Mysteries of Udolpho* and *The Italian*, had appeared, as well as countless "blue books", abridgements or imitations of Gothic novels, selling very cheaply and bearing cheap titles.[15]

These were the sort of fictions made fun of by Jane Austen in *Northanger Abbey* and Peacock in *Nightmare Abbey*. But fashion was everything; the poet Shelley himself wrote two such novels, *Zastrozzi* and *St. Irvyne*, while still at school.

Thomas Love Peacock (1785–1866) was no Gothic novelist. However, he used the Gothic mise-en-scène, and the very titles of his remarkable novels look back ironically to the fiction of his youth, from *Headlong Hall* (1816) to *Gryll Grange*, published forty-four years later, in 1860. Peacock's form of discussion novel, in which characters in remote country houses discouragingly discuss the world situation, and anything else that enters their heads, while eating and drinking well, provides a format for later writers such as Aldous Huxley.[16]

Mary Wollstonecraft Shelley read Peacock's *Melincourt*, published two years before *Frankenstein*. The dangers of a critical method which would explain everything in terms of influence and derivation are well exemplified by Peacock's little-read novel. For the central character in *Melincourt* is an orang-outang called Sir Oran Haut-Ton, who does not speak but performs well on flute and French horn. Peacock was satirizing an early pioneer of anthropology, Lord Monboddo, who cherished a pet orang-outang as an example of "the infantine state of our species". So is Sir Oran a symbol of the natural man, harking back to Rousseau? Is he a literary precursor of Frankenstein's monster? Is he a precursor of Poe's orang-outang in "Murders in the Rue Morgue"? Is he, indeed, with his title and rolling acres, a precursor of Tarzan? We perhaps do better to turn back to Gothic.

In the Gothic mode, emphasis was placed on the distant and unearthly, while suspense entered literature for the first time—Mrs Radcliffe was praised by Scott for her expertise in suspense. Nowadays, this quality in her work has worn thin, and what remains to attract in her best work is a dreamy sense of the exotic. Gothic's brooding landscapes, isolated castles, dismal old towns, and mysterious figures can still carry us into an entranced world from which horrid revelations start.

The revelations may prove a disappointment, as they do in *The Mysteries of Udolpho*. Then we rouse from our dreams to indigestion. We know that some Gothic-Romantic authors relied heavily on dreams for inspiration: Mrs Radcliffe herself consumed indigestible food in order to induce dreams of terror, just as Fuseli ate raw meat towards the same end, in order to feed his voracious muse. Appropriately, Fuseli's most famous canvas is *The Nightmare*.

The methods of the Gothic writers are those of many science fiction and horror writers today. Stephen King is Modern American Gothic, the Radcliffe of the Greyhound Bus. The horrid revelations will not lie down. It would be as absurd to suggest that most SF writers were serious propagandists for the cause of science as that the author of *Romano Castle: or, The Horrors of the Forest* was a serious critic of the evils of the Inquisition—however much both sides may have considered themselves in earnest.

Other planets make ideal settings for brooding landscapes, isolated castles, dismal towns, and mysterious alien figures[17]; often, indeed, the villains may be monks, exploiting a local population under the guise of religion.[18] The horrid revelations may be on an imposing scale: that mankind has been abroad in the universe long ago, but was beaten back to his home planet by a powerful adversary[19]; that Earth is merely a sort of Botany Bay or dumping ground for the disposal of the vicious elements of the galaxy[20]; or that mankind is descended from rats which escaped from some interstellar vessel putting in at Earth.[21]

Again, for both Gothic and science fiction writers, distance lent enchantment to the view, as the poet Campbell put it. If something unlikely is going to happen, better to set it somewhere where the reader cannot check the occurrence against his own experience.

For this reason, locations in Gothic novels lie in a distant and misty past. Mrs Radcliffe sets *The Mysteries of Udolpho* in the late sixteenth century; her château commands views of a river, with fine trees (she always particularizes about trees, and many passages in her novels remind us that this was the age of Gilpin's *Forest Scenery* and Repton's *Landscape Gardening*), and "the majestic Pyrenees, whose summits, veiled in clouds, or exhibiting awful forms . . . were sometimes barren . . . and sometimes frowned with forests of lofty pine". Mrs Radcliffe is careful with her locations; her imitators were often less precise.

So with science fiction novels. Distance lends enchantment. They may locate themselves in distant futures on Earth, on one of the planets of the solar system, or anywhere in our galaxy, even a distant galaxy; though enchantment is not in direct proportion to distance. Or they may occupy a different sphere or another time-track entirely. We then find ourselves cut off from our present, in an alternate universe.

There are several brilliant alternate universe novels. In Ward Moore's *Bring the Jubilee*[22], the South won the American Civil War. In Harry Harrison's *A Transatlantic Tunnel, Hurrah!*, George Washington was shot and the American Revolution never happened. In Philip K. Dick's *The Man in the High Castle*, the Axis powers won World War II. In Keith Roberts's *Pavane*, Queen Elizabeth I was assassinated and England remained a backward Catholic country. In Kingsley Amis's *The Alteration* (which wittily pays tribute to the two preceding titles), the Reformation never happened. In all these novels, history (rather than science) is used as incantation, according to a prescription dreamed up by Walpole.

The Gothic novel was part of the great Romantic movement. Its vogue declined early in the nineteenth century. But terror, mystery, and that delightful horror which Burke connected with the sublime—all of them have remained popular with a great body of readers, and may be discovered, sound of wind and limb, in science fiction to this day. Undelightful horror is also in vogue, in movie and video particularly. Perhaps this taste set in with the decay of that calm eighteenth-century confidence in rationality expressed by Pope in the phrase "whatever is, is right". Shelley was born in 1792, and his is a different outlook with a vengeance!

> While yet a boy I sought for ghosts, and sped
> Through many a listening chamber, cave and ruin,
> And starlight wood, with fearful steps pursuing
> Hopes of high talk with the departed dead.[23]

This is the Gothic Shelley, always in quest for mystery.

The new age had a passion for the inexplicable, as we have in ours; its uncertainties were soon memorably enshrined in the pages of the novel written by Shelley's young second wife.

Frankenstein: or, The Modern Prometheus was published anonymously on 11th March, 1818, in the same year as works by Shelley, Peacock, Scott, Hazlitt, Keats, and Byron. The Napoleonic Wars were over; *Savannah* crossed the Atlantic, the first steamship to do so; the early steam locomotives were chuffing along their metal tracks, Boulton's iron foundries were going full blast; the Lancashire cotton factories were lit by gas, and gas mains were being laid in London. Telford and McAdam were building roads and bridges, Galvani's followers and Humphry Davy were experimenting with electricity. "So much has been done," exclaimed the soul of Frankenstein, "more, far more, will I achieve!" (Chapter III)

As with Erasmus Darwin's reputation, the reputation of the modest author of *Frankenstein* has been too long in eclipse.

Mary Wollstonecraft Godwin was born in August 1797. Her intellectual and beautiful mother died ten days later, after an ague and a severe haemorrhage, leaving the impractical Godwin to care for the baby and for Fanny, Mary Wollstonecraft's three-year-old child from an earlier liaison.

Later, when Percy Bysshe Shelley took to calling at Godwin's house, he and Godwin became friends. Mary fell in love with Shelley and eloped with him to the Continent in 1814. In the following year Mary[24] bore Shelley a son, who died. By then, her destiny was linked with the poet. Her eight brief years with Shelley, until his death by drowning in 1822, were the decisive ones in her life. Theirs remains one of the most fascinating marriages in literary history.

1816 marked a vital period in Mary's affairs. A son, William, was born in January. In May, Shelley and Mary, with Mary's half-sister, Claire Clairmont, left England for the second time, to stay in Switzerland, near Geneva. Here Mary began writing *Frankenstein*, before her nineteenth birthday. Shelley's first wife, Harriet, drowned herself in the Serpentine early in December, and Shelley and Mary were married before the end of that year.

Here is the portrait Trelawny paints of Mary: "The most striking feature in her face was her calm grey eyes; she was rather under the English standard of woman's height, very fair and light-haired, witty, social, and animated in the society of friends, though mournful in solitude."[25] This is a portrait of the first writer of science fiction; Mary had imbibed the philosophical ideas of Locke and the scientific ideas of Darwin, Humphry Davy, Joseph Priestley, and others.[26] She had read Condillac's *Treatise on the Sensations*. These helped shape her intellectual life and she set about applying her ideas to paper within a loose Gothic structure of suspense and pursuit.

Frankenstein was completed before Mary was twenty. She lived to write other novels, eventually supporting herself by writing. She never remarried, and died in 1851, the year of the Great Exhibition, aged fifty-three. She is buried in a churchyard in Bournemouth.[27]

Of her two sons and two daughters by Shelley, only Percy Florence survived beyond childhood. As Shelley put it in a poem to her:

> We are not happy, sweet! Our state
> Is strange and full of doubt and fear.

As if in response, Mary Shelley says that she wished her novel to "speak to the mysterious fears of our nature". This *Frankenstein* certainly does.

Mary Shelley's later novels should be listed. They are *Valperga* (1823), *The Last Man* (1826), *The Fortunes of Perkin Warbeck* (1830), *Lodore* (1835), and *Falkner* (1837); all were published anonymously.[28] Her story "Matilda" remained unpublished until 1959.[29] Godwin, Mary's father, had greeted this manuscript with coldness and silence. It tells of motherless Matilda who is brought up by an aunt until, when she is sixteen, her father returns from abroad. All Matilda's emotions are lavished on him, and reciprocated—until she realizes that his love for her is physical as well as paternal. Overcome by horror, the father drowns himself in the sea. When a poet, Woodville, comes along offering love, Matilda cannot accept him. Neglecting herself, she contracts consumption, most romantic of nineteenth-century maladies, and dies.

Some commentators have seen in this piece of self-dramatization proof of Mary's incestuous feelings. More cautiously, her latest biographer says, "It is her father who incestuously desires Matilda, but the father in many ways resembles the forceful side of Shelley and his death by drowning and Matilda's nightmare pursuit in search of news of him find a parallel in Shelley's own death, a prognostication that Mary recognized in retrospect."[30]

The sea, the drowning, echo back and forth in Mary's writing. Both motifs emerge in a neglected story, "The Transformation"[31], which throws light on the events of Frankenstein's wedding night.

A monstrous dwarf who is also a magician survives a shipwreck. Swimming to the Italian shore, the dwarf encounters Guido wandering along the beach. Guido was engaged to Juliet until his wicked behaviour became too much for her. Guido and dwarf change bodies. The dwarf (as Guido) goes to Genoa, charms Juliet, and is accepted in marriage. Guido (as dwarf) discovers Juliet and his double whispering together. He springs from the shadows and puts his dagger to the real dwarf's throat.

Dwarf (as Guido) says, "Strike home! Destroy this body—you will still live."

The dwarf (as Guido) then draws a sword. Guido (as dwarf) throws himself on the blade, at the same time plunging a dagger into the other's side.

Guido revives, to find himself in his own body once more and the dwarf dead. Juliet tends him lovingly. But he has to live with the knowledge that it was the monstrous dwarf who won back Juliet's love and the creature she now reviles who was himself.

This doppelganger theme bears affinities with the Frankenstein-monster confusion; here as there, the misshapen partner has no name. Both stories express the struggle Mary felt within herself between the loved and unloved side, the light and the dark. We understand that Shelley's death must have seemed to her like her own.

Readers and commentators alike are agreed that *Frankenstein* is Mary Shelley's great original novel. It is hardly surprising. *Frankenstein* is the one novel she wrote during Shelley's lifetime. As he in his poems was opening up new ground, she—wrapped in the aura of intellectual excitement which existed between them—also ventured into startling new territory.

Although Mary Shelley's reputation was long eclipsed by the fame of Byron and Shelley, the binary stars burning near her, *Frankenstein* was a success from the first.

One of the few joyous moments in her letters for 1823, when she returns to England from Italy, following Shelley's death, comes when she exclaims, "But lo and behold! I found myself famous!—*Frankenstein* had prodigious success as a drama and was about to be repeated for the 23rd night at the English opera house."[32]

The story of *Frankenstein: or, The Modern Prometheus* is familiar in outline, if distortedly, from film, stage and TV versions. Victor Frankenstein assembles a body from various parts of fresh corpses and then endows it with life. He quickly rejects the new being, which disappears and becomes a threat to him and others. The novel is long and considerably more complex than brief synopsis suggests; it is stocked with political and philosophical observations which film versions ignore.

Frankenstein opens with letters from a Captain Walton to his married sister at home. Walton's ship is exploring in unfamiliar Arctic waters near the pole. Walton is a man with a love for the marvellous. Just as well, for he sights a monstrous being driving a sledge across the ice floes. Next day, the crew rescues a man from the ice. This proves to be Victor Frankenstein, a scientist of Geneva. He is close to death. Recovering from exhaustion, he tells his tale to Walton.

Frankenstein's narrative comprises the bulk of the book. At the end, we return to Walton's letters. His quest abandoned, Walton recounts the death of Frankenstein to his sister.

Contained within Frankenstein's narrative are six chapters in which his creation gives an account of its life, with emphasis on its education and its rejection by society because of its repellent aspect. Within the creature's account is a briefer story of injustice, the history of the De Laceys, beneath whose roof the creature finds shelter.

The novel contains few female characters, a departure from Gothic practice. Victor's bride to be, Elizabeth, remains distant and cold. The characters passionately seek knowledge; this quest means everything to Frankenstein and Walton; they are never disabused. Frankenstein, indeed, praises the voyage of discovery as an honourable and courageous undertaking even as the creature's hands are about to close round his throat. The constant litigation which takes place in the background represents another kind of quest for knowledge, often erroneous or perverted.

One of the attractions of the novel is that it is set, not in the shabby London Mary Shelley knew from childhood, but amid the spectacular alpine scenery she visited with Shelley. The puissance of the monster gains force by being associated with the elements presiding over the mountains, storm, snow and desolation. Its first speech with its creator is on the glacier below Mont Blanc.[33]

What exactly is uniquely innovative about *Frankenstein*?

Interest has always centred on the creation of the nameless monster. This is the core of the novel, an experiment that goes wrong—a prescription to be repeated later, more sensationally, in *Amazing Stories* and elsewhere. Frankenstein's is the Faustian dream of unlimited power, but Frankenstein makes no pacts with the devil. "The devil" belongs to a relegated system of belief. Frankenstein's ambitions bear fruit only when he throws away his old reference books from a pre-scientific age and gets down to some research in the laboratory. This is now accepted practice, of course. But what is now accepted practice was, in 1818, a startling perception, a small revolution.

The novel dramatizes the difference between the old age and the new, between an age when things went by rote and one where everything was suddenly called into question.

Jiggery-pokery magic, of which Wells was to speak contemptuously, achieves nothing in this new age. Victor Frankenstein goes to the University of Ingolstadt and visits two professors. To the first, a man called Krempe, a professor of natural philosophy, he reveals how his search for knowledge led him to the works of Cornelius Agrippa, Paracelsus, and Albertus Magnus. Krempe scoffs at him: "These fancies, which you have so greedily imbibed, are a thousand years old."

This is a modern objection; antiquity is no longer the highest court to which one can appeal. "Ancient wisdom" is supplanted by modern experiment.

Frankenstein attends the second professor, Waldman, who lectures on chemistry. Waldman is even more scathing about ancient teachers who "promised impossibilities, and performed nothing". He speaks instead of the moderns, who use microscope and crucible, and converts Frankenstein to his way of thinking. Only when Frankenstein turns away from alchemy and the past, towards science and the future, is he rewarded with a horrible success.

In Wright of Derby's air pump, the white bird fluttered and died. Now something flutters and lives.

The "vital spark" is imparted to the composite body. Life is created without supernatural aid. Science has taken charge. A new understanding has emerged.

The Byron-Shelley circle understood themselves to be living in a new age. They felt themselves to be moderns. The study of gases was advanced; much was understood about the composition of the atmosphere; that lightning and electricity were one and the same was already clear—although that it was not a fluid was still so indefinite that Mary was able to use that misconception as a metaphor. Shelley had a microscope while at Oxford, and the study of morbid anatomy was well advanced. Mary lived in a thoroughly Newtonian world, in which natural explanations could be sought for natural phenomena. It is for this reason she sends Victor Frankenstein to Ingolstadt University; it was renowned in its time as a centre for science. Mary knew more of the science of her time than has been generally granted. But Samuel Holmes Vasbinder's useful researches in this area should change this uninformed opinion.[34]

Why, then, is so much time spent by Frankenstein with the alchemists, with Cornelius Agrippa and Paracelsus?

One practical answer is that Mary Shelley wished to make it plain that the old authorities who "promised impossibilities and performed nothing" had to go. She had to show that they were useless, outdated, and without merit in a modern age. Krempe's contempt is clear: "I little expected," he tells his student, "in this enlightened and scientific age, to find a disciple of Albertus Magnus and Paracelsus. My dear sir, you must begin your studies entirely anew."

Waldman summarizes the miracles the modern researchers have achieved.

"They ascend into the heavens: they have discovered how the blood circulates, and the nature of the air that we breathe. They have acquired new and almost unlimited powers; they can command the thunders of heaven, mimic the earthquake, and even mock the invisible world with its shadows."

Thus Mary Shelley, like a practised modern SF writer, prepares us beforehand for what is to follow. Of course she cannot show us how life is instilled in a dead body, any more than a modern writer could, but she can suspend our disbelief. The only problematic item in Waldman's listing of scientific wonders is "mocking the invisible world with its shadows".

This could be a reference, not to magic lanterns, or de Loutherbourg's Eidophusikon, or all the other devices relying on mechanics and optics which were popular at the time, but to the Spectre of Brocken. The Spectre of Brocken was just the sort of natural optical effect to attract the Shelleys and the Romantics. Like the Fata Morgana, the Spectre was a kind of mirage. It was seen in mountainous districts. One of the best accounts of it was given by M. Haue, who saw it in 1797, the year Mary was born. The sun rose at four one morning. At four-fifteen, Haue saw a human figure of monstrous size, apparently standing on a nearby mountain. An innkeeper was called. The two men saw two monstrous figures, which mimicked their movements.[35] Though explicable in natural terms, such gigantic doppelganger figures created awe in all who beheld them. They too may have played a part in the creation of the monster.

As if to dispel any doubts about her aversion to "jiggery-pokery magic", Mary makes it plain that her central marvel shares the essential quality of scientific experiment, rather than the hit-and-miss of legerdermain. She has Frankenstein create life a second time.

Frankenstein agrees to make a female companion for the monster, subject to certain conditions. When his work is almost finished, Frankenstein pauses, thinking of the "race of devils" that might be raised up by the union between his two creatures (a curious moment, this, for science fiction, looking back towards Caliban's snarl to Prospero in *The Tempest*—"I had peopled else the isle with Calibans!"—and forward to the monstrous legions of robots which were to tramp across the pages of the twentieth-century world). Victor destroys what he has begun, the monster discovers the breach of contract, utters his direst threat—"I shall be with you on your wedding-night"—and disappears.

The rest is a tale of flight and pursuit, punctuated by death and retribution, with everyone's hand turned against the wretched monster. This section contains much of Godwin's thinking, and of his novel, *Caleb Williams*, which, as its preface announced, was a review of "the modes of domestic and unrecorded despotism by which man becomes the destroyer of man".

The influence of Godwin and *Caleb Williams* is very strong. Frankenstein's friend, Clerval, is probably named after Mr Clare, the one good man in *Caleb Williams*—as, in Mary Shelley's later novel, Lord Raymond is named after the Raymond, a kind of eighteenth-century Robin Hood, in her father's novel.

No celestial vengeance here. No devils, no retribution from God. Mankind is left alone, scheming to take over the vacant premises. Like *Caleb Williams*,

Frankenstein becomes a story of implacable lay revenge, hatred, judicial blunder, pistols fired from open windows, a thwarted voyage of discovery, exhausting journeys without map or compass. There is nemesis but no promise of afterlife—unless it is the miserable hounded afterlife suffered by the monster.

Despite the powerful Godwin influence, Mary was her own woman. Her letters reveal an early preoccupation with politics.[36] They display, says her editor, an abiding belief in the freedom of the individual.

One enduring attraction of the book is its series of ambiguities, not all of which can have been the intention of an inexperienced novelist. We never see Frankenstein in his laboratory, throwing the fatal switch. That was the film. The book tells us only of the creature bending over his master. Again, in the pursuit, pursuer and pursued take turns. In particular, the language of the novel invites us to confuse the main roles. Perhaps we are meant to believe that the creature is Frankenstein's doppelganger, pursuing him to death. Which of them is "restored to animation"? "We . . . restored him to animation . . . As soon as he showed signs of life we wrapped him up in blankets. I often feared that his suffering had deprived him of understanding . . . He is generally melancholy and despairing. . . ."

This is not the monster but Victor, before Victor tells his story to Walton. We have only his word for the story's accuracy, just as, finally, we have only the monster's promises, as he disappears into darkness and distance, that he will destroy himself. The outcome of all the trials (there are four in the book) are unreliable; are we then encouraged to trust our witnesses?

"I am the assassin of these most innocent creatures; they died by my machinations"; again not the monster but Victor is speaking of the deaths his creature caused. He seems unsure of the creature's actual physical existence (this uncertainty is here reinforced by his use of the term "assassin", which suggests hashish and an altered state of mind). There is a reason for the way the world has confused which is Frankenstein, which monster; the confusion seems to have been part of Mary's intention.

In 1831, a slightly revised edition of *Frankenstein* was published. The 1818 edition contains a Preface, the 1831 edition an Introduction. From these prefatory pieces, something of Mary's inspiration and intentions can be gathered.

In her Introduction to the 1831 edition Mary reveals that her story, like *The Castle of Otranto*, began with a dream, those signals from our inner selves. In her dream, she saw "the hideous phantasm of a man stretched out, and then, on the working of some powerful engine, show signs of life, and stir with an uneasy, half vital motion." It was science fiction itself that stirred.

The dream followed on late-night conversations with Shelley, Lord Byron, and John Polidori, Byron's doctor. Their talk was of vampires and the supernatural. Polidori supplied the company with some suitable reading material[37]; Byron and Shelley also discussed Darwin, his thought and his experiments.[38] At Byron's suggestion, the four of them set about writing a ghost story apiece.

Mary's dream of a hideous phantasm stirring to life has the emotional coloration of a nightmare recorded in her journal a year earlier. In February 1815, she lost her first baby, born prematurely. On the fifteenth of March, she wrote: "Dream that my little baby came to life again; that it had only been cold, and that we rubbed it before the fire and it had lived."

From its very inception, the monster was a part of her.

In one of its aspects, *Frankenstein* is a diseased creation myth, prototype of many to come—an aspect we consider when we light upon *Dracula*.

Here we confront the more personal side of the novel. The struggle between Victor and his fiend is Oedipal in nature. Like André Gide's Oedipus, the fiend seems to himself to have "welled out of the unknown": "Who was I? What was I? Whence did I come?" it asks itself. (Chapter XV) The muddying of generations and generation reflects the confusion Mary Shelley felt regarding her own involved family situation, surrounded by the half-sisters of both her mother's earlier and her father's later liaisons.

Some critics have read into the more macabre scenes of *Frankenstein* undertones of vampirism (a favourite with Lord Byron) and incest. "I shall be with you on your wedding night," cries the creature to Victor, who is in a sense its mother and father. Sexual tensions move throughout the book.

As she had to give birth alone, so—as she claims in her Introduction—Mary gave birth to her "hideous progeny" alone.

Through her own complexities Mary gained a deep understanding of Shelley, because their mutual passion was strong. One critic, Christopher Small, suggests that Frankenstein and Frankenstein's monster between them portray the two sides of the poet[39]—the side that was all sweetness and light, and the charnel side, the knowledgeable side and the irresponsible side.

The metaphorical quality of a good novel permits more than one interpretation. Small's interpretation does not rule out my own conviction that Mary's hurt and orphaned feelings are embodied in the unloved creature; it is because Mary felt herself monstrous that her monster has had such power for so long. Part of the continued appeal of her novel is the tragedy of the unwanted child.

The average first novel commonly relies for its material on personal experience. It is not to deny other interpretations to claim that Mary sees herself as the monster. As it does, she too tried to win her way into society. By running away with Shelley, she sought acceptance through love; but the move carried her further away from society; she became a wanderer, an exile, like Byron, like Shelley himself. Her mother's death in childbirth must have caused her to feel that she, like the monster, had been born from the dead. Behind the monster's eloquence lies Mary's grief.

But of course *mere* science fiction novels are not expected to contain autobiographical material!

In referring to *Frankenstein* as a diseased creation myth, I have in mind phrases in the novel with sexual connotations such as "my workshop of filthy creation", used by Frankenstein of his secret work. Mary's experience brought her to see life and death as closely intertwined. The phraseology employed to describe her dream, already quoted, is significant. She saw "the hideous phantasm of a man stretched out, and then, on the working of some powerful engine, show signs of life, and stir with an uneasy, half vital motion". The vigorous line suggests both a distorted image of her mother dying, in those final restless moments which often tantalizingly suggest recovery rather than its opposite, as well as the stirrings of sexual intercourse, particularly when we recall that "powerful engine" is a term serving in pornography as a synonym for penis.

Ellen Moers, writing on female gothic[40], disposes of the question of how a young girl like Mary could hit on such a horrifying idea (though the author was herself the first to raise it). Most female authors of the eighteenth and nineteenth century were spinsters and virgins, and in any case Victorian taboos operated against writing about childbirth. Mary experienced the fear, guilt, depression and anxiety which often attend childbirth, particularly in situations such as hers, unwed, her consort a married man with children by another woman, and beset by debt in a foreign place. Only a woman, only Mary Shelley, could have written *Frankenstein*.

Great events were afoot between the publication of the first and second editions of *Frankenstein*. The first volume of Lyell's *Principles of Geology* had just appeared, drastically extending the age of the Earth. Mantell and others were grubbing gigantic fossil bones out of the ground, exhuming genera from the rocks as surely as Frankenstein's creature was patched together from various corpses. Already awakening was that great extension to our imaginative lives which we call the Age of Reptiles—those defunct monsters we have summoned back to vigorous existence.

The 1831 Introduction makes reference to galvanism and electricity. The preface to the first edition of 1818 is also instructive. Although Mary had set herself to write a ghost story, according to Byron's decree, her intentions soon changed; she states expressly in the Preface, "I have not considered myself as merely weaving a series of supernatural terrors." The Preface is an apologia, and Mary Shelley's chief witness for her defence, mentioned in her first sentence, is Erasmus Darwin.

Far from being supernatural in nature, the bestowal of new life to a corpse is to be regarded as "not of impossible occurrence".

The changes made to the novel between editions are also significant, and probably tell us something of Mary's sad emotional make-up. Different relationships are ascribed to Victor and his fiancée Elizabeth. In the first edition, Elizabeth is the daughter of his aunt. In the revision, she is brought into the family by adoption. In both versions, she is often referred to as "cousin". Mary's disastrous early years had bred a confusion in her mind. The incestuous pattern of two children brought up under one roof almost as brother and sister and then falling in love recurs elsewhere.

In *The Last Man*, Mary's later scientific romance, it is Adrian and Evadne, both residing in Windsor. In a short story, "The Invisible Girl" (1833), it is

Henry and Rosina: "They were playmates and companions in childhood, and lovers in after days."

Incest and necrophilia surface in the scene where Victor dismembers that hideous Eve, the female he is building for his macabre Adam. But incest was in fashion at the time, and not only as a reliable literary titillator: Byron and his dearest Augusta, his half-sister, provided living examples which must have interested Mary with her half-brothers and half-sisters in mind.

If Mary had read De Sade's novel *Justine*, as seems likely, she would find fathers raping and ruining their daughters[41], while in her husband's own verse-drama, *The Cenci*, the same theme holds court. Old Cenci rants over his daughter for all the world like one of the divine Marquis's heroes.

Algolagnia was certainly not absent from Mary's make-up. She wrote *Frankenstein* with her baby son William by her side; yet she makes the monster's first victim a little boy called William, Victor's younger brother. "I grasped his throat to silence him, and in a moment he lay dead at my feet. I gazed on my victim, and my heart swelled with exultation and hellish triumph." Which William was this, her father or her son? Her little William ("Willmouse") died in the summer of 1819.

Mary herself, in her Introduction to the 1831 edition, appears to invite a psychological interpretation of her story when she says "Invention . . . does not consist in creating out of a void, but out of chaos; the materials must, in the first place, be afforded: it can give form to dark, shapeless substances, but it cannot bring into being the substance itself."

This remark shows an acute understanding of literature, whatever else underlies it.

For every thousand people familiar with the tale of Frankenstein creating his monster from various cadaver spares and electrifying them into new life, only one will have read the novel. The cinema has helped enormously to disseminate the myth while destroying its significance.

Shortly after its original publication, *Frankenstein* was made into a play. Various versions were performed with great success until the nineteen-thirties. By that time, the cinema had moved in. There were short silent versions, but the monster began his true movie career in 1931, with James Whale's Universal picture *Frankenstein*, in which Boris Karloff played the monster. The dials in the castle laboratory have hardly stopped flickering since. The monster has spawned Sons, Daughters, Ghosts, and Houses; has taken on Brides and created Woman; has perforce shacked up with Dracula and Wolf Man; has enjoyed Evil, Horror, and Revenge, and has even had the Curse; on various occasions, it has met Abbott and Costello, the Space Monster, and the Monster from Hell.

The Whale film borrowed much of its style from German Expressionism. The first Hammer Frankenstein, the 1957 *Curse of Frankenstein*, had sumptuous Victorian settings and a chilly Peter Cushing as Frankenstein. But all the films simplify. They allow only literal meanings.

They omit the social structure which greatly strengthens the novel, while giving it the leisurely pace movies must reject. In combining social criticism with new scientific ideas, Mary Shelley anticipates the methods of H. G. Wells—and of many who have followed in Wells's footsteps.

After *Frankenstein*, a pause. The idea of looking into the future was yet to be properly born in anything but a religious sense. Such writings about future developments as there were tended to be of a political or satirical nature, such as the anonymous pamphlet *One Thousand Eight Hundred and Twenty-Nine*, first published in 1819, which attacked the claims for Catholic emancipation and predicted the restoration of the Stuart kings in 1829.

An intuitive work, however, came from the poet who, next to P. B. Shelley, had been closest to Mary Shelley.

While *Frankenstein* was being written, Lord Byron was exiling himself from England forever. He took a house on the shores of Lake Geneva, the Villa Diodati (where John Milton had once stayed), during that cheerless summer of 1816. The Shelley entourage was nearby. It was then that Byron wrote his poem *Darkness*—the word again—a sort of grim evolutionary vision, the imagery of which, for our generation, carries promptings of nuclear winter. Like Mary's novel, *Darkness* too begins with a dream or at least a hypnoid fantasy.

> I had a dream which was not all a dream.
> The bright sun was extinguished, and the stars
> Did wander darkling in the eternal space
> Rayless, and pathless, and the icy earth
> Swung blind and blackening in the moonless air.

The Earth is in ruins, barbarism descends, whole populations starve. The last two men alive die of horror when they meet.[42]

The poem speaks of a deserted world, "treeless, manless, lifeless". That was the theme Mary Shelley was to explore in the best of her later novels, after both Byron and Shelley had died, one in Greece, one in Italy.

In Mary Shelley's lifetime, six of her novels and two travel journals were published. *The Last Man* (1826) appeared anonymously, as being "By the author of *Frankenstein*". Like the earlier work, it carried on its title page a motto from *Paradise Lost*, this time the grim

> Let no man seek
> Henceforth to be foretold what shall befall
> Him or his children.

Novels at this period were not the major literary force they were later to become; the luminaries of the eighteen-forties were still below the horizon. It was a transitional period. For all its power, *The Last Man* strikes one as a rather transitional novel. Landscape forms a considerable part of it, used without the great allegorical power that landscape ("foreign parts") takes on in *Frankenstein*, reminding us how much prose fiction and travel literature, evolving together, are indebted to each other.[43] For all that, *The Last Man* can still hold our interest on more than literary-historical grounds.

It is the story of Lionel Verney, set towards the end of the twenty-first century. The king of England has abdicated, bowing to popular feeling. His son, Adrian, now known as the Earl of Windsor, befriends Verney and later becomes Lord Protector of England. Verney's father was a favourite of the king's but fell from favour, since when Verney has "wandered among the hills of civilised England as uncouth as a savage". He is converted to finer feelings by his friendship with Adrian.

Enter Lord Raymond, a youthful peer of genius and beauty. The date is AD 2073, but the Turks are still lording it over the Greeks; Raymond eventually becomes commander of the Greek army and besieges Constantinople.

This much, with many complications concerning the various sisters and mothers of the various parties, occupies the first third of the narrative. A modern reader hews his way through it by recalling that Mary was drawing portraits of people she knew, Shelley being Adrian, Byron Raymond, and Claire Clairmont Perdita, Verney's sister. Several of the infants are also identifiable. This cast is deployed in an England evolving peacefully from a monarchy into a republic—though all is swept away when plague arrives.

The *roman à clef* involvement is partly abandoned when Constantinople falls to its besiegers. They walk in unopposed, Raymond at their head. The defenders have died of plague: the city is empty.

With the introduction of the plague, the narrative gains pace, dire events and forebodings of worse flock one after the other.

> What are we, the inhabitants of this globe, least among the many that people infinite space? Our minds embrace infinity; the visible mechanism of our being is subject to merest accident. (Volume 2, Chapter 5)

Raymond is killed by falling masonry, Perdita commits suicide by drowning. The plague spreads all over the world, so that "the vast cities of America, the fertile plains of Hindostan, the crowded abodes of the Chinese, are menaced with utter ruin".

Back in Windsor, Verney fears for his wife and children, although refugees from plague-stricken spots are allowed to find shelter within the castle walls; the parks are ploughed up to provide food for everyone. Adrian is working for the general good in London, where plague has secured a footing. After helping him, Verney returns to Windsor, to find plague in the castle.

> Death, cruel and relentless, had entered these beloved walls . . . [Later] quiet prevailed in the Castle, whose inhabitants were hushed to repose. I was awake, and during the long hours of dead night, my busy thoughts worked in my brain like ten thousand mill-wheels, rapid, acute, untame-able. All slept—all England slept; and from my window, commanding a wide prospect of the star-illumined country, I saw the land stretched out in placid rest. I was awake, alive, while the brother of death possessed my race. (Volume 2, Chapter 7)

Winter halts the advance of plague. Next summer brings renewed onslaughts, and England is invaded by hordes of Americans and Irish—an invasion force which Adrian quells with peaceful talk.

Adrian and Verney eventually lead the few English who survive from England to France. By then, one of Verney's sons is dead; his wife dies during a snowstorm.

Fifty survivors, their number dwindling, move southwards from Dijon. Mary Shelley leaves not a wither unwrung. "Images of destruction, pictures of despair, the procession of the last triumph of death, shall be drawn before thee," she warns her gentle reader.

Adrian and Verney, with two children, Clara and little Evelyn, reach Italy. Typhus claims Evelyn by Lake Como. The three survivors find nobody else alive. The country is desolate. They reach Venice, only to find it ruinous and slowly sinking under the lagoon.

Prompted by Adrian's wish to see Greece again, they set sail down the Adriatic. A storm rises, the boat sinks. They are plunged into the water—and eventually Verney flings himself ashore, alone. He is the last man alive.

Verney indulges in some bitter comparisons between his state and Robinson Crusoe's, after which he makes for the Eternal City (where Shelley's ashes lie buried). Still he finds no living soul. In Rome, he gluts himself with Rome's treasures of the past, wandering in its art galleries and its libraries, until settling down to write his history. Our last glimpse of Verney is when he sets out with a dog for company to sail south through the Mediterranean, down the African coast, towards the odorous islands of the far Indian Ocean.

Surprisingly, the novel ends on a tranquil note. Instead of *Frankenstein*'s final darkness and distance, distance here embraces the light, the glorious light of the south, the equator. The one survivor is another sort of Adam, more solitary than ever Frankenstein's creature was.

The name Verney is probably a tribute to Volney, the French count, Constantin François de Chasseboeuf, whose revolutionary book, *Les ruines, ou Méditations sur les révolutions des empires* (1791), describes the rise and fall of ancient civilizations and the prospects for a future in which tyranny will be abolished. Volney's book was known in English as *Ruins of Empires*. It is the book from which Frankenstein's creature learned "the science of letters".[44] It also formed the springboard for Shelley's ambitious poem, *Queen Mab*[45], in which Shelley (like Godwin before him) claims that

> Power, like a desolating pestilence
> Pollutes whate'er it touches.

Volney may be responsible for that remarkable and contradictory preoccupation with ruins and ruin which haunts those who write of the future. Once Volney's philosophical superstructure is established, Mary Shelley's story takes on powerful suspense as we arrive at Constantinople. Some of the moralizing and rhapsodizing—Mary Shelley's prose has become fleshier since

Frankenstein—may strike a modern reader as tedious, but there are moments of lurid truth, for instance in the dream in which Raymond's body becomes the pestilence itself.[46] Here to perfection is Burke's "delightful horror".

The gloom of *The Last Man* is also striking—and strikingly expressed. Here is Raymond speaking to Verney:

> You are of this world; I am not. You hold forth your hand; it is even as a part of yourself; and you do not yet divide the feeling of identity from the mortal form that shapes forth Lionel. How then can you understand me? Earth is to me a tomb, the firmament a vault, shrouding mere corruption. Time is no more, for I have stepped within the threshold of eternity; each man I meet appears a corse, which will soon be deserted of its animating spark, on the eve of decay and corruption. (Volume 2, Chapter 2)

This obsession with corruption is alarming; the impulse behind *Frankenstein* has grown like a cancer, until revulsions which once applied to an exceptional case now condemn the whole human race. It is the race, rather than the individual, which is now hunted down to exile and extinction.

How are we to regard these two novels of Mary Shelley's? They are not merely subjective tales. *The Last Man* is not merely "a vast fantasy of entropy".[47] Nor can we pretend that it cannot be "placed in any existing category"[48], since many poems, tales, and paintings of the period devoted themselves to variations on the theme.[49] As has been pointed out elsewhere, *The Last Man* is in many of its aspects a transposition of reality, rather than fantasy.[50] Mary Shelley wrote of what was happening. Hers is a scientific romance.

Critics like chasing literary influences. Creative writers use the great world beyond books for their material. Entrenched behind this division, critics have hitherto failed to observe that a virtual plague was raging even as *The Last Man* was being written. When *Frankenstein* first appeared, in 1818, news was reaching England of a terrible epidemic in India. The inhabitants of Jessore, near Calcutta, had died or fled, spreading the contagion. In the spring of 1818, the epidemic broke forth again, more violently. Three years later, it crossed the Arabian Sea. The victims were so numerous their bodies were thrown into the waters. In Basra, 15,000 died in eighteen days. The disease was cholera—then regarded as untreatable.

By 1822 the infection had reached southern Russia. It had also spread eastward—Burma 1819—Siam 1820—then onwards, to the islands which now form Indonesia, as far as the Philippines. It slipped through the portals of China.

By 1830 the plague was in Moscow. It swept across Europe. The deaths became uncountable. The British watched uneasily as the plague approached their shores. Summer of 1831 was exceptionally fine and warm; then it was that cholera arrived in the North of England. Soon it infested London.

Almost as frightening as the pandemic itself was the civil disorder which accompanied its remorseless advance. Foreign doctors and the rich were often blamed. In Hungary, the homes of the nobility were stormed. Troops were called out in many cities.[51]

Mary Shelley, in *The Last Man*, was hardly doing more than issuing a symbolic representation, a psychic screening, of what was taking place in reality. In that, at least, she was setting an example to be followed by the swarming SF scribes of the twentieth century.

The last word on *Frankenstein* will never be said. It contains too many seemingly conflicting elements for that. A consideration of some of them concludes this chapter.

The Outwardness of science and society is balanced in the novel by an Inwardness which Mary's dream helped her to accommodate. This particular balance is perhaps one of *Frankenstein*'s greatest merits: that its tale of exterior adventure and misfortune is accompanied by—encompassed by—psychological depth. Mary might have claimed for her drama what Shelley said in his Preface to *Prometheus Unbound*: "The imagery which I have employed will be found, in many instances, to have been drawn from the operations of the human mind, or from those external actions by which they are expressed."

Love, fear, the cruelty of parents and lovers—such familiar acquaintances are stirred up by the introduction of the central novelty.

Victor's lowly unique creature, outcast from human kind, takes a lofty view of itself and—in contrast with the almost dumb fiend to which the movies have accustomed us—is articulate regarding its sorrows.

Here we are given an educational prescription which looks both backward and forward—to a time when mankind does not judge merely by appearances.

Shelley read *Paradise Lost* aloud to Mary in 1816.

The monster likens himself to Adam in the poem—but how much less fortunate than Adam, for in this case the creator rushes away from "his odious handywork, horror-stricken". The creature's career has something in common with Adam's, with the vital exception of the missing Eve. He is first created, and then brought to full intellectual awareness of the world in which he lives—at which stage, "benevolence and generosity were ever present before me". (Chapter XV) He then undergoes his version of the Fall, when "the spirit of revenge enkindled in my heart". (Chapter XVI) Now the creature is frequently referred to as "the fiend". In many ways, it becomes less human, more a symbol of inhumanity. "I saw him," says Frankenstein, "descend the mountain with greater speed than the flight of an eagle, and quickly lost him among the undulations of the sea of ice." (Chapter XVII)

The fiend increasingly speaks of itself in Miltonic terms, saying of itself at last, over Victor's corpse, "the fallen angel becomes a malignant devil".

This change in the nature of the monster enables Mary Shelley to bring out two aspects of the struggle which are subordinate to the eschatological theme.

The first aspect is man's confrontation with himself, which the power of creation necessarily entails. The diseased creation myth prefigures Jekyll and Hyde, as Frankenstein struggles with his alter ego; their obsessive pursuit of one another makes sense only in metaphysical terms.

The second aspect is the disintegration of society which follows man's abrogation of power. One perversion of the natural order leads to another. *Frankenstein* is loaded with a sense of corruption, and "the fiend" moves about the world striking where it will, like a disease which, beginning naturally enough in a charnel house, can be isolated and sterilized only on a drifting ice floe.

The rejection of a just Heavenly Father, the concern with suffering, the sexual obsessions, have helped preserve *Frankenstein*'s topicality. Not only does it foreshadow our fears about the two-edged triumphs of scientific progress; it is also the first novel to be powered by the evolutionary idea. God, however often called upon, is an absentee landlord. The lodgers have to fight things out between themselves.

Herein lies the force of the novel's sub-title. In Shelley's lyrical drama, *Prometheus Unbound*, mighty Jupiter has chained Prometheus to a rock. Prometheus suffers terrible torture, but is eventually freed when Jupiter is dethroned, to retire into obscurity.

What is mankind to seek, if not God? Answers to this modern conundrum include objectives like knowledge, power, and self-fulfilment. According to one's reading of the novel, Victor Frankenstein can be understood to seek all three.

The use of this modernized Faust theme is particularly suited to the first real novel of science fiction: Frankenstein's is *the* modern predicament, involving the post-Rousseauvian dichotomy between the individual and his society, as well as the encroachment of science on that society, and mankind's dual nature, whose inherited ape curiosity has brought him both success and misery. His great discovery apart, Frankenstein is an over-reacher and victim, staggering through a world where virtues are few (though the fiend *reads* of them). Instead of hope and forgiveness, there remain only the misunderstandings of men and the noxious half life of the monster. Knowledge brings no guarantee of happiness.

For this critic's taste, the Frankenstein theme is more contemporary and more interesting than interstellar travel tales, since it takes us nearer to the enigma of man and thus of life; just as interstellar travel can yield more interest than such fantasy themes as telepathy.

Since the publication of *Billion Year Spree*, many scholars have been at work on *Frankenstein* from within and without the science fiction field. One of the most creative and ingenious is David Ketterer[52], though he seeks to deny that the novel is science fiction at all, on the grounds that it is much else beside. But so indeed is all good SF, which can live only on its appetite. Ketterer also implies that *Frankenstein* cannot be SF since SF was not a category in 1816. Nor, in 1816, did the word scientist exist: yet the world has adopted Frankenstein as the model of the irresponsible scientist.

Despite this, Ketterer's arguments regarding this extraordinary novel, and the centrality of the quest for knowledge ("knowledge is what *Frankenstein* is all about") are stimulating and thought-provoking. *Frankenstein* is also "all about" a parent/child relationship.

It is appropriate that "darkness and distance" should be the closing words of *Frankenstein* just as "darkness" is almost its first word, presented on the title page within the quotation from *Paradise Lost*. SF is often haunted by that same sense of corruption and loss. When we turn to the writer who is the subject of our next chapter, we find again an emphasis on incest, darkness, fear, and "the tremendous secrets of the human frame".

CHAPTER II

Something Monomaniacal:
Edgar Allan Poe

I was alone, and the walls were checkered by shadowy forms.
—Charles Brockden Brown: *Wieland*

Pessimism or optimism? Black or white?

Are we going to make it to the stars? Or—to put the question in other terms—can our salvation come through material things?

Do we hope or fear for the future?

SF novels and stories divide into those which are optimistic about the improvement of life and those which are entirely more sceptical. For historical-economic reasons, American SF still attempts to enforce a prevailing optimistic tone. Publishers and editors, in the main, hate anything they can label "downbeat". The result has often been a lot of enforced cheeriness.

Science fiction and scientific romances which have accepted a darker view of life have proved more durable. Such is certainly the case with the immarcescible romances of Edgar Allan Poe. That lover of the grave's pained felicities still retain their power.

Assumed pessimism is as bad as assumed optimism. Where did the vein of darkness come from which runs through Mary Shelley's work, through Poe's, Lovecraft's, Shiel's, Dick's work onwards—a vein quite at odds with the utopianism from which the optimistic side of science-fictional thought issues?

Does national disposition enter the matter?

Paris, 1771. France, the first country of the Enlightenment, the home of Diderot and the Cyclopaedists. The Enlightenment view of the future was one of Happiness and Order—two qualities Romantics were to hold antithetical. The Enlightenment aspirations are enshrined in a remarkable utopian fiction, Louis-Sébastien Mercier's *L'an deux mille quatre cent quarante*, published in 1771. The book was translated into several European languages, including English, and eventually published in the newly independent America as *Year 2440*. Fountains and fine buildings, noble sentiments and innocuous musics, fill Mercier's vision. All actual and metaphorical Bastilles have vanished. Justice has replaced them.

England in 1771. By contrast, a much more sober view of the future. See, for instance, an anonymous squib by one "Antonius" appearing in *Lloyd's Evening Post* for 25th–28th November, the year in which Mercier was published. "Antonius's" article looks two centuries ahead to a ruinous Britain overcome by an American Empire.

Two Americans are guided round London by a poor Briton. The latter
provides a running commentary as follows:

> Yonder is a field of turnips, there stood the Palace of Whitehall; as to St.
> James's there are no traces of that left, it stood somewhere near that pond.
> Here stood that venerable pile of antiquity, Westminster Abbey, which
> was founded in the year 796; at the west end was the famous Chapel of
> Henry the Seventh, in which were interred most of our English Kings.
> That on the right is the remains of Queen Elizabeth's tombe; that on the
> left, those of King William the Third; all the rest are swept away by time.
>   The whole church had been ornamented with monuments of Admirals,
> Generals, Poets, Philosophers, and others, two of which only we found
> legible, that of Locke and Newton, some being quite defaced, and others
> we could not come at on account of the ruins fallen in upon them.—What
> a melancholy sight, we exclaimed, that this venerable dome, dedicated to
> God, should now be converted into a stable!

South Sea House is a mere jakes, its infamy well known. India House was
destroyed one hundred and sixty years earlier, "for the blood they shed in India
called for vengeance, and they were expelled the Country". And so on.

Why this dark vision? Only a generation after Antonius, a young woman was
writing the melancholy and perverse *Frankenstein*—an English woman of
nineteen. Later, other generations would queue to inflict on England all the
miseries and disasters imaginable.

Poe is a Hamlet of letters. There is always something rotten in his state. He
remains isolated, dandyish, tormented. The ghost of his father calls to him from
the cellarage.

Edgar Allan Poe (1809–1849) is a writer whose literary merits are still being
debated a century and a quarter after his death, though he often figures among
the ten great writers of nineteenth-century American literature.

A striking early judgement was passed by the Goncourt brothers in their
Journal for 1856:

> 16 July—After reading Edgar Allan Poe. Something the critics have not
> noticed: a new literary world pointing to the literature of the twentieth
> century. Scientific miracles, fables on the pattern A + B; a clear-sighted,
> sickly literature. No more poetry, but analytic fantasy. Something
> monomaniacal. Things playing a more important part than people; love
> giving way to deductions and other sources of ideas, style, subject, and
> interest; the basis of the novel transferred from the heart to the head, from
> the passion to the idea, from the drama to the denouement.[1]

A confused remark in some ways. But it points to one factor Poe's writing has
in common with Mary Shelley's, an attempt to balance Inwardness with
Outwardness. Poe is the great hierophant of the Inward; yet he could not resist
the scientific miracles, the A + B of which the Goncourts speak. Poe's dark
chambers are littered with the gadgets of his age.

Those who enjoy science fiction above all other kinds of writing must enjoy its vitalizing bastardy, its immoral interdisciplinary habits, as it feathers its nest with scraps of knowledge seized from the limits of an expanding world-view. We can only agree with the Aldous Huxley who said, "I have a taste for the lively, the mixed and the incomplete in art, preferring it to the universal and the chemically pure."

Poe's chemical impurities were built into his fibre from birth.

It is sometimes difficult to separate the facts of his life from fiction. Poe was born in Boston in 1809, not 1811 as he later stated, of itinerant parents. His father was a travelling actor. His mother was Elizabeth Hopkins, an English woman and leading lady in the company of actors. She died in poverty—of the consumption which stalks through nineteenth-century artistic history—when Poe was only two years old; by then, his father had disappeared. These early disasters isolated him from society, as similar disasters had done with Mary Shelley.

Poe was adopted by a Scottish tobacco merchant, John Allan. Their relationship appears to have been an affectionate one throughout Poe's boyhood, although some critics dispute this. He entered the University of Virginia, but was expelled for gambling debts. Now began his quarrels with Allan.

Poe's first verses were published in 1827 (*Tamerlane and Other Poems*— forty copies only); by then, he had enlisted in the Army, perhaps prompted by the knowledge that his paternal grandfather had fought in the War of Independence.

Always a great embroiderer, Poe made out this period of his life to be full of adventure and travel; in fact, he never left North America. He entered West Point in 1830, and was discharged only a few months later, for disobedience and absenteeism. His movements are often obscure. He appears to have suffered from the difficulties in sustaining personal relationships which characterize children bereaved of their mothers in early years. Slowly, he began building a reputation with his fiction and acquiring status with an editorial job on the *Southern Literary Messenger*. Much of his excellent literary criticism was written at this time, during the late eighteen-thirties and early forties.

In 1836, Poe married his cousin Virginia. She was not then fourteen. Literary theorists have smacked their lips over this conjunction; but, however terrible his pleasures, Poe's pains seem to have been more terrible. If we are allowed to call as evidence in this relationship Poe's tale "Eleonora"[2], then Poe and his cousin loved each other deeply, and by no means celibately ("No guile disguised the fervour of love which animated her heart, and she examined with me its inmost recesses"). Of course poor Poe may have found it necessary here, too, to embroider.

However that might be, of his suffering there is no doubt. Virginia wasted before his eyes; she had ruptured a blood vessel while singing and on several occasions fell into a deathlike trance. She died of tuberculosis in 1848. During this game of hide-and-seek with death, Poe took to drink and possibly to opium;

he also underwent a lesion on one side of his brain, which rendered him unable to take alcohol without becoming drunk.

It is as well that Poe was the least materialistic of men, for he remained materially poor even when his reputation as poet, critic, and short-story writer was high. During the last year of his life, 1849, he became emotionally involved with three women, and was busy with lecture tours and editing. He died in Baltimore in mysterious circumstances, from brain fever, epilepsy, or a fatal drinking bout. One version of his last days suggests that he was the victim of local press-gang politics—that on his way to a new life in New York, having signed the pledge, he was set upon, drugged, forced to vote at a number of election booths. Was he a fated victim or an incurable soak? Or perhaps something of both?[3]

More ill luck attended Poe's choice of executor, a literary villain named the Reverend Rufus W. Griswold, who spread many calumnies about Poe, working on the fertile ground of Poe's own inexactitudes.

Poe's reputation is as entangled as his career. His writing was renowned in France, as the extract from the Goncourt Journal indicates, at a time when the English-speaking world cared little for its merits. This was in part due to the obsessive attention lavished on his work by Charles Baudelaire. The great poet devoted some sixteen years of his creative life to translating Poe into French. It is difficult to think of a parallel to such literary devotion!

The absence of moralizing in Poe had much to do with Baudelaire's hero worship, in an age when morality and literature were becoming increasingly confused. He admired Poe's exploration of mental and moral disease and the terror that was "not of Germany but of the soul".[4] It is on this view of Poe's writings that his best reputation now rests; but English critics have been reluctant to accept it. They regard Poe either as hopelessly immature[5] or as a stage manager, concerned with little beyond immediate effect—and unfortunately there are a host of tales and poems that support this attitude, which D. H. Lawrence called "the bad taste of sensationalism"[6], and which Aldous Huxley said contained "those finer shades of vulgarity that ruin Poe."[7] Philip K. Dick identified it, more simply, as "the schlock factor".

Poe's most successful tales are those in which some airless room is haunted by the memory of a pale woman, loved yet feared. Then Poe does achieve a haggard grandeur which uniquely mingles immense muffled silences and jangled nerves. The least successful tales—judged as literature—are those in which Poe's predilection for ugly horseplay takes over: the murdered and decomposing Mr Shuttleworthy popping up out of a crate in "Thou Art the Man"; the homicidal orang-outang, which provides a denouement for "The Murders in the Rue Morgue"; the grotesque mass-drowning in ale in "King Pest"; the setting fire to a party dressed as orang-outangs in "Hop-Frog". This horseplay side of Poe recalls the work of an ill-natured schoolboy.

His most valid tales include "The Fall of the House of Usher", "Ligeia", "Eleonora", "The Masque of the Red Death", "The Facts in the Case of M. Valdemar", "The Pit and the Pendulum", "The Purloined Letter", "The Cask of Amontillado", "The Gold Bug", "The Mystery of Marie Roget", "The Tell-Tale Heart", and "William Wilson". They show a remarkable ability to survive, despite their often over-strained language. Their windowless or curtained chambers are a valid metaphor for a sunken aspect of the human spirit which had rarely found such intense utterance. Edgar Allan Poe is the first Poet of the Great Indoors; his is an unlikely figure to appear when it did, when the Great Outdoors was being celebrated so heartily by Fenimore Cooper and others. It is this which enables Poe's portrait to be hung in the board room of modernity and science fiction, along with other defunct directors such as Verne and Wells and Mary Shelley.

Nevertheless, Poe had his predecessors in the United States. Charles Brockden Brown (1771–1810), the first professional American writer, dwelt extensively on morbid subjects and died of tuberculosis at the age of thirty-nine. His *Wieland* (1798) is a Gothic study of mania, while *Arthur Mervyn* (1799/1801) is the story of a plague, Brown himself having survived two epidemics of yellow fever. This latter novel is mentioned in Mary Shelley's *The Last Man*.

Nathaniel Hawthorne (1804–1864) is a more distinguished literary figure, though his most famous novels, such as *The Scarlet Letter* (1850), *The House of the Seven Gables* (1851), and *The Marble Faun* (1860), were all published after Poe's death. Hawthorne was a New Englander whose writings contain a deal of allegory and tend, in such short stories as "The Artist of the Beautiful" (1844) towards science fiction. Amid a great display of sensibility, Warland creates an exquisite insect; it may be a steam-driven butterfly. When the girl he admires sees it and asks if he made it, his reply is, "Wherefore ask who created it, so it be beautiful?" Among similar impressive manifestations of the subjunctive, the insect is clobbered by an unfeeling child; but Warland does not mind. He has his Art.

Hawthorne really lies beyond our scope, but his continued interest for the critics if not the readers of science fiction is well warranted. His work might best be described as psychological allegory. He can be regarded as a non-generic contemporary not merely of Poe but of a whole range of Modernist writing, including much SF from writers as different as Disch, Bishop and Benford. Hawthorne was obsessed with "the dark problem of life made plain" (*The Scarlet Letter*), as such stories as "Rappaccini's Daughter" (1844) show.

Hawthorne's novel, *The Blithedale Romance* (1852) concerns the corrupting effects of unexamined power-drives and the flaws inherent in practical utopianism—why an early commune fails to work. Hawthorne had actual experience of such an institution—something few modern writers of utopian SF could claim. The novel tells of conflicts involved in "our effort to establish the one true system".

The theme of evil's permanent existence in a society dedicated to the idea of infinite progress is obviously of central relevance to SF today.

As a student of morbid psychology, Poe strikingly presents his characters through pictorial descriptions of their surroundings. Most popular representations of Poe's works—the cinema in particular—treat him as a horror-merchant. But Poe's horror is of a special order. He uses none of the supernatural machinery, the framework of evil gods, manipulated so vigorously by such successors as Machen and Lovecraft. His are the domestic horrors, the glimpses of little lives riddled with fears of life and sex, with only an occasional occult visitation; any revenants from the grave are likely to be female. Ill-health has become the badge of aesthetic principle.

Even hell-fire has died; the terrible frenzies of human desire are banked down under chilling languors and the leukaemias of isolation; the world of Poe is frightening because it is a world of deprivation and of a love that does not dare to breathe its pseudonym. So heavily is the course of love perverted that the inaction (one would hardly speak of action in a typical Poe tale) generally takes place below ground, to symbolize the depths to which the psyche has foundered.

In his essay *Eureka*, Poe speaks of Laplace's nebular hypothesis (that the planets of the solar system were ejected from the sun as the latter cooled) with great amateur enthusiasm. "From whatever point of view we regard it, we shall find it *beautifully true*. It is by far too beautiful, indeed, *not* to possess Truth as its essentiality." But Poe was confusing Keats's dictum about beauty being truth with scientific verities. Laplace's hypothesis has gone the way of phlogiston and the luminiferous aether, though Voyager 2's recent findings regarding Uranus and that planet's ring and moon systems have re-introduced it to consideration.

The pages of science fiction are littered with broken theories, like a nursery floor littered with broken toys. It is no disgrace; the speculative seizes on what it will. All the same, it remains hard to think of Poe as centrally a science fiction writer, except in the impatience of his imagination.

True, there is the French connection. Paul Valéry said of Poe that he was teaching a doctrine in which "a kind of mathematics and a kind of mysticism became one". Mallarmé wrote the verses carved on the stone erected over Poe's grave. Hubert Matthey in 1915 called him "le créateur du roman merveilleux-scientifique". And, of course, Jules Verne himself acknowledged his debt to Poe.

According to Dr Bruce Franklin[8] the first person to hail Poe as "the father of science fiction" was an anonymous writer in *The Saturday Review* in 1905. The notion has rattled about ever since, like the living dead. There is more substance in Harold Beaver's ranking of Poe[9] as a believer in human imperfectibility and an escape, by whatsoever means, from normal limitations of perception. Certainly Poe was no subscriber to scientism.

And Poe has another claim on our gratitude, distinct from the debt we owe him for some of the fertilizing terrors of our childhood. Poe holds, with Hawthorne, one of the patents on the short story as an artistic mode. At least until yesterday, the short story was an ideal form for science fiction, where the Notion, the Effect, could appear naked, without accoutrements.

Among his stories, those most likely to pass muster as science fiction are "The Conversation of Eiros and Charmion" ("where the approach of a giant comet brings a hideous *novelty* of emotion"), "A Tale of Ragged Mountains", "A

Descent into the Maelström", "The Facts in the Case of M. Valdemar", *The Narrative of Arthur Gordon Pym of Nantucket*, "The Unparalleled Adventures of One Hans Pfaall", "The Balloon-Hoax", "Mellonta Tauta", "Mesmeric Revelation", "The Colloquy of Monos and Una", and "The Thousand-and-Second Tale of Scheherazade". A handful of tales, and the roll call establishes this: that Poe's best stories are not science fiction, nor his science fiction stories his best.

Certainly Poe shows remarkable prescience. For instance, in a neglected story, "The Colloquy of Monos and Una", he perceives certain laws of conservation which were only widely acknowledged in the 1960s. In this potted history of a technologically overwhelmed future, he says, "Meantime huge smoking cities arose, innumerable. Green leaves shrank before the hot breath of furnaces. The fair face of Nature was deformed as with the ravages of some loathsome disease. . . ." He also makes the equation between global pollution and global ageing: "Prematurely induced by intemperance of knowledge, the old age of the world drew on."

In a letter, he said, "I live continually in a reverie of the future." But those stories which are most like science fiction are least like stories, more resembling essays or conversations, and often tumbling into the facetious (one of Poe's besetting sins, linked with a habit of giving characters names like von Underduk), as if he found his material intractable.

He may use scientific flavouring, much as Lawrence Durrell does in our day; but this makes him no more a science fiction writer than it does Durrell—in fact, rather less, when we remember the latter's *Nunquam*, with its transvestite Frankenstein motif.

There are excellent stories which are kin to science fiction: "MS. Found in a Bottle", featuring a splendid 'Flying Dutchman', which has often been turned into a derelict spaceship; "William Wilson", with a doppelganger, which has often been turned into an android since Poe's time; but Flying Dutchmen and doppelgangers are not in themselves science fiction and were only later smuggled into the genre. Poe wrote stories in which scientific or quasi-scientific theories are present, as mesmerism is in the horrific "The Facts in the Case of M. Valdemar". That story is his most successful science fiction.

"M. Valdemar" concerns the hypnotizing of a sick man. He dies, but his soul cannot leave his decaying body until the hypnotic bond is released. Poe's biological details are good, his manner cool and clinical. He regarded mesmerism as a strange but legitimate new science. But the emotional charge of the story, which is the well-spring of its horrifying success, comes from the fact that Poe is here treading on his favourite unhallowed ground, the territory between life and death.

Cases could also be made out for the curious kind of time-travel in "A Tale of Ragged Mountains" or the mock psychiatry in "The System of Dr Tarr and Prof. Fether"; and there is Hans Pfaall's balloon journey to the Moon, painstakingly described; and *Arthur Gordon Pym*, to which we shall turn shortly.

But none of these triumph like those Poe mainliners of horror, "The Pit and the Pendulum", "The Tell-Tale Heart", "The Masque of the Red Death", the majestic "The Fall of the House of Usher", and so forth. And, on such a modest science fictional showing, Poe would receive little longer mention in a history of science fiction than his contemporaries and near contemporaries such as Brockden Brown, Hawthorne, and Oliver Wendell Holmes[10], born the same year as Poe. But there is more to Poe than this.

Beneath Poe's stage machinery, beneath the mock Gothic and his transplanted bits of a never-never Europe, beneath his melodrama, is a retreat from, a sabotaging of the so-called rational world in which he with such difficulty found his way. In his fiction, Poe discards most of the trappings of this world, its politics, its finances, its day-to-day affairs, and most of its people. For he knows of Another World. He cannot tell us where it is: perhaps it is beyond the tomb, perhaps in a lost continent, perhaps through a mirror, perhaps in another stage of mind, another time, another dimension. But he knows it is there.

This knowing and being unable to say—it is the essence of Poe, and lends a necessary ambiguity to what might otherwise seem too obvious. That remarkable prose poem, for instance, "The Masque of the Red Death"—what is it really about? Is the Red Death a plague like the Black Death? But the opening words of the tale appear to contradict this idea ("The 'Red Death' had long devastated the country. No pestilence had ever been so fatal, or so hideous. . . .") Could 'Red Death' be Poe's sardonic way of describing, not death, but life itself?[11] Remembering Poe's ecological interests, and his identification of the colour white with death, we may judge this reading tenable. The story is Poe's brilliant palindrome on life.

Knowing and being unable to say: it is for this reason that Poe's works are scattered with puzzles and cryptograms and cyphers[12], that baffling clock symbols recur again and again[13], that strange fragments of foreign tongues are put into the mouths of animals and birds[14], that he was fond of hoaxes[15], that he writes stories as articles, using the persona of first-person narrators[16], that he is full of tricks and curiosities[17], that his characters have speech impediments[18], that he could never master anything as long-winded as a novel. All his considerable eloquence points towards a central inarticulacy. He knew of Another World, and could express it only in symbols, with a slightly self-conscious mellifluousness.

It is in the techniques Poe developed to skirt this central inarticulacy that he has made most impact on other writers. The symbols he uses, the worm-riddled furniture of his sentences, appealed to Mallarmé, Valéry[19], and the Symbolists[20]; while his pervasive sense of something waiting just out of sight—in the wings, the tomb, or the head—has been reproduced in the writings of such authors as H. P. Lovecraft, Ray Bradbury, Richard Matheson, Robert Bloch, Harlan Ellison, Ramsey Campbell, Robert Aickman, and Stephen King. And, of course, in Bram Stoker's *Dracula*.

Consideration of Poe's work brings us to a consideration of the whole nature of fiction. We may regard fiction as play, though often play of a serious nature. When children play, they frequently imitate adult situations (mothers and fathers, or doctors), scaling them down so as to come to terms with potentially painful or threatening confrontations. Literature for adults reverses the effect: it produces a play situation in which painful or threatening confrontations are scaled up. This is true of both farce and tragedy.

Science fiction is a particular example of scaling, in which one of the axes of the graph is exaggerated, so that threatening situations become particularly precipitous: as if in compensation, the congruence with reality then becomes somewhat less. It is Poe's especial merit—shared with few other writers—that when he is at his best he threatens us with something never precisely defined, in which a part of us must compulsively believe. The resolution of the story leaves that belief intact.

Poe's game is one of literary hide-and-seek. It is too easy to say that he is obsessed with death. He is an obsessive writer, but the goal of his quest lies just beyond the clutch of death. The narrator in "MS. Found in a Bottle" says that he is "hurrying onwards to some exciting knowledge—some never-to-be imparted secret. . . .", and many of Poe's other characters are trapped in the same predicament. This it is which sets them apart from society. Their conscious minds dilate, they become, like Roderick Usher, possessed of extrasensory perceptions. The unsociable are in search of the unspeakable. Their knowledge, like Faust's, must be paid for dearly; its "attainment is destruction".

So Poe's heroes in extremis often find themselves in oddly similar situations, bathed in luminous meteorological phenomena (which may be accompanied by Poe's ubiquitous water symbols). The eponymous character in "Metzengerstein" is enveloped in "a glare of preternatural light" as he rides to destruction; the old Norwegian who describes his descent into the maelstrom sees, in the moments of crisis, "the rays of the moon" shining on "a thick mist in which everything there was enveloped"; the traveller to "the Domain of Arnheim" meets with "an effulgence that seems to wreathe the whole surrounding forest in flames"; just before Madeline Usher appears in her shroud and falls upon her brother, he sees "the unnatural light of a faintly luminous and distinctly visible gaseous exhalation which hung about and enshrouded the mansion"; while the wretched Arthur Gordon Pym, drawn towards that "shrouded human figure, very far larger in its proportions than any other dweller among man", is swept along while "out of the milky depths of the ocean a luminous glare arose", to disappear from our ken in a limitless cataract, without sound, which ranges along "the whole extent of the southern horizon". In "The Conversation of Eiros and Charmion" the entire Earth is snuffed out with the same lurid lighting effect: "the whole incumbent mass of ether . . . burst at once into a species of intense flame". That the Undefined should be a blaze of white light is at once a religious and a scientific concept. There are moments when Poe reminds us of another poor visionary, William Blake.

Knowing but being unable to say, Poe is forced to terminate his narrations with these veils of white. Only once does he venture further, in "The Colloquy of Monos and Una", then to return to his favoured theme of love in or beyond the grave. Yet a new universality is added. This time, the light is "*that* light which alone might have power to startle—the light of enduring *Love*." And the climax of the story carries us movingly into all time and space, away from material things!

> The sense of being had at length utterly departed, and there reigned in its stead—instead of all things—dominant and perpetual—the autocrats *Place* and *Time*. For *that* which *was not*—for that which had no form—for that which had not thought—for that which had no sentience—for that which was soulless, yet of which matter formed no portion—for all this nothingness, yet for all this immortality, the grave was still a home, and the corrosive hours, co-mates.

Such quests for the unknown and the infinite are very much in the science fictional vein. Yet the nearer Poe moves towards the actual trappings of science fiction, the less successful are his effects; such stories as "Mellonta Tauta", which is set in the year 2848 and contains cosmological speculations, and "The Thousand-and-Second Tale of Scheherazade", which shows how the Sultan put his wife to death for telling one extra and unbelievable story (which contains nothing but sober nineteenth-century technological achievements) are limp and jocular and without revelation, as are the descriptions of lunar landscape in "Hans Pfaall". It is as if Poe needed to master a science fictional mode but failed, seeing, despite himself, that there was no solution to his personal problems within the realm of science—or rather, within this life.

Yet Poe is of the limited company of the world's great short story tellers, and the short story hardly existed as a genre when he wrote, certainly not in America or England. He reached the largest international audience of any of his countrymen last century, proving—to paraphrase his own words—that terror was not of America but of the soul. He was an innovator in both content and form, and in more than one field, for tales such as "Thou Art the Man" and "The Gold-Bug", and his stories about Auguste Dupin ("The Murders in the Rue Morgue", "The Purloined Letter", and "The Mystery of Marie Roget") entitle him to be regarded as an originator of the tale of pure deduction and detection. His best stories—"The Fall of the House of Usher" is his masterpiece—are as alive today as when they were written.

In Poe, so extravagant is his method, success and failure lie close together. His longest work, *The Narrative of Arthur Gordon Pym*, finds room for both failure and success and, in its relationship to science fiction, merits closer inspection.

Pym, first published in 1836, is one of Poe's rare excursions away from the Great Indoors. It begins as a story of sea voyage and shipwreck, of stowaways and mutineers, of villainous cooks and men overboard, in the worst traditions of the sea. Poe also crams in a live burial, a man-eating dog, blood-drinking, cannibalism, an impersonation of a corpse (at which sight, one of the hardened villains of the crew falls back "stone dead"), and a sort of ghost ship manned by a crew of grotesque dead men.

To compensate for all this frantic activity by the author, his hero is as passive as a limbless child in a womb. Only when Pym gets aboard a second ship, the schooner *Jane Guy*, does the narrative gain other than risible interest. As the vessel sails for southern latitudes, the story takes on impetus and becomes SF.

There is a reminder of Coleridge's great poem as the *Jane Guy* makes her way among the ice floes of the Antarctic. The captain hopes to find new lands to the south; Poe responds to the theme of the quest, his prose tightens, and we take in our stride polar bears and an increasingly warm climate, for now we are embarked on a marvellous voyage.

The schooner arrives at an island called Tsalal, on which everything is black— another colour reversal, as in "The Masque of the Red Death"—soil, vegetation, birds, and human beings, the latter being "the most wicked, hypocritical, vindictive, bloodthirsty, and altogether fiendish race of men upon the face of the globe". These people have black teeth; their fear of anything white extends even to flour and the pages of a book. Not unnaturally in these circumstances, they kill all the crew of the schooner—except Pym and a fiendish half-caste, who escape massacre by accident.

Pym and the half-caste find themselves at the bottom of the words of God (another cryptogram), graven deep into the rocks. They manage to climb out of this tangible evidence of the world's damnation and get away from the island in a canoe. It is then that they are swept "with a hideous velocity" over the face of the ocean towards that never-to-be-imparted secret ahead, where there is "a chaos of flitting and indistinct images". That shrouded figure, larger than any man, looms out of the unknown. They rush towards it. The screen goes white.

After its abysmal beginning *Pym* is marvellous Poe, atmospheric and baffling. It is useless to complain that the end is unsatisfying, or that Poe makes no connections (as Henry James complained); if God speaks only in cryptograms, how should Edgar Allan Poe be more explicit? Pym has reached the end of his quest, and that is that. Destruction is all we may expect—the common and often desired lot of a Poe hero!

Pym is an early model of a Poe hero, the alienated man. Leslie Fiedler[21] calls *Pym* "the archetypal American story, which would be recast in *Moby-Dick* and *Huckleberry Finn*". Even allowing that the inner meaning of *Pym*—as Fiedler sees it—rests on a fear of black men, a hatred of women, or a longing for the womb, or all three, and that the whole thing is a parody to boot, it is a remarkably ill-executed, blemished, and melodramatic narrative. If Poe had conceived a science fictional form more clearly, he could have cast the story more effectively. This stricture applies to most of his few other gestures towards the genre.

Poe pre-empted a science fictional content, particularly its transcendental content, yet mishandled its form, owing to perverse qualities in his own temperament. Far from being the Father of Science Fiction, this genius bodged it when he confronted its themes directly. Yet he brought off some of its best effects, more or less when looking the other way.

For Poe's is the power to flood a dismal scene with burning light and show us a man on his own besieged by a malignant power he can scarcely understand, let alone master. The evil that confronts the Poeian protagonist is not simply external; it is a part of his destiny, if not of himself. This is not an untruthful view of reality. Later science fiction authors who change the terms of Poe's equation, making the protagonists gigantic and heroic, conquering the universe, or making the evil purely external—and so cast in opposition to an innocent mankind—falsify reality. Poe may exaggerate; but, in these respects at least, it is the truth he exaggerates.

The Gothic mode—itself a branch of the Romantic movement—took deeper root and flourished longer in the United States than elsewhere. Its characteristic ingredients—ruined landscapes, haunted characters, persecuted females, the flight from domesticity—might change in the hands of successive practitioners, from Charles Brockden Brown, Fenimore Cooper, and Nathaniel Hawthorne, through Melville, to William Faulkner, John Steinbeck, and Tennessee Williams, but were never abandoned, as witness Stephen King's novels.

These characteristics appear most strikingly in a sub-genre, the Western, the first literary form to find its true strength in another medium: as film. In the cinema, with dusty cow towns taking the place of Renaissance piles and the dated personae of monks, aristocrats, and torturers transformed into sheriffs, good guys, and outlaws, the Western became a vehicle for the endless discussion of the role of the individual and law and order in society. So universal is its appeal that Ranch-House Gothic is one of America's gifts to the rest of the world.

The other remarkable sub-genre is science fiction. As cinema, on the large screen, it first rivalled then surpassed the Western in popularity. In modern America, the spaceship has overtaken the stage-coach. The stranger in town is probably back from the future.

On the printed page, science fiction has proliferated enormously. Its special success is to have diversified the Gothic tale of terror in such a way as to encompass those fears generated by change and the technological advances which are the chief agents of change.

On the VDU, science fiction has become the predominant language of adventure; we are space pilots before we are teenagers.

In role-playing games, SF and fantasy have exploded into psychotherapy.

In all media, Gothic comes belting back in technological armour.

The Renaissance piles are transformed to subterranean war rooms, fortresses on distant worlds, cities under limitless oceans, or overblown metropolises, hundreds of thousands of years into the future.[22] The Gothic impulse is still at work and, behind it, Burke's dictum about beauty and the sublime, which inspired awe and terror!

It is this holocaust of Gothic which leads to the sort of confusion whereby critics can claim that all or most nineteenth-century authors wrote at least some science fiction. Washington Irving, Melville, Oliver Wendell Holmes, Silas Weir Mitchell, Ambrose Bierce, Mark Twain, Henry James, and all—all are called to serve! Perhaps some of the territorial ambitions which would seek to draw Dante, Shakespeare, and the author of Genesis into the ranks of science fiction writers are at work. We have to recognize that science fiction is a mode, identity uncertain. However often the features that make it attractive are espied elsewhere, these are features it has imitated and adapted. The converse applies rarely.

Once this distinction is grasped, we have less trouble in perceiving where science fiction begins and ends. In the past, inordinately large claims have been made for the genre—one thinks, laughingly, of Robert A. Heinlein's dictum: "For the survival and health of the human race one crudely written science fiction story containing a single worth-while new idea is more valuable than a bookcaseful of beautifully written non-science fiction."[23] This is to rate Dick above Dickens, or Priest above Proust.

But, with modesty and realism intervening, we are now able to turn to those earlier writers, the Pilgrim Fathers, whose speculations on an unfolding world about them make them still so attractive, and enjoy their works as cathedrals of an earlier epoch, whose stones were often appropriated for the hastier buildings of later ages. Although they stand outside the science fiction field, no history of science fiction would make sense without reference to them.

CHAPTER III

Honourable Ancestors:
Good Places and Other Places

> I was questioning him . . . and had incautiously said, "Of
> course I realise it's all rather too vague for you to put into
> words," when he took me up rather sharply . . . by saying,
> "On the contrary it is words that are vague. The reason why the
> thing can't be expressed is that it's too *definite* for language."
> —C. S. Lewis: *Perelandra*

It is impossible to list in one chapter the honourable ancestors to whom the
science fiction field pays lip service, if nothing more. Each writer, in his way,
sought the thing of which C. S. Lewis spoke, something too definite for
language, something strange which we feel close to us. The thing was sought in
many different places.

When we launch ourselves on these earlier seas of speculative thought, our
finest catches will be in the eighteenth century.

The eighteenth century was the age of the Enlightenment, the century when
the viewpoints of Romanticism came to be formulated. A continuity exists
between the eighteenth century and the present day which we can readily
appreciate, and not only because from that time onwards new knowledge was
regarded as cumulative and inherently verifiable by experiment. A vague but
crucial barrier had gone down in human minds. The nature of civilization had
been transformed by science, and by one science in particular, the science of
astronomy. It is not for nothing that of all the sciences astronomy has dominated
science fiction. The perception represents a fundamental truth. Copernicus,
Kepler, Galileo, altered the European—and hence the World—mind. They
altered it by painstaking observation and by an aggregation of facts rather than
fiats. We live off their earnings.

Systematic observation favoured the invention of better instrumentation, and
vice versa. Science began to move forward, thought to change.

Isaac Newton is best remembered for his theory of universal gravitation,
which sought to explain the natural world in terms of a single physical
principle.[1] One modern commentator says of Newton, "He gave men grounds
for hoping that the mysteries of nature could, given time, all be explained,
because they must be manifestations not of incomprehensible, arbitrary will,
but of ordered, regular principles. In the end, those principles might reveal even
the nature of the Creator himself."[2] Such understanding is in Victor Frankenstein's mind as he says, "When I considered the improvement which every day

takes place in science and mechanics, I was encouraged to hope my present attempts would at least lay the foundations of future success . . . It was with these feelings that I began the creation of a human being." (Chapter IV)

Before this time, such perilous meditations were impossible. True science fiction was impossible.

As we have seen, Poe had trouble with the *form* of his science fiction. In most of his forays into the genre, we witness him abandoning his usual Gothic-fiction narrative line, employing instead a sort of straightforward didacticism thinly disguised as fiction, or served up as dialogue; examples are "Mellonta Tauta", "The Colloquy of Monos and Una", and "The Conversation of Eiros and Charmion".

In this, Poe shows kinship with his literary ancestors, the utopianists, the marvellous-voyagers, and the moralists who use the fantastic to make their point. These older writers do not seek to involve us in the sufferings of their heroes by tricks of suspense and character-drawing, as do Ann Radcliffe and her heirs; their intentions lie elsewhere. This holds true even when we look back towards the beginning of the Christian Era to Lucian of Samosata.

The dialogue form of his *Icaro-Menippus* reminds us that Lucian had something of the Socratic spirit. In the *True History*, some of the episodes—particularly the ones in which the adventurers are swallowed, ship and all, by a whale—look forward to Baron Munchausen, as well as back to the tall stories in Homer; while the spirit of Aristophanes's comedies presides fitfully over the whole.

Mention of Socrates and Aristophanes must suffice to recall the truism that much is owed to the Greeks, in science fiction as in science and civilization generally. Many of the staple themes of science fiction were familiar to the Greeks.

Plato's *Republic*, cast in the form of Socratic dialogue, ranks as the first utopia. Aristophanes' comedies sprout utopian ideas and fantastic notions. In his play *The Birds*, war-weary citizens join the fowls of the air in making a Cloud-cuckooland between heaven and earth, and the birds become masters of the universe. In the *Lysistrata* we find a theme which has proved viable in this century, where the women refuse to let their men have sexual intercourse with them until the war is brought to a close. In *The Frogs*, Aristophanes takes his audience on an excursion into another world—to Hell. In *Peace*, performed first for an Athens that had been ten years at war, Trygaeus rides up to heaven on the back of a giant beetle to see Zeus. (Perhaps Lucian was thinking of this flight when his Menippus also ascends.)

Such flights of fantasy, permissible in comedy, were forbidden in tragedy. So it still is today.

In the *True History*, waterspouts and winds carry a Greek ship to the Moon, which proves to be inhabited. The travellers find that the King of the Moon and the King of the Sun are at war over the colonization of Jupiter. Fantastic monsters are employed in the battles; and the minions of the Sun build a double wall between Sun and Moon, so that the Selenites live in permanent eclipse. They surrender.

One of the clauses of the peace treaty is that both sides shall send a colony to the Morning Star (Venus). The travellers sail their ship to the new colony and then steer for the Zodiac, leaving the Sun to port, until they reach Lycnopolis, a city inhabited by lamps that speak. They also see Cloudcuckooland, witness a battle of giants, and visit a city built of gold and precious stones. Later, they come to the Isle of Dreams, where Antiphon invents dreams of different kinds:

> Some long, beautiful and pleasant, others little and ugly; there are likewise some golden ones, others poor and mean; some winged and of an immense size, others tricked out as it were for pomps and ceremonies, for gods and kings; some we met with that we had seen at home; these came up to and saluted us as their old acquaintance, whilst others putting us first to sleep, treated us most magnificently, and promised that they would make us kings and noblemen; some carried us into our own country, showed us our friends and relations, and brought us back again the same day. Thirty days and nights we remained in this place, being most luxuriously feasted, and fast asleep all the time. . . .[3]

Thus the first portrayal of a Dream Palace, which has made several appearances in the fiction of our day.

Many translators of Lucian, anxious to preserve the pure Anglo-Saxon world from dirty Mediterranean habits, have omitted the more titillating passages from his text—for instance his description of the custom of Lunar inhabitants of wearing artificial private parts, which apparently work well. The rich have theirs made of ivory, the poor ones of wood. This phallic ingenuity establishes Lucian's claim to be, not only the first writer of interplanetary fiction, but the first writer to describe prosthetic limbs and cyborgs.

Lucian's tales are now perceived as pure fantasy, although for centuries they were highly regarded as speculative fiction. An example of these attitudes in transition occurs in a little Victorian edition of Lucian's two trips to the Moon (Cassell's National Library). This edition contains the following editorial footnote with supplement by a later editor, inserted at the point in the text where the travellers observe Earth hanging in the lunar sky like a Moon: "Modern astronomers are, I think, agreed that we are to the moon just the same as the moon is to us. Though Lucian's history may be false, therefore his philosophy, we see, was true (1780). (The moon is not habitable, 1887.)" The disappointments of progress. . . .

We no longer expect anything but entertainment from Lucian, and that he still provides.

Under the drift of centuries, interplanetary voyages were forgotten. Spiritual voyages were another matter. The progression of mankind in his frail coracle of civilization is itself a spiritual voyage, which naturally finds its embodiment in tales of difficult journeyings. But the finest mediaeval minds were in quest for a unity between life on Earth and the Heavenly Father. In the words of Sir

Kenneth Clark, "Behind all the fantasy of the Gothic imagination, mediaeval man could see things very clearly, but he believed that . . . appearances should be considered as nothing more than symbols or tokens of an ideal order, which was the only true reality."[4]

Perhaps the form of those times closest to science fiction was the bestiary, derived from Greek sources, in which animals were endowed with human attributes and enacted moral or satirical tales, like aliens in today's science fiction. The history of Reynard the Fox is the best known of these tales in English-speaking countries, thanks to a translation printed by Caxton in 1481. Reynard and Chanticleer the Cock also figure in Chaucer's "Nun's Priest's Tale" in *The Canterbury Tales*. Another popular beast was *The Golden Ass* of Apuleius, a contemporary of Lucian. This is a satire in which a man is turned into an ass and tells the tale of the follies and vices of his various owners. The transformation takes place accidentally, through the carelessness of an enchantress's servant. Such tales, always plentiful, take us too close to magic and too far from science fiction.

Came the dawn of the Renaissance, men developed new ways in which to think and feel. They rediscovered the classical past and, among the tally of its treasures, the writings of its poets, historians, and philosophers, including Lucian.

Lucian's writings in Greek and Latin ran through several editions in the late fifteenth and sixteenth centuries, and in 1634 were translated into English by Francis Hicks. The translation was widely read; the influence on later writers, both of the *True History* and *Icaro-Menippus*, was considerable. Lucian is said to have inspired Rabelais's *Voyages of Pantagruel*, Cyrano de Bergerac's *Voyage dans la Lune*, and Swift's *Gulliver's Travels*. No doubt all those eminent authors read their great predecessor avidly, for writers instinctively seek out others of their own persuasion; but there is a great deal of difference between imitation and emulation, and the most original authors often begin on premises laid down by others. Thus, Lucian himself conceived the *True History* as a parody of those Greek historians who magnified every detail into something grander than it began; while Swift's *Gulliver's Travels* began as a minute lampoon on the politics of Queen Anne's reign. Great authors appropriate; little authors steal.

The early seventeenth century was a fantastic age, a time of great voyages and discoveries; of the writing of utopias and death-enriched plays; of a widening universe and the first use of the decimal point; of the sailing of the Pilgrim Fathers; of the discovery of the circulation of the blood and the invention of cribbage; of the founding of colleges and universities, the establishment of colonies, and the perfection of the flintlock. Exploration clearly had an appeal and may be blamed for the increase in fictitious Moon voyages.

Kepler's *Somnium* (or *Dream*) was published in Frankfurt in the same year as Hicks's translation of Lucian. Kepler had then been dead four years. Johannes Kepler (1571–1630) was the German mathematician, astrologer and astronomer who laid the foundations of modern astronomy. Kepler's narrative is cast as a dream, and his observer, Duracotus, ascends to the Moon by supernatural means. On the Moon, however, science takes over, and Duracotus expatiates on that globe as recently revealed by telescope. Cold and heat are more extreme than on Earth. There are dreadful nights a fortnight long, unrelieved by moonlight. As the climate differs from Earth, so does the landscape: mountains are higher, valleys deeper. The ground is perforated by caves and grottoes. Cloud cover and rain prevail over the near side of the lunar globe.

Although Kepler introduces life to the Moon, the living things are made to conform to the lunar environment. They are not drawn in detail; an impression of variety and grotesquery is given. One sentence allows a foretaste of Wells's *First Men in the Moon*: "Things born in the ground—they are sparse on the ridges of the mountains—generally begin and end their lives on the same day, with new generations springing up daily."[5]

We acknowledge this as fantasy now. But Kepler conformed to his own hard-won scientific theories. That claim of scientific accuracy was made on behalf of Jules Verne, two centuries later, as if it were a great novelty.

Kepler had a scientific vision of the Moon; his *Somnium* is straightforward astronomical exposition. He established no utopias there. But utopias were still being built.

The conjunction of wonderful voyages with utopias is of long standing; once a writer has got his travellers to his obscure region on Earth, or to another world, or to the future, he must find something for them to do. On the whole writers divide fairly sharply between those who have their protagonist lecture and listen to lectures, and those who have them menaced by or menacing local equivalents of flora, fauna, and Homo sapiens.

If this division of interest is still with us, at least the problem of how to reach the Moon has been solved. It has in actuality proved far more costly than any storyteller ever dared guess. Lunar-voyage devices come very inexpensively until we reach the days of Verne and Wells and, even then, the Baltimore Gun Club can finance its own vehicle, while Cavor has comfortable private means. Before those days, nature, or a balloon, could be relied on to do the trick at minimum expense.

Supernatural means of travel were the cheapest of all. Athanasius Kircher, in his *Itinerarium Exstaticum* of 1656, produced an angel who takes the chief protagonist on a Grand Tour of the heavens to complete his education—a pleasant idea that could still be made to work fictionally today.

Another means of travel which proved cost effective was to ascend with the aid of birds; Bishop Francis Godwin's *Man in the Moone: or A Discourse of a Voyage Thither by Domingo Gonsales* appeared in 1638 and remained popular for something like two centuries. Godwin's Gonsales trains swans until, by degrees, they learn to carry him through the air. The swans or "gansas", twenty-five of them teamed together, save Gonsales from shipwreck. Unfortunately, Gonsales has overlooked the migratory habits of gansas, and his team carries him to the moon, where gansas hibernate.

Gonsales finds the lunar world a utopia inhabited by giants. The giants are long-lived and any wounds they receive quickly heal again; even if you get your head cut off, apply a certain herb and it will join together once more. Murders are unknown, along with all other crimes; while the women are so beautiful that (claims Gonsales) no man ever wants to leave his wife. This peaceful state of affairs comes about because the Moon-dwellers detect potential sinners at birth and ship them off to Earth, where most of them are deposited in North America (the first appearance of an idea to enjoy fresh currency in twentieth-century fiction).

Despite these delights, and the beautiful colours on the Moon, Gonsales wants to get back to his family. The Prince Pylonas gives him jewels, he sets off for Earth with his gansas—and lands in China, where he is imprisoned as a magician.

In the same year that Godwin's pleasant fiction was published, John Wilkins's *Discovery of a New World in the Moone* appeared. This is a speculative work concerning the possibilities of travelling to the Moon, with discussions of what life there might be like—what we could call popular science. As with Godwin's book, it was immensely popular. The times were ripe for it and, with many a reference back to Daedalus, the more *au fait* citizens of the seventeenth and eighteenth centuries began to discuss the possibilities of flight.

Wilkins's book influenced many, including the remarkable Margaret Cavendish, a friend of Wilkins, who teased him about his imaginary flight. That forgotten but admirable lady is truly an honourable ancestor of Mary Shelley.

Probably other women wrote something like early science fiction, which further research will reveal. The present authors' researches have turned up the once-illustrious name of Margaret Cavendish, Duchess of Newcastle, born Margaret Lucas in the Year of Our Lord, 1623. According to Samuel Pepys and others, she was an eccentric as well as a fashionable beauty. All of London turned out to see her when she was received at Court by Charles II. She died in 1673, having survived both the Great Plague and the Great Fire.

Margaret Cavendish was interested in science. She argued with Thomas Hooke over his experimental methods. Her *Philosophical Letters: or, Modest Reflections upon some Opinions in Natural Philosophy* was published in 1664. It is a response to the works of Hobbes, Descartes, and others. Her strong analytical mind preferred "untrammelled speculation" to the growing experimentation of her age. To this end, she published *Observations upon Experimental Philosophy* in 1666, the year of the Great Fire of London. To which, as an appendix, she added a short (160 page) book entitled *The Description of a New World, called The Blazing World*, published separately in 1668. This she referred to as "meerly Fancy; or (as I may call it) Fantastical".

Halfway down page two, we are already in the blazing world. A young man absconds with his lover in a ship, which is blown northwards in a great tempest. At the pole, it passes through a bridge between this world and the blazing one, which is very close. The blazing world has its own sun, but the brightness of ours stops us seeing it. The two worlds are balanced pole-to-pole.

The blazing world is a place full of creatures half-man, half-beast: bee-men, wolf-men, bear-men, etc., rather like Dr Moreau's island. Margaret Cavendish had a very avant-garde notion that we might be ruled over by a non-human—animal—Intelligence. The capital of her world is called Paradise, entered only by a labyrinthine gate; it is a place of reason and riches. This allows the duchess to conduct a kind of utopian exercise, arguing about the greed and avarice which exist in our own world.

In her introduction to this remarkable piece of speculation, the author declares, "That though I cannot be Henry the Fifth, or Charles the Second; yet I will endeavour to be, Margaret the First: and, though I have neither Power, Time, nor Occasion, to be a great Conqueror, like Alexander, or Caesar; yet, rather than not be Mistress of a World, since Fortune and the Fates would give me none, I have made One of my own."

A reasonable apologia for a private universe.

This eagerness to extend our dimension of experience is often mocked; yet it lies deep in many hearts, and is summed up in John Keats's words, "Ever let the fancy roam, Pleasure never is at home." In present context, Milton perhaps puts it better: "Headlong joy is ever on the wing."

We prize the imaginative leap. Nevertheless, imagination and originality, like their more prosaic brother, logic, progress best by short steps. Only by these short steps can we trace what is daring and worthwhile (as opposed to what is merely daring) in science fiction.

From imagining wings which would assist human flight it is a short step to imagining humans born with wings. Robert Paltock's *The Life and Adventures of Peter Wilkins* appeared in 1751, and remained in demand for many years. Shipwrecked, Peter Wilkins discovers the country of flying men and women. He marries a woman called Youwarkee, and the loving pair rear seven children, some winged, some not, rather on Mendelian principles.

Also in 1751, *The Life and Astonishing Adventures of John Daniel*, by Ralph Morris, was published, in which human flight is achieved by a veritable "engine", a platform on which two can stand and work the wings by means of levers; John Daniel and his son Jacob take themselves up to the Moon in this machine.

The daftest way of getting to the Moon was the one chosen by Cyrano de Bergerac, in *Voyage dans la lune*, a comic history first published in 1657, to be followed later by *L'histoire des états et empires du soleil*. The two are known together as *L'autre monde*.[6]

Cyrano makes himself his own hero, and fastens a quantity of small bottles filled with dew to his body. The Sun sucks him up with the dew, and he lands on the Moon in a couple of paragraphs.

So begins the jolliest of all lunar books, with Cyrano spouting unlikely explanations for amazing phenomena for all the world like a modern SF writer. He does the same in the second book, when he lands on the Sun, glibly explaining why he has no appetite in space, why the Sun's heat does not burn, what causes sleep, how he became invisible, how the inhabitants of the Sun grow from the ground in a sort of spontaneous generation, and so forth.

Cyrano meets Campanella, author of *Civitas Solis*, and together they encounter a woman whose husband has committed a crime which makes the arguments of modern anti-abortionists seem tame.

"Since you are a philosopher," replied the woman, addressing Campanella, "I must unburden my heart to you before I go any further.

"To explain the matter that brings me here in a few words, you must know that I am coming to complain of a murder committed against the person of my youngest child. This barbarian, whom I have here, killed it twice over, although he was its father."

We were extremely puzzled by this speech and asked to know what she meant by a child killed twice over.

"You must know that in our country," the woman replied, "there is, among the other Statutes of Love, a law which regulates the number of embraces a husband may give his wife. That is why every evening each doctor goes the rounds of all the houses in his area, where, after examining the husbands and wives, he will prescribe for them, according to their good or bad health, so many conjunctions for the night. Well, my husband had been put down for seven. However, angered by some rather haughty remarks I had addressed to him as we were getting ready to retire, he did not come near me all the time we were in bed. But God, who avenges those who are wronged, permitted this wretch to be titillated in a dream by the recollection of the embraces he was unjustly denying me, so that he let a man go to waste.

"I told you that his father had killed him twice over, because by refusing to make him come into existence, he caused him not to be, which was the first murder, but subsequently he caused him never to be able to be, which was the second. A Common murderer knows that the man whose days he cuts short *is no more*, but none of them could cause a man *never to have been*. Our magistrates would have dealt with him as he deserved if the cunning wretch had not excused himself by saying that he would have fulfilled his conjugal duty, had he not been afraid (as a result of embracing me in the height of the rage I had put him in) to beget a choleric man."

Cyrano is known to a wide audience as the comic character in Rostand's successful but meretricious play, *Cyrano de Bergerac*. But there are no difficulties for a modern reader in the enjoyment of his Moon and Sun books, unless the reader himself puts them there by expecting a coherent philosophy. This Cyrano does not provide. What he does provide is a conspectus of all the exciting prospects opened up by contemporary science and exploration.

For Cyrano (1619–55) is a younger contemporary of the English poet, John Donne (1572–1631), another man who celebrated the fact that "The new philosophie calls all in doubt". Donne could not quite bring himself to believe in the Copernican system; but all theories could be pressed to serve his metaphysical wit. As a recent biographer says, "The fact is, he did not care whether the new theories were true or not, so long as they supplied material for his speculation. He wanted to feel free to entertain or dismiss them."[7] This pleasant confusion remains true of our minds today. How are we as individuals to verify or deny the latest astrophysical theories? I suspect it was the same with Cyrano.

On the Moon, Cyrano is escorted by the Demon of Socrates, some of whose remarks retain their original force, penetrating to the heart of curiosity and its limitations.

> "If there is something you men cannot understand [says the Demon of Cyrano], you either imagine that it is spiritual or that it does not exist. Both conclusions are quite false. The proof of this is the fact that there are perhaps a million things in the universe which you would need a million quite different organs to know. Myself, for example, I know from my senses what attracts the lodestone to the pole, how the tides pull the sea, and what becomes of an animal after its death."

All writers of fantastic tales feed on their predecessors. Swift took a pinch of wit from Cyrano—about whose book Geoffrey Strachan, its translator, justly says, it "is a poem from an age when poetry, physics, metaphysics, and astronomy could all still exist side by side in one book".

There is no need to detail further flights of fancy to the Moon. Marjorie Hope Nicolson has produced a definitive account[8], readable and scholarly, of the subject, which is hardly likely to be bettered. Philip Gove has defined the genre and provided a list of two hundred and fifteen such voyages published in the eighteenth century alone.[9]

It may be that we still have need of utopias. Or it could be that the belief that mankind can create a perfect state for itself, like the current belief in the right of every individual to perfect happiness, causes misery by the falsity of its assumptions. However that may be, we revere the great utopias as attempts to improve our lot, on paper if nowhere else. As Bernard Shaw said, perfection has been achieved only on paper.

Utopianism or its opposite is present in every vision of the future. There is little point in inventing a future state unless it contrasts in some way with our present one.

This is not to claim that the great utopias are science fiction. Far from it. Their intentions are generally moral or political. But they point to a better world in which the follies of our world are eliminated or suppressed.

Plato's *Republic*, written four centuries before the Christian era, concerns itself with justice and injustice, and with the ideal state, which Plato makes a city-state like Athens. "Our purpose in founding the city was not to make any one class in it surpassingly happy, but to make the city as a whole as happy as possible."

The society of this state is divided into three classes: the ruling class, who are virtuous because wise; a guardian class, consisting of public officials and so on; and the workers and tradesmen. Slaves are taken for granted. They are the androids and brief chronicles of their time.

Great emphasis is laid on education. Private property is abolished, and the state controls marriage and child-bearing.

Nowadays, we are sceptical of such arrangements. The *Republic* would work, we feel, only if all its inhabitants were over fifty years old. The place lacks two items on which we set great store, passion and a check on the activities of our rulers.

Nevertheless, the influence of Plato remains, a part of our rich inheritance. Incidentally, the *Republic* includes Plato's striking image for ignorance and the perception of reality, the great extended metaphor of the prisoners in the cave, who can see only the shadows of real objects, cast on the wall of the cave. (Book vii)

Utopias sometimes took on dialogue form. This is the case with Sir Thomas More's *Utopia*, from which the form derives its name. The word means "no place" or, arguably, "good place". More's *Utopia* was first published in Latin in 1516 and translated into English in 1551 after More's death by beheading in 1535.

More's England was a place of ferocious injustice. Such notions as freedom of speech were unheard of. More himself was not even allowed freedom of silence by his King (as Robert Bolt's play, *A Man for All Seasons*, later made into a film, bore out). Such conditions should be kept in mind when we read *Utopia*.

Utopia, for all its originality, owed more than its form to Plato's work, then almost two thousand years old.

> "Now am I like to Plato's city
> Whose fame flieth the world through"

Utopianists, like town-planners, wish to produce something that is orderly and functions well. Citizens have to fit into this pattern as into a town plan. More's Utopia is quite a friendly and sensible place, yet its restrictions often sound a chilly note to readers who live in a world of flourishing police states.

When More's Utopians go outdoors, they all wear the same kind of cloak, of one colour. There are a number of cities in Utopia, but all are alike; "whoso knoweth one of them knoweth them all". Citizens must get a licence to travel from one city to another. Furthermore, "dice-play and such other foolish and pernicious games they know not". Farewell, Earth's bliss! Goodbye, Las Vegas! It is of small consolation to learn that they "use two games not much unlike the chess".

More offers higher things. His little world has sane laws and is wisely ruled. The citizens have fine gardens and hospitals. Bondmen perform all the drudgery, mercenaries fight all the wars. Conversation, music and banquets are welcome, although ale houses and stews are forbidden, as is astrology. Many passages show the human side of More, not least in the question of courtship.

> For a sad and honest matron sheweth the woman, be she maid or widow, naked to the wooer. And likewise a sage and discreet man exhibiteth the wooer naked to the woman . . . The endowments of the body cause the

virtues of the mind more to be esteemed and regarded, yea, even in the marriages of wise men.

This proves a useful precaution—breakers of wedlock are sternly dealt with in Utopia. (Campanella has matings arranged by the state.) Utopia is a religious land and, although one's own faith may be followed without persecution, only the pious are allowed to teach children and adolescents.

Such sober and worthy plans as More's for a better life on Earth have become remote from us nowadays; our belief in the perfectibility of man and the triumph of altruism over self-interest is less strong than was the case in earlier centuries; a desperate environmentalism has become the new utopianism.

We have seen the noble line of utopias—such as Johann Valentin Andrea's *Christianopolis* (1619), Francis Bacon's *The New Atlantis* (1627), Tommaso Campanella's *Civitas Solis* (*City of the Sun*) (1623) (an instrument of his radical political campaigning, for which he was several times imprisoned), James Harrington's *The Commonwealth of Oceana* (1656), and those of the nineteenth century, such as Samuel Butler's *Erewhon* (1872), W. H. Hudson's *A Crystal Age* (1887), and Edward Bellamy's *Looking Backward* (1888)—we have seen this noble line of utopias slide down like sinking liners into the cold depths of dystopianism. This dire progression is epitomized by Yevgeny Zamyatin's *We* (1920) and Orwell's *1984* (1949). Morality, the system whereby man controls himself, has become another weapon in the state armoury, whereby it controls its citizens.

Most utopias start with a description of the journey there. The travel element is important, whether by ship as in More's *Utopia* or by time machine to some future state. Movement is a biped's *sine qua non*. As I. F. Clarke says, "The fabulous element was a necessary constituent of the seventeenth-century utopias. Even at their most perceptive and original, as in *The New Atlantis*, the authors concerned themselves with aspirations rather than with anticipations."[10]

A decline in the general belief in political systems; a profound questioning of the effects of technology; even the retreat from so much as lip service towards established religion; these are some of the factors which render unlikely the creation of utopias in the immediate future. Aldous Huxley's *Island* (1962)—in common with its distinguished predecessors, more a polemic than a novel—may be among the last of the considerable utopias until the world climate alters. Even on Huxley's well-favoured island the people sustain themselves with drugs and acknowledge how transient is the *status quo*, threatened with immediate collapse by the end of the book.

The trouble with utopias is that they are too orderly. They rule out the irrational in man, and the irrational is the great discovery of the last hundred years. They may be fantasy, but they reject fantasy as part of man—and this is a criticism which applies to most of the eighteenth-century literature with which we deal in this chapter. However appealing they may be, there is no room in them for the phenomenon of a Shakespeare—or even a Lovecraft.

And yet, among the distinguished seventeenth-century utopias, there is one which could almost contain both Shakespeare and Lovecraft, as well as E. E. Smith for that matter. Of course, we have to stretch our terms somewhat to think of John Milton's *Paradise Lost* (1667) as a utopia, but of the power of this great poem there is no doubt. Particularly appealing are its vistas of an unspoilt Earth, while the passages which deal with Hell, and Satan's lonely flight from Hell across the gulfs of space to God's new world, retain their magnificence. Satan in particular is as puissant as a present-day Apollo when he

> Springs upward like a pyramid of fire
> Into the wild expanse, and through the shock
> Of fighting elements, on all sides round
> Environ'd, wins his way. (Book II)

Like his near contemporary, John Donne, Milton infuses his poetry with "the New Philosophie".

From Milton's imagined worlds and exalted poetry, we bring ourselves back to Earth with the aid of Peter Wilkins, the adventurer who married a winged lady and had seven children by her. Paltock's *The Life and Adventures of Peter Wilkins* remained popular for so many years that it was played as a pantomime at Sadler's Wells when Dickens was a boy.

Wilkins's adventures encompass another science fictional device, the subterranean journey which discovers human beings living underground. Later—and not much later—this gambit will develop into journeys to the centre of the Earth.

Wilkins's ship gets into trouble near Africa. A strong and remorseless current draws it towards the South Pole and eventually through an archway under an island, into a strange underground world. "I could perceive the boat to fall with incredible violence, as I thought, down a precipice, and suddenly whirled round and round with me, the water roaring on all sides, and dashing against the rock with a most amazing noise." The boat drifts in complete darkness down a subterranean river, delivering Wilkins into an immense cavern, where flying people live.

Here is more than one incident found later in Poe. The subterranean descent also carries reminders of a book published ten years before *Peter Wilkins*—Holberg's *A Journey to the World Underground*. Holberg's is one of the books, together with Campanella's utopia, *The City of the Sun*, which Poe lists as being in Roderick Usher's library—"the books which, for years, had formed no small portion of the mental existence of the invalid".

In turn, Holberg's work owes much to *Gulliver's Travels*, as well as to such earlier subterranean voyages as Athanasius Kircher's *Mundus Subterraneus* of 1665. But Holberg has curious ideas of his own.

Baron Ludvig Holberg was born in Bergen, Norway, in 1684. He was a great traveller, and his writings, particularly his plays, brought him fame. I was pleasantly surprised to find one of his comedies being performed in an obscure corner of Austria a year or so ago.

Nicolai Klimii Iter Subterraneum (Holberg wrote it in Latin) was first published in Germany in 1741. It won immediate popularity and was translated and published—and is still being translated and published—into many languages.

Again a travel element predominates. Niels Klim is potholing in the mountains near Bergen when he falls down a steep shaft, and keeps falling for some time, for all the world like Alice. He emerges into a wonderland no less remarkable than Alice's, tumbling into the space at the centre of the Earth to become one more heavenly body circling about a central Sun.

Klim lands unhurt on the planet Nazar, which proves to be amazingly like Earth, except that night is almost as light as day. "Nay, the night may be thought more grateful than the day, for nothing can be conceived more bright and splendid than that light which the solid firmament receives from the sun and reflects back upon the planet, insomuch that it looks (if I may be allowed the expression) like one universal moon." Another difference from Earth is that the intelligent species on Nazar is a sort of perambulating tree.

This novelty is rather a distraction than otherwise, since, apart from their arboreality, the creatures serve a similar function to Swift's Lilliputians and Brobdingnagians: to make reasonable man reflect on his own unreasonableness, and to make what appears natural seem topsy-turvy. Trees do not effectively serve didactic purposes. Their bark is better than their bite.

The trees exhibit local differences from land to land. Their paradoxes are paraded for Klim in a series of mini-utopias: farmers are the most highly regarded citizens in one land; in another, the more honour the state piles on a citizen, the more he acts with humility, since "he was the greatest debtor to the commonwealth"; in another, only the young are allowed to govern, for the older people grow the more wanton and voluptuous they become; and so on.

In one of the most curious countries, the inhabitants never sleep. As a result, they are always in a hurry and confusion, and are obsessed by details. Klim looks into a local bookshop and notices a *Description of the Cathedral* in twenty-four volumes, and *Of the Use of the Herb Slac* in thirteen volumes. None of these curious situations is developed as Holberg flicks them past our eyes like colour slides. Klim is involved in them, for the most part, merely as observer.

Some adventures befall Klim. He is banished by bird to the Firmament, which he finds full of monkeys. There he is wooed by an attractive lady monkey. "I thought it better to be exposed to the vengeance of disappointed love than to disturb the laws of human nature by mixing my blood with a creature not of the human species."

The slings and arrows of outrageous fortune form Klim's lot. He is sent for a galley slave; gets shipwrecked; wins a war; becomes Emperor of the Quamites, Niels the Great; grows overbearing; suffers revolution; escapes; and falls back up the same hole down which he fell twelve years previously!

Klim's journey is now a curiosity and little more. Overshadowing it are the two great books of fake travel which precede it, Defoe's *Robinson Crusoe* and Swift's *Gulliver's Travels*. Both books hinge on shipwrecks in remote parts of the globe, both are honourable precursors of the science fiction genre, both are written in the sound style of their age which has guaranteed them wide readership even in ours.

Often when talking of science fiction and the ur-science fiction preceding it, one is like a traveller walking down an unkempt lane, over the other side of the hedge from which lie the cultivated gardens of Literature. Occasionally lane and garden become one. Then the prospect widens out, to the benefit of both wild and sown. So it is in the age of Defoe and Swift, when the enormous advances in pure science of the previous century, the findings of Galileo and Isaac Newton, were still providing speculative fuel.

Swift and Defoe are writers very different in character. Swift, a clergyman, belongs to the mandarin tradition of his friend Pope, the great Augustan poet; Defoe, a journalist, is much more of the people. We resist the temptation here to discuss them and the variety of their writings, Defoe's especially, and concentrate on what we may term the science fictional element in their books.

Daniel Defoe (1660–1731) was the son of a butcher in Cripplegate. His life was filled with cross currents of religion, politics and economics. He travelled widely in Europe. He was a Puritan, born on the eve of the Restoration, who lived through the bursting of the South Sea Bubble. All these influences are apparent in his best novel. As for literary influence, this is the place to mention, belatedly, that wonderful journey which was to be found in almost every English home from its first appearance in the sixteen-seventies until the end of Victorian times: Bunyan's *Pilgrim's Progress*, written, like Campanella's utopia, in prison.

After a crowded life, enormously productive as a journalist, Defoe in his sixties took to writing novels, or rather fake memoirs[11], such as *Moll Flanders* and—a book which Poe and Mary Shelley knew—*A Journal of the Plague Year*. In his busy life, Defoe produced over 550 books, pamphlets and journals.

The Life and Strange and Surprising Adventures of Robinson Crusoe, of York, Mariner was published in 1719. It was an immediate success. Popularity and merit ran hand in hand. The book has never been out of print since, despite all the changes of taste in the past two hundred and fifty years. Crusoe on his lonely island at the mouth of the Orinoco (and he was there for twenty-five years before setting eyes on his man Friday) has as perennial a fascination as Prospero on his island, also marooned in the same quarter of the world.

If some kind of global ballot were taken to determine the best-known incident in all English literature, then Crusoe's discovery of the solitary footprint in the sand would be voted first, or at least very soon after the apparition of the ghost of Hamlet's father, Oliver Twist's asking for more and the death of Little Nell. That alien imprint has proved indelible.

The science fictional attractions of *Robinson Crusoe* are obvious: the desert-island theme is eternal, whether transposed to William Golding's island in *Lord of the Flies* or to another planet (as was expertly done by Rex Gordon, paying eponymous tribute to sources, in *No Man Friday*, set on Mars). But beyond these attractions lies a deeper one.

In the slow plodding of Crusoe's mind, as he creates amid the wilderness of his island a model of the society he has left, and as solitude forces him to come to terms with himself, Defoe builds up a picture of isolation which still stalks our overpopulated times. No imagined planet was ever such a setting for the drama of Man Alone as is *Robinson Crusoe.* Though the emphasis on religion may hold little appeal for modern tastes, a patient reading of the text reveals a book that lumbers to real greatness. As one critic has said of Defoe, "He was never brilliant; but he employed dullness almost magically."[12]

Defoe dropped religious orders; Swift took them.

Jonathan Swift (1667–1745) was born in Ireland of English parents. His father died before his birth; he was separated from his mother soon after birth. How far these facts, which find an echo in the life history of Edgar Allan Poe, influenced Swift's sense of separation from humanity, we cannot determine. He was brought to England as a baby, later returning to Ireland to complete his education at Trinity College, Dublin. Thereafter, his hopes, like his life, vacillated between the two countries. He was ordained in 1694.

Swift became a great pamphleteer, and was deeply involved in the politics of his time. Disappointed in his political ambitions in England, he returned to Ireland, where he eventually won great popularity as Dean of the Cathedral of St Patrick. The last few years of his existence were tormented by increasing madness, a fate that sometimes overcomes those otherwise most sane.

Swift's was a mysterious life, full of ironies. Romantics and psychiatrists have been attracted to the riddle of Swift's relationships with the two women in his life, his "Stella" and his "Vanessa". His remains lie now in the cathedral of Dublin, beneath the epitaph he composed for himself: *Ubi saeva indignatio ulterius cor lacerare nequit:* "Where fierce indignation can no longer tear the heart".

Most of his many writings, like his women, appeared under guises, anonymously or pseudonymously. As if in retaliation, the public has always rejected the title of his most famous and living book, *Travels into Several Remote Nations of the World: in Four Parts* (1726), and insists on calling it familiarly *Gulliver's Travels.*

It is fortunate that this masterly work does not count as science fiction, being satirical and/or moral in intention rather than speculative, for, if it did so count, then perfection would have been achieved straightaway, and the genre possibly concluded as soon as it had begun. But Swift's magical book defies any category into which critics try to place it.

Swift uses every wile known to Defoe, and more besides—the use of maps, for example—to persuade a reader that he holds yet another plodding volume of travel in his hand. Swift knew his Lucian. His mind was also stocked with a variety of imagery from travel books. As did Defoe and Coleridge, Swift used such imagery to his own purpose, as do the SF writers of today. Indeed, the link between SF and travel is probably as close in the eighties as the link between SF and science.

Gulliver seems at first to resemble Crusoe, of York, Mariner—a solid man, a surgeon in this case, using a good plain prose, and as shipwreck-prone as his predecessor. But Gulliver proves to be one of the cleverest heroes a writer ever set up in a work of fiction, at once simple and sly, rash and cowardly, a man who likes to think himself unwaveringly honest and yet who is all too ready to trim his sail to whatever wind prevails. It is a mistake to identify Gulliver with Swift.

But Swift makes it difficult for readers not to identify with Gulliver. He spins so many layers of irony that we are bound to get caught somewhere.

The four voyages lead us ever deeper into Swift's web. We share Gulliver's amusement at the Lilliputians and their petty affairs, so that we are bound to share Gulliver's humiliation at the court of Brobdingnag. In these two first voyages, scale is considered in the worth of human affairs; in the third voyage, to the flying island of Laputa, we see what intellectual endowments are worth; while in the last voyage, to the land in which Houyhnhnms and Yahoos are contrasted, we see what our animal nature is worth.

This splendid fourth part has acted like a lodestone on satirists since—on Holberg, as we have seen, and on Wells, Huxley, and Orwell. To the courteous race of horses, the Houyhnhnms, the filthy Yahoos are animals or, at best, peasants and servants. The Yahoos overwhelm Gulliver with disgust. Yet, when his clothes are off, he is almost indistinguishable from them; indeed, once while swimming, he is set on by a lust-mad female Yahoo. The Yahoos are humanity.

And this is true in somewhat more than a metaphorical sense. The Yahoos almost certainly derive from a number of accounts of Hottentots and Central American monkeys. John Ovington's 1696 descriptions of Hottentot women with ugly dangling breasts led to the Yahoo females with "their dugs hung between their Forefeet".[13] Swift's creative faculties leap upon facts and transpose them into a narrative from which a new imaginative structure emerges.

It is as if Swift, when drawing his portrait of the Yahoos, had a horror-comical vision of Stone Age hordes, long before theories of evolution had uncovered such an idea to human contemplation. Or the Yahoos are the Id in contrast to the Super-ego of the Houyhnhnms. One of the books's strengths is its openness to differing readings.

Certainly Swift's mighty satire has gained power and meaning with age. It is indestructible, defying time and final exegesis.

Thackeray, in mid-Victorian times, spoke for the opposition when (referring in particular to the fourth part) he called Gulliver's Travels, "A monster, gibbering shrieks and gnashing imprecations against mankind—tearing down all shreds of modesty, past all sense of manliness and shame; filthy in word, filthy in thought, furious, raging, obscene." In another category entirely is the Irish bishop—or so Swift claimed in a letter to Pope—who read the book and declared he scarcely believed a word of it.

What book can compare with Swift's? It unshakeably has the vote of humanity, selling ten thousand copies in the first three weeks of its long life, and being translated and pirated at once all over Europe. So it has gone on ever since, bowdlerized, truncated, serialized, cartoonized, animated, plagiarized—and read over and over, like a dark obverse of Pilgrim's Progress.

Swift intended to amuse a cultivated audience. Readers have recognized a strong salting of truth in his view of humanity; and the fantasy of big and little people, of civilized horses, races of immortals, and the quizzing of the dead, all have a perennial appeal. And, one must add, this is some of the rarest wit delivered in some of the finest language.

Many of Swift's best effects are achieved through Gulliver's blind pride, which insists on appealing to something base or petty to bolster what he feels is a worthy claim.

Talking of trade in England ("the dear place of my nativity") Gulliver tells his master, the Houyhnhnm, how European ships go out to all oceans and bring all sort of provisions back. "I assured him, that this whole globe of earth must be at least three times gone round, before one of our better female Yahoos could get her breakfast, or a cup to put it in." This is the reductive method of Pope's *Rape of the Lock*; Belinda opens her toilet box:

> Unnumbered Treasures ope at once, and here
> The various offerings of the World appear.

The question is one of reasonable scale.

Again, when "my master" is wondering at the Yahoos' disposition towards dirt and nastiness, compared with a natural love of cleanliness in other animals, "I could have easily vindicated human kind from the imputation of singularity upon the last article, if there had been any *swine* in that country (as unluckily for me there were not), which although it may be a *sweeter quadruped* than a Yahoo, cannot, I humbly conceive, in justice pretend to more cleanliness. . . ."

Again, in Laputa, Gulliver's interpreter remarks that he has "observed long life to be the universal desire and wish of mankind. That whoever had one foot in the grave, was sure to hold back the other as strongly as he could."

Such brief examples could be infinitely multiplied. They show a kind of *mistaken reasonableness* at work. If we accept *Gulliver* (among all the other things it is) as a great debate on Reason, many of the problems that have confronted commentators in the fourth part will vanish. Consider the end of his four-decker maze, where we meet with the Houyhnhnms, Swift's creatures of pure reason. This is the climax of Gulliver's search, and he is converted to their outlook on life, lock, stock and barrel—so much so that, when he returns to England, he cannot bear the proximity of his loving wife and children, regarding them as Yahoos.

We must always beware of Gulliver when he admires anything; his name does not begin with "Gull" for nothing. This is part of Swift's "fierce and insolent game", as F. R. Leavis calls it. These horse-shaped children of Reason are cold, uninteresting, and condescending—indifferent alike (as Gulliver becomes) to the lives of their children or the deaths of their spouses. They have limited vocabularies and limited imaginations, which is a fairly strong clue to Swift's real attitude to them. As George Orwell says, they are also racists.[14]

Orwell, who numbers *Gulliver* among his six indispensable books, yet makes the mistake of confusing Swift with Gulliver and believing that it is Swift who admires the Houyhnhnms. That is surely incorrect.

What Swift presents in the Houyhnhnm culture is a warning. This, he says, is what a utopia would be like if governed by pure reason: the nearest thing to death. Horrible though the Yahoos are, they are the oppressed, they have more life and vitality than their oppressors—and they probably have more of Swift's sympathy than is generally allowed. Orwell should have got the message, since he appears to feel sympathy as well as distaste for his *1984* Proles, literary offspring of the Yahoos.

In *Gulliver's Travels*, black is never opposed to white: even in despicable Lilliput, wise laws are passed for rewarding virtue. Swift supposes us cultivated enough to be able to compare faulty states of living, and to understand (as we do when reading Aldous Huxley) that civilized virtues may be represented only covertly in the text, for instance in a pure and urbane prose style. As his subject is Reason, so reason is needed to enjoy his entertainments to the full.

This is why *Gulliver's Travels* works so well over the centuries, why it continues to delight: paralleled by its pure vein of fantasy expressed in terms of naive realism goes its intellectual paradox. We have to be better than Yahoos to recognize that they are us, we they. So we are raised to the level of Swift's own ironical vision. Despite the subject matter that Thackeray so disliked, the effect of this great book is to exalt us.

From the two masterpieces of Augustan prose, *Robinson Crusoe* and *Gulliver's Travels*, we move on over thirty years to glance at two other masterpieces which appeared at the same time. A glance will have to suffice, for neither stands directly in the literary line developing towards science fiction, although, in their concern for the modern human predicament, they contain much of interest to science fiction readers.

Voltaire's *Candide* was published in February 1759, to be followed less than two months later by Samuel Johnson's *The History of Rasselas: Prince of Abissinia*. Johnson was later heard to say that "if they had not been published so closely one after the other that there was no time for imitation, it would have been in vain to deny that the scheme of that which came latest was taken from the other". Coincidentally, Bulwer-Lytton's *The Coming Race* was published just before Butler's *Erewhon* in the following century, when Butler was at pains to deny that the scheme of his book was taken from the other.[15]

Like *Robinson Crusoe* and *Gulliver's Travels*, *Rasselas* and *Candide* were both immediate successes. Neither has been out of print since. Johnson's book was written in about a week, Voltaire's in three days: facts which should cause the modern denizens of Grub Street to take fresh heart.

Both are cautionary tales against optimism. Voltaire's is much the more sprightly, but any reader susceptible to the cadences of prose will be attracted instantly by the noble melancholy with which Johnson embarks upon his narrative:

Ye who listen with credulity to the whispers of fancy, and pursue with eagerness the phantoms of hope; who expect that age will perform the promises of youth, and that the deficiencies of the present day will be supplied by the morrow: attend to the history of Rasselas, prince of Abissinia.

More English optimism!

In his attempts to escape from the happy valley in which he lives, Rasselas meets a man "eminent for his knowledge of the mechanic powers", who builds a flying machine. The machine absorbs a lot of work and time, and crashes in the end—not before the designer has made the perceptive remark, "What would be the security of the good, if the bad could at pleasure invade them from the sky?"

Whatever begins well, ends badly. Aspiration is always defeated. Travelling is as bad as arriving. The only consolation is the rueful moral to be drawn from every contretemps.

In *Candide*, matters begin badly and get worse; the comedy is in the way Candide and his companions, Pangloss and Cunégonde, draw idiotically optimistic conclusions from each fresh disaster. Estrangement between hope and performance is complete; facts exist by the teeming multitude—they are interpreted according to individual temperament.

The nearest the utopian Candide gets to Utopia is in El Dorado, where the streets are paved with gold. There, pleasures are purely material, dinners always excellent. Courts of justice and parliament buildings do not exist; there are no prisons. But the Palace of Sciences has a gallery two thousand feet long, filled with mathematical and scientific instruments. Furthermore, the king's jokes are witty even in translation.

Voltaire, industrious philosopher whose works fill many seemly volumes, had indulged his sense of surrealism before writing *Candide*, most notably in the two *contes*, *Zadig, ou La Destinée* and *Micromégas* (1747 and 1750). In the former, Zadig's observation of clues which lead him to deduce that the queen's dog and the king's horse have passed qualify him as a predecessor of Poe's Auguste Dupin.

In *Micromégas*, a gigantic visitor from one of the planets of Sirius and his hardly less gigantic friend from Saturn arrive on Earth. They lift a ship out of the Baltic. Holding it in the palm of one hand, the two giants examine it through a microscope and observe the human beings aboard, with whom they talk. Rabelais was probably an influence here; Swift is also mentioned; but the inversion of having the space journey done *to* Earth rather than *from* it is characteristically Voltairean; so is the conversation. In the end, the two enormous visitors present the creatures of Earth with a volume in which, they promise, the explanation of the universe will be found.

When the secretary of the Academy of Sciences in Paris opens the volume, he finds it contains nothing but blank pages. Later, in Vonnegut's *Sirens of Titan*, the message delivered across the galaxy at such great inconvenience, will be found when opened to contain the single word, "Greetings."

A reminder of the *Micromégas* incident comes in *Candide*, in a passage of philosophical conversation between Candide and Martin which flows like Marx Brothers' dialogue:

> "While we are on the subject, do you believe that the Earth was originally sea, as is stated in that great book which belongs to the captain?" asks Candide.
>
> "I believe nothing of the sort, any more than I do all the other fancies that have been foisted upon us through the centuries."
>
> "But to what end, think you, was the world formed?"
>
> "To turn our brains."
>
> "Were you not astonished by the story I told you, of the two girls in the country of the Oreillons, who had monkeys for lovers?"
>
> "Not in the least. I see nothing strange in such an infatuation. I have seen so many extraordinary things that now nothing is extraordinary to me."
>
> "Do you think that men always slaughtered one another, as they do nowadays? . . ."
>
> "Do you think that hawks have always devoured pigeons at every opportunity?"[16] (Chapter 21)

Candide was written soon after the Lisbon earthquake, an event which shook civilized Europe as severely as the sinking of the *Titanic* rattled Edwardian society. In *Candide* and *Gulliver* especially we derive a strong impression of the times, and of those weaknesses of the flesh eternally with us—then much complicated by the prevalent scourge of syphilis, to which both authors pay tribute.

These two remarkable books, together with *Robinson Crusoe* and *Rasselas*, are not quite classifiable as novels by any strict accountancy. Novel, travel, dystopia—they cross genres. In that respect, many of today's science fiction "novels" resemble them. They are, all four, good examples of masculine intellect at work, sketching in character with economy, not concerned with ambivalences of human relationships, interested in telling a tale and, above all, looking outward and drawing conclusions about the world in which the authors find themselves.

In this respect, this brilliant eighteenth-century quartet resembles some of today's science fiction—say Bruce Sterling's *Schismatrix*, or Robert Sheckley's *Dimension of Miracles*—more closely than the somewhat wishy-washy Moon voyages immediately preceding them.

A more feminine sensibility was to arise, and would dominate much literary criticism if not the novel itself. Jane Austen in the early years of the nineteenth century, Henry James in the late; and E. M. Forster, Iris Murdoch, and the many miniaturists of our century; these tropes and totems have been frequently preferred by critics to more robust canvases. The great nineteenth-century novelists, Balzac, Stendhal, Dickens, Melville, Dostoevsky, Tolstoy, Hardy, are of a different kind, aiming to produce works or series of works which achieve a kind of totality.

In the latter category of "great works" can be perceived the outlines of what the critic Georg Lukacs has described as the "bourgeois epic", in which a solitary and generally alienated hero is set against his society or his environment.

This pattern also applies generally to science fiction. The tradition of looking outwards and measuring a man against the world he has made or found—linked to the custom of telling a bold tale, even if it may be no more prodigal of incident than Crusoe's long years on his desert island—has continued generically. Shunned by critics, SF maintains a narrative tradition which offers much vitality, however socially unacceptable it may be.

The wonderful journeys, the utopias, the adventures and satires herded together in this chapter, point towards the birth of what is unmistakably science fiction. To claim that they are themselves science fiction is to break down boundaries of useful definition.

All are time-locked—not recognizing change as the yeast of the societies they depict. Gulliver could sail on forever, discovering strange communities lost in the wilderness of untraversed ocean. Their view of man in relation to nature is modest, governed by the modesty of good eighteenth-century common sense; nature operates on him or him on it randomly. Careers and shipwrecks collide with friendly frequency.

Although the authors use what we might be tempted to call pragmatic fantasy, fantasy as other than an end in itself, they do not acknowledge fantasy as an internal force; Crusoe's Inwardness is all directed outwards, towards his Maker. Even the ingenious Candide operates in the present, without reference to a wider canvas of past or future.

The greatest of these books would be the greatest of science fiction if they were science fiction. But only the growth of the genre, the mode, in our century, has made them seem to resemble it as much as they do. They may have been used as models, their arguments and ingenuities redeployed—but those who plunder the Pyramids do not make themselves relations of the Pharaohs thereby.

Candide displays the enticing rottenness of the world. Only five years later comes the story which began as a dream and begat a new genre, Horace Walpole's *Castle of Otranto*, to which we have already referred. The new genre, closeted, cloistered, complex, advances atmosphere at the expense of action. As Gothic mists draw across the Age of Reason, we come closer to dreamland than to the world of soldiers, politicians, mariners, surgeons, and travellers.

Turning to the nineteenth and twentieth centuries, we find a mingling of introspection and outwardness. Sometimes the one predominates, sometimes the other. A balance between the two came early, in *Frankenstein*. But a whole new generation of writers was pressing at Mary Shelley's heels, and very soon making many of her techniques look as old-fashioned as Crusoe's musket.

CHAPTER IV

The Gas-Enlightened Race:
Victorian Visions

Here about the beach I wandered, nourishing a youth sublime
With the fairy tales of science, and the long result of Time
—Alfred Tennyson: *Locksley Hall*

There are many conceptions of science fiction. On the one hand, it may be
regarded simply as entertainment, each story or novel having no possible
connection with any other. On the other hand, it may be regarded, more loftily,
as one way in which a civilization sees itself: though to regard all authors as
holding identical intentions is most certainly an error. Our Western culture,
which now affects most people on Earth, from African tribal chiefs to Korean
violinists, contains many myths and beliefs—including the perception that
there are separate civilizations.

One Western myth, if that is the right word for it, is that men and women are
in some way able to take charge of their own destinies. This realization may be
observed during the last century in its science fiction. The slaves which made
possible the well-being of the inhabitants of Plato's ideal city-state are replaced
by machines. Chance adventures brought about by migratory gansas are
replaced by an increasing sense of direction in history: the idea of Progress.

To some, the idea of Progress is a doctrine which allows no argument, though
many writers like Samuel Butler and William Morris were to argue against it.
Alexis de Tocqueville, in his Introduction to *Democracy in America*, written in
1831, observes that the drive in Christian society has been towards social
equality. He predicts that for better or worse this will come about.

Since de Tocqueville wrote, slavery has been abolished, at least in the West.
The privilege that goes with birth has been challenged, as has discrimination on
racial grounds. Universal franchise has been established, educational opportunities have opened for all. Equal rights for women are at least in view.

All these advances we accept; they are written into the idea of Progress.

There's a trade-off. From these advances comes the tyranny of the mass mind,
which wishes to adjudicate in all things. With its inherent mediocrity, its lack of
specialized knowledge, it threatens to dictate all we see and hear and experience.

We must believe that all men are equal, while knowing it is not so.

These are the doubts against which we live and writers write. They have led
to the false polarity which beggars literary judgement, that what is good cannot
be popular and what is popular cannot be good. This dichotomy is quite
modern: we inherit it only from the last century, and remain unable to resolve it.

The wide expanses, the hidden valleys, of the nineteenth century lie like a great continent before any explorer of yesterday's fiction.

A critic gazing at this territory is aware of the falsity of that popular view which regards science fiction as "beginning with H. G. Wells". Wells stands at the end of the century and at the end of the Victorian Age; behind him lie sixty glorious and congested years.

A roll call of all the writers whose works were undoubtedly science fiction, or scientific romance, or marginally science fiction, or even far from science fiction and yet of central interest (such as the works of Lewis Carroll) would be a long one. The popular view is correct to this extent, that many of the names on the roll call have been forgotten to all but specialists, except Verne's and Wells's.

Yet the townscape, the morphology, of SF was laid in the last century, in an act of town-planning enforced by pressures under which, if to a greater degree, we must pass our lives today. Some cities are Babylons of the mind, some New Jerusalems. The themes that inhabit them were used over and over again, to be drawn together—to be re-focused in Wells's work.

Piety and materialist optimism were once features of Victorian life about which a good deal was heard; today, as we remake that multi-coloured period in our own image, we hear more about scepticism, agonized atheism, and the sort of doubts about a growing mass society as are expressed in de Tocqueville's *Democracy in America*. Most of these grey notes find an echo in the science fiction of the period; from *Frankenstein* on, it has remained most typically a literature of unease.

Typical too is that other *Frankenstein* theme, the duality of man, expressed markedly in Victorian times by a duality of society—the Rich and the Poor, dramatically labelled by Disraeli "the two nations".

The eighteen-thirties, as literary historians have remarked, were a time of decline for the novel in general, as well as for the Romantic movement.[1] After the death of Sir Walter Scott in 1832, fiction was in recession, to come bouncing back in the forties with a power that rendered the novel the dominant form in imaginative literature for the rest of the century. Among the remarkable new novels of the eighteen-forties were Thackeray's *Vanity Fair*, several of Dickens's novels—including *Martin Chuzzlewit* and *Dombey and Son*—Disraeli's *Coningsby* and *Sybil*, novels by all three of the Brontë sisters—*Wuthering Heights*, *Jane Eyre*, and *Tenant of Wildfell Hall*—as well as novels by Mrs Gaskell, Harrison Ainsworth, Herman Melville, George Borrow, Charles Kingsley, and Anthony Trollope.

Most of these names were new to the reading public. A few novelists, by reason of age or stamina, bridged the ebb tide of the thirties. Among them were Shelley's friend, Thomas Love Peacock, and Bulwer-Lytton.

The life-cycle of the Bulwer-Lytton is almost as complicated as an insect metamorphosis; and his name underwent as many changes. He ended as Edward George Earle Lytton Bulwer, First Baron Lytton, after beginning life as a fairly simple Bulwer and somewhere along the line narrowly avoiding becoming Lord South Erpingham. Having started as a young Regency sprig who imparted ideas of dandyism to Disraeli, he finished life as one of the dullest pillars of Victorian society.

Two years after the fashionable publisher Henry Colburn had published Mary Shelley's *The Last Man* in three volumes, Lytton's dandy novel, *Pelham*[2], appeared from the same house in the same format. Later, Lytton turned successively to novels about crime and criminals (such as *Eugene Aram*), historical novels (such as *The Last Days of Pompeii*), the occult (such as *Zanoni*), and novels of peaceful everyday life in the manner of Trollope (such as *My Novel*); he also wrote plays.

"What will Bulwer become? The first author of the age? I do not doubt it. He is a magnificent writer"[3], wrote Mary Shelley. But our interest in him must here be confined to *The Coming Race* (1871), his novel about supermen.

The Coming Race is the story of a human being who enters a coal mine, stumbles down a ravine, and discovers a human-like race living peaceably under the Earth's crust in well-lit caverns. This race has air boats, automata, mechanical wings, formidable weapons, and grand buildings. And scenery that seems to owe much to John Martin[4]:

> My host stepped out into the balcony; I followed him. We were on the uppermost story of one of the angular pyramids; the view beyond was of a wild and solemn beauty impossible to describe—the vast ranges of precipitous rock which formed the distant background, the intermediate valleys of mystic many-coloured herbage, the flash of waters, many of them like streams of roseate flame, the serene lustre diffused over all by myriads of lamps, combined to form a whole which no words of mine can convey adequate description: so splendid was it, yet so sombre; so lovely, yet so awful. (Chapter 5)

Burke's sublime with a vengeance!

The race that lives in these caverns is called the Vril-ya, after a beneficent and all-purpose force, *vril*, with which they control their world. Vril is a "unity in natural energetic agencies". The coinage lent its name to Bovril, a fortifying beef beverage, and Virol, a fortifying toffee-like substance, both liberally poured into this critic when young, to his great benefit. The Vril-ya are far from warlike. Hunting dangerous animals (a few antediluvian monsters still survive) is left to children, because hunting requires ruthlessness and "the younger a child the more ruthlessly he will destroy". Lytton spoke as a family man.

Most of the novel is taken up by pedestrian descriptions of how the subterranean world differs from ours, in the manner of all utopias. There is a slight humorous element, since one of the alien women falls in love with our hero—and these women are larger and altogether more formidable than human women, taking the initiative in courtship. Our anonymous hero admits that Zee "rather awed me as an angel than moved me as a woman".

He admires the subterranean world but finds it dull, and eventually escapes back to his own world, carried in the arms of the woman who loves him. The somewhat philosophical narrative ends on a subdued note of menace:

> The more I think of a people calmly developing, in regions excluded from our sight and deemed uninhabitable by our sages, powers surpassing our most disciplined modes of force, and virtues to which our life, social and political, becomes antagonistic in proportion as our civilisation advances—the more deeply I pray that ages may yet elapse before there emerge into sunlight our inevitable destroyers.

Here is a submerged nation, perhaps an echo of Disraeli's.[5]

The Coming Race was descended from tribes living on the Earth's surface. Records suggest that their retreat underground took place "thousands of years before the time of Noah". But that does not accord with current theories in geological circles, "inasmuch as it places the existence of a human race upon earth at dates long anterior to that assigned to the terrestrial formation adapted to the introduction of mammalia". In this way and in others, Lytton shows a somewhat confused interest in evolutionary theory.

The year after the publication of his novel, a much bigger gun was turned towards the same target.

Samuel Butler (1835–1902) is one of those brilliant writers who never lives up to his brilliance. The two books for which he is now best remembered are his posthumous novel *The Way of All Flesh* (1903) and his satirical utopia, *Erewhon* (1872), in which Butler's wit combines with his interest in science (and particularly in Darwinism, with whose adherents Butler skirmished through many books and many years) into a somewhat Swiftian whole. The result is a much more living book than *The Coming Race*, though Butler recognized their similarity. Nor need plagiarism be suspected; when it is time to think about a subject, a lot of people will be thinking about it.

Whereas the use of *vril* and all its forces has made Lytton's people strong and impressive, the Erewhonians are strong and impressive because they have banned the use of machines.

Butler deploys his arguments with something of Swift's skill, though without the same liveliness:

> There is no security against the ultimate development of mechanical consciousness, in the fact of machines possessing little consciousness now. A mollusc has not much consciousness. Reflect upon the extraordinary advance which machines have made in the last few hundred years, and note how slowly the animal and vegetable kingdoms are advancing. The more highly organized machines are creatures not so much of yesterday, as of the last five minutes, so to speak, in comparison with past time. Assume for the sake of argument that conscious beings have existed for some twenty million years: see what strides machines have made in the last thousand! May not the world last twenty million years longer? If so, what will they not in the end become? Is it not safer to nip the mischief in the bud and to forbid them further progress? (Chapter 23)

Such reasoning would not have been possible a generation before Butler; nowadays it is far more common among scientists. And there are other pleasant reversals of what we regard as normal, the best known being the way in which Erewhonians are treated as criminal when they are sick, and sick when they are criminal. Higgs, Butler's protagonist, sees these methods working at first hand, for his host, Mr Nosnibor, is a respected embezzler.

> I do not suppose that even my host, on having swindled a confiding widow out of the whole of her property, was put to more actual suffering than a man will readily undergo at the hands of an English doctor.

Erewhon has a love affair—the standard one. Higgs falls in love with a girl called Arowhena and, despite all obstacles, eventually manages to escape with her by balloon.

Witty though *Erewhon* is, it rarely rises above the level of a spirited debate on current themes, the nature of society, etc. We see an immense difference if we contrast it with the books H. G. Wells was writing twenty-five years later, where we catch vivid glimpses of a Butlerian society in which machines have reached supremacy, from *The Time Machine* onwards.

Samuel Butler speaks of machines reproducing themselves[6], and of men becoming their slaves: "Consider also the colliers and pitmen and coal merchants and coal trains, and the men who drive them, and the ships that carry coals—what an army of servants do the machines thus employ! Are there not probably more men engaged in tending machinery than in tending men?" (Chapter 24)

H. G. Wells *shows* us, for instance in *When the Sleeper Wakes*, what happens when men are slaves to technology. What Wells imagines, Butler merely fears.[7]

The difference between the two methods lies not only in the changes which took place between the publication of *Erewhon* and Wells's novel, but in radical differences of temperament: Butler cautious and—when all is said—ever looking back; Wells the new man, eager—when all is said—for the next thrilling chapter in human history, whatever it might bring. Yet the contrasts between the two men are not so great. Butler's is a keen sardonic eye. Both he and Wells would have concurred with Tennyson's great line: "Better fifty years of Europe than a cycle of Cathay."

Speaking as one who had experienced more than fifty years of Europe, the old novelist Peacock presented a thoroughgoing scepticism to modern improvements of any kind in his last novel, *Gryll Grange* (1861). There he invoked an ancient spirit to return from the dead with the wish that

> with profoundest admiration thrilled,
> He may with willing mind assume his place
> In your steam-nursed, steam-borne, steam-killed
> And gas-enlightened race. (Chapter 28)

Butler and Lytton seized eagerly and early on the theory of evolution, to employ it in their fiction as essentially an aesthetic object (the phrase is Butler's). This is the way in which most scientific theories, whether invented for the occasion or not, are employed in science fiction.

Evolutionary speculation has become, and remains, one of the staples of science fiction. It lends secular perspective to the human drama. The glacier-like grandeur of natural selection and adaptation colours our thought. This, and such obsessions as The Wilderness Comes Again—to which we proceed later this chapter—can be revisited continually, as long as the potential prompting them remains. Genre ideas do not wear out if they have truth behind them; they are the genre, its reason for being.

Here perhaps mention should be made of an early successor to Poe, Fitz-James O'Brien. O'Brien was an Irishman who came to America at a young age, where he enjoyed life to the full. Between flirtations and binges, O'Brien wrote several short stories which have the authentic science fiction flavour. His best-known piece is "The Diamond Lens", published in a newspaper in 1858. This story of a man who falls in love with a beautiful woman living in a drop of water, whom he sees through a microscope, proved very popular, as its later imitators (Ray Cummings, Henry Hasse) show.

There the inaccessible woman is! "Her long lustrous hair following her glorious head in a golden wake, like the track sown in heaven by a falling star. . . ."

The drop of water, unlike the prose, dries up. The voyeur dies in frustration. It's a happy ending really, because he is a murderer.

One needs a head of stone not to find O'Brien's callow tale risible nowadays. If the idea works no more, it is because the theory on which it was based—the false analogy of the "worlds of the atom" being like the worlds of the solar system—is long discarded. *And* because the treatment, the language, fails to rise to the occasion; were the language not false, the story might survive as fantasy.

The Coming Race and *Erewhon* rank among the nineteenth century's best utopian novels. (*Erewhon Revisited* in 1901 is less of a success.) Like the seventeenth century, the nineteenth yields many utopias, most of them occasioned by the weight of increasing industrialization. We can do no more than nod towards such utopian philosophers as John Ruskin, Carlyle, Thoreau, Emerson, and, to some extent, William Morris. But a word should be said about *Looking Backward*, because its theories are somewhat more than aesthetic object; they are its very existence.

The author of *Looking Backward* (1888) is Edward Bellamy (1850–98). Bellamy was born and died in Chicopee Falls, Massachusetts, but his novel is set in a Boston of the future. The protagonist, Julian West, suffers from insomnia and passes his nights in a subterranean chamber, where a mesmerist occasionally puts him to sleep. This is presumably a late echo from the world of Poe and M. Valdemar. But when West awakes he is no corpse; he fell asleep in 1887, and the year is now 2000.

A socialist utopia unfolds, in which nineteenth-century Boston is unfavourably compared with a Boston of the future. "The glorious new Boston with its domes and pinnacles, its gardens and fountains, its universal reign of comfort. . . ." Industrial organizations have evolved into something larger, resulting in a sort of state socialism where every man is worthy of his hire. In consequence money is abolished. So how does a man pay his way abroad? "An American credit card is just as good in Europe as American gold used to be."

There are other touches which prove the shrewdness of Bellamy as a thinker. But his optimism got in his way; marriages are not made only for love, any more than machinery provides us with nothing but pleasure. Nor do we occupy our leisure time peacefully and profitably, listening to sermons or whatever. The human animal, forced to operate within a non-human scheme of affairs, will always defy the rationalist.

With Bellamy we find as with later writers that he may hit with seeming precision on a future technological development while failing to grasp its social repercussions, rather in the same way that the first team to land on the Moon in the film *Destination Moon* (1950) walk around in their crater for a while before thinking to give the President of the United States a call on the radio-phone. The July 1969 moon event is predicted, but not the social factor of its being a global tele-event, watched by millions of viewers. And what is it that makes Bellamy's Year 2000 Boston a paradise?

> If we could have devised an arrangement for providing everybody with music in their homes, perfect in quality, unlimited in quantity, suited to every mood and beginning and ceasing at will, we should have considered the limit of human felicity already attained. . . .

Electronics and the Sony Walkman have now brought just such an enviable situation, and not only to Boston. Yet even Bostonians do not claim to have reached the limits of human felicity thereby. Here again is the problem we saw in operation earlier, of a writer's aspirations taking precedence over anticipations. Yet we are nowhere—even the nowhere of utopia—unless our writers aspire.

Thinkers in the nineteenth century were conscious as never before of the contrast between poverty and riches all round them, and aspired to vanquish that difference. The wealth which capitalism brought to the world made possible the hope that poverty could be abolished. The very notion of such a possibility was born some time in the last century or the previous one; it inspired Karl Marx, and it inspired Bellamy too.

Dusty though Bellamy's book has become in our more violent and pragmatic century, there is a touching faith in it, an honest hope, which we can only envy.

Looking Backward was taken up by followers of Henry George, the revolutionary economist, and by socialist groups then struggling for coherence inside the United States. The influence of the book spread to Europe, and provoked attack and counter-attack. Its effect was not only on the literary.

While we are talking of utopias, mention must be made of one of the best of them, a witty and sly story which lay forgotten for many years in the pages of an obscure magazine. It was written by a woman, and featured a land populated only by women. There is no crankiness about it, no bitterness, just a broad good humour conveying a humane appeal. We know of no other story like it.

Charlotte Perkins Gilman's *Herland* is the most sprightly of American, of all, utopias. Which wears its didactic message lightly. Three men stumble on an isolated land somewhere in South America which is inhabited by a race of parthenogenic females. The women have established a fruitful and pleasant land, dominated by the idea of Motherhood. It is no land of Cockayne. Everyone works. And gradually the men are "tamed".

Humour is apparently on the banned list in any utopia, but in *Herland* fun is derived from the differing responses of the three men to the situation in which they find themselves. They are baffled by the fact that the women, though comely, are uninterested in sex. "Feminine charms" are in fact merely reflected masculinity. According to their responses to this amazing society, the men meet with differing fates.

Herland is to be cherished. The energetic Gilman was a feminist and a socialist. She established her own magazine, *The Forerunner*, and wrote every word of it herself for some years. *Herland* appeared in it in 1915, where it was forgotten until rescue came in book form only in 1979. It was then accompanied by an excellent introduction by Ann J. Lane. An English reprint was published in 1986 by the Women's Press, who have established a line of science fiction by women writers.

Charlotte Perkins Gilman must be an inspiration to all the lively female SF authors now active. What mainly informs her book is an acute sense of observation of social conditions. We see also that she owed something to the ideas of Bellamy and Henry George.

The same can be said of two other socialist-inclined utopias of the period, one British, one Austrian, both published in 1890, two years after Bellamy's fable. William Morris, influenced by Ruskin as well as Bellamy, depicted a twenty-first century in *News from Nowhere* which contains many of the features of the mediaeval world Morris reverenced.

William Morris was a poet first, a designer of many things, a political writer, and a creator of prose romances last. In 1884 he had founded the Socialist League, and it was in this League's journal, *The Commonweal*, that *News from Nowhere* was first published. Morris designed and made furniture and fabrics—his wallpapers have never gone out of fashion. He espoused what he regarded as a mediaeval ideal of craftsmanship, that work should be done for the love of it. His Kelmscott Press produced, almost beyond argument, the most beautiful books to be printed last century.

News from Nowhere, in book form in 1890 and occasionally reprinted since, is a dream vision of man in harmony with nature and himself. The state has withered away. Machines have been destroyed.

Critics find Morris hard to deal with. Eric S. Rabkin dismisses *News from Nowhere* as "a Communist tract".[8] As might be expected, the best understanding comes from C. S. Lewis[9], whose essay on Morris should be read as a defence of all imaginary worlds. First, as to language: "The question about Morris's style is not whether it is an artificial language—all endurable languages in longer works must be that—but whether it is a good one." Then, that the old fashion for "living men and women" in a naturalistic setting is obsolete: "All we need demand is that this invented world should have some intellectual or emotional relevance to the world we live in." Also, and finally, that Morris's worlds have truth at their core. Or, as Lewis finely puts it, "He seems to retire far from the real world and to build a world out of his wishes; but when he has finished the result stands out as a picture of experience ineluctably true."

Lewis had the art of praising well. He also says of Morris's fantasies, "No mountains in literature are as far away as distant mountains in Morris."

Theodor Hertzka described a perhaps more practical utopia in *Freeland: A Social Anticipation* (as the English translation of 1891 is called). The utopia of Freeland, established in Africa, is a modified capitalist state which makes full use of modern inventions, plus a few of its own. Many societies sprang up—D. H. Lawrence's planned Rananim among them—trying to put Hertzka's propositions into effect. One even set sail for Africa, but the experiment was not a success.

Hertzka's is essentially a capitalist utopia. Published in the same year as *News from Nowhere* and *Freeland*, 1890, was Ignatius Donnelly's *Caesar's Column*, published under the pseudonym Edmund Boisgilbert. The book was as famous in its time as Bellamy's *Looking Backward*. Donnelly's is a socialist future. The workers revolt against their masters in 1988, and a civil war breaks out which brings civilization to an end. Here is the "two nations" theme again, with the proles rising instead of sinking, as they were soon to do in H. G. Wells's imagining.

Writers like Donnelly, aware of social injustice, impelled by strong socialist desires for reform, see through to the fragility of civilization, a less easy perception in the eighteen-nineties than in our century, after the experience of the Great War (as it was once called). Their books, often didactic, may now be merely the study of specialists. In their time, they moulded public opinion, as they intended to do, and helped ameliorate the worst vagaries of materialism. They represent an adventure in ideals unique to our culture.

Evolution was used opportunistically by Lytton in *The Coming Race*. It was more central to Samuel Butler's work. He devoted four volumes to discussion of it.[10] We shall see how large a part it played in Wells's writing; but there is a writer greater than any of them in whom the evolutionary revelation works throughout most of his literary life.

In 1873, a novel was published which contains a situation not unfamiliar to readers of thrillers, although this was no thriller. A man has fallen part way down a cliff, and is clinging there, the sea below him, with slender chances of rescue.

> By one of those familiar conjunctions of things wherewith the inanimate world baits the mind of man when he pauses in moments of suspense, opposite Knight's eyes was an imbedded fossil, standing forth

in low relief from the rock. It was a creature with eyes. The eyes, dead and turned to stone, were even now regarding him. It was one of the early crustaceans called Trilobites. Separated by millions of years in their lives, Knight and this underling seemed to have met in their place of death. It was the single instance within reach of his vision of anything that had ever been alive and had had a body to save, as he himself had now.

The creature represented but a low type of animal existence, for never in their vernal years had the plains indicated by those numerous slatey layers been traversed by an intelligence worthy of the name. Zoophytes, mollusca, shell-fish, were the highest developments of those ancient dates. The immense lapses of time each formation represented had known nothing of the dignity of man. They were grand times, but they were mean times too, and mean were their relics. He was to be with the small in his death. (Chapter 22)

The passage continues with a lecture on life before man—poetic and striking as well as learned, but out of key with the rather trivial love-story-with-ironies in which it is embedded.

The author is Thomas Hardy, the novel, *A Pair of Blue Eyes*. It is one of the weakest of the Wessex novels. Wessex is, in Hardy's hands, an example of a dream world, although its boundaries lie very near the boundaries of reality. Hardy himself referred to Wessex's "horizons and landscapes of a partly real, partly dream-country", in the Preface to *Far from the Madding Crowd*. *A Pair of Blue Eyes* has faults and defenders. Tennyson much admired it and Proust declared it to be "of all books the one which he would himself most gladly have written."[11] It provides early evidence of Hardy's tremulous awareness set against the encompassing mysteries of space and time. This sensibility he would develop more fully in other novels and in poems, and in his mighty verse-drama, *The Dynasts*.

F. R. Southerington's perceptive guide to Hardy's thought emphasizes the effects Darwin's writings had on him.[12] Hardy's is the loneliness of the long-distance eye; his is perhaps the first zoom lens in literature, and from the picture of ancient Egdon Heath, where "the distant rims of the world and of the firmament seemed to be a division in time no less than a division in matter", in *The Return of the Native* (1878), through such novels as *The Woodlanders* (1887) and *Tess of the D'Urbervilles* (1891), to the exalted poetry of *The Dynasts*—less a historical play than a long meditation on the evolution of consciousness—Hardy presents mankind in perspective: a unique panorama of men and women in relationship to their environment, where time and chance are as influential as the seasons.

An extract from *Two on a Tower* (1882) shows Hardy's method. It is a monologue by Swithin St. Cleeve, the astronomer hero, punctuated by Lady Constantine's comments, as they stand at the top of his tower and gaze at the night sky:

"You would hardly think, at first, that horrid monsters lie up there waiting to be discovered by any moderately penetrating mind—monsters to which those of the oceans bear no sort of comparison."

"What monsters may they be?"

"Impersonal monsters, namely, Immensities. Until a person has thought out the stars and their inter-spaces, he has hardly learnt that there are things far more terrible than monsters of shape, namely, monsters of magnitude without known shape. Such monsters are the voids and the waste spaces of the sky . . . Those are deep wells for the human mind to let itself down into, leave alone the human body! . . . So am I not right in saying that those minds who exert their imaginative powers to bury themselves in the depths of that universe merely strain their faculties to gain a new horror?"

Standing, as she stood, in the presence of the stellar universe, under the very eyes of the constellations, Lady Constantine apprehended something of the earnest youth's argument.

"And to add a new weirdness to what the sky possesses in its size and formlessness, there is involved the quality of decay. For all the wonder of these everlasting stars, eternal spheres, and what not, they are not everlasting, they are not eternal; they burn out like candles. . . ." (Chapter 4)

In *The Dynasts* (1904)[13], Hardy presents his final grand development of those evolutionary speculations present in the passage quoted from *A Pair of Blue Eyes*, concerning the growth of consciousness and intelligence.

The scene in *The Dynasts* moves from Earth to the Overworld—where the final stage of evolution will occur when the Immanent Will that rules us all (with "eternal artistries in Circumstance") eventually achieves consciousness and fashions a better universe, more in accordance with human thoughts and wishes. No bolder speculation than this comes our way until Olaf Stapledon's works in the nineteen-thirties.

Thomas Hardy's work is alive with observations honed on his peculiar temperament by the scientific findings and developments of his time. The wounded man of a new age, wandering compressed landscapes, presents himself in Hardy's novels. Yet it would be absurd to regard Hardy as a science fiction writer.[14] And for three main reasons.

Firstly Hardy does not introduce his changes in the natural or the old order for the sake of novelty or sensationalism, though he is not averse to sensationalism in other respects. The changes he records go to buttress deep feelings and movements in the novels and remain subordinate to the lives of his characters (who in any case live in surroundings where most changes appear transitory).

Secondly, and more subtly, there is a question of *tone*. The tone of science fiction is characteristically rapid and light, and this is far from Hardy's voice—Swift, for instance, is several degrees nearer to it. Nor is Hardy a great espouser of Progress. The novelty of the threshing machine in *Tess of the D'Urbervilles*, for instance, is a sinister one. The machine enslaves rather than frees the workers.

Thirdly, there is the matter of genius. Genius does what it must; talent does what it can. Hardy, for all his faults, is a genius; while science fiction—as yet at any rate—has only attracted writers of talent, with one or two exceptions. Those with greater or lesser attributes work elsewhere.

The most immediate shaping force on the range of verse in *The Dynasts*, on its different metres, its various spirit voices, and, to some extent, its subject matter, is Hardy's favourite poet, Percy Bysshe Shelley, in particular his *Prometheus Unbound*. This poem, as we noted, bears certain filial duties to Erasmus Darwin's poetry. The tenor of Hardy's prose links him with later novelists, Jefferies, Powys, Lawrence, Golding, who do not belong in the Gothic tradition.

Hardy's novels are novels of character, not novels that rely on a gadget, a marvel, or a *novum*, for their central attraction. Published about the same time as *A Pair of Blue Eyes* was a dime novel entitled *The Steam Man of the Plains* (see Chapter 6). Even the most biased reader could hardly regard the two novels as in any way equivalent as regards emotional depth, intellectual scope, or power of expression. Yet the unavoidable impression is that much of twentieth-century SF was to follow the way not of the Wessex man but the Steam Man. The imposition of hastily written genre products on the public led them to accept what was less than the best. They accepted eagerly. This was the tyranny of the mass mind that de Tocqueville feared. The way was paved for Hugo Gernsback. A whole new public discovered the rapture of eternal adolescence.

Both space and the haste of critics force us to concentrate on Anglo-Saxon contributions to science fiction. The Japanese now lead the world in many areas of technology, as the USA did until recently, as Britain once did. Fortunately, the Japanese have yet to write a science fiction which the world will embrace as an essential part of its vocabulary. That honour is reserved for the Anglophone world. It travels everywhere, on one-way tickets.

It may be that the flexibility of the English tongue, its appetite for foreign words and concepts, its adaptability, have made it uniquely able to coin phrases and visions, to go in quest of definitions of mankind and its status in a changing universe.

Increasingly, though, other countries are originating science fiction, in modes designed to satisfy or stimulate local requirements. In France, however, science fiction has long spoken with its own unique voice; and there can hardly be a tongue on Earth into which the works of its most renowned practitioner have not been translated.

With Jules Verne looming ahead of us like Poe's monstrous figure in the ice fields, we should remind ourselves that science fiction was never a national prerogative.

The French could probably claim a figure as considerable as Erasmus Darwin in the writer best known to the English-speaking world for *Monsieur Nicolas*,

Restif de la Bretonne (1743–1806). One of Restif's biographers salutes him as "a prophet who foreshadowed the atom, the sputnik, flying men and air squadrons, interplanetary missiles, bacteriology, atomic energy, Communism, etc".[15] Most of this claim derives from Restif's work, *La Découverte australe, par un homme-volant* (four volumes, Paris, 1781).

Of this work, which may have been suggested by *Peter Wilkins*, a distinguished French scholar has written that it "not only described a heavier-than-air-flying machine which was a combination of helicopter and parachute, and foretold the creation of airborne fleets whose bombs would leave 'in the immense space of future time a trail of infamy, fear and horror', but looked forward beyond that period of war to the creation of a communist society in which property should be abolished".[16] This last vision was no vague utopian daydream: in *La Découverte australe* and other works Restif elaborated detailed practical plans for the institution of collective farms, a five-hour day, a five-and-a-half-day week, communal refectories, organized leisure activities, and changes in the penal system, all designed to achieve "a general reform of manners and through that reform the happiness of mankind". Restif was always aware of the sexuality of human beings. In this, his contribution to utopian literature is unique. He seems to have perceived the stubborn paradox which bedevils all our societies. Only when a society is designed to correspond to the basic motivations of human nature can a civilization become utopian. Nature and civilization are at odds. Yet both must find accommodation in a morally effective community.[17]

Finally, not content with describing the present and prophesying the future, he looked back to the very springs of life, sketched out a theory of microbes a hundred years before Pasteur, described a system of creative evolution which foreshadowed Bergson, and asserted his belief in "a divine electro-magnetico-intellectual fluid", which in our times Teilhard de Chardin was to call the "noosphere".[18]

From Restif de la Bretonne, a sedulous scholar may trace a thread to surrealism and Dadaism and the pop art movements that feed on them. That scholar may one day write a history of a hitherto undiscerned modern movement, its current intermingled with—but perhaps flowing against—the commercial genre of "space fiction". A European "scientific romance".

Certainly the pains and raptures of alternative worlds are contained in the writings of the man who called himself Gérard de Nerval. Nerval found inspiration in Restif's work. He endured the same generation gap as Thackeray and Dickens, being born in 1808—but in France, following the Revolution, the gap was wider, more dangerous, and the gulf between writer and society perhaps also deeper than in England.

Nerval was a poet, traveller, eccentric, and suicide. His body was found one morning in a Paris street, hanging by a piece of kitchen cord from the bars of a window, just before the second part of his most famous work, *Aurelia*, was published in 1854.

The opening of *Aurelia* is justly praised: "Our dreams are a second life. I have never been able to penetrate without a shudder those ivory or horned gates which separate us from the invisible world. . . ."[19] In its disorganized way, *Aurelia* presents many striking images, not least when it bursts into a kind of evolutionary fantasy:

> . . . I imagined myself transported to a dark planet where the first germs of creation were struggling. From the bosom of the still soft clay gigantic palm trees towered high, poisonous spurge and acanthus writhed around cactus plants: the arid shapes of rocks stuck out like skeletons from this rough sketch of creation, and hideous reptiles snaked, stretched, and coiled in the inextricable network of wild vegetation. Only the pale light of the stars lit the bluing perspectives of this strange horizon; yet, as the work of creation proceeded, a brighter star began to draw from it the germs of its own future brilliance.

Nerval's strange landscapes are presented as interior visions, a product in part of an anguished mental state which had no other outlet—although the story is still told of Nerval, perhaps apocryphally, that he would take his walks with a live lobster on a leash, which is indicative of a certain unusual state of mind. He described his trials as comparable with "that which the ancients understood by the idea of a descent into hell".[20]

Another romantic of slightly later date whose work, like Nerval's, seems to presage another age, is Villiers de l'Isle-Adam. He is generally regarded as the first symbolist. He lived and breathed in the exotic world peopled by the spectral presences of Byron, Hoffmann, Baudelaire, Hugo, and Poe.

Despite these illustrious shades, de l'Isle-Adam had his own original viewpoint, embodied in his famous play *Axel* (1890), with its well-known line, "Vivre? Les serviteurs feront cela pour nous", and writings which more closely approach science fiction, as they approach surrealism.

Notable among these are the *Contes Cruels* and *L'Ève future*. In the latter, published in 1886, de l'Isle-Adam tells of an inventor who creates a beautiful automaton, whom he christens Hadaly. Hadaly closely resembles a real woman; she can sing and carry on conversations, being powered by electricity and carrying a stack of gramophone records inside her metal breast.

This splendid creature looks back to the beautiful but mechanical Olympia in E. T. A. Hoffmann's "The Sandman", who dances and sings to clockwork perfection. Olympia was given an extension of life in Offenbach's opera *The Tales of Hoffmann*.[21]

De l'Isle-Adam's *Cruel Tales* (first published in book form in 1883) have a Poe-like strangeness and Poe's mistrust of materialism, together with a wider spectrum of interest than Poe could command.

The *Cruel Tales* are less cruel than unusual. They concern a duke suffering from a rare kind of leprosy, a duel which one of the seconds persists in regarding as a stage performance, a beautiful woman isolated from her lovers by deafness, a new machine for guaranteeing a play's success, the use of the night sky for advertising, and so on. In this latter story, "Celestial Publicity", as in many others, de l'Isle-Adam turns his sense of humour against the mercenary traits of the *bourgeoisie*:

A moment's reflection is enough to allow one to imagine the consequences of this ingenious invention. Would not the Great Bear herself have cause for astonishment if, between her sublime paws, there suddenly appeared this disquieting question: "Are corsets necessary?"[22]

In his sonnet to de l'Isle-Adam, Aldous Huxley concludes with the words:

> you bade the soul drink deep
> Of infinite things, saying, "The rest is naught."

Jules Verne (1828–1905) was born ten years earlier than de l'Isle-Adam. On him, as on the younger man, the writings of Poe in Baudelaire's translation had a stimulating effect; one of Verne's earliest stories *Cinq semaines en ballon* (*Five weeks in a Balloon*), published in 1863, bears a clear relationship to Poe's "The Balloon-Hoax" of 1844.

Poe's use of scientific detail must have attracted Verne; he would have liked, too, the way in which the Poeian protagonist stands outside society, as do Verne's great heroes. But where Poe is the doomed poet of the Inward, Verne is the supreme celebrant of the Outward.

In Verne, as in Nerval, we find descents, even to the earth's core. The symbolic significance is nil. The subterranean chamber gives way to the sea, the elements. Yet, even towards the end of Verne's career, he still fishes in Poe's wake. In 1897, he published *Le Sphinx des glaces* (known in English as *The Sphinx of the Ice Fields* or *An Antarctic Mystery*), a sequel to *The Narrative of Arthur George Pym*, which Verne believed to be incomplete.

Verne's career began in the theatre. He wrote plays, light opera, and sketches, and met Dumas *fils*, collaborating with him on several occasions.

Voyage au centre de la terre (*Journey to the Centre of the Earth*) (1864) was an early success. From then onwards, Verne wrote prolifically and enjoyed immense fame in a line "which I have invented myself", as he put it. That line was science fiction. Even if Verne did not invent science fiction, he was the first to succeed in it commercially, which is perhaps as great a thing. And he was the first and last to be blessed by the Pope for so doing. Even L. Ron Hubbard did not achieve as much.

Verne was born at Nantes, and so was familiar from birth with ocean-going ships and the traffic of ports. As a boy, he tried to run away to sea, was caught and beaten; but his father seems to have been an understanding man, who subsidized Verne's early writing. Although a misogynist, Verne had the sense to marry well and raise a large family. He went into local government, became a pillar of society, and enjoyed sailing his own yacht on that sea which comes breaking in as a symbol of freedom throughout many of his books. A prosperous and preposterous late nineteenth-century life. . . .

On the surface Verne remained as good a Catholic as de l'Isle-Adam was a bad one. On one of his cruises in the Mediterranean, he was received by the Pope, who praised him as a moral and didactic writer.[23] He died full of years and honours at Amiens. There his remains are interred under a grandiose tomb which depicts him rising again in full marble, but naked. This vision used to adorn the title pages of early *Amazings*.

One of Verne's critics, Marcel More[24], has argued that behind Verne's industrious and bourgeois facade lay a more anguished personality. The key to this perception is the way the novels concern only masculine relationships, where women, the few there are, are mere cyphers. In the words of a British biographer, Verne "never sullied his pages by descending to scenes of lust".[25]

Michel Butor, novelist and critic, takes another view of Verne, seeing him as "a cryptologist of the universe", composing imaginative variations on the themes of the four elements, earth, air, fire, and water, with electricity as a pure form of fire.[26] His characters forever oppose the unruliness of the world with logic; the poles are sacred places because they form still points in a turning world.

Such theories illuminate some aspects of the novels. A light is certainly needed to guide one through the toilsome mountain ranges of *Les Voyages extraordinaires*, the collective title of Verne's novels. They span the last four decades of the nineteenth century, and cover the globe, moving from one place to another in which struggles for liberty were being waged. Verne wrote in the great imperialist age. Like Wells, he is not on the side of the imperialists; yet he devours the world bit by bit as if it were an old *baguette*. Unlike later SF writers such as the Robert Heinlein of *Starship Troopers*, and the Pournelle school, Verne is quietly against conquest. His typical hero is a rebel or outcast from society, the most notable example being Captain Nemo, the nationless figure at the centre of *Twenty Thousand Leagues Under the Sea* (1870).

More amazing than the lack of women is the lack of religious feeling; throughout the great turbulent landscape of the novels, there is scarcely a priest or a church to be had. In extremities, the protagonists utter only a conventional cry to Providence. True, Milliard City has a church, St Mary's. Milliard City is the capital of *Une ville flottante* (1871, translated as *A Floating City*, 1876), a man-made island four and a half miles long and three broad, which travels about the oceans like a piece of floating geography. As with Verne's other machines, it works like mad. But no one visits the church. Verne is a utilitarian, a French Gradgrind.

In the early novels, detailing tremendous voyages to the centre of the Earth, to the bottom of the sea, to the Moon, or off on a comet, Verne celebrates man's progress. Both machines and machine-builders exist apart from society as a whole. But society comes creeping up. The tone of the novels changes, the atmosphere darkens with time. The later novels clog with satanic cities instead of super-subs, with Stahlstadt, Blackland, Milliard City. Even the brave scientists show signs of deterioration, eccentricity, blindness. The heroic age of the engine is done. Things fall apart, the centre will not hold.

Verne's great land of the future, America—setting of twenty-three of his sixty-four novels—develops increasingly negative aspects, a sickness Dr de

Tocqueville could diagnose. Dollar diplomacy enters, expansionism takes over, the machine-mentality triumphs. Robur, benevolent hero of 1886's *Robur le conquérant* (generally translated as *Clipper of the Clouds*) returns in a sequel as a destroyer (*Maître du Monde—Master of the World*). Men and societies are going down into eclipse, driving and driven by their dark angels, the machines.[27] Sam Smiles has moved out to make room for Nietzsche.

Pedestrian English translations of Verne have not diminished his popularity, merely his chance of better critical appraisal. His tone is flat, his characters are thin, and he pauses all too frequently for lectures; his is a non-sensual world, choked with facts. These are his negative features, and very damaging they are, even if his books are regarded as fit merely for boys as for years they were.

His positive features include a fascination with scientific possibilities, a passion for geography on the hoof, his undying affection for liberty and the underdog, an awareness of the political realities of his own time which parallels H. G. Wells's, and his relish for a good story. These qualities have rightly carried his books to treasured and meagre bookshelves round the world. Of course, it is his negative qualities which have been found most available for imitation by his successors.

There is little point in discussing *Les Voyages extraordinaires* individually.[28] A characteristic passage from an early novel must serve instead.

This is from *Hector Servadac* (1877), sometimes known as *Off on a Comet*. A comet has grazed the Earth, carrying a portion of North Africa, the Mediterranean, and the Rock of Gibraltar off into space. Along with this chunk go Captain Hector Servadac and his orderly, Ben Zoof. At first they are unable to account for the strange phenomena which surround them, but the truth of their exceptional situation gradually becomes clear to them. They meet other survivors of various nationalities in their travels, as they are whirled further from the Sun and the temperature becomes chillier.

> Telescopes in hand, the explorers scanned the surrounding view. Just as they had expected, on the north, east, and west lay the Gallian Sea, smooth and motionless as a sheet of glass, the cold having, as it were, congealed the atmosphere so that there was not a breath of wind. Toward the south there seemed no limit to the land, and the volcano formed an apex of a triangle, of which the base was beyond the reach of vision. Viewed even from this height, from which distance would do much to soften the general asperity, the surface nevertheless seemed to be bristling with its myriads of hexagonal lamellas, and to present difficulties which, to an ordinary pedestrian, would be insurmountable.
>
> "Oh for some wings, or else a balloon!" cried Servadac, as he gazed around him. And then, looking down at the rock upon which they were standing, he added, "We seem to have been transplanted to a soil strange enough in its chemical character to bewilder the savants at a museum."
>
> "And do you observe, Captain," asked the count, "how the convexity of our little world curtails our view? See, how circumscribed the horizon is!"

Servadac replied that he had noticed the same circumstance from the top of the cliffs of Gourbi Island.

"Yes," said the count. "It becomes more and more obvious that ours is a very tiny world, and that Gourbi Island is the sole productive spot upon its surface. We have had a short summer, and who knows whether we are not entering upon a winter that may last for years, perhaps for centuries?"

"But we must not mind, Count," said Servadac, smiling. "We have agreed, you know, that, come what may, we are to be philosophers."

"True, my friend," rejoined the count, "we must be philosophers and something more; we must be grateful to the good Protector who has thus far befriended us, and we must trust His mercy to the end. . . ."

Before the evening of this day closed in, a most important change was effected in the condition of the Gallian Sea by the intervention of human agency. Notwithstanding the increasing cold, the sea, unruffled as it was by a breath of wind, still retained its liquid state. It is an established fact that water, under this condition of absolute stillness, will remain uncongealed at a temperature several degrees below zero, while experiment, at the same time, shows that a very slight shock will often be sufficient to convert it into solid ice.

. . . Servadac . . . assembled his little colony upon a projecting rock at the extremity of the promontory, and having called Nina and Pablo out to him in front, he said:

"Now, Nina, do you think you could throw something into the sea?"

"I think I could," the child replied, "but I am sure that Pablo would throw it a great deal further than I can."

"Never mind, you shall try first."

Putting a fragment of ice into Nina's hands, he addressed himself to Pablo:

"Look out, Pablo; you shall see what miracles Nina can accomplish! Throw, Nina, throw as hard as you can."

Nina balanced the piece of ice two or three times in her hand, then threw it forward with all her strength.

A sudden thrill seemed to vibrate across the motionless waters to the distant horizon, and the Gallian Sea had become a solid sheet of ice![29]

Absurd perhaps, but colourful and dramatic. And of course based on scientific fact. And to be echoed in later writings. Burke's sublime gets its first chromium-plating. A myth-making trait in Verne's novels has allowed them to survive—dated though their details may be—when more serious work has died. The cinema has mined him extensively, following Walt Disney's successful Cinemascope production of *20,000 Leagues Under the Sea* in 1954, with James Mason playing Captain Nemo. The novel was first filmed as early as 1905. Verne has a long publishing life still before him.

Verne's huge initial success is coincidental with the establishment of railway bookstalls with their proliferating cheap editions, of popular lending libraries, and of various education acts.[30] Sensationalism, often coupled with a vague air of uplift, was much in demand, and sermons on science were becoming as respectable as sermons on morality.

Verne's sermons of work and militant liberty do not go down well at present, but a good translation of his best novels might effect a revaluation of his vast *oeuvre*, as seems to be happening presently in France, with critics of the stature of Butor and Chesneaux.

Before leaving France, mention must also be made of the draughtsman, engraver and writer, Albert Robida, one of the first men to grasp how the technologies of the nineteenth century might be turned to total warfare. Robida's visions began to appear in a periodical, *La Caricature*, in 1883; they were published in Paris in book form in 1887 as *La guerre au vingtième siècle* (*The Twentieth Century War*) and provide an extraordinary panorama of new weapons of the future, illustrated in Robida's delightful and spectacular style. Also in the 1880s, Robida produced a second serial, *La vie électrique*. Both novels are set in the 1950s. I. F. Clarke has said of Robida that his is "the first major vision of technological warfare ever presented". But Robida's outlook is essentially light-hearted, his illustrations have panache, and many of his incidents are comic—for instance, food kitchens on a mammoth scale supply the needs of his future city, the nutrients being pumped through enormous iron pipes; but a pipe bursts and floods Robida's hero's home with soup.

Despite this blithe approach, Robida made many remarkable forecasts. It was a game that all could play. At the turn of the century, in particular, looking forward became a hobby. Although would-be inventors or cartoonists could easily dream up a personal flying-machine with pack and propellor strapped on the back and flapping wings above, they could scarcely imagine what wide-scale effects such an innovation would have on society. Instead, they contented themselves with picturing the appliance simplifying courtship or complicating a game of tennis.[31]

From the ascent of the first hot-air balloon, despatched by the brothers Montgolfier in 1783, onwards, it was a pleasant exercise of the imagination to visualize aerial warfare. Those first paper novelties were soon recognized as omens of something less pleasant—yet the tone is generally half facetious, for men were still not trained to regard the future with great seriousness.

In this respect, one of the earliest balloon paintings remains the most striking. Towards the end of his long life, Francesco Guardi, the contemporary of those other Venetian masters, G. B. Tiepolo and Canaletto, painted the *Ascent of the Montgolfier Balloon, 1784*. There it sails over the Giudecca, while the Venetians watch it under their colonnades; dressed in their finery, they huddle and gawp at the new thing as helplessly as any bunch of peasants. Through Guardi's brushstrokes, we watch the old order confronted by the ascendance of the new.

Balloons were soon being used in reality for military ends. The first air raid in history took place in 1849, when the Austrians used pilotless *montgolfières* to bomb Venice. Gas balloons were extensively employed during the siege of Paris, 1870–71.

A more earnest note enters speculation on future warfare during this period, coinciding with the growing imperialism of the European powers. Critics owe a debt to the researches of I. F. Clarke for his exhumation of the literature of this subject[32], and for his resurrection of the pamphlet *The Battle of Dorking*, published in 1871, when the balance of power in Europe had been so remarkably altered by the German invasion of France.

The Battle of Dorking, published anonymously, was by Colonel George Tomkyns Chesney, and his story is purely didactic in intent: to warn England of Germany's rearmament and of her own unpreparedness.

His narrator is a volunteer who fought in the engagements he is describing to his grandchildren. He tells of an invasion of England in the near future, in which modern Prussian forces sweep away a native army still attempting to fight as it did at Waterloo. It is beaten and broken. Fortitude is not enough. At Guildford, the First Army Corps is falling back; everywhere, British troops have to retreat in disorder; Woolwich, the country's only arsenal, is captured by the enemy. London falls, the country surrenders and is stripped of its colonies.

Darwinism gave new point to the knowledge that only the fittest army will survive; it also produced the perspectives into which a tale of the future could be painted. But a more immediate inspiration for *Dorking* was those new breechloaders rolling out of Krupp's.

Chesney tells his story with vigour and sure military knowledge. Even his polemics come in the same forthright prose, without waste of words.

> Truly the nation was ripe for a fall; but when I reflect how a little firmness and self-denial, or political courage and foresight, might have averted the disaster, I feel that the judgment might have really been deserved. A nation too selfish to defend its liberty, could not have been fit to retain it. To you, my grandchildren, who are now going to seek a new home in a more prosperous land, let not this bitter lesson to be lost upon you in the country of your adoption.

Chesney's story was immediately effective. Fear and interest were aroused on all sides. Gladstone spoke out against the pernicious pamphlet: "Unfortunately these things go abroad, and they make us ridiculous in the eyes of the whole world."

Go abroad they did. For Chesney had hit upon a formula and a nerve centre. The device of future war, sudden invasion, beggarly unpreparedness, inevitable defeat, and national disgrace was open to all. Counter-arguments, translations, imitations, parodies, appeared at home and in European countries; while in the United States, Canada, Australia, and New Zealand, more editions of Chesney's story were rapidly printed. A new fashion in Dreadful Warnings has begun.

As I. F. Clarke puts it, "Between 1871 and 1914 it was unusual to find a single year without some tale of future warfare appearing in some European country." France, the mood of *la revanche* upon it, was the first country to produce a revised version of Chesney, with *La bataille de Berlin en 1875*—a story of comfort rather than discomfort.

Such was the prestige of Chesney's story that, almost thirty years later, in 1900, another colonel, also anonymously, published *The New Battle of Dorking*—clearly confident that the reference would be widely understood. The last edition of Chesney's story was a German translation—published by the Nazi regime in 1940, as England lay awaiting possible invasions.

That the Chesney syndrome is by no means exhausted was shown by the wide success of General Sir John Hackett's *The Third World War* (1978). Even in his choice of viewpoint, it is evident that Hackett has learnt from the earlier military man. The Prologue of his story commences, "The publication of this book so soon after the cessation of hostilities between major participants in the Third World War will mean that much of what it contains will be incomplete. . . ." etc.

Last century's tales of future wars which never took place make dusty reading now. It is hard to say whether these Dire Warnings are really SF. Sufficient to note that the tradition was a flourishing one, and that H. G. Wells's *The War of the Worlds* belongs to that tradition. Wells wrote many books about war, and was not alone in that. He may be contrasted with William Le Queux, who specialized in war scares. A new Le Queux was the by-product of every European crisis. Franco-Russian amity in 1893 produced Le Queux's *The Great War in England in 1897*, published in a journal that year. It was widely popular, was issued in book form, and inspired many imitations, including several by Le Queux himself. We find him still going strong just before the outbreak of war in 1914.[33]

Scientific rationalism coupled with a general authoritarianism in society had set up diluted realism as the proper channel for the novel in the eighteen-sixties. As respectability sought to smother its opposite, so a rich vein of fantasy flowed beneath the sort of realistic social novel of which Trollope was a successful exponent.[34]

> The whole great wicked artificial civilized fabric,
> All its unfinished houses, lots for sale, and railway outworks

as Clough called it, might be laid bare in the novels of Dickens, Charles Reade, and Mrs Gaskell, but the best fantasy did not entail an entire abandonment of reason and responsibility. Hawthorne and Melville were great American influences. The reforming novelist Charles Kingsley turned to *The Water Babies* (1863). Meredith's *The Shaving of Shagpat* (1856) is a mixture of Arabian Nights and Gothic. George MacDonald entered the lists with his symbolic fairy tale *At the Back of the North Wind* (1871). Uncanny fantasy reposed in the hands of

Sheridan Le Fanu, the Irish poet and journalist whose writings include *The House by the Churchyard* (1863) and *In a Glass Darkly* (1872), which contains much-anthologized short stories, such as "Green Tea" and "Carmilla".

Le Fanu's sinister masterpiece, *Uncle Silas*, was published in 1864 and is still justly enjoyed today. Also at high table with Le Fanu sits Wilkie Collins, the friend of Dickens. Collins published *The Moonstone* in 1868, when half awash with laudanum—a powerful early tale of detection with fantastic elements, untrustworthy Orientals, double lives, crime committed under the influence of drugs, and a strong undercurrent of superstition, which was not without its impact upon Dickens's last and unfinished novel, *The Mystery of Edwin Drood* (1870).

In the next decade, the eighteen-eighties, a storyteller of a different kind emerges, with a dark and powerful fantasy containing several layers of meaning. This is Robert Louis Stevenson, whose *The Strange Case of Dr Jekyll and Mr Hyde* was published in 1886.

Framed in a narrative contributed by three different hands, it relates, as every schoolboy worth his salt must still know, how an Edinburgh doctor discovers a concoction which releases his baser nature. Unhappily, the drug is habit-forming. The baser nature, Mr Hyde, takes over, commits murder, and is finally hunted down. Like several other works we have noted, *Dr Jekyll* began as a dream, which RLS wrote down when he awoke.

> Late one accursed night, I compounded the elements, watched them boil and smoke together in the glass, and when the ebullition had subsided, with a strong glow of courage, drank off the potion.
>
> The most racking pains succeeded: a grinding in the bones, deadly nausea, and a horror of the spirit that cannot be exceeded at the hour of birth or death. Then these agonies began swiftly to subside, and I came to myself as if out of a great sickness. There was something strange in my sensations, something incredibly new . . . I knew myself, at the first breath of this new life, to be more wicked, tenfold more wicked, sold a slave to my original evil.

Even in a volume like this, dedicated to strange stories, *Dr Jekyll* remains very strange. Stevenson was conscious of its allegory; but what exactly is the allegory? Is it concerning the duality of man's nature, with "angel and fiend" (in Jekyll's words) in one flesh? Is it about the struggle between rationality and instinct? Or is what Jekyll calls "the brute that slept within me" playing its "apelike tricks", a mythical reinterpretation of the Descent of Man? Whichever of these readings Stevenson favoured (and there is no reason why they should not all have been in his mind), there is little doubt that the doppelganger relationship between Jekyll and Hyde parallels the one between Frankenstein and *his* bundle of retribution, the monster.[35]

We see Stevenson now through time's diminishing glass, but he achieved great fame in his day, partly for his personal history of illness and retreat to the South Seas. H. G. Wells was later to admit to his influence, for Jekyll is one in the line of meddling savants from Frankenstein to Wells's Moreau and Griffin and so on to yesterday's "mad scientist" and today's horribly sane ones.

Before *Dr Jekyll*, Stevenson had written other fantasies, *The New Arabian Nights* and a real heart-knocker, "Thrawn Janet", among them. "Thrawn Janet" is about a black man who takes over—and occasionally takes off—a dead woman's body. It is a sort of ur-Jekyll. But Stevenson's main influence was as a teller of splendid romantic tales, such as *Treasure Island* and *Kidnapped*, and we shall come across several novelists of the nineties in a later chapter who emulate something of his swashbuckle, if not his vein of dark fantasy.

Lewis Carroll's kind of fantasy stands apart, not only from Stevenson's, which it predates, but from everyone else's.

For the SF buff, 1871 is a vintage year. It saw the publication not only of *The Battle of Dorking* and Lytton's *The Coming Race* but of an adult fantasy masquerading as a child's book, *Through the Looking Glass*.

> . . . And certainly the glass was beginning to melt away, just like a bright silvery mist.
>
> In another moment, Alice was through the glass, and had jumped lightly down into the looking-glass room. The very first thing she did was to look whether there was a fire in the fireplace, and she was quite pleased to find that there was a real one, blazing away as brightly as the one she had left behind . . . Then she began looking about, and noticed that what could be seen from the old room was quite common and uninteresting, but that all the rest was as different as possible.

Through the Looking Glass is inseparable from its predecessor, *Alice's Adventures in Wonderland* (1865). Though nominally addressed to children, these two unique Victorian dreams contain profound veins of symbolism, imagination, satire, and metaphysical terror, as well as a reinterpretation of the Victorian submerged-nation theme noted in Disraeli, Kingsley, and Lytton. (The first Alice book was originally called *Alice's Adventures Underground*.) Adults discern these veins below a delightful surface play of up-ended logic.

> Alice laughed. "There's no use trying," she said: "one *can't* believe impossible things."
>
> "I daresay you haven't had much practice," said the Queen. "When I was your age, I always did it for half an hour a day. Why sometimes I've believed as many as six impossible things before breakfast."

Compare:

> "How many fingers, Winston?"
>
> "Four. I suppose there are four. I would see five if I could. I am trying to see five."
>
> "Which do you wish: to persuade me that you see five, or really to see them?"

"Really to see them."

"Again," said O'Brien.

Alice and her immortal adventures form no part of science fiction. Equally, her ventures into other dimensions and her experience of situations where the commonplace is weirdly distorted ("Now, here, you see, it takes all the running you can do, to keep in the same place. If you want to get somewhere else, you must run at least twice as fast as that," says the Red Queen) relate to the surreal aspect of science fiction. Carroll's various amazing animals, often mythological, often grotesquely dressed, stand between the worlds of Beatrix Potter and the universe of Gray Lensman.

Carroll's logical inversions have had a marked effect on the field, though his adroit mixture of fantasy, seriousness and wit is less easily imitated. It has surfaced occasionally in the writings of Henry Kuttner, Ray Bradbury, Eric Frank Russell and Robert Sheckley, among others.

Carroll's method has also been assimilated. "Gulliver is a commonplace little man and Alice a commonplace little girl," says C. S. Lewis in his essay on science fiction.[36] "To tell how odd things struck odd people is to have an oddity too much." This rule has generally been observed.

Beside the major figure of Carroll we may set a minor one, another scholar with an interest in mathematics, Edwin A. Abbott. Abbott was a Shakespearian scholar and theologian, now best remembered for that slender sport *Flatland*, first published in 1884 and surviving still by reason of its wit and originality.

Flatland—subtitled *A Romance of Many Dimensions* (and published as by A. Square)—describes a world where the inhabitants live in two dimensions; they are of various shapes, triangles, squares, circles, pentagons, and so on, but can see each other only as straight lines because they have only length and breadth. It is a terrible place in many other ways; law and order are major preoccupations in Flatland, and women, being sharp-pointed, are penalized.

This slender work is hardly science fiction, conforming to our original definition in content but not form, which is of the straight expository kind, aided by blackboard diagrams. But it has always attracted SF readers, not least because its lucid account of two dimensions reminds us that we may be relatively as imperceptive of the reality of our universe as were the inhabitants of Flatland.

A recent amusing gloss on *Flatland* is Rudy Rucker's story, "Message Found in a Copy of *Flatland*", reprinted in the story collection *The 57th Franz Kafka* (New York, 1983). Rucker is also a mathematician.

Our rapid survey demonstrates that science fiction and many of its themes were flourishing by the end of the 1890s. The diversity of the nineteenth century—its achievements and disappointments under which we still labour—guarantees that.

It has been possible to point only to a title here and there. Yet many of these titles, from the earliest times until our day, have been immensely influential, not only on the literati, but in moving the minds of practical men unused to books. As Dickens's *Great Expectations* would be different without *Frankenstein*, so the shape of Brasilia, Washington, Canberra, would be different without Plato. The history of SF is largely the history of an unwritten culture, full of lost hopes. As one eminent critic puts it, "in view of the largely suppressed SF tradition, the achievement of each such major writer (such names as Plato, Lucian, More, Verne) not only *has to* but legitimately *can* indicate and stand for the possibilities of a largely mute inglorious epoch".[37]

How are we to live? What sort of animal are we that we live as we do?

To set science fiction down as something beginning with Hugo Gernsback's lurid magazines in the nineteen-twenties, as some histories have done, is a wretched error. Science fiction must call to account our deepest fears and aspirations.

As the nineteenth century drew to a close, as the dark cities spread on every continent, as metal roads were driven through jungles, questioning minds among the gas-enlightened race asked themselves opposed sets of questions: was the millennium round the corner? What was being lost to Progress?

All over Europe in the 1890s, it is safe to say, opposed utopian and dystopian visions were being written and read. The sense of a new age dawning, an old age dying, was felt. In Slovenia, for example, on the sunny side of the Alps, in what is now Jugoslavia, Ivan Tavĉar, a respected author and Mayor of Ljubljana, published *4000: Ĉasu Primerna Povest iz Prihodnjih Dob* (1891). *4000* presents an optimistic view of the world of the future. Tavĉar is still honoured today, at least to the extent that there is a tavern in Ljubljana named after him, where his writings are preserved.

Far north of Slovenia, Tyko Hagman wrote the first Finnish science fiction story, "Matkustus Kuuhun", published in 1887. Finland was then an agricultural country under Russian rule. Hagman wrote of a more advanced civilization on the Moon. He hoped for better times in the next century, as did Tavĉar.

The idea of utopia has grown dull since Tavĉar's time. The theme of nature coming back into its own has never died.

For all its pains, civilization is to be preferred to barbarism, isn't it? The two oppositions present themselves to us vividly today. Barbarism is filled with boredom, slavery, drudgery and fear. But there are writers who present barbarism as a luring alternative to the technological state.

W. H. Hudson's *A Crystal Age* (1887) has affinities with Morris's reveries. Hudson's narrator undergoes a classical metamorphosis, awakening from sleep to find himself in an undated future where industry is no more. *A Crystal Age* is a pastoral, sickly to some tastes. Society is now stable because the sexual impulse has waned. Hudson wrote better things—*A Shepherd's Life*, for instance, and *Green Mansions*.

The theme of nature reasserting its dominance can be clearly related to evolutionary thought. If humanity does not prove fit to rule the world and itself, then it will be overwhelmed. Earth will be green once more. The wilderness will come again.

This particular variation on the theme of nemesis was given memorable expression by a naturalist and journalist suffering from a terminal case of consumption. Richard Jefferies's *After London* (1885) begins with a survey, Hardyesque in tone, of what happens to the land "after London ended". Jefferies hated London and the age in which he lived. He shares none of Hardy's or Tennyson's cautious welcome of change and "the thoughts that shake mankind". He sat defeated in Brighton, phthisically writing off change, thought, and the metropolis.

Jefferies could not visualize a catastrophe devastating enough to demolish a whole capital city. Our fancies are much clearer in that respect. Jefferies dispenses with all explanations. London has ended. This lends his text an agreeably sinister and Kafkaesque taking-the-unaccountable-for-granted air.

The triumph of nature is described in grand style:

Footpaths were concealed by the second year, but roads could be traced, though as green as the sward, and were still the best for walking, because the tangled wheat and weeds, and, in the meadows, the long grass, caught the feet of those who tried to pass through. Year by year the original crops of wheat, barley, oats, and beans asserted their presence by shooting up, but in gradually diminished force, as nettles and coarser plants, such as the wild parsnips, spread out into the fields from the ditches and choked them.

Aquatic grasses from the fields and water-carriers extended in the meadows, and, with the rushes, helped to destroy or take the place of the former sweet herbage. Meanwhile, the brambles, which grew very fast, had pushed forward their prickly runners farther and farther from the hedges till they now had reached ten or fifteen yards. The briars had followed, and the hedges had widened to three or four times their breadth first, the fields being equally contracted. Starting from all sides at once, these brambles and briars in the course of about twenty years met in the centre of the largest fields.

Hawthorn bushes sprang up among them, and, protected by the briars and thorns from grazing animals, the suckers of elm-trees rose and flourished. Sapling ashes, oaks, sycamores and horse-chestnuts lifted their heads. Of old time the cattle would have eaten off the seed leaves with the grass so soon as they were out of the ground, but now most of the acorns that were dropped by birds, and the keys that were wafted by the wind, twirled as they floated, took root, and grew into trees. By this time the brambles and briars had choked up and blocked the former roads, which were as impassable as the fields. (Chapter 1)

Interest fades when Jefferies introduces characters into his feral landscape; his people enjoy less animation than his plants. Perceptive naturalist though he was, Jefferies's gifts as a novelist are small, and—as many later writers bear witness— imagination is of little use unless teamed with the other necessary talents of a writer.

The ruins of ancient Athens and Rome still impress us. They have power over our minds still, representing as they do the historic cradle of so many Western traditions. Similarly such staple SF ideas as the Wilderness Come Again can be revisited continually as long as the possibility prompting the idea remains—in this case the costs of Progress.

While Jefferies was writing and dying, another tubercular young man was living and working in the sooty, hammer-and-tongs London Jefferies was busy destroying. This young man, Herbert George Wells, was attending Professor Thomas Huxley's lectures in biology and zoology. Time was approaching when he would prove himself to have in superabundance the necessary talents of a writer—and a towering and ferocious imagination besides.

CHAPTER V

The Great General in Dreamland:
H. G. Wells

And here like some weird Archimage sit I,
Plotting dark spells, and devilish enginery,
The self-impelling steam-wheels of the mind
Which pump up oaths from clergymen
—P. B. Shelley: Letter to Maria Gisborne

Increasing industrialization brought increasing power into play in the West. Much could be done that had never been done. Yet technology, or its misappliance, increased an ordinary citizen's feeling of helplessness and alienation.

In the year that H. G. Wells's first book was published, Sigmund Freud's *Studien über Hysterie* laid the cornerstone for psychoanalysis. Freud's teaching dominated thinking in ways later generations will scarcely credit. Like industrialization, Freud undermined belief in the power of reason. His work on the interpretation of dreams and their sexual content, shocked and fascinated the Western world. Under the gilt and plush of late Victorian times gathered the tide of uncertainty on which we ride today. Wells was ideally placed to embody that uncertainty in a series of dream-like images, which distil the paradoxical hopes and fears of his age.

The attention psychoanalysis has drawn to the few but powerful archetypal figures in the psyche paved a way for the acceptance of diverse arts—surrealism, photography, cinema, and science fiction, where aliens, robots, spaceships, planets, and so on act as counters in a complex mental game. A character landing on the moon can be a symbol of conquest, of fulfilment, or of alienation, depending on context. Writers perhaps understand this more readily than mainstream critics, who do not always distinguish between characters and personages.

Wells had the new language off from the start.

Herbert George Wells was born in Bromley, Kent, in 1866, into his parents' little china shop. He made his way in the world with no assets but his genius. Life long remained a battle for health and success.

Wells's mother had been in service when she met and married H. G.'s father, then working as a gardener. The shop was their first hopeful matrimonial venture together; it failed by degrees, year after year. Wells wrote with love and some exasperation of his mother, "Almost as unquestioning as her belief in Our Father was her belief in drapers." After some elementary schooling, his first job

118 TRILLION YEAR SPREE

was in a draper's shop in Windsor. He was no good at it, and they told him he was not refined enough to be a draper. He got the sack.

This was the man who wrote two books in 1905 of which the great Henry James said in a letter, "Let me tell you, simply, that they have left me prostrate with admiration, and that you are, for me, more than ever, the most interesting 'literary man' of your generation."[1]

Wells became a teacher, educating himself as he went along, and so moved into journalism and authorship. His first books appeared in 1895, when he was almost thirty. Around him, a raw new London was emerging, consciously the Heart of Empire—an expanding capital trapped in the contracting housing Wells described with such hatred. The central figures of many of his novels are chirpy Cockney "little men" with whom he was entirely familiar—their accents came to him through the flimsy bedroom partitions of his various digs. Wells exhibits them for inspection rather than admiration.[2]

In this submerged metropolitan world, taking lessons from Thomas Huxley, thinking great thoughts and struggling with great illnesses, Wells lived and survived. In 1895, he was paid one hundred pounds by W. E. Henley for his short novel *The Time Machine*. Its sceptical view of the present, and its pessimistic view of the future of mankind—and of life on Earth—challenged most of the cosy ideas of progress, as well as the new imperialism, then current.

Except for a collection of essays, *The Time Machine* was the first of Wells's one hundred and twenty-odd books, and it is very nearly his most perfect. It was an immediate success.[3]

Here is part of the famous passage in which the time-traveller stands alone at the end of the world—the Last Man theme again—and looks about him:

> The darkness grew apace; a cold wind began to blow in freshening gusts from the east, and the showering white flakes in the air increased in number. From the edge of the sea came a ripple of a whisper. Beyond these lifeless sounds, the world was silent. Silent? It would be hard to convey the stillness of it. All the sounds of man, the bleating of sheep, the cries of birds, the hum of insects, the stir that makes the background of our lives— all that was over. As the darkness thickened, the eddying flakes grew more abundant, dancing before my eyes; and the cold of the air more intense. At last, one by one, swiftly, one after the other, the white peaks of the distant hills vanished into blackness. The breeze rose to a moaning wind. I saw the black central shadow of the eclipse sweeping towards me. In another moment the pale stars alone were visible. All else was rayless obscurity. The sky was absolutely black.
>
> A horror of this great darkness came on me . . . I felt giddy and incapable of facing the return journey. . . .

As Bernard Bergonzi has stressed in his excellent study of Wells's science fiction[4], *The Time Machine* is very much a *fin de siècle* book. One glimpses in it some of the despairs of Hardy's vision; while the Eloi, those pale, decadent, artistic people that the time-traveller discovers, carry a flavour of the aesthete from the eighteen-seventies, and are echoed in those pale lost lilies of people who haunt Beardsley's and Walter Crane's drawings and Ernest Dowson's poems.

The Eloi live above ground, in idyllic surroundings. Below ground live the dark and predatory Morlocks, appearing at night to snatch the helpless Eloi. The innocence and laughter of the Eloi are only an appearance; below the surface lies corruption. The theme is a familiar Victorian one; it had vivid meaning for urban generations striving to install efficient modern sewers under their towns. One finds it, for instance, in Oscar Wilde's *The Picture of Dorian Gray*, published in 1891, where the sinner stays young and fair; only his portrait, locked away from prying eyes, ages and grows dissipated and obscene.

But the Eloi and Morlocks have historically deeper roots. They are a vivid science fictional dramatization of Disraeli's two nations. Wells tells us as much in a later book, *The Soul of a Bishop*:

> "There's an incurable misunderstanding between the modern employer and the modern employed," the chief labour spokesman said, speaking in a broad accent that completely hid from him and the bishop and every one the fact that he was by far the best-read man of the party. "Disraeli called them the Two Nations, but that was long ago. Now it's a case of two species. Machinery has made them into different species . . . We'll get a little more education and then we'll do without you. We're pressing for all we can get, and when we've got that we'll take breath and press for more. We're the Morlocks. Coming up."

This "submerged-nation" theme, coupled with the idea of retribution, is essentially a British obsession, occurring in writers as diverse as Lewis Carroll, Charles Dickens, S. Fowler Wright, and John Wyndham. The essential American obsession, as we shall see, is with the Alien—and thus perhaps with self-identity.

Wells in his thirties was prodigious. Most of his best books were published before his fortieth birthday: *The Island of Doctor Moreau, The Invisible Man, The War of the Worlds, When the Sleeper Wakes* (later revised as *The Sleeper Awakes*), *The First Men in the Moon, Tales of Space and Time, The Food of the Gods*, and the two novels before which the Master was prostrate, *A Modern Utopia* and *Kipps*, as well as such non-SF works as *Love and Mr Lewisham* and *Anticipations*.

Still to come after that first decade of writing were many good things, among them *The History of Mr Polly, The New Machiavelli, The War in the Air, Ann Veronica*, and a number of lesser and later books which would have looked well in the lists of a lesser writer: *Tono-Bungay, The World Set Free, The Dream, The Shape of Things to Come, All Aboard for Ararat*, and *Men Like Gods* (about which more will be said in Chapter 7), as well as his excursions into popular education, such as *The Outline of History, The Work, Wealth and Happiness of Mankind*, and *The Rights of Man*.

We also remember Wells for a number of remarkable short stories. He was one of the forgers of this genre in England, following the example of de l'Isle-

Adam, de Maupassant, and others in France. Among his stories are some that won immense popularity in their time, such as "The Country of the Blind", "The Door in the Wall", "The Truth about Pyecraft", "The Crystal Egg", and "The Man who Could Work Miracles". Most of them belong to Wells's early creative phase.

In many of these stories Wells proved himself the great originator of science fictional ideas. They were new with him, and have been reworked endlessly since. He seems to have been the first fiction writer to use the perspectives of evolution to look backwards as well as forwards. His "The Grisly Folk" (1896) is a tale of humankind struggling against the Neanderthals as the glaciers retreated. "Great Paladins arose in that forgotten world, men who stood forth and smote the grey man-beast face to face and slew him."

Tales of prehistory have always remained a sort of sub-genre of science fantasy. Wells also wrote "A Story of the Stone Age" (1897), and Jack London dealt with the confrontation of human with pre-human, but it is not until William Golding's *The Inheritors* (1955) that this theme yields anything like a masterpiece. Wells's mind is the first to venture so far into the past as well as the future.

Among science fiction writers past and present, Wells, with Olaf Stapledon, is one indisputable giant. His debt to Hawthorne, Poe, and Swift, which he acknowledged, is apparent; he mentions also the novels of Oliver Wendell Holmes and Stevenson[5] in this context. It is true that Wells lacks the Inwardness we perceive in Mary Shelley; but he has an abundance of imagination as well as inventiveness—the two are by no means identical.

The virtues which lift Wells above his successors (and above Verne) are threefold. Firstly, he inherited something of the enquiring spirit of Swift—and science is, when all's said, a matter of enquiry. From this spring the other two virtues, Wells's ability to see clearly the world-as-it-is (for without such an ability it is impossible to visualize any other world very clearly), and his lifelong avoidance of drawing lead characters with whom readers will uncritically identify and thus be lulled into acceptance of whatever is offered.

To see how these virtues work in practice, we may examine two of the early novels, *The War of the Worlds* and *The Island of Doctor Moreau*.

The War of the Worlds was published in serial form in 1897 and in book form a year later. It describes what happens when Martian invaders land on Earth. The story is told by an English observer, who sees the invaders move in on London against all the Army can do to hold them off. London is evacuated before the invaders die, killed by common microbes.

As even this brief outline shows, *The War of the Worlds* is part of the literary lineage which includes Chesney's *The Battle of Dorking*. But Wells makes a twofold progression. This time the invader is from another planet. This time, the invader is effortlessly more powerful than the invaded.

These two steps forward are not merely a projection of wandering fantasy; they form a development of the moral imagination. For Wells is saying, in effect, to his fellow English, "Look, this is how it feels to be a primitive tribe, and to have a Western nation arriving to civilize you with Maxim guns!"

An element of *fable* or oblique social criticism in Wells's early work is marked, from the novels to such short stories as "The Country of the Blind" and "The Door in the Wall". Yet it remains always subservient to the strong flow of his invention; only when invention flagged did moralizing obtrude and the narrative become pedestrian.

Certainly Wells was aware of the change which overtook his writing. He spoke of two kinds of thinking, directed and undirected thought. In *The Work, Wealth and Happiness of Mankind* (1931), Wells talks in Chapter 2 of directed thought as something which enters philosophy with Plato and which defines the scientific aspect of modern civilization. Undirected thought is a sort of muzzy version of thinking, imaginative play, almost what we would call a hypnoid state.

Wells's writing moves gradually from undirected to directed thought. From a fiction capable of ironic and ambivalent tolerances to a functional fiction directed towards proof and prediction. Fiction cannot be justified by its power to predict. Even science fiction is not a science. (And is at its weakest when it pretends otherwise.)

A useful discussion of these two antithetical ways of thought, by John Huntington[6], is followed by a searching analysis of *The Time Machine* which, if taken further, would reveal a Wells of greater—and more extended—artistry than he himself allowed.

The ambivalences continue in *The Invisible Man*. We are not intended to identify with Griffin in his strange plight. Nor can we exactly side against him with the village of Iping, where Griffin takes refuge, for the village proves to be ruled by money. They tolerate their seclusion-loving guest only until he "shows signs of penury".

Even when we are used to the extraordinary wealth of detail which grows from the central invention, the story holds us.

The moral beneath the fable is that scientific knowledge should not be used for selfish gain (as Moreau uses his knowledge for personal satisfaction and so is damned just like Dr Jekyll); but this moral is so profoundly part of the fabric of the story that many reviewers and readers missed the point, and complained that Griffin was "unsympathetic". Similar obtuseness confronts a science fiction writer today. His audience is accustomed to powerful heroes with whom they can unthinkingly identify. A mass audience expects to be pandered to. Wells never pandered.

Of course, Wells provides plenty of sensationalism in *War of the Worlds*. There is the carefully detailed destruction of the London of his day, followed by the horrible appearance of the Martians. Cunningly, Wells refrains from describing his invaders—we have seen them only in their machines—until over halfway through the book. They are then as ghastly as you please.

After a description of their external appearance comes an account of their internal anatomy when dissected. Wells's manner is cool and detached. From description, he turns to a discussion of the way in which the Martian physiology functions ("Their organisms did not sleep, any more than the heart of man sleeps") in matter-of-fact detail, going on to consider Martian evolution. The telling stroke, when it comes, lifts the whole remarkable passage to a higher level. "To me it is quite credible that the Martians may be descended from beings not unlike ourselves, by a gradual development of brains and hands . . . at the expense of the rest of the body." It is this linking of the Martians with humanity, rather than separating them from it, which shows Wells's superior creative powers. At the same time, he prepares us for the surprise and the logic of his final denouement.

C. S. Lewis was later to attack Wells for peopling our minds with modern hobgoblins. The hobgoblins were already there. It was Wells's successors in the pulp magazines, the horror merchants with no intent but to lower the reader's body temperature as fast as possible, who served up horror for its own sake. Wells's non-humans, his Martians, Morlocks, Selenites, and Beast-People, are creatures not of horror but terror; they spring from a sophisticated acknowledgement that they are all part of us, of our flesh. It was the later horror merchants who made their creatures alien from us, externalizing evil. Wells's position is (malgré lui) the orthodox Christian one, that evil is within us. His non-humans are not without Grace but fallen from Grace. Freud would have understood.

In The War of the Worlds we can distinguish Wells using three principles to produce this masterly piece of science fiction. Firstly, he begins by drawing a recognizable picture of his own times, "the present day". While we acknowledge the truth of this picture, we are being trained to accept the veracity of what follows. Secondly, he uses the newer scientific principles of his times, evolutionary theory and the contagious and infectious theories of microorganisms, as a hinge for the story.[7] Thirdly, he allows a criticism of his society, and possibly of mankind in general, to emerge from the narrative.

This remains a classic ground plan for an SF novel. Veracity, capacity, universality.

To these three principles must be added Wells's ability to write. There are few openings in science fiction more promising, more chilling, than that first page of The War of the Worlds, including as it does the passage, "Across the gulf of space, minds that are to our minds as ours are to those of the beasts that perish, intellects vast and cool and unsympathetic, regarded this earth with envious eyes, and slowly and surely drew their plans against us." How beautifully underplayed is that adjective "unsympathetic"!

Yet Wells's early readers were puzzled over the question of his originality. How original was he? This question of originality is bandied about with regard to today's writers, all of whom stand in Wells's portly shadow. Wells himself has an amused word to say on the subject in his autobiography.

In the course of two or three years I was welcomed as a second Dickens, a second Bulwer Lytton and a second Jules Verne. But also I was a second Barrie, though J.M.B. was hardly more than my contemporary, and, when I turned to short stories, I became a second Rudyard Kipling. I certainly, on occasion, imitated both these excellent masters. Later on I figured also as a second Diderot, a second Carlyle and a second Rousseau[8] . . . These second-hand tickets were very convenient as admission tickets. It was however unwise to sit down in the vacant chairs, because if one did so, one rarely got up again.[9]

These remarks indicate a certain amorphousness in the character of Wells, an amorphousness which was to stand him in good stead in his writing, where he could be many things, whatever difficulties it produced in his emotional life. Some writers have a need to be protean.

As a result, Wells was not above a little posturing. He enjoyed charades and the company of those who posture (at one time, he was friendly with Charlie Chaplin). Making an attempt to sum himself up, he once claimed that he was "a sentimentalist, a moralist, a patriot, a racist, a great general in dreamland, a member of a secret society, an immortal figure in history, an impulsive fork thrower and a bawling self-righteous kicker of domestic shins".

All these things Wells was and more. To most of the readers of this book, however, he is most cherished as—in that fine phrase of his—"a Great General in Dreamland".

The War of the Worlds enjoyed an immediately favourable reception from readers and critics. Yet many of its aspects were ignored or misunderstood. It was felt in some quarters that the novel was not very *nice*. The reviewer in the *Daily News* declared that some episodes were so brutal that "they caused insufferable distress to the feelings". *The Island of Doctor Moreau* had had the same effect two years earlier.

Despite its merits, *The War of the Worlds* contains at least two aspects of Wells's writing which tell against it increasingly as time goes by. They turn out to be aspects of the same thing, Wells as a delineator of "the little man". I mean his penchant for humour, particularly Cockney humour, and the general scrubbiness of his characters.

An old man is rescuing his orchids as the Martian invasion force draws near. "I was explainin' these is vallyble," he says. Wells's London is populated by shop assistants, cabmen, artillerymen, and gardeners. There is a curate, too, but he, like most of the clergy in Wells's work (and in his disciple Orwell's), is used as a comic butt and talks nonsense. "How can God's ministers be killed?" he asks. There are no characters in *The War of the Worlds*, only mouths.

In Wells's best book, this fault does not obtrude.

The Island of Doctor Moreau, published in 1896, contains for all practical purposes only three human beings: Moreau, the scientist ahead of his time; Montgomery, his assistant, a drunken doctor in disgrace; and Prendick, the common man, the narrator. Prendick has none of Bert Smallways's or Mr Polly's or Kipps's cocky chirpiness, while the Beast-People hardly crack a joke between them. If the characters are in part cliché, this is in part because they serve symbolic roles; they are personages. A symbolic quality about the whole gives it a flavour of Poe or the French writers.

Moreau begins in a businesslike way, in the manner of *Gulliver's Travels*, with a sea voyage and a shipwreck. Prendick survives the wreck and arrives at an unnamed island, owned by Moreau. A mystery surrounds the place, there are strange shrouded creatures, cries in the night. If this is Prospero's island, it is peopled by Calibans. In the way Prendick's mind leaps to terrible nameless conclusions, we come to that nervous playing on unvoiced things which is the essence of science fiction.

Incident flows smoothly on incident, each preparing us for the next; Prendick's unwelcome arrival; the mystery of the "natives"; Prendick's suspicion that Moreau experiments on human beings to bestialize them, and then the revelation that Moreau is in fact creating something like humanity from animals by the extreme application of vivisection techniques; then we meet the grotesque population of the island, the fruits of Moreau's surgery, the Hyæna-Swine, the Leopard man, the Satyr, the Wolf Bear, the Swine Woman, the faithful Dog Man. Then we have the death of the Leopard Man; the escape of the female puma on which Moreau is operating; the death of Moreau himself in the ensuing hunt through the forest; Prendick's shaky assumption of control; Montgomery's carousal with the Beast-Men, in which he is killed; the destruction of the stronghold; and the whole awful decline, as Prendick is left alone with the Beast-People while they slowly forget what language they have learned, and lapse back into feral savagery.

Nobody has quite decided what *Moreau* is, apart from being a splendid and terrifying story. But it is clear that Wells has something more in mind, something larger, than a thrilling adventure: just as one of this novel's descendants, Golding's *Lord of the Flies*, is more than a thrilling adventure.

In the main, Wells's first critics and reviewers expressed shocked horror at the whole thing, and would look no further; in short, he was condemned rather than praised for his artistry—a reception which was to have its due effect on Wells's future writings. Yet it is not difficult to see what he intended.

For some time, we are kept in suspense with Prendick about the nature of the island's population. Is it animal or human? This is not merely a plot device; as with the scientific hinge on which *The War of the Worlds* turns, Moreau's experiment links with the entire philosophical scheme of the novel. And even after we learn the true meaning of the Beast-People, Wells carefully maintains a poignant balance between animal and human in them. At their most human, they reveal the animal; at their most animal, the human.

The point may be observed at the moment when Prendick, now in the role of the hunter, catches up the Leopard Man in the forest:

> I heard the twigs snap and the boughs swish aside before the heavy tread of the Horse-Rhinoceros upon my right. Then suddenly, through a polygon of green, in the half-darkness under the luxuriant growth, I saw the creature we were hunting. I halted. He was crouched together into the

smallest possible compass, his luminous green eyes turned over his shoulder regarding me.

It may seem a strange contradiction in me—I cannot explain the fact—but now, seeing the creature there in a perfectly animal attitude, with the light gleaming in his eyes, and its imperfectly human face distorted in terror, I realized again the fact of its humanity. In another moment others of its pursuers would see it, and it would be overpowered and captured, to experience once more the horrible tortures of the enclosure. Abruptly I slipped out my revolver, aimed between his terror-struck eyes and fired.

It is clear that *Moreau*, at least in one sense, speaks against transplant surgery, the consequences of which are revealed in the ghastly Law which the Beasts chant (a Law which some critics have seen as a parody of the Law of the Jungle in Kipling's *Jungle Book* and the Ten Commandments, though the dry, sublimated humour of Swift is also present):

> Not to suck up Drink: *that* is the Law. Are we not Men?
> Not to eat Flesh or Fish: *that* is the Law. Are we not Men? (etc.)
> *His* is the Hand that wounds.
> *His* is the Hand that heals.

We are put in mind—not accidentally—of liturgical chant. "For His mercy is on them that fear Him: Throughout all generations." We recall that Wells labelled the novel "an exercise in youthful blasphemy". Moreau is intended to stand for God. Moreau is a nineteenth-century God—Mary Shelley's protagonist in his maturity—Frankenstein Unbound.

Furthermore, Moreau's science is only vaguely touched on; the whole business of brain surgery, on which the novel hinges, has none of Wells's usual clarity. We can infer that he wanted to leave this area sketchy, so that we no more know what goes on in Moreau's laboratory than in God's. This vagueness, by increasing our horror and uncertainty, is a strength rather than otherwise.

When God is dead, the island population reverts to savagery, though he hovers invisible above the island. Prendick tells the Beasts: "For a time you will not see him. He is . . . there [pointing upward] where he can watch you. You cannot see him. But he can see you."

Blame for the wretched state of the Beasts is set firmly on Moreau. "Before they had been beasts, their instincts fitly adapted to their surroundings, and happy as living things may be. Now they stumbled in the shackles of humanity, lived in a fear that never died, fretted by a law they could not understand."

At this moment, Wells is trying to create a synthesis between evolutionary and religious theory. Not to put too fine a gloss on it, he does not think highly of the Creator. Nor does he of the created. Moreau says it for Wells, declaring that he can "see into their very souls, and see there nothing but the souls of beasts, beasts that perish—anger, and the lusts to live and gratify themselves". There is that Biblical phrase which echoes in the opening of *The War of the Worlds*: "beasts that perish". As for the two real humans, Prendick is certainly not there for us to identify with, any more than the Invisible Man is. His shallowness, his lack of understanding for Montgomery, his lack of sympathy for the Beasts, is perhaps a mark against the book—the darkness of any painting can be enhanced by a highlight here and there. Or perhaps it is just that Prendick is a commonplace little man, as Gulliver was a commonplace little man and Alice a commonplace little girl.

Moreau stands in an honourable line of books in which man is characterized as an animal. *Gulliver's Travels* is one of the best-known examples of the genre, and the one to which Wells paid homage—the Beast-People are kinfolk to the Yahoos—but such stories stretch back to the Middle Ages and beyond. Wells, however, revived the old tradition, gaining additional power because he and his audience were aware of evolutionary theory. They are the first generation to understand that it was no mere fancy as hitherto to regard man as animal; it was the simple betraying truth, and formalized religion began to decay more rapidly from that time onwards.

Prendick eventually returns to "civilization", rescued from the island by a boat with dead men in it. His fears pursue him back to England. (Perhaps something of these passages went into Conrad's *Heart of Darkness*.) "I could not persuade myself that the men and women I met were not also another, still passably human, Beast People, animals half-wrought into the outward image of human souls; and that they would presently begin to revert, to show first this bestial mark and then that." The Leopard Man, *c'est moi*.

This is the final triumph of *Moreau*: that we are transplanted from the little island, only seven or eight square miles in extent—say about the size of Holy Island—to the great world outside, only to find it but a larger version of Moreau's territory. The stubborn beast flesh, the beast mentality, is everywhere manifest.

Here indeed is the "search for a definition of man and his status in the universe" of our definition. Moreau represents a new mythology for the dawning century, in which terror and dispossession are prominent.

The ending has a sombre strength. (Not least, one would imagine, for George Orwell, who may have found in the passage last quoted inspiration for what was later to become *Animal Farm*.) As with the climax of *The War of the Worlds*, it comes not just as a surprise but as a logical culmination. Wells has subtly prepared us for it, so that it is revelation rather than punch line, for instance in his remark at once Hardyesque and Darwinian, that, "A blind fate, a vast pitiless mechanism, seemed to cut out and shape the fabric of existence."

In this early novel, Wells amply fulfilled his conscious intentions. The exercise in youthful blasphemy worked. It is apparent that he also exorcized something that obsessed him during that period. Although *Moreau* is the darkest of his novels, it is not strikingly different in attitude from several others. We find a horror of animality, an almost prurient curiosity about flesh, and the culture shock of evolution stamped across all Wells's early science fiction. As the Beast-

People are our brethren, so the Martians could be us at another stage of our development; while the Morlocks, that submerged nation in *The Time Machine* whose *vril* is flesh of Eloi—they are descended from us, our flesh could grow into such nocturnal things. "I grieved to think how brief the dream of human intellect has been," says the Time Traveller.

The cannibalism practised by the Morlocks is paralleled by the flesh-eating of the Beast-People. Although the Invisible Man divests himself of flesh, he does not lose a vicious competitive streak. The Selenites of *The First Men in the Moon* are one long nightmare of distorted flesh; like the Morlocks, they live underground. They are forced into arbitrary shapes by social usage almost as cruelly as if they came under Moreau's scalpel. In *The Food of Gods*, flesh runs amok—like *Moreau*, this novel, too, is in part an allegory of man's upward struggle.

With a frankness remarkable for its time, Wells has told us much about his early sexual frustrations. He was a sensuous man and, with success and wealth, found the world of women open to him. It may be that this gradually assuaged his old obsessions; though he never achieved peace of mind, his later books do not recapture that darkly beautiful quality of imagination, or that instinctive-seeming unity of construction, which lives in his early novels, and in his science fiction particularly. Perhaps it was just that he fell victim to success.

The rest of Wells's career must be looked at briefly, bearing in mind the question of why the hundred books that followed do not share the complex imagination of the early crop.

As soon as Wells's public became accustomed to one Wells, up would pop another. There was *A Modern Utopia*, the first of its kind to declare that from now on, with improved communications, no island or continent was big enough to hold a perfect state—it must be the whole world or nothing. Later, he developed the idea of a World State.

Read today, Wells's outline of the "fundamentals of the coming world state" appears intoxicatingly idealistic. There will be a universal religion (not Christianity nor Buddhism nor Islam but religion "pure and undefiled"); universal education; vast free literature of criticism and discussion; much scientific research; democratic organization. There will be no armies or navies, no unemployed, no rich or poor.[10]

Here we see surfacing again many of the ideals first formulated in Plato's Republic.

Such has been the persuasive power of Bernard Bergonzi's book on Wells that critics have come to hold that there are no good scientific romances after *The First Men in the Moon* in 1901. But later books, though creatively less inspired, still have power.

Very few critics seem to have thought well of *In the Days of the Comet* (1906), a rare exception being Frank McConnell[11] who, calling the book brilliant, points out the skill of its opening line ("I saw a grey-haired man, a figure of hale age, sitting at a desk and writing") and of the symbol of the concave speculum above this man's head, in which a vision of the future is magnified and distorted—a telling image of Wells's art.

In the Days of the Comet is in form essentially not a novel but a novella.[12] The characters are few and symbolic: the tortured hero, the girl, the rival in love, the suffering old mother. The real centre of the novel, the one thing vividly portrayed, is the condition of mind of the England of that day, where the approaching comet shines down on "dark compressed life" with its "cities men weep to enter". In a well-argued essay[13] on *Tono-Bungay* (which was to appear three years later in 1909) David Lodge puts the case for a way of reading that novel which differs from the way of reading (to give his example) Henry James. The argument is similar to those adduced within the SF field by critics such as Samuel Delany. Lodge points to *Tono-Bungay* as a Condition of England novel. The principle applies to some extent to the novella, coming as it does between *A Modern Utopia* and *Tono-Bungay*. It is clear that Wells's creative vein was by no means exhausted, although he had almost twenty books behind him.

A utopian element enters with the Comet. The Comet transforms life. Wars cease. An era of free love begins. The Comet is merely the device enabling the scene to be changed and Wells to say, "Look here upon this picture, and on this." The device is disarmingly effective, although—as is usual in such novels, for instance Marge Piercy's *Woman on the Edge of Time* (1976)—present discontents are more vivid than future promises.

In 1924, Wells contrived an interesting reversal of the situation in *In the Days of the Comet* with a short novel entitled *The Dream*. People of a happier future are going into the mountains when one of their number, Sarnac, falls asleep and "dreams" himself into the distant past, our present, where he assumes the identity of Harry Mortimer Smith. The emphasis here is on the activities of people of today. The characterization is mocking but affectionate.

The Dream in its turn relates to *Christina Alberta's Father*, published the following year, 1925. Here, the eponymous father believes himself a reincarnation of a king of ancient Sumeria.[14] Wells's remarkable ability to make us keep turning the pages is still in evidence.

The theme of free love which emerges at the end of *Comet* is used again in a contemporary novel, *Ann Veronica*, first published in 1909. It caused a storm of protest. If it seems mild today, we forget the suppressions against which Wells fought.

In 1914, just before the outbreak of hostilities, *The World Set Free* was published. It contains some of the most amazing of Wells's predictions, in particular of atomic warfare, but also—more accurately and horribly—of trench warfare. His speculations on tank warfare had already appeared in a short story, "The Land Ironclads". We have seen how Wells's warfare books were written very much in the *Battle of Dorking* tradition—yet he was remarkably more successful in predicting what actually happened than his rivals, perhaps because he was no reactionary (as were most of the rivals), and therefore tended less to view the future in terms of the past; and also because he actually hated war (though with the ambivalent feelings many people experience) unlike such men as Le Queux, who pretty clearly longed for it.

The World Set Free is full of shrewd preachments, exciting home truths writ large, and radical diagnoses of human ills, all of which made the book (novel it hardly is) exciting and immediate at the time.

Here is Karenin in the future, when London is being cleared up after extensive bombing. He is looking and talking about a 1914 which bears a resemblance to the 1980s.

> "It was an unwholesome world," reflected Karenin. "I seem to remember everybody about my childhood as if they were ill. They were ill. They were sick with confusion. Everybody was anxious about money and everybody was doing uncongenial things. They ate a queer mixture of foods, either too much or too little, and at odd hours. One sees how ill they were by their advertisements . . . Everybody must have been taking pills . . . The pill-carrying age followed the weapon-carrying age. . . ." (Chapter 5 §4)

The World Set Free is successful in every way but the ways in which the early Wells books were successful. It is full of lively ingredients; it has no organic life. Wells the One-Man Think-Tank has burst into view. His books are no longer novels but gospels.

After World War I, this more solemn Wells developed further into the Wells who produced solid and effective works of scientific popularization and started the vogue for one-volume encyclopaedias. Wells was on the way to becoming the most popular sage of his day. An edition of *The World Set Free* published in the twenties heralds Wells, on the cover, as "The most widely read author in the world".

He was still producing novels every year.

During the thirties, Wells the Novelist faded out before Wells the World Figure. He was a famous man, busily planning a better world, chatting with Gorki, feuding with George Bernard Shaw, flying to the White House to talk to Roosevelt, or to the Kremlin to talk to Stalin. Remembering the muddle of the London of his youth, he visualized a World State as the tidiest possible way of governing mankind for its own happiness.

Later in life, in 1940, when Britain stood alone against Nazi Germany, Wells undertook a lecture in the USA, flying some 24,000 miles to present the British cause to the American people. His agent Peat arranged some young ladies for him. Wells enjoyed what he called "a last flare of cheerful sensuality". He was seventy-four. Free love was still an active principle.

Unlike Jules Verne, Wells was never in danger of being blessed by the Pope.

Wells proved himself one of the few men capable of spanning the great gulf between the mid-Victorian period when he was born and our modern age. He had grasped the principle of change. He was a visionary and not a legislator, yet he worked for the League of Nations during World War I and, during the Second, helped draw up a Declaration of the Rights of Man which paved the way for the Universal Declaration of Human Rights adopted by the United Nations after Wells's death. He died in 1946, having witnessed the dropping of an atomic bomb he had predicted many years earlier.

Not uncharacteristically, H. G. Wells left a time bomb behind him. One of his most engaging books is his *Experiment in Autobiography*, published in two volumes in 1934. At the same time, he was secretly composing a companion-piece which, because it involved figures—mainly women—still alive, could not be published until 1984.

H. G. Wells in Love: Postscript to an Experiment in Autobiography is edited by his son, G. P. Wells, now dead. It is an honest and good-natured account of Wells's energetic sex life. "To make love periodically," Wells remarks, "with some grace and pride and freshness, seems to be, for most of us, a necessary condition to efficient working." A comic way of putting it. Wells loved women for their own sake, and the love was often ardently returned.

His illegitimate son by Rebecca West, Anthony West, also had an unshakeable love for his father. His *H. G. Wells: Aspects of a Life* (1984) presents a close-up view of Wells's life and times. This book and Wells's own time bomb give any interested reader a good insight into this likeable and extraordinary man, for whom change was a necessity in all things, including partners.

To the Establishment, the idea of courage is always anathema.[15] It never took Wells to its lordly bosom, just as it has never taken science fiction, possibly for the same reason. It disliked him for the things he did best, and thought him a cad. So did the literati, perhaps with more reason. Wells's ill-timed attack on his old friend Henry James in *Boon* (1915) was a poor thing; most orthodox writers sided with James.

The literati still do not accept Wells to the sacred canon. In a volume such as Cyril Connolly's *The Modern Movement*, which claims to list books "with the spark of rebellion", there is room for Norman Douglas and Ivy Compton-Burnett but none for Wells, except in an aside. However, some real writers like Nabokov and Borges appreciated his true worth as innovator and creative spirit.

A prevalent idea of Wells seems to be that he began modestly and well as an artist (*The Time Machine* and all that) and then threw it all up for journalism and propaganda.[16] There is a grain of truth in the charge. Many of his books were hastily written or scamped; he says himself, "It scarcely needs criticism to bring home to me that much of my work has been slovenly, haggard and irritated, most of it hurried and inadequately revised, and some of it as white and pasty in texture as a starch-fed nun." Lesser writers today would not dare admit anything of the sort.

The facts do not entirely bear out either the prevalent idea or Wells's own admission (what writers say of themselves should always be greeted with scepticism). Wells began as a teacher and continued as one. He had a strong didactic example from his teacher, Thomas Huxley, one of the great controversialists of the century. For a while, in those earlier novels, Wells followed the doctrine of art for art's sake (in favour with those writers and artists who were, like Wells, against the "done thing").

When he took care to incorporate his central point into the imaginative whole, when his point was so well integrated as not to be obvious, his audience misunderstood him or failed to get to the point, as was the case with *Moreau*, *The Invisible Man*, and *The War of the Worlds*.

Wells hated muddle and misunderstanding. He took to making the message clearer and clearer. His characters became mouth-pieces, the fiction became lost in didacticism. Wells gained volume and lost quality, but he was always a man with an amplifier, not content to whisper in corners. Indeed, the controversial nature of science fictional themes is such that only careful control—the control Wells found and lost—deflects the fantasy from the sermon.

Despite his fecundity and his joy in producing a different-coloured rabbit from his hat with each performance, Wells was consistent in his career. As early as 1912, he turned down an invitation to join the Academic Committee of the Royal Society of Literature. He wanted to deal with life, not aesthetics. Perhaps he failed to recognize that he was a creator, not an administrator. He could exhort but not execute. Eventually, the exhortations took over from the imagination. Yet who is to say that the exhortations, the aspirations, were unnecessary?

Much of Wells's work has been filmed. *The Time Machine* was not filmed until 1960, in an indifferent version produced by George Pal for the MGM Studios. *The Island of Doctor Moreau* was filmed as *Island of Lost Souls* in 1932. Paramount made it with Charles Laughton as the doctor. Considerable liberties were taken with the story. The 1977 version, starring Burt Lancaster, was not much better.

In 1933, Universal filmed *The Invisible Man* directed by James Whale, who made the original *Frankenstein*. Both Universal and Whale were full of expertise in the matter of horror, and the tricks of invisibility—long grass crushed under unseen footsteps—were remarkable for their time. Claude Rains, unseen for most of the film, played Griffin. Universal made a sequel in 1940, with Joe May directing and Sir Cedric Hardwicke in the eponymous role. This was *The Invisible Man Returns*. The same year saw a saucy comic variation on the theme, *The Invisible Woman*, with the delightful Virginia Bruce revealing generous amounts of leg as she unexpectedly becomes visible again.

Paramount made *War of the Worlds* in 1953, with George Pal producing. The story was updated and the location shifted from England to California. The machines are altered radically, and the comic curate becomes one of the film's (incinerated) heroes. It is generally agreed that this is a successful SF film, by the standards of the day.

Most famous is the October 1938 CBS adaptation of *The War of the Worlds*. This was an early venture in the career of young Mr Orson Welles. So effective was the broadcast that a wave of hysteria swept the United States. Although consistently dismissed as nonsense, science fiction has always been effective on the "unknown fear" level, as was demonstrated on this occasion.

The British *First Men in the Moon*, made in 1964 and directed by Nathan Juran, was a poor thing, despite special effects by Ray Harryhausen and jovial performances from Lionel Jeffries and Edward Judd as Cavor and Bedford. There was an early version in 1919—the first of Wells's books to be filmed.

AIP released a lame version of *Food of the Gods* in 1976, at a time when there were better movies around.

In 1936, two Wells films appeared, *The Man Who Could Work Miracles*, and, more importantly, *Things to Come* under Wells's supervision, both with screenplays by Wells. For *Things to Come*, Alexander Korda was in charge of production, William Cameron Menzies directed. A particularly fine musical score was provided by Arthur Bliss. The design of the film was stunning, while Raymond Massey and Ralph Richardson and the other actors did not allow themselves to be entirely dwarfed by the impressive sets, or a story that moved many years into the future. However shaky some of *Things to Come*'s ideas have proved (the reign of technocracy, for example), the film remains grand and striking, one of the classics of the cinema, and certainly Wells's best memorial film.

Many of his non-SF novels have also been filmed, among them *Love and Mr Lewisham*, *Kipps* (a memorable performance from Michael Redgrave), *Ann Veronica*, and *The History of Mr Polly*. *Kipps* also turned up as a musical entitled *Half a Sixpence*, with Tommy Steele.

Wells himself appeared, portrayed by Malcolm McDowell, in *Time After Time* in 1979.

Wells did not change the world as he would have wished. He did alter the way millions of people looked at it. He was the first of his age to see clearly that our globe is one, the people on it one—and the people beyond this globe, if they exist. He helped us understand that present history is but a passing moment, linked to distant past and distant future. It was Wells who said, "Human history becomes more and more a race between education and catastrophe". As the human race struggles and sinks beneath its own weight of numbers, we see how his words remain contemporary.

Perhaps a writer who views human history as a race between anything and catastrophe is doomed to write hastily and carelessly, as Wells often did. Yet Wells was loved by men and women far beyond his personal acquaintance, far beyond the normal readership a novelist gathers if he merely has staying power. He was witty and honest, he spoke for his generation—and for more than one generation. George Orwell conveyed something of what a symbol H. G. Wells became:

Back in the 1900s it was a wonderful thing to discover H. G. Wells. There you were, in a world of pendants, clergymen, and golfers, with your future employers exhorting you to "get on or get out", your parents systematically warping your sex life, and your dull-witted schoolmasters sniggering over their Latin tags; and here was this wonderful man who could tell you all about the inhabitants of the planets and the bottom of the sea, and who *knew* that the future was not going to be what respectable people imagined. [17]

Orwell was speaking of the beginning of the century. Thirty years later, as this writer can vouch, the same state of affairs held true. Wells was still at it, stirring everyone up.

He spread his energies widely. It was in his nature to do so.

Much of his activity has been dissipated. His novels remain. The science fiction is read more than ever.

Wells was born in the year dynamite was invented; he lived to witness the inauguration of the nuclear age. Inaccurately, Orwell characterized Charles Dickens's novels as "rotten architecture but wonderful gargoyles"; it is Wells's gargoyles, his Martians, the Selenites, the Morlocks, the Beast-People, we most relish today, when Lewisham and Polly grow faint. We may no longer share Wells's faith in the potentialities of education, but we long ago conceded his point that we show "first this bestial mark and then that".

Within his own domain, Wells is *sui generis*. Within the domain of scientific romance, he managed three unique achievements. He elevated the freak event— a visit to the Moon, an invasion from another planet—into an artistic whole. In consequence, he greatly extended the scope and power of such imaginings. And he brought to the genre a popularity and a distinctness from other genres which it has never lost since, despite the blunders of many following in his wake.

Wells is the Prospero of all the brave new worlds of the mind, and the Shakespeare of science fiction.

CHAPTER VI

The Flight from Urban Culture: Wells's Coevals

Of all things human which are strange and wild
This is perchance the wildest and most strange,
And showeth man most utterly beguiled,
To those who haunt that sunless City's range:
That he bemoans himself for aye, repeating
How time is deadly swift, how life is fleeting,
How naught is constant on the earth but change.
—James Thomson: *The City of Dreadful Night*

The inhabitants of the congested cities of Europe and America found themselves increasingly in need of distraction. Not only religion but fiction also became the opiate of the people. SF is the hard stuff of fiction.

As the nineteenth century drew to its close a literary revolution was taking place of as much importance as the paperback revolution of the nineteen-fifties. Wells and his contemporaries enjoyed expanding markets. New journals and periodicals were springing up every week, to cater to a new reading public. Disraeli's submerged nation was coming up for air.

This was the age when many of the great newspapers were founded, and with them the fortunes of their proprietors. In London, this was the day of Newnes, Pearson, and Northcliffe. Among his other good and profitable works, George Newnes started the first modern magazine, the *Strand*, in 1890. Pearson started *Pearson's Magazine* and *Pearson's Weekly*.

The new public devoured newsprint. The number of novels published in England in 1870, the year of Dickens's death, was 381; by the turn of the century, it had swollen to over two thousand. This tremendous increase is traditionally ascribed to the Education Act of 1870. In fact, a similar, though proportionately smaller, increase in novels published may be observed at the end of the eighteenth century. The *Monthly Review* for 1796 notices twice as many novels as in 1795. By 1800, novels were so numerous and so bad that some magazines (e.g. *Scots* and the *Gentleman's Magazine*) ceased to notice them at all. Later, in the eighteen-fifties, Railway Library and Yellow Back novels were exploiting a less cultivated reading public.

In the United States, the dime novel flourished. August 1868 saw the publication of *The Huge Hunter: or, The Steam Man of the Prairies*, written by Edward S. Ellis. Thus indigenous science fiction entered the States, unfolding a theme which was to prove a lasting attraction. The steam man is the invention of a hunchbacked boy. It steams across the land, fighting off Indians and bad men, an inhuman hero of the frontier. Mechanization fights the vicious primitive without the law, and wins.

This semi-juvenile adventure was not of any high literary order. The famous Frank Reade series started up in imitation of Ellis, with *The Steam Man of the Plains* (1876). This new dime novel series ran, with variations, until 1898. All but the first four titles were written pseudonymously by Luis Philip Senarens. Senarens was nineteen years old when he turned out the first of his science fictions. This industrious hack produced something like forty million words over the next thirty years.[1] Senarens died in 1939.

Transportation was a prominent theme in the Senarens series, as it was in Verne's concurrently unfolding novels.

After Frank Reade were to come whole successions of boy inventors[2], invading a stratum of American juvenile tales, eventually to emerge into semi-adulthood in such narratives as Gernsback's *Ralph 124C 41 +*. Following on from Frank Reade, Sr and Jr, came the "Tom Swift" stories, many titles of which were written pseudonymously by H. R. Garis under the house name Victor Appleton, a good healthy outdoor label. In these and many similar stories, distance lent enchantment to the tale.

Nor were girls entirely ignored. There were "Motor Maid Series" and "Girl Aviator Series". Wonder Woman was on her way.

The arrival of the pulps, with a less unsophisticated ethos, forced the dime novels out of existence, just as the slicks later eclipsed most of the pulps and paperbacks the slicks. The laws of evolution apply to newsprint.

The pace of progress was quickening. The cities were growing. The wildernesses were being tamed. Trees were turning into paper before you could say Productivity.

New publishers, new magazines, new writers! It is hardly surprising that many authors regarded their potential audience as merely one to be exploited. It is evident, then as now, that the authors most eager to write for the quick buck are the ones most easily exploited by publishers.

A diversity of publications meant a diversity of themes, and a slow stepping up of the luridness of the content, as well as the emergence of a type of modern power fantasy which has less to do with the conditions of life than the fairy story, traditionally a cautionary form. We call such fantasy "escapism"—the escape, probably, from the repressed "civilized" self. It relates to day-dreaming and is found in its purest form in areas which border closely on science fiction. Its appearance has bedevilled the history, the criticism, and the writing of science fiction ever since.

The main characteristic of the work of some of the fantasy and science fiction writers who were active between the 1890s and the 1920s is a wish to escape from claustrophobic urban culture.

At the same time, the escape is often shown to be the proverbial one, from frying pan into fire. It's nice to get away for a quiet weekend in the Amazonian jungle—where the ferocious Stone Age tribes will capture you! Such seems to be the moral of Conan Doyle's *The Lost World*, typical of its time.

The other characteristic tale of the period is the one that deals with war—often the real war that came about in 1914, but sometimes a war against nations in the Far East. War, too, is an escape from personal responsibilities and problems, from the "civilized" self.

The savage hero has a real function—to defy the march of Progress.

Such escapes represent a way of dealing with man's anxieties about his ability to cope with day-to-day existence. Some of the authors of the period, from Rider Haggard onwards, express a common anxiety about death. Fantasy painlessly lets us acknowledge our deepest fears, of inadequacy or death or whatever it may be; science fantasy lets us acknowledge more recent cultural fears, as androids often symbolize a fear of depersonalization.

Between 1890 and 1920, we find a sort of neutral time zone, where tale-telling has no particularly focused infra-structure of significant new myth, except in the earlier works of Wells; that is to come. On the Eastern shores of the Atlantic, the British appear to be forgetting their obsession with submerged nations—again, except for Wells. While on the Western shores, the Americans have not yet become obsessed with the vanished Red Indian, who will later return to haunt their science fiction.

Even of such a neutral period, one appreciates the force of what Susan Sontag has said of SF as a life-normalizing agent. It is true that her statement was made with reference to the SF film; yet it seems to me one of the most effective—in its deliberately refraining from claiming too much or too little—explanations ever made of the function of science fiction:

> Ours is indeed an age of extremity. For we live under continual threat of two equally fearful, but seemingly opposed, destinies: unremitting banality and inconceivable terror. It is fantasy, served out in large rations by the popular arts, which allows most people to cope with these twin spectres. For one job that fantasy can do is to lift us out of the unbearably humdrum and to distract us from terrors—real or anticipated—by an escape into exotic, dangerous situations which have last-minute happy endings. But another of the things that fantasy can do is to normalize what is psychologically unbearable, thereby inuring us to it. In one case, fantasy beautifies the world. In another, it neutralizes it.
>
> The fantasy in science fiction films does both jobs. The films reflect world-wide anxieties, and they serve to allay them. They inculcate a strange apathy concerning the processes of radiation, contamination, and destruction which I for one find haunting and depressing. The naive level of the films neatly tempers the sense of otherness, of alien-ness, with the grossly familiar. In particular, the dialogue of most science fiction films, which is of a monumental but often touching banality, makes them wonderfully, unintentionally funny . . . Yet the films also contain something that is painful and in deadly earnest.[3]

Deadly earnestness, between 1890 and 1920, was not greatly in favour with the Great Reading Public. Their heroes are strong and serious and correct; it is a time for John Buchan's men, and Bulldog Drummond. By and large the crises in which they are involved concern only their own immediate circle and not the great globe itself; their job is to save themselves and not the world. Action is the thing, within decent limits. RLS is more of an influence than LSD.

Dr Jekyll and Mr Hyde, that strange tale which has gained power since the dark star of psychoanalysis rose over the horizon, is something of a sport in Robert Louis Stevenson's output. Stevenson's main influence was as a romancer. The impact of his *Treasure Island* (in book form in 1883) and *Kidnapped* (1886) is reflected in the novels of his contemporaries—in Henry Rider Haggard's *King Solomon's Mines* and its successors; in Anthony Hope's *Prisoner of Zenda* and its sequel, *Rupert of Hentzau*; and in the once popular novels of Stanley Weyman, such as *Under the Red Robe*. Also of the nineties are Conan Doyle's early historical novels such as *The White Company*, and Doyle's greatest creation, the unlikely but mesmeric Sherlock Holmes, issuing from his fog-swathed lodgings in Baker Street.

William Morris published *The Wood Beyond the World* in 1894 and *The Well at the World's End* two years later. These fantasies of an imaginary Middle Ages have none of the grossness of that period and some of the anaemic grace of the paintings of Morris's friend, Burne-Jones. *The Wood Beyond the World* belongs to the tushery school ("She said, in a peevish voice: 'Tush, Squire, the day is too far spent for soft and courtly speeches; what was good there is naught so good here.'" Chapter 14). It has been hailed as "the first great fantasy novel ever written".[4] The Chinese with more reason might claim that honour for the sixteenth-century novel *Xiyouji*, featuring the famous Monkey King, whose exploits may be viewed nowadays on Western TV screens.

In mid-decade, Rudyard Kipling published his two *Jungle Books*. These, and Kipling's vision of India in his short stories and (later) *Kim*, and the other colourful tales and genres, all contain elements soon to be incorporated into science fiction. Exotic territories ruled over by exotic women, remote countries contested by doubles, quests for kingdoms, pretty uniforms, mad adventures, hard riding, talking animals—not to mention a sackful of latter-day tushery— all could be accommodated within the happy hunting grounds of later science fantasy.

Of this group of romantic writers, one was to have an influence on science fantasy at least as strong as Wells's. As we have seen, Wells's was mainly an analytical fiction, not the sort of thing craved by broadest public taste. To satisfy that taste, brave and good heroes, stirring exploits and pageantry, and an escape from the prodromic troubles of the present (Wells's hunting grounds) were needed. These ingredients Rider Haggard (1856–1925) supplied in abundance, staging them far from the overcrowded cities of London and New York.

Haggard himself never wrote science fiction, unless one counts the post-humously published *Allan and the Ice-Gods* (1927), Haggard's version of the Ice

Age, or *When the World Shook* (1919), with its lost Atlantis myth. As a young man, he went to South Africa as secretary to Sir Redvers Bulwer, the governor of Natal; there he explored the country which provides the background for the best of his long string of romantic novels set on the Dark Continent.

The first of Haggard's many novels was written as the result of a shilling bet with his brother that he could come up with a better book than Stevenson's *Treasure Island*. It was published in 1885—*King Solomon's Mines*—and became an immediate and striking success. Like Kipling, and unlike his imitators of later date, Haggard knew whereof he spoke, and the best of his novels, like *She* and *Allan Quatermain*, still have vigour, even if their punctilious mores have dated.

The lost-race novel bears Haggard's patent. As Neil Barron's[5] *Anatomy of Wonder*, always a reliable guide in these matters, remarks, when some of the interest in utopias died, the lost-race took its place, especially when it dramatized the themes of neoprimitivism and the flight from urban culture.[6] Haggard's novels were popular for this reason; nor was a covert interest in the attractions of exotic women an impediment to their success.

The episode in *She* (1887) in which the immortal Ayesha bathes herself in life-giving flame and then dies when it fails her—dies and dwindles to a ghastly thing—is memorable (it impressed Jung).

"She, who but two minutes gone had gazed upon us—the loveliest, noblest, most splendid woman the world has ever seen—she lay still before us, near the mass of her own dark hair, no larger than a big ape, and hideous—ah, too hideous for words!" The corpse is referred to as "the little hideous monkey frame".

Echoes of the scene rattled through science fiction for many years. See, for instance, the Clark Ashton Smith story, "City of Singing Flame", and the last chapter of John Russell Fearn's *The Golden Amazon* (1944).

In a critical essay, Richard Kyle has this to say of the famous passage: "Pale Ayesha . . . died after two thousand years of life, turned into a large and ancient ape—even as Haggard's generation saw divine, God-created Man dying with the birth of evolution, after two thousand years of Christianity, leaving behind only a large and ancient ape."[7]

Kyle presents an argument for some of the substance of Edgar Rice Burroughs's early Mars books being derived from *She* and *Cleopatra*.[8] From Haggard on, crumbling women, priestesses, or empresses—all symbols of women as Untouchable and Unmakeable—fill the pages of many a "scientific romance". And the reels of many a silent film.

Haggard is remembered. Edwin Lester Arnold is forgotten. But that is not entirely true; in the SF field, nobody is ever totally forgotten, not even Otis Adelbert Kline.

The fame of Edwin Lester Arnold (1857–1935) was eclipsed by that of his father, the Sir Edwin Arnold whose much reprinted *Light of Asia* brought Buddhism into many an antimacassared Anglican home. The son wrote two novels on the theme of reincarnation, *Phra the Phoenician* (1890) and *Lepidus the Centurion* (1901), in both of which souls journey across the centuries.

Mysticism, like crumbling women, is something close to SF's adolescing heart. We shall meet it again. Roger Lancelyn Green calls *Lepidus* "a far finer book"[9], but *Phra* has its merits, and the story of the Phoenician trader who survives to chat with Good Queen Bess is told in appropriate language:

> So I was a prisoner of the Romans, and they bound me, and left me lying for ten hours under the side of one of their stranded ships, down by the melancholy afternoon sea, still playing with its dead men, and rolling and jostling together in its long green fingers the raven-haired Etrurian and the pale, white-faced Celt. (Chapter 1)

Phra was reprinted in the magazine *Famous Fantastic Mysteries* for September 1945, and nobody found its presence there incongruous.

Reincarnations also awaited Arnold's third novel (after which he gave up). *Lieut. Gulliver Jones: His Vacation* was published in 1905 and was destined to lie fallow until Richard Lupoff discovered it in 1963. Lupoff persuaded Donald Wollheim, then at Ace Books, to publish it, in its first American edition, as *Gulliver of Mars*.

Jones gets to Mars by wish and magic carpet, and finds there a gentle race, not quite male or female, which lives in the ruins of a long-decayed civilization, rather like the Eloi in *The Time Machine*. It, too, is threatened by a submerged nation. The Martian Morlocks are the dreaded Thither-folk, who ascend every so often to extract goods and lovely slave girls from the decadent culture. The beautiful princess whom Jones is going to marry is carried off by nasty ape-like Ar-hap. Jones, in true fairy tale fashion, sets off to rescue her.

Even today—but why the "even", when in the dream worlds of SF nothing changes?—passages of Arnold's amazing book come over with force.

Here's what he sees when he is cast upon an alien shore:

> All the opposite cliffs, rising sheer from the water, were in light, their cold blue and white surfaces rising far up into the black starfields overhead. Looking at them intently from this vantage-point I saw without at first understanding that along them horizontally, tier above tier, were rows of objects, like—like—why, good Heavens, they were like men and women in all sorts of strange postures and positions! Rubbing my eyes and looking again I perceived with a start and a strange creepy feeling down my back that they *were* men and women!—hundreds of them, thousands, all in rows as cormorants stand upon sea-side cliffs, myriads and myriads now I looked about, in every conceivable pose and attitude but never a sound, never a movement amongst the vast concourse.
>
> Then I turned back to the cliffs behind me. Yes! they were there too, dimmer by reason of the shadows, but there for certain, from the snowfields far above down, down—good Heavens! to the very level where I stood. There was one of them not ten yards away, half in and half out of the ice wall, and setting my teeth I walked over and examined him. And there was another further in behind as I peered into the clear blue

depth, another behind that one, another behind him—just like cherries in a jelly. (Chapter 14)

A whole nation in ice! Arnold's picture is reminiscent of an Yves Tanguy or a Max Ernst canvas. Lupoff argues that this novel was the formative influence on Burroughs's Mars.[10] Is this derivation correct, or is Kyle's through She? Perhaps the answer is that neither is incorrect. All fantasy ideas are amazingly alike. No man is an island. No fantasy writer is a continent.

The real Mars was, at the end of the last century, a striking and mysterious object for speculation, just as black holes or the moons of Uranus are in our time—though Mars was more accessible than black holes, with respect both to proximity and popular comprehension.

When the Red Planet was in opposition in 1877, 1879, and 1881, the Italian astronomer G.V. Schiaparelli made studies and charts of its surface. Schiaparelli noted straight lines running across the surface, which he labelled "*canali*"—a word generally meaning "channels". Translated into English as "canals", it started a whole new train of thought. . . .

The canals were confirmed by French astronomers in 1885. A few years later, the American Percival Lowell built his famous observatory at Flagstaff, Arizona, in order to study Mars and its mysterious features. Lowell, too, saw the canals, and firmly believed that Mars was the abode of life. His two books, *Mars* (1895) and *Mars and Its Canals* (1906), aroused considerable interest. Lowell perhaps raised a red gleam in the eyes of Wells and Arnold; Percy Greg's *Across the Zodiac*, however, predates Lowell's books.

Across the Zodiac was published in 1880. It is possibly the first interplanetary journey to be made by spaceship which wears an aspect of credibility. Like Verne, Percy Greg produces painstaking facts and figures for his remarkable craft. It even carries a rudimentary hydroponic system to recycle air, and boasts walls of metal three feet thick. Greg's space travellers find an advanced civilization on Mars, with polygamy and atheism the established thing. A doctrinaire utopianism prevails in which, unusually, a monarchy has succeeded a communist state. The plot involves an underground subversive movement in which the narrator, by marrying a Martian woman, Eveena, becomes entangled. Eveena is killed. The hero comes back to Earth, brokenhearted.

Greg's ship was powered by a mysterious force called "apergy", a form of anti-gravity, another SF dream of long-standing. The same driving force is used on the interplanetary trips featured in *A Journey in Other Worlds* (1894) by John Jacob Astor. In order to escape the monotony of the utopian Earth of the year AD 2000, a venturesome party visits Jupiter and Saturn. The former is stocked with the giant reptiles of prehistory; the latter contains spirits, and the travellers enjoy some Biblical experiences. Perhaps Astor was undecided between the rival attractions of *The Descent of Man* and the Old Testament.

George Chetwynd Griffith-Jones (operating under a pseudonym for obvious reasons) is less escapist and employs the powerful themes of war and revolution. As George Griffith, he was immensely popular for a time, his two best remembered romances being *The Angel of the Revolution* and its sequel, *Olga Romanoff*, both serialised in *Pearson's Weekly* and appearing in hardcover form in 1893 and 1894. At the centre of these stories is a colossal power struggle. A British-German-Austrian alliance is almost defeated in warfare by a French-Russian alliance. When London has been reduced to rubble, the British-German alliance is saved by a socialist America. Aerial warfare is conducted with dirigibles, airplanes, poison gas, and so forth.

In the sequel, set some years later, a socialist utopia has been established. A successor of the last Czar—the redoubtable Olga herself—stages a comeback. War breaks out again. Olga is about to take over the world when a passing comet burns almost everything to a cinder.

One escape route from urban culture is to destroy it. . . .

Later Griffith turned to more peaceful subjects with *A Honeymoon in Space* (1901), in which newlyweds (perhaps significantly an English lord and an American millionaire inventor's daughter) trip round the solar system, getting as far out as Saturn. To the angels who live on Venus, the happy couple sing "Home Sweet Home" and "The Old Folks at Home".

Another Anglo-American alliance features in *The Great War Syndicate* (1889), following a war between the two sides. This was by Frank Stockton.

The name of Stockton grows faint, but still rings pleasantly, mainly because of one clever and teasing short story, "The Lady or the Tiger?". His novel *The Great Stone of Sardis* was published in 1898. It is based on the remarkable premise that there was once a comet consisting of a huge diamond. It was captured by the Sun, whereupon the surface of the diamond burnt to ashes and became soil; the main body of the diamond became the Earth. Twentieth-century men bore down beneath the crust and find the great diamond still intact. Stockton's work, as one encyclopaedia puts it "was very unequal in interest".

"Grant Allen and I were in the tradition of Godwin and Shelley," said Wells.[11] Grant Allen was a Darwinian. Like Wells, he used the future to mirror the evils of the present. His *The British Barbarians* (1895) presents a scientist from a distant future working as an anthropologist among a savage tribe in an English suburb, while he investigates the current shibboleths on class, sex, property, and creed. Grant Allen's best-known novel is *The Woman Who Did*, also published in 1895, about a woman who bears and cares for an illegitimate child—a daring theme at the time, which may have moved Wells towards the writing of *Ann Veronica*.

In 1897, a thousand-page novel was published in Germany: *Auf zwei Planeten* (*On Two Planets*), by Kurd Lasswitz. It became very popular and was translated into several European languages, although its appearance in an English version had to wait until 1971. As in *The War of the Worlds*, appearing serially in the same year, Martians land on Earth—at the North Pole. They capture two Earthmen, taking them back to Mars. Lasswitz's Martians are much more humane than the Wellsian variety. Prettier, too. La, daughter of the engineer Fru, has large eyes, which change colour, and hair of "a reddish shimmering blonde like that of a tea-rose".

Mass slaughter does not appeal to the Martians—although they don't draw the line at wiping out the entire British Navy. After several forays they establish a utopian world state, with Martians and Earthmen working together.

We may regret that Lasswitz's great novel does not exist in a better translation. Lasswitz is an important figure in German SF—or rather in the mysterious lack of German SF. There is a gap after Kepler in the seventeenth century, scarcely filled by Jean Paul Friedrich Richter, an eighteenth-century figure whose *Leben des Quintus Fizlein* (1796) contrasts old views of the cosmos with scientific ones.

Lasswitz, whose Martians are based, like Wells's, on Lowell's supposed findings, had a clear idea of what SF should be and do. His prescription was set out in a remarkable essay published in 1910, entitled "Unser Recht auf Bewhoner anderer Welten" ("Our Claims on Inhabitants of Other Worlds"). Parts of it might be taken to heart today:

> Everything that occurs in a novel which is intended seriously as art must be capable of being related to our own experience, i.e. the contemporary view of natural laws and psychology; in short it must be explicable and plausible. An effect which occurred simply by magic and could not be explained scientifically would be just as unusable poetically as a sudden, psychologically unmotivated transformation of a character. . . .
>
> Our sense of veracity tolerates no postulates which directly and absolutely contradict previous scientific and psychological experience. . . .[12]

Unfortunately, events since Lasswitz's time have eroded our natural sense of veracity.

Kurd Lasswitz was a humanist in the mould of Goethe. Few writers in Germany followed him. Hans Dominik was a prolific supplier of the *Zukunft-roman* or novel of the future, inspired by zeppelins and other technological advances. Dominik continued to be published under the Nazis, although other writers were suppressed. Of course, Fritz Lang was one of the great figures of early SF cinema. Only after World War II did SF in Germany make a new start, at first imitating or being translated from eminent Anglo-American models, as has been the case in so many countries.

In the same year that *War of the Worlds* and *Auf zwei Planeten* appeared, 1897, a romance of another kind was published. As *Frankenstein* had been at the beginning of the century, this dark melodrama coming at the century's end was an immediate success. Its theme, that the living dead prey upon the living, is the reverse of scientific, while its horrid concoction of ruinous castles, blood, and coffins was by no means a suitable dish to set before populations bracing themselves for that most Modern of centuries—so far, at least—the Twentieth.

Yet Bram Stoker's *Dracula* was undeniable. It has never been out of print since. Wretched must be the language which contains no translation of it. It has been endlessly parodied, travestied, and filmed. It has spread the legend of the vampire far and wide.

Well, *Dracula* is a remarkably good book of its sensational kind, floridly well written, deftly constructed of diaries and letters, carrying more conviction by far than any of Stoker's other rather feeble novels, and crammed with dramatically conceived terrors which are scarcely diminished by re-reading.

The Morlocks coming up at night to devour the dainty Eloi are not half as imaginatively appalling as Lucy Westenra's coming out at night to suck the blood of London children.

The question is, why was such a tale taken up with such enthusiasm? In part, the answer must lie with the blatant sexual connotations of the theme.

> With his left hand he held both Mrs Harker's hands, keeping them away with her arms at full tension; his right hand gripped her by the back of the neck, forcing her face down on his bosom. Her white nightdress was smeared with blood, and a thin stream trickled down the man's bare breast, which was shown by his torn-open dress. The attitude of the two had a terrible resemblance to a child forcing a kitten's nose into a saucer of milk to compel it to drink.

Another answer is offered by the novelist and biographer, A. N. Wilson[13], who says, "This widespread horror of the living dead, whipped up for purely sensational purposes, began at a phase when, for the first time in Christian history, there was a widespread doubt about the real likelihood of a resurrection of the Body."

Many thoughtful people in the nineteenth century, men and women, underwent agonies of religious doubt, grappling with fading beliefs, groping for new certainties. The ethical problems raised by the Incarnation had troubled sensitive spirits since the start of the century. But it is difficult to read *Dracula* as a novel with primarily religious undertones.

My own theory is that in fact *Dracula* is only metaphorically and euphemistically about vampirism. Its real subject is that obsession of the *fin de siècle*, syphilis. *Dracula* is the great Victorian novel about VD, for which vampirism stands in as Stoker's metaphor.[14]

If this theory, which has not been advanced before, may seem extravagant, the facts of Stoker's life must be considered. Stoker was married to Florence Balcombe in 1878. Florence was a great beauty; she was sketched by Burne-Jones and Oscar Wilde, to whom she was at one time engaged. She was a cold woman, who evidently refused sexual relations with her husband after the birth of their one son. Stoker was a hearty, active man, who must have formed liaisons elsewhere. His constant travelling with Henry Irving's theatrical group would have given him many opportunities to do so.

An early biographer of Stoker, Harry Ludlam, writes of his death in 1912, "On the death certificate appeared the word 'Exhaustion'. He was sixty-four."[15] The later biography by Daniel Farson, who was Stoker's great-nephew, is more frank.[16] Farson reveals that the death certificate reads in full: "Locomotor Ataxy 6 months Granular Contracted Kidney. Exhaustion. Certified by James Browne MD." Locomotor ataxia is GPI, the tertiary stage of syphilis.

Farson adds, "(Stoker) probably caught syphilis around the turn of the century, possibly as early as the year of *Dracula*, 1897." He had a reputation as a womanizer. With such facts in mind, Stoker's masterpiece acquires a new dimension, the intense sexual threat-and-submission of the women a new significance. One recalls Maurice Richardson's comment on the novel: "It is a vast polymorph perverse bisexual oral-anal genital sado-masochistic timeless orgy."[17]

Van Helsing is the doctor with the syringe. The Count, largely off-stage, represents the disease itself, Renfield, the lunatic, its tertiary stage. The women, Lucy Westenra and Mina Murray, are the vectors of syphilis. "Unclean! Unclean!" cries Mina, "Even the Almighty shuns my polluted flesh!"

But the Wilson theory has one great advantage. It explains why *Dracula*—clearly not SF—and *Frankenstein*—clearly SF—are linked in the popular mind. The popular mind is correct in perceiving a similarity.[18] Doubts about the Resurrection entered well before the end of the century. *Frankenstein* at the beginning of the century is also a gruesome Resurrection myth—a parody, as was Dracula's, of what Christians had been taught to regard as truth.

Last century is bracketed between these two sinister tales. Our century, caught in inherited dilemmas, still perpetuates their myths.

Nobody would rank Mary Shelley and Bram Stoker with the great novelists, with Tolstoy or Scott or Melville. Yet both achieved something which escaped beyond literature entirely: the creation of new archetypal figures.

There are times when a diligent chronicler of out-moded novels wonders if the lives of the authors he glancingly surveys were not more compulsively interesting than the books themselves. This reflection certainly comes to mind when the opportunity arises to speak of M. P. Shiel, one-time King of Redonda, mystery man, philosopher, probable lunatic, and author of thirty-one books.

Matthew Phipps Shiel (1865–1947) was born in the West Indies. His father was an Irish Methodist of strict persuasion. His mother may have been a mulatto and freed slave. Mystery shrouds the details. Was Shiel, for instance, "a physical culture nut, reportedly homosexual"[19], as suggested by one critic, or "a lover of women—and therefore a realist", as suggested by another?[20] It does seem likely that he was crowned, at the age of fifteen, king of a pretentious rock in the Leeward Islands called Redonda, and that he was sent to be educated in England at an early age. There he made a precarious living as a professional author. Like many writers, he died in poverty and squalor.

Shiel's brain seems to have encompassed many of the ideas swilling about in the Europe of his day: socialism, evolution, new messiahs, conquest, Schopenhauer, industrialism, the yellow peril, revolutions, orgies of blood, overpopulation, Nietszcheism, spiritualism, eugenics, insanity, disease, miscegenation, and "the biology of war"—in short, all the ingredients that go to make life in the West such a heady experience.

By common consent, the two most interesting vehicles for these conflicting notions are *The Yellow Danger* and *The Purple Cloud*.

The Yellow Danger (1898) contains a world-wide war which ultimately, as in the manner of Wells's later novels, leaves the globe open to a better state of affairs in future. A great warlord rises in the East, and a Chinese army 100 million strong invades Russia and Europe. The Europeans reply by spreading cholera among the enemy; the Kaiser defeats them in a final great battle. The inscrutable British become masters of the world.

Better remembered is *The Purple Cloud* (1901), which owes something to Mary Shelley's *The Last Man*, while being executed entirely in Shiel's own megalomaniac spirit. The malign Adam Jeffson reaches the North Pole after great hardship. On the way back to England, he finds only death. An erupting volcano somewhere in the Pacific has extinguished all life.

Returning to London, Adam sets fire to it—arson, the solitary vice—and

> now the whole area which through streaming tears I surveyed, mustering
> its ten thousand thunders, and brawling beyond the stars the voice of its
> southward-rushing torment, billowed to the horizon one grand Atlantic
> of smokeless and flushing flame; and in it sported and washed themselves
> all the fiends of Hell, with laughter, shouts, wild flights, and holiday; and
> I—first of all my race—had flashed a signal to the nearer planets.

Years pass. Adam puts the torch to Calcutta, Peking, San Francisco. He comes across a mysterious young woman. His first impulse is to eat her, but they become reconciled, so that the human race can begin again.

Hartwell's judgement is that *The Purple Cloud* is "neither Vernian nor Wellsian but one of the few Poesque science fiction novels". Bleiler commends the "mad activities on a spoiled planet".[21]

Other products of Shiel's imagination are even less appetising. In *Lord of the Sea* (1901), for instance, the Jews have been almost exterminated in Europe. The survivors flee to England for refuge, where the strange "hero", Hogarth, himself Jewish, becomes a Lord Protector and enacts a harsh series of anti-Jewish laws, including forcible conversion.

Although Shiel is now the centre of a small cult, charges of anti-Semitism stick. Sam Moskowitz, who has studied the matter, says that Shiel, "through the entire length of his career . . . (displays) an unending barrage of insult, innuendo, curses, misrepresentations, lies and canards aimed at Jews individually and collectively."[22] Then there was the business of the yellow hordes— Shiel is credited with the coinage, "the yellow peril".[23] He was always obsessed with matters of race, possibly because of his own racially mixed blood. For a writer as strange as Shiel, the King of Redonda, there was perhaps no recourse open but a career in science fiction!

When the century turned, it affected little but the calendars. For well over half its length, the twentieth century was secretly the nineteenth, re-run, script by M.P. Shiel. World War I—the end of an old civilization—lay ahead, with the gas ovens of Hitler's camps and the fiery destruction of whole cities beyond that.

One immediate effect of World War I on fiction was to kill dead the future-war story—though resurrection came with the thirties, for instance in the air-warfare stories of Robert Sidney Bowen.[24] Men like William Le Queux were put out to grass, although in 1906 he is still going strong with *The Invasion of 1910*, later highly successful in book form.

The Germans invade again. Aided by maps and proclamations, Le Queux relates the progress of the war until the all-conquering German armies take London. The Kaiser sends a telegram to his commander in chief: "Your heroic march, your gallant struggle to reach London, your victorious attack and your capture of the capital of the British Empire, is one of the greatest feats of arms in all history."[25]

It would be wrong to suggest that Le Queux just petered out when the war he had dreamed of proved so much less fun in fact than in imagination. He went on writing[26], and among his daunting output are such titles as *Tracked by Wireless* and *The Voice from the Void*.

Many stories such as Le Queux's play upon the jingoism, fears, and prejudices of readers. Better and more lasting examples of the obsession with war are H. G. Wells's *The War in the Air* (1908), in which Bert Smallways, "a vulgar little creature", becomes involved with a mighty German fleet of airships which destroys New York; Wells's prophetic *The World Set Free* (early 1914); Conan Doyle's short story, "Danger!" (published in the *Strand Magazine* just one month before hostilities broke out in Europe), which predicted submarine warfare, with merchant ships being sunk until food supplies give out and Britain sues for peace; and H. H. Munro's *When William Came*, published early in 1914, a few months before William (the Kaiser) actually started to march. 1909 marked a spate of future war films. Slightly earlier than these is a remarkable novel pitched in a different key, Erskine Childers's *The Riddle of the Sands*, published in 1903.

The Riddle of the Sands, as its subtitle says, is "A Record of Secret Service". There are superb passages in it, and a great feel for the pleasures of sailing and the open air, as well as a well-founded German invasion plot which is gradually unravelled. Childers reads like the precursor of Buchan, which he was; his book became a minor classic, still being reprinted in the nineteen-seventies.

When William Came is a pungent tale of German occupation of Britain, as much domestic as military in tone. H. H. Munro is better known by his pseudonym, "Saki", under which name he wrote many spiky and clever short stories in the Edwardian era—stories which enjoyed a long vogue. He enlisted in the Army when war came, and was shot in the trenches on the Western Front in 1916. His apotropaic vision had not preserved him from evil, and it remains a debatable question whether talking about or preparing for such a dire event as war averts it or merely hastens its fulfilment.[27]

Future wars apart, the period was a welter of variously coloured plagues, invisible airships, mysterious civilizations under volcanoes, poisonous clouds of gas, new versions of the Flood, bouts of immortality, and Mars splitting in two. Slightly nearer to reality are the warnings about New York being destroyed, socialism taking over, women ruling the world, radium power bringing the millennium, and a transatlantic tunnel being built.

Some of the authors of the period still have a faithful band of followers. Konrad Lorenz has shown how young ducklings become imprinted by their mother's image at a certain tender age (when even a false mother will do the trick), after which they can accept no substitutes for her. The same effect is observed in many species, not excluding our own. Tastes in the arts may be formed in this way. It is hard to understand otherwise the furore that greeted the early works of Abe Merritt, Lovecraft, and Otis Adelbert Kline. Nevertheless, these and other writers had their audiences, often to be numbered in millions.

A few of the better authors who wrote some science fiction made their reputations in other fields.

Among them is numbered Rudyard Kipling, with such stories as "With the Night Mail" (1905), a glimpse of the world of the year 2000, in which flying has become so important that the ABC (Aerial Board of Control) rules the world. A sequel "As Easy as ABC" (1912) continues the same theme, showing how it develops, with the ABC ruthlessly trying to maintain law and order. In general terms, Kipling's fancy was not incorrect: international scheduled flying has changed the world, just as scheduled railway services changed it in the 1830s and 1840s.

G. K. Chesterton, that master of paradox, wrote a number of fantasies, among which the best-known and most enjoyable is *The Man Who Was Thursday* (1908), a story of a group of anarchists who have been interpenetrated entirely by detectives until no anarchists are left. The narrative itself is free-flowing and ingenious.

> Syme was increasingly conscious that his new adventure had somehow a quality of cold sanity worse than the wild adventures of the past. Last night, for instance, the tall tenements had seemed to him like a tower in a dream. As he now went up the weary and perpetual steps, he was daunted and bewildered by their almost infinite series. But it was not the hot horror of a dream or of anything that might be exaggeration or delusion. Their infinity was more like the empty infinity of arithmetic, something unthinkable, yet necessary to thought. Or it was like the stunning statements of astronomy about the distance of the fixed stars. He was ascending the house of reason, a thing more hideous than unreason itself. (Chapter 9)

Not science fiction, perhaps, yet nearer to science and rationality than the science fantasy which is the hallmark of the period.

Arthur Conan Doyle's science fiction belongs to this time: *The Lost World* was serialised in 1912, while *The Poison Belt* appeared the year after. There are other, later, novels, which pass for science fiction (*The Land of Mist*, *The Maracot Deep*), but it is the earlier two which are remembered with pleasure. There are also some short stories, of which the most reprinted is "When the World

Screamed", in which the thrusting Professor George Challenger penetrates the Earth's crust to pierce living matter below.

The Poison Belt is a tepid performance, much under Wells's influence. Challenger and Co. spend a night sipping oxygen while the Earth ploughs through toxic interstellar gas. Next morning, the whole world is dead, and the surviving party tours the picturesquely deserted London we shall meet again in *The Day of the Triffids*. It turns out that the gas induces not death but catalepsy; people revive, and everything returns to normal. After the 1914–18 war, such meek reversions to the prosaic would no longer be possible.

Like Conan Doyle's more famous creation, Sherlock Holmes, Professor Challenger is an unlikely and inhuman figure; but he does permit a certain crispness in the dialogue.

Challenger is the first to diagnose what is about to happen. Gathering his friends about him in his house, he explains the threat poised by the gas in lofty terms:

> "You will conceive a bunch of grapes," said he, "which are covered by some infinitesimal but noxious bacillus. The gardener passes it through a disinfecting medium. It may be that he desires his grapes to be cleaner. It may be that he needs space to breed some fresh bacillus less noxious than the last. He dips it in the poison and they are gone. Our Gardener is, in my opinion, about to dip the solar system; and the human bacillus, the little mortal vibrio which twisted and wriggled upon the outer rind of the earth, will in an instant be sterilized out of existence."
>
> Again there was silence. It was broken by the high trill of the telephone-bell.
>
> "There is one of our bacilli squeaking for help," said he, with a grim smile. (Chapter 2)

The Lost World is a great adventure story to rank with the best of Rider Haggard's—to which it is probably indebted. Challenger and his cronies find a mighty volcano in the Amazon basin. In the dead crater, isolated from the outside world, a fragment of prehistory has survived. Stone Age tribes, ape men, dinosaurs, and all, alive alive-o! Conan Doyle happened on the perfect setting for adventure.

Filmed more than once—most recently with Michael Rennie negligently dropping half-smoked cigarettes into the jungle and exclaiming "There goes a brontosaurus now" as a stegosaurus lumbers by—*The Lost World* is an imaginative romp that no schoolboy in his right mind can resist. The atmosphere of the lost world is vividly conveyed, its creatures gustily described, as we move towards the final battle when Challenger and Lord John Roxton lead "a host of the stone age" into victorious battle against the ape men.

In the end, they escape from what Doyle by this time calls "a dreamland of glamour and romance", and return safely to London and Roxton's chambers in the Albany. We have enjoyed the literary equivalent of a good hard game of Rugger before tea.

The last author we need name whose reputation was made beyond the science fantasy field is the redoubtable Jack London (1876–1916). There is something engaging in the story of this self-made man of letters, "at fifteen a man among men"[28], to quote his own words. He lived hard, gulping down Washington Irving's *The Alhambra* and Ouida's novels while working on ranches, selling newspapers, becoming an oyster pirate, going seal-hunting in the Pacific, joining in the rush for gold in the Klondike and other characteristically American occupations of the period.

London was only forty when he died, his fifty-odd titles all appearing during the last seventeen years of his life. Such books as *The Call of the Wild*, *White Fang*, *The People of the Abyss* (which is informed by London's strong socialist sympathies), and *The Sea Wolf*, many times filmed, were tremendously popular, and won him world-wide reputation. They contain something of London's own rough kindness, something of his imaginative and empathic response to life, and a lot of his vitality.

His place in the history of science fiction is secured by three books, among which the most eminent in reputation is a dystopian tale of future dictatorship, *The Iron Heel* (1907). Alas for reputation, *The Iron Heel* is hard to take today. Its honest sympathies with the poor and the oppressed are never in doubt, but they come clothed in clichés with alternate spates of denunciation and sentimentality. "This delicate, aristocratic-featured gentleman was a dummy director and a tool of corporations that secretly robbed widows and orphans" (from Chapter 5), combines both modes. London has no real vision of a future; his future is just the present in trumps.

Though time has not improved *The Iron Heel*, it still retains sporadic life, notably towards the end, where London's heroine, Avis, witnesses the revolt of the proletariat in Chicago. In a manner that brings to mind Dickens's revulsion for the mob in *Barnaby Rudge* and *A Tale of Two Cities*, Avis, loyal supporter of the popular struggle, suddenly sees the horde with fresh insight:

> The inner doors of the entrance were locked and bolted. We could not escape. The next moment the front of the column went by. It was not a column, but a mob, an awful river that filled the street, the people of the abyss mad with drink and wrong, up at last and roaring for the blood of their masters. I had seen the people of the abyss before, gone through its ghettos, and thought I knew it; but I found that I was now looking at it for the first time. Dumb apathy had vanished. It was now dynamic—a fascinating spectacle of dread. It surged past my vision in concrete waves of wrath, snarling and growing carnivorous, drunk with whisky from pillaged warehouses, drunk with hatred, drunk with lust for blood—men, women, and children, in rags and tatters, dim, ferocious intelligences with all the godlike blotted from their features and all the fiendlike stamped in, apes, and tigers, anaemic consumptives and great hairy beasts of burden, wan faces from which vampire society had sucked the juice of life, bloated forms swollen with physical grossness and corruption, withered hags and

death's heads bearded like patriarchs, festering youth and festering age, faces of fiends, crooked, twisted, misshapen monsters blasted with the ravages of disease and all the horrors of chronic malnutrition—the refuse and the scum of life, a raging, screaming, screeching, demoniacal horde. (Chapter 23)

London certainly knew how to pile on the agony. In *The Star Rover* (1915) the hero goes berserk and slays some two hundred seals. "Indeed, quite bereft was I of all judgment as I slew and continued to slay." (Chapter 19)

The Star Rover is an uneven book; its hero is Darrel Standing, whose soul can flip from one existence to another, reliving his past lives. He works his way back through one period of time to another, remembering such gods as Ishtar and Mitra, until he becomes a prehistoric man.

I was Ushu, the Archer, and Igar was my woman and mate. We laughed under the sun in the morning, when our man-child and woman-child, yellowed like honey-bees, sprawled and rolled in the mustard, and at night she lay close in my arms and loved me, and urged me, because of my skill at the seasoning of woods and the flaking of arrowheads, that I should stay close by the camp and let the other men bring me the meat from the perils of hunting. (Chapter 21)

Ouida was evidently a lasting influence. The story is told within the framework of Standing's confinement to a strait jacket in a death cell in San Quentin, where a sadistic warden tortures him. He escapes from the torture by skipping back in time.

London himself had skipped back in time before this. His *Before Adam*, published in book form in 1906, is a story of the Stone Age. Racial memory again plays a part. A city child dreams he is Big-Tooth, growing up with the Cave People, braving the terrors of the past world. Anthropologists may find fault with many of the facts of London's reconstruction, but the book has a sort of wild lyric truth, and some of his guesses about prehistory still appear sound— for instance that inventions might come about through the necessities of old age; the use of gourds to store water is credited to old Marrow-Bone, who kept a store of water in his cave to save him visiting the stream; gourds had previously been mere playthings.

Big-Tooth himself had racial memory dreams:

For Big-Tooth also had an other-self, and when he slept that other-self dreamed back into the past, back to the winged reptiles and the clash and the onset of dragons, and beyond that to the scurrying, rodent-like life of the tiny mammals, and far remoter still, to the shore-slime of the primaeval sea. I cannot, I dare not, say more. It is all too vague and complicated and awful. I can only hint of those vast and terrific vistas through which I have peered hazily at the progression of life, not upward from the ape to man, but upward from the worm. (Chapter 9)

Other writers before London had ventured into the neolithic world. H. G. Wells's forays have been mentioned. And there was Stanley Waterloo's *The Story of Ab* (1897), a romance of the uniting of palaeolithic and neolithic cultures.

London was accused of plagiarism by Waterloo; but, from this time onwards, the sheer bulk of publication and the contemporaneousness of writers makes the question of plagiarism almost irrelevant (though in a field naturally dependent upon surprise and sensationalism, it remains an interesting question). At any time, there are common moods, currents of thought, even catchwords— "atavism" being one catchword that runs through the science fiction of this period as "entropy" would later—which give society a mysterious unity. The prospect of nuclear doom which transfixes the nineteen-fifties, the fascination with drugs and over-population in the sixties and seventies: such general preoccupations are naturally reflected in the fiction of the period.

Before Adam reflects London's wish to escape from urban civilization. Drugs are often a defeatist symbol of the same longing. At the beginning of the present century, that longing more healthily found refuge in the still untamed regions of Earth. Hence the success of Kipling's *Jungle Books* and *Kim*, followed by the African tales of Edgar Wallace in *Sanders of the River*, and Edgar Rice Burroughs's Tarzan novels, also set in Africa.

So we come to two writing prodigies of the period, one British, one American—Edgar Wallace and Edgar Rice Burroughs. Burroughs belongs far more centrally to the history of science fiction, and lords it over our next chapter. But Wallace has an honoured place, for his name, with Merian C. Cooper's, adorns the credits of the greatest monster-science-fiction movie of them all, *King Kong*. He was finishing the script in Hollywood when death overtook him—a fittingly bizarre place in which to end an amazing career.

Wallace was born in the same year as Burroughs, 1875, the illegitimate son of an actress. He ran away to sea as a youth, soldiered in the Boer War, and worked as a reporter before beginning to write stories and plays. He had an immediate success with *Sanders of the River*.

He became tremendously prolific in middle age, writing one hundred and sixty-seven novels in fourteen years—a rate just one short of one a month. The *Sanders of the River* stories, set in the Congo, were wildly popular, and based on firsthand knowledge of Africa. They ran from 1909 until well into the nineteen-twenties. Wallace also wrote some science fiction, such as *The Day of Uniting* (1926), a Wellsian tale about the threat of a large comet which, in its close approach to Earth, causes humanity to unite as never before. In 1929, he published *Planetoid 127*, about the discovery of a planet "on the far side of the sun"—the traditional location of the hypothetical planet Vulcan.

His main output was devoted to crime, his favourite locale being the London underworld and the race track. Wallace knew both much better than Vulcan. His biographer relates how, when Wallace stood for Parliament at the height of his success, he did not endear himself to his constituency by admitting in a public speech that one reason why he wanted to get into the House of Commons was that "a writer of crook stories ought never to stop seeking new material".[29]

During the most prolific period of his life, there was a joke current about the appearance of "the noonday Wallace". In England, in the late twenties, he became the second biggest seller after the Bible. He was made chairman of British Lion Films, sometimes directing his own scripts from his own novels. A Rolls would wait outside the Carlton, London's most expensive hotel, in case Wallace felt like taking a drive. He liked to live well, was magnificently generous, and enjoyed his success to the full.

It is estimated that Wallace's sales have topped twenty million, while some one hundred and ninety films have been made, silent and talkie, from his books and plays, in the United Kingdom, the United States, Germany (an especially faithful market) and elsewhere.[30] His biographer was guilty of no exaggeration when she called him a phenomenon.

Among Edgar Wallace's successors is Ian Fleming, with his redoubtable hero, James Bond. Both these authors set their protagonists in the contemporary world, or a version of it, however fantastic the goings-on therein. Wallace's coeval, Burroughs, opted for the wide-open spaces, the remote. Burroughs utilizes that urge to escape from the trammels of civilization only casually pressed to serve by RLS, Haggard, Doyle, and their ilk. When he arrives at his formula, the unique prescription of present-day SF is almost fulfilled.

CHAPTER VII

From Barsoom to Beyond the Borderlands: Swords, Sorceries, and Zitidars

> The most poignant sensations of my existence are those of
> 1896, when I discovered the Hellenic world, and of 1902, when
> I discovered the myriad suns and worlds of infinite space.
> Sometimes I think the latter event the greater, for the grandeur
> of that growing conception of the universe still excites a thrill
> hardly to be duplicated.
> —H. P. Lovecraft (in letter to Edwin Baird)

The relationship between travel literature and the novel in all its forms is
intimate. Ever since the Greeks, an intermediate literature of fantasy travel has
flourished. Journeys to other planets are plainly extensions of this tradition as
exotic terrestrial locations succumb to nature reserves and housing estates. As
much can be said of journeys underground or beyond life. The search for white
space on the map has hotted up.

Within science fiction, there have always been attempts to separate SF proper
from fantasy, and to draw a line between what is remotely possible and what is
almost certainly impossible. To follow, in other words, the view propounded
by Kurd Lasswitz, quoted in the preceding chapter, to tolerate no postulate
which directly and absolutely contradicts previous and psychological experience.

Such rulings cannot be made to apply to groups of writers. If individual
writers wish to follow them, that is for their own practice. General prescriptions
can never be applied.

Indeed, it might be argued that one of the stimulations we derive from SF is in
deciding whether what we read is SF or fantasy. Could Venus really be as Edgar
Rice Burroughs would have us believe, choked with giant trees? Are there really
worlds where humans communicate with dragons and fly them like animated
Boeings? Perhaps our answers depend on what Lasswitz called "our sense of
veracity", and how many feet we have planted firmly on the ground.

But questions of categorization arise again in the nineteen-eighties, when
many novels announced on publishers' lists as SF are undisguised fantasy, and
SF which does not affront our sense of veracity is harder to find than at any time
since the twenties.

A time never existed when SF was "pure". There is, for instance, the case of
the remarkable Edgar Rice Burroughs.

Burroughs published some seventy books, fifty-nine of them in his lifetime.
World sales have topped one hundred million. His Tarzan character alone has

appeared in countless films, comic strips, and comic books, and been imitated in endless variations. Tarzan, Lord of Men and Apes, sophisticate and savage—he is the perfect urban fantasy. Tarzan, boy child brought up by the apes, is one of the most pleasantly innocuous of all modern pop myths, making even Superman slightly sinister by comparison, though Superman too is more syndicated than sinning.

Yet Burroughs's stories, even at the end of his life, his fame assured, were being rejected by *Cosmopolitan* and *Collier's*. He himself remained an endearing mixture of modesty and boastfulness. Burroughs's unease is plain in a response he made to the formidable critic Queenie Leavis: "I wish you to know that I am fully aware of the attitude of many scholars and self-imagined literati toward that particular brand of deathless literature of which I am guilty."[1]

And what was this deathless literature? Fantasy. Fancy. "Fantasies of eroticism and power," says the reliable E. F. Bleiler.[2] Burroughs's Mars, his Venus, his world at the Earth's core, even his Africa, bore only the slightest tinge of veracity. Nobody appeared to mind. Only the sedulous critic need observe distinctions to which readers are blind.

Burroughs's first published story was a six-part serial which ran in one of the grand old pulps, the *All-Story*, in 1912. This was "Under the Moons of Mars", better known by its later book title, *A Princess of Mars*. With this first effort, Burroughs brought the novel with an interplanetary setting into science fiction to stay.

Burroughs launched out on a series of interconnected novels set on the Red Planet, known to its inhabitants as Barsoom. *A Princess of Mars* was published in book form in 1917, soon to be followed by two sequels, *The Gods of Mars* (1918) and *The Warlord of Mars* (1919). As one of his more literate admirers puts it, "To the schoolboy in his early teens, Burroughs can open magic casements with the best . . . Those who read him at the right age owe a great debt of gratitude to Edgar Rice Burroughs." (Roger Lancelyn Green, *Into Other Worlds*)

Wafted by mystical and Blavatskian means across the gulfs of space, John Carter finds himself on Barsoom.[3] In no time, he is confronting a fifteen-foot-high Martian, green, four-armed, and sharp-tusked. Action and blood follow thick and fast in all Burroughs's books. A hasty ingenuity is his.

Yet the world of Barsoom, its history and geography, is painted in with a generous brush. Barsoom is dying, its seas drying; of the old civilizations little is left but ruin and deserted cities; its tribes, which vary in skin colour, are deadly enemies. In the first book Carter falls in love with the princess, Dejah Thoris, a beautiful red woman. All Martian women are oviparous, although this does not stop them mating with Earthmen.

Here is a colourful passage where a company of green Martians and their animals, together with Carter and Dejah Thoris, move across one of the dried-out sea beds:

> We made a most imposing and awe-inspiring spectacle as we strung out across the yellow landscape; the two hundred and fifty ornate and brightly

coloured chariots, preceded by an advance guard of some two hundred mounted warriors and chieftains riding five abreast and one hundred yards apart, and followed by a like number in the same formation, with a score or more of flankers on either side; the fifty extra mastodons, or heavy draft animals, known as zitidars, and the five or six hundred extra thoats of the warriors running loose within the hollow square formed by the surrounding warriors. The gleaming metals and jewels of the men and women, duplicated in the trappings of the zitidars and thoats, and interspersed with the flashing colours of magnificent silks and furs and feathers, lent a barbaric splendour to the caravan which would have turned an East Indian potentate green with envy.

The enormous broad tyres of the chariots and the padded feet of the animals brought forth no sound from the moss-covered sea bottom; and so we moved in utter silence, like some huge phantasmagoria, except when the stillness was broken by the guttural growling of a goaded zitidar, or the squealing of fighting thoats. The green Martians converse but little, and then usually in monosyllables, low and like the faint rumbling of distant thunder.

(from the chapter "Sola Tells Me Her Story")

This passage also shows Burroughs's carelessness—to speak of turning potentates green gives the game away, for this is clearly what he is doing, by transposing an Eastern sumptuousness to Mars. Nevertheless, the first three novels make an enormous paella of colour, mystery, and excitement for hungry adolescent stomachs.

Unfortunately, Burroughs could never resist ruining a good thing. The success of his trilogy of Martian novels led him to continue with eight sequels. We find him still spinning them out into the 1940s, with *Synthetic Men of Mars*. But Burroughs claimed never to write for anything but money.[4]

As the self-imagined literati would say, Burroughs was a slave to the wicked god of productivity.

The creator of Tarzan was born in the same year as the creator of King Kong, in 1875, on Chicago's West Side. As a young man, he enlisted in the US Cavalry, and saw something of a West that was still wild, meeting men who had fought Sioux and Apache. Later, he was discharged, tried gold-prospecting, and then ran through a series of miserable jobs, including railroad policeman in Salt Lake City and candy salesman. He was in his thirties, married, and with a family to support. "Economise as we could, the expenses of our little family were far beyond my income," wrote Burroughs. Then he tried his hand at writing. Success was immediate.[5]

Eight years after writing his first story, Burroughs was able to purchase rolling acres and a press baron's palace near Los Angeles. This site is now the township known as Tarzana—the word made flesh, or at least bricks and mortar. In his sixties, in World War II, Burroughs was appointed war correspondent, and spent some while in Hawaii. When he died in 1950, he left behind a flourishing town and millions of ardent readers.

Tarzan of the Apes was Burroughs's second story. It was published in 1912, also in *All-Story*. It reflects to perfection the wish to escape from urban civilization, where there are lousy jobs like railroad cop going. The story and the characters made Burroughs's fortune.

Mystery surrounded John Carter's birth. Tarzan's origins provide a perfect invitation to day-dreamers; in Burroughs's immortal words, "the son of an English lord and an English lady was nursed at the breast of Kala, the great ape". Rousseau's Noble Savage has been ennobled. Tarzan is not only the great killer of the jungle; he is also Lord Greystoke, heir to a fortune in England, and the plot of the first Tarzan novel juggles effectively between these incongruities.

Tarzan is not science fiction. Even his ability to talk "apish" does not make him a borderline case. But there is no doubt that he is a magnificently successful embodiment of fantasy. If the blood of Mowgli, child of the wolves, runs in his literary veins, then Tarzan in turn has fathered many fictional progeny, and must be accounted godfather to Otis Adelbert Kline's *Jan of the Jungle* and Robert Grandon series (set on Venus), to Howard's Conan series, just as Barsoom is elder planet to Marion Zimmer Bradley's Darkover, and a myriad other worlds of loincloth and luxury.

ERB's reincarnation of noble savagery (bad ideas never die) came swinging through the trees on to cinema screens early in his career. The first Tarzan movie was produced in 1917, since when ape-man movies have proved more permanent than custard pies. At one time, Tarzan was played by Buster Crabbe, who then went on to the title role in Universal's Flash Gordon serials, inspired by Alex Raymond's elegant science fantasy strip. There was also a syndicated comic strip based on Burroughs's novels, scrupulously drawn by Hal Foster; this strip was later taken over by Burne Hogarth and other artists.

At first, Burroughs seemed genuinely interested in working out the complex, if fictional, problems which would confront someone with such a conflicting inheritance as Tarzan's. In *The Return of Tarzan*, these problems are already being laid aside in favour of a rather trite exposure of the decadence of civilization compared with the ethical codes of the jungle. Already, duelling Frenchmen, beautiful Russian countesses, unsavoury Europeans, brutish black men, survivors of Atlantis, and lost treasure cities ruled over by lovely priestesses, are oozing through the undergrowth, until Africa bears about as much relationship to reality as does Barsoom.

Burroughs could resist anything but success.

Tarzan of the Apes was followed by some two dozen sequels, straggling on throughout ERB's career—and after. Tarzan also makes a guest appearance in a third series he was hatching at the same time as the first two, the Pellucidar series, which commenced with *At the Earth's Core*, first published as a serial in 1914.

The *donnée* of this series is John Symmes's theory that the Earth is hollow. Earth's lining supports a whole world of savage tribes and amazing creatures, some of whom enslave humans. (Slavery is never far from Burroughs's mind.) This is Pellucidar. Pellucidar is lit by a miniature Sun burning in the centre of the hollow; the Sun has a small satellite revolving round it in a twenty-four-hour orbit. Inner Space indeed!

To enquire whether Burroughs derived this idea from Niels Klim is idle, though the similarity of concepts is striking. The truth is, that when one is hard up for secret worlds, one can find them under the Earth, in a puddle, in an atom, up in the attic, down in the cellar, or in the left eyeball. All of these vantage points have been explored by hard-pressed fantasists. Furthermore, we need no longer enquire whether extrapolations of Mars or Venus derive from such astronomers as Lowell or Arrhenius; the generations of writers now close ranks and begin to derive their ideas from one another. This is known as a continuing debate.

David Innes, Burroughs's new hero, arrives in Pellucidar via a giant mechanical mole, boring down through the Earth's crust. There Innes undergoes a number of remarkable adventures which parallel fairly closely the crises, hairbreadth escapes, and cliff-hangers of Carter and Tarzan. Only the cliffs are different. In the first two novels in this series, *At the Earth's Core* (book form 1922) and *Pellucidar* (1923), something of ERB's excitement and interest in creating a new world is communicated.

Here is a passage from the first of the two novels, which shows, even in slight abridgement, the dextrous way Burroughs had of moving along from one exotic focus of interest to another, with a smoothness that perhaps no other fantasy writer has managed. David Innes and his friend Perry are taken to an arena to witness the punishment of two slaves—man and woman—watched over by the ruling race, the Mahars:

For the first time, I beheld their queen. She differed from the others in no feature that was appreciable to my earthly eyes, in fact all Mahars look alike to me; but when she crossed the arena after the balance of her female subjects had found their bowlders, she was preceded by a score of huge Sagoths, the largest I ever had seen, and on either side of her waddled a huge thipdar, while behind came another score of Sagoth guardsmen. . . .

And then the music started—music without sound! The Mahars cannot hear, so the drums and fifes and horns of earthly bands are unknown among them. The "band" consisted of a score or more Mahars. It filed out in the centre of the arena where the creatures upon the rocks might see it, and there it performed for fifteen or twenty minutes.

Their technique consisted in waving their tails and moving their heads in a regular succession of measured movements resulting in a cadence which evidently pleased the eye of the Mahar as the cadence of our own instrumental music pleases our ears. Sometimes the band took measured steps in unison to one side or the other, or backward and again forward— it all seemed very silly and meaningless to me, but at the end of the first piece the Mahars upon the rocks showed the first indications of enthusiasm that I had seen displayed by the dominant race of Pellucidar. They beat their great wings up and down, and smote their rocky perches with their mighty tails until the ground shook. . . .

When the band had exhausted its repertory it took wing and settled upon the rocks above and behind the queen. Then the business of the day was on. A man and woman were pushed into the arena by a couple of Sagoth guardsmen. I leaned far forwards in my seat to scrutinize the female—hoping against hope that she might prove to be another than Dian the Beautiful. Her back was toward me for a while, and the sight of the great mass of raven hair piled high upon her head filled me with alarm.

Presently a door in one side of the arena wall was opened to admit a huge, shaggy bull-like creature.

"A Bos," whispered Perry excitedly. "His kind roamed the outer crust with the cave bear and the mammoth ages and ages ago. We have been carried back a million years, David, to the childhood of a planet—is it not wondrous?"

But I saw only the raven hair of a half-naked girl, and my heart stood still in dumb misery at the sight of her, nor had I any eyes for the wonder of natural history. (Chapter 6)

The conclusion of this passage, with irony reinforcing sorrow, is very effective.

Again, Burroughs never knew when enough was enough. Six Pellucidar novels were published in his lifetime, and a seventh, *Savage Pellucidar* (1963), was cobbled together after his death. One of the six is *Tarzan at the Earth's Core* (1930).

In 1932, *Argosy* began to serialize the first novel in Burroughs's fourth major series. This time the setting is Venus. Carson Napier is a typical Burroughs hero, even down to the oddities surrounding his birth. He was the son of a British army officer and an American girl from Virginia, born in India and brought up under the tutelage of an old Hindu mystic who taught Carson many odd things, "among them telepathy"!

Conforming to precedent, Burroughs frames his narrative in introductory matter which mentions real names and places, to ease one into the incredible happenings which are to follow. The framework in *Pirates of Venus* mentions David Innes and Pellucidar, for the author seems to have a vague idea of linking his entire *oeuvre* together, rather in the way that Anthony Trollope provided links within his Barchester novels.

This new Barsoomian Barchester, although generously supplied with strange topography, people, and adventures, never has the zip of the Martian series. But then, Venus has never been the best planet for the imagination. Its shrouded surface has damped the creative urge. Drawing out a very slender thread of reasoning, the Swedish astronomer Arrhenius proclaimed in 1917, "Everything on Venus is dripping wet"—and the depressing thought stuck.[6] The writerly imagination has been clouded ever since.

Right: Reginald Easton's portrait miniature of Mary Wollstonecraft Shelley was painted from a cast made after the author's death. Her novel, *Frankenstein: or, The Modern Prometheus,* has now taken on the status of archetype for the socially irresponsible scientist. As if to prove that her first venture into scientific romancing was no accident, she went on to write *The Last Man,* the seminal treatment of a human being alone in a ruined world.

Below: Joseph Wright of Derby is the first painter of scientific experiments. His *An Experiment on a Bird in the Air Pump,* dating from about 1767-68, shows a scientific demonstration in progress. A laboratory assistant pulls down the blind on the moon showing through a rear window. At this time, there was no division between science and the arts.

Left: Jules Verne depicted as one who triumphs over mortality and says "Hi!" to later readers. This engraving featured on the contents page of Hugo Gernsback's magazine, *Amazing Stories* Although Verne was born almost 160 years ago, his name is still known throughout the world. His novels show a slowly increasing pessimism concerning human nature.

Below: H.G. Wells on the set of Alexander Korda's film, *Things to Come*, the most Wellsian of the many films made from Wells's writings; it contains much of his political and utopian thought. With Wells are Raymond Massey as John Cabal and Margaretta Scott as the voluptuous Roxana. The sets and costumes of this mid-thirties film had a considerable influence over later SF artwork.

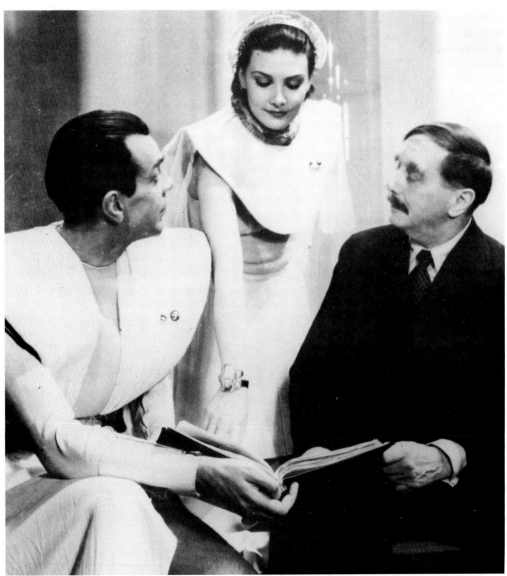

Edgar Rice Burroughs achieved best-sellerdom almost overnight with his Tarzan stories. His is one of the great popular success stories of the century. SF readers remember him best for his romances set on Mars, fabled Barsoom. Here he reads one of his own stories with apparent enjoyment.

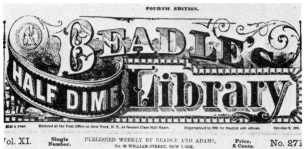

FOURTH EDITION.

Vol. XI. Single Number. PUBLISHED WEEKLY BY BEADLE AND ADAMS, No. 98 WILLIAM STREET, NEW YORK. Price, 5 Cents. No. 271

THE HUGE HUNTER; or, THE STEAM MAN OF THE PRAIRIES

BY EDWARD S. ELLIS.
AUTHOR OF "THE BOY MINERS," "SETH JONES," "BILL BIDDON," ETC., ETC., ETC.

Indigenous science fiction entered the United States with the publication of Edward S. Ellis's *The Huge Hunter: or, The Steam Man of the Prairies*, in 1868. This impressive metal figure, the invention of a hunchbacked boy, forges across the land, ridding the West of bad men and Injuns. It began a vogue for Frontier-adventure SF which has never died.

The Anglophone world is reluctant to acknowledge the existence of science fiction elsewhere in the world. Yet these two magazines, *Hugin* and *Der Orchideengarten*, began publication in 1916 and 1919 respectively, and included in their pages many authors we now recognize as writers of science fiction, including illustrious names such as Poe, de Maupassant, de l'Isle Adam, and Čapek.

Facing page: Hugo Gernsback published several magazines, including *Your Body* and *Modern Electrics*, the world's first radio magazine. His *Amazing Stories* is widely regarded as the first science fiction magazine. Here Gernsback the inventor is shown listening through his teeth on his new patent — the Osophone.

Hearing Through the Teeth

By H. GERNSBACK

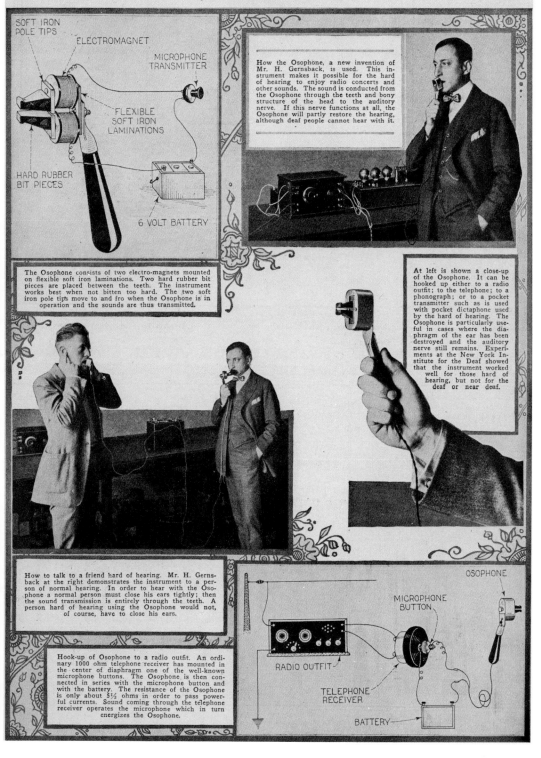

How the Osophone, a new invention of Mr. H. Gernsback, is used. This instrument makes it possible for the hard of hearing to enjoy radio concerts and other sounds. The sound is conducted from the Osophone through the teeth and bony structure of the head to the auditory nerve. If this nerve functions at all, the Osophone will partly restore the hearing, although deaf people cannot hear with it.

The Osophone consists of two electro-magnets mounted on flexible soft iron laminations. Two hard rubber bit pieces are placed between the teeth. The instrument works best when not bitten too hard. The two soft iron pole tips move to and fro when the Osophone is in operation and the sounds are thus transmitted.

At left is shown a close-up of the Osophone. It can be hooked up either to a radio outfit; to the telephone; to a phonograph; or to a pocket transmitter such as is used with pocket dictaphone used by the hard of hearing. The Osophone is particularly useful in cases where the diaphragm of the ear has been destroyed and the auditory nerve still remains. Experiments at the New York Institute for the Deaf showed that the instrument worked well for those hard of hearing, but not for the deaf or near deaf.

How to talk to a friend hard of hearing. Mr. H. Gernsback at the right demonstrates the instrument to a person of normal hearing. In order to hear with the Osophone a normal person must close his ears tightly; then the sound transmission is entirely through the teeth. A person hard of hearing using the Osophone would not, of course, have to close his ears.

Hook-up of Osophone to a radio outfit. An ordinary 1000 ohm telephone receiver has mounted in the center of diaphragm one of the well-known microphone buttons. The Osophone is then connected in series with the microphone button and with the battery. The resistance of the Osophone is only about 5½ ohms in order to pass powerful currents. Sound coming through the telephone receiver operates the microphone which in turn energizes the Osophone.

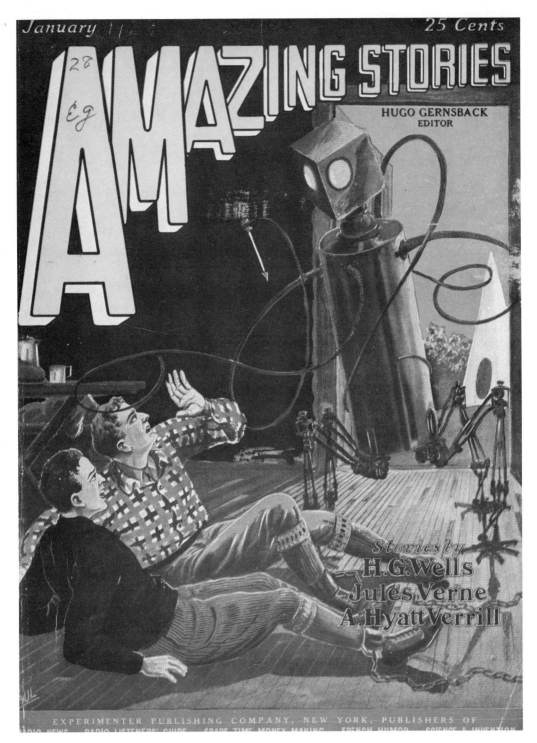

One of Gernsback's greatest discoveries was the artist Frank R. Paul, an Austrian who had trained as an architect. His futurist scenes have a special enchantment approached by few artists since, even if a certain weakness in Paul's early figure-drawing confined many of his protagonists, as here, to jodhpurs. Note that this issue of *Amazing* carries reprints by Wells and Verne.

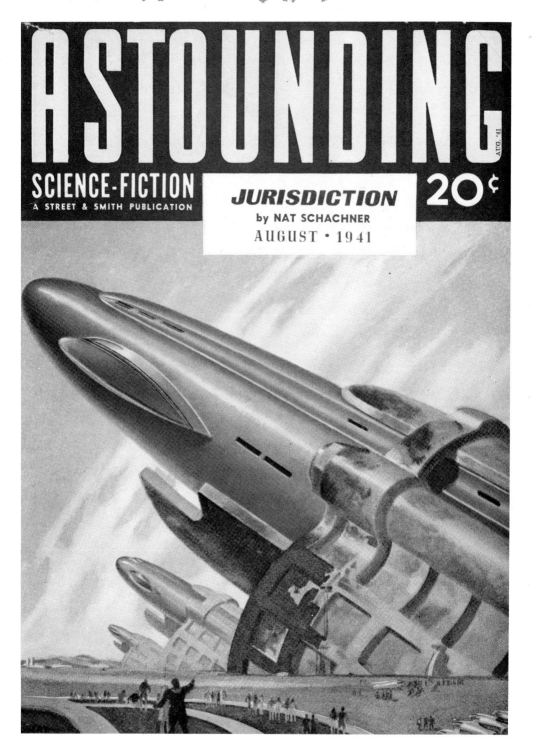

ASTOUNDING

SCIENCE-FICTION
A STREET & SMITH PUBLICATION

JURISDICTION
by NAT SCHACHNER
AUGUST · 1941

20¢

AUG. W.

This *Astounding* cover, with its gigantic rusting spaceships, is by the Canadian-born artist, Hubert Rogers. His style appears to have been influenced by the Wells film, *Things to Come*. The elegant sans serif lettering of the magazine's title represented the last word in modernity at the time.

John Wood Campbell, indisputably the greatest editor the SF field has known. After writing many fantastic science fiction stories, he took over the editorship of *Astounding* in 1937, remaining there until his death in 1971. The portrait is by one of *Astounding*'s most popular artists, Kelly Freas.

A pensive Olaf Stapledon. So individual is his voice that his writing has never been properly accepted in either the history of literature or of science fiction. Yet his two major works, *Last and First Men*, and, more especially, *Star Maker*, are unrivalled for scope, beauty, and aspiration.

Burroughs's Venus possesses a year-long axial rotation, so that it always turns to face the sun, and regions of ice surround the hot equatorial region. Mile-high trees grow in the tropics. (Think of that, lads!)

Three more Venus novels followed the first, in true Burroughs fashion, and a fourth was started but not completed. World War II got in the way. Burroughs died in bed one day, while reading a comic book—a man of seventy-four still dreaming up wild refuges for his somewhat garish imagination.

For all their faults, Burroughs's stories have a power more pretentious novels sometimes lack—a quality which has little to do with veracity and much with the simple and ancient art of telling an engagingly tall story. Before that art, Queenie Leavis's scorn has no power.

Besides the novels mentioned, ERB wrote many others, some of them also in series. *The Moon Maid* (serialized in 1923) launched a series which depicts an inner world on the Moon. No wonder that Burroughs—like Walter Scott before him—founded his own publishing house to cope with his massive output!

Many readers consider Burroughs's best novel to be *The Land That Time Forgot* (first published in book form in 1924). It consists of three novelettes, each purportedly written by a different person; they are, "The Land That Time Forgot", "The People That Time Forgot", and "Out of Time's Abyss". The beginning of the story contains echoes of both Poe and Conan Doyle, where a submarine is drawn towards an uncharted magnetic island, sighting icebergs as it goes. On one of the island's rare beaches, a dead man is sighted, reminding one of the crew of a prehistoric man. They find the subterranean channel of an inland river flowing into the sea; the submarine navigates its channel, thus entering the world of Caprona, or Caspak as it is known to its inhabitants.

And what inhabitants! The mystery of this lost world is solved, typically enough, by a story told to Bradley while he is imprisoned in a foul pit in the Blue Place of Seven Skulls. Evolution is not a unitary process involving all phyla on Caspak, but an individual one. The tribes through which the sailors have passed from south to north are each representatives of an upwards evolutionary process; all individuals pass through this process, recapitulating in their own bodies a whole cycle from tadpole to fish or reptile, to the ape, and then— if they are lucky—to Man. The women lay their multitudinous eggs into warm pools.

It is another "mystery of sex and birth" story. But the fantasy is nicely worked out, the stages well visualized, although the novel is blemished by its cast of disagreeable Germans and stage Cockneys ("Wot s'y we pot the bloomin' bird, sir?").

All Burroughs's novels are vaguely similar, wherever they are set, heroes and incidents being often transposable, as clips of crocodile fights were transposed from one Tarzan movie to the next. After his first burst of creativity, from 1912–14, when Barsoom, Tarzan and Pellucidar appear, Burroughs strings sequels on to these three kites. Since his characters are almost characterless—little but exotic names—they experience nothing of the difficulties of personality with which we all wrestle in real life. ERB specialized in unreal life. His novels offer to a remarkable degree every facility for identifying with the hero and daydreaming through his triumphs.

No harm in such facility, perhaps; but self-exploration is at least as important as self-indulgence, and there is always the possibility of becoming permanently drugged by such brightly coloured pipe dreams.[7]

What, finally, are we to make of ERB, that supreme example of the dichotomy of taste, between critics who see no virtue in him, and fans who see no fault?

One peculiar feature of Burroughs's output is the frequency with which mystery surrounds birth. The lead figures in the major series all have oddities attending their infancy, except for David Innes. This is most extreme in the hero of the best series, John Carter of Mars, who could almost pass for Ayesha after a sex-change. Carter recalls no childhood, has always been adult, and remains at about the age of thirty. Other instances of children, like Tarzan, lost to or estranged from parents, are many. A comic example is the eponymous cave girl in a lesser series which begins with *The Cave Girl* (published in book form in 1925); she is revealed to be the daughter of a vanished count and countess. The women of Mars, like the women of Caspak, are oviparous; in other terms, children are born away from or rejected by their mothers, rather as Tarzan is fostered by an inhuman creature.

Was there confusion as well as an attempt to glamourize his own origins in ERB's statement that "I was born in Peking at the time that my father was military adviser to the Empress of China, and lived there, in the Forbidden City, until I was ten years old."? (*Edgar Rice Burroughs, Fiction Writer*)

Sexual dimorphism is common in Burroughs's world. The hideous males of Opar in the Tarzan series differ markedly from the beautiful females. (Though in *Tarzan and the Ant Men*, 1924, it is the females, the Alalis, who are hideous because they have achieved sexual dominance.)

Despite a considerable amount of nudity in ERB's novels, sexual intercourse is neither mentioned nor implied; we might be in a prepubertal world. This is bowing to more than the literary conventions of the times. Thuvia, maid of Mars, spends fifteen years as a "plaything and a slave" of the egregious White Martians, and runs around naked to boot, yet survives to flaunt her virginity in the very title of the novel!

Yet the *danger* of sex is always there. One industrious critic, Richard D. Mullen, has calculated the omnipresence of the threat of rape in Burroughs's world, and found female virtue in danger no less than an obsessive seventy-six times in the novels written between 1911 and 1915! The menaces include a marvellously miscegenously-inclined throng of apes, usurers, black sultans, Negroes, green, white, and yellow Martians, cavemen, hairy men, orang-outangs, and Japanese head-hunters.[8] In every case, chastity is successfully preserved.

In Carl Jung's *Memories, Dreams, Reflections*, Jung recounts the vivid psychosis of one of his female patients, who believed that she had lived on the Moon. She told Jung a tale about her life there. It appears that the Moon people were threatened with extinction. A vampire lived in the high mountains of the Moon. The vampire kidnapped and killed women and children, who in consequence had taken to living underground. The patient resolved to kill the vampire but, when she and it came face to face, the vampire revealed himself as a man of unearthly beauty.[9]

Jung makes a comment which could stand on the title page of this book: "Thereafter I regarded the sufferings of the mentally ill in a different light. For I had gained insight into the richness and importance of their inner experience." Without imputing mental illness to Burroughs, I believe that Jung provides a key to fantasy writing in general, and to the echoing of themes. He does illuminate something compulsive and repetitive in Burroughs's output.

It is idle to protest that the Burroughs books depart from facts—that an oviparous woman is a contradiction in terms, that Mars has no breathable atmosphere, that a child raised by apes would be incapable of learning human language when older, that Venus rotates and is intolerably hot, that a sun inside Earth would turn it into a nuclear bonfire, and so on. Burroughs is not interested in the facts of the external world.

As one critic has observed, by this blindness Burroughs throws away advantages—for instance, by not preserving the distinction that Lowell clearly made between old Martian sea beds and barren plateaux, thus forfeiting a sharper realization of his Barsoom.[10] But Burroughs was reporting from his own internal Pellucidar. Burroughs's Mars, like Ray Bradbury's later Mars, reports on areas which cannot be scrutinized through any telescope.

A failure to make a simple distinction between two sorts of vision, the Wellsian and the Burroughsian, or the analytic and the fantastic, bedevils all criticism, especially SF criticism—as well it might, for the distinction is particularly hard to draw in science fiction. Lowell's Mars—in its time the latest factual study science could produce—is now itself as much a fantasy world as Barsoom.

Comparing a Wells and a Burroughs novel makes the distinction between the strategies plain. It happens both authors published novels in 1923.

In *Men Like Gods*, one of Wells's little men, a Mr Barnstaple, drives his car into the fourth dimension, there to find a utopia of beautiful, powerful, and frequently nude people. With him is a diverse group of his contemporaries who do their best to wreck the utopia. Barnstaple defeats them with utopian aid, and eventually returns through the dimensional barrier, back to the real world.

Pellucidar, after a brief prologue intended to establish the "reality" of what follows, is the story of a world at the hollow centre of the Earth, where David Innes searches for his lady love. He is reunited with her after many strange adventures, travelling through savage country populated by monsters and primitive creatures.

Described like this, the two novels sound not dissimilar. Both are fantasies, both use people as symbols, both have their excitements. Yet their differences are many.

The fourth dimension is about as unlikely as a hollow earth, and Barnstaple's adventures no more probable than Innes's. However, Wells's fantasy device, the fourth dimension, serves merely to lead us to his utopia. The utopia is so much the thing, that the feasibility of the device which gets us there does not much matter, provided it is dealt with briefly and interestingly. On the other hand, Burroughs's Inner World is the whole story, and the narrative is largely taken up with the stones and arrows loosed there, and the fangs and claws bred there.

Burroughs's characters are exotic and bear strange and beautiful names, of which perhaps the best is Pellucidar itself. Barnstaple is allowed his handle "Mr" throughout, while the characters he is involved with are based on real politicians of the day, such as Balfour and Winston Churchill.

Action in *Men Like Gods* is leisurely. There is plenty of time for discussion, which mainly consists of contrasting our world unfavourably with utopia and airing Wells's ideas about world government. In *Pellucidar*, events move fast; one threat succeeds another, one scrape succeeds another; conversation is practically limited to threats, or to explanations of what has happened or is about to happen. Incident is all-too-frequent, but plot is non-existent.

When Barnstaple returns in his battered old car to our world, it is a recognizable dull world of hotels with waitresses serving tea, the *Daily Express*, *The Times*, chat about Poland, the Chinese, and sport. Our world in *Pellucidar* is represented by a telegram from Algiers, the finding of a mysterious telegraphic instrument buried in the Sahara, a call to action!

In short, Wells's is a serious tale, enlivened by a little humour. Its aim is to discuss entertainingly ways in which mankind might improve itself and its lot. Burroughs's story is fantasy adventure without structure which we do not for one minute take seriously.

The publishing history of the two novels is also interestingly in contrast. Wells's novel was published in hard-cover in 1923 and only achieved paperback publication forty-seven years later.[11] Burroughs's novel was serialized in *All-Story Cavalier Weekly* in 1915, to appear in hard-cover in 1923, since when it has made many paperback appearances.

Which of the two is the "better" book? If the question has any meaning, my answer would be that *Pellucidar* is the better. If one's choice of company lies between a fatigued schoolmaster and an inspired anecdotalist, the better bet is the anecdotalist.

Burroughs, in this novel, writes about as well as he can write, not well but serviceably, while his fertile imagination pours out lavishly the details of his preposterous world. Wells appears constipated beside him. Wells's novel is laborious, and, whatever it was in 1923, takes an effort to read now. Burroughs still slips down easily. With Burroughs you have (moderate) fun; Wells here gives off what Kingsley Amis categorizes as "a soporific whiff of left-wing crankiness".[12]

So why does one obstinately respect Wells the more? It must be because, whatever else his failings, Wells is trying to grapple with what he sees as the real world. Burroughs, however expertly, is dishing out daydreams.

Wells does not expect anyone to identify with his stuffy little central character; Barnstaple is just an ordinary fellow, not held up particularly for approval or ridicule. The characters who surround him are mildly satirized, though no grotesques. This may account for the reason why Wells was never a popular author as popular authors go, liable to speak of his work as "that particular brand of deathless literature of which I am guilty", as Burroughs did. All Burroughs's main characters can claim the old title "hero"—not only in the Pellucidar novels but in all the other Burroughs series, Tarzan's jungles, Napier's Venus, Carter's Mars. Burroughs wants us to identify, to sink into his dream countries and exclude the outside one.

Wells is teaching us to think. Burroughs and his lesser imitators are teaching us not to think.

Of course, Burroughs is teaching us to wonder. The sense of wonder is in essence a religious state, blanketing out criticism. Wells was always a critic, even in his most romantic and wondrous tales.

And there, I believe, the two poles of modern fantasy stand defined. At one pole wait Wells and his honourable predecessors such as Swift; at the other, Burroughs and the commercial producers, such as Otis Adelbert Kline, and the weirdies, and horror merchants such as H. P. Lovecraft, and so all the way past Tolkien to today's non-stop fantasy worlders. Mary Shelley stands somewhere at the equator of this metaphor.

At the thinking pole stand great figures, although it is easy to write badly. At the dreaming pole stand no great figures—though there are monstrous figures—and it is difficult to write well. In the eighties, the dreaming pole is in the ascendant.

Although reading is primarily for pleasure, one should try to be pleased by whatever rewards with the highest pleasure. A swimming pool is a poor place in which to swim when there is a great ocean near by. Unless, of course, you are slightly afraid of the water. . . .

Burroughs, in his proliferating series and sequels, is one of the most commercially successful authors of this century, certainly the most commercially successful science fantasy author. His sales continue. His influence has been immense, and often damaging.

One further general point before leaving Burroughs. ERB's stories are much like Westerns, and the Chicago in which he was born still retained elements of a frontier town. The vanishing redskin was not far away in space or time. Burroughs often wrote about him, directly or indirectly; his writings are a welter of racial fantasy—even Tar-Zan means White Skin in the language of the apes.

Burroughs fits very neatly into Leslie Fiedler's synthesis of the myths which give a special character to art and life in America. Fiedler's synthesis culminates in *The Return of the Vanishing American*. The one passage in that volume which deigns to mention Burroughs is so apropos to the hordes of odd-coloured and shaped creatures which were about to descend on twentieth-century man via science fiction that it deserves quotation.

Fiedler, putting his case against the American male, shows how the image of a white girl tied naked to a stake while redskins dance howling round her appeals to both our xenophobia and a sense of horror. Often such images were used as crude magazine illustrations.

> And, indeed, this primordial image has continued to haunt pulp fiction ever since (often adorning the covers of magazines devoted to it); for it panders to that basic White male desire at once to relish and deplore, vicariously share and publicly condemn, the rape of White female innocence. To be sure, as the generations go by, the colour of her violators has changed, though that of the violated woman has remained the same: from the Red of the Indians with whom it all began, to the Yellow of such malign Chinese as Dr Fu Manchu, the Black of those Africans who stalk so lubriciously through the pages of Edgar Rice Burroughs's Tarzan books, or the Purple or Green Martians who represent the crudest fantasy level of science fiction.[13]

This theory does not hold water—or rather, holds more water than Fiedler thinks, for Sax Rohmer, the creator of Dr Fu Manchu, was an Englishman, and we have noted that two most likely sources of Burroughs's Mars lie in *Gulliver of Mars* and *She*, both written by Englishmen. Americans are not alone in obsessional fears about sex and colour. Indeed such fears are also observed in deepest Africa. Suffice it to say that Pocahontas and Ayesha really started something. With those mother-figures, the guilts of their respective doomed continents merge. Burroughs let the spectral Red/Black/Yellow/Green men into SF, and they have been on the warpath ever since—all the way to the stars on zitidars.

Burroughs marks a retreat to the primitive. Other writers took other paths in their flight from urban culture and the burdens of rational thought.

Otis Adelbert Kline's imitation of Burroughs seems fairly open. Kline's *Planet of Peril* is Venus. It was published in serial form in 1929. An inevitable sequel followed. Later, Kline moved on to Mars with *The Swordsman of Mars*, and on to Tarzan with *Tam, Son of the Tiger* and *Jan of the Jungle*—made indiscriminately into a Universal film serial, just as Tarzan had been. And so on.

Others of the great obscure include Austin Hall and Homer Eon Flint, authors of *The Blind Spot* (*Argosy*, 1921), polished off adequately by Damon Knight in a chapter entitled "Chuckleheads" in his *In Search of Wonder*; and Ralph Milne Farley, an ex-state senator from Wisconsin, whose *The Radio Man* of 1924 was followed up (or down) by *The Radio Beasts*, *The Radio Planet*, and "The Radio Minds of Mars". There are also Ray Cummings, best remembered for *The Girl in the Golden Atom*—Gulliver down the microscope—Charles B. Stilson, Victor Rousseau, and J. U. Giesy, author of the attractively titled *Palos of the Dog Star Pack*, which ran as a serial and of course spawned sequels.

Croft, the hero of *Palos*, travels to that distant star by astral projection, the means by which John Carter reached Mars—or the anonymous traveller in the

1741 *A New Journey to the World in the Moon* reached the lunar world. Mysticism in one form or another never dies, and SF carries its due freight.[14] It may be regarded either as another form of retreat from the materialist problems of today, or as a plot device to remove a hero far and fast from an everyday situation to a bizarre one. These alternatives do not necessarily conflict.

One escape route lay through the macabre, to the shadowy worlds where the rational could be set aside by the supernatural. Whatever we care to say about Burroughs's worlds, he does present us with a great frieze of capering beings, full of pulp life, and engaged in hearty struggle with their enemies. On Hodgson, Merritt, Lovecraft, and their ilk, the shadow of the grave lies as heavy as it did across Poe. These practitioners stand nearer to what we have termed the dreaming pole than does ERB.

William Hope Hodgson, born in Essex in 1877, served in the British Merchant Navy. He was a courageous and active man, shot in the trenches in 1918, in the war which killed Saki and millions of others. Hodgson's total output is modest. He never wrote a perfect book; yet he produced two scientific romances which have embedded in them visions as impressive as any mentioned in this volume. They are the basis for a reputation that has grown slowly since Hodgson's death.

The House on the Borderland (1908) is a strange house indeed, a massive stone affair in which the narrator lives with his old sister. The house is built over a pit, from which swine-things (another submerged nation?) emerge and go through the traditional uncanny, nocturnal, and nauseous antics of all swine-things.

So far, so undistinguished. But the centre of the story is something different. The pit is in some vague fashion connected with the universe. The narrator stands transfixed at his window while time accelerates outside. The Sun begins to whirl across the heavens until it is an arc of fire, a Sun stream.

> From the sky, I glanced down to the gardens. They were just a blur of a palish, dirty green. I had a feeling that they stood higher, than in the old days; a feeling that they were nearer my window, as though they had risen, bodily. Yet they were still a long way below me; for the rock, over the mouth of the pit, on which this house stands, arches up to a great height.
>
> It was later, that I noticed a change in the constant colour of the gardens. The pale, dirty green was growing ever paler and paler, towards white. At last, after a great space, they became greyish-white, and stayed thus for a very long time. Finally, however, the greyness began to fade, even as had the green, into a dead white. And this remained, constant and unchanged. And by this I knew that, at last, snow lay upon all the Northern world.
>
> And so, by millions of years, time winged onward through eternity, to the end—the end, of which, in the old-earth days, I had thought remotely, and in hazily speculative fashion. And now, it was approaching in a manner of which none had ever dreamed.
>
> I recollect that, about this time, I began to have a lively, though morbid,

curiosity, as to what would happen when the end came—but I seemed strangely without imaginings.

All this while, the steady process of decay was continuing. The few remaining pieces of glass, had long ago vanished; and, every now and then, a soft thud, and a little cloud of rising dust, would tell of some fragment of fallen mortar or stone.

I looked up again, to the fiery sheet that quaked in the heavens above me and far down into the Southern sky. As I looked, the impression was borne in upon me, that it had lost some of its first brilliancy—that it was duller, deeper hued.

I glanced down, once more, to the blurred white of the world-scape. Sometimes, my look returned to the burning sheet of dulling flame, that was, and yet hid, the sun. At times, I glanced behind me, into the growing dusk of the great, silent room, with its aeon-carpet of sleeping dust. . . .

So I watched through the fleeting ages, lost in soul-wearing thoughts and wonderings, and possessed with a new weariness. . . .

It might have been a million years later, that I perceived, beyond possibility of doubt, that the fiery sheet, that lit the world, was indeed darkening.

Another vast space went by, and the whole enormous flame had sunk to a deep, copper colour. Gradually, it darkened, from copper to copper-red, and from this, at times, to a deep, heavy, purplish tint, with, in it, a strange loom of blood.

Although the light was decreasing, I could perceive no diminishment in the apparent speed of the sun. It still spread itself in that dazzling veil of speed.

The world, so much of it as I could see, had assumed a dreadful shade of gloom, as though, in very deed, the last day of the worlds approached. (Chapters XVI–XVII)

As the house crumbles, the Sun begins at last to grow dull. Finally, it hangs in the sky, stationary, like a bronze shield. The air falls as snow round the shell of the house. The Central Suns approach. Earth itself is a forgotten thing.

What did this overpowering spectacle of the Remote mean to Hodgson?

His mystical vision carries an echo of the initiation of Harmachis, in the fourth chapter of Haggard's *Cleopatra* ("Behold the world that thou has left," said the Voice, "behold and tremble"); but Hodgson's scope and verve are his own. The whole vision, a mingling of astronomy and psychic experience, extends through several chapters—a bravura piece of writing, full of wonder, excelling in its scope anything written up to that date, and bursting far beyond the tawdry horror story in which it is set.

The Night Land (1912) flares into magnificence and dies into unreadability. Hodgson makes the strategic error of embedding his main story, which is set far into the future, within a preposterous seventeenth-century framework, written in mock-antique. It is a very long book, and a reader may be forgiven if he never gets to the end even of the abridged edition, issued in 1921; yet within it lies a drama of great and powerful splendour, the drama of the Last Redoubt.

The residue of humanity waits under siege in the Redoubt. The old world has been laid waste by "Monsters and Ab-human creatures", which have been permitted, through the agency of long-past human science, to pass "the barrier of Life". The Last Redoubt is a pyramid, seven miles high, set on a desolate plain.

The Redoubt is powered by electricity drawn from the Earth. Fantastic creatures gather on the plain from the Night Lands, awaiting the exhaustion of this power. Greatest among these creatures are the Watchers. The Watchers are enormous, immobile, silent, and have been so throughout unknown thousands of years, awaiting the end that must come.

Before me ran the Road Where The Silent Ones Walk; and I searched it, as many a time in my earlier youth had I, with the spy-glass; for my heart was always stirred mightily by the sight of those Silent Ones.

And presently, alone in the miles of that night-grey road, I saw one in the field of my glass—a quiet, cloaked figure, moving along, shrouded, and looking neither to right nor left. And thus was it with these beings ever. It was told about in the Redoubt that they would harm no human, if but the human did keep a fair distance from them; but that it were wise never to come close upon one. And this I can well believe.

And so, searching the road with my gaze, I passed beyond this Silent One, and past the place where the road, sweeping vastly to the South-East, was lit a space, strangely, by the light from the Silver-fire Holes. And thus at last to where it swayed to the South of the Dark Palace, and thence Southward still, until it passed round to the Westward, beyond the mountain bulk of the Watching Thing in the South—the hugest monster in all the visible Night Lands. My spy-glass showed it to me with clearness—a living hill of watchfulness, known to us as The Watcher Of The South. It brooded there, squat and tremendous, hunched over the pale radiance of the Glowing Dome.

Much, I know, has been writ concerning this Odd, Vast Watcher; for it had grown out of the blackness of the South Unknown Lands a million years gone; and the steady growing nearness of it had been noted and set out at length by the men they called the Monstruwacans; so that it was possible to search in our libraries, and learn of the very coming of this Beast in the olden-time.

This compelling situation has a brooding quality reminiscent of the tale Jung's woman patient told him about the monster—in her case a vampire—tyrannizing everyone on the Moon. The situation in *The Night Land* is never resolved, as perhaps some trauma in Hodgson's personal life was never resolved. We are left with the image of those monstrous things, implacably sitting out the span of humanity's existence.

What can one say of the great A. Merritt? It is a name that still stirs the pulses of old-time fans. His dreamy, suffocating tales were reprinted in science fiction magazines and well received.

Abraham Merritt (1884–1943)[15], a newspaper man and keen traveller, went much further along the fantasy trail than Burroughs. At least one may look into the night sky and observe Mars and Venus, and have something to speculate upon. Merritt fled to never-never lands without benefit of Morris. His heroes are forever stepping through strange jewels, galloping through great doorways in mountains, discovering stairways leading down into extinct volcanoes, or arriving at temples full of unhallowed mysteries in some lost oasis. He is right up the dreaming pole.

Merritt's best-known titles, "The Moon Pool" (and its inevitable sequel, "The Conquest of the Moon Pool"), *The Ship of Ishtar*, *Seven Footprints to Satan*, *Dwellers in the Mirage*, and *Burn, Witch, Burn!* all appeared in the flourishing pulps from 1918 to 1932. Two were filmed.

That haunting title, *The Ship of Ishtar*, was voted the most popular story ever to appear in *Argosy All-Story*. The influence of its exoticism on younger writers was strong. This and other of Merritt's writings were published later in SF and fantasy magazines. Merritt's overheated style matched his plots, which were up to here in serpents, feathers, fur, great black stallions, freaks, naked women, evil priests, golden pigmies, talismans, monsters, lovely priestesses, sinister forces, gigantic Norsemen, and undefined longings. Merritt believed in fairies.

> I heard a sweet, low-pitched voice at the other side of the tower trilling the bird-like syllables of the Little People—And then I saw Evalie.
>
> Have you ever watched a willow bough swaying in spring above some clear sylvan pool, or a slender birch dancing with the wind in a secret woodland and covert, or the flitting green shadows in a deep forest glade which are dryads half-tempted to reveal themselves? I thought of them as she came towards us.
>
> She was a dark girl and a tall girl. Her eyes were brown under long black lashes, the clear brown of the mountain brook in autumn; her hair was black, the jetty hair that in a certain light has a sheen of darkest blue. . . . [etc. etc.]
>
> But it was the grace of her that made the breath catch in your throat as you looked at her, the long flowing line from ankle to shoulder, delicate and mobile as the curve of water flowing over some smooth breast of rock, a liquid grace of line that changed with every movement.
>
> It was that—and the life that burned in her like the green flame of the virgin forest when the kisses of spring are being changed for the warmer caresses of Summer. . . . [etc. etc.]
>
> I could not tell how old she was—hers was the pagan beauty which knows no age. . . .
>
> The small soldiers ringed her, their spears ready.
> (*Dwellers in the Mirage*, Chapter 8)

As the critic Moskowitz perceives, Merritt was "escaping from the brutalities and injustices of the world". His world ends not with a bang but a simper. His reputation, once high, now lies about him like a shattered cut-glass totem pole.

Merritt's later stories turned progressively to the darker side of the occult, which was just about where H. P. Lovecraft began.

Clouds of sunset gather. We come upon that kind, lonely, influential man, Howard Phillips Lovecraft. Born 1890, departed this life 1937. With Lovecraft, the retreat to the irrational has become complete. A dank, airless darkness rules at the dreaming pole. Lovecraft's literary ancestry includes Poe and the remarkable Lord Dunsany (1878–1957), who wrote delicate fantasies of never-never lands (while soldiering in the Coldstream Guards in the Boer War and the Royal Inniskillin Fusiliers in World War I, and living at other times a sporting outdoor life).

Lovecraft is a prisoner of the library and the cold damp hand. Horror, the abnegation of personality, is his one permanent interest. Although horror can make a good literary seasoning if sparingly used, like salt it makes an indigestible banquet. The conclusion of "Dagon" (1919), one of Lovecraft's earliest stories, shows how he means to go on:

> The end is near. I hear a noise at the door, as of some immense slippery body lumbering against it. It shall not find me. God, *that hand!* The window! The window!

The macabre, the eldritch, is Lovecraft's province. He developed a demoniac cult of hideous entities, the spawn of evil, which were seeking to take over Earth, Cthulhu, Shub-Niggurath, Yog-Sothoth, Nyarlathotep, the Magnum Innominandum, and other titles like anagrams of breakfast cereal names. He had a fondness for the device used by Hodgson to conclude the main manuscript of *The House on the Borderland*, the first-person narrator who continues desperately scribbling his journal until the very moment when he goes insane or his head is bitten off by the menace. (Indeed, the conclusion of *The House on the Borderland* manuscript is perhaps the model of "Dagon" a few years later: "There is something fumbling at the door-handle. O God, help me now! Jesus—The door is opening—slowly. Somethi——").

Here, even Merritt's world of titillation and adventure has faded and gone. The only culture possible in Lovecraft's universe is a search for old books of black magic. Attempt anything livelier and monstrosities start tramping dankly up from the foundations.

Predictable though the horrors are, buried in Lovecraft's writing is a core of power which remains disconcerting when all the adjectives have fallen away like leaves. Colin Wilson indicates this quality when he says that Lovecraft's writing holds interest as a psychological case history, even if it fails as literature. "Here was a man who made no attempt whatever to come to terms with life. He hated modern civilization, particularly in its confident belief in progress and science. Greater artists have had the same feeling, from Dostoevsky to Kafka and Eliot . . . Possibly future generations will feel that Lovecraft is 'symbolically' true."[16]

The point is arguable. Lovecraft's hatred of science and progress is part of a hatred of life. The mistrust of science, its ends and means, finds more rational expression in later science fiction authors such as Ray Bradbury, who has acknowledged his debt to Lovecraft. Indeed, Lovecraft's influence on the field has often been through later authors—not always fortunately. Talented and sensitive writers such as August Derleth (whose memoirs in *Walden West* are much to be cherished), Fritz Leiber, Lord of Lankhmar, and Robert Bloch (perhaps best known for his novel *Psycho*) may have been deflected from their course by Lovecraft's too easy vein of grave-haunting. Perhaps as much is true of the sesquipedalian Clark Ashton Smith.

Modelling himself on writers of the past, Lovecraft had a contempt for money. His career is a decline from richer to poorer. This is the attraction of Lovecraft in a mercenary age, that he was both good-natured and helpless. If he wrote few stories, he wrote many letters. His letters to Clark Ashton Smith alone averaged about 40,000 words a year. He kept anything up to a hundred correspondences going at once.

Some of his correspondents remained forever grateful, convinced they had been in touch with a genuine literary force.[17]

L. Sprague de Camp's interesting biography of Lovecraft claims the latter wrote over 100,000 letters, totalling ten million words.[18] Lovecraft loved writing letters. He was a master of the private communication.

One or two of Lovecraft's stories rank as science fiction, for instance "Herbert West—Reanimator", an exercise on a Frankenstein theme (filmed in 1985 as *Reanimator*). West's lifework is the reanimation of the dead. The First World War provides him with plenty of corpses. Lovecraft is about his old business of chilling the blood, however ludicrously:

> For that very fresh body, at last writhing into full and terrifying consciousness with eyes dilated at the memory of its last scene on earth, threw out its frantic hands in a life and death struggle with the air; and suddenly collapsing into a second final dissolution from which there could be no return, screamed out the cry that will ring eternally in my aching brain: "Help! Keep off, you cursed little tow-headed fiend—keep that damned needle away from me!"
> (From *Dagon and Other Macabre Tales*)

One may find Lovecraft funny, and his most dramatic effects overloaded. But he had and still has staunch supporters. August Derleth and Donald Wandrei founded a publishing imprint, Arkham House, in 1939, simply to publish Lovecraft in book form; and those early publications are now valuable, scarce, and much sought after. Truly, friends are better than critics.

Many of Lovecraft's tales appeared in the celebrated and long-lived pulp magazine *Weird Tales*. Two fellow-haunters of those ghoulish pages also deserve tangential mention, if only for the things they represent.

Robert E. Howard (1906–1936) created a brawny bone-headed hero called

Conan, whose barbarian antics are set in the imaginary Hyborian Age, back in pre-history when almost all woman and almost no clauses were subordinate. Conan's adventures have been successfully continued by L. Sprague de Camp and others.

Clark Ashton Smith (1893–1961) was a much more pretentious writer, whose stories are stuffed with hard words and titles ("The Weird of Avoosee Wuthoqquan"). Smith followed Howard in conjuring imaginary ages and countries, notably Hyperborea, which is a polar continent still free of ice. His terms of reference are wider than Lovecraft's.

Here is a passage from Smith's "The Abomination of Yondo":

> Hidden by the low ridges, where cities of which no stela remained unbroken—immense and immemorial cities lapsing shard by shard, atom by atom, to feed infinities of desolation, I dragged my torture-weakened limbs over vast rubbish-dumps that had once been mighty temples; and fallen gods frowned in rotting psammite or leered in riven porphyry at my feet.[19]

And of course there are also fallen gods in yesterday's SF. Yet one still remembers one's first reading of Smith's "City of Singing Flame" (1931 and oft reprinted).

The flight from urban culture and rational thought continues. Hyperborea can stand for all the lost lands in which readers still take refuge. The cities perpetually decay, the gods tumble, the mongrel nations go down into dust. We have no space to speak of Lost Race novels, virtually a category in itself, a library in its own right. Most are metaphors for childhood and happy irresponsibility, with hardly an exception. When you've found one lost race, you've found them all. . . .

CHAPTER VIII

In the Clutches of the Zeitgeist:
Mainly the Thirties

It would be impossible for anyone who has not experienced it to
understand the sense of violation that I felt when I found
another mind in possession of mine, overpowering it, seizing
my will, laying hands on my personality.
     —Joseph O'Neill: *Land Under England*

Another age was rushing towards its demise. The Nazi party was in power in
Germany, greedy to take advantage of the human weaknesses of individuals,
greedy to take over men's minds, to lay hands on personality. Thomas Mann
said, "The really characteristic and dangerous aspect of National Socialism was
its mixture of robust modernity and an affirmative stance towards progress,
combined with dreams of the past: a highly technological romanticism."

Much of science fiction must face similar accusations. The same seemingly
opposed attitudes were held by many of the writers already examined, where a
sturdy show of modernity is linked up with a dream of a past when mores were
simpler. Nor are present-day writers immune from this affliction. Indeed, as the
stresses of society increase we may expect the affliction to spread. Dreams of the
past are common enough. So is a robust modernity. The two combine in stories
set after nuclear catastrophe when—by some miracle—survivors of the disaster
enact harsh pastorals for our entertainment.

We must not be seduced by such technological romanticism. Civilization,
with all its flaws, is precious. Whatever succeeds it will be worse.

SF's tonic schizophrenia is in evidence in the Thirties. High SF is full of
zeitgeist, mirroring uneasily the forthcoming global conflict with all its lost store
of lives. Low SF dabbles contentedly in the marvels of technology and the
purple things that loom beyond the Beyond.

This division echoes a division of experience which existed between writers
of American and British science fiction.

As we have seen, different traditions had developed between the two
countries. The scientific romance, which enjoyed its heyday in the works of
Shiel, Griffith, and H. G. Wells, was shortly to merge with the science fiction of
the SF magazines. Its traditions had been weakened by the World War of
1914–18, and by the shrinkage of the world.

Its appeal, though limited, had always been to an intelligent middle-class
audience.

American science fiction came from different roots, appealing to simpler audiences. As we saw in Chapter VI, the roots lay mainly in the boys' science-adventure stories written by Senarens, Garis, and others, in the old dime novels. At a time when American scientifiction was becoming capable of infiltrating higher intellectual levels in the USA, the scientific romance in England was lapsing into boys' literature, for instance in such weekly magazines as *Hotspur*, *Adventure*, *Wizard*, and *Champion*, and the more up-market *Modern Boy*, which featured the scientific adventures of Captain Justice.[1]

Much of the scientific romance had been sturdily dark in tone, just as a robust optimism dominated scientifiction. In part, the marked contrast is attributable to different life-experience in Britain and the United States.

"The Great War", as it was called until a greater world war broke out, lasted for four years, as far as the European powers were concerned. Total war casualties amounted to 12,000,000, of which only 325,876 were American. British casualties were 744,702—several times larger than American losses if relative populations are taken into account—or over three million for the British Empire. The sense of outrage in Britain and the experience of disillusion after the war went deep.[2] Every town and village in the country erected a war memorial.

In the Second World War, British casualties were lighter (only 450,000, against America's figure of 290,000), but damage to towns and the infrastructure was much greater. Hardly a town in England and Wales escaped some ruination; the mainland of the USA was never touched by enemy action.

Britain was slow to recover from wars that were the making of the USA and a direct cause of its development into superpower status. Economic decline in the one country was counterbalanced by economic ascendancy in the other.

When we look at the writings we now label science fiction, we confront a variety of different works, coming from different intentions and different intellectual climates, all contributing to a common literature. The authors who assemble in this chapter present a challenge to catholicity. Between the humanitarian pre-occupations of a Čapek and the gadgetry of a Gernsback lie light-years of culture. While novelists like Aldous Huxley and Olaf Stapledon are elitist in their perception, it would be idle to expect any such thing from magazines moulded by consumerism and adversity.

These divisions are inevitable, given the date. The world of ordinary fiction has long been divided into high- and low-brow; so why not SF? All tastes can be catered for. There was strong pressure on the SF of the pulps to remain simple in vocabulary, ideas, and structure (though remarkably enough it took only a decade for that situation to begin changing). A million immigrants steamed into New York harbour through Ellis Island in 1905 alone. The pulps offered an immediate chance of cheap and easy escape from the harsh verities of life, not criticism of those verities. The steamship ticket was in itself a sufficient criticism. Authors who appeared in Munsey's *All-Story* magazine, as did Edgar Rice Burroughs, became famous overnight.[3] Monocultural magazines arose, to specialize in one type of story alone, to maximize sales. The pulps are sentimentalized over today. It is the fate of all sweat-shops.

The establishment of magazines which specialized in SF alone—excluding all else—institutionalized the division between highbrow and lowbrow. Such classification, never openly acknowledged, led eventually to some prodigies; but for a short period it debased the product by appealing to an ardent and uncritical readership; while in the long run it induced an "SF ghetto" mentality from which both readers and writers still scheme to escape (or imagine they have escaped).

Writers who appeared in the *Strand* or *All-Story* had to compete with a variety of other writers on other themes. Writers in *Amazing Stories* were thrown among themselves (or among twenty-year-old reprints of Wells stories).

With the coming of *Amazing* in 1926, and for many succeeding years, the more analytical type of story appears outside the magazines, which are devoted to gosh-wowery. Many kinds of fantasy appeared there. Older fans still remember the Richard Shaver stories about an underground world, appearing in *Amazing* as late as 1945, which gullible readers believed as gospel. Many fantasies imitated Burroughs, while others were anti-Burroughsian and in consequence less attractive. They believed in a technology-dominated world and are conveniently labelled Gernsbackian. Neither dreams nor culture can warm Gernsbackian sci-fic. It exists as propaganda for the wares of the inventor. Screwdrivers substitute for vision.

Although there are exceptions, the authors of the thirties whose names retain our respect had most probably never heard the sacred words, science fiction.

It is as difficult to imagine Franz Kafka, Aldous Huxley, Karel Čapek, et al., submitting their works for serialization in *Amazing Stories* or *Weird Tales*, as it is to think of E. E. Smith, creator of the Gray Lensman, as a moulder of Western thought. The gulf between two similar sorts of reading matter is absolute. But SF is a literature of surprises. In fact, *Amazing Stories* for August 1927 published "The Tissue-Culture King", a story by Aldous Huxley's elder brother, Julian Huxley.

The two streams. This salient fact in the history of modern SF remains open for further investigation. Meanwhile—to leap ahead of our narrative—we must marvel at the way SF writers of the 1970s and 1980s have attempted a synthesis of such opposed modes.

This chapter is a survey of the writers who wrote for their peers rather than for the magazines. It includes some great names, among them the most brilliantly imaginative writer science fiction has known. And it concludes bathetically by inspecting the first "scientifiction" magazines.

Immortality is but one traditional theme to filter from folk tales into science fiction. In particular, the legend of the Wandering Jew, who must tarry on this earth until Jesus returns, persisted through the centuries. Maturin's *Melmoth the Wanderer* has elements of this legend, which was particularly strong in German literature. Immortality (given quasi-scientific respectability by means of an elixir which must be drunk every century) is what afflicts Emilia Marty.

178   TRILLION YEAR SPREE

Emilia Marty is the central figure of the opera *The Makropoulos Case*. Although she is several hundred years old when the curtain goes up, she presents a radiantly youthful appearance. She drank the elixir of longevity first in 1565. We meet her in 1907, the year in which the action of the opera is set. Emilia is torn between a need to recover the secret of the elixir (buried in the complicated documentary files of the Makropoulos estate) and a wish to yield to the death she has so long eluded. Her existence, once so bright and warm, has come to depend on a formula; even her lover can no longer reach her heart.

Eventually, this brilliant but alarming figure collapses. All that remains is a little broken burden in her latest lover's arms.

Anyone who saw one of the few performances that the English National Opera gave of *The Makropoulos Case* in 1971 was more privileged than he or she knew. By the end of that year, the gorgeous Marie Collier, who played the immortal woman, was dead.

The musical score of the opera is by Janaček, based on a play translated into English in 1925 as *The Makropoulos Secret*. The play was one of several written by the Czech dramatist and man of letters, Karel Čapek (1890–1938).

As the curtain rises on the first act, we are taken into a dusty office filled with wooden desks and files. In these cobwebby pigeonholes, valuable documents are lost for years, or fogrotten secrets suddenly materialize. This is Prague in the fusty days of the Austro–Hungarian Empire, the Prague of secrets and conspiracies. It may have reminded the Coliseum audience of similar gloomy rooms to be found in the strange unfinished novels appearing in the very year that Čapek's play was translated into English.[4] The novels of Franz Kafka.

Kafka's unique mystery-dramas were pieced together only after his death. It was Čapek's reputation which spread first, although he was Kafka's junior by seven years.

Čapek was a great humanist—and a humorist as well, two characteristics he shared with that other internationally popular Czech writer Jaroslav Hašek, author of *The Good Soldier Schweik*—born the same year as Kafka. Čapek's humour was gentler than the anarchistic wit of Hašek, and has worn less well. But there is still force in his best-known work, the play *R.U.R.*, first performed in the capital of the new Czechoslovakia in 1921, and shortly thereafter all round Europe and the United States.

R.U.R. stands for Rossum's Universal Robots. The play is a satire on capitalist methods and, more deeply, an embodiment of Čapek's fears that increasing automation and regimentation will dehumanize mankind. Old Rossum has invented a formula whereby artificial people can be made in a factory. His robots are simplified versions of human beings; they have no soul and do nothing but work (the word "robot" which is Čapek's coinage, comes from a Slav root meaning "work"). In the end, the robots take over and wipe out humanity. They cannot breed, but two aberrant robots, a male and a female, are left to start all over again.

Nowadays, the word robot is reserved for creatures of metal; Čapek's robots are what we would regard as androids or clones. His theme is a logical development of the Frankenstein theme. Victor's solitary product has become the staple of a conveyor belt.

The Insect Play was written in collaboration with Karel's eldest brother, Josef, a painter of some renown whose reputation was made in the Cubist school. It proved another success of the early twenties, again concerned with the theme of regimentation.

Karel Čapek was art director of the National Theatre of Prague, later establishing his own theatre (staging Shelley's *The Cenci* among other plays). He was editor of an eminent cultural periodical. He travelled a great deal, and wrote many travel and gardening books; he was also a close friend of Thomas Masaryk, the first Czech president, writing the latter's life story in the thirties.

His versatility was as tremendous as his fondness for themes bordering on science fictional was constant. *Továrna na Absolutno* is a novel, published in 1922 and translated into English a few years later as *The Absolute at Large*. This is a Wellsian discussion of the relativity of human values, with a company setting itself up to manufacture and sell—not robots this time, but atom-powered machines, locomotives, cars, ships, guns.

As in *R.U.R.*, war breaks out. Civilization is destroyed. Čapek would have agreed with Erskine Childers's conclusion that "preparedness induced war". His novel *Krakatit* (1924; also translated as *An Atomic Phantasy*), relates how atomic energy is discovered and, through human dishonesty, causes widespread destruction.

Concern with the spread of fascism, which was soon to engulf his unlucky country, inspired Čapek to write *Válka s Mloky* (translated as *War with the Newts*) in 1936.[5] The "newts" are small and docile-seeming when first discovered. There are hopes that they may serve, like the robots, as a new proletariat. Mankind is depicted as both greedy and short-sighted. Eventually the newts, which multiply fast, start to undermine the continents in order to gain more living room. Many men help them to bring about the destruction of human life. The theme is not unlike that of *Frankenstein*: a desire for knowledge, however admirable in itself, is destructive when allied with indifference to the consequences of that knowledge. The newts are not merely Nazis but the dark side of our own nature.

"This is not a speculation about the future, but a mirroring of what exists," said Čapek, thus putting in a strong plea for relevant science fiction. His novel is formed of a mosaic of independent reports, though the mixture of satire and allegory is not entirely successful. Bestowing high praise on *War with the Newts*, Darko Suvin claims that Čapek is, "together with Yevgeny Zamyatin—the most significant world SF writer between the World Wars".[6]

In the real world, Hitler's robots were undermining the Continent. Masaryk's republic was well prepared for war; but France and Britain were not, and the United States was isolationist in attitude. Czechoslovakia was persuaded to give in to Hitler's threats, the Wehrmacht rolled into the Sudetenland in 1938. The dismemberment of the Czech state commenced. Čapek, a great and liberal man, died on Christmas Day in 1938, a mere atom in the general darkness engulfing Europe. Like his beautiful Emila Marty, he had lost the will to live. As for his elder brother, Josef, he was sent to German concentration camps, to die in Belsen in 1945.

Prague harboured a greater writer than Čapek. Franz Kafka (1883–1924) was Austrian, born in Prague, son of a forceful Jewish businessman. By dying young he avoided the horrors that awaited so many of his compatriots. But his novels seem to look, not only backwards to the dusty files of the Dual Monarchy, where precious documents could be lost forever, but forward to the *Nacht und Nebel*[7] of Nazi Germany, where precious individuals and families could be lost forever.

The world of Kafka's two major novels, *The Trial* and *The Castle*, is as coherent and as original as the world of Swift or Lewis Carroll, and so formidable that it has become the target of a whole library of interpretations. It is not simply that both novels deal with a puzzle never resolved, or that Kafka's manner of relating the puzzle is oblique, but that, on the surface, the furniture of his novels is an ordinary world with which we are all familiar: yet we are adrift in it.

As one of his commentators, Erich Heller, puts it, the Kafka universe is "like the reader's own; a castle that is a castle and 'symbolizes' merely what all castles symbolize: power and authority; a telephone exchange that produces more muddle than connections; a bureaucracy drowning in a deluge of forms and files; an obscure hierarchy of officialdom making it impossible ever to find the man authorized to deal with a particular case; officials who work overtime and yet get nowhere; numberless interviews which are never to the point; inns where the peasants meet, and barmaids who serve the officials. In fact, it is an excruciatingly familiar world, but reproduced by a creative intelligence which is endowed with the knowledge that it is a world damned for ever."[8]

It is not necessary to agree with that final phrase (Kafka's world is too humdrum for the drama of damnation, being more concerned with corruption) to accept the truth of the rest. Alice was a commonplace little girl. Kafka's is a commonplace little world; yet the spell of terror—an oddly comic terror—lies over it.

Kafka does not seem to be writing allegory, although many commentators would not agree, nor does he fit into the symbolist camp. He goes about his own business—and so thoroughly and so convincingly that an ordinary reader might be scared off by the litanies of scholarly praise which have risen like incense on all sides, from W. H. Auden's "Had one to name the author who comes to bearing the same kind of relation to our age as Dante, Shakespeare, and Goethe bore to theirs, Kafka is the first one would think of", onwards.

Against the higher criticism one arms oneself with the recollection of Kafka's friend, Max Brod, reporting how Kafka's friends laughed as he read passages of *The Trial* aloud to them, while Kafka himself could scarcely continue for tears of laughter. Kafka's atmosphere of foreboding is shot through with his unique humour. His diaries[9] reveal a constipated, father-dominated, slyly amusing man. Dickens, the Dickens of the Circumlocution Office, stands prominent in Kafka's literary ancestry.

Little of Kafka's work was published in his lifetime, although he had gained a reputation in Czechoslovakia and Germany by the time of his death. His executor, Max Brod, had instructions to burn his literary remains, but fortunately disobeyed orders. So his three posthumous novels appeared, *Der Prozess* (*The Trial*, 1925), *Das Schloss* (*The Castle*, 1926), and *Amerika* (1927, translated under the same title). These were all unfinished works set into order by Max Brod.

The Trial is the story of Joseph K., perplexingly arrested on a charge which is never specified, and eventually executed on the sentence of a judge he has never seen, despite his efforts to clear himself.

The Castle is the story of K., who claims to be a land surveyor and arrives in a village dominated by a castle, in which K. seeks work; but the forces in the castle are impressively passive, and never accept him, so that the situation remains unresolved.

These are Kafka's two long works, which come near to a spirit of science fiction. Manifestly, they are not SF, although it would need only the revelation (but Kafka's is, of course, not a literature of revelation) that the judge is K.'s doppelganger, or that the Castle has been taken over by aliens, to reduce both novels to traditional science fiction.

The baffling atmosphere, the paranoid complexities, the alien motives of others, do make the novels a sort of *haute* SF. The stature of Kafka's writing, particularly since World War II, relates it to several kinds of writing by the influence it has had. Yet its oneirocritical faculties are so powerful, that one has only to contrast it with more orthodox kinds of science fiction—say Wells's *Mr Britling Sees It Through* or Burroughs's *Jungle Tales of Tarzan*, both written when Kafka was writing *The Trial*—to see how Kafka had a terrifyingly different kind of imagination, which has haunted a whole generation. Like Poe, he has the three "I"s—Inwardness, Imagination, and Invention.

Because one of his strengths is to weave a web of suspicion, propitiation, and innuendo, Kafka's potent effect is not easily conveyed by extracts. Here, however, is a quotation from early in *The Castle*, when K. is exploring the village and passing the school.

The children were just coming out with their teacher. They thronged round him, all gazing up at him and chattering without a break so rapidly that K. could not follow what they said. The teacher, a small young man with narrow shoulders and a very upright carriage which yet did not make him ridiculous, had already fixed K. with his eyes from the distance, naturally enough, for apart from the school-children there was not another human being in sight. Being the stranger, K. made the first advance, especially as the other was an authoritative-looking little man, and said: "Good morning, sir." As if by one accord the children fell silent, perhaps the master liked to have a sudden stillness as a preparation for his words. "You are looking at the Castle?" he asked more gently than K. had expected, but with the inflexion that denoted disapproval of K.'s occupation. "Yes," said K. "I am a stranger here, I came to the village only last night." "You don't like the castle?" returned the teacher quickly. "What?" countered K., a little taken aback, and repeated the question in modified form. "Do I like the Castle? Why do you assume that I don't like it?" "Strangers never do," said the teacher. To avoid saying the wrong thing K. changed the subject and asked: "I suppose you know the Count?" "No," said the teacher turning away. But K. would not be put off and asked again: "What, you don't know the Count?" "Why should I?" replied the teacher in a low tone, and added aloud in French: "Please remember that there are innocent children present." K. took this as a justification for asking: "Might I come to pay you a visit one day, sir? I am to be staying here for some time and already feel a little lonely. I don't fit in with the peasants nor, I imagine, with the Castle." "There is no difference between the peasantry and the Castle," said the teacher. "Maybe," said K., "that doesn't alter my position. Can I pay you a visit one day?" "I live in Swan Street at the butcher's." That was assuredly more of a statement than an invitation, but K. said: "Right, I'll come."

The exchange has the lucidity and enigmatic quality of an actual encounter. Kafka offers plenty of data, little interpretation. In this respect, he contrasts markedly another Central European Jew whose work was set amid the obfuscations of Franz Josef's Dual Monarchy: Sigmund Freud.[10]

More directly science fictional are some of Kafka's short stories, of which the best known is "Metamorphosis" ("Die Verwandlung", first published in 1916), about the man who wakes up one morning and finds himself transformed into a gigantic insect. The family is a little stuffy about it at first, but rapidly adapts to the change. This story looks forward to Ionesco's *The Rhinoceros* and the Theatre of the Absurd. "In the Penal Colony", with its horrendous torture machine, also approaches science fiction. "The Giant Mole", which concerns exactly what the title claims, is a sort of humorous fantasy; J. G. Ballard produced a pastiche of it, "The Drowned Giant", which is a Kafka story in its own right.

Kafka always felt himself helpless, threatened by imponderable forces, unable to approach women even when attracted to them. He reports on this condition with absolute truthfulness. Kafka is a refutation to all those writers who claim that fiction should lie. Of course it was in his early years that his vulnerable psyche was formed, though others have argued that his Jewishness was a contributory factor.[11] He saw little of his parents in infancy, which was further disrupted by changes of home and nurses. His younger brother died in early childhood. Only with his younger sister, Ottla, was he on confidential terms. Franz and Ottla would meet to write letters and whisper secrets to each other in the bathroom.[12]

Kafka's relationship with Prague is intimate, and interesting in terms of SF's involvement with cities. The old gaslit houses and alleyways, the mouldering magnificence of the buildings and courtyards of Prague, no less than its function as a human melting pot, helped awaken Kafka's eloquence. "Prague does not let go—either of you or of me." So said Kafka.[13] "This little mother has claws. . . ."

Another thing Prague had was the golem. In 1580, a man was supposedly made out of clay on the banks of the River Moldau. A Rabbi pronounced an incantation, whereupon the figure came to life. It was without the gift of speech. No doubt Mary Shelley was familiar with this tale, although it was not given modern form until Paul Wegener's film interpretation, *Der Golem*, in 1914.[14] Gustav Meyrink's novel of the same name was published in Leipzig in 1915, during the war. Both novel and film give a vivid picture of the streets and houses of old Prague.

Working in Prague today is another highly individual science fiction writer, Josef Nesvadba. Although his stories, told with a sardonic and labyrinthine humour, are unmistakably his own, it is easy to see him also as heir to the grim comedies of Kafka and, to a lesser extent, Čapek.

In lighter mood, Nesvadba wrote the screen play for the amusing *Slenca Golem* (*Miss Golem*), a feature film directed by Jaroslav Balik in the early seventies. The delectable Jana Breichova plays a double role, the nice girl and her naughty duplicate, a female golem made by accident. The film is set in the happier Prague of the twenties. At one point, the protagonists break into a theatre, where they interrupt a performance of Čapek's *R.U.R.*, a nice literary allusion.

The famed reluctance of the Anglo-Saxon world to translate from or become conversant with languages other than English means that many writers celebrated in their own countries are unknown in the parts of the world which chiefly concern us. To give an instance, while Kafka was writing *The Castle*, Mihaly Babits was publishing his fantasy *The Nightmare* in Hungary (1916). This short novel is about a case of split personality and clearly owes much to philosophical thought and new scientific findings.[15]

Another Hungarian writer, the popular Frigyes Karinthy, added two further books to the four of *Gulliver's Travels*, one of which (*Voyage to Faremido*, 1916) features an automated robot culture, and the other (*Capillaria*, 1921) a country ruled by women. The latter book was accompanied by an introductory letter to H. G. Wells on its first appearance.[16]

The culture on Faremido is far more advanced than the rough-and-ready world Čapek later dreamed up. The "*solasi*" robots are all metal. "Not even the tiniest fragment of their body consisted of that certain matter which, according to our conception, was the only possible carrier and condition of life, and which was called, in common parlance, organic matter." Karinthy's latter-day Gulliver describes the brains of these strange beings, and goes on to explain how they reproduced:

A glance at the face of the *solasi* convinced me that it was manufacturing this same product which it needed—eyes. Now it became evident how these amazing creatures or mechanisms came into being: they themselves manufactured their equals from metals and minerals, and they themselves activated the finished *solasi* through the sources of energy (electric accumulators, steam, gases, etc.) placed within their bodies. (Chapter 4)

The *solasis* live a calm and pleasant life. Thought, inward thought, is an infection; organic life on Earth is no more than a disease. In true Swiftian fashion, Karinthy's Gulliver is converted to his hosts' point of view, and begs to be turned to metal. He is given an injection, after which he saw "heat, thermal energy flowing around me in a multicoloured, wavering stream, lapping over my body", and other remarkable things besides. But his body and mind are too immature for the shot to have its desired effect, and Gulliver returns sadly to Earth.

It is truly astonishing that *Faremido*, with its sophisticated early treatment of robots, is not more widely known and admired. Karinthy's is a satirical technological utopia, still without equal. The *solasis* make all other robots until Philip Dick's seem like country cousins.

All generations think themselves modern, but some generations are more modern than others. The *solasis* were free from sex, manufacturing each other from minerals.[17] The Bright Young Things of the Twenties wished to be free for sex. One of their graduate members produced a bleak utopia where sex was reduced to an innocent pastime, separated from the reproductive function. Automation was extensive, extra-uterine babies were produced in factories, education was a matter of stratification of function, and untidy emotions like misery—which was closely related to art—were swept away.

Aldous Huxley's *Brave New World* was published in 1932, to astonished acclaim. In part, it was a reply to H. G. Wells's utopian ideas, and superseded the overpraised "The Machine Stops" (1909), by E. M. Forster, described by its author as "a reaction to one of the earlier heavens of H. G. Wells".

Forster's story is all very back-to-the-wombish. There is an underground world in which everyone lives in separate rooms, completely tended by the Machine. In the end, the machine breaks down, most people die, including the central character with his body of white pap, but a few lucky ones are left to tramp about in "the mist and the ferns". Humanity has learnt its lessons. So much for English middle-class dreams of a quiet garden suburb! *Brave New World* has a lot more punch, no easy solutions, no moralizing.

Brave New World is arguably the Western world's most famous science fiction novel.[18]

All these years later, and in a world which has seen many changes, Huxley's novel retains its interest. This is not only because of the lively, counterpointed style in which it is composed, but because its dramatized debate on how far we must sacrifice our individuality in the face of proliferating technology, and how far we should push the quest for pleasure, remains of concern. While Huxley's atheist state may contain some of his feelings on the Soviet Revolution, he wrote the novel shortly after a visit to the USA. *Brave New World* reflects the coming

Americanization of the world. It is after all 632 AF—the year of Our Ford, not Our Lenin.[19] The future world may be cosmopolitan—the names of the characters signify as much—but it is horrifyingly narrow. To be young and superficial is everything.

Isn't one of the delights of *Brave New World*, when all is said and pontificated, that it is told with a perfect balance of wit and humour? How many times, as faithfully reported in these pages, is not a sledgehammer despatched to crack the nut of the future? Here it is prized open with a rapier.

"If you want to get men to act reasonably, you must set about persuading them in a maniacal manner," says Mr Scrogan, in Huxley's earlier novel, *Crome Yellow*. *Brave New World* persuades us with the agreeable weapon of Swift, Peacock, Voltaire—satire.

Aldous Huxley (1894–1963) opens his masterly novel without compromise. In the future, at least six centuries in the future. This is something none of his predecessors had done; even Wells liked to begin his novels cautiously, in the present day. Huxley is also wholehearted about his future civilization. Instead of introducing one major change, for instance the extra-uterine production of babies, or the cloning methods of obtaining identical people ("Bokanovsky's Process" it is in the book), or the disappearance of Christianity, and so on, Huxley draws an altered society where several such major changes interact.

On the first page, we are swept into the London Hatchery, on a dazzling and polemical tour of this atrocious but well-reasoned future. Unlike poor E. M. Forster, Huxley shows us a world that indeed does have its insidious attractions. We can believe in it.

The weakness of the book (apart from an occasional descent into facetiousness) lies in the character of the Savage, whom Huxley introduced to symbolize the world of the spirit which the Ford-founded utopia has banished. The Savage is never entirely credible; in all Huxley's novels, there is generally a wise old figure who spouts at length, like Propter in *After Many a Summer* or Rontini in *Time Must Have a Stop*, who comes on strong about Vermeer, Pergolesi, Pascal, the Spirit, and kindred topics of enlightenment. The Savage is a wise young man who quotes Shakespeare too much and never ceases to be a twenties stereotype of untrammelled youth drawn by a man who has known D. H. Lawrence personally.[20]

One takes this in one's stride, assisted in so doing by the jazzy arrangement of the blocks of prose. The book bubbles with invention and aphorism, as the smug society, with its ever-available girls and the slugs of *soma* when needed, parades its monstrous virtues. The saxophones wail, the feelies go full blast ("There's a love scene on a bearskin rug; they say it's marvellous. Every hair of the bear reproduced"), everyone talks, everyone copulates, Ford's in his Flivver, all's right with the world.

"All men are physico-chemically equal."

"When the individual feels, the community reels."

"Was and will make me ill. I take a gramme and only am."

Art has gone by the board. It would rock the boat too much. "That's the price we have to pay for stability. You've got to choose between happiness and what people used to call high art." Scientific progress too has had to go. Knowledge and truth are dangerous. "What's the point of truth or beauty or knowledge when the anthrax bombs are popping all round you?" God also has been abolished for the general good. "Anybody can be virtuous now. Christianity without tears—that's what *soma* is."

The Controller sums it up. "Industrial civilisation is only possible when there's no self-denial. Self-indulgence up to the very limits imposed by hygiene and economics. Otherwise the wheels stop turning." The philosophy of conspicuous consumption.

The moulded personalities of Huxley's new world may owe something to Wells's Selenites in their inspiration, but on the whole the novel has a pleasing originality still evident today, long after all the "shocking" aspects which helped or retarded sales in the thirties have evaporated.

Huxley was a noted essayist as well as novelist, covering not merely a wide range of subjects, but covering them—and often dramatically juxtaposing them—in a single essay. He wrote other novels which qualify as his own special kind of science fiction.

After Many a Summer (1939), the wittiest of his novels, includes a view of Los Angeles which was later expanded by Evelyn Waugh in *The Loved One*, a beautiful pastiche of an eighteenth-century diary, and Huxley's acerbic comment on evolution.

Underlying *After Many a Summer* is a deep pessimism concerning man's nature.[21] The wretched English poet Jeremy Pordage goes out to California to catalogue a millionaire's book collection. The lusts of the flesh are all about him (Huxley was always keen on *them*); even the tame baboons in the grounds rut for human delight, and when the dumb blonde calls dreadful Dr Obispo an "ape-man", both she and he are aware of the flattery involved.

The millionaire, Stoyte, dreads death. When Pordage discovers that the lecherous Fifth Earl's two-centuries-old journal discloses the secret of immortality, Stoyte takes the whole party to England. There, beneath the Fifth Earl's mansion, in a stinking cellar, they find the old boy still alive—two hundred years old, and apelike in appearance and habit. The foetal anthropoid has been able to come to maturity! What a long way this cruel joke is from Čapek's handling of the immortality theme!

Ape and Essence (1949) shows man again surrendering to the ape in him. This novel, cast as a screenplay with a foreword relating its ironic provenance, uses a post-World War III society in which God and Devil have reversed roles to point to the twin evils of Progress and Nationalism. Radiation has upset mankind's genetic structure, so that "romance has been swallowed up by the oestrus" and mating is a seasonal mass orgy (which Huxley views with his usual lip-licking disgust).

Admittedly, *Ape and Essence* does not make pleasant reading. It has an occasional shrillness of tone. But the chill of its initial reception was undeserved. Huxley has to a large extent overcome his old difficulty of the omniscient

Propter-figure who lectures on art and morality by introducing two such figures, both slightly comic. One is the Narrator of the scenario, whose incursions are always brief and pointed. The other is the Arch-Vicar, a comic-sinister figure who can munch pig's trotters while he lectures.

Even Poole, the central character, who begins from the usual ineffectual-intellectual Huxleyan position—though quoting Shelley to good effect—retrieves himself vigorously by opting for the well-padded No's of sex!

The novel, in its concern for ecological damage to the planet, is ahead of its time.

Another reason for the book's cool initial reception is one which applies to many works falling within the science fiction category. Huxley's prophetic vein runs a good deal deeper and stronger than that of his critics. They may think he is indulging in exaggeration or fancy. In fact, he is diagnosing a condition to be widely recognized only after his death. Here is the Arch-Vicar, swigging from his bottle and chatting familiarly of the Devil:

> From the very beginning of the industrial revolution He foresaw that men would be made so overwhelmingly bumptious by the miracles of their own technology that they would soon lose all sense of reality. And that's precisely what happened. These wretched slaves of wheels and ledgers began to congratulate themselves on being the Conquerors of Nature. Conquerors of Nature, indeed! In actual fact, of course, they had merely upset the equilibrium of Nature and were about to suffer the consequences. Just consider what they were up to during the century and a half before the Thing. Fouling the rivers, killing off the wild animals, destroying the forests, washing the topsoil into the sea, burning up an ocean of petroleum, squandering the minerals it had taken the whole of geological time to deposit. An orgy of criminal imbecility. And they called it Progress. Progress!

Huxley here is as perceptive, as prophetic, as previous, and as impressive, as ever H. G. Wells was.

There, I believe, comparison between the two writers ends. Wells never quite abandoned a faith in Reason. Huxley was suspicious of Reason from the first. For instance, as early as *Crome Yellow* in 1921, he offers us, satirically, Mr Scrogan's Rational State.[22] Huxley saw, as a prime necessity, the reunification of humanity with the natural world. Indeed, according to one witness, Isaiah Berlin, he became almost totally preoccupied with this subject.[23] Only such a reunification would save both humanity and the planet.[24]

Towards the end of his life, his utopian novel, *Island* (1962) appeared. Far from perfect—indeed, soppy in parts—*Island* can never win wholehearted praise. Yet one hopes it will never be forgotten. At the very least, it stands as an endearing example of something of which Jung would have approved, the sense of a man, knowing his life was coming to a close, drawing together with wisdom and forethought the many strands of his psyche into a final harmony. Even death, in *Island*, is no longer the malign torturer but rather a culmination.

Indeed, *Island* is filled with all those pressing matters which preoccupied Huxley, and which crowd *Brave New World* and the Bright Young Thing novels. Here, thirty and more years later, they are stood on their heads.[25]

For instance, drugs are now valued as gateways to new perception, and free love is advocated as opening the personality; even the children's mindless rhymes of the previous book are here made delightful, an easy way of learning. And the precarious little state of Pala, an island somewhere near Indonesia, is indeed a utopia, full of happiness.

Unfortunately, it is full of slop too. The old Huxleyan disgust and irony have been put away. Here his people talk their big ideas in baby talk. Chapter 6 begins:

> "Golly!" the little nurse exploded, when the door was safely closed behind them.
> "I entirely agree with you," said Will.
> The Voltairean light twinkled for a moment on Mr Bahu's evangelical face. "Golly!" he repeated.

An earlier Aldous Huxley could never have written the sort of dialogue which fills *Island*. Was he trying to show us that the inhabitants of this utopia are not priggish just because they are perfect, or had he by this date gone soft? I prefer to believe the case as Philip Toynbee stated it at the time *Island* was published:

> This book, then, is an act of genuine virtue and love. Mr Huxley has renounced his natural material because he no longer believes that mere disgust is enough to change us. He has deliberately stepped into an area where he is automatically turned into a stutterer and crude fumbler with words. He has done this, I believe, because he is far more concerned with helping the world forward than with writing a praiseworthy book. And it seems to me that it is our duty to look beyond the evident failure . . . to hear what it is that he means us to hear. If we do this I think we shall find a great deal of wisdom, and indeed help, in these awkward pages.[26]

Aldous Huxley was the grandson of the great T. H. Huxley, the supporter of Darwin who became Wells's instructor late in life. He achieved at least three reputations, as a cynic in the day of the Bright Young Things, as a mystical philosopher, and, after his death, as a sort of godfather of the hippies. He was erudite, saintly, and a man of marvellous gifts, which showed through more in his life, possibly, than in his books.

That enquiring spirit of Huxley's never allowed him to rest on any one plateau of achievement. He could without much distortion be made to stand as one shining and eccentric example of the way the twentieth-century world has gone. For this scion of a noted English family, this son of Eton and Balliol, likened to Noël Coward during the period of his post-war success, moved ever outwards, rejecting accepted religion and much else, until he worked his way through Hindu faiths to a philosophical position of detachment and concern.

It was in 1954 that Huxley published *The Doors of Perception*, an account of his experiences with mescalin. How much it and its successor, *Heaven and Hell*, have contributed to the widespread use of drugs cannot be assessed; but Huxley's delighted account of his experiences made at least one reader hasten round to his local chemist next day (but mescalin was not in the Pharmacopoeia).

After Huxley's first wife, Maria Nys, died, he married an American, Laura Archera, in 1956, and they settled in California, not too far from Sin City. There, his library, with a lifetime's collection of books and manuscripts, was destroyed by a canyon fire—a disaster which Huxley seems to have accepted with serenity. He and Laura took LSD together (by now he was regarded as the father-figure of hippiedom), enjoying many happy psychedelic experiences. It was in this atmosphere that *Island* was written.

When he died, he went out on a tide of *moksha*-medicine, talked into the beyond by a loving wife whispering to him.[27] To the last he was by no means cut off from the world. Only eighteen months before his death, he was fulfilling a demanding timetable of lectures and seminars, in California and further afield.

He always maintained a distance from other people, his erratic blindness perhaps acting as a creative malady. This distancing was doubtless reinforced by the death of his mother during his adolescence. His first wife conspired in his brief love affairs, with a devotion rather reminiscent of "Jane" Wells. His sweet nature, as well as his remoteness, is amply testified to.[28]

What Huxley left behind was a considerable body of work which—at least at present—is considerably undervalued. His mistrust of either spirituality or sensuality without counterbalancing factors is clear. Because he was no great hand at drawing character, his essays are as much to be valued as his novels; nobody who reads Huxley's essays on art, music, and personality could help feeling in his debt. The unceasing quest for the nature and enrichment of individual life is clear.

Huxley's life, graduating from Bright Young Thing to near-sainthood, embodies much of the history of our times; it is the trajectory leading from the strictness of a Victorian free-thinker's upbringing, through immense popularity and controversy, to the luminous Californian freedom of gurudom.

Huxley died on 22nd November 1963, the day that President J. F. Kennedy was assassinated. Almost within twenty-four hours, Professor C. S. Lewis also was dead. He died in Headington, Oxford.

Like Huxley, Lewis was a seeker after truth; he found its illuminations within the Christian belief. Like Huxley, he called forth affection and respect from all who met him, even those opposed to his views. Again like Huxley, he was drawn to science fiction as a medium of expression.

With the possible exception of Huxley, C. S. Lewis was the most respected champion of science fiction the modern genre has known.

Clive Staples Lewis (born 1898) spent most of his working life at either Oxford or Cambridge. He served in the infantry in the First World War, and was wounded in 1918. He was elected Fellow and Tutor in English Literature at Magdalen College, Oxford, in 1925, a position he held until 1954. It was during his Oxford period that he wrote the trilogy which has earned him an enviable place in science fiction history, *Out of the Silent Planet* (1938), *Perelandra* (1943) and *That Hideous Strength* (1945).

No journey from Earth to another planet was ever of more consequence than the one which took Devine and Weston to Lewis's world of Malacandra (Mars). For their voyage broke the ages of quarantine which have kept Thulcandra, the Silent Planet (Earth), from the converse of the planets and of the solar system— known to the *eldila*, the angel-like beings who tend it, as the Field of Arbol. Great questions are now open again as a result of the voyage.

The first volume of the trilogy has Ransom kidnapped and taken to Mars by Devine and Weston. The latter two are caricatures of the progressive scientist.

Ransom is at first terrified by the whole idea of Malacandra and its inhabitants. "His mind, like so many minds of his generation, was richly furnished with bogies. He had read his H. G. Wells and others." But Malacandra's inhabitants are entirely amiable, as he finds on his first encounter with a *hross*, a seal-like being. Later, Ransom meets the tall *sorns*, the froglike *pfifltriggi*, and the great Oyarsa, the *eldil* who rules Malacandra.

As a philologist, Ransom learns to speak the language of Oyarsa with some ease. Weston and Devine have only a toehold in the language, which leads to one of the most comic and telling scenes in the book. Weston, a keen evolutionist, addresses Oyarsa in the sort of terms H. G. Wells or Olaf Stapledon might use, and Ransom interprets for him. Only the terms come out a little strangely in translation:

> "Life [says Weston] is greater than any system of morality; her claims are absolute. It is not by tribal taboos and copy-book maxims that she has pursued her relentless march from the amoeba to man and from man to civilization."
>
> "He says," began Ransom, "that living creatures are stronger than the question whether an act is bent or good—no, that cannot be right—he says that it is better to be alive and bent than to be dead—no—he says, he says—I cannot say what he says, Oyarsa, in your language. But he goes on to say that the only good thing is that there should be very many creatures alive. He says there were many other animals before the first men and the later ones were better than the earlier ones; but he says the animals were not born because of what is said to the young about bent and good action by their elders. And he says these animals did not feel any pity."
>
> "She—" began Weston.
>
> "I'm sorry," interrupted Ransom, "but I've forgotten who She is."
>
> "Life, of course," snapped Weston. "She has ruthlessly broken down all obstacles and liquidated all failures and today in her highest form— civilized man—and in me as his representative, she presses forward to that interplanetary leap which will, perhaps, place her for ever beyond the reach of death."
>
> "He says," resumed Ransom, "that these animals learned to do many

difficult things, except those who could not; and those ones died and the other animals did not pity them. And he says the best animal now is the kind of man who makes the big huts and carries the heavy weights and does all the other things I told you about; and he is one of these and he says that if the others all knew what he was doing they would be pleased. He says that if he could kill you all and bring our people to live in Malacandra, then they might be able to go on living here after something had gone wrong with our world. And then if something went wrong with Malacandra they might go and kill all the *hnau* in another world. And then another—and so they would never die out." (Chapter 20)[29]

Oyarsa decides to return the humans to Earth, though Ransom may stay on Malacandra if he so desires. His answer, "If I cannot live in Thulcandra, it is better for me not to live at all," might be a reproof to John Carter of Mars. So he returns unharmed, completing one of the most delightful space voyages in literature.

The whole mythology is informed by the powerful religious nature of Lewis's mind. He takes great pleasure in invention, like any good storyteller, although a wish to be improving sometimes gains the upper hand. Both invention and preachment are stronger in the second volume, although Lewis categorically denied that he wrote primarily for a didactic purpose.[30]

Perelandra is Venus, on which watery planet the scene is set. The description of the planet, its floating and flexible rafts of islands contrasted with the Fixed Land, set in the midst of a summery and non-salt ocean, is delightful.

Ransom is transported from Thulcandra by Oyarsa's powers. On one of the floating islands he meets the Green Lady. She is at present separated from her king, who is elsewhere. Perelandra is as yet a sinless world, and the Green Lady its Eve (though we are warned that history never repeats itself exactly). The Serpent arrives in the form of Ransom's old enemy, Weston, who is taken over bodily by the Bent One, the devil himself. "Weston" tries to tempt the Green Lady to stay on the Fixed Land, which Maleldil has forbidden her to do.

The temptation goes on for many days, with Ransom speaking up, not always effectively, for good. Eventually, it comes down to a physical battle between him and "Weston", and the Bent One is vanquished. Ransom then has some adventures in a subterranean world before rejoining the Green Lady and her king for a grand finale at which the *eldils* are also present. Perelandra has been preserved from evil.

Lewis manages to convey both the horror of the thing that is no longer Weston, together with the misery of all things concerned with it, and, in contrast, the beauty and happiness of things Venerian, or Perelandrian; he also displays with considerable skill the force and truth behind Christian myth—i.e. the importance of individual life, however puny-seeming. What he cannot do is make non-Christians believe in his overall design, though it is undeniable that he can sometimes make them squirm with embarrassment, as in the psalm-singing ending.[31]

Much original work shows traces of its ancestry, as Shakespeare's dramas exhibit their debts to Holinshed's chronicles and old Tudor plays. The first two Lewis novels reveal fairly clearly one line of their descent.

Out of the Silent Planet was in some measure inspired by a favourite novel of Lewis's, *A Voyage to Arcturus*, by David Lindsay. Lindsay roars along like a late member of *Sturm und Drang*, although his extravagant story was published in 1920. It relates how one Krag persuades Nightspore and Maskull to travel in a spaceship to Tormance, a planet where weird metaphysical adventures confront them. Read as allegory, these adventures defy interpretation; they have to be accepted as vision.

Perelandra is much more allegory than vision. But it derives power from that great allegory *Paradise Lost*, a poem with which Lewis was thoroughly familiar. How far this is from saying that *Perelandra* is similar to *Paradise Lost* (although it does have its similarities) we can see when we recall that a very different novel, Mary Shelley's *Frankenstein*—as dark and atheistic as Lewis's Venus is religious and well lit—also owes much to Milton. The more one considers it, the greater is every English fantasy writer's debt to Milton; and that includes Lindsay.[32]

The forces of "Progress" which will ruin the world have become much more powerful in *That Hideous Strength*, the third book of the trilogy. Devine is now Lord Feverstone, backing a National Institute for Co-ordinated Experiments. N.I.C.E.'s programme is vague and grandiose, including a massive programme of vivisection and the re-education of man, together with pre-natal education. N.I.C.E. begins to take over the town of Edgestow, using a mixture of circumlocution and secret police. Victory would be theirs, had they not already broken Earth's quarantine, thus permitting good *eldils* to enter from outside and help man to frustrate them.

The somewhat ragged forces opposing N.I.C.E. include Ransom, now a man of some power. Happily, Edgestow is the site of ancient Logres. Merlin is resurrected and he and Ransom, operating as the Pendragon, rout N.I.C.E. utterly by using Earth-magic.

This is a curious novel which seeks to operate on several different levels, from realistic through to symbolic. H. G. Wells appears as Jules, the figurehead of the Institute, and is shot. The Institute for Co-ordinated Experiments is full of Kafkaesque obfuscation, making it difficult for us to believe that it could represent a major threat to anything. Moreover, its grasp on science is too nebulous for the sort of villainy Lewis seeks to portray. Devine has visited Mars, and one of his objectives through N.I.C.E. would surely have been to duplicate Weston's space flight and to attempt to control the forces there, forces of whose presence he is dimly aware.

On the other side, it is hard to believe in the Christians, trailing clouds of Arthurian romance with them and subscribing to both a high moral creed and a love of bucolic little England.

The total effect is rather as if C. P. Snow and Charles Williams took turns to rewrite Rex Warner's *The Aerodrome*: remarkable rather than successful. Frankly, *That Hideous Strength* is not very good.

What remains vital about *That Hideous Strength*, and the trilogy of which it is part, is that it tries to answer the Wellsian position in vaguely Wellsian terms. It is not dystopian; it is simply against the idea of utopia. As such, it represents a genuine minority viewpoint.

In a short book on C. S. Lewis[33], Roger Lancelyn Green, Lewis's noted disciple, quotes a letter from Lewis in which the latter says:

> What immediately spurred me to write was Olaf Stapledon's *Last and First Men* and an essay in J. B. S. Haldane's *Possible Worlds*, both of which seemed to take the idea of such (space) travel seriously and to have the desperately immoral outlook which I try to pillory in Weston. I like the whole interplanetary idea as *mythology* and simply wished to conquer for my own (Christian) point of view what has always hitherto been used by the opposite side. I think Wells's *First Men in the Moon* the best of the sort I have read. . . .

Nevertheless, Lewis's attitude to Wells was ambivalent[34]; Wells awoke Lewis's imagination and his moral dislike at one and the same time. So with Stapledon: "I admire his invention (though not his philosophy) so much that I feel no shame to borrow," says Lewis in his preface to *That Hideous Strength*.

An interesting footnote to *That Hideous Strength* is that it shows another influence besides the Wells-Stapledon axis, the influence of two of Lewis's close friends at that time in Oxford, J. R. R. Tolkien and Charles Williams. The latter is present in the Logres material, the former in rather cryptic references to Numinor and the True West, with a tantalizing word in the Preface about "the MSS of my friend, Professor J. R. R. Tolkien".

Tolkien, Williams, and Lewis were great conversationalists. At one time, they liked to meet with other cronies in an Oxford pub, The Eagle and Child, and were known as the Inklings.[35]

Tolkien's *Lord of the Rings*, when it finally began its monstrous appearance, proved every bit as anti-Wellsian as Lewis's trilogy, and every bit as fantastic. By the way it was clutched to the chests and bosoms of SF readers, one can see that their true interest is not in the writer's viewpoint, but in his imagination. Lewis or Wells, Stapledon or Tolkien, Burroughs or Asimov—in one sense all are equal in the eyes of the reader; what they have in common is greater than what they have against each other; the medium is the message.

Wells, escaping from the horrors of a lower-class Victorian environment, saw the hope that science offered of a better world. Those who argued against him, like Lewis and Huxley, saw only the eternal human condition, which science could not improve when regarded from the spiritual viewpoint. Wells also saw the human condition, and loathed it—hence his strong vein of pessimism—but he believed it was malleable, not eternally the same.

Wells both hopes and fears. Since his day, his fears have been accepted, his hopes rejected—or, where challenged, as by Huxley, Forster, and Lewis, challenged largely in Wells's terms.[36] For such was Wells's influence that for many years to speak of the future was to attack or defend Wells.

We turn now to the greatest of Wells's followers, who said of his influence, "A man does not record his debt to the air he breathes." This is Lewis's *bête noire*, W. Olaf Stapledon.

Stapledon was born in 1886, in the Wirral, Cheshire. Much of his childhood was spent in Egypt. He received a good education, and was a rather unlikely product of Balliol. He served in an ambulance unit in World War I. He lectured in philosophy at Liverpool University and wrote several works of philosophy. All his novels may be classified as speculative fiction, even his slender last book, *A Man Divided*, which has autobiographical elements. It was published in 1950, the year Stapledon died.

The atmosphere Stapledon generates is chill but intoxicating. Reading his books is like standing on the top of a high mountain. One can see a lot of planet and much of the sprawling uncertain works of man, but little actual human activity; from such an altitude, all sense of the individual is lost.

The best of Stapledon is contained in two long works of fiction and two shorter novels. His most famous work is the first he published: *Last and First Men: A Story of the Near and Far Future*. It appeared in 1930.

The author himself regarded—or said he regarded—his chronicle as expendable; for the next generation, it would "certainly raise a smile". Well, there is no doubt that Stapledon's version of events from 1930 to the present is ludicrous. It is worth close attention if one wishes to savour how wrong prediction can be, in both fact and spirit. Almost anything Stapledon says about Germany and America is incorrect. Only when one climbs through the leaden opening chapters of the book does one start to soar on the wings of inspiration—"myth", Stapledon called it. Politics then gives way to an enquiry into life processes.

One thing is never at fault: the invention. The Second Men, for instance, are bothered by Martian invasions; although the idea may have been derived from Wells, the Martians are cloudlike beings and derive only from Stapledon.

If the periodical catastrophes become mechanical, the successive panoramas of life which Stapledon unrolls are always varied and striking. They are variations on the theme of mankind as a creature like any other, fatally victim of its surroundings, so that whatever is godlike in the creature is brought to nothing by blind happenstance. Like Hardy, Stapledon was influenced by Schopenhauer's philosophy of being, as well as Spengler's philosophy of the cyclic nature of history; his view is at once more prideful and more pessimistic than Hardy's. The time-scale of the novel is unmatched in science fiction, except by the later Stapledon.

Here is one of his final visions, which science fiction readers find moving— though it is the kind of passage which annoyed C. S. Lewis:

> But in the fullness of time there would come a far more serious crisis. The sun would continue to cool, and at last man would no longer be able to live by means of solar radiation. It would become necessary to annihilate matter to supply the deficiency. The other planets might be used for this purpose, and possibly the sun itself. Or, given the sustenance for so long a

voyage, man might boldly project his planet into the neighbourhood of some younger star. Thenceforth, perhaps, he might operate upon a far grander scale. He might explore and colonize all suitable worlds in every corner of the galaxy, and organize himself a vast community of minded-worlds. Even (so we dreamed) he might achieve intercourse with other galaxies. It did not seem impossible that man himself was the germ of the world-soul, which, we still hope, is destined to awake for a while before the universal decline, and to crown the eternal cosmos with its due of knowledge and admiration, fleeting yet eternal. We dared to think that in some far distant epoch the human spirit, clad in all wisdom, power, and delight, might look back upon our primitive age with a certain respect; no doubt with pity also and amusement, but none the less with admiration for the spirit in us, still only half awake, and struggling against great disabilities. (Chapter 16)[37]

Such a chilly vision is best conveyed as fiction or music; as architecture or government, it would be intolerable. Note how the eschatology of this passage takes us a long way beyond the passage we quoted from William Hope Hodgson's *The House on the Borderland*. We may suspect that Stapledon's alienation was at least as severe as Hodgson's; but Stapledon's powerful intellect has shaped his mental condition into a metaphysic.

In 1932, Stapledon published *Last Men in London*, a pendant to the earlier book. His greatest work appeared in 1937, when the shadow of another war was stretching over Europe. In his Preface, Stapledon makes an apology for writing something so far removed from the sounds of battle, and says of those in the thick of the struggle that they "nobly forgo something of that detachment, that power of cold assessment, which is, after all, among the most valuable human capacities"—a very suspect claim; there is no denying that he set great store by a detachment he probably could not help but feel. His was among those "intellects vast and cool and unsympathetic" to which Wells made reference in another context.

Star Maker begins, in some respects, where *Last and First Men* left off. An unnamed human being, the disembodied "I" of the book, falls into a kind of trance, a "hawk-flight" of the imagination", while sitting amid the heather on a hill close to his home. The "I"'s essence is drawn away from Earth, into the solar system and then beyond, farther and farther, and faster.

This is a new—and so far unsurpassed—version of the spiritual voyage. A fresh generation has brought fresh knowledge. Einstein's perceptions, and the findings of astronomers, add calibre to Stapledon's new model of the universe. As in this poetic vision of the doppler effect:

After a while I noticed that the sun and all the stars in his neighbourhood were ruddy. Those at the opposite pole of the heaven were of an icy blue. The explanation of this strange phenomenon flashed upon me. I was still travelling, and travelling so fast that light itself was not wholly indifferent to my passage. The overtaking undulations took long to catch me. They therefore affected me as slower pulsations than they normally were, and I saw them therefore as red. Those that met me on my headlong flight were congested and shortened, and were seen as blue.

Very soon the heavens presented an extraordinary appearance, for all the stars directly behind me were now deep red, while those directly ahead were violet. Rubies lay behind me, amethysts ahead of me. Surrounding the ruby constellations there spread an area of topaz stars, and round the amethyst constellations an area of sapphires. Beside my course, on every side, the colours faded into the normal white of the sky's familiar diamonds. Since I was travelling almost in the plane of the galaxy, the hoop of the Milky Way, white on either hand, was violet ahead of me, red behind. Presently the stars immediately before and behind grew dim, then vanished, leaving two starless holes in the heaven, each hole surrounded by a zone of coloured stars. Evidently I was still gathering speed. Light from the forward and the hinder stars now reached me in forms beyond the range of my human vision.

As my speed increased, the two starless patches, before and behind, each with its coloured fringe, continued to encroach upon the intervening zone of normal stars which lay abreast of me on every side. Amongst these I now detected movement. Through the effect of my own passage the nearer stars appeared to drift across the background of stars at greater distance. This drifting accelerated, till, for an instant, the whole visible sky was streaked with flying stars. Then everything vanished. Presumably my speed was so great in relation to the stars that light from none of them could take normal effect on me. (Chapter 2)

The traveller moves ever on in quest for planets that might support humanlike life, and eventually arrives on Other Earth. A full description of its societies is given before the traveller passes on; there is some mild satire of terrestrial behaviour as well as occasional comments which foreshadow the writings of more intelligent modern SF writers, including C. S. Lewis and James Blish. "Shortly before I left the Other Earth a geologist discovered a fossil diagram of a very complicated radio set", suggests the extraordinary reality-reversions of Philip K. Dick.

Travelling faster than light, the traveller meets other mental cosmic adventurers. They explore endless worlds, endless modes of life, in which Stapledon's ingenuity in creating varied species of men as demonstrated in *Last and First Men* is completely eclipsed. Here, under all sorts of alien conditions, he shows us many "strange mankinds", as he calls them—among them centaurs, which are fairly common in the universe (recalling Van Vogt's comment in his novelette "The Storm" that the centaur family is "almost universal"), human echinoderms, and intelligent ships, as well as symbiotic races, multiple minds, composite beings, mobile plant men, and other teeming variants of the life force. Utopias, interstellar-ship travel, war between planets, galactic empires, terrible crises in galactic history, telepathic sub-galaxies going down in madness

. . . until a galactic utopia becomes a possibility. In all this, the history of *Last and First Men* appears as a couple of paragraphs, lost among greater things. Stapledon is truly frightening at times.

He keeps turning the volume up. We move to para-galactic scale. Stars also have mentalities, and the minded worlds establish contact with them. As the galaxy begins to rot, there is perfect symbiosis between stars and worlds. Meanwhile the "I" observes "the great snowstorm of many million galaxies". A full telepathic exploration of the cosmos is now possible, yet the "I" still remains a mystery to itself.

The scale increases. The "I" is now part of the cosmic mind, listening to muttered thoughts of nebulae as it goes in quest of the Star Maker itself. This Supreme Creator is eventually found, star-like and remote. It repulses the raptures of the cosmic mind. The created may love the creator but not vice versa, since that would merely be self-love of a kind. This emphasis that God is Not Love was bound to upset Christians such as C. S. Lewis.[38]

This encounter brings a sort of dream to the cosmic mind. In the most fantastic part of the book, the cosmic mind visits earlier models of the cosmos with which the young Star Maker experimented, now cast aside like old video cassettes in a cupboard. These are toy versions of the universe. They cannot be detailed here; their place is exactly where Stapledon sets them. Suffice it to say that one of these "toy" cosmoses consists of three linked universes which resemble a Christian vision of the world. In the first of these universes, two spirits, one "good" and one "evil" dice or play for possession of souls of creatures. According to whether they are won or lost, the souls plunge into the second or third linked universes, which are eternal heavens or hells, and there experience either eternal torment or eternal bliss of comprehension. We in our cosmos retain a dim memory of this regime.

The range of cosmoses is continued, up the scale, as the Star Maker's own skill and perception are improved by his models. Perpetually and tragically he outgrows his creatures. Later creations show greater economy of effort than ours, but suffering is always widespread. The creations pour on successively, until the cosmic mind is fatigued; then it comes to the ultimate cosmos.

Beyond that, the cosmic mind wakes from its "dream" and understands that it has encountered the consciousness of the Star Maker, which comprehends all lives in one timeless vision. Such contemplation is its greatest goal.

The "I" now returns to Earth, is back in the present, may take refuge in littleness. The man may go home to his wife. Yet private happiness remains mocked by public calamity. The world is faced with another crisis. All we can do is fight for a little lucidity before ultimate darkness falls.

Time scales complete this magnificent and neurasthenic vision.

Not only is the vision in *Star Maker* wider than in *Last and First Men*; it has become less coarse. Not only does a continuity operate among its parts which is much more various than the somewhat crude cause-and-effect which serves to perform changes of scene in the earlier book, but a concomitant flexibility works through the prose itself. The personal viewpoint, however attenuated it becomes, is a help in this respect, adding a cohesion which *Last and First Men* lacks.

Last and First Men is just slightly an atheist's tract, based largely on nineteenth-century thought, and in particular on Winwood Reade's *Martyrdom of Man*. In *Star Maker*, the atheism has become a faith in itself, so that it inevitably approaches higher religion, which is bodied forth on a genuinely new twentieth-century perception of cosmology. It therefore marks a great step forward in Stapledon's art, the thought unfolding with little sense of strain through chapter after chapter. It is magnificent. It is almost unbearable.

Stapledon also published several slightly more orthodox novels, of which mention need only be made of *Odd John* (1935) and *Sirius* (1944). *Odd John* is a pleasant superman tale, relating how John grows up, experimenting with his special powers until he discovers others of his kind and founds a community on an island in the Pacific. Although this small and somewhat crazy utopia is eventually wiped out, the mood of the book is light and cheerful. The histories of all the supermen are different, and Stapledon clearly enjoys himself inventing past histories for them. Since this is the nearest the author ever came to "a good read", it is a suitable Stapledon for beginners, a vernal hill before tackling the dizzy and formidable heights beyond.

Sirius is the most human of all Stapledon's novels, perhaps because its central figure is a dog. Sirius is a sheep dog that has the brain and consequently the perceptions of a man, although in other respects it remains dog. The product of a scientific experiment, the dog gradually wins its independence. The scientist who develops Sirius's intelligence exclaims, "I feel as God ought to have felt towards Adam when Adam went wrong—morally responsible." By this and references to Milton's poem, the theme of *Sirius* is linked to *Frankenstein*, as another critic has observed.[39]

Unlike Frankenstein's monster, the great dog is allowed a mate. Its life is made tolerable by a reciprocated love for the girl Plaxy. Love is a rare thing in Stapledon's world; here, reaching across species, it finds the warmest and most touching expression, to live on even when the mutated dog is killed.

The ordinary clamour of human affairs, the rattle of coffee spoons, the marrying and begetting, lie beyond Stapledon's compass: yet this harried canine life, with its struggle for self-realization on lonely hillsides, does grow to represent, as Fiedler declares, "the condition of all creatures, including ourselves".[40]

These two novels are fine of their kind; the name of Olaf Stapledon would be commemorated by them alone in the science fiction field, where memories are long. But *Last and First Men* and *Star Maker* soar far beyond the accepted limits of science fiction. Or rather, one might say, Stapledon is the great classical example, the cold pitch of perfection as he turns scientific concepts into vast ontological epic prose poems, the ultimate SF writer. In particular, *Star Maker* stands on that very remote shelf of books which contains huge foolhardy endeavours, carried out according to their author's ambitions: Hardy's *Dynasts* stands there, the writings of Sir Thomas Browne, C. M. Doughty's epic poems, and maybe Milton's *Paradise Lost*.

How it is that the funeral masons and morticians who work their preserving processes on Eng. Lit. have rejected Stapledon entirely from their critical incantations is a matter before which speculation falls fainting away. His prose is as lucid as his imagination is huge and frightening.

Star Maker is really the one great grey holy book of science fiction—perhaps after all there is something appropriate in its wonderful obscurity and neglect!

The writers assembled in this chapter created their work in response to forces fermenting in society and to the ideas of their times. Most of them retain at least a shadowy fame today. Others have been almost completely forgotten, and should have their trophies hung in the halls of SF; or, in the case of two novels we must glance at briefly, in that older hall, now mildewy and taken over by the more modern premises next door, the hall of the scientific romance.

They are *Land Under England* and *The Strange Invaders*.

Joseph O'Neill's *Land Under England* (1935) is a remarkable mixture of psychological novel and warning. The encroaching tide of totalitarianism was clearly in O'Neill's mind when he wrote; he was a man of affairs, with a position in the Irish government, the author of several books.

Like Lytton's *The Coming Race*, *Land Under England* is set underground, near Hadrian's Wall in the North of England, where a Roman legion has remained in limestone caverns for centuries. Cut off from external stimulae, subjugated by a kind of telepathy, the army has become a mindless machine. The central character, Anthony, is trapped there, in a desperate search for his father. Gradually, his understanding reaches out to embrace the situation:

> In this survey it left nothing unexamined, nothing untouched. It saw this underworld State clearly as the monstrous machine that it was—a blind thing, with no vision, no pity, no understanding, not even an understanding of that human need to love that it used to enslave its victims.
>
> It saw that I was the only human being left in that world outside the machine; that, under that dome, which was the land of England, I must make a stand for humanity against the Frankenstein monster which, having devoured the highest as well as the lowest, now functioned mechanically in a world in which man, as we know him, had ceased to exist.
>
> It saw that, if this machine that had come alive could obtain knowledge—not wisdom or real knowledge, for of that it was incapable, but the technical knowledge that I had stored in my brains—if it could force this knowledge into its possession, with me as the controlling and directing robot, and add our scientific powers to its tremendous discoveries, then a new and ghastly era might open up for mankind.

Against this slightly conventional menace is set Anthony's relationship with his father. Only when the power of the father is shaken off can the son mature.[41]

Alun Llewellyn's *The Strange Invaders* was published in 1934. Llewellyn, like O'Neill, was in politics, and had visited the Soviet Union. He responded less favourably to what he saw than did Bertrand Russell, H. G. Wells, and other intellectuals.

The Ice Age is returning. The scene is somewhere in the south of Russia, where cold winds speak of coming winter; Moscow is already under the ice. Interest centres on a mediaeval community whose religion has likewise undergone a long freeze. Marx, Lenin, and Stalin are worshipped superstitiously as gods. All details are intense, like a novel by Ursula le Guin. And then the big reptiles return.

They turned. At first they could see nothing.

The walls stood bare of guards, for those set there had come down to ward off the attack of Tartars upon the gate, and men had been too much preoccupied to station sentinels there again. The crenellations jutted raggedly against the sky of thick and rolling cloud. But there was something unfamiliar about their pattern, in one place.

A dark shape thrust above the walls, a shape they could not make out; a shape that seemed of stone, so motionless it was. The day broadened.

A head, long and narrow and flat. Shoulders that humped as if about to thrust the arms for a mighty leap. A head covered with horny scales that glittered and winked with a sheen of smooth polished colour. Hands that gripped the top of the battlements with clawed fingers, glowed with the same shining scales. From the base of the head, over the shoulders, it appeared as if some supple mail were stretched, wrinkled and gleaming. Stiff, unbreathing it stood; it seemed immaculate, bright, shaped of some strange metal by an inhuman, precise craftsman. Its scales were laid with a cunning geometry of design. The nostrils were bored in its snout in horny circles; its ears, or what seemed its ears, were also incised hollows. The grim line of its mouth slit its head and curled up with the hint of an emotionless grin far back from the nostrils. It did not appear to look at them, and yet it watched. Sidelong it gazed with an eye close to the top of its brainless head, an eye that had a glassy shimmer over a hint of twinkling green. An eye that witnessed without consideration, like a mechanism that would catch apprehension of what was about it and instruct some mighty, cold and purposeful force to action. It watched.

Its long shadow spread hugely over the city. One hand in its jewelled mail curved down into the fortress; the other rested on the wall and they saw the fourth finger, three feet long, longer than its fellows, curl slenderly into the air.

Their breath was stopped in their nostrils.

The creature moved. Its jaws opened silently and shut; a black tongue flickered, forked, out and in.

The people shuddered and they sighed like a moaning wind. The Chief of Fathers neither stirred nor breathed.

Karasoin swayed upon his steed; then sprang from the saddle. (Chapter XI)

An alien scene, alien creatures, and alien faith—all were staple diet of magazine fiction. Never were they so hauntingly combined as here. Many other writers produced science fiction or scientific romances, with greater or lesser conviction. Some of S. Fowler Wright's novels, such as *The World Below* (1929), written while Wright was translating Dante's *Inferno*[42], still have remarkable power. E. C. Large put the emphasis on science in *Sugar the Air* (1937), in which the prospects of resolving the world's food shortages are mooted. The scientist involved sees his plans thwarted by human stupidity. There was a sequel, *Asleep in the Afternoon* (1938), but Large's most wonderful novel, *Dawn in Andromeda* (1956), seems to have been forgotten. Large was a scientist himself. In *Dawn in Andromeda*, ten men and woman walk naked out of the ocean of a distant planet and begin to create a civilization from nothing, along scientific lines. Within twenty-five years, they progress from flint implements to a seven-valve, all-wave, superhet radio.

John Taine, a mathematician and science popularizer, wrote such novels as *Before the Dawn* (1934), a prehistoric romance, and *The Time Stream* (1946), first serialized in 1931–2 in the magazine *Wonder Stories*.

Although such lists do not add greatly to the sum of human knowledge or entertainment, mention should be made here of prolific popular novelist Dennis Wheatley. As well as his endless supernatural novels, Wheatley wrote *Black August* (1934), long remembered by young impressionables, and lost-world-type novels such as *They Found Atlantis* (1936) and *Uncharted Seas* (1938), the last of the Great Sargasso novels. There was also Philip Wylie, whose collaboration with Edwin Balmer, *When Worlds Collide* (1933), was later made into one of the more successful of the 1950s cycle of SF movies. James Hilton's sentimental *Lost Horizon* (1933), owing much to Haggard, was also filmed, and more than once. J. B. Priestley, who spoke in praise of Stapledon, wrote plays based loosely on the theories of J. W. Dunne, the best being *Time and the Conways* (1937) and *I Have Been Here Before* (1938).

One of the strangest novels to spring from a hope that great new engineering enterprises would improve the world is *The Diamondking of Sahara* by Sigurd Wettenhovi-Aspa, a Finnish writer whose book was published in Helsinki in 1935, in English. Since it was never reprinted elsewhere, it represents a treasured rarity for the bibliophile.

The Diamondking of Sahara concerns a group of worldly people who work for the general good. Mr King has an empire in Africa bigger than Italy. He has his own fliers, and is converting the Sahara into forests. The climax of the whole affair comes when the group alters the Niagara Falls, placing them a few miles further upstream in order to generate much more electricity. All of North America is illuminated at night. Crops prosper. The inhabitants of both Mars and Venus see the lights and signal back. Obviously, a reign of interplanetary prosperity is about to dawn as the novel closes.

The narrative is to be treasured for Wettenhovi-Aspa's idiom as well as his optimism.

But it was the greater talents, the Kafkas, Huxleys, Čapeks, and Stapledons, who most ably put the salt on the tail of the *zeitgeist* and, by capturing it, seem to defy it and live on.

Most of the writings designed for the SF magazines of the period, however, have by now lost what savour they possessed. They tell us less about the world and more about the tricks of their lowly trade. They created the popular SF medium, digested the scientific romance, and inevitably lowered SF's "once-for-once-only" quality. Many readers are content with this trade-off.

It is easy to argue that Hugo Gernsback (1894–1967) was one of the worst disasters ever to hit the science fiction field.

Gernsback's segregation of what he liked to call "scientifiction" into magazines designed to contain nothing else, ghetto-fashion, guaranteed the setting up of various narrow orthodoxies inimical to any thriving literature. A cultural chauvinism prevailed, with unfortunate consequences of which the field has yet to rid itself. Gernsback, as editor, showed himself to be without literary understanding. The dangerous precedents he set were to be followed by many later editors in the field.

When these modest statements were first made in *Billion Year Spree* I believed they merely expressed a truth apparent to any reasonable mind. Instead, they aroused fury. My book was widely condemned. Holy relics had been disturbed.

However, it seems I trod too gently. I made no attempt to demolish the myth that Gernsback, with *Amazing Stories* in 1926, published the world's first SF magazine. Here are some predecessors.

Stella was published from April 1886 through August 1888 in Sweden, although it managed only four issues in that time. It featured most of the leading European authors, including Kurd Lasswitz and Jules Verne. *Hugin* was launched in 1916; when it ceased publication in 1920, eighty-six issues had appeared, glorifying the wonders of the future. It was mainly the work of one man, Otto Witt, a Swedish engineer and author. *Der Orchideengarten* was an Austrian-German-Swiss magazine published from 1919–21, and included all the leading Continental writers within its fifty-four issues. Such are the facts.[43]

Der Orchideengarten published 18 issues in 1919, twenty-four in 1920, and twelve in 1921. 9/10 and 11/12 were double issues. There were never more than twenty-eight pages per issue, of which a proportion were adverts. While the original fiction was weak, many authors were represented by reprints. They included Čapek, Guy de Maupassant, Poe, Hawthorne, de l'Isle Adam, Kipling, Wells and others.

Curiously, Karl Hans Strobl, managing editor of *Der Orchideengarten*, Otto Witt, publisher of *Hugin*, and Hugo Gernsback all studied at Bingen, in Germany, at the same time. Maybe they met, and each decided to launch SF magazines. Only Hugo, seeking the New World, made it to the Big Time.

Naturally, European feelings are slighted by the gradual (and to my mind inevitable) American usurping of science fiction.

Sam J. Lundwall, the Swedish editor, publisher, and science fiction writer[44] was good enough to support my criticisms of Gernsback. He says:

As a European, I find myself having a peculiar love-hate relationship with the US science-fiction scene, particularly the side of it represented by its magazines. I was born in 1941, and like many other Europeans of my generation I found SF first through the writings of Jules Verne and Hans Dominik, and then through US SF magazines. It took me many years to realize that there actually was a European heritage of this literature, that the genre actually had originated in Europe—and, in a sense, I felt that the USA had stolen this heritage, transforming it, vulgarising it and changing it beyond recognition. A generation of European science fiction scholars and readers are now rediscovering their own background, and it is a quite painful process. We find hundreds of eminent science fiction works hidden beyond insurmoutable language barriers, hidden beyond all those British and US works which during the years have been all too easily available, to such a degree that everything else has disappeared from view. What is worse, we find that we are now so used to the particular US way of writing science fiction that some of our own heritage seems strange and even alien to us. Like a child revolting against its parents, this is bound to result in unjustified down-playing of the merits of US SF—I am probably guilty of that myself—while some European works might find themselves unjustly praised.[45]

Gernsback was born in Luxembourg, received a technical education, and emigrated to the United States in 1904, determined to make good as an inventor. In no time, he was marketing home radio sets and publishing such magazines as *Your Body* and the world's first radio magazine, *Modern Electrics*. In that journal, in 1911–12, he serialized his novel *Ralph 124C 41+: A Romance of the Year 2660*—a novel which gives us a pretty broad hint as to his lack of interest in anything but technical marvels and gimmicks.

A sample of this unique document is in order. This the opening of Chapter 3, "Dead or Alive?":

An apologetic cough came through the entrance of the laboratory. It was nearing one o'clock of the following day.

Several minutes later it was repeated, to the intense annoyance of the scientist, who had left orders that he was not to be interrupted in his work under any circumstances.

At the third "Ahem!" he raised his head and stared fixedly at the empty space between the doorjambs. The most determined optimist could not have spelled welcome in that look.

Peter, advancing his neck around the corner until one eye met that of his master, withdrew it hastily.

"Well, what is it?" came from the laboratory, in an irritated harsh voice.

This tawdry illiterate tale, which drifts into space and back, is packed with all sorts of technical predictions, each one of which has apparently been invented just before the story opens in 2660. But society is unchanged. Boy meets girl in the same prissy 1911 way, and Ralph has a manservant. Sleep, in this hideous world, is regarded as wasted time, so that during the night children are fed lessons, and adults—of all miserable things—the contents of newspapers.

This is simple-minded Victorian utilitarianism. Gernsback's philosophy, far more than Stapledon's, is what C. S. Lewis would have loathed, had he known it; but Stapledon would have loathed it, too, had *he* known it.[46] The worst Gernsbackian SF neither thinks nor dreams.

Gernsback's sorry concoction met with great success. Its flow of inventions went down well, the dearth of Inwardness and Imagination notwithstanding. Gernsback began to publish more science fiction—mercifully by other hands—in his magazine. In April 1926, he launched *Amazing Stories*, with a first issue featuring reprints of stories by Verne, Poe, and Wells. Full of confidence, he launched *Amazing Stories Annual* in 1927, replacing it with *Amazing Stories Quarterly* in 1928—and reprinting *Ralph 124C 41+* in the latter in 1929.

He lost control of *Amazing Stories* early in 1929 after thirty-seven issues. The sense of wonder had been activated. Publication of *Science Wonder Stories* began in the summer of 1929, with a speed which says much for his initiative. Gernsback was an energetic and courageous publisher, always ready to follow up success. He also circulated the term "science fiction"[47], after juggling with the unpronounceable Gernsbackian uglyism "scientifiction". For all that, it is very difficult to understand why he should ever have been spoken of as "The Father of Science Fiction".[48] Doubtless the naïvety of fans who swallowed all the hype is to blame. But we have met enough of these false claimants to realize that Gernsback was just a midwife disguised as a Young Pretender.[49]

The very existence of Gernsback's magazine attracted new writers. Names such as Murray Leinster, David H. Keller, Stanton A. Coblentz, Jack Williamson, Bob Olsen, Harl Vincent, and Philip Francis Nowlan, who wrote of the Buck Rogers later to be immortalized in comic strip, were associated with his imprint. He also imported German writers in translation, so that such exotic names as Otfrid von Hanstein and Bruno H. Burgel appeared in his pages.

Much uncritical praise has been loaded on Gernsback. A pleasantly objective view was recently taken by a veteran editor of the field, Robert A. W. Lowndes[50], who points out that, in *Science Wonder Quarterly*, Gernsback presented readers with translations of SF novels from German and French. Between 1929 and 1935, fifteen such novels were published. "Thus the reader of the time who had no language but English had his or her first exposure to science fiction written by Europeans," says Lowndes, and stresses the poverty of the times, during the depression.

Gernsback laid great emphasis on the need for scientific accuracy in stories, and later competitors felt bound to copy him. Although this dictat was more honoured in the breach than the observance, it did have the effect of introducing a deadening literalism into the fiction. As long as the stories were built like diagrams, and made clear like diagrams, and stripped of atmosphere and sensibility, then it did not seem to matter how silly the "science" or the psychology was.

A typical story might relate how a scientist experimenting in his private laboratory found a new way to break up atoms so as to release their explosive power. In so doing, he sets up a self-perpetuating vortex of energy which kills either the scientist or his assistant, or else threatens the career of his beautiful daughter, before the vortex rolls out of the window and creates great havoc against which the local fire brigade is powerless. The vortex grows bigger and more erratic all the while. Soon it is destroying New York (or Berlin or London or Moscow) and causing great panic. Tens of thousands of lunatics roam the open countryside, destroying everything in their path. The CID (or the militia or the Grenadier Guards or the Red Army) is helpless.

Fortunately, the scientist's favourite assistant, or the reporter on the local paper, or the boyfriend of the beautiful daughter, has a great idea, which is immediately taken up by the President (or the Chancellor or the King or Stalin). Huge tractors with gigantic electromagnets are built in every country, and these move in on the vortex, which is now very large indeed, having just consumed San Francisco Bridge (or Krupp's works or Buckingham Palace or the Kremlin). Either everything goes well, with the hero and the beautiful daughter riding on the footplate of one of the giant machines as the energy vortex is repulsed into space—or else things go wrong at the last minute, until a volcanic eruption of unprecedented violence takes place, and shoots the energy vortex into space.

The hero and the beautiful daughter get engaged (or receive medals or bury Daddy or are purged) by the light of a beautiful new moon.[51]

The effect of this sort of story was to kill the vogue for the Burroughsian interplanetary romance. The bright colours of the latter were replaced by the grey contretemps and armistices of technocracy.

But talent will out, even in adverse circumstances. Gradually a synthesis between the Burroughsian and Gernsbackian was reached.

The synthesis was reached by way of the "Gosh-wow!" type of story, and not through Gernsback's magazines alone. (*Amazing*—which amazingly still survives—has in fact contributed little to the field).

Farnsworth Wright's grand old pulp, *Weird Tales*, published a considerable amount of science fiction—without always calling it that—ever since its first number in March 1923. And in January 1930, a new magazine joined the lists. It was named *Astounding Stories of Super-Science*. In it the synthesis would appear, making a new sort of sense, and a better kind of wonder.

CHAPTER IX

The Future on a Chipped Plate:
The Worlds of John Campbell's "Astounding"

"I hate a story that begins with the *atmosphere*. Get right into the story, never mind the *atmosphere*."
—John W. Campbell, quoted in
The Way the Future Was by Frederik Pohl

This chapter is really about one man, and a man remembered chiefly as an editor, not an author. One of the hardest-working men in the business. John W. Campbell.

"The dozen years between 1938 and 1950 were *Astounding* years. During these years the first major science fiction editor began developing the first modern science fiction magazine, the first modern science fiction writers, and, indeed, modern science fiction itself."

So says James Gunn in his genial pictorial album-chronicle of SF, *Alternate Worlds: The Illustrated History of Science Fiction* (New Jersey, 1975).

"Science Fiction has had a great many idiosyncratic editors. Some have wound up on the funny farm. One or two have landed in jail. A few have been very good, many have been competent, and a lot have brought to their craft the creativity of a toad and the intelligence of a flatworm. John stands above them all. By any measure you can name, he was the greatest editor science fiction ever had."

So says Frederik Pohl in his generous memoir, *The Way the Future Was* (New York, 1978).

So it must have been so.

Most of the magazines of the thirties, hastily written, hastily thrown together, make lame reading half a century later. And why not? Campbell's *Astounding*—and it can't be just nostalgia speaking—is different, and we shall come to it shortly.

In a fashion, all the old treasured magazines have survived. They survive as microfiche duplicates. They survive as collector's items. They survive as artefacts of that now remote period. They are strange and individual to look at. Their covers are gaudy and gorgeous.

The artwork, in fact, has survived well, for some of the artists such as Frank R. Paul—a Gernsback discovery—Wesso, Virgil Finlay, and Elliott Dold, projected a genuine outré personality. They are now antiques, valued by connoisseurs, much as Meissen porcelain or English watercolours are valued.

These connoisseurs are, in the main, science fiction fans.[1] Gernsback soon discovered and made use of an active fandom, lads who read every word of the magazine with pious fervour and believed every word of editorial guff. These fans formed themselves into leagues and groups, issued their own amateur magazines or "fanzines", and were generally a very vocal section of the readership. Many writers and editors later rose from their ranks.

This particular factor of a devoted and enthusiastic readership is peculiar to science fiction, then and now. The fans founded their own publishing houses, instituted their own international awards (called, of course, the "Hugos"), and organized their own conventions on local, state, national, and international scales.

Nowadays, there is a convention or a conference most weekends of the year, and very glamorous some of them are.

No writer can be other than grateful for this attention in an age when writers by and large complain of isolation from their audience. But there is an obverse side of every coin, and the truth is that several promising writers have been spoiled by seeking popularity exclusively from the fans who—like any other group of enthusiasts—want more of what they have already been enjoying. To attain true stature as a writer, one must look beyond the fervid confines of fandom—however cosy it may seem by the campfire, yarning of old times and old mistresses.

How far that campfire was from civilized arts, back in the late twenties and thirties! Those gaudy covers, for instance, which in time became an art form of their own, were totally divorced from all the exciting new movements of the early twentieth century.

Cubism, futurism, surrealism, exerted no influence. At the time when Burroughs began to write of Barsoom, the Italian painter Giorgio de Chirico was founding metaphysical painting; one of his inspirations was Jules Verne[2], and surely those strange paintings of his would have touched the imagination even of Gernsback's stable. Yet it was not until the early sixties that modern science fiction met art, when English Penguin Books launched their new science fiction series with surrealist and other covers. Bradbury and Blish came decked with details of Max Ernst canvases, Picasso adorned Roy Lewis's *The Evolution Man*. Hal Clement was paired with Yves Tanguy, Frank Herbert with Paul Klee.[3]

By that time, science fiction and fantasy had produced many artists whose names and works were bywords within the field, even if they were unknown beyond it. Virgil Finlay, Paul, Wesso, and Dold have already been mentioned. Later came Orban, Charles Schneeman, Roy Krenkel, Hubert Rogers, Timmins, Edd Cartier, Alex Schomburg, John Schoenherr, Kelly Freas, Jack Gaughan, Vincent di Fate, and two exceptionally fine artists, Richard Powers, whose rise is roughly coincidental with the growth of SF in paperback, and the use of freer techniques, and "Emsh"—Ed Emshwiller, later to become famous as a film-maker (his *Relativity* was one of the early successes of the Underground cinema). Among their British contemporaries are Brian Lewis, Bruce Pennington, Chris Foss, Jim Burns, and Patrick Woodroffe.

The Japanese have also produced excellent SF artists, the wit and style of Hiroshi Manabe being especially impressive. The Italians have published some of the most striking art. The beautiful surrealist covers of Karel Thole, the Belgian artist, would stand out in any company. The Frenchman Philippe Druillet's fantasy strips are magnificent creations.

Today's artists are true professionals, who can command professional prices.

The history of science fiction art deserves to be written.[4] In some respects, it has been less provincial than the science fiction of the magazines—to which we now return.

What we see in the thirties, after the rise of *Amazing*, is minor competence. No writer or editor seems to have a clear idea of what he is doing, beyond producing safe variations on what has gone before. Basically, two disciplines predominate, the fantasy mode of Burroughs and Merritt, and the *Popular Mechanics* mode of Gernsback and his merry men.

The authors who most interest us today are those who somehow managed to embrace the two modes and add some quality of their own. Three names stand out above the morass of the thirties. Two of them, within the limits of the field, are innovators: Edward E. Smith, Ph.D, and John W. Campbell. Jack Williamson, a disciple of Merritt's, survives because he operates powerfully at the dreaming pole.

Within SF fandom—that is the coterie of readers to whom science fiction virtually meant the magazines—E. E. Smith, Ph.D (known as "Doc" Smith), was one of the greatest names, if not the greatest of all.

Well, we have met many superlatives by now, and E. E. Smith (1890–1965) certainly introduces us to many more. His is the logical development of Gernsbackian thought, the infinite extension of technology for its own sake, the glamorous disease of giantism. It was E. E. Smith who started science fiction off on the trillion year spree which is now an integral part of its image.

Beneath Smith's advance, the light-years went down like ninepins and the sober facts of science were appropriated for a binge of impossible adventure. Smith set the Injuns among the stars.

Smith was a doughnut-mix specialist when he had his first novel, *The Skylark of Space,* accepted by *Amazing* in 1928. It was full of super-science. Interstellar travel was taken for granted, and the heroes were super-heroes. At the onset of his career, Smith found a formula which he never abandoned. His hero was an inventor-adventurer, and things had to move fast.

The first Skylark novel was followed by three sequels. The last of them, *Skylark DuQuesne,* was serialized in a magazine (*Worlds of If*) in 1965. Here the hero single-handedly destroys an entire galaxy of fifty thousand million suns, plus an undisclosed number of inhabited planets. Smith has a brief but cheerful description of all the deaths involved. Such callousness is one of the features of SF which naturally precludes its acceptance by an ordinary readership.

Whatever his faults, Smith was energetic and inventive. The Skylark series spawned the Lensman series, Smith's magnum opus, the trillion year spree personified. The Skylark series eventually spanned six volumes, running from

Triplanetary (serialized in *Amazing* 1934) to *Children of the Lens*, serialized in *Astounding* in 1947.[5]

This series postulated two extremely ancient cultures, mutually incompatible, the Arisians and the Eddorians, the former being good, the latter horrendously evil. They lived in separate galaxies, unknown to one another until the galaxies happened to drift into each other. The Arisians are gentle and For Civilization, the Eddorians are utterly sexless and For Power. Lovely Dreamers versus Horrid Intellectuals.

The tale of their struggle, with certain Earthmen and other alien life aiding Arisia, fills the six books. *Triplanetary* begins: "Two thousand million or so years ago two galaxies were colliding; or rather, were passing through each other . . ." and goes on from there. Such events as the sinking of Atlantis, the decline and fall of the Roman Empire, and the world wars, have been but incidents in the long struggle against the Eddorians.

Doc Smith, in short, wrote the biggest game of Cops and Robbers in existence. His various aliens proved irresistible, while his smooth talk of ion-drives and inertialess drives—to avoid the little problem of light possessing ultimate velocity—went down like a tonic with those readers wishing to accelerate their grey cells. His saga is loaded to its armpits in unstoppable forces and immovable objects, in hyper-spatial tubes and super-weapons and planets full of stupefying life armed with terrible mental capabilities.

And then the doors and windows crashed in, admitting those whom no other bifurcate race has ever faced willingly in hand-to-hand combat—full armed Valerians, swinging their space-axes!

The gangsters broke, then, and fled in panic disorder; but escape from Narcotics' fine-meshed net was impossible. They were cut down to a man.

"QX, Kinnison?" came two hard, sharp thoughts. The Lensmen did not see the Tellurian, but Lieutenant Peter vanBuskirk did. That is, he saw him, but did not look at him.

"Hi, Kim, you little Tellurian wart!" That worthy's thought was a yell. "Ain't we got fun?"

"QX, fellows—thanks," to Gerrond and to Winstead, and "Ho, Bus! Thanks, you big, Valerian ape!" to the gigantic Dutch-Valerian with whom he had shared so many experiences in the past. "A good clean-up, fellows?"

"One hundred percent, thanks to you. We'll put you. . . ."

"Don't please. You'll clog my jets if you do. I don't appear in this anywhere—it's just one of your good, routine jobs of mopping up. Clear ether, fellows, I've got to do a flit."

"Where?" all three wanted to ask, but they didn't—the Gray Lensman was gone.

The whole gigantic road show works by magic. The Lenses of the Lensmen, which resemble fantastic jewels, are semi-sentient life forms bestowed by

Arisia, providing their wearer with amazing paranormal powers. Spaceships travel across hundreds of light-years at faster than light speed. They become non-detectable when required, can evade thought-screens, can be converted to perform amazing feats and hitherto unheard of marvels in the realm of physics. The Lensmen wear non-detectable armour, can enter the minds of sinister aliens or harmless insects. They are unkillable, and encounter the most formidable situations with schoolboy glee.

Smith took great pains with his epic, rewriting its earlier parts to hang together in one entire enormous concept. And the concept is impressive. Unfortunately, everything moves at such breath-taking speed—or else stops entirely while everyone talks and the plot catches up—that what is good in theory is by-passed in practice. The author conveys no visual experience and does not make his immense distances real; his banal hearty style is obvious from the extract quoted.

Nevertheless, for youngsters, the entire astounding edifice held a lot of joy and excitement, mainly because, whatever else Doc Smith could or could not do, he clearly *enjoyed* spinning out this doughnut mix of galactic action.

He died in 1965, loaded with honours by the science fiction field, unknown beyond it.[6] And in the 1970s, the whole Lensman saga started to sell millions all over again, in paperback to a new audience.

It must have been a painful experience to write for the pulps in the thirties. One had to conform to formula or get out. There was no sort of cultural tradition or precedent to appeal to. Low rates of pay engendered much hack-work.

Perhaps things would never have changed, had not editors often been short of material and published stories which, to their amazement, readers liked . . . However that may be, a few writers did spring up among such super-hacks as John Russell Fearn, who pillaged ideas from all quarters, including the cinema, and wrote under various names.[7] Many of them, such as Edmond Hamilton, chronicler of "Captain Future", are worth a chapter in their own right, but we must take as our representative the redoubtable Jack Williamson.

Williamson, born 1908, began writing in Gernsback's *Amazing* and never looked back. He was much influenced by Abe Merritt, and managed to assimilate Merritt's sense of colour and movement without taking over the fairies as well. His output was fairly prolific, as outputs needed to be if one was to live by writing in a field where *Amazing* and *Wonder* were paying half a cent a word on publication. His greatest early success was with a serial in a 1934 *Astounding*, *The Legion of Space*, a Gosh-wow! epic which thundered along on the cloven heels of Doc Smith. But there are later novels of Williamson's which have more to offer, and which—unlike some of the so-called "classics" of the field—have not been reprinted as often as they might be.

The Legion of Time was a serial in a 1938 *Astounding*. Its plot, while being philosophically meaningless, is a delight. Lanning, a Harvard man who becomes a reporter, is thinking of time. Because of this, he is visited by the fair Lethonee. Lethonee comes from far in the future; she carries an immense jewel, which allows her to travel back in time to Lanning. Later, Lanning is visited by the sexy Sorayina, also from the future. Lethonee's and Sorayina's futures are mutually exclusive. One will materialize at the expense of the other. Either Jonbar, Lethonee's capital, or Gyronchi, the tawdry capital of Sorayina, inhabited mainly by anthropoid ants, will come into being, depending on how their potentialities for realization are strengthened in Lanning's own time.

After many desperate struggles, which Lanning's Legion of Time generally wins, it is discovered that the crucial moment at which the time-lines divide is a day in 1921. The Legion's timeship heads for 1921, closely pursued by Sorayina's dreaded black Gyronchi ship.

In 1921, they find a boy in a meadow. This is John Barr, who will either pick up a magnet in the grass and thus be moved to become a scientist (making great discoveries from which will develop Jonbar), or will fail to pick it up, will pick up a pebble instead and become a migratory worker. In the latter case, his great discovery will be made by an "exiled engineer from Soviet Eurasia and a renegade Buddhist priest", who will turn the discovery (something about mentally released atomic power) to evil ends, thus developing Gyronchi.

Lanning battles through despite all the enemy can do, pitches the magnet at Barr's feet, and sees the "very light of science" dawn in the boy's eyes. So Gyronchi is defeated. Lanning sails the time-streams to Jonbar to get the girl, and is agreeably surprised (though not *very* surprised) to find that Lethonee and Sorayina have become merged into one. He's got them both!

Fairy tales have a way of revealing hard truths about everyday life. Science fiction so often turns out to be a fairy tale—never more so than in this instance! The significance of some of the inconsistencies in this tale has been discussed elsewhere[8]; but its romantic charm obstinately remains. Like Doc Smith's saga, this one also works on magic. Most traditional SF does. The magical spells are given such names as "mentally released atomic power"; the hyper-drives light the way to Babylon.

Hardly surprisingly, Williamson's best novel deals directly with magic. *Darker Than You Think* was published in *Unknown* in 1940. Barbee, like Lanning, is a reporter. He goes to cover the return of a scientific expedition from the interior of Asia, the members of which he knows. They return with an ironbound box containing some terrible secret they guard with their lives.

Barbee gets mixed up with a beautiful girl called April Bell, who sends odd little shivers down his spine. She presents a Lethonee-Sorayina duality: by day, a beautiful girl; in his dreams, a superb wolf bitch. And Barbee finds he has the power to change to a wolf in his dreams and pursue her into the wilds. In that dream state, she leads him to enter houses and kill. Barbee soon has proof that his dream state is no dream.

In the chest that Dr Mondrick and his colleagues are guarding so anxiously is evidence that Homo lycanthropus once existed—a witch people, whose genes merged with mankind and may now, by skilful interbreeding, become dominant again. One by one, Mondrick, his expedition members, his wife, are killed. Barbee is there. Despite his efforts, he feels himself responsible for their deaths. Only his closest old friend, Sam Quain, survives, lugging the chest with its deadly secret. Barbee tries to help him, but Quain will not trust him. Despite the mounting crisis, Barbee attempts to remain human. The taunting wolf with her green eyes and red tongue calls to him. Soon the Child of Night, the great new witch, will emerge and start a new reign of his kind.

Barbee is the Child. He turns into a pterosaur, kills Quain, and destroys the evidence that might make mankind rise against his kind. Then he follows the white wolf into the forest.

Preposterous though this sounds in outline, it is well worked out, full of genuine suspense and excitement, and primed with a good hefty sense of evil. The characters, though obvious, are clearly drawn; but the major advantage of the novel is that it is full of the pleasure of wild life, of running free in the dark, of the forests, the mountainside, and of the scents of the breeze. The novel works like a *novel*, not a diagram, showing us without lecturing how splendid it would be to chase a white she-wolf through the night. Here is a happier escape from the human than poor Jekyll achieved.

And suddenly he was free.

Those painful bonds, that he had worn a whole lifetime, were abruptly snapped. He sprang lightly off the bed, and stood a moment sniffing the odours that clotted the air in the little apartment—the burning reek of whisky from that empty glass on the chiffonier, the soapy dampness of the bathroom and the stale sweaty pungence of his soiled laundry in the hamper. The place was too close; he wanted fresh air.

He trotted quickly to the open window, and scratched impatiently at the catch on the screen. It yielded, after a moment, and he dropped to the damp, hard earth of Mrs Sadrowski's abandoned flower bed. He shook himself, gratefully sniffed the clean air of that tiny bit of soil, and crossed the sidewalk into the heavy reek of burned oil and hot rubber that rose up from the pavement. He listened again for the white she-wolf's call, and ran fleetly down the street.

Free—

No longer was he imprisoned, as he had always been, in that slow, clumsy, insensitive bipedal body. His old human form seemed utterly foreign to him now, and somehow monstrous. Surely four nimble feet were better than two, and a smothering cloak had been lifted from his senses.

Free, and swift, and strong!

"Here I am, Barbee!" the white bitch was calling across the sleeping town.

The plot hinge of *Darker Than You Think* is characteristic of the period: humanity, or reality, is revealed by some accident of scientific research or discovery to be other than we have assumed. The revelation is always unpleasant. The great exemplar is Charles Fort's dictum, "We're property!" which was embodied in a novel by Eric Frank Russell, *Sinister Barrier* (published in *Unknown*, like *Darker Than You Think*). Slightly later, van Vogt's "Asylum" depicts Earth as a dumping ground for the scum of the universe, just as Thulcandra is the dumping ground for the Bent One. As the psychiatrist Glenn says in Williamson's novel, "The unconscious mind does sometimes seem a dark cave of horrors, and the same unpleasant facts are often expressed in the symbolism of legend and myth." Faced by the horrors of a global war, the SF writers were fashioning their own kinds of myth. Despite a slight clumsiness, *Darker Than You Think* still works in this manner.

Perhaps one should not compare Williamson's story with a subtle literary treatment of the lycanthropy theme. Nevertheless, Hermann Hesse's 1925 novel, *Steppenwolf,* is content to leave an alternative human line of evolution as metaphor for the outsider in society.

Williamson's *The Humanoids* is less successful. As a novel-length sequel to a short story called "With Folded Hands", it appeared in *Astounding* in 1948 under the title . . . *And Searching Mind*. Williamson presents a well-constructed plot, buttressed with learned bits of pseudo-science, which centres around the coming of robots to a planet geared for war with its neighbour. The first robot that the hero, Forester, sees, strikes him as attractive when it drops its human mask.

> There was nothing really horrible about what emerged from that discarded mask.
> Rather, it was beautiful. The shape of it was clearly human, but very slim and graceful, with no mechanical awkwardness or angularity whatever. Half a head shorter than Forester, it was nude now, and sexless. The sleek skin of it was a shining black, sheened with changing lights of bronze and blue. (Chapter 9)

The humanoids arrive by the thousand and take over in the midst of the crisis. They are units of a cybernetic brain many light-years away, and their prime directive is "To Serve and Obey, and Guard Men from Harm". In effect, they bring peace by rendering men powerless—in the most benevolent possible way. Unlike Čapek's humanoids, Williamson's are utterly subservient, and he wisely leaves the ending open, as the humanoids lay their benevolent plans for Andromeda—is their peace-keeping a triumph or tragedy? As Damon Knight says in Chapter 4 of *In Search of Wonder*, the book is important because its theme is important.

Unfortunately, the impact is muffled by having it set far away across the galaxy. To have set it on Earth would have been dramatically better. And, of course, the philosophical implications take second place to a tale of adventure. All the same, *The Humanoids* has plenty of readability, because Williamson's strong visual sense is at work, here as in *Darker Than You Think* (we are constantly reminded of the *presence* of the androgynous metal creatures), and his characters are not thick-ear supermen like Doc Smith's but pretty ordinary fallible people, in need of some sort of prop just like the rest of us.

Under his own name and pen names, Williamson wrote many other novels and stories. In the fifties, he wrote undersea novels of SF adventure with Frederik Pohl, and the Starchild trilogy in the sixties. And several more novels since then. Williamson has been much involved in the expansion of academic studies of SF. For his versatility he is much to be honoured.

The third author who rose to eminence in the thirties' magazines is a controversial figure who had a greater effect on magazine science fiction than any other man.

John W. Campbell (1910–71) was one of the field's intellectuals. He had strong ideas, some of them erroneous, but his positive side triumphed over many of his mistakes. He encouraged and trained many of the field's strongest genre writers.

Campbell's own first story was published in the January 1930 *Amazing*— "When the Atoms Failed". He rapidly made his name in the realm of megalomaniac galaxy-busting being pioneered by Doc Smith, with stories whose very titles can still light the dim eyes of senior fans: "Piracy Preferred", "The Black Star Passes", *Islands of Space*, *The Mightiest Machine*, *Invaders from the Infinite*, and so on. Most of these stories show deep interest in complex machines and are studded with explanations of their workings.

In 1934, Campbell changed his approach. Taking on the pseudonym of Don A. Stuart (derived from his first wife's name), Campbell produced a series of short stories in a much more meditative mood. The first was "Twilight"; it imitates the dying fall of Wells's *The Time Machine*, and features a man who goes into the far distant future when man is extinct because his curiosity is dead. A civilized regret is the mood aimed at. Campbell adopts a kind of singsong intonation and a faux-naïve style.

> Can you appreciate the crushing hopelessness it brought to me? I, who love science, who see in it, or have seen in it, the salvation, the raising of mankind—to see those wondrous machines, of man's triumphant maturity, forgotten and misunderstood. The wondrous, perfect machines that tended, protected, and cared for those gentle, kindly people who had—forgotten.

When "Twilight" was gathered into a collection by Shasta Publishers, Campbell claimed that it was "entirely different from any other science fiction that had appeared before". That is totally incorrect; the Wells influence is clear. It did, however, bring into magazine science fiction another alternative to utilitarianism, talking animals and Gosh-wow; its "all passion spent" mood was imitated by other writers such as Lester del Rey and, later, Arthur C. Clarke.

Even in his lachrymose vein, Campbell continued to write about huge engines and the vanishing tricks of supernormal power, interspersing them with rather plodding technical detail. Belief in incredible forces of ESP was to dog him all his life.[9] Here are four paragraphs from "The Cloak of Aesir", first published in 1939, which demonstrate several of his literary characteristics. The Sarn-Mother, one of the rulers of a defeated Earth, is talking:

"Aesir spoke by telepathy. Mind to mind. We know the humans had been near to that before the Conquest, and that our minds are not so adapted to that as are the humans'. Aesir used that method.

"He stood before me, and made this statement that was clear to the minds of all humans and Sarn in the Hall of Judgment. His hand of blackness reached out and touched Darnell, and the man fell to the floor and broke apart like a fragile vase. The corpse was frozen glass-hard in an instant of time.

"Therefore, I released Grayth and Bartell. But I turned on Aesir's blackness the forces of certain protective devices I have built. There is an atomic blast of one-sixteenth aperture. It is, at maximum, capable of disintegrating half a cubic mile of matter per minute. There was also a focused atomic flame of two-inch aperture, sufficient to fuse about twenty-two tons of steel per second.

"These were my first tests. At maximum aperture the blackness absorbed both without sound or static discharge, or any lightening of that three-dimensional shadow."

By the time "Aesir" was published, Campbell was editor of *Astounding*. He took over in 1937, at the age of twenty-seven, to begin what proved to be a thirty-four-year reign.[10] As Donald Wollheim points out, Campbell could begin to draw on the first generation of young writers, raised on magazine SF; "science fiction builds on science fiction".[11]

Incidentally, Campbell took the editorial chair from F. Orlin Tremaine, who had produced fifty issues of *Astounding Stories* (as it was). Tremaine had already introduced improvements in the magazine.

The new editor was confronted by new competition. A promising and colourful *Marvel Science Stories* appeared on the stands in 1938, to be followed by *Startling Stories*, *Dynamic Science Stories*, and *Science Fiction*. Thick and fast they came at last, and more and more and more. *Fantastic Adventures* arrived as a stable mate to *Amazing*, at that time owned by the Ziff-Davis chain—then *Planet Stories*, pursued by two magazines edited by a teenage Frederik Pohl, *Astonishing Stories* and *Super Science Stories*. *Future Fiction*, *Comet Stories*, *Cosmic Stories*, and *Stirring Science Stories* pop up around the same time. Most of these magazines were in the Burroughsian mode, *Planet Stories* especially.

Astounding itself acquired a sister magazine in the Street and Smith group. This was *Unknown*, which appeared on the news-stands in the spring of 1939 and ran for less than forty issues. Campbell edited both magazines in tandem. *Unknown* specialized in bizarre fantasy, which frequently operated close to reality but stood it upside down—*Darker Than You Think* is a good example. When *Unknown* died, so, it seems, did Campbell's love of that particular genre, and a wartime mood of "realism" spread over stories that were often far from realistic in essence.

Campbell soon proved himself a good and ambitious editor. He forced his writers to think much harder about what they were trying to say, and clamped down on Gosh-wowery, although, when a genuinely inspired madman like A. E. van Vogt came along, Campbell was wise enough to let him have his head. Also, he had the fortune to take over at a good time, when the monstrous footprints of Burroughs and Gernsback had, to some extent at least, obliterated one another. The stiffening breeze from Europe also introduced a more responsible note.

He worked, too, on logic—a quality his competitors had always been short of. It was Campbell's own peculiar sideways logic (which accounted for his fondness for Lewis Carroll), but it led him to reject the Bug-Eyed Monsters—known in the trade as BEMs—and many of the trashy plots that went with them. As he remarked at a later date, while thinking genially about the unthinkable:

Two motives standard in BEM-style science fiction can be dismissed quickly. Aliens aren't going to invade Earth, and breed human beings for meat animals. It makes a nice background for horror-fantasy, but it's lousy economics. It takes approximately ten years to raise one hundred pounds of human meat, and at that it takes high-cost feed to do it. Beef cattle make better sense—even though that louses up the horror motif.

And that is, of course, assuming the improbable proposition that the alien's metabolism can tolerate terrestrial proteins at all.

If they can, of course, it's much easier to get local natives, ideally adapted to the planet's conditions, to raise the cattle. Inherently much cheaper than trying to do it yourself. Besides, the local yokels can be paid off in useless trinkets like industrial diamonds, or tawdry little force-field gadgets, children's toys that won't cut anything with any accuracy better than a microinch.

Then there's the old one about raiding Earth and carrying "Earth's fairest daughters" away as love-toys on some alien planet. Possible motive . . . if you'd define "fairest" adequately. If the aliens happen to come from a bit heavier planet, the proposed raids on "Earth's fairest daughters" might turn out to be very distressing to the gorilla population. In those "Earth's fairest daughter" bits, I've noticed, nothing whatever is said about the intellectual capabilities of the "fairest"; a charming young gorilla maiden would pass the only test proposed . . . if your eye for looks were slightly different. And obviously those interstellar harem-agents aren't interested in offspring anyway; there couldn't possibly be any.[12]

A team of new writers, or old writers operating under pseudonyms—often a surprisingly effective way of altering writing habits—began to gather round Campbell. Unlike many editors before and after, Campbell knew when a story made sense and when it didn't. He argued strongly with his contributors—and his arguments were often well informed and fair. Thus he laid the foundations for what the gentle hearts of fandom call "The Golden Age".

One authority on the subject, Alva Rogers, is definite about the date. When he reaches 1939 in his chronicle, he says, "The July issue was unquestionably the first real harbinger of *Astounding*'s Golden Age."[13] This issue carried a story by A. E. van Vogt, "Black Destroyer", which later became part of his book *The Voyage of the Space Beagle*. Other new writers appeared that year, soon to become famous, among them Robert A. Heinlein, Isaac Asimov, and Theodore Sturgeon.

Heinlein's first short novel, *If This Goes On . . .*, was published early in 1940—a brisk tale of total dictatorship in the United States operating under the cloak of religion. This was followed by a serial from L. Ron Hubbard, *Final Blackout*, which supposed that the war in Europe dragged on until civilization broke down. Hubbard had previously been known as a fantasy writer. His story and Heinlein's were at the time much more plausible than the lead stories *Astounding* had hitherto been publishing.

In 1941, Heinlein revealed the plan of his scheme for a Future History series, while Asimov formulated the three laws of robotics, which prevent robots from harming men.

Asimov's famous *Foundation* series, too, is in marked reaction against the slam-bang space opera preceding it.[14] "Violence is the last refuge of the incompetent" is quoted with great approval. Readers have complained that Asimov's characters talk too much. At least they are not blasting each other down.

In such respects, Heinlein and Asimov brought literary law and order into magazine science fiction. Asimov's robot stories are amusing little puzzles, without the philosophical implications of Williamson's *The Humanoids*, Čapek's robots, or Frankenstein's monster, from which they ultimately derive. But Asimov's achievement—which should not be forgotten—is that he banished those slavering metallic hordes, or those single mechanical men forever reaching for the nearest axe, which had been a boringly predominant feature of the magazines until Campbell's day.

Both Asimov and Heinlein brought intelligence and knowledge to their storytelling. Heinlein's preoccupation with power was sometimes to express itself disastrously, as in his novel *Starship Troopers*. But that was later; in the early forties, he could do no wrong. In 1941 alone, *Astounding* published three of his novellas which can still be read with pleasure, "Logic of Empire", set on Venus, "Universe", set on a gigantic interstellar ship, and "By His Bootstraps", a time-paradox story which still delights by its ingenuity, as well as several excellent short stories.

It seemed that the cosmos was his oyster, so diverse was his talent. But no author has more than one secret central theme, or needs it; "Logic" is about resistance to authority; "Universe" is about what happens when authority breaks down; and "Bootstraps" is a good-humoured demonstration of the trouble that can come when the father-figure is removed.

Heinlein's Future History was gradually outshone by Asimov's future history, the centuries (actually only 350 years) covered by the series of short stories, novellas, and serials published in *Astounding* between 1942 and 1950, which eventually became known as *The Foundation Trilogy*. The story of the

Foundation and the workings of psychohistory was to prove just about the most popular writing ever to emerge from the magazines, despite severe structural faults.

Once free of Campbell's orbit, Asimov and Heinlein were to prove alarmingly prolific. Almost half a century after publication of the original short story, *Foundation*, Asimov is still—as we shall see—piling up wordage on the same subject.

Theodore Sturgeon, on the other hand, was to become known later in life for his silences. His stories had an engaging twist to them, were generally set on Earth, and were written in what could be recognized as a style. Perhaps because of his interest in the psychology and oddity of human beings, he seemed more of a real writer than the big guns booming about him. About twenty-five stories by Sturgeon appeared in *Astounding* and *Unknown* until the latter ceased publication at the end of 1943 and Sturgeon disappeared into the armed forces.

Among the best-loved Sturgeon stories of this period are "Microcosmic God" and "It". Later came "Killdozer!" and "'Thunder and Roses". Asimov had sound, Heinlein had fury; Sturgeon had music.

L. Ron Hubbard began as a pulp writer and ended as a millionaire and a legend. Which makes his fiction hard to judge. But no one who read "Fear" (in *Unknown*, 1940) during their impressionable years would ever forget it. It portrays a man who must go back in time to face what he most fears. "Typewriter in the Sky" (also *Unknown*, 1940) is more amusing, and concerns a popular author whose swashbuckling character in the story he is writing takes him over. Funnily enough, the same thing seemed to happen to Hubbard.

From 1947 to 1950, Campbell published the series of Ole Doc Methuselah stories by Rene Lafayette, who was Hubbard lightly disguised. Ole Doc is a medic, one of the Soldiers of Light, "more dreaded than the Law itself", who travels round the galaxy like a one-man Starship *Enterprise*, putting things to rights with a pinch of Freud and a dollop of good old American know-how. Thus was foreshadowed Dianetics and the Church of Scientology. Like Asimov, Hubbard took to SF again following a long break. Shortly before his death in 1986, *The Invaders Plan* appeared, the monstrous first volume of a planned decalogy.

Then there was A. E. van Vogt. Hardly a typical Campbell man. Your typical Campbell author put you right about this or that. Van Vogt proceeded to beat your brains into scrambled egg.

A. E. van Vogt was talking confidently of interstellar winds back in 1943, and dropping in casual word of large pockets of space—as when a survey ship reports that a small system of stars "comprises two hundred sixty billion cubic light-years, and contains fifty million suns."

Van Vogt was the ideal practitioner of Doc Smith's trillion year spree. He was not hard and cold and unemotional, in the manner of Clement, Asimov, and Heinlein. He could balance his cubic light-years and the paraphernalia of super-science with stretches of tenderness and pure loony joy. Intimations of humanity surfaced now and again among all his frenetic mental powers and titanic alien effects.

Van Vogt was not seen at his best in longer works. Among his short stories, one of the best—because it exhibits all his talents in dynamic balance—is "The Storm" (1943), which contains some moments of love between Maltby and the Lady Laurr (Van Vogt was a sucker for a title). Indeed, there's a hint that the story's title is intended to refer also to an internal storm of emotion. Very sophisticated! But, of course, it was the intergalactic storm which interested readers, and that was what they got.

> In those minutes before disaster struck, the battleship *Star Cluster* glowed like an immense and brilliant jewel. The warning glare from the Nova set off an incredible roar of emergency clamor through all of her hundred and twenty decks.
>
> From end to end her lights flicked on. They burned row by row straight across her four thousand feet of length with the hard tinkle of cut gems. In the reflection of that light, the black mountain that was her hull looked like the fabulous planet of Cassidor, her destination, as seen at night from a far darkness, sown with diamond shining cities.
>
> Silent as a ghost, grand and wonderful beyond all imagination, glorious in her power, the great ship slid through the blackness along the special river of time and space which was her plotted course.
>
> Even as she rode into the storm there was nothing visible. The space ahead looked as clear as any vacuum. So tenuous were the gases that made up the storm that the ship would not even have been aware of them if it had been travelling at atomic speeds.
>
> Violent the disintegration of matter in that storm might be, and the sole source of cosmic rays, the hardest energy in the known universe. But the immense, the cataclysmic danger to the *Star Cluster* was a direct result of her own terrible velocity.
>
> If she had had time to slow, the storm would have meant nothing.
>
> Striking that mass of gas at half a light year a minute was like running into an unending solid wall. The great ship shuddered in every plate as the deceleration tore at her gigantic strength.
>
> In seconds she had run the gamut of all the recoil system her designers had planned for her as a unit.
>
> She began to break up.

The writing has clarity and brevity, ably conveying van Vogt's excitement at his immense drama. Later, and beyond the pages of Campbell's magazine, van Vogt was never to recapture his first fine careless rapture. Nor that mixture of kookie science—half a light year per minute, indeed!—with lyric excitement.

Van Vogt was Philip K. Dick's spiritual forefather. Dick admitted as much. His emotional impact, his complexities, were what Dick took from him.

Slan was van Vogt's first novel-length success, in *Astounding* in 1940. The following year produced *The Weapon Shops of Isher*. These successes were eclipsed by *The World of Null-A* (1945), and its sequel, *The Pawns of Null-A* (1948–49). Null-A purported to be a form of non-Aristotelian logic which would make us all cleverer, based on the theories of General Semantics.

The Null-A serials caused a sensation within the small circle of Campbell's audience. They were colourful, confusing, fast-moving, and appeared to be saying something profound—no one has yet discovered what.

After that, van Vogt had only a quieter serial to offer, *Empire of the Atom* (1946–47), before lapsing into silence for some while. In fact, he joined Hubbard over at the Dianetics Institute.

Much followed from that first Null-A serial. It became the first novel from the SF magazines—the first of many—to emerge later from a major hardcover company, in this case Simon & Schuster (1948).[15] It alone—according to one authority, Jacques Sadoul—created a French SF market when translated (and van Vogt was fortunate to be translated by surrealist writer Boris Vian) and published in Paris. Any publisher anywhere in the world who wanted to start up an SF line made sure he had a van Vogt title to begin with.

Even the General Semantics Institute benefited. Its founder, Count Korzybski, was photographed clutching van Vogt's book and—but what else?—*smiling*.

After this inordinate success, an inevitable downgrading. It is now impossible to take the Null-A books seriously; the schlock ingredient is too high. Yet there were gold nuggets in all those cubic light-years of candy floss. The observer is inevitably part of the observed Gilbert Gosseyn, van Vogt's hero, who has false beliefs about himself, from which he must be freed.

"This is true of all of us," said van Vogt later.[16] "Only, we are so far gone into falseness, so acceptant of our limited role, that we never question it at all."

Well said—and well-suited to Campbell's expansionist philosophy.

One thing *Astounding* had which can never be recaptured. It had faith. The peculiar faith that space travel was possible and would come about. This belief has long ago been translated into fact. At the time, however—in the forties and fifties—it was greeted with almost universal scepticism or ignorance. To be a part of Campbell's audience was to feel oneself a member of a privileged minority who knew in their bones what was going to happen in future.

Space travel was the major chord, with war and telepathy as minor ones.

The exciting developments under Campbell may be read in the covers of the magazine.

Symbolism always precedes actuality, just as a belief in space travel preceded the space programmes. A concept must be visualized before it can be realized. So the art side often flies ahead of the contents. The 1938 covers of *Astounding* span a wide range of subjects, are interesting, but have no unity. From 1939, a kind of coherence appears. The Campbell orchestra tunes up. The January covers for both 1939 and 1940 romanticize industrial processes (i.e., organizational action as opposed to individual action)[17] and might be used with perfect propriety as factual illustrations two or three decades later.

The age of the boy-inventor is over, while the all-action scientist adventurer, so popular from *Ralph 124C 41 +* onwards, is waning. Mythology was getting an overhaul. The Canadian artist Hubert Rogers was ideal for Campbell's purposes; his sombre scenes and muted colours, coupled with modern *sans serif* lettering, formed *Astounding* covers into a new generic proclamation of intent. Rogers produced fifty-nine covers for *Astounding* between 1939 and 1952, and at least as many interior illustrations. He was influenced by art director Vincent Korda's costumes and set for the 1936 movie, *Things To Come*. The aerodynamic interiors and shortie cloaks Rogers used were made in Korda's studios.

While magazine science fiction could produce no Swifts, no Mary Shelleys, no Wellses, it nourished a stream of accomplished entertainers who were also thought-provoking and imagination-stirring, however reach-me-down the prose. Finesse would have sunk the ship.

Whereas Kafka, Huxley, Stapledon, and authors of that ilk were critics who arose to deal with a specific socio-technological situation, the very nature of the magazine SF field—its month-by-month continuity—nurtured something of another order: a dialogue between writers. The conditions had been there in embryo in the thirties; in the forties, under Campbell, they bore fruit. The constant cribbing of ideas became instead something of a genuine exchange.

If some of the excitement generated then has evaporated several decades later, it is because one of the electrifying factors was precisely that creative exchange, building from issue to issue, year by year, conducted by Campbell and other later editors such as Pohl—and nobody knew quite what was coming next. Every month brought the promise of something wilder and stranger—and the promise was always kept!

A similar fecundating situation occurred in the mid-sixties, when Michael Moorcock took over *New Worlds*. As Moorcock did later, Campbell seized on his editorial column to expound his theories, hoping that writers would pick up the trail. It is typical of the whole success story of *Astounding* that it is not only the fiction which has been anthologized again and again; a selection of Campbell's editorials has also been published.[18]

Magazine SF writers differed from the Huxleyan kind of writer in one other important way. That difference is implicit in what has already been said. They did not question the basic value of technology. They saw that technology would bring big troubles (wasn't that what SF was all about?), but they were secure in the belief that more massive, more organized, doses of technology would take care of the problem. Such a formalized credo helped make Campbell's magazine—their bastion until his death in 1971—much more of a force to be reckoned with than its predecessors.

The spaceships that Heinlein and van Vogt dreamed up would have drained the energy systems of Earth many times over had they been built, as well as swallowing all its metallic ores. But what *symbols* the spaceships were!

For many years, science fiction fans were fond of saying jocularly, "A spaceship is just a phallic symbol." So it often may have been in terms of cover art—Emsh for one often used spaceships deliberately as phallic symbols.[19] But they symbolized a great deal more. In the thirties, they took the place of tramp steamers or ocean liners. In the writings of Campbell's new wave, they might variously stand for a spirit of dedication, manly togetherness, or a romanticized industrial process of gigantic proportions.[20]

While symbolizing such matters, the spaceships, of course, served also as a convenient way of hefting their heroes across the paper light-years. But one need not be an avid searcher for symbols to see that, whatever else they stood for, spaceships meant the conquest of nature. Or vice versa.

> Long rows of shops and warehouses stood deserted. Doors yawned open. Neglected roofs were sagging. Ruined walls, here and there, were black from old fire. Every building was hedged with weed and brush.
>
> Far across the shattered pavements stood the saddest sight of all. A score of tall ships stood scattered across the blast aprons, where they had landed. Though small by comparison with such enormous interstellar cruisers as the *Great Director*, some of them towered many hundred feet above the broken concrete and the weeds. They stood like strange cenotaphs to the dead Directorate.
>
> Once they had been proud vessels. They had carried the men and the metal to build Fort America. They had transported labor battalions to Mars, dived under the clouds of Venus, explored the cold moons of Jupiter and Saturn. They had been the long arm and the mighty fist of Tyler's Directorate, and the iron heel upon the prostrate race of man.
>
> Now they stood in clumps of weeds, pointing out at the empty sky they once had ruled. Red wounds marred their sleek skins, where here and there some small meteoric particle must have scratched the mirror-bright polish, letting steel go to rust. And the rust, in the rains of many years, had washed in long, ugly, crimson streaks down their shining sides.

An excerpt from Jack Williamson's "The Equalizer", in a 1947 *Astounding*. This story is about a power beyond the atomic which makes every man his own master, so that the social contract is dissolved. Williamson appears to be in some confusion here—the rockets were used for oppression, yet their abandonment is "the saddest sight of all"—but the connection between spaceships and mastery of the environment is abundantly clear.

Astounding developed into a hymn to this connection. The hymn is less fashionable nowadays; but fashions come and go.

So the magazine SF writers became able to do many things that the writers outside the field could not do. Above all, they could depict a technological culture as a continuing process—often continuing over thousands of millions of years. Although the writers (optimistically or blindly) neglected the vital factor of depletion of Earth's mineral and other resources, they perceived that Western civilization rests increasingly on a non-random process of innovation.

This continuity of culture has its analogue in the continuity of *Astounding* over its vital years. *Astounding* was a collaborative work, the first think-tank. And was followed in that role by such later magazines as *Galaxy* and *The Magazine of Fantasy and Science Fiction*.

The stellar empires postulated by Asimov in his *Foundation* series or van Vogt in his *Empire of the Atom* series—though both may have been based on older models (such as Gibbon or Robert Graves's Claudius books)—owe a superior vitality over previous empires to their basic premise that technology demands continuity and expansion. The Manhattan Project, involving specialists from many countries, drove the lesson home—but the lesson is foreshadowed in science fiction before it emerges fully in society. That the way to the Moon lay through a door marked R&D is a perception one first encounters in Campbell's *Astounding*.[21]

Campbell's own special field was atomic physics. This proved a rapid growth area in the period after he took over in *Astounding*'s editorial office. It was no accident that Military Intelligence agents visited that office in 1944, to investigate the background to Cleve Cartmill's story "Deadline" which Campbell had just published.

"Deadline" deals with the development of an atomic bomb; Cartmill assembled facts which were known at the time. What Cartmill did not know was the existence of the Manhattan Project, dedicated to lines of research identical with the one in his story. The story of this invasion of Campbell's office was immensely popular in SF circles. It was cherished as proof that SF was not just fairy tales, but seriously predicted coming nuclear weaponry. As significant is the fact that the Manhattan Project itself, that grandiose and secret conspiracy of talent, had also been foreshadowed in *Astounding*. The industrialization of science, the rise of the industrial spy, the anxious guarding of new processes, the paranoia of high-funded laboratories—these themes emerge in pre-imago state in story after story.

As a corollary, the typical *ASF* story was rather cold and impersonal in tone. Its contents often displayed callousness, disguised as manliness. It could degenerate into a sort of illustrated lecture.

Before many years were past, the gimmick or gadget story had fallen from popularity. At least one reader gave up reading (for a couple of months) after a confrontation with the glib superficiality of Harry Stine's "Galactic Gadgeteers" in 1951. In its heyday, the gimmick was best devised by writers such as Hal Clement, an MIT man whose novel *Mission of Gravity* (an *ASF* serial in 1953) remains a great favourite.

Clement's short story "Fireproof", in 1949, presupposes launcher satellites girdling the Earth in a continued East–West confrontation, with an Eastern spy aboard a Western satellite. The spy is going to blow up the launcher, but fails to do so because fire will not burn where there is no convection of air, as in the gravity-free conditions of the satellite (a fact on which the spy has not been briefed, happily for the West!). The story hardly exists as a story; nor does Campbell regard it as a story, but as part of the continuing *Astounding* debate. The evidence for this lies in the wording of Campbell's blurb for the story, a minor art of which Campbell was master:

This yarn, gentlemen, introduces a brand new idea in the field of spaceship operation. There's twenty years of discussion gone by—and this beautiful, simple and exceedingly neat point has been totally missed! Before you reach the end, see if you can figure the answer!

There were times when *Astounding* smelt so much of the research lab that it should have been printed on filter paper.

Nevertheless, the research lab approach generated ideas. No popular magazine has ever been such an intellectual delight. Many later problems were foreshadowed in general terms and chewed over excitingly. Such superman stories as Mark Clifton's "What Have I Done?" discussed the relative meaning of equality in human society. Clifford Simak's *City* series investigated new relationships among living things. Eric Frank Russell imagined strange new symbiotic forms of life in stories such as "Symbiotica". Old hand Murray Leinster visualized a time when people might lose interest in maintaining the strenuous arts of civilization. It's true that in this particular story, "Trog", interest is artifically occulted by a fiendish enemy brain wave, but the general thrust of the story points to a stage of culture which sometimes seems only now to be approaching.

Writers argued about the role of the computer long before the computer cut its first transistor, wondering how it would alter man's world. One of the most brilliant and pithy answers was contained in the one-page story by Fredric Brown, "Answer". (Though it did not appear in *Astounding*, its punch line, "*Now* there is a God!" became a password in some circles.)

As for aliens, they were everywhere. In *Astounding* at least, the Burroughs emphasis sank below the surface, as the writers realized increasingly that man's behaviour, alone among species, was not species-specific, and that that plasticity could best be expressed by using aliens as if they were merely behaviourly different kinds of men (though disguised maybe by fangs or scales). Simak's aliens are generally just men without sin. Later, in the fifties, this balanced attitude fell away, perhaps under pressure of Campbell's xenophobia—as Wollheim says, "No internationalist he"—and the aliens became warped symbols of fear. But, in the forties, all seemed well.

Of many other able writers who matured in the pages of Campbell's first decade, there is room to mention only one more in any detail.

Henry Kuttner (1914–58) was another great producer. His work seems to have been enriched by his marriage to another writer, Catherine Moore, in 1940. Her bloodthirsty "Shambleau" was widely admired. Together, Kuttner and Moore wrote under such pen-names as Lawrence O'Donnell and Lewis Padgett, publishing in *Astounding*. "Clash by Night", and its serial-length sequel, *Fury* (1947), are vividly remembered; the vein of sensuality in the latter was not characteristic of the rather coldly masculine *Astounding*. *Fury* is set in the decadent undersea "keeps" of the planet Venus, after Earth has been destroyed by atomic fire.

Kuttner's and Moore's was a sensuous world, non-diagrammatic, blurred at the edges. Whereas Asimov concerned himself with robots and androids which men could not tell from fellow men, and other writers fostered the dangerous cult of the superman, Kuttner rejected such non-resonant themes. Like Sturgeon, he was for the underdog.

He posited a human society in which there was a persecuted sub-species of telepaths, all linked to each other by thought and sensation. The telepaths could be distinguished from ordinary men by their bald heads. Hence the series was known as "The Baldies", to be gathered into book form under the title *Mutant* (1953).

In Kuttner's world, people marry and have babies and cry and upset milk. They enjoy the Earth and the Sun. Donne-like, they understand that no man is an island, not even a mechanical island. "Each time a telepath dies, all the rest within minds' reach feel the blackness close upon an exhausted mind, and feel their own minds extinguish a little in response."

Even at a time of tension, Kuttner's telepathic minds are open to random impressions. In "Humpty Dumpty", a "Baldy" story, in a 1953 *Astounding*, we read:

> By now Cody was at the little park before the long Byzantine building. Trees were wilting above brownish lawns. A shallow rectangular pool held goldfish, who gulped hopefully as they swam to the surface and flipped down again. The little minds of the fish lay open to Cody, minds thoughtless as so many bright, tiny, steady flames on little birthday candles, as he walked past the pool.

An image like that can burn in a reader's mind for decades after he has read it. Kuttner died in 1958, at the ripe young age of forty-three. Our own minds were extinguished a little in response.

Kuttner was given little recognition by pre-WWII fans, who could not accept his attempts to coax a little sex and sensuality into the genre, whether in *Astounding* or *Marvel Science Stories*.[22] Of the two original trusty writer-critics within the SF field, only James Blish puts in a really strong word for Kuttner.[23] Faced with the terrors of earning a living in a field where the editor was all-powerful (and economical to boot), Kuttner did admittedly turn in a lot of hack-work; yet he was voted favourite living SF author at an 1947 SF convention.

Kuttner was exceptional. Campbell liked to give the impression that all stories were machine-turned off a lathe of truth. *Astounding* stories were tested for popularity monthly and ranked in order by readers, in a department labelled the Analytical Laboratory—or An Lab—as if scientism might also speak for literary merit.

Nevertheless, *Astounding* wisely never confined itself to what was merely likely.[24] The technicalities of Hal Clement and George O. Smith with his Venus Equilateral stories were counterbalanced by one more chunk of the Lensman saga, the wildness of A. E. van Vogt, or the doomed psychiatric fun of Theodore Sturgeon.

Campbell enjoyed a joke. Eric Frank Russell was for years his licensed jester.

There were also "spoof" articles by Isaac Asimov, and, later, John Brunner's "Report on the Nature of the Lunar Surface", which proved that the Moon really was made of green cheese.

The impossible was not ruled out, if only because nobody knows what is possible and what is not. Also, there is some evidence that SF writers are particularly prone to confuse science with magic. Arthur C. Clarke put it this way: "Any sufficiently advanced technology is indistinguishable from magic."

Even the hardheaded Campbell, who saw in science and applied science "the salvation, the raising of mankind", even Campbell believed that the impossibility of getting something for nothing might be transcended by a formula or incantation—hence his extraordinary notion that seventy-five per cent of the brain (and the most powerful part) lay unused, his belief in psionics, and his pursuit of cults such as Dianetics (later Scientology, founder L. Ron Hubbard), which caused a breach between editor and readers.[25]

There was also the Dean Drive, a neat little device which was supposed to generate thrust without producing an equal and opposite reaction. The Dean Drive sounded suspiciously like the device Jack Williamson had written about a few years earlier in "The Equalizer", a solenoid wound in special way which generated almost unlimited electrical power, thus enabling every man to be independent and ending dictatorship forever. Campbell, convinced of the profound worth of science fiction, tried to live some of it.

John Campbell was a bit of a philistine, and a bit of a chauvinist. But first and foremost he was a bit of a miracle.

By general consent, *Astounding/Analog* was the best and most influential of all popular SF magazines. During 1960, Campbell changed the title over from *Astounding* to the more anodyne *Analog*. He continued to edit until his death in 1971. By then, the heat had gone off the stove, although excellent writers like Frank Herbert, Harry Harrison, Mack Reynolds, and Robert Silverberg still appeared there. The first appearance of James Tiptree Jr was in *Analog* in 1968; Anne McCaffrey's Pern dragon stories, beginning with "Weyr Search", made their debut in 1967.

Despite an increasing crankiness, Campbell was a man of great personal kindness and charm. In that respect, his successor in the editorial chair resembled him. Ben Bova tackled the difficult job with energy, and introduced more flexible policies which gained the magazine a new lease of life. At the end of the seventies, Bova handed *Analog* over to Stanley Schmidt, moving on to edit the new glossy *Omni*.

Space is short in which to deal with all the other magazines, that jostling throng. Some of them contributed little to the general good, some a great deal. Some of their editors are honoured; others had, in Fred Pohl's immortal words, "the creativity of a toad".

Among the most eminent of those magazines lacking toads in the editorial chair is the *Magazine of Fantasy and Science Fiction*, still with us and known familiarly as *F&SF*. Launched in 1949, *F&SF* was edited originally by Anthony

Boucher, with J. Francis McComas as co-editor. Since 1965, the magazine has been edited by Edward L. Ferman.

Galaxy Science Fiction was launched in 1950, shortly after *F&SF*. Under four editors, it lasted for thirty mainly glorious years.

And there was a company of other magazines, some evanescent, some longer-lived. Those which established a clear identity of their own, such as *If* and *Planet Stories*, were best loved. SF magazines have managed to survive long after other related kinds of magazines have perished.

They are still remembered with affection, years after their demise, by those who bought and collected them in their youth. And they have their chroniclers, perhaps most notably the four-volume *The History of the Science Fiction Magazines*, by Mike Ashley[26] and the recent, extraordinary, indispensable *Science Fiction, Fantasy, & Weird Fiction Magazines*, edited by Marshall B. Tymn and Mike Ashley.[27]

"Cultural background" is a term much loved by literary critics. The reality behind the term is something that should never be forgotten when we look back at Campbell's achievements with *Astounding*.

But Campbell's magazine began as just one of many hundreds of pulp magazines, most of them short-lived, short-sentenced, and short-changed. They were considered to be beyond the pale of literacy. Moreover, when Campbell arrived, the great era of the pulps was already dead—some say it closed with the paper shortages induced by World War II.[28] Campbell had no *incentive* to improve matters beyond his own acumen, which was considerable.

The pulps are slowly gaining recognition as a new common culture, growing in place of one that had been shattered. Certainly they were churned out for a lower middle or working class—in many cases immigrant—entirely without privilege (another contrast with the prosperous audiences of a stable society addressed by the Huxley-type science fiction writer). The pulps gave a whole stratum of the American public, hit by the Depression and other economic evils, a sort of unified viewpoint, a voice.

Tony Goodstone points out that the "latent pyscho-sexual drama of the Depression" depended in part on the era's "unusually emasculating effect on the breadwinner".[29] More straightforwardly, we can agree that the effect on a man of being unemployed or underpaid is a feeling of powerlessness.

All the successful pulps used strong, tough, all-action heroes with whom the underprivileged could identify. All the air aces, cowboys, detectives, Tarzans, Conans, and mighty avengers such as Doc Savage and the Shadow (let's not mention Superman, Batman, and the extraordinary mob of comic-book heroes who followed) are in this succession. Science fiction offered an unusual and almost limitless extension of the hero role and of power. Campbell must have seized instinctively on this function. His response to his times was intuitive.[30]

Nick Carter might set the New York underworld to rights. All the brave adventurers and aviators might vanquish their enemies. Doc Savage might own an inexhaustible gold mine under a mountain in South America. But only

Campbell's heroes had the real equalizer: the infinite policing powers of the mind, the inexhaustible forces beyond the atom!

So SF transcended the pulps, by extending their simple strong-arm formulas and inventing new protagonists big enough to take on the universe. At the same time, very subtly, the problems those protagonists faced could be shown to have close bearing on day-to-day problems in a technological society, problems on both a "realistic" and a "mythological" level. Where other magazines messed about with the present, Campbell gave you the future on your chipped plate.

Even more, you could grow up still believing in the Campbellian magic. You couldn't grow up believing in Doc Savage's ludicrous gold mine, but it needs a very sophisticated mind to sort out prediction from fantasy. *Astounding* was a mag for all seasons.[31]

Part Two

INTO THE BIG TIME

CHAPTER X

After the Impossible Happened: The Fifties

The claws got faster, and they got bigger. New types appeared, some with feelers, some that flew. There were a few jumping kinds. The best technicians on the moon were working on designs, making them more and more intricate, more flexible. They became uncanny; the Ivans were having a lot of trouble with them. Some of the little claws were learning to hide themselves, burrowing down into the ash, lying in wait.
—Philip K. Dick: *Second Variety*

Since World War II ended, and the dropping of the atomic bomb on Japan became the first move in the Cold War, science fiction has diversified in a number of ways. That diversification leads us directly to the present.

Once magazine science fiction began to spread to traditional publishing, and to appear in hard-cover, it reached a general public and the libraries. Success attended such pioneering anthologies as Raymond J. Healy and J. Francis McComas's *Adventures in Time and Space* and Groff Conklin's *The Best of Science Fiction* (both 1946). The way was open for SF to take itself more seriously. That growing seriousness has been one of its more significant characteristics of recent years, for better or worse.

Outcrops of SF include think-tanks, such as Herman Kahn's Hudson Institute, which have to some extent taken over SF's predictive role, much as ICBMs have taken over from the old-fashioned bombers of SAC. Frederik Pohl, however, has a good argument to show that SF's role can still be fruitfully predictive, since it injects into the picture the emotional tone that the statistics leave out, thereby allowing us all to see whether we want to accept the futures the planners posit for us. To some of us steeped in the SF of the time, space flight itself—and the launching of the first sputniks and satellites—seemed like an extension of SF, just as the Wellsian atomic bomb had done.

For several years before the first space rockets lumbered up to lodge a human being in orbit, the SF magazines issued propaganda on the subject; when success came, one might almost have been forgiven for believing that "thinking made it so". Space flight had been the great dream, the great article of faith; suddenly it became hardware, and was involved in the politics of ordinary life.

The first sputnik went into orbit in October 1957, and the Space Age had begun. It is hard for people now to realize how stubbornly the idea of any form of space travel was opposed before that date, and not only by the supposedly ignorant. There was the British Astronomer Royal, who declared in 1956, "The future of interplanetary travel is utter bilge!" (He later compounded his error by saying that what he *really* said was that stories about interplanetary travel were utter bilge.)

Space travel was a dream, the precious dream of SF fans. It was part of the power fantasy of the SF magazines. When space travel became reality, the dream was taken away from them. At least for two decades. *Star Wars* gave it back, and our screens have been cluttered with the dream objects ever since. However, in the late fifties the sales of magazines dropped dramatically. Commentators have always found difficulty explaining that fact, but the reason is simple— withdrawal symptoms were in progress.

If the transformation of dream to hardware brought disillusion to many SF fans, it also meant that SF and the general idiom of a life style that courted the unlikely became much more of a commonplace. The impossible had happened. People began to expect the unexpected.

As a result the SF ghetto walls crumbled from outside; there was no longer reason to feel persecuted inside. The decor of new cities, the design of world's fairs and expos, the feel of offices and community centres, the gaga sophistication of TV ads, the sheen on hundreds of motion pictures from the James Bonds onwards—all merged with the slick worlds of science fiction. The term "science fiction" increasingly became used as a sort of okay jargon term, meaning something futuristic, unlikely, and high-powered.

Moreover, evidence began to emerge during the late fifties that the USSR— that dark Communist alter ego of the capitalist Western world—harboured its own science fiction writers. Later, Russian SF found its way to the West in translation, while Western SF found its way to the socialist camp. Some of us found friends on the other side of what was once called the "Iron Curtain" whose greatest need—as desperate as ours several years earlier—was for science fiction magazines. Later still, an International SF Symposium was held at which Russian and Western SF writers met, exchanged views, and became closer friends.[1]

To say this is to anticipate to some extent the contents of this and the following chapters. To make sense of the present, we should look at developments after World War II, when science fiction was still a minority cult, little known to any but its devotees.

Astounding after the war was a very black magazine. Its writers and readers— to say nothing of its editor—were digesting the implications behind the nuclear bomb, its unlimited powers for greatness or destruction. It was a painful process: the old power fantasies were rising to the surface of reality. Many stories were of Earth destroyed, culture doomed, humanity dying, and of the horrific effects of radiation, which brought mutation or insidious death. Nor were things depicted as much cheerier beyond the solar system.

Titles of late forties and early fifties stories in *Astounding* reinforce the point: "Tomorrow and Tomorrow" (Kuttner), "The End is Not Yet" (Hubbard), "There is No Defence" (Sturgeon), "Dawn of Nothing" (Chandler), "Space Fear" (Schmitz), ". . . And Then There Were None" (Russell). In Simak's *City* series, humans had passed from the Earth, leaving it to a rabble of dogs and miniature robots. The news was no more encouraging on Trantor, where the Mule was threatening Asimov's galaxy with thousands of years of slavery and barbarism. But the absolute supremacy of *Astounding* was almost at an end; new magazines, new writers, were assembling in the wings.

Terms such as "pessimism" and "optimism" are loosely used in the science fiction debate. There was plenty of pessimism in *Astounding*; that is a simple emotion. What it lacked was the natural and decent despair which has always characterized much of ordinary literature. But, even in 1985, editors in the SF field reject stories because they are "too down-beat"—a curious rejection, since SF has always been, on the whole, a gloomy literature when not aimed at the nursery.

We find that natural and decent despair in the writings of such authors as Bester, Sheckley, Harrison, and—later—Spinrad, Ballard, and Disch, a despair which lends zest to the rest of life. In our present decade James Morrow and Russell M. Griffin might be said to be the inheritors of the mantle of decent despair. These authors relish humour, and have a reverence for other people and a regard for sex, vital elements often found with despair. Of these writers, only Harry Harrison found his métier in *Astounding*. His first two novels were published in the early sixties just as the magazine's name was changing to *Analog*. They were *Deathworld* and *Sense of Obligation* (book form as *Planet of the Damned*), and marked Harrison out as one of the few authors capable of carrying the old vigour of earlier days forward into a new epoch.

As for Bester and Sheckley, they found their niche in *Galaxy*, edited by Horace Gold, which, with the *Magazine of Fantasy and Science Fiction*, sprang up lustily in the early fifties. (Gold had written for *Astounding* as early as 1934; with L. Sprague de Camp, he contributed the haunting "None But Lucifer" to Campbell's *Unknown*). Alfred Bester produced two novels, both containing gaudy and exciting glimpses of future societies, *The Demolished Man* (serialized 1952) and *The Stars My Destination* (serialized 1956–7, and known also as *Tiger! Tiger!*).

The latter novel in particular is a definitive statement in Wide Screen Baroque—a kind of free-wheeling interplanetary adventure, full of brilliant scenery, dramatic scenes, and a joyous taking for granted of the unlikely. Bester writes with natty panache, a style more encouraged by Gold's type of madness than Campbell's.

> He jaunted.
> He was aboard the *Nomad*, drifting in the empty frost of space.
> He stood in the door to nowhere.
> The cold was the taste of lemons and the vacuum was a rake of talons on his skin. The sun and the stars were a shaking ague that racked his bones.[2]

There are passages in Durrell's later *Alexandria Quartet* which are not dissimilar, and tied also to exotic backgrounds ("Long sequences of tempera. Light filtered through the essence of lemons. An air full of brick-dust—sweet-smelling brick-dust and the odour of hot pavements slaked with water").

Bester had written science fiction in the forties and had a number of short stories published in the magazines—stories which he retrospectively dismissed as being fairly awful—and for most of the forties he found himself writing comic book scripts for Standard Magazines, a four year experience which gave him the opportunity to get a lot of lousy writing out of his system. What it also gave him was an acute sense of dramatic effect and pacing. His next job was as a scriptwriter for radio, where he utilized his comic book experience in visualization, attack, dialogue, and economy. He turned to writing SF again as a safety valve, even though the pay was far lower than he'd become accustomed to. From that safety valve came the two SF novels of the fifties, and the TV-showbiz novel *The Rat Race* (1955, titled *Who He?* in the USA) whose taut opening line, "Every morning I hate to be born, every night I'm afraid to die", earned it such adjectives as "hard-boiled" from reviewers.

After these wild novels, Bester fell silent for almost twenty years, returning to the genre with *Extro* (also known as *The Computer Connection*) in 1975 and *Golem[100]* in 1980. Neither attains the heights of earlier work. Perhaps Bester himself recognized that his earlier statement was definitive, leaving it to others with a tenth of his perception and wit to churn out pale imitations.

His few short stories are also cherished. Most of them concern long odds of one sort and another, a good example being "Time is the Traitor" (1953), in which one John Strapp travels round the galaxy in quest of a duplicate of the girl he loved ten years ago. He finds her at last, but he has changed. "The mind goes back, but time goes on, and farewells should be forever." So run the story's closing words. For a long time they seemed to represent Bester's personal philosophy—and in most of our minds he is still linked strongly to those two bright flashes in the fifties.

Robert Sheckley's appearances in the pages of *Galaxy* were less marked but not less cherished than Bester's. As a novelist he emerged strongly in the sixties and will be dealt with there, but as a short story writer he sparkled from the first:

During breakfast, Thurston explained in pedantic detail why a trap could not function unless it had an opening to admit the prey. Dailey smiled and spoke of osmotic section. Thurston insisted that there was no such thing. When the dishes were washed and dried, they walked over the wet, springy grass to the trap.

"Look!" Dailey shouted.

Something was in the trap, something about the size of a rabbit, but coloured a bright green. Its eyes were extended on stalks and it clicked lobsterlike claws at them.

"No more rum before breakfast," Thurston said. "Starting tomorrow. Hand me the canteen."

Dailey gave it to him and Thurston poured down a generous double shot. Then he looked at the trapped creature again and went, "Brr!"

"I think it's a new species," Dailey said.

"New species of nightmare. Can't we just go to Lake Placid and forget about it?"

"No, of course not. I've never seen anything like this in my zoology books. It could be completely unknown to science. What will we keep it in?"

"*Keep it in?*"

"Well, certainly. It can't stay in the trap. We'll have to build a cage and then find out what it eats."

Thurston's face lost some of its habitual serenity. "Now look here, Ed, I'm not sharing my vacation with anything like that. It's probably poisonous. I'm sure it has dirty habits." He took a deep breath and continued. "There's something unnatural about that trap. It's— inhuman!"[3]

This from "Trap", an ingenious alien invasion tale, more comic than sinister, and one which, like so much of Sheckley's early work, turns out to have marital problems at the back of it. Even aliens can wish to dispose of their wives and lust after another slender-tentacled and delectable little creature. The grass—indeed, the woman herself!—is always greener. . . .

A blurb on the same collection which includes "Trap", *Pilgrimage to Earth* (1957), describes Sheckley as "an extrapolating philosopher", and that's a fair description. Within the limitations of generic fiction, Sheckley produced dozens of telling short stories—stories like "Specialist", "Pilgrimage To Earth", "Ask A Foolish Question", "A Ticket to Tranai" and "The Store of the Worlds"— which did far more than simply entertain. There was intelligence and genuine insight, often for satirical purpose.

Galaxy, under the editorship of H. L. Gold, and *F&SF* under the editorship of Anthony Boucher, provided several other writers with a congenial platform. The original version of that slender modern classic, Ray Bradbury's *Fahrenheit 451* (1953), appeared in *Galaxy*'s fifth issue as "The Fireman". Theodore Sturgeon's extraordinary "Baby is Three" appeared in *Galaxy* in 1952, and later was built into the novel, *More Than Human* (1953). The story is about six outcasts of society who together make a viable Gestalt entity; it transcends its own terms and becomes Sturgeon's greatest statement of one of his obsessive themes, loneliness and how to cure it.[4]

Galaxy brought into the sunlight a number of excellent satirists, comedians, and ironists, among whom Frederik Pohl has proved to have the greatest survival value. His story, "The Midas Plague" (1954) remains as an acid comment on the consumer society as, to a lesser degree, do "The Tunnel Under the World" and several other stories of the time.

That Cold War epoch brought forth another noted satirist in Damon Knight, whose macabre humour found voice in "To Serve Man" in *Galaxy*'s second issue, (1950). Among the excellent stories which followed, perhaps "Four in One" (1953) and "Country of the Kind" (1956) are best remembered. Knight also shone as a critic. His reviews were gathered into *In Search of Wonder* (1956).

Only those who read that volume at time of publication can judge the remarkable effect it had on both writers and readers; Knight had had the courage to say, as truthfully, clearly, and amusingly as possible, what he thought about both the classics and contemporaries of SF. Gardner Dozois does not exaggerate when he calls Knight "the founder of science fiction criticism".[5]

In the mid-sixties, Knight went on to found the Science Fiction Writers of America, becoming its first president. He had by then initiated the Milford Science Fiction Writers' Conference, a kind of teach-in for the professionals. His anthology series, *Orbit*, ran from the mid-sixties on to 1980. It featured unconventional writing, not least the stories of his elegant third wife, Kate Wilhelm. Altogether, twenty-one volumes of *Orbit* were published. They were models of how such anthologies should be run.

The fame of Walter M. Miller nowadays rests securely on his novel, *A Canticle for Leibowitz* (1960). His short stories reveal a conscious ironist at work, an element far from absent in the novel. In 1952 alone, Miller produced three fine short stories, "Anyone Else Like Me?", "Dumb Waiter", concerning the negative effects of technology, and "Command Performance", a study of a woman who finds she is telepathic.

But of all the fifties satirists working in the short story field—at a time when the SF short story was surely at its peak—none had a sharper wit than William Tenn.

Tenn liked to work on a small scale, although his targets were often commendably large. The majority of his work is confined to a comparatively brief period. Little appeared after "The Liberation of Earth" in 1953 and "Down Among the Dead Men" in 1954 (two of his most memorable stories), although a novel *Of Men and Monsters* surfaced rather unexpectedly in 1968. His best collection is *Of All Possible Worlds* (1955).

Awful confrontations with the future or with aliens form Tenn's most congenial subject matter. "Down Among the Dead Men" has corpses revived to fight again in Earth's battle against a repulsive insectlike alien aggressor. "Eastward Ho!" (1958) is a neat inversion story, with the white men in America setting sail to colonize Europe, because the Amerinds, in this post-holocaust world, have adapted better than they. As Malcolm Edwards has pointed out, "The Liberation of Earth" is Tenn's most satisfying and durable satire.[6] The wretched inhabitants of Earth have allied themselves with first one side and then the other in a vast galactic war. Every alliance brings further grief and destruction, until the planet is ruined and humanity devolves into a small burrowing creature. The concluding line of the story is harshly memorable: "Looking about us, we can say with pardonable pride that we have been about as thoroughly liberated as it is possible for a race and a planet to be." The moral remains relevant.

This story appeared not in *Galaxy*, but in a lesser magazine, *Future Science Fiction*.

Commenting on his writing, Tenn said in an interview, "The humorous angle is the human angle as far as I'm concerned. And when I say the human angle I am thinking not of man in the form of a statue standing on tiptoe, pointing towards the stars, but . . . of man in a smelly urinal, scratching under his left armpit."[7] This scathing comment, which clearly would have precluded Tenn's regular appearance in Campbell's magazine, perhaps accounts for the comparative modesty of Tenn's output. The incentive to write for men in urinals is limited.

In general, 1952 was a good year at *Galaxy*. It also saw the serialization of Frederik Pohl and Cyril Kornbluth's *Gravy Planet*, known in book form as *The Space Merchants* (1953), and the start of the serialization of Clifford Simak's best book, *Ring Around the Sun. Astounding* had nothing equivalent to offer. Asimov's serial, *The Currents of Space*, based itself on the plot, old-fashioned even then, that the fate of Earth depended on one man, and he had lost his memory! Asimov's "The Martian Way", appearing in *Galaxy* at the same time, was much more forward-looking, besides being a critical comment on what Senator Joseph McCarthy was even then doing with his Committee on UnAmerican Activities.[8]

Pohl and Kornbluth made one of the greatest combinations in the science fiction field, and the death of Kornbluth in his thirties was a minor disaster— perhaps not least for Pohl. Together, they produced some excellent novels. *Space Merchants* apart, *Gladiator-at-Law*, set in and out of the slummy Belly Rave, *Wolfbane*, and *Search the Sky* also have their supporters. All except *Search the Sky* appeared in *Galaxy*.

The strangest of them is *Wolfbane* (serialized in 1957; book form 1959), in which Earth is moved out of its orbit by a runaway planet whose inhabitants are Pyramids. One Pyramid slices off the top of Everest and settles there. The central character, Tropile, is captured by the Pyramids and used as one component in their gigantic and grotesque computer. He wakes to find himself in a tank, floating spreadeagled and doing *something* automatically. Looking about, he finds he can see all round without moving his head. He has been given total vision. Then he looks at his hands.

He could see them, too, in the round, he noted; he could see every wrinkle and pore in all sixteen of them. . . .

Sixteen hands!

That was the other moment when sanity might have gone.

He closed his eyes. (Sixteen eyes! No wonder the total perception!) and after a while he opened them again.

The hands were there. All sixteen of them.

Cautiously, Tropile selected a finger that seemed familiar in his memory and, after a moment's thought, flexed it. It bent. He selected another. Another—on a different hand, this time.

He could use any or all of the sixteen hands. They were all his, all sixteen of them.

I appear, thought Tropile crazily, to be a sort of eight-branched snowflake. Each of my branches is a human body.

He stirred, and added another datum. *I appear also to be in a tank of fluid, and yet I do not drown.*

There were certain deductions to be made from that.

Either someone—the Pyramids?—had done something to his lungs, or else the fluid was as good an oxygenating medium as air. Or both.

Suddenly a burst of data-lights twinkled on the board below him. Instantly and involuntarily, his sixteen hands began working the switches, transmitting complex directions in a lightning-like stream of on-off clicks. (Chapter 10)

In *New Maps of Hell* (1960), Kingsley Amis refers to Pohl as "the most consistently able writer science fiction, in the modern sense, has yet produced". He perhaps gets nearer the truth when he calls Pohl "some sort of novelist of economic man". The best of Pohl's early work—a distinctively surrealist best—comes in his collections of short stories with the attractive titles, *Turn Left at Thursday* (1961), *The Man Who Ate the World* (1960), and *Day Million* (1970). His contribution to the field has been enormous—and not least for his editorial skills. Pohl edited *Star, If, Galaxy,* and other magazines, taking over the last-named from Horace Gold, when his sanity proved just as effective as Gold's messianic drives. Pohl reassessed his written work in the mid-seventies and began to produce a series of award-winning novels in an unique personal renaissance. We shall come to that in its place. Suffice it to say here that Pohl is one of those giant figures who have substantially shaped the genre about them, growing as the field grew, from child to man to grandfather of the field.

Another maturing talent in the fifties was that of James Blish, known mainly for his galaxy-spanning series of stories about the Okies in their flying cities.

James Blish's output is considerable, and ranges from rather acid critical articles published in two collections, *The Issue at Hand* and *More Issues at Hand*[9], to contributions to the Star Trek canon with novels like *Spock Must Die!* (1970). Blish is best known, however, for the stories and serials which became *Cities in Flight* (1970)[10], complete with a learned Afterword by Richard D. Mullen, examining the role of Oswald Spengler's philosophical thought in Blish's work.

Cities in Flight is a rather lumpy collection of stories. The four "novels" of which it is basically composed tell a large chunk of future history—to the end of our universe, in fact—in which the discovery of anti-death drugs and the invention of a space drive, the spindizzy, permit mankind to uproot its terrestrial cities and travel about the universe. The original stories appeared in *Astounding* over the decade of the fifties; unlike the galactic adventures written by the rest of Campbell's stable, Blish's are peaceful. The "Okies" travel round the galaxy seeking work, peddling their knowledge.

Knowledge was Blish's passion. He was an irreplaceable mixture of savant, plain hack, and visionary, and it is a case for sorrow that his individual contribution to SF has on the whole been disregarded.

The Frozen Year (1957, also published as *Fallen Star*) was Blish's own favourite among his novels. It was designed to celebrate International Geophysical Year, and falls within the honourable SF tradition of voyages to the poles: in this case the North Pole. The shadow of the Martians falls over the expedition. The expedition's leader, Farnsworth, preserves a pebble in an ice cube. The pebble is a tektite from the region of the asteroid belt, which Farnsworth discovers in the Arctic snows. The stone is formed of sedimentary rock.

The implications of this find resonate throughout the novel. An asteroidal planet existed which must have supported oceans for a considerable period. Therefore it must have had an atmosphere and its climate must have been warmer than that of Mars . . . A later discovery amplifies these theories: there was life on the planet, and it was destroyed by a Martian civilization within the period of mankind's existence on Earth. As Farnsworth says, "Cosmic history in an ice cube!"

This war in Heaven is echoed in many of Blish's other writings. Devils and angels feature prominently. Blish relished archaic systems of thought in conflict with modern scientific belief. This is perhaps most evident in the linked novels, *Black Easter* (1968) and *The Day After Judgement* (1971), both written with an enviable bleakness. The legions of hell are conjured up, the infernal city of Dis rises from below ground in Death Valley. Amid the Boschian spectacle, the Day of Judgement may be listened to on transistor radios. Satan himself walks the Earth and is forced to take over the Throne God has abdicated.

Religion is the subject of Blish's most famous short novel, *A Case of Conscience* (1958). The planet Lithia seems perfect and delightful, the amphibian race dwelling peaceably there appears benevolent and free of sin. But among the terrestrial exploration team which lands on Lithia is Father Ramon Ruiz-Sanchez, who looks beyond appearances. Eventually, he decides that Lithia is a creation of the Devil, designed to seduce Earthmen. A Lithian, Egtverchi, is taken back to Earth, precipitating a moral crisis there. Ruiz-Sanchez is forced eventually to perform an exorcism, with apocalyptic results.

Also worthy of attention are Blish's short stories. Particular favourites are "Surface Tension" (1952), "Common Time" (1953) and "Beep" (1954)—all appearing in what was certainly a vintage period for SF short fiction, though Blish himself was then living in difficult circumstances in a New York undertaker's parlour. "Beep" is about the Dirac transmitter, which provides instantaneous communication throughout the galaxy. It was later extended to form a short novel, *The Quincunx of Time* (1973).

Great popularity eluded Blish, though he never sought it. He seems to be a major writer, and his work repays study. No doubt he will survive to please and puzzle future generations. His life also has interest. He escaped from New York to live in the English countryside, where he died in 1975. His ashes are buried within sight of the University of Oxford.

SF readers, on the whole, thrive on multiple units and gigantic objects like galaxies. These, Blish could provide. He was also a master of the telling detail, without which the gigantic has no meaning. Although he is not always adept at handling human drama, a sense of inhuman drama is never far from his intricate surfaces. This example comes from his favourite novel, *The Frozen Year*:

> My post gave me a direct view of the magnificent photograph, about four by six, which was hanging over Ellen's desk. It looked like a star caught in the act of blowing up—as, in miniature, it was; the photo was an enlargement from a cosmic-ray emulsion-trace, showing a heavy primary nucleus hitting a carbon atom in the emulsion and knocking it to bits, producing a star of fragment-traces and a shower of more than two hundred mesons.
>
> Nobody with any sense of the drama implicit in a photograph like that—a record of the undoing of one of the basic building blocks of the universe, by a bullet that had travelled unknowable millions of years and miles to effect the catastrophe—could have resisted asking for a closer look.

Of all contemporary writers, Blish is most notable for the persistence with which he moved into new areas of exploration. Too many writers pretend to invent futures when they are busily rewriting past SF, with its tattered backdrop of telepathy, FTL drives, galactic conquest, and other shoddy goods; Blish stubbornly chose difficult themes and pursued his own course.[11]

In the early fifties, the SF field—as far as it was known at all—was generally misunderstood and condemned. Pornography got a better press. Yet the truth was, it was reforming itself from within, shuffling off the last of the Gernsback tradition.

Behind the violence of Harrison's writing, the power drives of Bester's, the comic reversals of Sheckley's, the eschatologies of Blish's, the social criticism of Pohl's, one senses the formation of liberal or liberal-minded societies. Harrison's *Make Room! Make Room!* (1966), for instance—later filmed as *Soylent Green*—is a highly credible portrait of an overcrowded New York, the society of which hangs together, not only through dogged police and governmental coercion, but through an unstated acceptance of the social contract by millions of hard-pressed inhabitants; so that, at the end of the book, the *status quo* still holds, the entity survives. (A masterly stroke, and not only because it defies a long-established SF convention that Everything Falls Apart in the Final Chapter.)

Such liberal inclinations represent a rejection, however unconscious, of the old pulps-through-*Astounding* tradition of indulgence in power fantasy.

"Make trade not war," say Blish's Okies, thereby taking a step towards less authoritarian attitudes.

So with *Tiger! Tiger!* (the better title, with its Blakeian reference): "There's got to be more to life than just living," says Bester's Gully Foyle, looking ahead to Moorcock's Jerry Cornelius. "Who are we, any of us, to make a decision for the world?"

This evolution in thinking was more than simply literary. In a world confronted by Hitler and Stalin—and the millions who made their rise to power possible—the old pulp ethos began to seem positively indecent. But something larger may have been involved. Our understanding of human behaviour continues to broaden and deepen, as it has done ever since Darwin's time. Western society is still liberalizing itself, tortuous though the process is (and threatened all the while). We used to hang people for stealing bread; now we pay unemployment benefits. We used to allow children to be used as slave labour; now we are extending the school-leaving age. We used to treat as criminal people who were merely sick. We may have many hang-ups, but socially we are more enlightened than we were at the beginning of the century.

We have painfully begun to understand that the way to reintegrate the rejects of society—whether rejected on grounds of race, poverty, low IQ, or whatever—is to express our concern, not our hatred; to bring them nearer rather than shutting them farther away[12]. As Mary Shelley pointed out a while ago, for it is one of the lessons of *Frankenstein*.

This moral progress comes as a result of scientific developments—a positive thing science does, often forgotten in a time when science's failures claim our attention. Human dignity does not go with an empty stomach, and it is science which feeds more mouths than ever before. The biological and biochemical springs of human action are still being examined; we can only say that they seem to undermine an authoritarian view of government, and equally to make moral judgements of the old kind irrelevant. The double helix of heredity may prove to be the next politico-religious symbol after the swastika.

Because this more understanding or science-based attitude has to fight its way to general acceptance—and has a painfully long way to go—we can expect to find it worked out in novel form, filtered through various aspects by various minds.

So it is. As well as the novels mentioned, which have to be taken as representative of many more, we can see a whole post-war range of fiction in which man's performance in an authoritarian society is examined. The range includes George Orwell's *Animal Farm* (1945), B. F. Skinner's *Walden Two* (1948), Orwell's *1984* (1949), George R. Stewart's *Earth Abides* (1949), Kurt Vonnegut's *Player Piano* (1952), David Karp's *One* (1953), Evelyn Waugh's *Love Among the Ruins* (1953), Pohl and Kornbluth's *The Space Merchants* (1953), Ray Bradbury's *Fahrenheit 451* (1953), and so on, through Anthony Burgess's two sixties novels, *A Clockwork Orange* (1962) and *The Wanting Seed* (1962), and such a novel as James Blish and Norman L. Knight's *A Torrent of Faces* (1967).

All these novels, whatever else they are, treat the predicament of the individual in societies that represent varying degrees of repression. They may be classed as utopias (or anti-utopias), which they undoubtedly are, but behind that classification stands a greater one. From the slogan "All animals are equal" down to F. Alexander's remark to Your Humble Narrator, in *Clockwork Orange*, "A man who cannot choose ceases to be a man", the authors are searching for a definition of man that will stand in the terrifying light of twentieth-century knowledge.

In this uncertain currency of the intellect, the SF writers are the unacknowledged bankers of the Western world. And it may be that their persistence in
drawing almost characterless central figures is no weakness of technique but
rather, as it were, a blank cheque, written against each reader's account of
himself.

To this debate, George Orwell (1903–50) brought little that strikes us as
startingly new. His *1984*, published in the year before his death, was an
immediate success; its fame waned and then peaked, understandably, in 1984
(real time). As Michael Radford's 1984 film cleverly showed, the novel
embodied all too effectively the depression prevalent in England and Europe at
the time of its composition, as an aftermath of war. Indeed, to re-read *1984* now
is to be struck with the truth of its psychic trace of British civilian life in World
War II, with the shifting populations, miserable housing, loosely packed
cigarettes, rationing, and the endless security restrictions—including those
alarming posters which said HITLER IS LISTENING.

Orwell's *1984* has also been under suspicion as a pastiche of the formidable
Russian anti-utopia, Yevgeny Zamyatin's *We*.[13] Although *We* was not published in Britain until 1970, it was written in 1920, published in English
translation in the United States in 1924, and done in various European languages
before Zamyatin died in exile in Paris in 1937. It seems very likely that Orwell—
and indeed Huxley before him—may have picked up a copy of *We* in France.

Be that as it may, the whole Orwellian paraphernalia of one man against a
super-state was not new. In particular, it was not new within the pages of SF
magazines.

It is entirely on the cards that Orwell, with his love of the outlawed in
literature, read a lot of science fiction.[14] His *1984* reads rather like a lobotomized
van Vogt, with its Newspeak standing in for van Vogt's General Semantics.
The thought police and the whole psychotic plot of the solitary good guy
against the universe is pure van Vogt, the twist in the tail being that in Orwell's
case the universe, represented by Big Brother, wins. Perhaps Winston Smith's
attempts to unravel the past reflect some past Orwellian attempt to unravel *The
World of Null-A*. If so, we feel a great deal of sympathy for him.

To say this is partly to poke fun at the legions of learned commentators who
find *1984* a nest of stolen ideas. For the novel possesses two cardinal virtues, one
intellectual and one emotional, which, taken together, make an original
contribution to the debate.

Firstly, Orwell states that the object of the party in power is to hold power.
His party holds power and glories in it; hence that memorable line, "If you want
a picture of the future, think of a boot stamping on the human face—for ever."
Unlike his predecessors—unlike even Wells, forever on his way up—Orwell
identified strongly with the lower classes, even when he found them repulsive[15];
and from this viewpoint, he saw lucidly that those who are down are kept
down. It is this perception which makes *Brave New World* seem namby-pamby;
for Huxley, secure in the upper classes, never thinks to give us a sight of the
whip.

The emotional virtue of *1984* is that Orwell's utopian desires are so much more human than those of his greater predecessors, of Plato, More and the others. His recipe for a good life is tender and fallen: something to eat, no nosey neighbours, a bit of comfort, and a girl to take to bed.[16]

Orwell succeeded in uniting intellectual and emotional. He shows what happens when power is all-powerful and what is human in man is eradicated in consequence:

> "What have you done with Julia?" said Winston . . . "You tortured her."
>
> O'Brien left this unanswered. "Next question," he said.
>
> "Does Big Brother exist?"
>
> "Of course he exists. The Party exists. Big Brother is the embodiment of the Party."
>
> "Does he exist in the same way as I exist?"
>
> "You do not exist," said O'Brien. (Part 3, Chapter 2).

Power obliterates character.[17]

An ability to unite intellectual and emotional is by no means simple. We would not want to suggest *1984* is a simple book. To whom is its warning directed? To the voters? If so, then it is an anti-prophetic book, in that the less this fictional world becomes reality—even after the test date—the better Orwell will have succeeded in his purpose. Against such an argument lies the fact that there are still totalitarian states in our world, and that Orwell's message is as accessible to right as to left on the political spectrum—as the British government proved in its 1983 General Election campaign.[18] Whatever Orwell's intentions may have been, there are wider aspects of the novel, which are beautifully brought out by Richard Rees in his book on Orwell, when he says:

> The core of Orwell's message in *1984*, stripped of Winston's tragedy and all the sadism, is simply that our industrial machine civilization is tending to deracinate and debilitate us, and will finally destroy us; and the consensus of opinion on this point among thinkers as diverse as Orwell, Huxley, Gandhi, Simone Weil, and D. H. Lawrence, to say nothing of the many others, such as Eliot and Koestler, who would go at least part way with them, is striking and depressing. All the more so because no one seriously believes that the rhythm of industrialization and mechanization could be relaxed or indeed that it can possibly fail to go on accelerating (unless interrupted by war) until the whole population of the world has been incorporated into the mass-civilization.[19]

Many of the more thinking science fiction writers found themselves stuck with this problem many years ago.[20]

Orwell's *Animal Farm* was published in 1945. It is a beautiful and brief book—of all the books mentioned in this volume, possibly the one most likely to get first to Pluto, tucked in microfiche edition in some visiting astronaut's pocket: a book with survival value.

Perhaps its meaning is little different from *1984*'s, but its impact is considerably different, and the story of the animals managing their own farm seems likely to live on to entertain future innocents, just as we enjoy Gulliver's troubles in Lilliput without bothering about the references to Queen Anne's court. Orwell's *1984* is much more time-bound.[21]

Clearly, *Animal Farm* is not science fiction in any accepted sense, despite a debt to *The Island of Doctor Moreau*. Equally clearly, it is one of those charming cases, such as *Alice*, which have intense appeal for anyone with that sort of mind. All animals are equal, but Orwell's animals are more equal than others.

Before World War II, such popular novels as were some kind of kissing kin with SF were mainly fantasy. The prime example is James Hilton's *Lost Horizon* (the last of the small-time Rider Haggards?), which made a smashing film with Ronald Colman in, and a dire musical (in 1972) with Charles Boyer.

In the long period after the war, we can point to a wide range of novels which have been just as popular and more serious in character, and nearer to many of the interests of SF.

One plunges into the list almost at random, but an interesting tally it makes, including Nigel Balchin's *The Small Back Room*; Nevil Shute's *No Highway*, *On the Beach* and *In the Wet*; C. P. Snow's *The New Men*; John Bowen's *After the Rain*; Constantine Fitzgibbon's *When the Kissing Had to Stop*; L. P. Hartley's *Facial Justice*; Kingsley Amis's *The Anti-Death League*, and his impressive later novel *The Green Man* (which contains a marvellous encounter with God); Michael Frayn's *The Tin Men*; all the near-future political thrillers of the *Fail Safe* category; Angus Wilson's *The Old Men at the Zoo*; the two Anthony Burgess novels already mentioned; some of J. B. Priestley's novels; William Burroughs's extraordinary fractured novels, such as *The Ticket That Exploded*; Lawrence Durrell's *Alexandria Quartet*, and his *Tunc* and *Nunquam*; Nabokov's dazzling *Ada*; the stories of Donald Barthelme; John Barth's *Giles Goat-Boy*; Iain Banks's *The Bridge*; Christine Brooke-Rose's *Xorandor*; the puzzles of Jorge Luis Borges; the extraordinary creations of Samuel Beckett; Gore Vidal's novels *Messiah*, *Kalki* and *Duluth*; Robert Coover's remarkable *The Public Burning*; Richard Adams's bestselling *Watership Down* and *Shardik*; *Duncton Wood* by William Horwood; *Waiting for the Barbarians* by Booker Prize-winning J. M. Coetzee; Denis Johnson's much-lauded *Fiskadoro*; and—most particularly— William Golding's novels, *Lord of the Flies* and *The Inheritors*, with its evocation of lost things . . . There one must halt, since one must halt somewhere. But what an impressive array of novels! All of them look towards a definition of man and his status. All of them approach the science fiction condition; just as, on its own side of the fence, science fiction approaches the modern novel.

Such a rapprochement is probably due as much as anything to a change in emotional climate. On the one side, the evolution of McLuhan's global village has involved increasing numbers of people in a forward-directed world outlook which features SF. On the other side, the same cultural effect has meant that SF writers have become more involved with the world, less content with the old artificial patterns of SF adventure.

Of course, SF adventure, redskins among the stars, will always survive. No medium is better equipped to deliver heart-wrenching surprises, desperate odds, and formidable mysteries—the whole Gothic package—than science fantasy. And, in the fifties, numerous practitioners rose to fame who specialized in such adventure, among them such prolific writers as Poul Anderson, Robert Silverberg, and John Brunner, all of whom sprouted pseudonyms. But there were signs elsewhere of diversification.

Ray Bradbury was the first to take all the props of SF and employ them as highly individual tools of expression for his own somewhat Teddy-bearish view of the universe. On the whole, the props of SF are few: rocket ships, telepathy, robots, time travel, other dimensions, huge machines, aliens, future wars. Like coins, they become debased by over-circulation (though it is true that some of them, adroitly used, acquire *baraka* by long association). This is crucial to an understanding of the seventies and eighties, but in the fifties, with many new outlets for SF, writers combined and recombined these standard elements with a truly Byzantine ingenuity—indeed, to *aficionados*, this permutational aspect becomes one of SF's chief attractions—but there were signs even then that limits were being reached. By the sixties, the signs could not be ignored.

Those who became successful in the fifties refurbished the worn props. Either, like Bradbury and Clarke, by using them with fresh insight; or, like Heinlein and Frank Herbert, by expanding the field of vision and using the props together with exotic elements. Philip K. Dick and Kurt Vonnegut, who belong to a future chapter, make the props subservient to their own brands of existential wit.

It was the first writer to recombine the old props in his own way who won the greatest fame. Ray Bradbury's flamboyant rocket ships took him into a high literary orbit. It couldn't, as they say, have happened to a nicer guy.

> One minute it was Ohio winter, with doors closed, windows locked, the panes blinded with frost, icicles fringing every roof, children skiing on slopes, housewives lumbering like great black bears in their furs along the icy street.
>
> And then a long wave of warmth crossed the small town. A flooding sea of hot air; it seemed as if someone had left a bakery door open. The heat pulsed among the cottages and bushes and children. The icicles dropped, shattering, to melt. The doors flew open. The windows flew up. The children worked off their wool clothes. The housewives shed their bear disguises. The snow dissolved and showed last summer's ancient green lawns.
>
> *Rocket summer.* The words passed among the people in the open, airing houses. Rocket summer. . . .

The first words, of course, of Bradbury's *Martian Chronicles* (1951, also published as *The Silver Locusts*). That was way back in the earliest of the fifties. How delicate and nice it is, and what an extraordinary poetical idea, that rocket exhausts could change climates! Well, they changed political climates and helped to defreeze the Cold War, so perhaps a prophetic symbolism may be detected.

And these tender, telling stories appeared first in the scorned *Thrilling Wonder*, edited by Sam Merwin, and *Planet Stories*.

What one did not realize at the time was that Bradbury dealt best with a prepubertal world, and that his stories read like translations of Ukranian folk tales. He seemed like a magician.

The Illustrated Man! The Golden Apples of the Sun! Fahrenheit 451! The October Country! How enchanting those early books were at the time, how we needed them.

They are perfect in their way, and their way is the way of *Wind in the Willows*. They belong to an imaginary American past where every town had wooden sidewalks, every house a verandah with a rocking chair, and every attic a dear old Grandma fading out under the rose-blossom wallpaper. In this milieu, rockets are just quaint novelties, like early Fords, Hudsons, and Packards. There are also sharp social comments, such as "The Pedestrian", about a man arrested for that un-American activity, walking.

Bradbury is of the house of Poe. The sickness of which he writes takes the form of glowing rosy-cheeked health. It is when he makes functional use of this, contrasting sickness and health in one story, that he is at his most persuasive. For instance, in "The Third Expedition", in *The Martian Chronicles*.

Here, an Earth rocket lands on Mars and finds that it is like Earth long ago when the rocket crew were children. There are cute old Victorian houses, and houses of red brick, and church steeples with golden bells. And plenty of trees and green grass. The inhabitants of the town prove to be all the characters you knew and (since this is Bradbury's reality) loved as a kid, particularly Grandma and Grandpa, and Mom, pink, plump, and bright, and Dad, all set in a context of victrolas playing and turkey dinners being eaten.

Then Captain Black has to go upstairs to sleep in the old brass bed with his brother, who has golden shoulders, and the mood changes. Black grows very frightened when the lights go down, and suddenly realizes that the whole setup is a terrible and evil alien trick.

> And suppose those two people in the next room, asleep, are not my mother and father at all. But two Martians, incredibly brilliant, with the ability to keep me under this dreaming hypnosis all of the time.

He never makes it to the bedroom door. His brother gets him.

Christopher Isherwood came along and announced that Bradbury was a poet. His name became famous overnight, and he has remained one of our eminent dreamers ever since, the Hans Christian Andersen of the jet age, a king on a bicycle.

Arthur C. Clarke is another dreamer to make good into the starry empyrean beyond the SF field. His escape velocity has been fuelled by reserves of technical knowledge, and his career resembles in many ways the schoolboy dream of success. It has been said, unfairly, that Bradbury's science fiction is for those who do not like SF; but no such monstrous charge can be levelled at Clarke's writing. More than any other SF author, Clarke has been faithful to a boyhood vision of science as saviour of mankind, and of mankind as a race of potential gods destined for the stars. If Stapledon has successors, Clarke is the foremost. Egotistical in many ways, he has throughout his career remained humblingly true to that early faith, and to science fiction as the literature of the gods.

His literary abilities are traditional, and his prose often workaday. But he rises to a certain strength when he manages to unite the thinking and dreaming poles of his nature (to amalgamate the Wellsian and Burroughsian as it were). This he achieves in several masterly short stories—especially in "The Nine Billion Names of God", justifiably famous—and in two novels, *The City and the Stars* (1956) and *Childhood's End* (1953). In the latter especially, a rather banal philosophical idea (that mankind may evolve into a greater being, an Overmind) is expressed in simple but aspiring language that vaguely recalls the Psalms, even down to the liberal use of colons; when this is combined with a dramatized sense of loss, Clarke's predominant emotion, the result has undeniable effect.

This passage is from the end of *Childhood's End*, when Karellen, a member of a menial alien race, has seen Man vanish from Earth, and prepares to return to his own distant planet:

> For all their achievements, thought Karellen, for all their mastery of the physical universe, his people were no better than a tribe that had passed its whole existence upon some flat and dusty plain. Far off were the mountains, where power and beauty dwelt, where the thunder sported above the glaciers and the air was clear and keen. There the sun still walked, transfiguring the peaks with glory, when all the land below was wrapped in darkness. And they could only watch and wonder: they could never scale those heights.
>
> Yet, Karellen knew, they would hold fast until the end: they would await without despair whatever destiny was theirs. They would serve the Overmind because they had no choice, but even in that service they would not lose their souls.
>
> The great control screen flared for a moment with sombre, ruby light: without conscious effort, Karellen read the message of its changing patterns. The ship was leaving the frontiers of the Solar System: the energies that powered the Stardrive were ebbing fast, but they had done their work.

Arthur Clarke's success story lies in the main beyond the scope of a mere literary critic. His early theoretical work on earth satellites in the mid-forties made him almost as much a part of the space race as Cape Canaveral itself. He is also celebrated as co-author of the Stanley Kubrick film, *2001*, one of the great cult successes of its day.[22] In the mid-seventies he was to return to SF writing with a number of impressive works. We shall come to them in their place.

Every few years, a great submerged theme moves through science fiction like a ground swell. There are always cross-currents, but, with insight or hindsight, we may catch the main drift. In the sixties, this ground swell was to move towards environmental topics. To elaborate, the most important work done tended to direct itself towards new socio-scientific attitudes, towards the complex factors involved in the technological culture's slow debasement of man and his natural world. This found its expression in many of the writings we shall deal with in the sixties, which characteristically dramatized affairs on this overpopulated world rather than any other, or with the role of malfunctioning or discontented individuals—what we shall term Life-Style SF.

Moreover, we believe that this sixties ground swell, which points the way to a general public concern in the seventies with these same issues, had its inevitable precedents in the SF of the fifties, in its most characteristic mood. The fifties ground swell might be called Fear of Dehumanization in the Face of the Stars.

Depersonalization was not a new fear. What was new was the characteristic science fictional form of expression it now achieved. And since it never achieved perfection of expression (or not on more than miniature scale), it came and passed, and has hitherto been unremarked.

Because the theme never crystallized, it remains somewhat surrounded by similar material. Nevertheless, its crest emerges clearly in 1953.

Robots can embody depersonalization fears. This is perhaps their most obvious psychological function. They then stand for man's anxieties about surviving the pressures of modern society, as in *R.U.R.* Since then, SF has taken the matter further and used symbols less accessible than robots to express anxieties about the blow to the psyche experienced by achieving space travel and confronting other worlds; or, to phrase it another way, the culture shock of the alien.

There were several SF precedents before 1953: John W. Campbell's "Who Goes There?", as far back as 1938[23], Eric Frank Russell's "Metamorphosite" in 1946 (a curious story with a frighteningly beautiful symbol of flowering nuclear power), and van Vogt's "The Sound" in 1950, provide three examples.

Then in 1952 came Alan Nourse's "Counterfeit", and there the theme was, almost full-grown. Friend indistinguishable from enemy.

"Counterfeit" appeared in *Thrilling Wonder*, and was necessarily melodramatic, but it made its point. A spaceship is returning to Earth from Venus. Aboard are men and an alien posing as a man, almost indetectable, right down to cellular level (Nourse was a doctor, and made the details convincing). The alien can imitate a human being to perfection. Dr Crawford detects one of them and kills the "man", whereupon it dwindles down into a little red blob.

But there is more than one alien aboard. The ship returns to Earth, the crew depart, and Crawford goes back to the ship on his own. He hears something. Another alien is there. He comes face to face with it. He is glaring at himself! The alien kills him, and heads into the city.

A perfect fable of dehumanization in the face of the stars.

In 1953, one finds several versions of the same fable, among them another tale by Nourse, "Nightmare Brother".

In Nourse's "Nightmare Brother", a man is being trained on Earth to confront the horrors on alien planets. These horrors are never described. All we know is that, as in the previous Nourse story, nothing is what it seems. The horrors can twist men's minds, inflicting illusions on them that may prove fatal.

Even the training is almost too much for Cox, Nourse's hero. His girl pleads for him.

"It may kill him! You're asking too much, he's not a superman, he's just an ordinary, helpless human being like anyone else. He doesn't have any magical powers."

And this was in *Astounding*, where magical powers had been the order of the day. Faced with the test case of actual space flight, the mask of pulp fantasy was slipping.

Cox learns to master the alien threat, but not all the characters facing similar peril in 1953 were as fortunate. For instance, the heroes of two Philip K. Dick variants, "Impostor" and "Colony"—in the first of which a man discovers he is an android manufactured on an alien world—a robot moreover, with a bomb in his chest! In the second, the engulfing alien takes on the form of a spaceship, into which the humans meekly troop, thinking to return to Earth.

James Gunn's "Breaking Point" appeared in Lester del Rey's short-lived but excellent *Space Science Fiction*. Here, the spaceship crew are subjected to intolerable mental forces, again expressed as hallucinations, by the aliens outside. Fear was the keynote. Curiosity rather than fear informs Damon Knight's "Four in One", in which Nourse's horrendous blob, now lying inert on Knight's planet, is big enough to absorb several rash Earthlings. The idea was used humorously twice by Sheckley, also in 1953, in "Diplomatic Immunity" and "Keep Your Shape". Always the alien took over, always he had an unfair advantage. The great powers enjoyed by Earthmen in the previous decade's fiction were now possessed solely by his enemies.

In the next year, the theme of dehumanization is already on the wane. But two good examples appear in *Galaxy*. Fred Pohl's "The Tunnel Under the World", where the man up against the inexplicable happenings discovers he is just a table-top robot, is the only one of this group of stories in which a menace from space is not involved. This is a Pohl story—the menace is Advertising. William Tenn's "Down Among the Dead Men" is the most gruesome of all. In Earth's battle against insect invaders from space, we are running short of men. But bits of bodies can be patched together and revived by new techniques.[24] The trouble is, the zombies smell a bit, which is unpleasant for the live men who lead them into battle . . . Dehumanization in the face of the stars can't go much further than this.[25]

Which is presumably why this theme now peters out in this particular form, re-surfacing a few years later in 1955 on celluloid, as *Invasion of the Body Snatchers*. Note that it is an essentially American form, possibly one culmination of the Injun-among-the-Stars obsession.[26]

In the nature of things, no theme becomes extinct in SF.[27] The aliens-turning-into-anything straggle on, for instance in Fredric Brown's *The Mind Thing*

(1961) and John Brunner's *Double Double* (1969), but by then the heat was off. However, back comes the theme in full creative force—i.e., transformed—in Stanislaw Lem's *Solaris* (English translation 1970, but first published in Polish in 1961), where his world-ocean can create human analogues which invade the satellite station. The Russian film *Solaris* (1972) very successfully re-creates the novel in cinematic terms. [28]

This Dehumanization in the Face of the Stars theme might be seen as one of the psychic birth pangs of the Space Age, a prodromus of the new stresses with which Russian and American space missions have faced society. The theme also functions within science fiction to prepare us for a movement away from the stars and towards Earth, which became the dominant theme of the most vital SF of the sixties.

The fears expressed in the fifties have led also to a much less glib readiness to pose and solve a major problem, once a characteristic of magazine SF. Or maybe life's just become trickier; as the problem of ending the Vietnam War demonstrated. (And in Vietnam, as on Procyon VI, it was hard to distinguish friend from foe. . . .)

Some of those elements that lead us to the present may be traced through the career of one writer who came to prominence in the fifties; a career which accurately graphs the state of SF (and the world) during its transitional phase.

The writer is John Wyndham. He changed his name and tune more than once. He went through several larval stages before emerging as a resplendent butterfly.

Wyndham had plenty of given names, all of which were utilized at one stage or another of his development. His full name was John Wyndham Parkes Lucas Beynon Harris, and he was born in 1903 in the Warwickshire countryside. His most famous novels would carry memories of the country, either wrecked or triumphing.

He started selling science fiction to the American SF magazines in the thirties under the name of John Beynon Harris, and became very popular. His manner was light and amused; he wrote about space flight but, one feels, without any burning faith in the possibility of its becoming reality. In "Exiles on Asperus" (1933), Earthmen are enslaved by the batlike inhabitants of an asteroid and grow to love their chains.

In 1935, a popular British family magazine called *The Passing Show* ran a serial in the summer months to catch the seaside trade. It was illustrated by a remarkable artist, Fortunino Matania, who had already done a sexy job on two of Edgar Rice Burroughs's *Venus* novels for the same magazine. *The Secret People* was by one John Beynon. Harris had dropped his "Harris".

The French, with Italian cooperation, have flooded part of the Sahara to create a huge new sea in an attempt to bring fertility to the barren land about its shores. Hero and heroine in plane crash into sea and are drawn by a swift-flowing current into vast subterranean caves. There they fall into the hands of a race of subterranean pigmies (the last of the British submerged nations?). They escape at the end of the story, bearing with them the pigmy secret of "cold light". The pigmies are all drowned when sea floods their caves. *The Secret People* was evidently popular with its audience; it had few unfamiliar elements in it to disturb them. It was published as a hard-cover book in the same year.

The Passing Show later serialized *Stowaway to Mars*, which also appeared in hard-cover (originally as *Planet Plane*). Both books were published in paperback later, and reprinted regularly. Wyndham was established as a success, although his literary talents had not revealed themselves as more than modest.

Other men who wrote science fiction in the mid- and late-thirties have since been almost forgotten. But they did not seek magazine publication, and their novels had more literary style.

R. C. Sherriff's *The Hopkins Manuscript* (1939) is now a period piece. Sherriff is the author of *Journey's End*. *The Hopkins Manuscript* is a cosy catastrophe, much in the style that Wyndham was to adopt two decades later. It reads now as a gorgeous parody of all things British and thirties-ish.

The hero, Hopkins, is in his fifties, has a Cambridge education, and comes of an old and honourable family. He breeds poultry. In true Edwardian style, he lives alone with his housekeeper in a large and comfortable house. When the Moon comes crashing down to Earth, says Hopkins, ". . . after careful reflection I decided to meet the crisis in the dining-room". He takes down the china ornaments and stacks them in cupboards.

The Moon splashes down in the Atlantic, raising the sea level, and bringing certain unpleasant problems with it.

> And how were we to live if, as I imagined, the whole fabric of civilization had collapsed? No butter, no milk, no bread, no meat? . . . The grim, unanswerable problems paraded before me in the dawn like spectres: no electric light—no sanitary services—no pure water . . .
>
> I missed the morning paper, too; I missed the dawn song of birds in the spring. And even the cheerful whistling of the milkman . . . (Chapter 22).

Rich mineral deposits are found on the Moon. War breaks out among the European powers. Hopkins, in desperation, goes to live in Notting Hill. His manuscript is presented as being found a thousand years later, by members of the Eastern races who invaded and conquered a divided Europe.

The divided Europe idea very soon became reality. War broke out, and eventually John Wyndham—like more than one British science fiction writer— found himself in the Royal Corps of Signals. He took part in the Normandy landings. After the war, when the fruits of victory were rapidly turning into the ashes of peace, he was without career or direction.

It was then that he embarked on the course that was to make him master of the cosy catastrophe. *The Day of the Triffids*, by John Wyndham, was serialized in *Collier's*, and appeared in hard-cover in England in 1951. Its success was immediate and prolonged, to nobody's surprise more than the modest Wyndham, who was having a sherry in a pub one day when he overheard two gardeners discussing their weeds over a pint of beer; one said, "There's one by my tool shed—a great monster. I reckon it's a triffid!" The word had entered the language, as unobtrusively as Heinlein's waldoes.

The triffids are huge perambulating vegetables with poisonous flails, who arrive on the scene just as everyone but the hero has been blinded by unusual meteors. Rarely has there been a less promising start to a story. Yet there is magic in *The Day of the Triffids*, and in the excitement of the hero and his girl moving through a collapsing London. It may be reminiscent of Conan Doyle's Poison Belt, but here everything goes to pot with no possibility of a subsequent cleaning up. The map has been irrevocably changed.

It changed again in 1953, when the krakens succeeded the triffids. *The Kraken Wakes* (plonkingly called *Out of the Deeps* in the United States) has the world invaded by things which settle in the ocean and melt the icecaps to give themselves more *lebensraum*. Motorboats in Oxford Street. Like the earlier novel, *Kraken* was an immense success, and adapted for radio—although it never made a (disastrous) motion picture like *Triffids*. Both novels were totally devoid of ideas but read smoothly, and thus reached a maximum audience, who enjoyed cosy disasters. Either it was something to do with the collapse of the British Empire, or the back-to-nature movement, or a general feeling that industrialization had gone too far, or all three. By contrast, "Consider Her Ways" (1956) and *Trouble with Lichen* (1960) are rich in speculation.

Wyndham's popularity continued. Short stories poured out, all urbane and pleasing. More novels appeared, one of which, *The Midwich Cuckoos* (1957), was later made into a very effective movie, *Village of the Damned*.[29] His best novel is *The Chrysalids* (1955, retitled *Re-birth* in the United States). *The Chrysalids* is set in a New England environment after nuclear war, when the fathers of the community sternly wipe out any mutated children. Not an original theme, but the characters and settings are beautifully realized. Much less successful was *The Outward Urge* (1959) by John Wyndham and Lucas Parkes—Lucas Parkes being more components of Wyndham's name. Wyndham died in 1969.

Many heroes besides Sherriff's decided to meet the crisis in the dining room, so to speak. The essence of cosy catastrophe is that the hero should have a pretty good time (a girl, free suites at the Savoy, automobiles for the taking) while everyone else is dying off. The best and most memorable example of this sub-genre is American: George Stewart's *Earth Abides*[30]; but it was the British writers—less preoccupied with aliens than their American counterparts—who specialized in Wyndhamesque comeuppances.

Among the afflictions visited on Earth by British writers are snow (John Boland's *White August* (1955)); gales (J. G. Ballard's *The Wind from Nowhere* (1962)); insanity (Dighton Morel's *Moonlight Red* (1960)); plague (John Blackburn's *A Scent of New-Mown Hay* (1958)); disappearing oceans (Charles Eric Maine's *The Tide Went Out* (1958)); super-beasts (J. T. McIntosh's *The Fittest* (1955)) and, more recently, mycelia (Harry Adam Knight's *The Fungus* (1985)).

Such novels are anxiety fantasies. They shade off towards the greater immediacy of World War III novels, a specialist branch of catastrophe more usually practised by American writers. Perhaps the extreme example here is Poul Anderson's *After Doomsday* (1962), which opens with the Earth already destroyed.

Master of the semi-cosy was John Christopher, whose name is often linked with Wyndham's, perhaps unfairly.

With Christopher, the catastrophe loses its cosiness and takes on an edge of terror. Though the terror is underplayed in his best novel, *The Death of Grass* (1956), in which a mutated virus attacks all grains and grasses, there is sound writing strategy in the way that a central character, Roger, operates less than well in the crisis which overtakes the world, and falls under the shadow of his friend, John, while both become almost subsidiary to Pirrie, a memorably formidable operator the others meet in a gunshop. The novel shows a grasp of political as well as psychological possibilities.

Christopher had already shown his mettle with a frolicsome intellectual novel, *The Year of the Comet* (1955). Under his own name, Sam Youd, and many pen names, he poured forth a stream of lucid and successful novels. After his great popular success, *Death of Grass*, his catastrophes grow increasingly dark and uncosy. Perhaps the best of these is *The World in Winter* (1962). *Pendulum* (1968), with the brutish young taking over, is merely painful. There is also the anti-cosy aliens-will-get-you shocker, *The Possessors* (1965), set in a decidedly chilly Switzerland.

Christopher has made a new reputation with his childrens' books, particularly after two TV series based on his trilogy, *The Tripods*. An intelligent and witty man, John Christopher seemed poised at one time to become the country's leading SF writer. But the race is not always to the swift, etc. etc.

Perhaps time was running against Christopher and Wyndham; for the catastrophe novel presupposes that one starts from some kind of established order, and the feeling grew—particularly in the mid-sixties—that even established orders were of the past.

Before we proceed to discuss the milestones cast by Tolkien, Peake, Heinlein, Miller, and Asimov, at least a mention must be given to the swarming talents of the fifties, all of whom have their followers, and whose stories still give pleasure.

Among them most assuredly are some of the senior writers of the field, active earlier and still active. Such as L. Sprague de Camp, a scholar whose main work is in fantasy.[31] Many recall with pleasure his Viagens Interplanetarias series, in which Brazil is top dog in the twenty-second century—an unlikely but not *too* unlikely conjecture. Charles Beaumont, great fun writer who merged horror and SF in equal measure, died in the old age of his youth, and is remembered for his collection, *The Hunger* (1957). Algis Budrys, once a power in the land, author of two fine novels, *Rogue Moon* (1960) and *Who?* (1958—and subsequently filmed in 1974). These days Budrys is the regular book reviewer for *F&SF* and trumpeter for L. Ron Hubbard. Kenneth Bulmer, stalwart of the Carnell magazines in the UK, who took over the long-running *New Writings in*

SF anthology series for the last few years of its existence in the seventies. His Dray Prescot series is in itself enough for any one writer.

Colonel Theodore Cogswell's "The Wall Around the World" is still being reprinted—one of the few convincing SF stories about workable magic. The pseudonymous Robert Crane's *Hero's Walk* (1954) enjoyed a vogue. David Duncan's novels had much to recommend them—*Another Tree in Eden* (1955); *Dark Dominion* (1954), with its strange new metal attracted to Jupiter; *Occam's Razor* (1957), with the great line, "Gentlemen, we are about to short-circuit the universe!" Jack Finney conveys a gentle and fantastic nostalgia; his *The Body Snatchers* (1955) was the basis of the Don Siegel film. Daniel Galouye, a follower of Heinlein's, found his most individual voice in a striking novel, *Counterfeit World* (1964, also as *Simulacron-3*), and is also remembered fondly for an ingenious post-nuclear holocaust story set underground, *Dark Universe* (1961).

James Gunn is a rare writer, who thrives in both the academic climate and the ragged-bannered world of commercial writing. His two early novels, *The Joy Makers* (1961) and *The Immortals* (1962) are evidence of a strong talent at work on important themes: how far mankind should pursue happiness and what the ethics are of enjoying near-immortality at the expense of others. Both suffered from a difficulty more widespread at that period than today: the problem of structuring a coherent novel from disparately published short stories and novellas on a common theme. Gunn's later novels include *The Burning* (1972), in which a scientist is hounded from his university during a general revolt against science, and *Kampus* (1975), in which several universities go up in flames. Gunn may be reckoned to know something of this subject matter, since he has been teaching English and SF at the University of Kansas since 1970.

Professor Gunn's good works include the four-volume teaching anthology, *The Road to Science Fiction* (1977–82) and an impressive album-chronicle on the field, *Alternate Worlds: The Illustrated History of Science Fiction* (1975), a lavishly illustrated account. Gunn sees science fiction as "the long journey . . . from Homer to Hamilton, Heinlein, Herbert, and Harlan".

Another author whose early novels pleased, but who has sunk somewhat from general recognition in pursuit of academic duty, is Chad Oliver. He began to teach anthropology at the University of Texas in 1955, and is now a professor there. *Shadows in the Sun* (1954) made good use of his learning; it vividly portrays a small Texas town where everything is so absolutely normal that visiting anthropologist Paul Ellery becomes suspicious—and finds that aliens have taken it over. *The Shores of Another Sea* (1971) also deals with an alien visitation of Earth. This time, the aliens take over the bodies of baboons. Professor Oliver treats his aliens sympathetically, rather in the manner of Simak.

Too little has also been heard of Daniel Keyes. His short story, "Flowers for Algernon" was an immediate and deserved success when it appeared in *F&SF* in 1959.[32] It tells of a near-moron (IQ 68), Charly Gordon, who is the subject of an intelligence-raising experiment. He is elevated to the intellectual level of a genius. Later, he has to suffer the deterioration of his new powers, knowing what he is losing. His pathetic friendship with a mouse is perhaps designed to recall the touching character, Lemmy, in Steinbeck's *Of Mice and Men*. This moving story lost something of its power when expanded to novel length.

Disappeared from view is J. T. McIntosh, once the hope of Scottish SF, who scored early success with *One in Three Hundred* (1954—the time when US and British SF were less far divorced). Charles Eric Maine was for some while a popular and prolific author, with a strong line in sensationalism. His best novel is perhaps the scary plague story, *The Darkest of Nights* (1962, also as *Survival Margin*). Maine is also remembered for *The Mind of Mr Soames* (1961), elegantly filmed in 1969 with Terence Stamp in the role of the thirty-one year old baby. Others of Maine's novels to be filmed include *Spaceways* (1953) and *Countdown* (1968).

The name of Richard Matheson has long been associated with Hollywood, to which lucrative Mecca he went to script his novel, *The Shrinking Man* (1956), into the successful film version, *The Incredible Shrinking Man* (1957). His novel *I Am Legend* (1954), the vampire story, has twice been filmed, with various degrees of implausibility. Matheson's early writing has something in common with Poe, in its love of the morbid, and he worked as a scriptwriter on three of Roger Corman's Poe films in the early sixties, *The House of Usher* among them. Later, he wrote the script for the Steven Spielberg TV movie, *Duel* (1971), that memorable piece of work. His debut, "Born of Man and Woman", was considered outrageous when it appeared in a magazine in 1950. The title was later used for Matheson's first story collection in 1954. A recurrent darkness and violence was entirely missing from the fantasy novel, *Bid Time Return* (1975), a romantic story of a man who travels back in time to meet an actress he loves.

Many other writers should be mentioned. Ward Moore's name lives on because of two novels, the satirical *Greener Than You Think* (1947), a great success in its time, and a classic alternative world story, *Bring the Jubilee* (1953), in which the hero lives in an America where the South won the Battle of Gettysberg; his interference in the battle, to which he time-travels, causes the North to win. So matters turn out as we know them today. The wit and ingenuity of this story influenced more recent excursions into alternative history such as Harry Harrison's *A Transatlantic Tunnel, Hurrah!*

Kris Neville was a satirical man who wrote too little; his *Bettyann* (1970) collects together stories about a little orphaned alien girl written in the fifties. Murray Leinster was an old-timer who wrote, dare one say, too much. His first story appeared in 1919 ("The Runaway Skyscraper"). His most popular story is probably "First Contact", in a 1945 *Astounding*. Many novels followed, many stories. Some of the later, about adventures on distant planets, were collected in *Colonial Survey* (1957—also published as *Planet Explorer*).

Some writers abandon SF for other genres, and thrive there. Alfred Coppel published in the pulps. "The Rebel of Valkyr" (1950) is a good swashbuckling example of his writing. Later, Coppel expanded the story into a trilogy. *The Rebel of Rhada* (1968), *The Navigator of Rhada* (1969), and *The Starkhan of Rhada* (1970) were published under the name of Robert Cham Gilman. Coppel made a different reputation with a near-future thriller, *The Dragon* (1977). Also appearing under the Coppel name is his latest novel, *The Fates Command Us* (1986), an historical novel of ample dimension set in Northern Spain.

Alan Nourse brings a doctor's understanding to his fiction; that fiction includes a bundle of striking stories, already mentioned, as well as several novels. Fletcher Pratt, historian of the American Revolution, preferred writing fantasy. His death in 1956 ended a long career in the magazines. Frank Robinson's exciting novel, *The Power* (1956), was filmed by George Pal and Byron Haskin in 1967—perhaps Pal's best film. James H. Schmitz, an *Astounding/Analog* regular, wrote one of the best exo-ecology stories, "Grandpa". Wilson Tucker was a great fan, the author of several excellent novels, among them *The Long Loud Silence* (1952, revised 1970) and the one with the beautiful title, *The Year of the Quiet Sun* (1970), one of the most striking time travel novels since Wells. James White's "Sector General" stories about sick extraterrestrials span a couple of decades; his best novel, *The Dream Millennium* (1974) centres on a giant decrepit spaceship while giving a vivid portrait of an Earth which has come to resemble White's native Belfast. Bernard Wolfe authored the massive amputee utopia, *Limbo 90* (1952), much praised by some.

A few women, such as C. L. Moore and Leigh Brackett, were working in the field earlier; Katherine MacLean entered the fray in 1949 in *Astounding*. On the whole they were romantics, though Katherine MacLean could do the hard stuff magnificently (as in "Incommunicado") or could be extremely funny (as in "The Snowball Effect" (1952), in which the Watashaw Sewing Circle takes over America). Leigh Brackett had many successes, among them *The Sword of Rhiannon* (1953), before becoming a high paid script writer in Hollywood.[33] Rhiannon is the most magical sub-Burroughs of them all, the best evocation of that fantasy Mars we would all give our sword arm to visit:

> Jekkara was not sleeping despite the lateness of the hour. The Low Canal towns never sleep, for they lie outside the law and time means nothing to them. In Jekkara and Barrakesh night is only a darker day.
>
> Carse walked beside the still black waters in their ancient channel, cut in the dead sea-bottom. He watched the dry wind shake the torches that never went out and listened to the broken music of the harps that were never stilled. Lean lithe men and women passed him in the shadowy streets, silent as cats except for the chime and whisper of the tiny bells the woman wear, a sound as delicate as rain, distillate of all the sweet wickedness of the world. (Chapter 1)

Catherine L. Moore began her writing career in 1933, publishing "Shambleau" in *Weird Tales*. Like many of her stories in the thirties and forties, it had a maturity few of her male contemporaries could match. Her 1939 story, "Greater Than Gods", for instance, presented a standard science fictional idea—that of a choice between two options, two alternative worlds, hanging upon one decision—in a highly personal form.

Dr William Cory, a 23rd century scientist, has to decide which of two beautiful girls he wants to marry. But he is granted a vision—pulsed back from the 30th century—of the two futures that might result from his choice—one a Matriarchal world of indolence, where science has ground to a halt, and the other a Machine-regimented future. These choices are presented not merely as future alternatives but potentialities within Cory.

A possible assassination from the future threatens to force Cory's hand—a "shotgun wedding from a mythical future", as he sees it. But in the end he makes his choice. He marries another woman, a third alternative: a woman who combines the attributes seen *in extremis* in the other two. It is at once thoughtful and emotional. The 1975 anthology, *The Best of C. L. Moore*, is an excellent showcase of one of the field's more neglected writers.

With the arrival of *Galaxy* and *F&SF*, more women writers appeared, attracted by less dour technology and wider audiences. Among the famous names were Zenna Henderson (whom we'll encounter later), Marion Zimmer Bradley, Rosel George Brown, Margaret St Clair (author of many novels as herself and as Idris Seabright), and the senior lady of them all, Miriam Allen deFord, an accomplished writer of sexual fantasy, as her collection, *Xenogenesis* (1969) proves. Also the best-selling Andre Norton, whose science fantasies are designed for teenagers and read by adults.

Dropping so many names at once is perhaps one way of conveying the wealth of talent that filled the magazines in the fifties and after. The list is by no means complete—and will be continued in the next few chapters.

In such an impersonal list, one passes too fast over many personal favourites. Here are two.

The first is L. Sprague de Camp, a writer who, like so many of his contemporaries, never produces masterpieces, but is nonetheless rarely dull. His books give the impression of being thrown off for fun while he equips himself for a second expedition to the delta of the Orinoco or wherever.

Many of de Camp's best books are collaborations, as are the two fantasies, *The Incomplete Enchanter* (*Unknown* again, in 1940) with Fletcher Pratt, and its follow-up, *The Castle of Iron* (1941, book form 1950). Or there's a *Planet of the Apes*-type novel, *Genus Homo* (1941, book form, 1950) with P. Schuyler Miller. But the saltiest de Camp is a solo effort, *Lest Darkness Fall* (*Unknown*, 1939), in which the ingenious Martin Padway falls back in time to sixth-century Rome and proceeds to wreck history with his premature inventions. We might see an echo of this tale in William Golding's 1958 play, *The Brass Butterfly* (in novella form as "Envoy Extraordinary"), in which another anachronistically-precocious inventor threatens to upset Roman history.

De Camp also writes non-fiction. He is author of *The Science Fiction Handbook* (1953, revised ed. 1975), as well as several books of historical and mythological travel—among them *Lands Beyond*, another collaboration, this time with Willy Ley. The first sentence of the Introduction to *Lands Beyond* reads, "Three colossal figures stride across the landscape of the mind of early man: the warrior, the wizard, and the wanderer." It is a sentence which also tells us much about the mind of early L. Sprague de Camp, as well as presaging his interest in the *Conan* books of the late Robert E. Howard.

And secondly, Charles Harness, a small producer whose novel *The Rose* (1953) frequently appears with recommendations from such connoisseurs as

Michael Moorcock, Judith Merril and Damon Knight. The importance of *The Rose* lies in the question it asks: "Can science and art be made compatible and complementary?"[34] Its complex symbolism is portrayed within a subtle and sensitive story of three very talented people, each searching for a rose of sorts. Its conclusion is at once tragic and triumphant—a new breed of Man is born, but at the cost of a life. One can trace the imagery and concerns of the story, however, through to Delany and Zelazny in the sixties, particularly Zelazny's "A Rose for Ecclesiastes", which is a variant on the same symbolic foundations (though as different as could be in story-line).

Our preference, however, is for Harness's *The Paradox Men* (1953). This novel may be regarded as one climax to the trillion year spree. It plays high, wide, and handsome with space and time, buzzes around the solar system like a demented hornet, is witty, profound, and trivial all in one breath, and has proved far too ingenious for the hordes of would-be-imitators to imitate. In my introduction to two British editions of this novel, I call it Wide Screen Baroque[35]; other novels in the same category are Doc Smith's and A. E. van Vogt's, possibly Alfred Bester's: but Harness's novel has a zing of its own, like whisky and champagne, the drink of the Nepalese sultans.

The fifties were a crucial period. SF came out of its shell, began to talk about the fullness of love as well as the emptiness of space, although interplanetary adventure still dominated all other themes. Magazines proliferated—later to dwindle again, after propagation had taken place. And what had been confined to magazine publishing became part of the ordinary publishing scene (including the burgeoning paperback market), so that SF would never again endure (or enjoy, depending on viewpoint) at least two decades out in a wilderness of its own.

Naturally, this major reorientation of audience had its effect. The whole operation became less ingrown. Another effect, to which we now turn in awe, was that authors were able to write large books which existed as books rather than serials. They could be visualized as a whole; the gains were sometimes enormous. Some of these giants had an immediate and powerful influence on our culture.

Beyond, or above, or outside science fiction—but watching over it as the Castle watched all that went on in the village in Kafka's novel—stands J. R. R. Tolkien's trilogy, *The Lord of the Rings* (1954–55).

The fame of this imposing structure grew throughout the fifties, although the Hobbit cult started only when Ace and Ballantine published their paperback editions in the States in 1965. Until then, the books had sold well, but Tolkien— a familiar Oxford figure, Merton Professor of English Language and Literature—was mainly known as editor of the set book, Oxford University Press's *Sir Gawain and the Green Knight*. The cult then spread back to England (the English write well, but borrow enthusiasm from others).

Presumably this large-scale work has been the main influence for the tremendous growth of fantasy and private-world fiction since then—the other influence being the dreadful state of the real world.[36]

One speaks of the Tolkien cult. To speak of the work itself is more difficult.

As Dr Johnson is reported apocryphally to have said of *The Oxford English Dictionary*, "It is an achievement which it would be irrelevant to admire, presumptuous to commend, and reckless to consult."

The saga takes the form of a quest, staged in a fictionalized early Earth compounded of elements of early Northern European legend and lore, Middle Earth. Moreover, it is not a quest to gain something (that was *The Hobbit*, a more juvenile and more straightforward tale) but to lose it: the ring.

Tolkien's learned apparatus helps to actualize his parallel world, establishing its language and cartography, as well as the full majestic regalia of its myths and fairy tales. We might view its individual elements as standard and rather twee fairy-tale fare: Hobbits living in cosy dens, eating as voraciously as schoolboys; elves; dwarves; trolls; talking, walking, thinking trees; dragons; black and white magicians; powerful swords; swift horses; and beautiful, ethereal and virginal ladies. The kindly Gandalf presides over the sylvan scene but, in the East, lies Mordor, ruled over by the dreaded Sauron and his army of the living dead. Frodo the Hobbit finally wins a tremendous victory, and the magic ring, which confers a dreadful and yet absolute power on its wearer, is destroyed, together with the powers of Sauron and all that is his.

Such a large scale work is open to many interpretations. There is no reason why it should be accepted at face value. One theory, now largely discredited, was that the work was an allegory on World War II. Lundwall describes it as "a conservative man's Utopia"[37], for the rigid class structure of Middle Earth, and the sense that the black industrial forces of Sauron (represented by the brickworks in the rural Shire) may overcome the fair lands carries a strong reminder of the England of Tolkien's youth—of Vaughan Williams's folk songs, mulled ale and honest yeomanry. Where else can all the best fantasies start but in one's youth?

This said, the whole exceeds its disparate parts, and *Lord of the Rings* involves the reader at an intense level. There is no sex in Middle Earth, despite its large population of sword-fodder, but there is a dark potency—a powerful sense of compulsion focused upon the ring itself. We might glimpse in this another, darker interpretation of the trilogy and of the ring itself: that the ring represents a suppressed sexuality and not merely the potency of evil. Gollum, an early wearer of the ring, calls it "My precious" and is forced, through compulsion, to follow its new wearer, Frodo Baggins, into the mouth of hell itself—Mount Doom—because of its shaping of his character. It causes Gollum to murder for its possession. And when Frodo encounters his uncle, Bilbo, another early wearer of the ring, there is a moment of stark revelation—of the corrupting force of the ring:

> "Have you got it here?" he asked in a whisper. "I can't help feeling curious, you know, after all I've heard. I should very much like just to peep at it again."
>
> "Yes, I've got it," answered Frodo, feeling a strange reluctance. "It looks just the same as it ever did."

"Well, I should just like to see it for a moment," said Bilbo.

When he had dressed, Frodo found that while he slept the Ring had been hung about his neck on a new chain, light but strong. Slowly he drew it out. Bilbo put out his hand. But Frodo quickly drew back the Ring. To his distress and amazement he found that he was no longer looking at Bilbo; a shadow seemed to have fallen between them, and through it he found himself eyeing a little wrinkled creature with a hungry face and bony groping hands. He felt a desire to strike him.

The music and singing round them seemed to falter and a silence fell. Bilbo looked quickly at Frodo's face and passed his hand across his eyes. "I understand now," he said. "Put it away! I am sorry; sorry you have come in for this burden: sorry about everything. . . ."

(*The Fellowship of the Ring*, Book II, Chapter 1; "Many Meetings")

This sense of burden increases—rather like the inverse square law—as Frodo approaches the Crack of Doom, and the intensity of the compulsion becomes almost unbearable. But to leaven the fantastic dough there is a second plot thread of mediaeval romance, complete with knights, heroic deeds, last battles and a whole songbook of unsingable songs (in Elvish!).

It is not a wholly fair comparison, yet there is something of P. G. Wodehouse in Tolkien's vision of Middle Earth. For both, time stopped some while before World War I broke out. The Hobbit dens might be likened to the Drones Club and other snug retreats, where chaps can gather for drinks and smokes and somewhat schoolboyish chat, secluded from the depraving company of women. The counterfeit gold of an Edwardian sunset lights the oeuvre of both men.

Where *Lord of the Rings* is like SF is in the way the heroes are almost all good (even Boromir), and evil is externalized and defeated—something which we know does not happen in real life, for evil is within us. That other, similarly titled novel, *Lord of the Flies*, published in the same year as the first two volumes of Tolkien's work, was more true to life in that respect. Golding has ingested the lessons of World War II and the concentration camps. Tolkien ignored them. Both novels are, it seems, equally popular—though some are more equal than others in the cult stakes.

The success of Tolkien and the failure of reality have brought popularity to other great fantasists, such as James Branch Cabell, or the revered Mervyn Peake—not as much popularity in Peake's case, because Peake's great Gothic trilogy, *Titus Groan, Gormenghast* and *Titus Alone* (1946–1959) needs much more concentrated reading than Tolkien.

Compare the two texts.

Frodo is journeying to Orodruin with the ring. His faithful servant Sam is with him, and they are surrounded by threatening things, thirsty and alone. Night falls.

They could not follow this road any longer; for it went on eastward into the great Shadow, but the Mountain now loomed upon their right, almost due south, and they must turn towards it. Yet still before it there stretched a wide region of fuming, barren, ash-ridden land.

"Water, water!" muttered Sam. He had stinted himself, and in his parched mouth his tongue seemed thick and swollen; but for all his care they now had very little left, perhaps half his bottle, and maybe there were still days to go. All would long ago have been spent, if they had not dared to follow the orc-road. For at long intervals on that highway cisterns had been built for the use of troops sent in haste through waterless regions. In one Sam had found some water left, stale, muddied by the orcs, but still sufficient for their desperate case. Yet that was now a day ago. There was no hope of any more.

At last wearied with his cares Sam drowsed, leaving the morrow till it came; he could do no more. Dream and waking mingled uneasily. He saw lights like gloating eyes, and dark creeping shapes, and he heard noises as of wild beasts or the dreadful cries of tortured things; and he would start up to find the world all dark and only empty blackness all about him. Once only, as he stood and stared wildly round, did it seem that, though now awake, he could still see pale lights like eyes; but soon they flickered and vanished.

The hateful night passed slowly and reluctantly.

(*The Return of the King*, Book VI, Chapter 3; "Mount Doom")

Now we visit Gormenghast Castle, and again it is night. The infatuated Irma has an assignation with Mr Bellgrove in the garden:

The night poured in on them from every side—a million million cubic miles of it. O, the glory of standing with one's love, naked, as it were, on a spinning marble, while the sphere ran flaming through the universe! Involuntarily they moved together into the arbour and sat down on a bench which they found in the darkness.

This darkness was intensely rich and velvety. It was as though they were in a cavern, save that the depths were dramatized by a number of small and brilliant pools of moonlight. Pranked for the most part to the rear of the arbour these livid pools were at first a little disturbing, for portions of themselves were lit up with blatant emphasis. . . .

From Irma's point of view the dappled condition of the cavernous arbour was both calming and irritating at the same time.

Calming, in that to enter a cave of clotted midnight, with not so much as a flicker of light to gauge her distance from her partner would have been terrifying even with her knowledge of, and confidence in, so reliable and courteous a gentleman as her escort. This dappled arbour was not so fell a place. The pranked lights, more livid, it is true, than gay, removed, nevertheless, that sense of terror only known to fugitives or those benighted in a shire of ghouls.

Strong as was her feeling of gratification that the dark was broken, yet a sense of irritation as strong as her relief fought in her flat bosom for sovereignty. This irritation, hardly understandable to anyone who has neither Irma's figure, nor a vivid picture of the arbour in mind, was caused by the maddening *way* in which the lozenges of radiance fell upon her body.

She had taken out a small mirror in the darkness, more from nervousness than anything else and in holding it up, saw nothing in the dark air before her but a long sharp segment of light. The mirror itself was quite invisible, as was the hand and arm that held it, but the detached and luminous reflection of her nose hovered before her in the darkness. At first she did not know what it was. She moved her head a little and saw in front of her one of her small weak eyes glittering like quicksilver, a startling thing to observe under any conditions, but infinitely more so when the organ is one's own. (*Gormenghast*, Chapter 36)

Tolkien's prose, the very shaping vehicle of his story, is bland and universalized, and often clumsy in its construction. It has no particular characteristic, apart from the joining of long sentences by "and", which can become wearying. Peake's prose is sharp and particularized. It cannot be mistaken for anyone else's writing or vision; wit moves through it, so that it is anti-sentimental—considerably less lulling than Tolkien's. On the other hand, it is decidedly quirky, too *dense*. A little at a time is all you need. Tolkien's prose is designed for the long, long empathic read. Nevertheless, Peake conjures the special flavour of a special night, and gets much nearer to the things that haunt shadows. It is, of course, a matter of taste, and both kinds of fiction can appeal— if to different faculties in the reader.

So to other milestones and large books that draw us closer to the sixties.

We have already met Isaac Asimov and Robert Heinlein, labouring lustily in the pages of *Astounding*. As this history continues we shall meet them again—for with their generation we have come upon a group of writers who have spent their whole lives within a recognizable (if developing) genre; a group who saw themselves as writing a specific form of fiction.

Like Bester, Asimov broke off from writing SF novels in the fifties and sixties with the exception of the novelization of *Fantastic Voyage*, and resumed only two decades later.

Asimov. What does one say in his praise that Asimov himself has not already said? "Why, man, he doth bestride the narrow world like a Colossus", says Cassius of Shakespeare's Julius Caesar, and many Cassiuses have risen to pay similar homage to Asimov. "For many people the name Isaac Asimov is science fiction." Thus spake Joseph F. Patrouch in 1974.[38]

He is a great producer. He enjoys enormous popularity. He has become monstrous. Yet there is still something sane, even likeable, about many of his utterances. Asimov is the great sandworm of science fiction, tunnelling under its arid places. And the critic's job remains that of a small termite, tunnelling under Asimov.

Asimov employed the wide-angle lens for his view of life and it is a pity that his largest milestone, the *Foundation* trilogy, was written before SF authors were able to think of their books as books, not as short stories or serials in cheap magazines (magazines that would have been ephemeral but for the dedication of fans). Conceived as an organic whole, the *Foundation* series might have risen to greater majesty. As it is, we must judge the original trilogy as it was conceived and presented to the readers of *Astounding* between May 1942 and January 1950.

The first part of the sequence, the novelette "Foundation"[39], was written by Asimov in August and September 1941 and bought by Campbell.

At once we are thrown into a situation where the Galactic Empire, a political unit involving tens of millions of inhabited planets, is in the first stages of collapse. A collapse brought about by indolence and complacency. The Foundation consists of a group of physical scientists established on the planet Terminus, on the galactic periphery. It is cut off from the centre of power, Trantor, by a revolt on Anacreon, and must maintain its independence by guile (because force is out of the question). The Foundation itself is the outward manifestation of "psychohistory", an exact social science which deals with the statistically predictable actions of vast numbers of human beings. This highly mechanistic sociological reductionism—a kind of quantum physics applied to human beings—has been developed with one aim only: to prevent a ten-thousand-year Dark Age wherein the Galaxy might fall into technological barbarism.

Neither of these ideas bears a minute's serious investigation. Yet upon these structures Asimov builds his huge house of cards. One cannot seriously believe that all tens of millions of human-settled planets would suffer the same fate—the loss of acquired human knowledge and technological know-how—or that the whole vast edifice could possibly have functioned as a political entity in the first place.

Psychohistory is the peg upon which Asimov hangs his theoretical coat. For all the grandeur of this unlikely vision, it's a coat of shreds and patches, yet undoubtedly psychohistory and its working out over centuries account for its enduring popularity. Most of the stories in the *Foundation* sequence depend upon individual action—by such as Salvor Hardin, Hober Mallow and others—and appear thus to run counter to psychohistorical theory. The "time vault" appearances of psychohistory's creator, Hari Seldon, at predicted moments of crisis, our "proof" of psychohistory at work, seem more incredible coincidence than accurate scientific planning.[40]

Even then Asimov, under Campbell's influence, was leaving each story open for a sequel. It was to prove the beginning of a chain of unresolved endings being maintained to this day.[41] Asimov's fiction is essentially of the puzzle-solving sort, detective novels of a very basic kind, set in a gimmick-ridden future not so very different from our own times in its psychology and social patternings. There is little genuine social or technological extrapolation (where is the complex computer technology of the future in *Foundation*, for instance?). All is modelled on the past, the known. Few imaginative risks are taken.

The models for *Foundation* were Gibbon's *Decline and Fall of the Roman Empire* and a 1907 24-volume work, *The Historian's History of the World*. For Asimov's final two volumes, Arnold Toynbee's *Study of History* was a major influence. All in all, then, what Asimov presents us with is Rome In Space. Not for the first time in Campbell's pages, but for the first time as epic. An epic in true Hollywood tradition, with extras hired for the day, rather wooden actors and plastic props. Very often Asimov didn't even bother with the wooden stage sets—his is a non-sensual universe. We see little of it. We can't touch it. His principal actors talk much more than they act, and notice very little of their surroundings. We can forgive the youthful Asimov such deficiencies—he was only twenty-one when he began the series—but lament their presence.

In case we forget this is science fiction and not a historical romance, Asimov provided us with a mutant telepath, Hitler with clout, in the mis-shape of the Mule. He's there to upset the smooth workings of psychohistory. A proof of the discipline in the negative.

Asimov recognizes his fictional limitations—and his immunity to twentieth-century literary influences, for instance—and his liberal views often emerge in his writings. He is a dove, not a hawk, and his vision of a galactic empire includes an abhorrence of nuclear weaponry which must be applauded. His most convincing work, however, is probably that which is nearest the detective format—with Conan Doyle's Sherlock Holmes as an obvious pattern. Two such SF detective novels appeared in the fifties, *The Caves of Steel* (1954) and *The Naked Sun* (1957). They are clever novels, extensions of his earlier robot stories—where Asimov, with John W. Campbell's help, created the "Three Laws of Robotics". They are murder mysteries involving logic, science and elements of futuristic psychology; the last founded in the agoraphobia of the Earthmen, shut away in their underground cities. Elijah Baley, the human detective, and his humanoid robot, R. Daneel Olivaw, are the Holmes and Watson of this future world—a team who, in one form or another, were still functioning in Asimov's two robot novels of the early eighties, *The Robots of Dawn* (1983) and *Robots and Empire* (1985).

The End of Eternity (1955) is a time travel novel, depicting "a universe where Reality was something flexible and evanescent". As such it falls into that sub-category of time travel books, the probability world tale. A group of humans outside of time, Eternals, act to ensure that mankind does not die out in the Galaxy. For much of the novel the pattern glimpsed in the *Foundation* series—of a steadily expanding *human*-settled galaxy—is denied. But by the end of the story the universe of *Foundation* has reasserted itself, thanks to the actions of the Eternals. There's also a love story—a Samson and Delilah story between Andrew Harlan and Noys Lambert—that culminates in a sexual relationship between them.

Asimov seemed at the height of his powers when he wrote *The End of Eternity*, and its merging of the personal and the abstract works perfectly:

> And he saw Eternity with great clarity as a sink of deepening psychoses, a writhing pit of abnormal motivation, a mass of desperate lives torn brutally out of context.

When returning to the genre in the late seventies, however, Asimov reverted to the patterns of the forties, and the complexity of *The End of Eternity* remains unique in his work. Asimov subsequently became one of the polymaths of our day, producing a stream of popularizations of various scientific and historical disciplines. The popularity of his novels continues. Like many another writer, Asimov began in a subversive vein, prophesying change and barbarism; but, generations later, such ideas lose their sting and become safe for a general public. Increasingly, one sees a solid conservative faith in technology in Asimov's novels. His short stories often err on the side of facetiousness.

Robert Heinlein's transition from magazine writer to novelist is dramatic. His great and rare virtue is that he has never been content to repeat a winner or rely on a formula; and this, as we know from our study of Edgar Rice Burroughs, is a way of defying popularity. Nevertheless, a special wide popularity has been his.

Heinlein is a pulp writer made good, sometimes with his strong power-drives half-rationalized into a right-wing political philosophy, as in *Starship Troopers* (1959), a sentimental view of what it is like to train and fight as an infantryman in a future war. Anyone who has trained and fought in a past war will recognize the way Heinlein prettifies his picture. But realism is not Heinlein's vein, although he has an adroit way of dropping in a telling detail when needed, sometimes giving the illusion of realism. This technique is notably effective in his boys' novels, such as *Starman Jones* (1953), where close analysis of character and motive is not demanded.

Heinlein's most enjoyable novel is *Double Star*, which first ran as a serial in *Astounding* in 1956. *Double Star* is a hymn to behaviourism. For once Heinlein begins with a "little" man, almost a Wellsian cockney, a pathetic failed actor, Lawrence Smith, who liked to style himself Lorenzo the Great.

Because of his chance resemblance to Bonforte, one of the leading politicians of the solar system, Lorenzo is forced to impersonate the politician and take on his powers, until he eventually becomes the man himself, clad in his personality and office. People in other Heinlein novels often have to fit into unaccustomed roles, become revolutionaries, become space troopers, wear slugs on their backs, or—like Smith in *I Will Fear No Evil* (1970)—live in a woman's body.

Heinlein's grasp of politics has always been frail, and the political issues concerning liberty which lie close to the heart of *Double Star* are absurdly falsified by the coarsely impractical methods the politicians employ. Thus, Lorenzo is shanghaied into playing his role, while Bonforte is kidnapped by the opposing party, the Humanists. This Chicago gangsterism is rendered the more silly because an effort is made to model political procedures on British parliamentary method: Bonforte is a Right Honourable, and "leader of the loyal opposition".[42]

Despite this monstrous drawback, *Double Star* survives somehow because at its centre is the process whereby Lorenzo becomes Bonforte, and Heinlein handles this with a clarity he is rarely able to sustain in his other adult novels. The scene on Mars where Lorenzo as Bonforte goes to be adopted into a Martian nest (rare honour for an Earthman) is effective. There are parallels between this novel and Hope's *Prisoner of Zenda*, and more than a touch of the "I Was Monty's Double" syndrome, too.

In a juvenile novel, *Red Planet* (1949), Heinlein presents another effective picture of Mars. Heinlein is obscurely moved by Mars. As a thinker, he is primitive[43]; perhaps that is the source of his appeal. The critic Panshin says that "Heinlein's idea of liberty is wolfish and thoroughgoing".[44] Although it is true that several of his novels are about revolution and wars, this does not make Heinlein a Zapata. The dark and blood-red planet shines only in the complex universe of his own mind; his ideas of liberty boil down to what a man can grasp for himself—a freedom *to* as much as a freedom *from*.

More nonsense has been written about Heinlein than about any other SF writer. He is not a particularly good storyteller and his characters are often indistinguishable. There is always a mouthpiece in his later work. His style is banal, highly colloquialized, and has not changed in its essence in the forty-odd years he has been writing. To compare him with Kipling is absurd. A better comparison is with Nevil Shute, who also loved machines and added mysticism to his formula. Like Shute, Heinlein can be highly readable. Unlike Shute, Heinlein is often verbose and pedantic.

Shute, however, is not as interesting as a character. The interest in Heinlein's writing lies in the complexity of Heinlein's character as revealed through the long autobiography of his novels. He is a particular case of that magic-inducing not-growing-up which marks so many SF writers, particularly at the heart of the genre. Thirty years on, as we shall see later, Heinlein remains the same, a straw-chewing technophile who would tell God himself that He was wrong.

We turn now to the last writer, and our final book in the parade of fifties giants. It is a novel which shows a central concern with religion.

In World War II, Walter M. Miller Jr, like his fellow American Kurt Vonnegut Jr, became involved with the hostilities in Europe. Vonnegut experienced the fire-bombing of Dresden and eventually produced *Slaughterhouse-Five* (1969). Miller experienced the assault on the Benedictine Monastery at Monte Cassino and wrote *A Canticle for Leibowitz*. So we digest our own experiences and offer them as nourishment for others.

Canticle has the dryness, toughness and nutritional value of *cordon bleu* pemmican. All SF writers are astonishing, but some SF writers are more astonishing than others. *Canticle* appears to be the rocky summit of Miller's brief writing career.

He came on strong with stories in—to mention it yet again—Campbell's *Astounding*—"Izzard and the Membrane", "Blood Bank", "The Big Hunger", using interstellar space as some sort of obscure private metaphor, in 1951 and 1952. But the stories that got turned into *Canticle* appeared in *F&SF*.

An aside about that magazine, since more has been said of *ASF* and *Galaxy*. It would be a shabby history of SF which held no warm word for the shade of Anthony Boucher, *F&SF*'s tremendous editor. Boucher's real name was William Anthony Parker White. He entered the SF field through Campbell's *Unknown*—as did his rival editor, Horace Gold.

As Gold, through *Galaxy*, brought in the divine razzmatazz of Bester, Pohl, Sheckley and Tenn, so Boucher, through *F&SF*, brought in literary standards and a much wider appreciation of what was implied by "science". As Judith Merril has said, "Until Boucher and McComas started *Fantasy and Science Fiction* in 1949, the Campbell-dominated speciality field had no place in it for the kind of stories Beaumont, Budrys, Clingerman, Cogswell, Dick, Henderson, Matheson, Miller, MacDonald, Moore, Nourse, Pangborn, Tenn, Vance, Vonnegut, and a score of others began to produce—as did Asimov, Bester, Leiber, Wyndham, and others, many of whom had virtually stopped writing until the necessary new magazine came along.[46]

Since Boucher's day, *F&SF* has been maintained successfully through the editorships of Robert P. Mills, Avram Davidson, and Ed Ferman, the present incumbent of the diocese and a veteran now of twenty-one years.

Canticle was first published in book form in 1960, and was immediately greeted with the warmest praise by reviewers—i.e., they said it was so good it couldn't possibly be SF.[47] It has its longueurs, but emerges as the best of the after-the-bomb novels.[48]

A Dark Age follows the nuclear holocaust, and such shreds of learning as can be picked from the ruins are preserved by the Catholic Church, and in particular by the holy men of the Order of Saint Leibowitz. This is far from being one more tedious exercise in revamped feudal history. Miller's sense of irony and of place ensure that. He takes us towards another Renaissance, when once more technology builds up to its previous level. Give or take a few mutants, everything is as before. Then the bombs begin to fall again.

In synopsis, this suggests an exercise in heavy message-dropping. *Canticle* is nothing of the sort.

> The two-headed woman and her six-legged dog waited with an empty vegetable basket by the new gate; the woman crooned softly to the dog. Four of the dog's legs were healthy legs, but an extra pair dangled uselessly at its sides. As for the woman, one head was as useless as the extra legs of the dog. It was a small head, a cherubic head, but it never opened its eyes. It gave no evidence of sharing in her breathing or her understanding. It lolled uselessly on one shoulder, blind, deaf, mute, and only vegetatively alive. Perhaps it lacked a brain, for it showed no sign of independent consciousness or personality. Her other face had aged, grown wrinkled, but the superfluous head retained the features of infancy, although it had been toughened by the gritty wind and darkened by the desert sun.
>
> The old woman curtsied at their approach, and her dog drew back with a snarl. "Evenin', Father Zerchi," she drawled.

This pathetic old creature wants the abbot to baptize Rachel. Which raises a nice theological point, for Rachel is her sleeping and mutated extra head. How many souls has an old two-headed woman?

Many years before this, Old Father Heinlein wrote a story called "Common Sense"[49], in which there is a tough two-headed mutant, Joe-Jim. Joe-Jim is the leader of a gang of mutants. Both heads, Joe and Jim, can talk and behave as brothers; in the end, one of them gets stabbed through the eye. Old Mrs Grales in *Canticle* represents an inspired improvement on the early model; Miller invests the sleeping head with mysterious significance.

The bombs drop. The monastery falls on Father Zerchi. Pinned down, he sees Mrs Grales approach. But no, the face of Mrs Grales is pale and withered; her eyes have closed; she appears to be dying.

Rachel has woken to transient life. Unlike that dull yellow eye of Frankenstein's creature, the eyes the bomb has opened are cool green eyes, alert with curiosity. Rachel is young and beautiful, only just born, full of wonder at the wounded world. The dying priest sees in her eyes a primal innocence and hope of resurrection as she kneels before him. More bombs fall.

Science fiction is like an ocean. The images come and go, mysteriously linked through transformation after transformation. Many rivers pour into the ocean, all the tributaries of our life, both waking and dreaming. These days, we all have two heads. Frankenstein's monster plunges along beside us, keeping just below the Plimsoll line of consciousness, buoyant with a life of its own.

CHAPTER XI

The Dawn of the Day of the Dumpbin: Cinemas, Computers, Colleges and Canticles

> Time hath, my lord, a dumpbin at his back
> Wherein he puts Ace for oblivion.
> —Shakespeare: *Troilus & Cressida*, III, iii

While the first edition of this volume was in preparation, John W. Campbell died. At the same time, something else was born. The popularity of SF. All that we had once hoped for came true. Wishes were granted—always a perilous process.

This chapter undertakes a survey of developments since the early sixties, before getting down to particulars. It records a time when SF novels reached the bestseller lists[1], when SF conventions became big business[2], when SF scholarship grew up, when even the publishing of SF criticism flourished in great diversity[3], and—this especially—when everyone went to SF movies.

Ah, the bad old days! The SF movie evolved like some dreadful growth from a gutter, creeping up from Saturday morning serials to B movies, and then to an occasional *Dr Cyclops* (1939) or *Forbidden Planet* (1956). In the mid-fifties a spate of SF movies brought forth some good things. We do not forget our first viewing of *Them!* (1953), *Invasion of the Body Snatchers* (1956) or *The Quatermass Xperiment* (1955). Only with the Kubrick-Clarke film *2001* in 1968 were the possibilities of SF realized in the cinema for a new generation. (The successes of *Metropolis* (1926), *The Tunnel* (1935), and *Things to Come* (1936) having been largely forgotten.) And then, and then, in 1977. . . .

"A real gee-whiz movie" was what George Lucas and his producer Gary Kurtz planned when making *Star Wars*, and a real gee-whiz movie was what they finished up with. There's no record of the total number of gee-whizzes it provoked, but we do know that the movie grossed more than $400 million at the world's box offices between first showing in 1977 and 1985, and TV and video appearances are uncounted.

Our opinion of *Star Wars*—followed by its sequels, *The Empire Strikes Back* and *Return of the Jedi*—may have changed in the intervening years since we first viewed it. Science fictional developments in that period have been extremely rapid. It was apparent from the first that *Star Wars* was an outsize elephant with the brains of a gnat; what has become more evident is how beautifully it was filmed, how sharp the editing, how clear the storyline, how refreshingly open the sets. Moreover, since *Blade Runner* (1982) and *Dune* (1985), we see that the morality of the film was comparatively innocuous.

Star Wars was space opera in the grand manner. A lad of lowly birth rises to defeat the evil Darth Vader and the forces of Empire. Computer graphics helped to enhance the excitement. The alien life-forms—often shown glancingly, to great effect—were new, amazing.

If only Luke Skywalker had had to suffer, to undergo long discipline, to submit to stern teachers, to fast, to train, to deny himself, in order to acquire The Force—as did the Samurai from whom, presumably, the idea of The Force is derived! We would then have felt an experiential counterpoise to the fantasy elements of the film, to that preposterous assumption that five brave guys and true—one of them a princess, one an overgrown Yorkshire Terrier—could save the galaxy. And the self-indulgence of Western culture would not have shown so nakedly.

Useless to complain. On its own level, *Star Wars* is no bad movie. It may be expected to gain in stature as the years and the duff videos drift by.

That same year, 1977, saw another massive SF blockbuster unroll across the world's screens. For many months previously, a publicity man at Columbia had been phoning to keep me informed of the progress of the film, possibly because he knew how I admired Steven Spielberg's early film, *Duel* (1971). "Yes, it sounds great," I'd say encouragingly. "Just as long as you remember to change that meaningless title before the première."

Well, we can all be wrong. Success sanctifies many things, including titles. *Close Encounters of the Third Kind* triumphed almost as greatly at the box office as *Star Wars*, despite its greater inner complexity.

Close Encounters shows humans and aliens meeting and establishing trust. The wonder generated by the arrival of the mighty UFOs lasts through to the end of the film, where the Earth child is welcomed aboard the mother ship which will carry him safely out into the galaxy. A barrage of Spielberg's special effects adds up to moments of genuine emotion—and of genuine hope that They might be like that, and We might be like that, if the moment came. No more crucifixions.

Whereas Luke Skywalker in *Star Wars* is a simple Disney-type young hero whose hair may occasionally be ruffled by Harrison Ford in a cynical elder-brother-type role, Richard Dreyfuss in *Close Encounters* plays an older and more complex character as the lead figure. Dreyfuss is an H. G. Wells man, a blue-collar worker none too successful at his job, stuck in a marriage without savour, who has a vision of better things. The film's ending apart, the most dramatic moment comes when Dreyfuss finds himself compelled to build a gigantic mudpie in the living room, thus desecrating the very centre of the home. His wife drives the kids away screaming in the estate wagon. Faith breaks up domestic bliss. Spielberg seems not to have grasped the power of his own theme, since much of this scene is omitted from the later revised version of the movie, *Close Encounters of the Third Kind—The Special Edition* (1980).

Wells, a realist despite his powerful imagination, would have had Dreyfuss settle down with the girl he meets in a riverside pub. Spielberg has him forget the girl and launch out to the stars. Utopia's where you find it.

Stars and space were back with a vengeance in the cinema. Old warhorses like *Gone With the Wind* and *The Sound of Music* never grossed as much as the *Star Wars* series, *Close Encounters*, Spielberg's later *E.T.* and *Back to the Future*, or even *Superman—The Movie* (1978).

Before *Star Wars*, George Lucas made an agreeably nostalgic movie called *American Graffiti* (1973). He surrounded himself with the popular music of the time while he went to work. Judging by the motifs and settings of *Star Wars*, he surrounded himself with old SF magazines while he went to work on that. It is a sensible way of proceeding, even if one thinks one catches glimpses of E. E. Smith's *Gray Lensman* Venusian bar, Harry Harrison's *Deathworld* and Frank Herbert's *Dune* as one goes along. *Nostalgie de la futur* is the order of the day.

On the heels of *Star Wars* came *Battlestar Galactica* (1978), shown as a tele-series in the States and as a movie in Europe. Like *Star Wars* (indeed, like *Superman* and *Star Trek*), the space operatic *Battlestar Galactica* has so far spawned two sequels, *Mission Galactica: The Cylon Attack* (1979) and *Conquest of the Earth* (1980), all with screenplays by the ubiquitous Glen A. Larson. For all their fireworks, and their theme of the quest for a far-distant Earth, the Galacticas move like lead and sink like the same. Superficial elements remind one of *Star Wars*, but they lack the mythic depths Lucas unconsciously tapped.

Lucasfilm and Fox brought an action for plagiarism against Universal, the studio which made *Battlestar Galactica*. Early in 1979 I was in California, advising a legal firm hired by Universal to defend the suit (which was never brought to court). It seemed to me at the time, and I have not changed my mind since, that both films derived from earlier models, to wit, from stories in the SF magazines of the forties and fifties. The films shared common ancestors.

The Los Angeles lawyers had summoned me from England for a good reason. To follow the publication of *Billion Year Spree*, I edited a book on science fiction art and a series of anthologies of what I called "Way-Back-When-Futures", the best-known of which is a two-volume anthology entitled *Galactic Empires*. The material for these volumes was culled from magazines I had collected since boyhood.

In the introduction to one volume I defined the essence of space opera. Here is what I said about space opera, in the anthology of that name:

Science fiction is a big muscular horny creature, with a mass of bristling antennae and proprioceptors on its skull. It has a small sister, a gentle creature with red lips and a dash of stardust in her hair. Her name is Space Opera. This volume is dedicated to her. . . .

Analogously with opera itself, space opera has several conventions which are essential to it, which are, in a way, its raison d'etre; one may either like or dislike those conventions, but they cannot be altered except at expense to the whole. Ideally, the Earth must be in peril, there must be a quest and a man to match the mighty hour. That man must confront aliens and exotic creatures. Space must flow past the ports like wine from a pitcher. Blood must run down the palace steps, and Ships launch out into the louring dark. There must be a woman fairer than the skies and a villain darker than the Black Hole. And all must come right in the end.

These comments and the anthology which contained them were published in 1974, three years before *Star Wars* excoriated our screens. The lawyers took my definition as a fair description of the essence of *Star Wars*. In other words, Lucas's film, however original a piece of film-making, derived from what was already an established genre on paper.

The lawyers' first formal question to me was this: "What was your initial response to *Star Wars*?" I replied, "I experienced the delights of recognition." They thought about it. Then they smiled.

Derivation is a feature too of most of the science fiction films made since *Star Wars*. Not all were as lacking in charm as *Battlestar Galactica*. *E.T.: The Extra-Terrestrial* (1982) suppurated charm, and is perhaps Spielberg's most successful film. *E.T.* is a story Disney has made many times before, with dogs, chipmunks or ponies playing the title role, which goes to prove that aliens are more fun. Once again, however, Spielberg added his own mysterious super-ingredient and surpassed his models. Not a dry eye in the house.

The Black Hole (1979) showed that Disney studios without Walt had lost their touch. Complete with cutesy, twittering robot, it was one of the least scientific SF films ever made. The descent into the aforesaid hole—curiously red—proves a bit of a downer. *Alien* (also 1979) carried many memories of old SF stories— good ones on this occasion. It had a simple but infallible storyline, a lot of terror, and good acting. A clever, memorable movie.

Mad Max (1979), *Mad Max II* (1981) and *Mad Max III: Beyond Thunderdome* (1985), Australian movies, starred brutal heartthrob Mel Gibson. They took the world of biking and car-crashes into the near future, but possessed a real sense of myth their countless imitators lacked. *The Final Countdown* (1980) was an under-rated time-adventure, with an American aircraft carrier time-stormed back to 1941 and the days directly before Pearl Harbor; a storyline straight from the pulps. *Saturn 3* (1980), with a script by Martin Amis and calisthenics by a frighteningly youthful-looking Kirk Douglas (is the man immortal?), is the one about a robot lusting, naturally enough, after Farrah Fawcett Majors.

Scanners (1980), by the idiosyncratic Canadian director David Cronenberg, had duelling telepaths and exploding heads—a fifties story given an eighties gloss. *Time Bandits* (1981) showed considerable originality by being comic. *Blade Runner* (1982), based on Philip K. Dick's cool novel, *Do Androids Dream of Electric Sheep?*, was an overheated farrago of SF crossed with private eye machismo and dragged down by pretentious sets. Part of its storyline and at least one of its characters was roped in from another Dick novel, *We Can Build You*.

So one might go on. An eye-catching bunch, though they brought few if any new ideas to the screen. Other movies, in an established Hollywood tradition, were re-makes of old ones, like *King Kong* (1976), *Invasion of the Body Snatchers* (1978), *The Incredible Shrinking Woman* (1981) and *The Thing* (1982). Only the last bears watching.

Some films were based on comic strips, like *Superman—The Movie* and *The Incredible Hulk*. And some films derived from TV series, such as *Star Trek—The Motion Picture*. None were movie versions of major SF novels, or not until we get to the disastrous *Dune* (1984). But more of that in its place.

One might briefly query why major directors have not searched out the riches of the written genre and snapped them up. Where is the film of Le Guin's *The Left Hand of Darkness*? Where a version of Mary Shelley's *Frankenstein* true to the spirit, atmosphere and intelligence of the original? Where are the films of *Tiger! Tiger!*, *Childhood's End*, *The Space Merchants*, *Odd John*, *Pavane*, *The Man in the High Castle*, *Earth Abides*, *A Canticle for Leibowitz*, *Bill, the Galactic Hero*, *More Than Human*, and many others? Some of science fiction's classics have been filmed—*Fahrenheit 451* and *The Martian Chronicles* by Bradbury are instances; the latter as a TV series—but there seems a profound ignorance in Hollywood of the written genre they are now mining for the raw materials of their money-spinning SF movies. It strikes one as either stupidity or rank amateurism—akin to drilling for oil without geological tests.

Along with the SF movies went the Horrors and the endless James Bond sagas, which contain flashy sci-fi elements. Most of them make a passable evening's entertainment. Few contain fresh ideas, or any sort of aspiring human values.[4] The studios' special effects department did not rise to power by spurning terror and destruction.[5]

Among these gaudy, noisy fairgrounds, technological novelty is offered, and often constitutes the most exciting part of the movie. The dazzling effects in *Star Wars*, not least the opening shot, with the immense Imperial battleship passing overhead, owe much to the computer-controlled camera. Technology begets technology. The most exhilarating moments in the Disney *Tron* (1982), with its computer programmer forced to run electronic gauntlets within the circuitry of a computer, are generated by the accelerated geometries of computer graphics. In *2010* (1985) the breath-taking shots of Jupiter's eternally storming cloudscape are the product of a Cray supercomputer's enhancement of Voyager's flyby photographs, courtesy of NASA.[6]

And what were Western civilization's younger generation doing when not gazing at these marvels in the cinema or on TV and video? During the late seventies they crouched tensely in amusement arcades, shooting down *Space Invaders*, or defending their mothership against encroaching asteroids. Let up on the destruction for an instant and one was wiped out.

In the twinkling of an eye, another gadget was upon us. The electronic carnage leaped from amusement arcade to home computer. Infants of tender age learned to fight off a succession of aliens, hunchbacks, blue meanies, missiles, insane dumper trucks, giant apes, intergalactic ravens, robots, and god-knows-what-else. And the older generation—slower on the joystick—sometimes slunk to their aid.

Early computer games required only speedy responses. Many had an SF base. Along came adventure games, in which the objective was, typically, to acquire treasure, by finding a way through the castle, hefting the correct weapon with which to defeat each oncoming terror—a red apple with which to distract the witch, and so on. Ingenuity and forethought were needed, as well as quick fingers on the keys. Such puzzles owed much to that other seventies craze, *Dungeons and Dragons*, and similar role-playing games. Gary Gygax's *Dungeons and Dragons* appeared in 1974; it in its turn owed much to that sixties craze, the works of J. R. R. Tolkien.[7]

Home computer games reach greater depths of sophistication as software multiplies. One participates in a welter of events. No characterization, no plot, no climax, just events.[8] But the player is, at least to some extent, making a story happen to himself. At home, we play *Elite* just now. It's SF, space opera. Planets must be held against enemies. Nice calculations are needed to fuel, provision and arm ships if one is to triumph. Then there are *Ancipital* and the jokey *Attack of the Mutant Camels*, where, as with the earlier *Chucky Egg*, which had an insidious attraction, humour creeps in. Before this volume sees print, these particular titles will be as forgotten as the current Number One in the pop charts. Ephemera have never been more transitory.

Even culture tries to creep into the realm of pattering pixtels. Commodore 64 users can play *Macbeth*. No soliloquies, but can you find the ingredients of the witches' cauldron in time?

Slippery little cassette boxes usurp the space on shelves once occupied by books. Under this welter of technological novelty, how has written SF, so far in this volume regarded as the mainstream of imagination, fared?

One thing is clear in the general confusion. The old SF field as, say, John W. Campbell knew it, has forever passed away. Theme parks, TV advertising, children's toys (what home is now without a robot somewhere?), rock music, military jargon—we live in a media landscape permeated with SF imagery. It has become impossible to remain ignorant of science fiction as a major factor in our world—even if only as a trite, misrepresented affair. SF books (by which is meant mainly those expendables of our culture, paperbacks) have also proliferated, to present in their full array a macaw-like down-market chic. By the beginning of the seventies it was almost impossible to read all the SF published. Nowadays it's impossible to assimilate half of what is produced.

We cannot in these pages explicate that amazing phenomenon, SF fandom.[9] Fandom has proved the sort of movement from which empires are born. Although our concern is to present SF as a literature, not as social activity, SF fandom at its best has a special and honourable distinguishing mark: the fans are omnivorous. Credit, tribal respect, was to be gained from reading and remembering. Literacy was rewarded. Pressure was on the new entrant to fandom to catch up, to become familiar with earlier writers as well as current ones. This was easy in the sixties, when anthologies were rife, rescuing old material for new audiences.[10] Harry Harrison and I contributed greatly to their number.

The technological advances of the seventies saw this reading tradition threatened. Anthologies are not the commercial propositions they were. Even the anthology series presenting new work, like Damon Knight's *Orbit* series, have died.[11] Instead, new writers and imprints spring up like weeds.

The seventies boom continued into the eighties. It competes with other media attractions and, inevitably, obliterates its own past by sheer weight of numbers. Those other media have nourished other fandoms which, like clones, resemble the original fandom—Trekkies, Dr Who fans, Sword and Sorcery buffs—but are different from it. The masquerades are great, the swordplay terrific, the Skywalker lookalikes fine. Lifestyle imitates art. But even the near past is forgotten when literacy becomes a minor category. There's no kudos in having read John Wyndham or Philip Dick's novels as they appeared. One of the main cohesive factors within the field has faded silently away. SF? . . . Who reads SF? . . . that seems a common modern fan's cry.

If the audience is different, so is the actual SF. How does today's SF shape up? On this subject we shall offer our verdict.

Age alters one's perspectives. But many readers by no means estranged from current trends will admit that they now only rarely find the stimulating new ideas, or those remarkable reversals of reality which made us look afresh at our own *umwelts*, which once reverberated through the pages of *Astounding* and *Galaxy*. Much of recent SF consists of retreads. It tends to obscure the work of genuine quality now being done.

There is more division within the extended ranks of SF than ever before. On the whole that division can be epitomized crudely by the question, Is SF better or worse than it was back in "the good old days" (wherever those days might be located)? The rest of this book is dedicated to a consideration of this question.

The day of the dumpbin has dawned. Must SF inevitably deteriorate, as so many honest critics believe?

Not to pre-empt our conclusions, we may say immediately that the diversification of the SF field, which has led to a splintering effect, means that increasing numbers of authors are now read in their own right. Their brand image is their individual name, not the generic label of yesterday. Widely dissimilar authors, such as Stephen Donaldson, Marion Zimmer Bradley, J. G. Ballard, and Joanna Russ, have their own followings. They do not think generically; they are not received generically. This may seem a bad thing to those who blindly follow the ragged banner of SF; but for the readership at large the effects will ultimately be nothing but beneficial.

A growing discernment ensures a decided preference as to which authors to read; and, among those authors, which of their books are of most value. This is another refinement antithetical to the old blind loyalties of fandom. But we shall find that refinement is one of the keys to an appreciation of today's diversity.

It is difficult to see the wood for the trees. There is, to an honest enquirer, the foremost problem of proliferating new titles, of endless retreads—the weight of numbers game. Several factors contribute to this situation.

The SF field harbours an ingrained philistinism in which many authors, publishers, critics and readers share. Whatever they may imagine, most people don't really want new approaches or ideas. They do not want the sort of fictions of which real literature is made. Fictions, that is, with central balance, which do not tell us we are living in the best of times, which do not pretend that materialism is all, which do not present the galaxy as a bauble for "conquest", and which traffic honestly with the tragic as well as the sunny side of life. Science fiction which presents any of these qualities separately or together is liable to be rejected out of hand as "too downbeat", "too pessimistic". That piddling word "pessimistic" has long kept SF hanging back at the nursery door.

A recent instance here. Under the editorship of Shawna McCarthy, *Isaac Asimov's Science Fiction Magazine* has, in the last few years, been publishing some of the more adventurous and literate SF. As expected, the letter column of the magazine shows the reaction to which we have referred. This from the January 1986 issue:

> It appears to me that *Isaac Asimov's* is being turned into a new *New Worlds—America*, or a resuscitated New Wave, à la J. G. Ballard, really mainstream with a slight veneer of SF and/or Fantasy. Now I enjoy both science fiction and fantasy, also an occasional good satire or symbolic piece. What I *don't* enjoy is issue after issue of very little else except downbeat gloom and woe and death, death, death. One can get this from any newspaper.

This plea, eloquent as it is, is a demand for escapism that avoids the real issues of contemporary or any envisionable future life. The question of realism versus escapism has raged throughout the genre's history.

Another factor. Science and technology no longer present simple issues which can be readily dramatized. We have seen striking novels about planetary exploration. There is no striking novel about cloning (unless we include Kate Wilhelm's attractive *Where Late the Sweet Birds Sang* (1976)). Clones do not speak to our dramatic sense, as the end of Joe Haldeman's *The Forever War* (1974) testifies. The November 1985 issue of *Science* announces boldly on its cover—"The Next Step: 25 discoveries that could change our lives". It's an exciting thought, but the individual pieces, knowledgeable as they are, prove remarkably lacking in real vision. Somehow specialization has removed the spark from science: the range of vision is too narrow, too obsessed with fine detail to see the larger perspectives, the greater implications. Modern science communicates poorly and few SF writers—Benford, Bear and Sterling amongst them—have found the metaphors to translate its ideas. The seed lies ungerminated, six feet down beneath the jargon and statistics.

SF began in an era of individualism; scientists and "inventors" were individual; now they work in teams in laboratories where findings are arcane, and where only a rare author can reach them.

An Awards system functions within the American SF field. The first such award was given out at the Philadelphia World Science Fiction Convention in 1953, and went to the novel voted the most popular of the previous year. That novel was Bester's *The Demolished Man*. The award was an irregular event for the next five years and was nicknamed the Hugo after Hugo Gernsback. 1959 saw the award formalized, and new categories added. Nominating ballots were held and voting membership was extended. But the broader franchise only reinforced the fact that what was being voted for was the most popular and acceptable, not the *best* piece of category fiction for that year.

In 1965 a second award was set up, the Nebula, awarded by the Science Fiction Writers of America, a body of active writers and critics working within the genre. It was to be a counterweight to the Hugos, providing a more literary judgement on that year's crop of fiction. Often the two awards overlapped, an indication, perhaps, that a work was well-honed as well as popular. Or so the theory went.

In the eighties we have a number of other awards: the John W. Campbell Memorial Awards, the Philip K. Dick Awards—the latter ostensibly to recognize new paperback writing. Great emphasis is placed on the winners of these awards. When publishers emblazon their paperbacks with "Hugo and Nebula Winner", sales can soar. For new writers the difference between obscurity and mass popularity can depend upon winning a Hugo or a Nebula.

It would be wrong to over-emphasize the effect of the awards on what is actually being written, but it would be crass to look upon a list of winners as a definitive guide to what has been happening in SF. Nonetheless, the awards cannot be ignored.

The awards also, generally, reflect what is happening in the American SF marketplace. Wherever SF came from, it is now, on the whole, an American pursuit. The main market is in the USA, the main financial rewards go to Americans. There are authors and publishers who live beyond the frontiers of the USA. There is SF published in other languages. These are the guerillas or the vassals of the central market place. That central market place demands a simpler product, easily packaged, something as reassuring as homogenized food bought in a shopping mall. SF has finally got into every home, just as the older fans hoped.

Even a cursory examination of the mass of SF currently being published reveals one striking phenomenon immediately. Much of it is not SF, despite its label. It is fantasy. Fantasy of various sorts. Moral/chivalric, amoral/heroic (to borrow two useful terms from David Hartwell), horrific, supernatural, conquest-addicted, hardwarist, elitist, and, of course, mixes of these kinds.

Many of these sub-genres owe their existence to the Tolkien cult of the sixties and to *Star Wars* and its successors. A million throats thirsting for escapism must be slaked (if not slit. . .).

To take an example from the nearest dumpbin. The *Horseclans* series by Robert Adams could be taken for SF. Certainly the premise contains what might be termed vaguely scientific concepts. A two-day war has plunged humanity (meaning the USA) into barbarism. Six hundred years later, the world has still not recovered. The Undying, immortal as a result of mutation, fight against evil scientists who can switch from body to body.

This setting is an excuse for scenes of torture, battle, and rape—and, of course, horses. Conan is the model, Howard's thick-armed Cimmerian hero, much more attractive on celluloid than on the printed page. Adams's series has proved popular, provoking more new adventures.

Unlike Howard, Robert Adams is as tough as his heroes. His publishers tell us that he is partial to "fencing and fancy swordplay, hunting and riding, good food and drink". He may be found "slaving over a hot forge to make a new sword". His heroes, equally, are no cissies. If it all takes place in some mythical future, where is the moral responsibility under which we labour today? Is it wise to chronicle a future in which our civilization has been wiped out of existence?

Other novels, less amusing, traffic in doom. The fate of the world depends on some poor slave girl and a man of low birth with—of course—mystic powers and an amulet from some distant future Neiman Marcus. Many romances of this kind opt for a feudal culture, the oldest favourite of all. They gloss over the real harshnesses of feudalism, where fiefs bore obligations to a lord, in cramped mediaeval societies where little freedom existed even for those who had large dispensations over the vassals below them.

Why does feudal life hold so great an attraction for writers of SF and fantasy? The answer in part is that the European Middle Ages need little research: one says "feudal life" as easily as one says "galactic empire" and, by long familiarity, a hazy picture is conjured up in the genre reader's mind. Similarly, galactic empires are often hazy reflections of the British Empire, where life was nasty, brutish, and in shorts.

Often galactic empires are revealed to have feudal bases—though how this politico-economic anomaly comes about is never explained. But perhaps the most compelling attraction of a feudal background is that money never has to change hands.

We are talking, after all, when we deal with this welter of fantasy, of the dreams of our society, our capitalist society. That society works by the circulation of money. What is the adolescent reader, the typical reader of these fantasies, most short of? Money. And the power that money brings. The attractions of societies where no money changes hands are obvious. A young fantasy hero cast up on a strange planet can go straight into the nearest tavern and obtain a tankard of ale or *bexjquth*. When did a fantasy hero ever fish a ten dollar bill from his pocket? When did milady seek alimony? When were travellers' cheques needed in Atlantis or Cathay? When was the lead villain simply slung into prison for debt? When did the mortgage ever fall due on one of those labyrinthine castles?

In the cities and taverns of idle fancy, young heroes neither pay up nor throw up. Instead, all their inner qualities are recognized and lauded, as never in life. The currency is flattery.

> A moment later, he was upon his mount once more, and riding on to Bombifale. In that ancient and most lovely of cities, where curving walls of the deepest burnt-orange sandstone were topped with pale towers tapering to elegant points, they had come to him one day, long ago when he had been on holiday alone, five of them, his friends, and found him in a tavern of vaulted onyx and polished alabaster, and when he greeted them with surprise and laughter they responded by kneeling to him and making the starburst sign and crying "Valentine! Lord Valentine! Hail, Lord Valentine!"

From *Valentine Pontifex* (1983), by the cunning old confectioner, Robert Silverberg.

In fantasies, banks—those bastions of capitalist society—are transformed into palaces or castles. Transactions take place in readily negotiable blood. It is not really science which yields to magic in these sagas, but the fiscal system. Hence the reason for their endless popularity. Witchcraft needs no bank loan. And, because such fantasies are always unsatisfying, it is also the reason why publishers need to keep up the supply of the drug, month by month. The Gor novels are for addicts, not adults. When economic policies weigh hardest on the people, dosages can be seen to increase.

It is perhaps hopeless to adumbrate the misty worlds of yesteryear which the fantasists have taken over. The land of the Norse gods, Atlantis, Greece, and anywhere smacking of ancientry—the Far East, the dunghills of Wales and Ireland, all have echoed to the clangour of miscellaneous hooves.

Even ancient Rome is called in. When David Drake, author of *Hammer's Slammers* (1979), came out with *Birds of Prey* (1984), his publishers explained what was going on in the Eternal City back in 262 AD: "One man stands between humanity and the Long Night, matching his savage determination against a hopeless future." Of course. We knew it, we knew it!

The land of King Arthur has been visited and revisited: yet even here, Marion Zimmer Bradley, famed author of the famed *Darkover* series, created a world-wide best-seller with her *The Mists of Avalon* (1983). Truly, fantasy is a Camelottery.

Out of these moneyless mists come heroes, heroines, and gods to satisfy an insatiable demand, accompanied by wizards, warlocks, unicorns and dragons, dwarves and faeries. It is hard to understand why the contemporary world should so desperately need these antiquated props from earlier ages, unless intellect is less secure on its throne than we had hoped.[12]

> Then Bres gave the signal to begin, and Lugh had no more time to consider. The woman was on him.
>
> Her attack was incredibly swift. She moved with sudden jerking movements, so fast she seemed to be coming from several points at once, driving in with both weapons. She poked and scratched at him and flapped around him continuously, while he moved and parried furiously, just to keep her off. . . .
>
> He tried to get his weapons up in defence, but she struck too swiftly. With a hoarse cry that was both hiss and shriek at once, she threw herself upon him. Her weight drove him back against the hearth. But as he fell, he realized with horror that it was now no human being who was upon him, but a giant raven, bigger than a hawk, black as a moonless sea.
>
> The bird was maddened by bloodlust. . . .

Kenneth C. Flint gets into his stride in *The Riders of the Sidhe* (1984), first of a series.

Though money rarely changes hands in fantasy novels, the novels are of course themselves objects of commerce, the better along with the worse. Individual novels or series, all must go through the check-out point. If they—if a whole year's harvest—if a dumpbin full of them—possess a corporate significance subject to analysis, then it is a disquieting one.

Brutality is a poor substitute for a tragic sense of life, plot for wit, or fancy for the genuine purging power of imagination. Yet something is being corporately bodied forth in the dumpbins of the mass-mind. If we are confronting the untutored consciousness, the unembarrassed outpourings of the mind of the US as it grows towards being the globe's dominating super-power of the Twenty-First Century—infinitely more strong, glittering, and expensive than any previous state—then we confront a mind almost wilfully irrational, technophobic, embracing the horrid, bugged by unknown superstition, and hypnotized by the infantile fantasy of owning the universe.

Fortunately, things are not as ill as they look. The increased commercialization of the field has opened the gates to cynical exploiters, who write their pile of rubbish, draw their pay, and move on into the sunset. The honest settlers sometimes tend to be ignored. But not always.

So to survey briefly some of the other strategies for survival within the fragmented and enlarged SF world of today.

Among the varieties of speculative fiction which abound, feminist fiction plays a major role. Inspired by the example of Ursula Le Guin, it has become almost a movement of its own during the seventies-eighties period.

Another great contribution to diversity has been the growth of SF scholarship, predicted in *Billion Year Spree*. The establishment of many courses in universities and colleges throughout the length and breadth of America has not been received with universal gratitude by SF writers. No doubt much of the criticism was drab at first. But the scholars are learning their new discipline rapidly. With the establishment of the SFRA (Science Fiction Research Association) and the IAFA (International Association for the Fantastic in the Arts), standards are improving.

Since the arrival of George Lucas's "real gee-whiz movie", science fiction books have appeared fairly regularly on the bestseller lists. Established authors have also sailed on to those tantalizing lists. Some now earn advances so sizeable they might be envied by novelists of any persuasion.

They certainly amaze writers of what we may call the literary novel. These large advances generally go to SF writers who have an established name and a nose for opportunity, such as Robert Silverberg or Jerry Pournelle. Older writers have also been attracted to the trough. While it is pleasant to see old warhorses like Robert Heinlein and Isaac Asimov raking in a million dollars at a go, it is saddening to read the resultant novels. To this curious phenomenon we devote a chapter later in this volume.

Large movies and large sums of money give the impression that SF is flourishing, commercially at least, though many authors of the middle range are in difficulties, or have turned to other fields, particularly in the UK. One strategy to overcome this and aid chances of publication is to launch out on a series. It was never easier to sell a trilogy, never harder to sell a single, difficult but well-crafted novel.

All publishers run such series. They are aware of the value of building up readers' allegiance. One of the more remarkable concoctions is the *Thieves' World* series, edited by Robert Lynn Asprin, sometimes with Lynn Abbey. Each volume contains various stories by various hands, all with a commonly invented universe as backdrop, a universe housing the usual mish-mash of murderers, aliens, unicorns, magicians, and so on, after the style of Fritz Leiber's celebrated Gray Mouser series. It is difficult to see how this kind of writing by committee can be successful in anything but a commercial sense; and in that sense it *is* successful. Money sanctifies many abominations. The publishers claim that over a million copies of the six *Thieves' World* titles (to date) are in print.

In the great welter of competition in a free market, gaudy covers are like stones on the seashore. Perhaps a Boris Vallejo piece of artwork catches the eye. An almost naked barbarian woman clutches her sword in one hand and the decapitated head of a man in the other. This is *Cheon of Weltenland, Book One: The Four Wishes* (1983), written by an English lady called Charlotte Stone—so we are told. Sub-Conan again, but with a lesbian heroine, whose adventures sometimes raise a smile. ("'I feel me a great desire of thrashing your ass on the bed, Theela—what say you?' he would say without shame.") But with several more books in the series still to go, the honest Ms Stone fairly warns the reader: "Thus did I lose Wanin who I thought never to see again. But I did, as you will learn if you read all my tale, be it ever so long." Aye, there's the rub.

A point about all these long series seems to have escaped general observation. Adolescent readers may be short of money—one reason to love stories where virtue and bravery win the princess's hand, not wealth as in the real world—but they are long on something else: time. Adolescents have time; time enough to consume a dozen *Dunes*, *Belgariads*, Covenants and the rest, just as their fathers sat in the apple tree all afternoon long, reading the adventures of John Carter on Mars.

That sense of time, of leisure, of security, perhaps of a log fire and bedtime delayed, are vital things threatened in our generation. It is too easy for an older generation to complain if what seems dull to them is satisfying to their children. The pleasures of reading are personal ones: something to be remembered when only two per cent of the population reads one book a year.[13] The readers of speculative fiction are to be cherished; and sometimes their authors must catch the very note they wish to hear, a note that older readers cannot. Possibly like this:

Late that night, refreshed and strengthened by a good dinner and much free laughter, Isaac Pen and Peter Lake sat down in the small study, staring at the fire. The heat ran around half a dozen logs that had become red cylinders of flame, changing their colours until they looked like six suns in a black universe of firebrick. Their glow was an invisible wind that irradiated the room and froze the two men in place—like deer in a forest which is burning all around them, who lift their heads to the highest and brightest flames and look into a tunnel of white light.

The magic of metaphor, which only the printed page is frail enough to bear, from Mark Helprin's *Winter's Tale* (1983). This aspect of the written genre cannot be stressed enough in an age where published material is often considered only as media fodder: fuel to stoke the ever-hungry furnaces of television— mini-series, TV movies, cartoons.

All of these factors have in some way distorted both what is expected from an SF writer and what is demanded by the readership. Awards and criticism on the one hand, the quest for large advances and blitzkrieg marketing—dumpbins and supermarket distribution—on the other, place pressures on writers that did not exist twenty-five years ago. Such pressures have grown phenomenally.

The SF field has never been *bigger*, nor has it ever—even in its infancy in the twenties—contained so much shoddiness and cynicism.

The pressure on a young writer to compromise his or her unique vision—to say something safe and acceptable, something *saleable*, something *proven* in financial terms, rather than risk new expression, new ideas—is enormous. New writers enter a genre that promises riches to those who will abide by its rules and nothing to those who will not, like Hollywood in the thirties and forties. There are exceptions, of course, but excellence is rarely an easily marketed commodity.

Few writers actually like starving in garrets. Discouraged, many stop writing, do something else. But what are the modern alternatives? Marketing— our most recent consumer sickness—creates a uniformity of demand and thus a standardized product. The unwary new writer too often becomes such a product overnight, his or her name bloated beyond all true worth. Such balloons rarely touch earth again. Those whom the gods wish to destroy, they hype too soon. . . .

In the chapters which follow we look at the new age of science fiction. An age in which SF became "popular", perhaps even respectable—a thing undreamed of back in the thirties. The Space Age. The Nuclear Age. A new age of Man. Years of aspiration and decline, of unprecedented luxury and immeasurable misery. The Drug Age. The Post-Industrial Era. The Punk Era. The day of the computer terminal. And of the dumpbin. . . .

CHAPTER XII

The Day of the Life-Style:
Into the Sixties

"Discorporate and come with me, shifting, drifting, cloudless, starless, velvet valleys and a sapphire sea. Unbind your mind, there is no time to lick your stamps and paste them in, discorporate and we will begin."
—Mothers of Invention: *'Absolutely Free'*.

And, even while fashion's brightest arts decoy,
The heart distrusting asks, if this be joy?
—Oliver Goldsmith: *The Deserted Village*

When did the dull, plodding world suddenly light up?

When did it fill with a vast, fast, cast of youth, all brilliantly playing roles only dreamed of previously in gaudy SF magazines?

What called into being all those glitzy, ritzy new classless culture-vultures, those hair-fashion stylists, those priests of the computer, those cookery experts, those dieticians, those instant ten-minute celebrities, those specialists in this and that (but especially in *that!*), those sanitized, austerely-sculpted models whose faces travelled across the globe's glossier and ever glossier newsprints? Those magazine pundits, those trendy swamis, those TV personalities, those hit-and-run satirists (shareholders now!), those Welsh sociologists, those authors of coffee-table books (just add the legs!), those pale interior decorators, those tanned jet-setters, pop mega-stars (twenty and over the hill!), spy-thriller chroniclers, maestros of the perfume bottle, playboy playwrights, transsexualists, drug-philosophers, acid-rockers, media men, Medean women, permanent partygoers, airline owners, beautiful people who never went to bed alone, and fore-doomed presidents?

What called them into being? When did they shimmer into life?

In the sixties.

In the sixties, when the concept of Image was all, and a euphoria of creativity and fake creativity bathed—nay, permeated—the Western world.

In the sixties, when Marshall McLuhan was the Son of God, or at least in a meaningful relationship with Him. Or, if not Marshall McLuhan, then Timothy Leary (a legend in his own mind). Everyone had meaningful relationships in the sixties—if only with their sex counsellors.

Austerity and drabness were out. A law was passed forbidding old age. The days of the holocaust were behind . . . and possibly ahead. But not NOW. NOW was for the Pill, for Peace, for Profile, for Pantheistic mysticism and violence in the streets. NOW was for the glowing images of television: by which flickering light whole societies seemed to radiate a more glowing image of themselves.

It was the Day of the Life-style, of Style itself.

And of course, such radical chic, such radical change, affected science fiction. It divided it radically. The old guard of SF writers who had grown up in the pulp tradition and were used to obeying its rules of play found themselves challenged by a new guard, a new generation of writers who wanted to break the rules, to import Life-style, philosophy, the trendier, so-called softer sciences, contemporary prose, and—of course—much heartier helpings of sex.

In the sixties, too, the Japanese started showering their Greek gifts on the West, those transistorized marvels which made earlier technologies of the West look about as spiritually uplifting as bakelite.

New technologies proliferated quantally. Future Shock was just around the corner—Alvin Toffler was compiling notes. The decade saw the development of the laser (1960), manned spaceflight (1961), communication satellites (1962), supersonic aircraft (1963), the discovery of quasars (1964), unmanned landings on the Moon (1966), the first heart transplant (1967), the discovery of pulsars (1968) and finally, a manned landing on the moon (1969).

The boundaries of known science were expanding more rapidly than ever before. Magazines like *Analog* (the re-vamped *Astounding*, still in the capable hands of John W. Campbell) reflected that ever-shifting frontier. But it was upon the social manifestations of those new discoveries—the spinoffs of the new high-tech age—that the SF writers focused their attention. They saw change all about them and mimicked that social metamorphosis in their extrapolated futures.

For all that it deals with hypothetical tomorrows, science fiction has always been of its age; more so, in fact, than any other literary form; for while the contemporary novel deals with social circumstances that are the result of past events—ideological, technical and historical—science fiction rides the crest of the wave of social and scientific thought, extrapolating the Now. The very diversity of its imaginings, which makes it a poor hunting ground for the futurologist seeking prophetic visions, tends to date it quickly. This was always the case, of course, but it was first evident in the heady, changeable days of the sixties.

The excesses of the sixties were passing shows. The accent on style—on *fashion*, simply another term for ephemerality of taste—seems, in retrospect, more dashing than important. Although that part of the science fiction genre which reflected fashion has dated, its experiments were not all fashionable capers but reflected a deeper dissatisfaction with the limitations of what was still, as the decade began, mainly a magazine form of fiction read by a limited coterie.

Style—it implies a degree of self-consciousness which wasn't there before, an element of outrageous showmanship, defiance, detachment, and just a touch of narcissism. Style—it is the heart of the science fiction controversy in the sixties. Style—reflecting a widening of choices rather than conformity of ideas, attitudes and expressions (the *consensus* of the Campbell stable as an instance) is the brand image of sixties' science fiction.

The sixties were also years of growing prosperity for science fiction writers. The revolution in publishing—paperbacks, anthologies, and regular hardback publication—meant more gasoline in the tank for some of those writers who'd ridden out the austerity years of the pulps. But for most it remained a case of produce or starve.

Over-production was a feature of the sixties. To meet demand, old as well as new SF poured from the presses in New York. Anthologies of old stories brought a shrinkage in time. Suddenly it seemed as if all the SF ever written was in print. And maybe it was.

It was good news for readers. But several of the major writers dealt with in this chapter and the next suffered from having to produce too much too quickly, without the opportunity of re-writing or polishing. Science fiction was still seen as ephemeral entertainment, although some fans had graduated to become editors and publishers. Growing stylistic awareness was, to a great extent, kept in check by economic necessity. But some authors—even those who were forced to over-produce—did grasp that entertainment and art weren't necessarily at odds, while others—Philip K. Dick perhaps foremost amongst them—produced art unconsciously from the schlock elements already to hand in the genre.[1]

But if there were some who had the vision, there were others who, had they even sniffed the idea, would have been after the rabbit, Art, with a twelve-bore and wide, barbarian grin. Foremost among them, perhaps, was the writer who cut his teeth in Campbell's *Astounding* back in 1939 and who had, in the decades since, built up a reputation as the "master" of the field, Robert Anson Heinlein.

In a symposium in 1947, Heinlein had produced an essay entitled, "On The Writing of Speculative Fiction".[2] There he laid down the five cardinal 'business habits' of a science fiction writer:

1. You must *write*.
2. You must *finish* what you start.
3. You must refrain from rewriting except to editorial order.
4. You must put it on the market.
5. You must keep it on the market until sold.

Such "rules" were, for the main part, unchallenged as the sixties opened—at two cents a word writers had to sell a *lot* of words to keep their heads above water. This, compounded by small audiences, was the chief reason why there were fewer than a dozen full-time science fiction writers as the Sixties began. It didn't pay to think of SF as art. It was like this year's car, this year's refrigerator, this year's nuclear shelter, made to be superseded, to be disposable.

Permanence crept in like anti-rust. Maybe the fans did it, working like Darwin's earthworms towards ends they could not visualize. Fans had always collected the magazines, treasured them, rather than throw them away. For them, obsolescence was a way of life. The fifties had seen some of their old favourites attaining the dignity of hard-cover publication. How about if SF took over all literature?

Heinlein himself, sagely anticipating revolutions both inside the genre and outside, cooled a typewriter still hot from *Starship Troopers*, slimmed a lengthy novel called *The Heretic* (to editorial order, of course) changed its title, and launched it on the seas of publication. A bid for universal acceptance was entered.

Stranger in a Strange Land (1961) is, perhaps, Heinlein's most eloquent novel, and it is one he says had to wait publication "until the public *mores* changed".[3] In certain respects it anticipates the dramatic change in attitudes towards sexuality that swept America (and thus the rest of the Western world) in the sixties, though without anticipating the accompanying misery, heartbreak and envy that the new morality brought in its wake. Although it is a heavily flawed book, Heinlein's energy and audacity are turned to full volume. It is also an ambitious book, and that deserves some respect.

As in much of his earlier work, Mars hangs just below the horizon.

The central figure of *Stranger in a Strange Land* is Valentine Michael Smith, twenty-five years old and a distant relation of Tarzan; he was born on Mars and brought up by Martians. Back on Earth, his strange Martian ways threaten political stability. He is even better equipped than Tarzan, materially and mentally—materially because oddities of his birth have left him heir to several considerable fortunes and have possibly made him owner of Mars as well; mentally, because he has picked up all sorts of psi powers, learned from his Martian parents.

Although the novel is by no means "a searing indictment of Western civilization" as the blurb of the First British edition (1965) would have it, *Stranger* does pitch in heartily against many of our idiocies, just as the early Tarzan books did.

But the odd attraction of *Stranger* is that it mixes the Burroughs tradition with the Peacock–Aldous Huxley tradition. It is filled with discussions of religion and morals and free love. For Smith comes under the protection of Jubal Harshaw, a rich old eccentric know-all, who holds forth about everything under the sun. Jubal is a distant and tiresome relation of Propter in *After Many a Summer* (and was later to spawn the even more distant and tiresome Chad Mulligan in *Stand on Zanzibar*, as well as that tireless and tiresome generator of aphorisms, Lazarus Long, in Heinlein's own *Time Enough for Love*).

Smith's ideas of sharing come from his Martian nest, which sounds much like the Martian nest in *Double Star*.

All the characters talk a great deal, their verbosity only exceeded by the characters in more recent Heinlein novels. Here's a sample, where Jubal and Ben discuss Smith's rejection of conventional moral codes, and Jubal calls Smith a "poor boy":

"Jubal, he is *not* a boy, he's a man."

"Is he a 'man'? This poor ersatz Martian is saying that sex is a way to be happy. Sex *should* be a means of happiness. Ben, the worst thing about sex is that we use it to hurt each other. It ought *never* to hurt; it should bring happiness, or at least, pleasure.

"The code says, 'Thou shalt not covet thy neighbour's wife.' The result? Reluctant chastity, adultery, jealousy, bitterness, blows and sometimes murder, broken homes and twisted children—and furtive little passes degrading to woman and man. Is this Commandment ever obeyed? If a man swore on his own Bible that he refrained from coveting his neighbour's wife *because* the code forbade it, I would suspect either self-deception or subnormal sexuality. Any male virile enough to sire a child has coveted many women, whether he acts or not.

"Now comes Mike and says: 'There is no need to covet my wife . . . *love* her! There's no limit to her love, we have everything to gain—and nothing to lose but fear and guilt and hatred and jealousy.' The proposition is incredible. So far as I recall only pre-civilization Eskimos were this naive—and they were so isolated that they were almost 'Men from Mars' themselves. But we gave them our 'virtues' and now they have chastity and adultery just like the rest of us. Ben, what did they gain?"

"I wouldn't care to be an Eskimo."

"Nor I. Spoiled fish makes me bilious."

"I had in mind soap and water. I guess I'm effete." (Chapter 33)

Smith's psi powers include the ability to slow his heartbeat, psychokinesis, and making objects vanish—which objects include clothes, guns, and human beings.[4] He is also represented as being both of high intellect *and* a great success with the girls. In fact, as James Blish knowingly put it, Smith "can work every major miracle, and most of the minor ones, which are currently orthodox in Campbellian science fiction".[5]

So Smith is ideally equipped by his author to found a new religion—and he does. After "discorporating" quite a few troublesome people, Smith allows himself to be killed by the mob, and discorporates on to the astral level himself.[6]

Stranger in a Strange Land has an odd fascination, despite its faults. It reminds one of Huxley's *Island* in its attempt to offer a schema for better living, but Huxley would have been horrified by its barely concealed power fantasy. Indeed, in his next two novels, Heinlein was to discard even the trappings of science fiction and present unabashed power fantasies in the Burroughsian tradition, with *Podkayne of Mars* (1963) and *Glory Road* (1963). The new leaf had been only partly turned. One might go even further than Blish (who was writing at the time of publication) and say that *Stranger* in fact represents one apotheosis of Campbellian science fiction.

Stranger also heralds a different movement within the field, one that Heinlein himself would later condemn.[7] Irrational quasi-mysticism mouths its lines in the wings. *Stranger* has a curious case history. When first published, it did not sell very well, although it collected a Hugo. It slowly built up a head of steam and became one of the campus best sellers, along with *Lord of the Flies*, *Siddhartha* and *Lord of the Rings*, spreading thence to Underground success.

Panshin, writing possibly in 1965, has a startlingly prophetic thing to say. Speaking of the fact that the religious premises of Heinlein's novel are untrue, and super-powers do not exist, he adds, ". . . without these anyone who attempts to practise the book's religion (which includes mass sex relations) is headed for trouble. In other words, the religion has no point for anybody."[8]

The sixties, so good for so many people in the West, began with the success of *Lolita* and the trial of *Lady Chatterley* and ended with the trial of the hippie murderer Charles Manson, whose family messily took care of Sharon Tate and other victims, and whose career encapsulates all the slummier manifestations of the decade. Manson's grotesque quasi-mystical "religion" was compounded of many straws drifting in the sixties air-currents, among them Bible texts, Beatle music and drugs. He also picked up some Scientology from a defrocked renegade from that movement—and we might recall with some misgivings that Scientology, too, was the brain child of another of Campbell's SF writers, L. Ron Hubbard, alias Rene Lafayette. *And*, in the words of Manson's biographer,

> . . . another book that helped provide a theoretical basis for Manson's family was *Stranger in a Strange Land* by Robert Heinlein. . . . Initially, Manson borrowed a lot of terminology and ideas from this book—not, hopefully, including the ritual cannibalism described therein. Manson, however, was to identify with the hero of the book, one Valentine Michael Smith (Manson's first follower's child was named Valentine Michael Manson)—a person who, in the course of building a religious movement, took to killing or "discorporating" his enemies . . . To this day Manson's followers hold water-sharing ceremonies. . . .[9]

Of course, only a moralist would be silly enough to imagine, during the Vietnam War, that the Sharon Tate murders and all the rest of Manson's odious mumbo-jumbo could be any sort of logical end result of the well-established pulp tradition of the all-powerful male, largely epitomized in Campbell's swaggering intergalactic heroes.

In any case, much cultural bric-à-brac was adopted by the hippie culture which had little or no relationship to its point of origin. Grokking and discorporating were simply "hip" terms, meaningless and harmless enough for the most part, though not as misleading as Timothy Leary's championing of the puritanical Hermann Hesse as a prophetic visionary of the drug culture with his *Journey to the East*. But as outer space made way for inner space within the genre—as the imaginary outward journey became the "trip" inward, a sinister blurring of fact and fiction began to take place. Heinlein's novel stands at the very beginning of this process—a process still occurring in the modern, eighties genre with its blurring of fantasy and science.

Before leaving Heinlein (for a time, at least) one thing more remains to be said. Old-time fans still think of him as a hardware specialist. In fact, Heinlein moved over very early to writing a different kind of SF, and one more in tune with the sixties and thereafter—a variant which we may call Life-Style SF.[10]

That is to say, a fiction which places the emphasis on experimental modes of living more in accord with contemporary pressures.

Heinlein kept a low profile after 1966's *The Moon is a Harsh Mistress*. Other, much younger, writers dominated the central years of the decade, winning the critical kudos and reshaping the nature of the genre with a stylistic panache only rarely seen in the genre prior to that time. There had been Bester, of course, and Theodore Sturgeon, but they were exceptions. The new shapers expressed themselves, quite naturally, in terms of style:

> A few months before I first went to Europe, a young woman music student came knocking at my door, waving a copy of *The Magazine of Fantasy and Science Fiction* with an absolutely obsessed expression: "Have you read this, Chip? Have you *read* this? Who is he? Do you know anything about him? What has he written before?" "The Doors of his Face, the Lamps of his Mouth" was headed by one of *F&SF.*'s less informative blurbs. I read it: that copy of the magazine went with me to Europe. I gave it to half a dozen people to read.[11]

The "Chip" of this reminiscence is Samuel R. Delany, and the author of the story was Roger Zelazny. Both proceeded to make dazzling names for themselves.

Unlike more radical shifts in attitude and approach which were to come a little later in the decade (from the British SF magazine, *New Worlds*), such changes as Delany and Zelazny made were embraced by the traditionally conservative American SF genre. Between 1966 and 1970 they were awarded nine of the major prizes in the field. In many ways they are—and were, even at the outset of their careers—poles apart as writers. Yet for the period of their greatest influence they seemed to share a number of concerns and were commonly linked in the minds of readers and critics alike. They were the new thing, the heralds of change.

Delany, almost five years younger than Zelazny, was the first to see his work into print. Unlike any previous writer working in the heartland of the science fiction field, Delany entered the field not as a producer of short stories for the magazines but as a fully-fledged novelist. His first novel was the ambitious and exuberant *The Jewels of Aptor* (1962). This book, prefiguring so many of the colourful traits of Delany's work, appeared when he was only twenty. In the six years that followed, a further eight novels were published, most of them trimmed to fit the Ace Books format.

Much has subsequently been written about the *meaning* of Delany's work— the underlying "Quest" pattern,[12] the experimentation in terms of language and perception, and the attempt to further Heinlein's Life-Style SF and create changing mores for changing times[13]—but what impressed at first reading was style, sheer *style*! The ideas were familiar fifties models—post-holocaust worlds of mutant beings—but the manner of expression transformed the tired images and scenes.

Fire leaped from the boy's hands in a double bolt that converged among the dark bodies. Red light cast a jagged wing in silhouette. A high shriek, a stench of burnt fur. Another bolt of fire fell in the dark horde. A wing flamed, waved flame about it. The beast tried to fly, but fell, splashing fire. Sparks sharp on a brown face chiseled it with shadow, caught the terrified red bead of an eye, laid light along a pair of fangs.

Wings afire withered on the ground; dead leaves sparked now and whips of flame ran in the clearing. The beasts retreated and the three men stood against the wall, panting. Two last shadows suddenly dropped from the air towards Snake, who still stood with raised arms out in the clearing.[14]

Such writing typifies Delany's early work, in which poets, the aristocrats of street-life, were frequently important actors. Delany's work was somewhere on the borderland between science fiction and fantasy—a middleground he was later to defend as "*speculative* fiction"—and its poetry was the poetry of excess, a form of rhetoric. Multi-armed heroes (some with only one sandal) stalk Delany's stories, along with a cast of giants and dwarves, geniuses and telepaths, incomprehensibly powerful aliens and galaxy-conquering villains, street punks and kings. Delany himself was there behind his mask, usually as the street poet in many of the early works, a criminal-outsider with a gang name—Snake, Vol Nonik, Lobey, Ni Ty Lee, Rydra Wong, The Mouse—and a strong sense of aesthetics, if not morals. But that too was part of the charm of these novels, with Delany a blend of Jean Genet and Cordwainer Smith, part cynical literateur, part wide-eyed fan. Realism entered Delany's work only with the lengthy (879 pages!) and long-laboured-over *Dhalgren* (1975). There we can see him crouched behind the figure of Kid, yet another poet of the streets.

From the outset there was a far greater emphasis on language than on ideas, although Delany's thoughts on hierarchies of perception, argued most cogently in his Nebula Award-winning novel *Babel-17* (1966), were something new in the genre. But it is for his intelligent approach to the actual business of writing, and his recognition of the sheer potentiality of science fiction's vast stock of ill-used and under-used metaphors, that Delany's work is valued.

Of Delany's early writing, the trilogy of novels which make up *The Fall of the Towers*[15] is perhaps his weakest. *Nova* (1968), with its re-casting of the Prometheus myth, is undoubtedly his finest, a work rising head and shoulders above contemporary SF novels like *Stand on Zanzibar* and Alexei Panshin's *Rite of Passage*, to stand on the level of *Do Androids Dream of Electric Sheep?*—all products of that same year. By comparison, *The Einstein Intersection* (1967), another re-telling of myth—this time of Orpheus in the underworld—is a slight and somewhat pretentious work, far too deliberate in its reconstruction and its levels of allusion and much too lightweight a story, anyway, to deserve all that mythical underpinning. Nonetheless, it too won a Nebula as finest SF novel of its year.[16]

Delany's short stories—almost as few as his novels—were collected in *Driftglass* (1971). Divorced from the quest formula that structures most of his novels, they show just how greatly Delany depends upon sheer style to carry his storytelling. There is a great deal of diversity in his shorter work and two of the stories won major awards; even so, a curious absence of dramatic tension or ideative innovation obtrudes. While Delany did bring an aesthetic sensibility to bear on what were standard genre materials, the end effect was one of disguise, not transformation.

Delany's central characters were of ambivalent sexual preference and, in stories like "Time Considered as a Helix of Semi-Precious Stones" (1969)[17], Delany explored a hip restructuring of society in the face of mass-media domination. In many ways, "Time Considered . . ." is archetypal Delany. It contains a name-changing semi-criminal narrator, another street-punk poet (Hawk, the Singer), cameo scenes of life with both the dregs and the elite— "Hell's Kitchen at ten; Tower Top at midnight"—and a style which, with its irritating parentheses, its obsession with colourful detail, and its total disregard for conventional genre means of story-telling ought to have been something truly experimental. It reads, in fact, like Heinlein on speed.[18] It is baroque, over-rich and garish. As pure story it is a piece of insubstantial and inconsequential work that suggests but never properly invokes a feeling of the criminal society it set out to depict.

For all his faults, however, Delany was *new*, and what was new was *in*, with writers like Fred Pohl and Theodore Sturgeon championing Delany's "cause". Delany was also *in* in a new way—he was the first SF writer to make himself at home travelling from campus to campus, relishing literary debate. Like all new things it soon became the fashion.

Delany's influence has been lasting.[19] Zelazny's influence was more immediate; he seemed at the time more accurately to reflect the mood of America's youth. Whilst Delany, in his move towards semiology and structuralism, travelled far from genre concerns, Zelazny was absorbed into the very heart of the body corporate that constitutes science fiction, rather like a slice of rich, alien gateau digested hungrily by tastes long deprived of such luxury. Part of his ready reception was due to the fact that for all its innovations of style (in terms of the magazine genre), Zelazny's work heralded a return to the pre-Campbellian mode of story-telling. It was a non-analytical, Burroughsian fiction. Stories like "A Rose for Ecclesiastes" (1963) called upon the settings of its fantastic precursors as unabashedly as did Heinlein's fantastic homages to Burroughs, *Podkayne of Mars* and *Glory Road*, clearly part of the same micro-climate.

One of the things that linked the work of Delany and Zelazny in the popular SF mind was their common use of myth as underpinning for their stories and novels. Of course, science fiction has often drawn on myth[20], but rarely so blatantly as these two "new generation" writers. Perhaps myth was grokked as the Image of Yesteryear.

Four of Zelazny's novels are re-workings of myth. *This Immortal*, which first surfaced as *". . . And Call Me Conrad"*, winning a share of the 1966 Hugo for best novel, is a confused and deeply flawed exhumation of old Greek myths, tangled up with a tale of aliens from Vega who want to turn Earth into a holiday resort. Thanks to charter flights, of course, we see exactly this happening to modern-day Greece, and so some claim might be made for Zelazny's prophetic insight in this minor regard, but as a science fiction novel it barely holds together. The mythic basis lies there, stodgy and undigested, in the stomach of the tale, and only Zelazny's innate sense of character makes this journeyman effort work. His hero, Conrad Nomikos (or Kallikanzares, or Karaghiosis), is one of many such in Zelazny's work—a man skilled in the martial arts, blessed with cunning, insight and a poetic tongue (almost, but not quite, a variant on Delany's street-punk poet). He proves, in this post-nuclear scenario, to be one of the old gods returned. Time and again the weight of allusion is a ball and chain, but the buoyant style, linked with a genuine concern for the first-person hero-narrator, brings Zelazny imaginative freedom. One senses here, in Zelazny's first novel-length work, how much in need of a good editor the early, undisciplined writer was.

The second and least overt of Zelazny's excursions into myth was *The Dream Master*, published the same year as *This Immortal* (1966). Like its predecessor, *The Dream Master* first appeared in a different form, under a different title; a shorter version, "He Who Shapes" (1965) won a Nebula. It is a more successfully structured novel than *This Immortal* and its central idea, about "Shapers", future psychiatrists who control dreams and thus cure the neuroses of their patients, is more compatible with Zelazny's imagination. Again it is a novel of character, the story of Charles Render, who plays God amongst his patients and proves, ultimately, to be more in need of his own treatment than they. Fortunately, Zelazny lets the story dominate the various strands of myth—Tristan and Isolde, the Grail Quest, Ragnarok—and concentrates on the interaction of his main characters. Jung is the off-stage Magus in this pointedly contemporary tale. With undiluted allusion thrust less frequently under the reader's often uncomprehending nose, the depth and richness of the brew comes through, flavoured by an occasional joy in recognizing those older patterns of thought which underlie Zelazny's modern fable.

Lord of Light (1967), Zelazny's third full-length work, was his most science fictional use of myth; a story which was, ironically enough, about the ossification of mythic patterns. Set in the far future and on an alien planet, *Lord of Light* is an investigation of Hindu mythology in a society where the gods are actualities amongst the technologically-repressed and medievalized masses. In fact—and in this lies the science fiction of the tale—these gods are mere immortals equipped with a few technological super-tricks like reincarnation into new bodies. As a tale it might be best described as an adventure story about form and chaos. It is fast-paced and intricate and more like an impressive comic book in prose than a genuine novel. The rigid, hierarchical structure of this alien society, mimicking the Hindu pantheon, is undermined by our hero, Sam (otherwise known as Mahasamatan), and the masses are, in effect, liberated to the blessed benefits of technology. Social concern plays back-seat to power-fantasy. The novel won a Hugo, of course. What wrong could Zelazny do in 1967, with such old turks as Theodore Sturgeon championing him?[21] But for all its mesmerizing glitter and excitement, *Lord of Light* remains a highly entertaining confection rather than the complex and homogeneous work of art some critics claim it to be.[22]

Lord of Light stands as a watershed in Zelazny's writing. From then on his work—with exceptions[23]—was to call more on the stereotypes of power fantasy than on genuinely envisaged characters and scenarios. The first clear sign of this deterioration can be found in his fourth dabbling with myth, *Creatures of Light and Darkness* (1969), where the Egyptian gods are wheeled out to do their party-pieces. But there's a sense throughout the novel of tiredness, of formularized responses to clichéd events.

Such degeneration shouldn't blind reader or critic to the impact of the early stories. It is with these, more than with the novels, that Zelazny established himself in the mid-sixties as a writer to watch. The novels reflected something happening in American culture at one level in the sixties—the struggle for identity as a cultural entity, we might call it: the search for a style that suited the inner man—which resulted in experimentation with old mythic patterns and behavioural systems as well as the development of cranky new cults. But the stories reflected another, perhaps stronger cultural element: the search for self and for individual expression.

Gallinger, the hero and first-person narrator of "A Rose for Ecclesiastes" (1962), is, like Conrad Nomikos, a mixture of great poet and man of action and proves, ultimately, to have been the alien saviour prophesied by Martian legend. Gallinger's development from self-obsessed elitist to love-sick and all-too-human catalyst of change, provides the small, individual perspective to a tale of an ancient Martian race who have succumbed to a profound and seemingly unshakable fatalism—in effect, a racial death-wish.

The story—with its rich embellishments and web of resonances centred upon the complex metaphor of the rose—has, for all its occasional clumsinesses, a potency that marks it out as something quite special in the genre. The sense of an old, tired culture encountering a new, vitally creative one is vividly created here. "It is our blasphemy which has made us great, and will sustain us, and which the gods secretly admire in us," Gallinger says, and we cannot help but agree. Gallinger, a frail, time-bound and highly singular and fallible human, defies—as Milton's Satan defied—the vast perspective of *what is*. By quoting the Book of Ecclesiastes (Man's own great fatalistic work) back at the Martians, with the message that pride and vanity are strong and necessary motivations for a living, growing culture, Gallinger achieves the status of germinating seed; of vital, creative catalyst.

These more universal comments aside, another aspect of "Rose" made it immediately popular. It made direct reference to and evocation of the sixties' ethos:

It was Greenwich Village I finally settled upon. Not telling any well-meaning parishioners my new address, I entered into a daily routine of writing poetry and teaching myself Japanese and Hindustani. I grew a fiery beard, drank espresso, and learned to play chess. I wanted to try a couple of other paths to salvation.

After that, it was two years in India with the Old Peace Corps—which broke me of my Buddhism, and gave me my *Pipes Of Krishna* lyrics and the Pulitzer they deserved.

The hip, modern man of the sixties, now an expert in tongues and no longer the competent engineer of earlier science fiction. This fashionable figure in effect encounters the ancient Mars of Burroughs and Bradbury and blunders into Self-Awareness. At the same time he plays symbolic corn-god to a dying race, thus fulfilling ancient prophecies.

Other stories share the verve and vitality of "Rose" while lacking its overall strengths—"The Doors of his Face, The Lamps of his Mouth",[24] "The Graveyard Heart", "Love is an Imaginary Number", "This Moment of the Storm", "For a Breath I Tarry", "The Man Who Loved the Faioli" and "The Keys to December". But very little of Zelazny's work after 1967 proved either as vivid or as imaginatively potent as these.

Another writer in the Burroughsian mould who had a great impact on mid-sixties' SF in the States, was Harlan Ellison.

Presented with a microphone, Zelazny leans back from it. Ellison grabs. He knows what Image is all about. Dynamic, garrulous, with something of the Archangel Gabriel and Quilp about him, swayed by his own gusty passions, Harlan Ellison is more a master of the hammer than the keyboard. Ellison is exclusively a writer in the essay or short story format. His work relies upon stylistic gaudiness—the shock of hyperbolic expression—to carry an essentially fabular kind of story-telling.

Stripped to their essence, Ellison's stories display a remarkable simplicity. "'Repent, Harlequin!' Said the Ticktockman" (1965) is pure fable, *modern* fable—a story about conformity, sterility and the stultifying effect of Time's dominion over Man's creative instincts. It's an undeniably powerful tale and yet, at the same time, it is ill-disciplined, raw-edged and—like much of Zelazny's work—in need of severe editing.

Between 1965 and 1969 Ellison, with Delany and Zelazny, dominated the genre's awards. Stories like "I Have No Mouth and I Must Scream", "The Beast that Shouted Love at the Heart of the World" and "A Boy and his Dog" did much to unsettle that part of the genre which was still preoccupied with hardware and problems in engineering and hyperspatial mechanics. All of Ellison's work of this period challenged the already weary belief that Technology was "a good thing"—particularly "I Have No Mouth. . . ." with its depiction of the world-encompassing computer, AM, which has swallowed its creators, and toys with them out of a vast malice formed of envy. Like so many of Ellison's stories, it is logically flawed. Why, for instance, couldn't AM build mobile extensions of itself and thus have the freedom of action it craves?—it does everything else bar this! Indeed, Philip K. Dick's 1960 novel *Vulcan's Hammer* posited just such a state. Ellison's story is also almost hysterically over-written yet remains powerfully effective. Like all good fables, it lingers in the mind far longer than other, calmer and more thoughtful stories. There are biblical cadences, almost the rhythms of evangelism in Ellison's work which outweigh the sometimes jumbled allegory. This is true particularly in "The Beast that Shouted Love . . ." and "Shattered Like a Glass Goblin", the latter a powerful anti-drugs story that fizzles out in its final page.

Ellison's masterpiece is "A Boy and his Dog" (1969), which won the Nebula for Best Novella that year. The boy of the title, Vic, and his dog, Blood, live in the ruins of a post-holocaust world where survival is paramount. These telepathically linked products of a stinking, morally degenerate environment are, in the story, contrasted with the citizens of "Topeka downunder", a thoroughly artificial picture-book, middle-class American, turn-of-the-century town. Topeka is built within a steel cave and is riddled with the cancers of hypocrisy, mean-mindedness and creative/sexual sterility. The story is, of course, a satire upon contemporary American mores—old stultifying values against new, amoral yet potent values: the literary equivalent of what Frank Zappa, with his group, the Mothers of Invention, was producing within rock music.[25] It is also a strong anti-sentimentalist, anti-love story, with the demands of survival outweighing all other demands and desires. A boy needs his dog, a dog has to eat, so Quilla June, the girl in the story, becomes food.

Ellison was important in the sixties for another reason—for his sponsorship and eventual editing of the anthology *Dangerous Visions*, which appeared amidst a thunderstorm of mock controversy in 1967. That this 33-story anthology could create such schisms in the genre is evidence of how cloistered the science fiction field was. The purpose of *Dangerous Visions* was, as Ellison painstakingly made clear to us, to challenge long-established taboos (mainly sexual, it seems) within the science fiction field and to write subversive material within the SF mode.

> But even more heinous is the entrance on the scene of writers who won't accept the old ways. The smartass kids who write "all that literary stuff", who take the accepted and hoary ideas of the speculative arena and stand them right down on their nose. Them guys are blasphemous.[26]

The thing has to be seen within context, of course. Some of the stories in the anthology—Spinrad's "Carcinoma Angels", and Philip José Farmer's "Riders of the Purple Wage" foremost among them—were of a very high quality.[27] Old and new wave writers were represented and many of them did write close to their best. But any comparison with "all that literary stuff" would have shown how uncontroversial most of it was set against writers like Henry Miller, William Burroughs and D. H. Lawrence, and how stylistically limited it was by comparison to writers like Herman Melville, James Joyce, B. S. Johnson and

William Golding: but such *real* comparisons were never popular within the genre.[28]

What *Dangerous Visions* actually was differed substantially from what it was claimed to be. What it *was* was an entertaining and thought-provoking collection, told with a care for the telling, and hyped dramatically. It was a marvellous showcase for some of the genre's better talents. What it was not was a genuine revolution. Within the American field, dominated by the artificially-sustained "family" values of the magazine ethos, these stories did appear quite shocking: but it was rather like shocking your maiden aunt with ribald limericks.

There was, however, a more genuine revolution going on at the same time— one which (for all Judith Merril's championing of it in the pages of *F&SF* and her intelligent annual anthologies) attracted less attention but which had more lasting and more profound effects on the genre. In Ladbroke Grove, in the heart of London, home of the Swinging Sixties, a British SF magazine was reshaping the materials and attitudes of the genre by producing work that was both genuinely radical and, within the larger context of the mainstream, literary.

New Worlds was founded by British fans. It made its first appearance in 1946 and, for the first eighteen years and 141 issues of its life, was a small circulation, fairly traditional British science fiction magazine, operating like an outpost of the American pulp tradition. It published the early works of British authors such as Arthur C. Clarke (his "The Sentinel", basis for *2001*, appeared there in no. 22 back in 1953); E. C. "Ted" Tubb (for many years the great producer of British SF and in recent years prolific author of the yet-multiplying *Dumarest* series, with about 30 titles to date); James White; John Rackham; Kenneth Bulmer; Philip E. High; Arthur Sellings; John Brunner (who was selling SF to *Astounding* at the age of seventeen); Brian Aldiss (a stalwart of *New Worlds*'s pages since 1955); and J. G. Ballard; as well as a number of American writers.[29]

Under E. J. "Ted" Carnell's editorship, anything experimental or new got in along with the hack work. But from issue 142, May–June 1964, all that changed. Carnell retired. Michael Moorcock took over the editorship of the magazine. Moorcock was twenty-four and the veteran of ten years' magazine editing and, in what was tantamount to a manifesto, began to alter radically the contents and direction of the magazine. The new god was not Edgar Rice but William Burroughs, of whom Moorcock wrote:

> And in a sense his work is the SF we've all been waiting for—it is highly readable, combines satire with splendid imagery, discusses the philosophy of science, has insight into human experience, uses advanced and effective literary techniques, and so on.[30]

Moorcock (and Ballard) saw Burroughs as the perfect mirror of "our ad-saturated, Bomb-dominated, power-corrupted times" and viewed him as the archetype for a new kind of unconventional SF which did not neglect the demands of entertainment. In the later sixties many could question whether the demands of entertainment *were* considered by the magazine at its most excessive. Yet Moorcock did not merely stick to his ideal of a new form of science fiction, one that wasn't simply a mimicry of Burroughs, but offered a variety of experimentation and themes; he also encouraged a good number of American as well as British writers. He was to prove the most dedicated and generous of editors.

In the mid-sixties, metamorphosis was necessary. England was *swinging* by then, with Beatlemania gripping the country, hair lengthening, consumerism thriving, and mini-skirts shortening; a new mood of hedonism was in the air. The British Empire had dissolved; the Romans were becoming Italians.

Moorcock's *New Worlds* had few taboos—something that often got it into trouble with distributors. It encouraged rather than rejected literary experimentation and steadily became the focus for a re-evaluation of genre standards and a crucible for new attitudes. The very first Moorcock issue contained the beginning of a two-part Ballard serial and an article by Ballard on William Burroughs.

> In *The Naked Lunch*, Burroughs compares organized society with that of its most extreme opposite, the invisible society of drug addicts. His implicit conclusion is that the two are not very different, certainly at the points where they make the closest contact—in prisons and psychiatric institutions . . .

It was to these extreme points that Ballard instinctively journeyed, the poles of mental inaccessibility, where normal and abnormal met on apotropaic neutral ground.

Moorcock's energy and the imagery of Ballard and Aldiss attracted a new audience to science fiction. It was, in fact, an audience already around, grokking the more way-out strata of the life of their time, but not at all tuned to the old pulp idiom, of which the Carnell magazines had been the tired inheritors.

The new *New Worlds* seized on an essential truth: that the speculative body of work contained in the SF of the past had been directed towards just such a future as the mid-sixties: the Sunday colour mags, proliferating LPs, drugs, promiscuity, cheap jet flights, colour TV, pop music that suddenly spoke with a living mouth—and the constant threat that the Middle East or Vietnam or South Africa or Somewhere would suddenly blow up and end the whole fantastic charade forever and ever amen—this actually *was* the Brave New World, nor were we out of it!

By 1967, while Harlan Ellison was trumpeting about how dangerous his anthology was, Moorcock was busy publishing Disch's *Camp Concentration*, Aldiss's *Report on Probability A* and *Barefoot in the Head*, Pamela Zoline's "The Heat Death of the Universe" and parts of John Brunner's *Stand on Zanzibar*, not to mention the more extreme experimentation of writers like Ballard, Michael Butterworth, Giles Gordon and Barrington Bayley.

Around *New Worlds* and the flamboyant figure of Moorcock gathered a staff who often doubled as writers, among them the redoubtable Charles Platt[31],

Langdon Jones, Hilary Bailey, Mal Dean, M. John Harrison, Diane Lambert, and the anthologist (and subsequently children's writer) Douglas Hill. Word got about. By 1967, however, matters were getting slightly out of hand. Anarchy collided with its creditors.

New Worlds had been in financial trouble but had been bailed out by a generous Arts Council grant, an appeal for which had been supported by such eminent figures as Edmund Crispin, Anthony Burgess, Roy Fuller, Kenneth Allsop, Angus Wilson (for years a staunch friend of science fiction and whose *Old Men at the Zoo* is peripherally SF), J. B. Priestley, and Marghanita Laski.[32]

The magazine was never far from trouble with officialdom, however. When Moorcock published American writer Norman Spinrad's thumping novel about cryogenics, the politics of power and the power of TV, *Bug Jack Barron*—serialized throughout most of 1968—its four-letter words and eleven-letter activities like cunnilingus, led to Spinrad's being referred to as a "degenerate" in the House of Commons—a notable if not singular honour—and to the magazine being dropped by W. H. Smith, the biggest distributor and retail outlet in Britain. Paradoxically, all this happened at the same time that the Arts Council—government funded—extended its grant for a further period.

As important as the medium, however, were the writers with the new message. Ballard—perhaps made slightly frenzied by having been so firmly nailed to the masthead of Moorcock's pirate ship—rejected linear fiction and was writing "condensed novels", impacted visions of a timeless, dimensionless world, lacerated by anguish, desiccated by knowledge, and illustrative of William Burroughs's dictum, "A psychotic is a guy who's just discovered what's going on."

> *Pentax Zoom.* In these equations, the gestures and postures of the young woman, Trabert explored the faulty dimensions of the space capsule, the lost geometry and volumetric time of the dead astronauts.
>
> (1) Lateral section through the left axillary fossa of Karen Novotny, the elbow raised in a gesture of pique: the transliterated pudenda of Ralph Nader.
>
> (2) A series of paintings of imaginary sexual organs. As he walked around the exhibition, conscious of Karen's hand gripping his wrist, Trabert searched for some valid point of junction. These obscene images, the headless creatures of a nightmare, grimaced at him like the exposed corpses in the Apollo capsule, the victims of a thousand auto-crashes.
>
> (3) *The Stolen Mirror* (Max Ernst). In the eroded causeways and porous rock towers of this spinal landscape Trabert saw the blistered epithelium of the astronauts, the time-invaded skin of Karen Novotny.

One "chapter" from "The Death Module", powerfully conveying some of the dislocation and unexpressed connections of its time. It is principally a question of style, once more, but style complementing its austere and haunting subject matter.

As a novelist, Ballard was less successful. *The Wind from Nowhere* has already been mentioned as a cosy catastrophe. The purest draught is contained in *The Drowned World* (1962), a picture of a landscape glowing in flood and heat, in which man is an amphibious thing, a native of disaster lured towards some ultimate nemesis.

The Drowned World sets the pattern for other Ballard novels of the sixties, all of which are novels of catastrophe, and in form—if form only—owing a good deal to John Wyndham; which may be why Ballard has cutting things to say about Wyndham. *The Crystal World* (1966) shows Ballard's style glittering darkly and reduplicating itself like the jewels encasing his saturnine forests. But the central problem of writing a novel without having the characters pursue any purposeful course of action—even more acute in *The Drought* (1965)—is not resolved. Ballard resolved it only in his novels of the seventies, *Crash!* (1973) and *Concrete Island* (1974) for instance, where obsession has usurped more normal plot criteria, or in his non-SF novel of the eighties, *Empire of the Sun* (1984), where the strength of autobiographical reminiscence powers the recasting of images familiar to the reader from Ballard's science fiction.

Ballard's short stories are *sui generis*. They hinge upon inaction, their world is the world of loss and surrender, their drama the drama of a limbo beyond despair where action is irrelevant. Early novels coin colourful doom-worlds; the best short stories stick (as do the seventies novels) to regions on the outskirts of London or Los Angeles only too bleakly familiar. Ballard's singular gift has been to identify this urban wilderness and give it a voice.

Some of Ballard's condensed novels were published together as *The Atrocity Exhibition* in England in 1970. American publishers took longer to bite and retitled the book *Love and Napalm: Export USA* (1972). Read together, the condensed novels become repetitive, and Ballard's habit of pushing jargon as others push dope becomes distracting. So is a repetitive use of what may almost be termed "Ballardian" imagery, setting and characterization. Indeed, in the last case *The Atrocity Exhibition* tends to illustrate the facelessness and colourlessness of a typical Ballard character. Interchangeable and anonymous in name and identity, he has no more significance than anything else in the obnubilated landscape.

Taken singly, as was originally intended, the condensed novels are more impressive; but it is perhaps the stories of Ballard's "Terminal Beach" period which will last the longest. His ferocious intelligence, his wit, his cantankerousness, and, in particular, his single-minded rendering of the perverse pleasures of today's paranoia, make Ballard one of the grand magicians of modern fiction. His is an uncertain spell, and not to all tastes, but it spreads—as Moorcock was among the first to perceive—far beyond the stockades of ordinary science fiction.[33] Ballard may have his weaknesses but his strengths are inimitable.

A passage from "The Terminal Beach" (1964) incorporates some of the symbols later to return in more impacted form to Ballard's fiction.

The Naval Party
When the search party came for him Traven hid in the only logical place.

Fortunately the search was perfunctory, and was called off after a few hours. The sailors had brought a supply of beer with them and the search soon turned into a drunken ramble.

On the walls of the recording towers Traven later found balloons of obscene dialogue chalked into the mouths of the shadowy figures, giving their postures the priapic gaiety of the dancers in cave drawings.

The climax of the party was the ignition of a store of gasoline in an underground tank near the air-strip. As he listened, first to the mega-phones shouting his name, the echoes receding among the dunes like the forlorn calls of dying birds, then to the boom of the explosion and the laughter as the landing craft left, Traven felt a premonition that these were the last sounds he would hear.

He had hidden in one of the target basins, lying among the broken bodies of the plastic models. In the hot sunlight their deformed faces gaped at him sightlessly from the tangle of limbs like those of the soundlessly laughing dead.

Their faces filled his mind as he climbed over the bodies and returned to his bunker. As he walked towards the blocks he saw the figures of his wife and son standing in his path. They were less than ten yards from him, their white faces watching him with a look of almost overwhelming expect-ancy. Never had Traven seen them so close to the blocks. His wife's pale features seemed illuminated from within, her lips parted as if in greeting, one hand raised to take his own. His son's face, with its curiously fixed expression, regarded him with the same enigmatic smile of the child in the photograph.

"Judith! David!" Startled, Traven ran forwards to them. Then, in a sudden movement of light, their clothes turned into shrouds, and he saw the wounds that disfigured their necks and chests. Appalled, he cried out. As they vanished, he ran off into the safety of the blocks.

If some of *New Worlds*'s writing was deliberately difficult, Moorcock's campaign converted a lot of fans and won new readers. Another major writer working regularly within the magazine's pages was Michael Moorcock himself.

Moorcock is a great, vital, generous figure, full of vigour and creative juice. He is also an awesome producer, though he over-produced throughout the late sixties and the first few years of the seventies. Much of that earliest work is hastily written sword-and-sorcery adventure (Hawkmoon, Elric and the Eternal Champion), which has proved durable in the popularity stakes. It was written in response to financial necessity—but of a kind different from the needs of most SF writers of the period. Moorcock had a towering, passionate disinterest in money for its own sake. He wanted money only to keep *New Worlds* going. Subscriptions and the Arts Council grant covered production costs, but Moorcock was often left with the problem of finding money to pay the contributors. His solution was to conjure a fantasy out of a bottle of whisky in three days flat.

Saying so much doesn't explain enough. Moorcock's sword-and-sorcery, for all its hasty construction, is not of the usual stereotyped kind. Edgar Rice Burroughs may have been an early hero of Moorcock's, but the young English writer switched Burroughs's formulae. Burroughs's swaggering heroes became Moorcock's uncertain, tormented victims-as-heroes, like Elric with his vampiric broadsword, Stormbringer. Blood and gore a-plenty flowed about Elric's saddle, but Moorcock's anti-heroes lived and breathed and had more personal problems than Conan would ever have dreamed of. As critic Colin Greenland has remarked, "Moorcock is the first sword-and-sorcery writer to build the psychological function of reading fantasy into the work itself."[34]

Moorcock did not confine himself to sword-and-sorcery. Perhaps his best known work from the *New Worlds* era chronicled the adventures of sixties' anti-hero Jerry Cornelius. The Cornelius books[35] were loosely structured and baroque, owing something to Bester's two fifties' novels[36] as well as to Burroughs (William, this time), Ballard and Wells. In a sense it was the same contemporary world coldly glimpsed in Ballard's work, but a world in which warm pastiche breathed, a world with far greater animation and personality. Cornelius himself was an attractive anti-hero, almost the hedonistic, amoral Everyman of his time. The novels themselves, cluttered with images and objects—vibrators, Sikorsky helicopters, Mars bars among them—are deliberately less meaningful. Of course, this was a kind of fictional in-joke amongst the writers of *New Worlds*: consequently, a comic book quality often pervades much of the writing.

Moorcock seems not to have taken his subject matter too seriously; the Cornelius adventures were a dark comedy set not just in space and time, but in all spaces and all times (though essentially *here* and *now* . . . Portobello Road, London, circa 1966)—in Moorcock's all-connecting "Multiverse", that realm of infinite possibilities:

> It was a world ruled these days by the gun, the guitar, and the needle, sexier than sex, where the good right hand had become the male's primary sexual organ, which was just as well considering the world population had been due to double before the year 2000.
>
> This wasn't the world Jerry had known, he felt, but he could only vaguely remember a different one, so similar to this that it was immaterial which was which. The dates checked roughly, that was all he cared about, and the mood was much the same. (*The Final Programme*, Chapter 6)

Perhaps ultimately more lasting was a novella Moorcock wrote for *New Worlds* 166 (September 1966) and subsequently revised for novel publication. "Behold the Man" won that year's Nebula for Best Novella and is the strongest argument against the view that Moorcock failed to practise what he so vehemently preached in the pulpit of *New Worlds*.

Behold the Man is *The Time Machine* as Wells would never have dreamed it. Part of the novel concerns the childhood and adult experiences of a young sixties male, Karl Glogauer. In its psychological portrait of Glogauer, *Behold the Man* is a superbly written mainstream novel concerned with how character is determined by event and vice versa. It was definitely *new* in this respect—in that it was concerned more with inner space than outer, with the effects of drugs on human life more than alien encounters, with psychology and not technology. But it is a science fiction novel, and an excellent vehicle for its ideas at that. For Karl Glogauer finds himself travelling back in time—in an experimental machine—to 28 AD. Back to the time of Jesus Christ, whom he finally meets:

> The figure was misshapen.
>   It had a pronounced hunched back and a cast in its left eye. The face was vacant and foolish. There was a little spittle on the lips.
>   "Jesus?"
>   It giggled as its name was repeated. It took a crooked, lurching step forward.
>   "Jesus," it said. The word was slurred and thick. "Jesus."
>   "That's all he can say," said the woman. "He's always been like that."
>   "God's judgement," said Joseph. (Chapter 12)

Glogauer's discovery that the "real" Christ is a congenital idiot results in his taking on the Christ role, recreating the life of Christ he remembers from his childhood scriptures—resulting, of course, in the crucifixion. Though the novel itself is a serious enough investigation of all the implications of this event and not a sensationalized account, the obvious blasphemy of the theme was attuned to the *New Worlds* experiment and did in reality what Ellison, in his introduction to *Dangerous Visions*, claimed to be doing. It is important to note also Moorcock's editorial presentation of *New Worlds* 166, which also contained the controversial "The Atrocity Exhibition" by Ballard:

> So, though we anticipate a certain response to some of the stories we publish in this issue, we hope that they will be accepted on their merits, on their own terms, and not regarded as "breakthrough stories" or "controversial" stories, or stories written to be sensational and to shock. They are seriously intentioned and deal with subjects that the authors felt deeply about. They are trying to cope with the job of analysing and interpreting various aspects of human existence, and they hope that in the process they succeed in entertaining you.

A wide gulf separates this from Ellison's "Them guys are blasphemous". And yet, for all the mumblings and grumblings of the "Golden Age" writers, Ellison's fake revolution was accepted without too much fuss, while most of what *New Worlds* attempted was—at least in immediate terms—rejected out of hand. Put it all down to showbiz razzamatazz, perhaps, but the emergent fact was clear—experiments with style were fine, perhaps even fun. Experiments with a style that reflected content matter was . . . well, it was different, unacceptable to most of the traditional readership.

Ironically, Ellison, Delany and Zelazny wrote some of their best material for publication in *New Worlds*.[37] Bright new American writers, sensing the importance of Moorcock's experiment, actually upped and moved to London. But we'll come to them in just a while.

Among the home-grown British talent were several names which deserve all-too-brief mention. Michael Butterworth, a fiercely intelligent writer, challenged *New Worlds*'s readers to untangle his literary conundrums, while Barrington Bayley—perhaps the most underrated short story writer in the genre—explored unconventional concepts with a remarkable ingenuity. His 1973 story, "An Overload", where future political constructs (named Sinatra, Bogart, Reagan!) control a multi-levelled city, is typical of his dark insights. Poets George Macbeth and D. M. Thomas were also drawn into the experiment. The latter extended the *New Worlds* lessons in his own novels, with great commercial success, *The White Hotel* (1981) becoming an international best-seller, while Macbeth's flamboyant novels seem to owe something to Jerry Cornelius. Pamela Zoline, with her exceptional "The Heat Death of the Universe", Langdon Jones ("Eye of the Lens"), Giles Gordon and M. John Harrison (to whom we shall return when talking of the seventies), all added to the flavour of *New Worlds*.

Before passing to those emigrés who graced the magazine's pages, brief mention must be made of David I. Masson, whose clutch of stories in the mid-sixties greatly enriched the *New Worlds* brew. He began spectacularly, in issue 154 (September 1965) with the story "Traveller's Rest", where H travels home from the war zone, the Frontier, and returns a few seconds later after his replacement has been killed. In the interim he has journeyed far south, away from the Frontier and its time-acceleration. The further he goes, the more slowly time passes. He has time enough to marry and have three children before he returns; time enough for normality before returning to the madness. Life as a long dream lived between moments of impacted madness. It suited the *New Worlds* idiom perfectly.

Masson's second venture was the powerfully evocative "Mouth of Hell" in January 1966, where atmosphere and idea are large enough to swallow any reader whole. It was science fiction of the most imaginative kind—metaphysical statements that touched one personally. Masson wrote only five more stories for *New Worlds* and wrote little fiction after 1967. His work, collected as *The Caltraps of Time* (1968), awaits rediscovery.

Two other writers, both Americans who moved to London in the sixties to be closer to the crucible of *New Worlds*, deserve more than a passing mention: Tom Disch and John Sladek.

Thomas M. Disch's science fiction rarely, if ever, left Earth. His first two novels, *The Genocides* (1965) and *The Puppies of Terra* (1966, also as *Mankind Under the Leash*) dealt with alien invasions in a far from conventional manner. People and their strange, alien ways mattered more to Disch than the aliens themselves. When Disch came to London and started contributing to *New Worlds* in September 1966, he was still very much an unknown commodity in terms of the SF audience. In the space of five years he produced a series of short stories—"The Squirrel Cage", "Casablanca", "The Asian Shore" and "Angoulême" foremost among them—and two novels, *Echo Round his Bones* (1967) and *Camp Concentration* (serialized 1967, book form 1968) which established him as one of the most intelligent and innovative of science fiction writers. With the intensity of a lapsed catholic he tailored science fiction's metaphoric richness to an investigation of the "human condition". Never more so, perhaps, than in *Camp Concentration*:

Enough of heaven, enough of God! They neither exist. What *we* want to hear of now is hell and devils. Not Power, Knowledge, and Love—but Impotence, Ignorance, and Hate, the three faces of Satan. You're surprised at my candour? You think I betray my hand? Not at all. All values melt imperceptibly into their opposites. Any good Hegelian knows that. War is peace, ignorance is strength and freedom is slavery. Add to that, that love is hate, as Freud has so exhaustively demonstrated. As for knowledge, it's the scandal of our age that philosophy has been whittled away to a barebones epistemology, and thence to an even barer agnoiology. Have I found a word you don't know, Louis? Agnoiology is the philosophy of ignorance, a philosophy for philosophers. (Book 2, Section 56)

The diarist of *Camp Concentration* is Louis Sacchetti, a minor poet and conscientious objector to the war in Vietnam. Transferred from a more regular prison to the deep caverns of Camp Archimedes, he is subjected to an experiment in intelligence raising. The "drug" used in the experiment, Palladine, is a derivative of syphilis; its effect is not merely to raise intelligence to new and giddy heights (some of which Disch strains to present in its own terms—a valiant if incomprehensible attempt!) but eventually to kill its subjects. Disch acknowledges his sources—Thomas Mann's study of syphilitic super intelligence, *Doctor Faustus*, undoubtedly lies behind the conception of Disch's novel—but shapes them to science fictional ends.[38] It is a harrowing, difficult book, more an intellectual treat than a good read, which in its last twenty pages proves as gripping as the most garish traditional SF yarn, as revelation follows revelation.

If Disch was shaping science fiction's metaphors to his own metafictional ends, John Sladek took the same bag of tricks and, with an intelligent and darkly humorous eye, turned the genre on its head. Although America and its contemporary inanities were often the butt of Sladek's humour, the science fiction story itself was just as likely to be subjected to Sladek's mischievous attentions. Parody and logical conundrum, blended with intelligent insight into the real problems behind SF's thoughtlessly-utilized themes—particularly that of artificial intelligence—marked Sladek's work from the first:

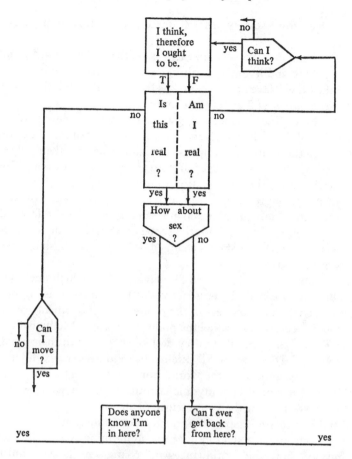

The novel that this delightful diagram is taken from, *The Müller-Fokker Effect* (1970), tells the story of Bob Shairp, who is reduced to computer data and stored on tape in a newly-discovered process. Like much of Sladek's work, it is a deeply satirical book, homing in on the US Army, evangelism, newspapers and the like for its targets, with an overall sense of fun reminiscent of the work of Kurt Vonnegut, Philip K. Dick and Sheckley. In recent years Sladek's stories of Roderick, a young, almost-human machine[39] have, in their thoughtful and funny way, provided an answer to the previous mechanistic views of robots.

In many ways *New Worlds* and its writers brought a cold sixties sophistication to the ideative content of the genre, together with some mere trendiness and a concern for a means of expression rather than simple stylistic showmanship. Delany and Zelazny gave you the icing but no cake; the *New Worlds* writers to a large degree provided both. In the States any writer with a freaky style became an honourable member of the New Wave—as Judith Merril publicized it—but the mistake was in assuming that style was all and meaning nothing. At the heart of *New Worlds*'s New Wave—never mind the froth at the edges—was a hard and unpalatable core of message, an attitude to life, a scepticism about the benefits of society or any future society. Merril demonstrated this in an early issue of *Extrapolation*.

Alarmed by the new hoo-ha (and it was, perhaps, pretty tiring unless you were young, high and living in Ladbroke Grove), Isaac Asimov said, "I hope that when the New Wave has deposited its froth and receded, the vast and solid shore of *science fiction* will appear once more."

What the New Wave deposited was much needed alluvial soil on that overtilled strip of shore. For the New Wave was but one of many tides and came much nearer to the source and impetus of creative writing than pulp formulae could. Its heroes did not swagger around in magnetized boots. They were generally anti-heroes, their destination more often bed than Mars.

To argue too strongly for either in such a controversy is a mistake. Failures and fatalities are thick on either hand, and good writers few. The new movement certainly widened both the scope of SF and its audience. For some years, at least, the image of SF was changed. It has become fashionable to write SF and even to read it.

The great mountain chains of old SF magazines, in which one may wander lost for a lifetime, may, in the perspectives of time, be seen as no more than a brief tectonic shrug of shoulders in the vaster plate movements of SF.

One should, nevertheless, recall the point that George Melly made about the Beatles in *Revolt into Style*, that "they destroyed Pop with their intelligence". The New Wave did the same to SF; intelligence and irreverence did it. Ballard's was not the sole perception of the world, nor Moorcock's the only approach to authorship, and it would be a myopic critical viewpoint which saw only the onset of the new and not the continuance of the old.

Shore and waves are inseparably linked in one function.

In the next chapter we shall look at the shore upon which the New Wave broke, and note both the continuances and changes in its ever shifting, tide-bound sands.

CHAPTER XIII

The Men in their High Castles:
Dick and Other Visionaries

Fortunately, in her kindness and patience, Nature never puts
the fatal question as to the meaning of their lives into the
mouths of most people. And where no one asks, no one need
answer.
—Carl Jung: *The Development of Personality*

What interested Jung was not the ordinary people who did not question their
lives, but the extraordinary ones whose nature compelled them to reject
conventional ways and views. Science fiction writers have a similar approach in
the main. The extraordinary, the monstrous, excites them. Many become
themselves monstrous. Their writings likewise. To their devoted readers they
become legendary monsters.

They sit in their high castles dreaming of alternatives. This is the story of what
some of them did in the sixties.

Firmly rooted in the old SF humus, but nevertheless highly susceptible to the
nutritious qualities of the new, were a pair of writers who had established
themselves in the fifties, Fritz Leiber and Philip José Farmer. Both were
interested in that amorphous realm, science fantasy—a hinterland of the SF
imagination. Their work cannot be classifed as "pure" science fiction in the
Campbell tradition, but it was exactly what the readers of magazines like *If,
Worlds of Tomorrow, Fantastic* and *Amazing* wanted: exotic and highly-coloured
glimpses of other worlds and other states of being.

Both were storytellers in some traditional senses. While the New Wavers
were conscious of breaking moulds in what they did, Leiber and Farmer were
happier transforming what they found—milking the metaphoric richness of the
genre as it existed, while yielding generously. This is not to say that they were
unaware of the larger literary context; both Leiber and Farmer were acutely
conscious of it and, when they put their minds to it, could beat the New Wavers
at their own game:

The Kid and his mate live in the old tree house now . . . surohc lakcaj fo
mhtyhr ot ffo kcaj chimps, Numa roar, Sheeta the panther cough like an
old junkie. Jane alias The Baltimore Bitch nag, squawk, whine about them
mosquitoes tsetse flies anti-things hyenas and them uppity gomangani
moved into the neighbourhood, they'll turn a decent jungle into slums in
three days, I ain't prejudiced ya unnerstan some a my best friends are
Waziris, whynt ya ever take me out to dinner, Nairobi only a thousand
miles away, they really swinging there for chrissakes and cut/

. . . trees chopped down for the saw mills, animals kilt off, rivers stiff stinking with dugout-sized tapewormy turds, broken gin bottles, contraceptive jelly and all them disgusting things snatches use, detergents, cigarette filters . . . and the great apes shipped off to USA zoos, they send telegram: SOUTHERN CALIFORNIA CLIMATE AND WELFARE PROGRAM SIMPLY FABULOUS STOP NO TROUBLE GETTING A FIX STOP CLOSE TO TIJUANA STOP WHAT PRICE FREEDOM INDIVIDUALITY EXISTENTIAL PHILOSOPHY CRAP STOP

. . . Opar a tourist trap. La running the native-art made-in-Japan concession and you can't turn around without rubbing sparks off black asses.[1]

Thus Farmer, writing a version of Tarzan as William and not Edgar Rice Burroughs might have written it for *New Worlds* 200, fulfilling with one foul blow Moorcock's formula for the new fiction. Then there's this from Leiber, prefiguring by a good eight years or so a more literary strain in the science fiction magazines:

There's a little window and the tops of trees that may be poplars when there's more light, and what there is shows cots like her own and heads under blankets, and hanging uniforms make large shadows and a girl is snoring. There's a very distant rumble and it moves the window a bit. Then she remembers they're Red Cross girls many, many kilometres from Passchendaele and that Bruce Marchant is going to die at dawn today.

In a few more minutes, he's going over the top where there's a crop-headed machine-gunner in field grey already looking down the sights and swinging the gun a bit. But she isn't going to die today. She's going to die in 1929 and 1955.

And just as she's going mad, there's a creaking and out of the shadows tiptoes a Jap with a woman's hairdo and the whitest face and the blackest eyebrows. He's wearing a robe and a black sash which belts to his sides two samurai swords, but in his right hand he has a strange silver pistol. And he smiles at her as if they were brother and sister and lovers at the same time and he says, "*Voulez-vous vivre, mademoiselle?*" and she stares and he bobs his head and says, "Missy wish live, yes, no?"[2]

The Big Time, from which this excerpt comes, won the Hugo for the best SF novel of 1958. The sudden, shocking juxtaposition of anachronisms and statements like "She's going to die in 1929 and 1955"—and this of a character who is patently "alive"—are symptomatic of a novel which is at one and the same time highly theatrical and acutely realistic. Its subject matter is the "Change War"[3], the vastest of all struggles, ranging through all space and all time. Our perspective, however, is a claustrophobic one, for all of the action in the novel takes place in "the Place", which, at one point in the novel, is cut off from all times, all space. Of all Leiber's work, it is the most deceptive and contains allusive riches that make it rather more experimental than those works—of Delany and Zelazny, in particular—which claimed that much for themselves. The science fictional struggle between the Spiders and the Snakes which makes up the pulp adventure element of the novel is transformed by the end of the book into a struggle within the mind of the Cosmos itself:

> In binding all possibility, the Demons also bind the mental with the material. All fourth-order beings live inside and outside all minds, throughout the whole cosmos. Even this Place is, after its fashion, a giant brain: its floor is the brain-pan, the boundary of the Void is the cortex of grey matter—yes, even the Major and Minor Maintainers are analogues of the pineal and pituitary glands, which in some form sustain all nervous systems.

Pulp influences overbalance artistic strivings, as ever in Leiber's work, but for once the struggle between the two is well worth the price of a ringside seat and art gets in a few cracking body-punches before the change commandoes finally triumph, singing their battle song as they go to blow ancient Egypt apart with an atom bomb.

The 6' 4'' Leiber—a somewhat Gothic figure in his dark costume—was the "only child of Shakespearean actors"[4] and his pulp origins as a writer[5] were counter-balanced by the knowledge that there was better writing elsewhere— the bard himself, Melville and Joyce. In the early sixties, however, Leiber was best known for his sword and sorcery tales of Fafhrd and the Gray Mouser, set in legendary Lankhmar, and what science fiction he did produce was often of a slightly humorous turn. But in 1964 he got hold of another vast concept and once more won himself a Hugo for the best SF novel of the year. The book was *The Wanderer* and it mixed in apocalyptic event, myth, pure science (of the Heinlein juvenile space-cadet variety) and a modernist multi-viewpoint technique—all to great effect.

A planet as large as the Earth and coloured a garishly vivid maroon and gold, appears suddenly from hyperspace and begins to dismantle the Moon for fuel. It's a successful recipe: disaster story meets love story meets tale of individual endeavour meets alien enigma. It's also a novel that inverts the normal science fiction formula—here everything falls apart at the beginning!—and has more in common with Bester's two baroque works of the fifties than the standard planet-splitting stories that appeared from time to time in *Analog*.

The Wanderer is also a book crammed to the teeth with science fictional references—particularly to Edgar Rice Burroughs's John Carter and his adventures on Barsoom. A number of the characters are science fiction fans— the exceptions seem to be saucer nuts or animals—and you have a real sense of reading a novel written specifically for a science fiction readership: something to be read out loud at a convention and rather too much of an in-joke to be entirely comfortable reading. Such playfulness is very much in character, however, coming as it does from the man who opened one of his 1951 stories with the sentence, "Pa had sent me out to get an extra pail of air".[6] There's rather more to

The Wanderer than playfulness and, like *The Big Time*, it ultimately transcends all jokes and genre clichés by the strengths of its imaginative undercurrents.

The Wanderer—principally through the character of the libidinous Sally Harris[7]—reflected new attitudes towards sex developing in American society. And there was that teasing Leiber title in a 1951 *Galaxy*, "Nice Girl With Five Husbands". It might almost have been a Farmer title.

As for Farmer himself, he was scandalous from the beginning. In "The Lovers" and *A Woman a Day* (a title if ever there was one to be graced with the most lurid of pulp covers rather staidly re-titled *The Day of Timestop* when it was revised in 1968) Farmer introduced sex to the magazine racks a good decade before they were ready for it. He went on in the late sixties to write a trio of sexually explicit SF novels.[8] It would be too easy, however, to see Farmer simply as a controversial writer and breaker of taboos, too easy to overlook the fact that he is one of the genre's finest entertainers. For various reasons Farmer has overproduced in the last three decades, with something like forty novels published. That said, there is little that's third-rate in Farmer's work. The best of it is imaginatively rich and highly memorable, a stir-fry of exotic ingredients.

Both Farmer and Leiber were working directly out of the Burroughsian adventure tradition, even in their best work, letting hectic coloration and fast-action plotting carry the reader smoothly through the tale. While their work was far from parodic (despite the fact that both have written Tarzan novels[9]), it must be said that Leiber was better at confronting the big imponderables than Farmer and less prone to turn aside into pure escapism.

In the mid to late sixties Farmer wrote a sequence of four novels, *World of Tiers*[10], a multi-levelled alternate universe tale which blended adventure elements with an intellectual puzzle. This picaresque-with-a-purpose presented an immortal Earthman, Kickaha, with a succession of adventures in different, fantastic environments reached through "gates" between the worlds (each of them straight from the pages of the twenties pulps—the dreaming pole of Burroughsian fiction in the ascendant). Unlike Burroughs's passive John Carter, transported suddenly and magically to Barsoom, Kickaha wants to know why he's there and what's going on.

This formula—a thinking man's variation on Burroughs—Farmer has used time and again, most successfully perhaps in his 1971 Hugo winning novel, *To Your Scattered Bodies Go*, the first of the Riverworld series. Here the nineteenth-century adventurer, Richard Burton, translator of the *Arabian Nights*, is the transported immortal Earthman, subject to the enigmatic doings of higher beings. *To Your Scattered Bodies Go* is an engrossing book. Much of its impact comes through the evocation of sheer scale.[11] "Imagine this!" Farmer seems to be daring us, and then presents us with an alien world where there is a river 25 million miles long, curling upon itself like the entrails of a giant. Along the banks of this mighty fluxion every human who ever lived has been reincarnated, naked and healthy—all 36 billion plus of them. It *is* a staggering notion, and, in a single, fast-paced book, Farmer's exploration of this marvellous metaphor— which reflects our own, *real* enigmatic existence here on earth—is successful.

Like Burton we want to know what's happening, why, and what exists at the end of the river.

Unfortunately, sequel syndrome set in. Farmer let his enjoyment of the world he had created tempt him to extend the journey. Four more volumes emerged before Burton finally discovers what the god-like humanoids are up to. It wasn't a tedious journey. Far from it; there was adventure all the way. But it was never again as memorable as at first, when Burton woke before time in the resurrection chamber with the sleeping billions suspended all about him, stretching away in almost infinite array. Nor were the shifting explanations of the final volume convincing. Faced with the Ultimate Questions, Farmer prefers to bundle his heroes into spaceships and thrust them out into the cosmos for further adventures. It is better to travel in hope . . . .[12]

Is Farmer more than a marvellous purveyor of escapist adventure? In his 1967 novella, "Riders of The Purple Wage"[13], there is an overt attack on the passive escapism practised by a whole section of the population of his envisaged future world:

> She has a hole in her head, and people addicted to fornixation seldom get fat. They sit or lie all day and part of the night, the needle in the fornix area of the brain delivering a series of minute electrical jolts. Indescribable ecstasy floods through their bodies with every impulse, a delight far surpassing any of food, drink, or sex. It's illegal, but the government never bothers a user unless it wants to get him for something else, since a fornic rarely has children. Twenty per cent of LA have had holes drilled in their heads and tiny shafts inserted for access of the needle. Five per cent are addicted; they waste away, seldom eating, their distended bladders spilling poisons into the blood stream.

Farmer's message here is to "rip out the umbilical cord" of dependency (of any kind), yet at the same time there's a sneaking suspicion that Phil Farmer is just a little in love with the "Purple Wage" of fornixation, the future's chemical Barsoom.

Another writer whose work exists at the dreaming pole is Jack Vance. Like Farmer, Vance has his own intense fandom round the world. Again like Farmer, Vance can be accused of producing too much too soon to satisfy. But here too there's intelligence behind the fast-paced action and exotic landscapes, while no trace of Burroughs's derangement can be discerned in Vance's imaginary worlds. Three major series have come from Vance's pen, *The Demon Princes*, *Durdane* and *Tschai* (also known as *Planet of Adventure* in a recent omnibus edition). In each case, Vance presents us with vividly imagined and highly idiosyncratic worlds. Durdane with its numerous Cantons (each with its own laws), its dirigibles and its Faceless Man as instrument of ultimate justice, is one example. The thinking self knows Durdane could never have come into being, but the dreaming self is glad it *does* exist . . . if only as a fiction.

Vance seems barely conscious in his work of what was happening in the real world, much less of the small scale generic revolution going on in Ladbroke

Grove. Changes in fashion and developments in the genre have left Vance unaffected, a gaudily painted coelacanth washed up on SF's shore.

That accusation cannot be levelled at Poul Anderson who, while being a *bête noire* of the New Wavers for his emphasis on hardware and militarism, deals with real issues quite often in his work, whether we agree with his conclusions or not. His first adult novel, *Brain Wave* (1954), a story of an Earth where all mammals experience increased IQ, brought Anderson early fame. He has won many Hugos and Nebulas since then, as a good writer with fannish orientation. A certain element of redskins among the stars marks Anderson's poorest work and he can seem quite inept at times: "It is Hloch of the Stormgate Choth who writes, on the peak of Mount Anrovil in the Weathermother. His Wyvan, Tariat, son of Lythran and Blawsa, has asked this. Weak though his grip upon the matter be, bloodpride requires he undertake the task."[14] One cannot help but wish that Tariat hadn't bothered, bloodpride or not!

We may regard Anderson's attempt to sketch out a future history—from our century to the seventy-second century—as slightly futile. The future is certain to be anything but what we imagine it will be.

This aside, what is often overlooked in the welter of space operas produced by Anderson, is his ability to present a balanced argument about militarism. Among his best work is "No Truce With Kings"[15] which counterpoints a Heinleinish bullishness—"I'd rather be dead than domesticated"—against a quite sensitive portrayal of a family ripped apart by Civil War. Then there's also *Tau Zero* (1970), an enjoyable novel about the relativistic effects on the spaceship *Leonora Christine* and its crew as it approaches the speed of light and becomes as big as the universe, counterbalanced by an admittedly rather soppy love affair. The voyage through space-time takes the ship beyond the dissolution of our universe.

Another future historian[16] whose work is set firmly in the heartland of the Campbellian tradition is Gordon R. Dickson, most notable for his sterling work on the six books of the Dorsai series[17], themselves part of a projected 12 volume scheme he has called the Childe Cycle, with three contemporary and three historical novels (all as yet unwritten) completing a unique examination of potential human development. Dickson's Dorsai is a genetically-enhanced future Sparta, a planet breeding sensitive military men. The young Dorsai heroes are confronted by situations on which hang the future of the human race.[18]

Dickson's ability to convey a genuine sense of their existence in a lean, uncluttered prose deserves admiration. As does his dedication—often through illness—to an almost impossible scheme.

Men like Gordie Dickson, Poul Anderson, Farmer, Vance, Leiber, embark on projects no mainstream author would attempt. They are true legendary monsters, worshipped by their readers as such, often to their detriment. So what, then, of Frank Herbert?

The charting of possible futures has become big business, as Frank Herbert discovered in recent years. A journalist with wide interests, Herbert had an impressive novel, *Under Pressure*, serialized in *Astounding* in 1955.[19] A number of fairly standard SF shorts followed before he started writing a very long work he called *Dune World*. It began serialization in the December 1963 large format *Analog* and ran for three issues, graced with some highly evocative illustrations by John Schoenherr. Many of the ideas were standard *Analog/Astounding* fare, but Herbert had sewn the familiar threads altogether into a tight, mesmerizing fabric, interwoven with a potent element of mysticism. Political intrigue in a harsh future Galaxy was a commonplace. So too were strange religions. But somehow Herbert merged the two strands with several new elements— primarily an interest in the eco-system of the planet Arrakis, the desert planet Dune—and produced something that is far greater than its parts.

Although Campbellian science fiction is still present, so, too, is an attention to sensuous detail which is the antithesis of Campbell. The bleak dry world of Arrakis is as intensely realized as any in science fiction. The shortage of water, for instance, is presented not just diagrammatically, but as a living fact which permeates all facets of existence.

In the dining hall of the Arrakeen great house, suspensor lamps had been lighted against the early dark. They cast their yellow glows upward onto the black bull's head with its bloody horns, and onto the darkly glistening oil painting of the Old Duke.

Beneath these talismans, white linen shone around the burnished reflections of the Atreides silver, which had been placed in precise arrangements along the great table—little archipelagos of service waiting beside crystal glasses, each setting squared off before a heavy wooden chair. The classic central chandelier remained unlighted, and its chain twisted upward into shadows where the mechanism of the poison-snooper had been concealed.

Pausing in the doorway to inspect the arrangements, the Duke thought about the poison-snooper and what it signified in his society.

All of a pattern, he thought. *You can plumb us by our language—the precise and delicate delineations for ways to administer treacherous death. Will someone try chaumurky tonight—poison in the drink? Or will it be chaumas—poison in the food?*

He shook his head.

Beside each plate on the long table stood a flagon of water. There was enough water along the table, the Duke estimated, to keep a poor Arrakeen family for more than a year.

Flanking the doorway in which he stood were broad laving basins of ornate yellow and green tile. Each basin had its rack of towels. It was the custom, the housekeeper had explained, for guests as they entered to dip their hands ceremoniously into a basin, slop several cups of water onto the floor, dry their hands on a towel and fling the towel into the growing puddle at the door. After the dinner, beggars gathered outside to get the water squeezing from the towels.

How typical of a Harkonnen fief, the Duke thought. *Every degradation of the spirit that can be conceived.* He took a deep breath, feeling rage tighten his stomach.

"The custom stops here!" he muttered.

He saw a serving woman—one of the old and gnarled ones the housekeeper had recommended—hovering at the doorway from the kitchen across from him. The Duke signalled with upraised hand. She moved out of the shadows, scurried around the table towards him, and he noted the leathery face, the blue-within-blue eyes.

"My Lord wishes?" She kept her head bowed, eyes shielded.

He gestured. "Have these basins and towels removed."

"But . . . Noble Born . . . ." She looked up, mouth gaping.

"I know the custom!" he barked. "Take these basins to the front door. While we're eating and until we've finished, each beggar who calls may have a full cup of water. Understood?" (*Dune*, Book 1)

And this from *Analog* in its maligned days!

The two Herbert serials about Arrakis ran in 1963, 1964, and 1965.[20] They are dense and complex books which repay careful attention and impress even on a fourth or fifth reading. As much cannot be said of the sequels which followed *Dune Messiah* in the seventies and eighties, but we shall come to them later. The success of *Dune* persuaded Herbert to throw in his lot with science fiction. The late sixties and early seventies were productive years for him, with a number of enjoyable, complex novels, including some about gods and god-making which remind one in theme if not in imaginative potency of *Dune*.[21]

Analog may well have seemed the complete antithesis to *New Worlds* during the sixties, though if we look back *Analog* seems less time-bound than *New Worlds*. But there were writers—miraculously enough—who did cross the seemingly impenetrable barriers between magazines and get published fairly regularly in both. Who were these schizophrenic creatures? Well, Harry Harrison for one. And English writer John Brunner for another.

Analog, like any other magazine, had its "names" in the early sixties, Murray Leinster, Christopher Anvil, Randall Garrett, James H. Schmitz and Mack Reynolds among them. Campbell's formula for good science fiction was still alive and, if not quite kicking, then certainly giving the occasional twitch. John Brunner, alone of the British writers who weathered the sixties, was able to produce work which fitted Campbell's bill. "Planetfall" in the May 1965 issue, for instance, was inoffensive and instantly forgettable, particularly when compared to work Brunner produced for *New Worlds*, like "The Last Lonely Man" in Moorcock's first issue, which Moorcock maintains "remains one of his very best short stories". But Brunner tried on many hats in the sixties and produced one of the giants—in size particularly—of the decade with *Stand on Zanzibar* (1968).

Zanzibar does not enter the matter; it is simply the area of land you would need on which to stand all the inhabitants of Brunner's 2010 world elbow-to-elbow. For this is a slick overpopulation novel, the crowded scene built up by slabs of close-ups, newspaper cuttings, coversation, jokes, and what the author calls "Contexts"—bulletins of one sort and another. All these buttress the narrative, and greatly increase its sense of density and complexity.

This is an extract from a party conversation, which shows some of the period slang at work:

> "One thing about this crazy party, I do depose—I never expected to see so many shiggies at Guinevere's place looking like shiggies instead of like sterile-wrapped machines. Do you suppose she's testing the temperature to see if she should move the Beautiques over to the natural trend?"

> "Happened all in a moment. One second, just a bunch of people walking down a street, not going any place in particular, and the next, these brown-noses clanging on big empty cans with sticks like drummers leading an army and all sorts of dreck flying through the air and windows being smashed if they weren't out already and screaming and hysteria and the stink of panic. Did you know you can actually smell terror when people start rioting?"

> "Louisiana isn't going to last much longer, you know. There's a bill up for next session in the state legislature which will ban child-bearing by anyone who can't prove three generations of residence. And what's worse they're only offering five to two against it being passed. The governor has his two prodgies now, you see."

> "I was in Detroit last week and that's the most eery place I ever did set foot. Like a ghost town. All those abandoned factories for cars. And crawling with squatters of course. Matter of fact I went to a block party in one of them. You should hear a zock group playing full blast under a steel roof five hundred feet long! Didn't need lifting—just stand and let the noise wipe you out."

> "It's more than a hobby, it's a basic necessity for modern man. It fulfils a fundamental psychological urge. Unless you know that if you have to you can kill someone who gets in your way, preferably with your bare hands, the pressure from all these people is going to cane you in."

Among all its diversions, *Zanzibar* produces three well-integrated stories, centering on present (sixties) discontents.

General Technics owns a computer called Shalmaneser, which is both vulnerable and unprotected, although tourists are allowed to view it. A girl tries to clobber it with an axe, and House—a black director of the company—has to come and sort out the trouble. He uses a liquid helium hose which snaps the girl's hand off her arm. This sort of unlikely and unpleasant melodrama militates against the lively intellectual dance going on elsewhere, and eventually overwhelms it. Before that, Brunner conducts a teach-in on modern moralities, aided by Chad Mulligan, a sort of hippie philosopher. As with all Propter-figures, as with Heinlein's Jubal Harshaw, Mulligan wearies, being an author mouthpiece. He puts us all to rights and even out-talks Shalmaneser. The book becomes too long.

Towards the end, faced with winding up a complex affair, Brunner takes refuge in a welter of action in which coincidences pile up, jaws drop, testicles hammer pavements, brains chill, and key scientists are smuggled out of police states at dead of night. The power of such well-observed details as casual terrorism—which has certainly become one facet of today Brunner foresaw—is dissipated.

But it is an interesting experiment, because it marks a stage along the road, midway between pulp and social commentary. Brunner had not prepared himself sufficiently in his previous writing for the creation of a major book: countless SF adventures—33 novels, many as Ace Doubles—before he slowed pace in 1966.

A man of intelligence and wit, Brunner seems unwilling to make a personal statement. His work has a cultivated distance to it. In *Zanzibar* he took courage from the new developments in SF, but it was as much style as social comment, as much pizazz as genuine perception of events, as later more didactic novels such as *The Sheep Look Up* (1972) demonstrate. Hip pessimism was also in style, as Michael Moorcock realized, presenting a more sober Cornelius in the last of Jerry's adventures, *The Condition of Muzak*, in 1977.

Harry Harrison negotiated with aplomb the rainbow-bridge between New and Old Waves. He has an enormous advantage over Brunner when it came to telling a tale—a sense of humour. Unlike many other writers, Brunner included, Harrison has a broad understanding of reality, coupled with a caustic acceptance of mankind as it is. He is the least probable author to have written *Childhood's End*: the Harrison version is *A Stainless Steel Rat is Born* (1985).

This legendary monster has his high castle in Ireland now and travels round the world every year—the world he has presented with a series of memorable entertainments, not missing a year for over three decades. Among them most notably is *Bill, the Galactic Hero* (1965), which, in its light-hearted way, has more than a lick of the New Tide in it, parodying as it does the megalomaniac worlds of Heinlein's *Starship Troopers* and Asimov's Trantor. *The Technicolor Time Machine* (1967) followed on the good work, to be capped by *A Transatlantic Tunnel, Hurrah!* (1972, wincingly re-titled *Tunnel Through the Deeps* in the United States). The latter is a parallel world novel in which George Washington was hanged after the Battle of Lexington and North America never broke away from Britain. One of the cleverest touches is the way in which the omniscient narrator thoroughly approves of the English class system and lordly British supremacy in this alternative twentieth century.

These three novels almost constitute a category of their own, buoyed as they are by Harrison's individual grasp of life.

Many of Harrison's lesser novels appear hastily written. Hardly surprising, for he has been one of the field's major editors, most notable among his productions being a decade of *Year's Best SF* (edited with the aid of a junior assistant) and the four volumes of *Nova*, in both of which series his sympathies with individual expression are expertly demonstrated.

His novel, *Make Room! Make Room!*—one of the definitive overpopulation novels—has already been mentioned. It was filmed in 1973 as *Soylent Green* with much more than the title changed in the process. But that's another story. . . .[22]

The Stainless Steel Rat books, featuring the exploits of one Slippery Jim diGriz, hardly add to his reputation, popular though they are. All the same, they burst out over and again with peculiarly Harrisonian virtues—for instance his love of horrible Paleo-Industrial artifacts. Here is the scene where diGriz (incognito, as ever) visits the smoke-filled castle of Count Rdenrundt on some remote and ill-visaged planet.

Something came in through the door and I recoiled, thinking the war was on. It was only a robot, but it made such a hideous amount of hissing and clanking that I wondered what was wrong with it. The Count ordered the ghastly thing to wheel over the bar, as it turned away I saw what could have been a *chimney* projecting behind one shoulder. There was the distinct odor of coal smoke in the air.

"Does that robot burn *coal*?" I gurgled.

"It does," the Count said, pouring us out a pair of drinks. "It is a perfect example of what is wrong with the Freiburian economy under the gracious rule of Villelm the Incompetent. You don't see any robots like this in the capital!"

"I should hope not," I gasped, staring bug-eyed at the trickle of steam escaping from the thing, and the stains of rust and coal dust on its plates. "Of course I've been away a long time . . . things change. . . ."

"They don't change fast enough! And don't get galactic-wise with me, Diebstall. I've been to Misteldross and seen how the rubes live. You have no robots at all—much less a contraption like this." He kicked at the thing in sullen anger and it staggered back a bit, valves clicking open as steam pumped into the leg pistons to straighten it up. "Two hundred years come next Grundlovsday we will have been in the League, milked dry and pacified by them—and for what? To provide luxuries for the King in Freiburbad. While out here we get a miserable consignment of a few robot brains and some control circuitry. We have to build the rest of the inefficient monsters ourselves."

He drained his glass and I made no attempt to explain to him the economics of galactic commerce, planetary prestige, or the multifold levels of intercommunication. He was still glaring at the robot when he leaned forward and suddenly tapped a dial on the thing's side.

"Look at that!" he shouted. "Down to eighty pounds pressure! Next thing you know the thing will be falling on its face and burning the place down. Stoke, you idiot—*stoke*!"

A couple of relays closed inside the contraption and the robot clanked and put the tray of glasses down. I took a very long drag on my drink and

enjoyed the scene. Trundling over to the fireplace—at a slower pace now
I'll admit—it opened a door in its stomach and flame belched out. Using
the coal scoop in the pail it shovelled in a good portion of anthracite and
banged the firedoor shut again. Rich black smoke boiled from its
chimney. At least it was housebroken and didn't shale out its grate here.

"Outside, dammit, outside!" the Count shouted, coughing at the same
time. The smoke was a little thick. I poured another drink and decided
right then that I was going to like Rdenrundt. (*The Stainless Steel Rat*,
Chapter 16)

The humour and imagination are characteristically Harrison. Grundlovsday
cannot come round too soon for many of his readers. "Harry is the iconoclast of
the known universe"—Philip K. Dick.

There was never a straight dichotomy between technophile and technophobe.
The interests of writers were too diverse for that. Antithetical to both the hard,
technological concerns of *Analog* and the stylistic, experimental emphasis of
New Worlds was a school of writing which we might term American Post-
Technology Pastoral. Traditional, comforting, and deeply humanistic in its
approach, it was typified by three writers, Clifford Simak, Edgar Pangborn and
Zenna Henderson. There were others, of course, but these three left their mark
on the decade, publishing in magazines like *F&SF* and *Galaxy*. Through their
influence they gave those magazines one element of their distinctive flavours.

Clifford Simak holds a special position in SF, enshrining as he does anti-urban
values and an open-air Midwest decency. He published his first science fiction
story, "The World of the Red Sun" in 1931 (the year before Huxley's *Brave New
World*) but was not an SF magazine regular until 1938, when he became part of
Campbell's *Astounding* stable. His *City* series of stories were first published in
Astounding in the forties, collected in volume form in the fifties, and completed
(with "Epilog") in 1973. They have already been mentioned.

In the sixties, Simak was highly active in the field, producing eight novels and
a large number of short stories. *Time is the Simplest Thing* (1961)[23] saw his return
to the novel after an eight year break, but it was not until the serialization of
"Here Gather the Stars" in *Galaxy* that Simak produced something as
impressive as *City* or *Ring Around the Sun*. It was published in novel form as *Way
Station* and won the Hugo Award for 1963.[24]

As before, Simak's central characters don't walk particularly tall, but they do
it amid corn or standing timber.

He stood on the rim of the cliff and looked out across the river and the dark
shadow of the wooded valley. His hands felt strangely empty with the rifle
gone, but it seemed that somewhere, back there just a way, he had stepped
into another field of time, as if an age or day had dropped away and he had
come into a place that was shining and brand new and unsullied by any
past mistakes.

The river rolled below him and the river did not care. Nothing mattered to the river. It would take the tusk of mastodon, the skull of sabertooth, the rib cage of a man, the dead and sunken tree, the thrown rock or rifle and would swallow each of them and cover them in mud or sand and roll gurgling over them, hiding them from sight.

A million years ago there had been no river here and in a million years to come there might be no river—but in a million years from now there would be, if not Man, at least a caring thing. And that was the secret of the universe, Enoch told himself—a thing that went on caring.

He turned slowly from the cliff edge and clambered through the boulders, to go walking up the hill. He heard the tiny scurrying of small life rustling through the fallen leaves and once there was the small peeping of an awakened bird and through the entire woods lay the peace and comfort of that glowing light—not so intense, not so deep and bright and so wonderful as when it had actually been there, but a breath of it still left.

He came to the edge of the woods and climbed the field and ahead of him the station stood foursquare upon its ridgetop. And it seemed that it was no longer a station only, but his home as well. Many years ago it had become a way station to the galaxy. But now, although a way station still, it was home again. (Chapter 25)

Time and again in Simak's books doors are opened on to strange, alien landscapes. It is a device he uses literally and which has its roots, perhaps, in Wells's "The Door in the Wall" or George MacDonald's *Lilith*. *Way Station* is, in this respect, the archetypal Simak book, for it deals with the keeper of such a door—"way station to the galaxy"—an immortal who meets strange travellers from every part of the teeming galaxy. Of course, this device is also a wonderful metaphor for the act of science fiction writing itself; this may be why Simak could breathe such life into Enoch Wallace, his civil war man who keeps lonely, ages-long vigil and tends the alien grave with its tombstone in an unknown, alien language.

Way Station is a book about substantial ghosts, about loneliness and about the sense of wonder itself and is, to many minds, Simak at his very best. Yet it ran against the general tide of the genre—that bipolarization of science fiction into colourful power fantasy and literary introversion. Not until Steven Spielberg came along with *E.T.* in a different medium, could Simak's ethos be said to be in the ascendant.

Simak was always weak on plotting but good on atmosphere and detail. This is true even of *Way Station*, which, like Leiber's *The Big Time*, is set mainly in a single room. Sound, if unremarkable novels followed, such as *All Flesh is Grass* (1965) and *Why Call Them Back from Heaven* (1967). But since *The Goblin Reservation* (1968) his novels have been less impressive. Even so, Simak in his seventies was still capable of producing a memorable and delightful novella, as is proved by his 1980 *Analog* story, "Grotto of the Dancing Deer" (another story of an immortal observer. It won the Nebula for that year).

Edgar Pangborn was New York born and bred. For all that, he is as much a country boy at heart as Simak.[25] In his work the humanistic element outweighs all the other traditional science fictional trappings. Science fiction allowed Pangborn a setting for his very human dramas and no more. As he himself wrote in the August 1974 issue of *Galaxy*, introducing the serial of his *The Company of Glory*:

> As in *Davy*, there are no gadgets, My raw material is just People and Possibilities and a touch of the Peculiar. In *Company of Glory* outer space stays right where it was when we last looked, and creatures with eyestalks remain at the bottom of the sea. The unexpected animals, here and in *Davy* could all be there without even a whisper about mutation.

If he had done nothing else, Pangborn would have been remembered for his elegant and moving pastoral, *Davy* (1964), to which *The Company of Glory* was a kind of prequel. One has only to open the book and read the first few paragraphs to get the flavour of Pangborn's writing.

> I'm Davy, who was king for a time. King of the Fools, and that calls for wisdom.
>
> It happened in 323, in Nuin, whose eastern boundary is a coastline on the great sea that in Old Time was called the Atlantic—the sea where now this ship winds her passage through grey or golden days and across the shoreless latitudes of night. It was in my native country Moha, and I no more than a boy, that I acquired my golden horn and began to learn its music. Then followed my years with Rumley's Ramblers into Katskill, Levannon, Bershar, Vairmant, Conicut and the Low Countries—years of growing with some tasty girls and good friends and enough work. And when, no longer with the Ramblers, I came into Nuin, I must have been nearly a man, or the woman I met there, my brown-eyed Nickie with the elf-pointed ears, would not have desired me.

Pangborn had won the International Fantasy Award in 1955 for his novel *A Mirror for Observers* which, for all its Martians, is a novel about human ethics, human values: "tasty girls and good friends and enough work" were always more important to Pangborn than inter-galactic warfare and planetary conquest. This healthy life response is shared by modern writers like Paul O. Williams and Kim Stanley Robinson, who have inherited Pangborn's concerns; it would be surprising if Pangborn's *Davy* were not a major influence.

Zenna Henderson was an Arizona teacher who always claimed that she wrote only what she knew about.[26] In the fifties she began publishing a series of stories in *F&SF* about the "People", a humanoid alien race, indistinguishable physically from Man, who had fled their edenic home planet and come to Earth. On Earth they were persecuted as witches by normal humankind who lacked some of their paranormal powers. As a sentimental portrait of the alien it out-Simaks Simak.

The aliens are essentially ourselves, with a few additional powers: their small, Midwestern community is modelled, it seems, on extant protestant communities, cut off from modern American culture. Henderson intended to end the sequence with "Jordan" in 1959, but sequelitis set in and she was still writing additional tales as late as 1975 ("Katie-Mary's Trip"). The stories were collected in two volumes, *Pilgrimage: The Book of the People* (1961) and *The People: No Different Flesh* (1966). As with Simak and Pangborn, Henderson was trying to deal with human potentiality and the capacity for caring rather than with Man-the-Tool-Maker. A sympathetic and intelligent film, *The People*, was made in 1971, with Kim Darby, William Shatner (Captain Kirk of *Star Trek* fame) and Dan O'Herlihy—a film notable in American SF cinema of the time for being neither shoddy nor sensationalized.

One further name, that of H. Beam Piper, might be added to the above. Piper was very much an *Astounding* man, with his Paratime Police series and such tough-jawed all-action novels as *Space Viking* (1963) and *Uller Uprising* (1953). Piper produced two other novels which fit within his "Federation" Future History series and fall more into the pastoral mould than his normal *Astounding* fare. These are *Little Fuzzy* (1962) and *Fuzzy Sapiens* (1964, also as *The Other Human Race*). Piper was of a school of writers—mainly technophile—who didn't question the notion that Man was the best thing that had happened to the Universe, and hanging wasn't good enough for anyone who disagreed. His was a literature of high organization and obscure knowledge; an auto-didact, Piper believed in the reconciliation of problems by logic, common sense or compromise—and, in the last resort, by justifiable force. The result was a series of conventional hardware stories, first-draft material prior to the revolution of style. But the two Fuzzy books[27] have a cosiness lacking in the rest of Piper's work. The cosiness consisted of a creature twelve to twenty-four inches tall, a ball of fur with large brown eyes and lacking all malice. A fuzzy.

Cynical readers, of course, had as little time for fuzzies as for Henderson's "People", and thought the author of "Omnilingual" (1957) had gone mad.

Fuzzies could be seen as a symbol of conscience, of lost innocence, of unfallen humanity. Take your pick. But in Piper's novels they were also *sapient*—not merely animals to be slaughtered and dealt with as part of Mankind's universal spoils. The struggle to prove and then assert the sapience of these creatures lifts these books above their pulp elements, prefiguring genre concern for ecology and the sentience of whales and dolphins.

The struggles evident in the novels, between unthinking military-type adventure and more thoughtful humanistic concerns, were, it seems, reflected in Piper's own life. Tragically, he committed suicide in November 1964, shooting himself with a handgun—one of over one hundred weapons in his collection. Poverty had reduced him to potting pigeons from his hotel window to ward off starvation.[28]

The questioning of technological progress has taken many forms since Mary Shelley's *Frankenstein*, among them the pastoral. One of the least known technophobe works is David R. Bunch's *Moderan*.

Now, to turn tedious for a time, this is what happened. Flesh-man had developed to that place on his random Earth-ball home where it was to be the quick slide down to oblivion. All the signs were up, the flags were out for change for man and the GO was DOWN. To ENDING. Flesh-man was at the top, far as he could climb as flesh-man, and from there he was certain to tumble. But he had the luck to have these brave good white-maned men in the white smocks, the lab giants, the shoulders, and great-bulged thighs of our progress (what matter if they were weazened, probe-eyed, choleric, scheming, little men sometimes—more often than not, REALLY?!) authors of so much of man's development and climb to that place where he was just due to die, expire, destroy himself and his home. These great good lab giants then froze man and his Earth-ball home at this grand stage of development to make new-metal man and set him in the Strongholds upon the plasto-coated Earth that had once been man's random and inefficient home. New-metal replaced flesh (down to the few flesh-strips and those, we hope, may soon be gone) the bones were taken out and new metal rods, hinges and sheets put in (it was easy!) and the organs all became engines and marvellous tanks for scientifically controlled functional efficiency forever. YAY! Don't you see?! Our Scientists made of life-man (the VERY-STRANGE-accident man) essentially a dead-elements man, one who could now cope with eternity, but he certainly was not a dead man. AH! Heavens no! He was alive! with all the wonderful science of the Earth ages, and just as functional as anyone could wish. YAY! science, take your plaudits now! You've shown what was meant from the beginning for the VERY-STRANGE-accident man.

As this extract shows, *Moderan* is about scientific dehumanization taken to its limits, yet told from a viewpoint which is superficially sympathetic towards this process. It is a darkly ironic book, where Man is seen reducing himself systematically to a brutal, callous, self-torturing machine. The theme has echoes of Nietzsche's Superman, a creature "beyond" a normal humane morality—beyond the pettiness of good and evil. Bunch's future humanity becomes the super-science men of Moderan, new-metal Men, at constant war with their neighbours, totally paranoid and mechanically immortal.

Bunch wrote the Moderan stories—mainly vignettes of two to five pages (the book version is comprised of 47 such pieces) throughout the sixties, publishing them in small literary magazines as well as in Cele Goldsmith's *Amazing* and *Fantastic*. One, "Incident in Moderan", appeared in *Dangerous Visions*. The vignettes provide tiny windows on a complex future society. In the book version (one hesitates to call it a novel) we trace the process of dehumanization as it affects Stronghold 10, once a man, slowly becoming a machine. The effect is as if Whitman and Nietzsche had collaborated to rewrite a typical Heinlein-Anderson-Niven-Pournelle future history story. As such it is a unique book in the science fiction field.

In his afterword in *Dangerous Visions*, Bunch revealed himself to be quite a rare creature himself—working for the US Air Force while pursuing an uncompromising career: "I wear no editor's and no publisher's collar when I sit down to that white paper."

Moderan appeared only once, in paperback in the USA in 1971. Like so many good books in SF's history, it vanished in the flood of hype which launches many lesser fictional craft.

The future is often delayed. Although Tolkien's great trilogy was first published in 1954, it was only with the paperback edition in 1965 that his great saga of Middle Earth became an almost universal read. *The Lord of the Rings*—the work and even more its staggering success—had a profound effect on SF. While not itself SF, it captured SF readers and writers. The power of its myth and its detailed picture of another world than ours prevailed; ever since, technological SF has been deposed from its central position.

While this may be regretted—not least by the compilers of this volume—the scholarliness of Tolkien, and the respect accorded him, have encouraged a rigour in the better writers (those who could profitably be encouraged) and brought about a wider outlook on the craft of science fiction.

Meanwhile, and perhaps correspondingly, the SF market was growing. Since, by the mid-sixties, it was no longer possible to read all the SF published, the old bibliomane pundits found their authority undermined. No longer was it necessary to memorize the contents of every old Gernsback magazine.

Very few factors ever improve conditions for writers in general. As individuals, they must fight their own fight, in large part. The bigger markets and higher prices being paid led to the hyping of new writers of slender talent and the overlooking of others, who, like Bunch or Harvey Jacobs in the States and David Masson in England, faded from view. But proliferation did mean that writers at the top of the scale were better paid for their work. So ended a long democratic tradition of everyone (bar three or four court-favourites) being in the same boat. Professional SF authors were still few in number.[29] Overproduction remained a hallmark of the field; its pride and its curse.

For this reason, revision of work was still as much the exception as the rule. That three-letter word, "Art", still evoked a philistine response in many quarters: the worst enemies of SF have always been its champions lurking within the field.

Critics like Alexei Panshin espoused a new, less parochial vision of science fiction. Although Panshin's novel *Rite of Passage* (1968) won the Nebula Award, it lacks the spark of life which might have fired its interesting subject matter, a *rite de passage* aboard a generation starship. For all its craft and its attempt to create an intelligent updating of a Heinlein juvenile, it proves tiresome rather than inspired. Style has become dullness.[30]

Less stylish but more enjoyable were the novels of Keith Laumer, an unabashed entertainer whose parallel worlds novels, beginning with *Worlds of the Imperium* (1962) are fresher than the formularized Retief novels that followed in the mid-sixties, though the latter proved more popular.[31] Hard to categorize other than as conjurors—singers of strange, sometimes acutely humorous songs—are Avram Davidson and R. A. Lafferty, both of whom have their addicts amongst the SF readership, and have shown genuine writerly attributes. But it is to three of the greatest entertainers in the field that we now turn. Entertainers whose dark, humanistic humour might be said genuinely to reflect the spirit of the decade: Robert Sheckley, Kurt Vonnegut Jr and Philip K. Dick. All three writers emerged in the fifties, to blossom in the sixties and continue writing into the eighties.

Sheckley at his best is Voltaire-and-soda. His fizzling nihilism expresses itself most pungently at short-story length. His stories poured into *Galaxy* in the fifties, when he could never write too much.

Sheckley has a wry inventiveness which skates him over profound depths, and a sense of playfulness even in his darkest moments. The "science" in Sheckley's work is not physics but metaphysics and his protagonists are wide-eyed innocents sent on journeys designed to disillusion the widest-eyed idealist. Thomas Blaine in *Immortality Inc.* (1959) and Joenes in *Journey Beyond Tomorrow* (1963) are typical of this Candide archetype. Religion and the existence/non-existence of God fashioned and perhaps obsessed Sheckley (in the way it did the later Phil Dick), but it was modern life and its absurdities which excited Sheckley's greatest interest and provoked his sharpest, wittiest responses.

> Joenes found this reply scarcely credible. He said, "Mr Watts, these people do not look dead. And in actual fact, all exaggeration aside, they are *not* dead, are they?"
>
> "I never put exaggeration aside," Watts told him. "But since you're a stranger, I'll try to explain a little more. To begin with, death is merely a matter of definition. Once the definition was very simple: you were dead when you stopped moving for a long time. But now the scientists have examined this antiquated notion more carefully and have done consider-able research on the entire subject. They have found that you can be dead in all important respects, but still go on walking and talking." (*Journey Beyond Tomorrow*, Chapter 5)

Echoes of Orwell's "We Are the Dead" aside, *Journey Beyond Tomorrow* is a novel which anticipated all that was to happen in America in the sixties and early seventies, a social fable. As unlike it as could possibly be—bar the infectious wit—was *Dimension of Miracles* (1968), Sheckley's best novel in the sixties. In that work Thomas Carmody finds himself—in true Simak fashion—involved in the wider galaxy of intelligent aliens, having won the Intergalactic Sweep-stakes. But as it transpires, he is the wrong Thomas Carmody, the prize itself is sentient—has wants and needs and berates Carmody for not satisfying them—and there is a special carnivore designed to hunt down the Carmodys. Insanely logical as it is, it puts the Big Questions as perhaps they ought be put—comically. Some of us grieved when Douglas Adams came along with his *Hitch-*

Hiker's Guide to the Galaxy and grew rich doing the Sheckleyan things which appeared to keep Sheckley poor.

Sheckley's charm is his irreverence, his iconoclastic shiftiness, his refusal to state an opinion and stick to it dogmatically. Everything is up for grabs, even God. In this he *is* the premier gadfly that Kingsley Amis termed him in *New Maps of Hell*. Sheckley is forever using phenomena for fun, so that science fiction's range of exaggerated metaphors are at their wildest in works like *Mindswap* (1966). The later Sheckley was to publish less often, *Options* in 1975, *The Alchemical Marriage of Alastair Crompton* (also as *Crompton Divided* in the States) in 1978 and *Dramocles* in 1983. Something of the effervescence of his earlier writings has vanished; besides, the galaxy of the eighties is less amusing. Overhead, without any fizz, the stars are going out. Sheckley is still, these days, wearing his Borges mask with its false tongue stuck firmly in its false cheek. His short stories still draw blood. Like P. G. Wodehouse's butler, Sheckley forms a procession of one.

Kurt Vonnegut Jr was an unavoidable figure on the American literary and campus scene in the sixties and cannot be said to have improved any since he was voted one of America's heap big gurus.

The purest Vonnegutian delights are to be found in his early novels, *The Sirens of Titan* (1959) and *Cat's Cradle* (1963), with its elegant new religion, Bokononism. *Sirens of Titan*, in particular, is a cascade of absurd invention, its hither-thither technique a sophisticated pinch from the Wide Screen Baroque school. The elaborations of plot make it read like an exceptionally sunny Dick novel (which is to acknowledge, too, Dick's father-figure, van Vogt); the spoof "explanations" of the origins of Stonehenge and the Great Wall of China are in that tradition. But the narrative is extremely well integrated—a perfect cartwheel of a performance.

The same complex plotting and infolding of event went into one of Vonnegut's best novels to date, the remarkable *Mother Night* (1962). It represents a triumph of ambiguity which even Dick never excelled. Is the central character a traitor or one of the country's great heroes? Even *he* does not know. Although this novel is not science fiction, its central character is called Howard W. Campbell Jr. Whether by this Vonnegut intended merely a jest at John W. Campbell Jr's expense, or whether he implied a profound commentary on Campbell as the greatest purveyor of pulp power fantasy, we must leave wiser critics to decide.[32] It is a fact that Vonnegut continues to harp on SF, its themes and characters, while denying that he writes anything of the kind.

An instance of this occurs in *God Bless You, Mr Rosewater* (1965). By now messages are replacing ambiguities. The message of *Mr Rosewater* is that non-conformists are more fun than conformists—hardly galvanizing news! Here the obsession with science fiction is embodied in the figure of Kilgore Trout, writer of interplanetary romances, author of eighty-seven paperbacks, unknown outside the science fiction field.[33]

Eliot Rosewater, the central character, visits the Milford Conference where Rosewater tells them

"I love you sons of bitches. You're all I read anymore. You're the only ones who'll talk about the really *terrific* changes going on, the only ones crazy enough to know that life is a space voyage, and not a short one, either, but one that'll last for billions of years. You're the only ones with guts enough to *really* care about the future, who *really* notice what machines do to us . . . You're the only ones zany enough to agonize over time and distances without limit, over mysteries that will never die, over the fact that we are right now determining whether the space voyage for the next billion years or so is going to be Heaven or Hell."

Vonnegut's tribute to the billion year spree—too long and lingering to be wholly satire.

Slaughterhouse Five (1969)[34] is a restless book; whether its hither-thither methods sufficiently emphasize the horrors of the bombing of Dresden, whether social conscience is not paraded a little too conspicuously, are moot points. The time-travel and other SF apparatus seem intrusive, fascinating though they are. Vonnegut's hither-thither technique worked better on the more frivolous subject matter of *Sirens of Titan*, where tremendous enterprises (such as a message brought right across the galaxy just saying "Greetings") are only pseudo-tremendous and carry none of the Death of Dresden with them. Tralfamadore and its super-intelligent aliens, common to both books, seem more pertinent to the earlier work.

The spiritual desiccations of Dresden were apparent before Vonnegut wrote. But Dick, as we shall see, gave us new insight into the desiccations of everyday. Despite these reservations, there is much in Vonnegut to admire—not least that exuberance of invention which he shares with most of the better SF writers.

Vonnegut sped right out of the SF field as soon as he had cash for the gasoline. For that he should not be blamed, though he cannot have failed to notice that he still lapses into SF, for instance in *Galapagos* (1985). The traffic is not one way. Other writers from other disciplines come in and make their contribution. To regard SF as some sort of closed shop is ridiculous, and the quickest way of getting the shop closed for good.

Later Vonnegut—the Vonnegut of concoctions like *Slapstick, or Lonesome No More* (1976)—displays a descent into farce which is at once sentimental and cute. Inventiveness has become woolly self-indulgence. It's the price to be paid for being elected popular guru. *Slapstick* was turned into one of the worst movies ever made[35]: a category in which the competition may be termed stiff. It is curious that writers with a genuine feel for vintage American idiocy, such as John Sladek and Robert Coover, receive much less attention than Vonnegut. Perhaps American readers, always wary of irony, prefer criticism wrapped, like Vonnegut's, in lovable Old Fartism.

Rejoicing, then, at the strong form shown in *Galápagos* (1985), Guru Vonnegut's latest. This sprightly, clever tale is purportedly told a million years in the future, and by the ghost of Kilgore Trout's son, when all who are left of the human race after The Disaster have landed on the celebrated eponymous isles and evolved into something rather more lovable and with Smaller Brains. Sprightly, funny, suspenseful, *Candide*-like, and endearingly ingenious in its telling, *Galapagos* was the best SF novel of its year, and could certainly teach whizkids like Gibson and Sterling a thing or two about the art of narrative.

Philip K. Dick, for all his pulp origins and pulp trimmings, is an intellectual— one of the Pirandello school. In his novels, things are never quite what they seem. Between life and death lie the many shadow lands of Dick, places of hallucination, perceptual sumps, cloacae of dim half life, paranoid states, tomb worlds and orthodox hells. All his novels are one novel, a fatidical *A la recherche du temps perfide*.

This multidextrous work is elegant, surprising, and witty, spilling out disconcerting artifacts, scarecrow people, exiles, street-wise teenage girls, Fabergé animals, robots with ill consciences and bizarre but friendly aliens. Dick published nineteen novels during the sixties, many for paperback, and as a result some are hastily written. Such prodigy demands an understanding editor; the inept start to *Ubik* all but cripples an exceptional novel.

From this period four titles deserve special attention. They are among the finest SF novels of the decade.

The Man in the High Castle (1962) best represents Dick's talents and his easy acquaintance with evil. It depicts a contemporary world in which World War II was won by the Axis Powers. North America has been divided into three strips. The large Eastern zone is occupied by the Nazis; the narrow Western seaboard is occupied by the Japanese. The middle section, the Rocky Mountain States, serves as a neutral buffer state. Dick populates this world with a number and variety of characters[36], some of whom can act with more effect than others, but all of whom are subservient to the currents of history.

In the Rocky Mountain States, however, lives Hawthorne Abendsen, a man whose vision runs counter to history. He is a novelist (rather a Heinlein figure in some ways) who has written a novel called *The Grasshopper Lies Heavy*. Abendsen is the man in the high castle. His novel postulates a world in which both Germany and Japan were defeated in the war; it is therefore subversive, and suppressed; but its message begins to revitalize a few defeated Americans. There is also the suggested possibility that only he sees clearly—that his vision is the truth—and that everyone else see things "through a glass darkly".

This last interpretation becomes possible when the novel is considered as a study of authenticity at every level of existence. Is this reality real or false? Does the *I Ching*, the Book of Changes used by several of the characters in the novel, present a real choice or an imitation? Throughout the novel there's an obsession with authenticity. Baynes, the Scandinavian, is in fact a German counter-intelligence agent. Joe, the Italian truck driver, proves to be a Gestapo assassin. Frank Frink pretends he's not a Jew. Childan, the American, imitates the cultural mores of the Japanese, while all of the Japanese in the book fanatically collect American cultural artifacts (themselves for the main part forged) and try to become as American as apple pie. The German philosophy of *Natur*, practised by these Nazis—an imitation of the process of Entropy, as Dick sees it—is false life. It is a world of creative sterility where the only thing that grows is death, the "Organisation Todt" (Todt being German for Death). The world in which Abendsen exists (and not the world he *sees*) is a hell world, evil, a counterfeit creation, like the Pandemonium of Milton's *Paradise Lost*, built by the fallen angels in mimicry of the marvellous city of Heaven.

One of the novel's attractive features is the way in which conqueror and conquered alike gain our sympathy. Juliana finds that killing the Gestapo man is a way to sanity. The central character, Mr Tagomi of the Japanese Trade Mission, is a good man who consults his *I Ching* at every turn. Like many good Dick characters, he is vouchsafed an actual glimpse of evil. Then, having killed two "bad" men for a "good" reason (with a fake Colt .44 which really works), Tagomi finds himself transported into our reality, not the world of Abendsen's novel. There are differences between our reality and the utopian alternative Abendsen describes. In both alternative worlds, Tagomi's dominant culture has been conquered.

Such twists and turns throughout the novel are part of the delight of Dick's work.[37] We can never be certain what is ground-level reality, and yet we never tire of these webs of maya—of illusion. What *is* unwavering in Dick's work is his moral sensibility. He recognizes and portrays the actuality of evil: a kind of being, lacking in empathy, sympathy or any sense of common humanity—be that being android, psychotic, junkie, autistic, paranoid or fascist. Such creatures are common in his work. Though Dick works hard to make us understand them, he spares little sympathy for them.

> This guy—Joe whatever—hasn't even got the right expression on his face; he should have that cold but somehow enthusiastic look, as if he believed in nothing and yet somehow had absolute faith. Yes, that's how they are. They're not idealists like Joe and me; they're cynics with utter faith. It's a sort of brain defect, like a lobotomy—that maiming those German psychiatrists do as a poor substitute for psychotherapy. (*The Man in the High Castle*, Chapter 3)

The Man in the High Castle is different in tone from most of Dick's work, with a sombre, rather sober ring to it. It was obviously not written on the run, as were many of his novels. But what it lacks in fizz it makes up for in after-taste. It is difficult to forget *The Man in the High Castle*, a worthy winner of the Hugo Award, surprisingly the only one of Dick's works to gain this accolade.

In *The Man in the High Castle*, Mars is off-stage, the unglimpsed new frontier, its sterile sands a new challenge to the Nazi death-dreamers. In Dick's 1964 novel, *Martian Time-Slip*[38], the dream has become exacting reality. The year is 1994 and disillusionment has set in. The first generation of Martians has been born, "a generation of schizophrenics". Among those new Martians is a young autistic boy, Manfred Steiner, trapped in "some divine and yet dreadful place beyond their own". Manfred is slowly shaping those about him and forcing them to see reality just how he sees it—

"It's the end," Jack said, "between me and Arnie—tonight. I know it, and I don't know why." He felt sick in his stomach. "It almost seems to me that Manfred does more than know the future; in some way he *controls* it, he can make it come out the worst possible way because that's what seems natural to him, that's how he sees reality. It's as if being around him we're sinking into his reality. It's starting to seep over us and replace our own way of viewing things, and the kind of events we're accustomed to see come about now somehow *don't* come about." (Chapter 10)

In Dick's imagined worlds mental illness is contagious: such seepage and replacement occurs time and again, from the reconstructed world of the fifties in *Time out of Joint* (1959) to the world in which Jason Taverner finds he does not exist in *Flow My Tears, the Policeman Said* (1974). The hallucination to which this particular passage refers is Jack Bohlen's own personal regression or time-slip, his own little slice of madness. This incident allows a glimpse of one of the processes continually occurring in Dick's work, a sudden peeling away of mundane perception, to reveal some other state of being, some alternative reality—and rarely one to be lived in permanently without sustaining severe psychic damage:

And then the hallucination, if it was that, happened. He saw the personnel manager in a new light. The man was dead.

He saw, through the man's skin, his skeleton. It had been wired together, the bones connected with fine copper wire. The organs, which had withered away, were replaced by artificial components, kidney, heart, lungs—everything was made of plastic and stainless steel, all working in unison but entirely without authentic life. The man's voice issued from a tape, through an amplifier and speaker system.

Possibly at some time in the past the man had been real and alive, but that was over, and the stealthy replacement had taken place, inch by inch, progressing insidiously from one organ to the next, and the entire structure was there to deceive others. To deceive him, Jack Bohlen, in fact. He was alone in this office; there was no personnel manager. No one spoke to him, and when he himself talked, no one heard; it was entirely a lifeless, mechanical room in which he stood. (*Martian Time-Slip*, Chapter 5)

This vision, recurring in Dick's work, can be reversed, so that machines become more human than real people.[39] We can relate the vision not simply to personal psychosis but to the estrangements of technological societies. It has affinities with other work already mentioned: with David Bunch's *Moderan* and its new-metal man[40], with Sheckley's walking dead in *Journey Beyond Tomorrow*, with Sladek's man trapped on tape in *The Müller-Fokker Effect*; with all androids, in fact.[41]

In each case the response is to the social process of dehumanization, a process for which the metaphor of machine-man is beautifully suited. It was, indeed, how many young Americans, and not only Americans, felt about the older generation, the "Plastic People" as Frank Zappa called them.

Reality-shapers, like Manfred Steiner, are another common element in Dick's novels of this period, in *Ubik* (1969), for instance, where another malevolent child, Jory, has infiltrated the half-life states of all the other frozen humans in the Beloved Brethren Moratorium and is warping their dream-like realities. This is, in part, a reflection of Dick's interest in Brahmin's Dream, the concept that our reality is only the ancient god Brahmin's dream and that when he wakes we shall all vanish.[42] Such themes are developed time and again in Dick's novels of the late sixties, perhaps most effectively in *The Three Stigmata of Palmer Eldritch* (1965). There a growing American obsession with hallucinogenic drugs is married to the reality-as-a-construct-in-god's-mind theme to produce a novel of some complexity.

In *The Three Stigmata* Dick hits the true apocalyptic note. The future depicted might appear far-fetched, with its truffle-skin currency, its argumentative automated cabs, its status-giving miniaturization "layouts", its evolution tampering E Therapy and its "precogs", but the good and evil within it are genuine enough. If the cluttered trappings and jargon of the novel are higher schlock, the sensibility behind the characterization is a mature and incisive one.

In its simplest sense, *Three Stigmata* is an alien invasion and takeover tale. After ten years in the alien Proxima system, Palmer Eldritch has returned to the Solar System. But something has taken him over, and that something is using Eldritch to gain its own insidious ends. On Earth and, in particular, on its colony worlds, a hallucinogenic drug named Can-D is in wide use, removing the tedious, oppressive reality of everyday living and substituting another where all is permitted because none of it is *really* real. In the Can-D drug dreams you can murder your neighbour, make love to his wife and get away with it. For colonists on the purgatory world of Mars it is the one thing that makes living bearable. However, Leo Bulero of Perky Pat Layouts holds the system-wide monopoly for Can-D (illicitly, of course), and the UN want to break that hold. Under their sponsorship, Eldritch is invited in with his new drug, Chew-Z.

The second level of the novel deals with the power struggle between Bulero and Eldritch. We quickly realize that it isn't a simple matter of massive corporations clashing over franchises but a battle for the human soul itself between a dark alien invader, Eldritch, and a rather frail and all-too-human being, Bulero. Nor are the two drugs comparable in their effects. Whereas Can-D allows human beings to come together in a shared experience (using the miniaturized Perky Pat Layouts as their constructed reality), Chew-Z isolates each user to his/her own solipsistic world. Chew-Z is also addictive. What's more, Eldritch himself is, like Jory, like Manfred Steiner, manipulating those closed worlds. Can-D is a positive experience, Chew-Z wholly negative and self-destructive. We glimpse, in this distinction, that what is at stake is not control merely of a commercial venture but of the very nature of the human world.

Underpinning this level of the book is a far more human story: the story of

Barney Mayerson and his ex-wife Emily, a potter. Mayerson, realizing how the ills of his present life stem from his mistakes in the past with Emily, tries to get her back. This level of things—of simple human relationships; of marital problems; of nostalgia for a better past—gives the novel a poignancy it would otherwise lack. The greater and the smaller are always delicately balanced in Dick's work.

We might say that Eldritch is once more Milton's Satan, playing at God with his Chew-Z imitations of reality, but Dick gives his modern-day Satan the trappings of this high-technology age:

> Gray and bony, well over six feet tall, with swinging arms and a peculiarly rapid gait. And his face. It had a ravaged quality, eaten away; as if, Barney conjectured, the fat layer had been consumed, as if Eldritch at some time or other had fed off himself, devoured perhaps with gusto the superfluous portions of his own body. He had enormous steel teeth . . . And—his right arm was artificial. Twenty years ago in a hunting accident on Callisto he had lost the original; this one of course was superior in that it provided a specialised variety of interchangable hands. . . .
>
> And he was blind. At least from the standpoint of the natural-born body. But replacements had been made—at the prices which Eldritch could and would pay . . . The replacements, fitted into the bone sockets, had no pupils, nor did any ball move by muscular action. Instead a panoramic vision was supplied by a wide-angle lens, a permanent horizontal slot running from edge to edge. (Chapter 10)

Dick has a specific symbolic use for these "stigmata", and at the novel's end he makes this quite clear, just as he clarifies where his own sympathies lie:

> I saw enough in the future not to ever give up, even if I'm the only one who doesn't succumb, who's still keeping the old way alive, the pre-Palmer Eldritch way. It's nothing more than faith in powers implanted in me from the start which I can—in the end—draw on and beat him with. So in a sense it isn't me, it's something *in* me that even that thing Palmer Eldritch can't reach and consume because since it's not me, it's not mine to lose. I feel it growing. Withstanding the external, nonessential alterations, the arm, the eyes, the teeth—it's not touched by any of those three, the evil, negative trinity of alienation, blurred reality, and despair that Eldritch brought back with him from Proxima. Or rather from the space in between. (Chapter 13)

The vision is frightening because convincing, convincing because Dick knew Eldritch was after *him* too.

Dick's world is but an outcrop of a universe in which good and evil battle, with evil always about to win. Dick professed himself not to be a Christian, yet his work is heavily permeated with Christian theological thought. In his later work—in particular in *Valis* (1981) and *The Divine Invasion* (1981) the Christianity became overt and swamped the science fictional element, to the detriment of the novels, but in the sixties it was just one of a number of complex strands that were woven richly into his novels.

Many of the novels read in isolation can seem like lumber-rooms of ideas, cluttered and over-complex, as if attempting too much at once. Perhaps the fault lies in market circumstances and the terse Ace format for which Dick wrote. One could also argue that Dick's novels were a quarter the length they ought to have been to contain such complexity and richness.[43] Even so, the marvellous, multi-levelled web of themes and concerns which emerges from this process of condensation gives Dick's work its specific feel, the very thing that makes it unique. Unrevised, eccentric and extravagant—even so, it's not too much to claim that Dick is perhaps the first real genius to have worked in the science-fictional mode since the days of Stapledon, a hybrid of Dickens and Dostoevsky, possessed of the comic delights and tragic depths of both, yet choosing work where his eccentricities were cherished.[44] In any case, like so many SF writers, he learned to love the genre through the magazines long before his literary tastes were formed. He never quite recovered from that first infatuation with the forbidden van Vogtian delights.

Dick is one of the masters of present-day discontents, in the grand tradition of despairers which runs through Swift and Huxley. There are no simple solutions for Dick, no easy identifications with all-powerful heroes. His often frail, often inadequate protagonists stand knee-deep in technological kipple, gazing at visions beyond their comprehension. The mood is often one of grey metaphysical comedy—Rick Decard, for instance, in *Do Androids Dream of Electric Sheep?* (1968), is brought to a final disillusionment by discovering that a toad he picked up in the desert is just another artifact, with a control panel in its belly, not the last living member of a species as he hoped. The toad brings us as much disgust and laughter as Harrison's coal-driven robot (though more pathos); perhaps we unconsciously set a toad and robot against a vision of Man, Son of God, seeing them as symbols at once of our achievement and failure—our Frankenstein inheritance reduced to painful farce.

Here is one paragraph from *Do Androids Dream*. Technological man—represented by the socially and mentally inadequate John Isidore—stands in an empty San Francisco apartment building.

Silence. It flashed from the woodwork and the walls; it smote him with an awful, total power, as if generated by a vast mill. It rose from the floor, up out of the tattered grey wall-to-wall carpeting. It unleashed itself from the broken and semi-broken appliances in the kitchen, the dead machines which hadn't worked in all the time Isidore had lived here. From the useless pole lamp in the living room it oozed out, meshing with the empty and wordless descent of itself from the fly-speckled ceiling. It managed in fact to emerge from every object within his range of vision, as if it—the silence—meant to supplant all things tangible. Hence it assailed not only his ears but his eyes; as he stood by the inert TV set he experienced the silence as visible and, in its own way, alive. Alive! He had often felt its austere approach before; when it came it burst in without subtlety, evidently unable to wait. The silence of the world could not rein back its greed. Not any longer. Not when it had virtually won. (Chapter 2)

Do Androids Dream is likely to be the only Philip K. Dick novel that a large number of non-SF readers will have encountered, under the title *Blade Runner* (an Alan Nourse title for a totally different novel). When Dick's novel was filmed in 1982 by Ridley Scott, its complex story-line was butchered to a single plot-strand of bounty hunter pursuing renegade humanoid robots. While it made effective SF cinema on that simplistic level, it nonetheless threw away the opportunity of making a brilliant and telling film. Gone was the level of the book which dealt with the moral problem of empathy. Gone were Rick Decard's marital problems and his fears about his own authenticity. Gone was the whole question of human worth as something not to be measured in simple IQ terms. Gone was the delicate humour, the sympathetic characterization, and one vital scene where Decard is forced to kill a female android who is the precise double of Rachel, the android woman he loves. In its place was a heavy-handed adventure-packed and sensationalized robot yarn with a tough-guy hero (Harrison Ford) from the school of Marlowe, who wins through and even gets the girl (admittedly artificial—but with all important distinctions ironed out) at the end.

Even so, the film serves to illustrate the richness of Dick's original. Scott's movie might have seemed an embellishment for most other genre novels. As an attempt to convey the essence of *Do Androids Dream* its two-dimensional paucity is readily evident. Dick's honest pessimism, lightened by a humanistic hope, was exchanged for a blue-jowled optimism. Why make a first-rate SF movie when it's so easy to make a second-rate one?

In novels like *The Simulacra* (1964), *Dr Bloodmoney* (1965), *Now Wait for Last Year* (1966), *Counter-Clock World* (1967) and *Galactic Pot-Healer* (1969), Dick amused, enthralled and astounded his readers, if not at his highest pitch. In the seventies he slowed his rate of production and re-cast his visions. His work of the sixties, rough-hewn and hasty as much of it was, created something both traditional and yet unique (which other SF writer could make us feel really bad at the death of a Ganymedean slime mould?[45]). There's no pomposity in Dick's work, no falseness. When the moment comes, Dick can pull all the stops out and sound the big, resonating chords, though calm, ironic understatement is his forte. His androids also dream.

The sixties, which began in hope, which were fired by an enthusiasm for mould-breaking and new life-styles, ended in pessimism and a sense of lost directions. The Vietnam War was escalating, the bills were piling up. No one knew where all the flowers had gone. Woodstock had vanished and Altamont was a dark scar on the memory. The Third World was dying all over again. Hippies who had dropped out found the need to drop back in again to pay the rent, raise kids, find status. It had been fun but it hadn't been real—it didn't last.

Reality closed like a rat-trap. Technology had grown vastly while the young and would-be-young played their games—like some monstrous Frankenstein-creation biding its time in the mountainous wastes. Some writers saw this, of course, and spoke of it in metaphoric ways. One such was a woman who, like Mary Shelley, wrote science fiction without knowing it and, in doing so, created one of the great science fiction novels.

> I should have to start searching for her all over again. The repetition was like a curse. I thought of placid blue seas, tranquil islands, far away from war. I thought of the Indris, those happy creatures, symbols of life in peace, on a higher plane. I should clear out, go to them. No, that was impossible. I was tied to her. I thought of the ice moving across the world, casting its shadow of creeping death. Ice cliffs boomed in my dreams, indescribable explosions thundered and boomed, icebergs crashed, hurled huge boulders into the sky like rockets. Dazzling ice stars bombarded the world with rays, which splintered and penetrated the earth, filling earth's core with their deadly coldness, reinforcing the cold of the advancing ice. And always, on the surface, the indestructible ice-mass was moving forward, implacably destroying all life. I felt a fearful sense of pressure and urgency, there was no time to lose, I was wasting time; it was a race between me and the ice. Her albino hair illuminated my dreams, shining brighter than moonlight. I saw the dead moon dance over icebergs, as it would at the end of our world, while she watched from the tent of her glittering hair.
>
> I dreamed of her whether I was asleep or awake. I heard her cry: "One day I'll go . . . you won't see me again. . . ." She had gone from me already. She had escaped. She hurried along a street in an unknown town. She looked different, less anxious, more confident. She knew exactly where she was going, she did not hesitate once. In a huge official building she made straight for a room so crowded she could hardly open the door. Only her extreme slimness enabled her to slip between the many tall silent figures, unnaturally silent, fantastically tall, whose faces were all averted from her.

In its terror and beauty, its mercurial shifts of mood, its cunning sliding panels which bring us abruptly from one level of reality to another, this is unmistakably a passage from Anna Kavan's *Ice* (1967).

Anna Kavan's story has been told already[46]—how she too was monstrous, how she had the heroin habit for several decades and came to terms with it, how she travelled from country to country, and how she committed suicide one week before the news arrived of *Ice*'s acceptance by Doubleday. The story of *Ice* in many respects bodies forth Kavan's inner life. It is the ultimate in catastrophe—the advance of the ice is real enough, but is also the ice of the soul, the heroin encroaching, the habit of death you can't kick. In this sense *Ice* represents one of the high points of science fiction, and so becomes unclassifiable.

And through the drifts the snowy clifts
Did send a dismal sheen:
Nor shapes of men nor beasts we ken—
The ice was all between. . . .

Some of *Ice*'s illustrious relations are clear. Kafka for a start. Anna Kavan's assumed name began with a K in his honour. There is also a surrealist vein, as exhibited in some of Cocteau's work and in the painter De Chirico's only novel, *Hebdomeros*. Again, *Ice* is a catastrophe novel that goes as far beyond Ballard as Ballard is beyond Wyndham, sailing into the chilly air of metaphysics. It looks sideways at its great contemporary among pornographic novels, Pauline Réage's *Story of O*. Even more, it is its own self, mysterious, in some ways unsatisfactory, an enigma—like all the greatest science fiction, approaching despair; but, in its acceptance of the insoluble, also full of a blind force much like hope.

As in our inner beings, there are only three persons in *Ice*. The pursued and the pursuer often change roles, become indistinguishable. In that respect, they remind us of Frankenstein and his monster, and remind us how Frankenstein and monster, and their many later progeny, come to us from the inner being, where religion, art, and science all begin.

CHAPTER XIV

The Stars My Detestation:
Sailing the Seventies

That picture of the Earth with the Moon in the foreground
should be in every classroom and home in the world. Plenty of
clouds and water are visible, but very little land. No national
boundaries are visible at all. Isn't that message clear enough?
—Harry Harrison: *Men on the Moon*

The grand official opening of the Space Age took place in October 1957, when
the first Earth satellite was lobbed into orbit. From then on, we could escape
from our planet. Or, at least, a specialized few could. A little later, with those
striking satellite photographs, came another realization which may stand us in
even better stead; that our planetary air, soil, water, are limited and must be
treated with proper respect if we are to survive. Looking back at the fecund
Earth from the void of space we recognized the fragility of our miracle of life.
Gaia, Mother Earth, was reborn in the human psyche.

In 1969, Donald Wollheim, then guiding light of Ace Books, published an
anthology called *Men on the Moon*. He persuaded twenty-seven writers to give
their views on the first lunar landing, which took place in July of that year. Isaac
Asimov, John Brunner, E. C. Tubb, Alan Nourse, and others had their say.
Only Philip K. Dick, Ray Bradbury, and Poul Anderson were full of
unqualified praise and excitement. Most of the authors took a very sceptical
view of the proceedings. The phrase on the plaque, "We Came in Peace for All
Mankind", stuck in their gullets; they started remembering the Indians.

Michael Moorcock quoted J. G. Ballard's wry remark: "If I were a Martian I'd
start running now!" Isaac Asimov hoped we might find a nobility in space of
which many dream and some practise. Bob Shaw thought that the plaque
should have borne not words but a symbol whose significance would have been
universally understood—"something like a grabbing hand with its fingers
clawed into the Moon's soil". Harlan Ellison talked about little old ladies getting
mugged. Harry Harrison was the one person who mentioned Vietnam,
pointing out that it was war, not the Apollo missions, which wasted everyone's
substance. Other writers felt that the lunar walk could have brought small cheer
to the oppressed and impoverished on Earth.

The general consensus was cautionary. Ever since the beginning of the Space
Age, SF writers have been less romantic about space flight, although there are
exceptions such as Poul Anderson. By and large, C. S. Lewis's view has
permeated the genre—that we are likely to spread destruction wherever we go,

although *Star Wars*, 1977's box office success, has had some effect in bringing space opera back into vogue. There may be something in Kenneth Bulmer's remark in *Men on the Moon*: "We're in the creative instant of the paleolithic man who's just hand-paddled a log across the estuary—now all the oceans lie beyond"; but the old joy in bigger and better logs is somehow less spontaneous than before—as NASA has discovered since the shuttle disaster of early 1986. Meanwhile, that Big Estuary in the Sky fills with high-tech hardware.

Now that the Moon has become real estate, can it so easily be dreamed about and handled as a symbol? Has the grandiose vision of interstellar flight lost its potency as it approaches reality? Do we now regard the stars in detestation rather than hope? Is the trillion year spree over?

Cinematic trends aside, the answer to this must be a personal one, and neither of the authors of this volume sets great store by the prophetic side of SF. To prophesy a war in 1999 means nothing in 1986; and it can make no difference in 1999. The gesture is even less meaningful if it happens to be the only correct one among ninety-nine failed prophecies. To prophesy as warning (as we believe Orwell did in *1984*) can be an entirely different matter.

But if SF as prophecy is out, SF as prodromic utterance is definitely in. We have seen how Mary Shelley has a prodromic gift. Our belief is that SF has something of the same ability. Submerged themes, as we've said already, move through science fiction, Fear of Dehumanization in the fifties, Life-Style in the sixties.

The New Wave writers were not the only ones to articulate clearly these manoeuvrings of the zeitgeist. "Strangely, it was becoming impossible for me to take that stuff of science fiction seriously any more—all those starships and androids and galactic empires," said Robert Silverberg, in his essay in *Hell's Cartographers* (1975). Silverberg is one of two contrasting writers who occupy the first part of this chapter, both of whom enlarged the territories of discussion as the seventies went their course.

The seventies brought many ground swells into prominence: ecology, computerization, proliferation of nuclear power, psychoanalysis, sexual liberation and feminism, and an adverse reaction to drugs. New technology fed new themes into the genre—cloning, biotechnology and computer science grew in importance as space flight diminished, though none had the same stark immediacy as symbol. Science was growing ever more complex, more specialized, harder to grasp. The reality of the world outside the SF magazines—harsher, more cynical, obssessed with marketing—was reflected inside the genre, exaggerated and extrapolated.

The early and mid seventies were a time of considerable maturation in the SF field. After the liberating and oft-times garish experimentation of the sixties, when style had seemed all-important and the desire to shock as great an impetus as the desire to tell a story well, the writing of the seventies was quieter, less ostentatious—but no less impressive. It was immediately evident that a greater sensitivity prevailed in the field, a restraint and care for craftsmanship matched by a desire to recapture the "sense of wonder" so marked in the SF of the thirties and forties. And not merely to recapture the sense, but to articulate it intelligently and evocatively. In a way to make good the fudged work of yesteryear.

> The only thing I set out consciously to do in the late sixties was to return to the classic themes of science fiction which I felt had largely been mishandled . . . in execution, not in thought; but in literary execution . . . and try to get them right, try to do them with a literacy, a grace that nobody seemed interested in doing . . . it was now time to re-examine those themes in a new light.[1]

The speaker is Robert Silverberg, who as a young writer in the fifties had produced "machine-written pot-boilers" as he himself termed them, along with innumerable stories for the SF magazines. By means of a prodigious work rate and intelligent investment, Silverberg had reputedly made himself a millionaire by his late twenties, but his capable pulp style had earned him a poor reputation in the field. It was against the grain of this reputation that his novels of the late sixties were written. *Thorns* (1967), an aptly named novel about pain, transformation and love, began the process of re-examination. It took most people by surprise—that is, those who even bothered to notice its publication. Old reputations die hard.

Today, Silverberg is one of SF's eminences, a quiet, kindly, yet sinister presence. He is valued not only for his knowledge and wit, but for the sense that he underwent many of the harsh inward experiences which are the lot of his central figures in the novels of his best period, which we now examine.

By the time he came to write *Nightwings* (1969)[2], Silverberg had, to a great extent, shaken off his early reputation. *Nightwings* is Stapledonian on a small scale, an exotic glimpse of a future Earth about to enter its fourth cycle of civilization—an Earth that has been conquered peacefully by humanoid aliens, the past hubris of its anthropocentricity punished by an exacting nemesis. Once the enslaver, Man becomes slave to one of his former servants. On a personal level it is the story of the Rememberer Tomis, who becomes a Redeemer, involved intimately in each stage of the process of conquest and racial redemption. Like so much of Silverberg's work of the period, it is a novel about rebirth and metamorphosis, about alienation and its cure:

> That night as on other nights I seized my stone and felt the chill and closed my eyes, and heard the distant tolling of a mighty gong, the lapping of waves on an unknown beach, the whisper of the wind in an alien forest. And felt a summons. And yielded. And entered the state of communion. And gave myself up to the Will.
>
> And slipped down through the layers of my life, through my youth and middle years, my wanderings, my old loves, my torments, my joys, my troubled later years, my treasons, my insufficiencies, my griefs, my imperfections.
>
> And freed myself of myself. And shed my selfness. And became one of

thousands of Pilgrims, not merely Olmayne nearby, but others trekking the mountains of Hind and the sands of Arba, Pilgrims at their devotions in Ais and Palash and Stralya, Pilgrims moving toward Jorslem on the journey that some complete in months, some in years, and some never at all. And shared with all of them the instant of submergence into the Will. And saw in the darkness a deep purple glow on the horizon—which grew in intensity until it became an all-encompassing red brilliance. And went into it, though unworthy, unclean, flesh-trapped, accepting fully the communion offered and wishing no other state of being than this divorce from self.

And was purified.

And wakened alone. (Part III, Chapter 4)

Silverberg's break with old pulp patterns took advantage of the freedoms gained by the *New Worlds* experiment, in particular those that involved character. Tomis, like so many of Silverberg's protagonists, proves to be flawed, inadequate and all-too-human, a traitor, in some respects afraid to act and plagued by desire. Such characters are neither heroes nor villains but reflect an almost autobiographical element which asks, "How might *I* have acted in such circumstances?" It is, as Silverberg recognized, a more literary approach, intensified in its effect by the first-person narrative he utilized for so many of the novels of this period.

In *Downward to the Earth* (1970), Silverberg again identified Man's isolation in his own skull as the reason for angst, and repeated the formula of *Nightwings* in an alien context. An Earthman, Gundersen, returns to Belzagor, a once-colonized planet restored to native control after the discovery that the aliens are a sentient species. Gundersen's obsession with the alien nildoror (elephant-like) and sulidoror (humanoid/ape-like) and their religion, leads him to trek up-country into the land of mists to share their rebirth ritual.

Gundersen's journey into the heart of an alien darkness is set against that of Kurtz, whose rebirth was into a grotesque form—an outward manifestation of his inner state. As a novel about guilt, sin, punishment and expiation, *Downward to the Earth* is more effective than *Nightwings*, though its depiction of Belzagor is simplistic. Gundersen is reborn not merely to a new form (ambiguously his own and yet not his own—it depends on how you see him) but to new powers—once again, to sharing in a common Will:

And he comes now to one that is neither nildor nor sulidor, a sleeping soul, a veiled soul, a soul of a colour and a timbre and a texture unlike the others. It is an Earthborn soul, the soul of Seena, and he calls softly to her, saying, awaken, awaken, I love you, I have come for you. She does not awaken. He calls to her; I am new, I am reborn, I overflow with love. Join me: Become part of me. Seena? Seena? Seena? And she does not respond.

He sees the souls of the other Earthmen now.

They have *g'rakh*, but rationality is not enough; their souls are blind and silent. (Chapter 16)

This religious merging of souls is, of course, a refurbishment of an old and highly familiar SF theme, telepathy. It is a device used again by Silverberg in his 1971 Nebula Award-winning novel, *A Time of Changes*.

The flawed but ultimately messianic figure of *A Time of Changes* is Kinnall Darival, son of the Septarch of Salla on the world of Borthan. Borthan is a harsh world, settled by stern, puritanical people some two thousand years or more before we encounter its society; a people bound to the Covenant, which expressly forbids expression of the self, or use of the words "I" and "me". Kinnall, a product of his society, unable to admit to his desire for his "bondsister", Halum, cut off from the love of father or brother, is tempted by an Earthman, Schweiz, into taking a sharing drug which opens one mind wholly to another's. His transformation is the beginning—its end unglimpsed as Kinnall's own story ends—of the transmutation of his rigid, codified and cold society.

One might glimpse similarities between the message of *A Time of Changes* and Heinlein's *Stranger in a Strange Land*. The impracticalities of each "solution" to the problem of alienation (mind-sharing drugs and super-powers) are self-evident. But *A Time of Changes* differs radically from Heinlein's power fantasy in that its depiction of Borthan and of Kinnall's struggle to free himself from the bonds of its rigid mores is only one stage removed from the inhibitive social customs we are accustomed to here and now, whereas Heinlein's exaggerations, bearing little relationship to reality, serve no real symbolic purpose. Silverberg's intention is to use science fictional metaphor to identify and clarify a tendency in Man: the tendency implicit in the socialization process—of hiding our true selves behind social masks.

Another factor which differentiates Silverberg's work from Heinlein's—which is symptomatic of this reworking of old themes in new, literary ways—is the vividness of his writing. When Kinnall finally "merges" with his beloved bondsister, Halum, Silverberg presents that merger in a lucid, convincing, and, in its beauty and tragedy, deeply moving way.[3] This quality of Silverberg's was never better demonstrated than in his 1972 novel, *Dying Inside*.

Dying Inside is another novel which uses telepathy, not in this instance as the catalyst or result of religious opening and transcendence, but as a genuine, functioning power in a contemporary human being. As such, *Dying Inside* is reminiscent of Saul Bellow's *Herzog*, told from a quirky viewpoint: its quirk is to make us feel, by its end, that *not* being telepathic is an abnormal condition.[4]

David Selig, the telepath of *Dying Inside*, is suffering in his forties from diminishing powers. His telepathy has isolated him from all but a few of his fellow humans, has provoked his sister's hatred, and broken apart the only two relationships he ever wanted. The powers that should have made him a god have been a curse, a blight on his life, and have, ironically, set him apart from his fellow man more effectively than prison walls or bars:

We had shared our shabby room nearly seven weeks—a bit of May, all of June, some of July—through thick and thin, heat waves and rainstorms, misunderstandings and reconciliations, and it had been a happy time, perhaps the happiest of my life. I loved her and I think she loved me. I haven't had much love in my life. That isn't intended as a grab for your pity, just a simple statement of fact, objective and cool. The nature of my condition diminishes my capacity to love and be loved. A man in my circumstances, wide open to everyone's innermost thoughts, really isn't going to experience a great deal of love. He is poor at giving love because he doesn't much trust his fellow human beings: he knows too many of their dirty little secrets, and that kills his feelings for them. Unable to give, he cannot get. His soul, hardened by isolation and ungivingness, becomes inaccessible, and so it is not easy for others to love him. The loop closes upon itself and he is trapped within. Nevertheless, I loved Toni . . . and I didn't doubt my love was returned. (Chapter 10)

Selig, trusting to that love, keeps out of her mind until, when sharing LSD with her, he has a bad trip and somehow transfers his distorted, malicious self-image to her. Like Halum with Kinnall, Toni is terrified by what she sees. The true reflection of the typical human soul is not ennobling. Later we see one of the consequences of this moment, as Selig glimpses the memories of the homosexual man to whom she fled for comfort; a man who, in charity, sympathy and simple human love, tried but failed to make love to her despite "her disturbing femaleness". It is a scene of great tenderness as well as empathy. *Dying Inside* is not merely a deeply imagined book but a deeply felt one.

As we noted when discussing the sixties, the rigid taboo against sex was a victim of the shake-ups within the genre. Magazine versions and book versions of stories might differ somewhat, but the barriers were coming down and have subsequently stayed down. It became odder to find a book without sex than with. Authors vied with each other to find new ways of making it in the stars; sex in free-fall, sex with clones! James Sallis even posited a future where you went to have a penis fitted when you came of age.[5] Silverberg, in his metamorphosed, messianic state, was explicit from the first, sometimes hilariously so:

> "It is life's most intense joy, what I do."
> I pictured a row of naked women lying side by side, reaching off to infinity. Every one of them had the wedge-shaped head and sharp features of Themistoklis Metaxas. And Metaxas was moving patiently up the line, pausing to stick it into this one, and the next to her, and the next, and the next, and in his tireless fashion he balled right up the line until the spread-legged women grew hairy and chinless, the womenfolk of Pithecanthropus erectus, and there was Metaxus erectus still jazzing his way back to the beginning of time. Bravo, Metaxas! Bravo!
> "Why don't you try it sometime?" he asked. (Chapter 27)

Up the Line (1969) was Silverberg's tongue-in-cheek reworking of the time travel story.[6] As in Heinlein's earlier "All You Zombies—" (1959) and later *Time Enough for Love* (1973), the incest motif is predominant.

Up the Line belongs to the second rank of Silverberg's work, like *Tower of Glass* (1970) and *The World Inside* (1971), those well-honed and intelligent entertainments providing new slants on old themes, androids in *Tower of Glass*, overpopulation in *The World Inside*. Somewhere between entertainment and insight lie the two novels *The Stochastic Man* (1975), a story of precognition set at the turn of the coming millennium, and *Shadrach in the Furnace* (1976), which depicts a near-future world suffering from the double blights of tyranny and genetic disease—"organ rot".[7] More remarkable was the novella, "Born with the Dead".[8]

In his search for truth, Silverberg went back to his Jewish roots. Sombre period Silverberg is often distinguished by an attractive prose style, quite different from the yard-goods of old, marked by a richness and a cadence which calls the Old Testament distantly to mind.

> Four priests station themselves at the corners of the mortuary house. Their faces are covered by grotesque wooden masks topped by great antlers, and they carry wands two feet long, effigies of the death-cup mushroom in wood sheathed with copper. One priest commences a harsh, percussive chant. All four lift their wands and abruptly bring them down. It is a signal; the depositing of the grave goods begins. Lines of mourners bowed under heavy sacks approach the mortuary house. They are unweeping, even joyful, faces ecstatic, eyes shining, for these people know what later cultures will forget, that death is no termination but rather a natural culmination of life. Their departed friends are to be envied. They are honoured with lavish gifts, so that they may live like royalty in the next world. . . .

"Born with the Dead" appeared in the April 1974 issue of *F&SF*, a special Robert Silverberg issue, complete with bibliography by Donald Tuck, critical overview by Thomas D. Clareson, and biographical profile by Barry N. Malzberg.

Set in the 1990s, "Born with the Dead" traces a Hardyesque obsession beyond death. Jorge Klein pursues his dead wife, Sybille—purged of all emotions and "rekindled" to a kind of life in Zion Cold Town—across the globe, breaking all conventions.

The "deads" are an emergent culture, yet to shape and change the world of the living, the "warms". They are reborn to youth and beauty as the "new aristocracy" of the Earth. But they are also somewhat indifferent to life itself, prove infinitely patient in their limited "immortality", and are subject to ennui.

Something of the quality of the deads and, indeed, of Silverberg's novella, is captured in a brief passage where Jorge looks at a holo-cube image of his re-kindled ex-wife.

> Her face was an expressionless mask, calm, remote, aloof; her eyes were glossy mysteries; her lips registered as a faint, enigmatic, barely percep-tible smile. It frightened him to behold her this way, so alien, so unfamiliar.

There is a particularized visual quality in this story, as in much of Silverberg's work of the early seventies, which is more reminiscent of Henry James than Henry Kuttner. And, in a mood at odds with the generally upbeat tone of American magazine SF, Silverberg brings his tale to a darkly pessimistic end. Jorge, reunited with Sybille through death and rekindling, inherits only an immense disinterest in her. Death is really death after all, for all that it resembles life. Love is for the warms. As it always was.

Another writer who began to exert a more literary influence on the SF field at the end of the sixties, and whose shadow fell large across the genre of the seventies, was Ursula Le Guin.

> Estraven did not answer for a while. He sat gazing at the fire, whose flames winked, reflected from his tankard and from the broad bright silver chain of office over his shoulders. The old house was silent around us. There had been a servant to attend our meal, but Karhiders, having no institutions of slavery or personal bondage, hire services not people, and the servants had all gone off to their own homes by now. Such a man as Estraven must have guards about him somewhere, for assassination is a lively institution in Karhide, but I had seen no guard, heard none. We were alone.
>
> I was alone, with a stranger, inside the walls of a dark palace, in a strange snow-changed city, in the heart of the Ice Age of an alien world.
>
> Everything I had said, tonight and ever since I came to Winter, suddenly appeared to me as both stupid and incredible. How could I expect this man or any other to believe my tales about other worlds, other races, a vague benevolent government somewhere off in outer space? It was all nonsense. I had appeared in Karhide in a queer kind of ship, and I differed physically from Gethenians in some respects; that wanted explaining. But my own explanations were preposterous. I did not, in that moment, believe them myself.
>
> "I believe you," said the stranger, the alien alone with me, and so strong had my access of self-alienation been that I looked up at him bewildered. "I'm afraid that Argaven also believes you. But he does not trust you. In part because he no longer trusts me."

This is from the first chapter of *The Left Hand of Darkness* (1969). The setting is another planet, and a magnificently visualized planet it is; but the writer's attention never wavers from the strange interplay of character between human and alien.

Le Guin is a rarity in the field in that she writes with artistry.[9] There is a haunting lucidity to her best work which is a result of clarity of thought, not simplicity of theme. *The Left Hand of Darkness* is a complex philosophical[10], political and personal statement, almost deceptively presented as a first contact story.

Genly Ai, the "I" of the quoted passage, is an envoy from the Ekumen, the League of All Worlds, that "vague benevolent government somewhere off in space". The strangeness of Gethen/Winter is experienced through his eyes, interpreted through his perception of events. But the strangeness of Genly Ai is seen through the eyes of his host, Therem Harth rem ir Estraven, the "King's Ear" of the kingdom of Karhide.

Gethen is a strange world. Its wintry condition has bred a hard, independent people. But more important than climatic determinants is the biological oddity of its native race. The Gethenians are androgynous, taking on a definite, polarized sexuality only once a month, during "kemmer"—sometimes male, sometimes female; able both to sire and gestate an infant. This peculiarity shapes Gethenian society in distinctive ways,[11] but Le Guin's skill is in making us accept the alien as familiar. Such was Silverberg's skill in *Dying Inside*. When we encounter normal human beings again, we see them from a changed viewpoint. Indeed, they seem more alien than the aliens.

> But they all looked strange to me, men and women, well as I knew them. Their voices sounded strange: too deep, too shrill. They were like a troupe of great, strange animals, or two different species: great apes with intelligent eyes, all of them in rut, in kemmer. (Chapter 20)

The tale of Genly Ai and Estraven is a story of misunderstandings, mistrust and betrayal, but it is also about bridge-building, trust and the marriage of alien cultures. The long passage towards the end of the book where the envoy and the exiled Estraven trek across the glacier—a desperate journey of 81 days and 840 miles, in foul conditions at the worst time of the year—vividly personalizes the issues of the novel. The extraneous is pared away and we come down to the essentials of human contact, as exemplified by the creed of the Ekumen in contacting other races. Genly Ai speaks both for himself and for the Ekumen:

> Alone, I cannot change your world. But I can be changed by it. Alone, I must listen, as well as speak. Alone, the relationship I finally make, if I make one, is not impersonal and not only political: it is individual, it is personal, it is both more and less than political. Not We and They; not I and It; but I and Thou. Not political, not pragmatic, but mystical. (Chapter 18)

Le Guin has an artist's understanding of the power of motif, of taking simple visual images—the keystone in the arch, a shadow on snow—and transforming them into complex metaphors. Her use of motif, a weaving of various strands into a whole, gives her writing a depth and richness that invites re-reading and growth in the reader's appreciation of her work. But, like Herman Hesse and Leo Tolstoy—writers whose simple, lucid styles Le Guin's writing often approaches—there is something of the preacher about her work which can irritate. She avoids this in her best work, but in stories like the novellas *The Word for World is Forest* (1972 in *Again, Dangerous Visions*; book form, 1976), and *The Eye of the Heron* (1978) Le Guin tends to oversimplify issues in her dramatization of them. She has, to borrow D. H. Lawrence's phrase, not just a finger in the pan but a whole fist, her idealism outweighing her sense of artistic balance.

At its best, however, Le Guin's work possesses not merely the intellectual muscularity and honesty of Orwell, but an entrancing lyricism wedded to an open-eyed realism. The ideal is set against the actual and we react to the work with both heart and mind.

Le Guin began humbly, publishing interesting but undistinguished SF and fantasy stories in the SF magazines during the sixties. Her first two novels, *Rocannon's World* and *Planet of Exile*[12] (both 1966) were well-crafted but simply-told hybrids of SF and fantasy elements. In all of this work there was little indication of how good Le Guin would become.

Her third novel, *City of Illusions* (1967), was a better book, and an indication of how Le Guin was treating her material with greater earnestness. It was set within the framework of the League of All Worlds and depicted a far future Earth which, like the rest of the Known Worlds, has fallen to another humanoid race, the Shing. Its strengths lie not merely in its visual clarity but in its creation of Falk, the novel's protagonist, and his quest for identity.

Le Guin's Ekumen, unlike so many other future historical backdrops, serves not to cement her stories into a chronological sequence, but to provide a philosophical context.[13] One might view all of Le Guin's work as utopianist in nature, and her alien Hain, those tall, elegant and intelligent humanoids who drift in and out of the background of these tales, as an evolutionary stage of Homo sapiens; Ethical Humanity, we might call it.

After *The Left Hand of Darkness*[14], Le Guin turned temporarily away from her Ekumenical setting to deliver a novel which, in its concerns, can be seen as a homage to Philip K. Dick, *The Lathe of Heaven* (1971). In *The Lathe of Heaven* the desire to create a utopia takes concrete form, as a man from the year 2000, George Orr, discovers he has the ability to change reality. It is a clever exercise in alternatives and ethics and the practical problems of utopia-building; like the best of Dick's work, it takes a stand for change and human choice over static perfection.

More powerful was Le Guin's trilogy of juvenile novels, collected as *Earthsea* and completed in 1972[15], which, in their use of dragons and wizardry, were fantasy in the Tolkien mode.

Le Guin's masterpiece appeared in 1974.

What are you doing here?

He had no answer. He had no right to all the grace and bounty of this world, earned and maintained by the work, the devotion, the faithfulness of its people. Paradise is for those who make Paradise. He did not belong. He was a frontiersman, one of a breed who had denied their past, their history. The Settlers of Anarres had turned their backs on the Old World and its past, opted for the future only. But as surely as the future becomes the past, the past becomes the future. To deny is not to achieve. The Odonians who left Urras had been wrong, wrong in their desperate courage, to deny their history, to forgo the possibility of return. The explorer who will not come back or send back his tale is not an explorer, only an adventurer; and his sons are born in exile.

He had come to love Urras; but what good was his yearning love? He was not part of it. Nor was he part of the world of his birth.

The loneliness, the certainty of isolation, that he had felt in his first hour aboard the *Mindful*, rose up in him and asserted itself as his true condition, ignored, suppressed, but absolute.

He was alone, here, because he came from a self-exiled society. He had always been alone on his own world because he had exiled himself from his society. The Settlers had taken one step away. He had taken two. He stood by himself, because he had taken the metaphysical risk.

And he had been fool enough to think that he might serve to bring together two worlds to which he did not belong. (*The Dispossessed*, Chapter 3)

The bridge-builder, the envoy here—playing the roles of both Genly Ai and Estraven, stranger and native—is Shevek, an award-winning physicist, whose Theory of Simultaneity gains him an invitation to visit Urras; the first man in seven generations to leave the anarchistic society of Odonians on Urras's moon, Anarres.

Disenchanted by the staleness and bureaucracy of his own austere world, embittered by the smallness and egotism of his fellow scientists, Shevek first sees the luxuriant world of Urras as a kind of Paradise. But his experience with the people and states of Urras sours him, bringing him to see why Odo and her followers left for Anarres and its hardships. However, the truth—as all truths seem to—lies somewhere between. For all his belief in his own failings, Shevek brings more than two worlds together. The practical application of his theory, the ansible—an instantaneous communicator that allows interstellar communication without any time lapse—is the tool which will allow the Ekumen to function effectively and extend the sphere of its harmonious activities.

Nor is Shevek alone, for all his sense of exile. Separate he is, for the element of *mindspeech* (telepathy) used by Le Guin in several of the other Ekumen novels (*The Left Hand of Darkness* amongst them) is absent here. But he has Takver, his female partner, his mate, his wife. Late in the book we see Shevek through her eyes, at dawn, after their first night together for some time.

He lay on his back, breathing so quietly that his chest scarcely moved, his face thrown back a little, remote and stern in the thin light. We came, Takver thought, from a great distance to each other. We have always done so. Over great distances, over years, over abysses of chance. It is because he comes from so far away that nothing can separate us. Nothing, no distances, no years, can be greater than the distance that's already betwen us, the distance of our sex, the difference of our being, our minds; that gap, that abyss which we bridge with a look, with a touch, with a word, the easiest thing in the world. Look how far away he is, asleep. Look how far away he is, he always is. But he comes back, he comes back, he comes back. . . . (Chapter 10)[16]

Bridges, return, distances—again Le Guin expresses these things as motifs: the wall about Abbenay spaceport; the thrown stone; Shevek's empty hands. But whereas *The Left Hand of Darkness* merely drew a certain life and potency from its motifs, they are central to the plot, characterization and structure of *The Dispossessed*.

The Dispossessed begins with the image of the wall about the only spaceport on Anarres and with Shevek's flight outward to Urras.[17] The story does not progress chronologically from that point. In alternate chapters Le Guin pursues two separate strands of narrative. The first strand begins with Shevek's arrival in Urras and follows his discoveries of its complex culture. The second begins in Shevek's childhood and traces his disillusionment on Anarres, ending at the point where he has decided to go to Urras. In this way, and by completing the novel with Shevek's journey back to Anarres from Urras, "with empty hands", Le Guin illustrates Shevek's cycle of return—the key to his theory of simultaneity—within the structure of her novel. This structure can be illustrated diagrammatically.[18]

The two stories interact with increasing complexity as the novel unfolds, permitting us a wholeness of vision which is an act of bridge-building in itself. We see not only the distinct societies, but the similarities, one might say the *constants* within human behaviour—the Yin/Yang nature of all things. Indeed, the Taoism of *The Dispossessed* is almost obtrusive; much more so than in *The Left Hand of Darkness*.

What impressed most readers and critics at the time of publication, however, was the novel's honest depiction of a working utopia, warts and all; perhaps the only attempt at realism in that category.[19] It is hard, dour work being an utopian, says Le Guin, but in small ways the rewards seem worth it—

> "Everything is beautiful, here. Only not the faces. On Anarres nothing is beautiful, nothing but the faces. The other faces, the men and women. We have nothing but that, nothing but each other. Here you see the jewels, there you see the eyes. And in the eyes you see the splendour, the splendour of the human spirit. Because our men and women are free—possessing nothing, they are free. And you the possessors are possessed. You are all in jail. Each alone, solitary, with a heap of what he owns. You live in prison, die in prison. It is all I can see in your eyes—the wall, the wall!"

Shevek's speech at a party on Urras is true enough, but not the only truth. Anarres is, in every sense, a prison world. Hard labour and a form of incipient censorship are shown to beleaguer Shevek's spirit effectively as any possessions, and his journey out from Anarres is clearly an escape from a prison of thought.

The Dispossessed forms a high water mark of modern science fiction, illuminating its medium. It is a novel of subtlety and power, and quintessentially science fiction: the story of the creation of an impossible device. A tale of two worlds. A nugget of future realism. It could not exist without its science fictional context—that concrete realization of a metaphysic. Its flowering was evidence that the much-tilled field of science fiction was far from barren in the seventies. Some, indeed, hailed it as a sign of a renaissance.

Le Guin's writing was always of a highly personalized nature. As she wrote in her essay, "Science Fiction and Mrs Brown"[20], "what good are all the objects in the universe if there is no subject?". Even so, *The Dispossessed* derives its potency as a novel from its marriage of subject and object, the abstract and the personal. In subsequent novels Le Guin never quite achieved this same marriage of elements, and, for all that they retain most of Le Guin's strengths as a writer, they lack the grand visionary touch of *The Dispossessed*.[21]

Indeed, in such writings as *The Eye of the Heron* (1978), we see a lapse into the preacherliness mentioned earlier—a failure in the author to balance idealistic fervour against pragmatic reality—which Le Guin's too immediate success probably encouraged. Critical praise is a frequent debaser of literary coinage. *Always Coming Home* (1985), depicting a future West Coast of America long after its ruination, though an attempt to return to creative strength, is too fragmentary and precious to convince totally. Nevertheless, it is far too soon to regard Le Guin as a spent force, and her second best equals the best of many.

Both Silverberg and Le Guin came to prominence in a genre undergoing what seemed like radical change. Future Shock had struck the SF field. The moon landing had shaken the dust on more than one arid surface.

Both writers wrote from strength of feeling, incorporating personal experience, perspicuity and intelligence, to produce a creative intensity which, of its nature, was not capable of being infinitely sustained. In some ways they were fortunate. Their separate visions came at the right moment in SF's history. There was a strong sense in the genre that, in a world where the reality of developing technology was day by day encroaching on the ability of SF's practitioners to extrapolate from trends, the old, hard-edged, pure-idea-based, technophilic SF had had its day. It hadn't, of course, and still flourishes, yet a search was needed for new ways of revivifying the genre, of de-emphasizing the technical and accentuating the literary, to achieve a balance of the two. The New Wave had laid the foundations for this attempt but had built a crazed, eclectic folly of disparate styles. Only in the seventies did the structure of a new SF begin to emerge, brick by brick, floor by floor.

The best of the new writers saw the weakness inherent in a purely ideative form of SF, and, attracted by the freedoms of the New Wave experiment, began to look for ways of properly melding Science and Fiction. The works of Silverberg and Le Guin are remarkable monuments in this new edifice.

Lord Valentine's Castle (1980) marks a retreat into safer fantasy. Perhaps Silverberg gave up too soon.

Le Guin suffered a different fate. She was temporarily canonized out of existence. She was adopted as the *ne plus ultra* of the new and proliferating critical community in SF. She alone washed whiter than white. She was, for a time, buried alive beneath a vast and ever-growing mound of criticism; laid out in fine gold vestments with amphorae of food and drink to nourish her on the journey to Godhead. Unsurprisingly, she turned away from SF and sought other avenues of expression.[22]

If the architects of this newer, subtler form absented themselves from the work of building upon their own foundations, there were still masons a-plenty to give their visions concrete form, among them Gregory Benford, Michael Bishop, George R. R. Martin and John Crowley.

Gregory Benford is a Professor of Physics at the University of California, Irvine. As the seventies opened he was a research physicist with a fascination for astronomy. Perfect material, it would seem, for a writer in the pure Campbellian mould of ideas first, action second, and characters be damned. The reality is something different.

> lungs panting with the effort he pauses and looks back toward the crosshair window and sees it as blowing him out, the inverse of the young lad's leaden shot, out into a billowing *swack* the blade bites into a rotten seam, wood frags showering up around him tumbling faceted a crash of crystal orbiting asteroids carving the cold, muscles clenching melting, heels biting the compacted snow as earth holds him in his fierce ageless grip of which he himself is a part, he has his own gravitational field, and thoughts flit like summer lightning through the streaming wash of feelings that float him through each moment, melting. Above was the galaxy, a swarm of white bees, each an infinite structure of its own, a spinning discus slicing space with its own definition; Nigel unable to see who threw the discus and uncaring, for there was enough here at the fragile axis of earth, each new truth melting into the old as their fraction of the world flowed through him, *let's slide out of here one of these nights* as continents against butted against each other *an' get an outfit, and go for howling adventures amongst the Injuns* chopping wood, trisecting Androm-eda *over in the territory* Oregon to Aquila *for a couple of weeks or two* all moments going, as he touched them, to smash and scatteration *and I says, all right, that suits me—*
>
> And it melts.
>
> "Nigel!" Nikka's voice comes "Have some more coffee." the cabin steaming melting with renewal
>
> "Of course," Nigel calls, "I'll be there."
>
> Eternally, it melts yes he turns and yes it melts and he falls through it melting and turning yes and yes eternally, it melts

This, with more than a passing nod to Joyce's *Ulysses* and Twain's *Huckleberry Finn*, is the final passage in Benford's 1977 novel, *In the Ocean of Night*.

Benford is another writer who readily admits to the influence of the New Wave on his writing. But he was also concerned with tradition. What Benford has brought to the science fiction field is an understanding of what it must *really* feel like to be a scientist working on the frontiers of discovery—"I tried to incorporate a good deal of science and its human dimensions in all my work."[23] This human dimension is most evident in his 1980 novel, *Timescape*, where the

FANTASTIC

STORIES OF IMAGINATION

35¢

OCTOBER

DELUGE II
By Robert F. Young

THE MOTHER
By David H. Keller, M.D.

LAST DRUM
By Joseph E. Kelleam

Two excellent covers from the science fiction magazines. John Schoenherr's painting for *Dune* depicts his interpretation of a giant sandworm, later closely copied in the film version. Alex Schomburg's career is long and varied, and includes work for Marvel Comics. His careful finish has won him a high reputation. This cover for *Fantastic* has an appealingly mythic quality.

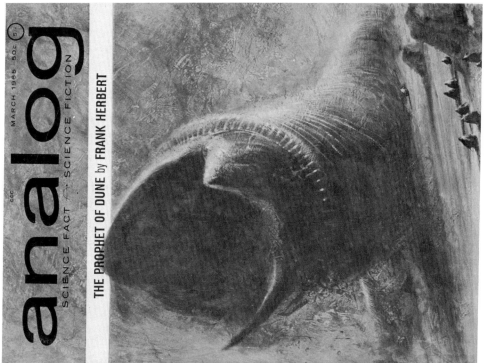

analog

SCIENCE FACT · SCIENCE FICTION

MARCH 1965 50c

THE PROPHET OF DUNE by FRANK HERBERT

Above: World War II, and a youthful Robert A. Heinlein and Isaac Asimov stand on either side of a youthful L. Sprague de Camp. Early in their careers, all three became eminent names in Campbell's *Astounding* stable. Between them, their careers span about one-and-a-half centuries.

Left: Arthur C. Clarke, appropriately surrounded by *2001* stills and space age relics.

SF conventions have been a feature of the life science fictional since the nineteen-thirties. Conferences of serious critical intent are of more recent vintage. Two scholarly bodies, the SFRA and the IAFA, hold annual conferences which are attended by SF specialists from all round the world. Some authors also come to make a contribution. Here one of the most eminent of them, Frederik Pohl, is seen at a recent IAFA meeting in Houston, Texas. The shot was taken at NASA HQ in Clear Lake.

Philip K. Dick was a Californian. His novels are filled with a distinctive mixture of black humour and wild imagination tied to a generally familiar setting. First appreciation of them came from Britain and France. However, since his death in 1982, a small American industry has grown up round his name. Here, Dick looks stern about the matter.

Left: The days of Marshall McLuhan, The Beatles, Swinging London, and Diane Lambert offering her back for art. This 1968 issue of *New Worlds* in its crusading heyday advertises some writers of the period, Spinrad, Disch, Sladek, and Aldiss. Censorship hovered in the wings.

Below: The first international symposium of SF writers and critics took place in Rio de Janeiro in 1969. In the steaming heat, a number of distinguished writers and critics foregathered, among them Fritz Lang, Jacques Sadoul, Marcial Souto, A. E. van Vogt, Robert A. Heinlein, Damon Knight, Robert Sheckley, Poul Anderson, J.G. Ballard, Alfred Bester, John Brunner, the three gentlemen shown here, Forrest Ackerman ("Mr Science Fiction"), Harry Harrison, and Brian Aldiss, *et al.*

Two stalwarts of speculative fiction, whose reputations as rebels and creators have travelled round the globe. J.G. Ballard *(below)* made his name as the chief exponent of the New Wave of the sixties. Michael Moorcock *(left)* is known not only for his prolific output of novels, but for his inspired editing of the magazine *New Worlds*.

Above: The Russian cinema produced an excellently enjoyable SF movie in the silent *Aelita*, in 1924. Not until *Solaris* in 1971 was it transcended. *Solaris*, based on Stanislaw Lem's novel of the same name, was directed by one of the geniuses of the cinema, Andrei Tarkovsky. Kris Kelvin is here seen on the haunted Earth observation satellite which orbits Solaris's sentient ocean.

Below: After Stanley Kubrick's *2001: A Space Odyssey* in 1968, there was a gap of nine years before another major SF box-office hit appeared; it was the less intellectual *Star Wars*, directed by George Lucas. Here Alec Guinness and Darth Vader cross light sabres on their way to fame and fortune. *Star Wars* and its two sequels, *The Empire Strikes Back* and *Return of the Jedi*, netted something like $700m by the end of 1984. Technological fairy tales whetted the public taste for more fantasy.

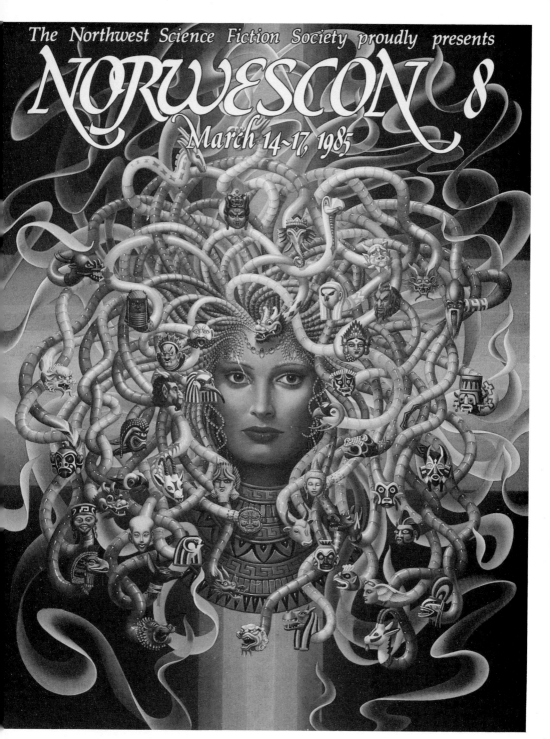

The Northwest Science Fiction Society proudly presents

NORWESCON 8

March 14–17, 1985

Science fiction has grown from an almost secret movement into a literature complete with critical apparatus. That growth has only been possible through the support and ramifications of SF "fandom", a loose-knit body of people from which have emerged many of the most engaged authors, editors, publishers, and critics. Not to mention artists. This splendid piece of artwork, by Ilene Meyer, formed the cover for the convention booklet of one of the major regional "cons", the Seattle Norwescon, an established annual event. Through Norwescon, local publishers specializing in SF have grown up.

Like any other literature, science fiction relies on an occasional infusion of whizz kids to maintain flying speed. Some of these whizz kids make spectacular early appearances and then vanish. Some are seen as disruptive, like J. G. Ballard, and are given a somewhat hostile reception. More recent groups of authors have been more warmly received. They include such prize-winners as William Gibson *(above left)* and Greg Bear *(above right)*, Margaret Atwood, and Bruce Sterling. It remains to be seen whether they will have the staying power and intellectual stamina of such authors as Ballard.

Below: A grounded Saturn rocket forms the background for a group of authors paying a visit to NASA HQ in 1986. Those present are, from left to right, Gregory Benford, Brian Aldiss, Elizabeth Anne Hull, Frederik Pohl, James Gunn, Jack Williamson and the photographer, Rosemary Herbert.

science fictional element—faster than light particles, tachyons, are being used to send messages back into the past to try to avert a catastrophe in 1998—is integrated with a portrait of the scientists involved and their domestic and working lives. In this regard it is unique in science fiction.

Timescape is a long, complex novel and reflects a far more realistic vision of our world than most SF novels. As in so much of Benford's work, it is set only decades away, where things are falling apart moment by moment, the eco-system dying, social institutions crumbling and absurd, millennial religions springing up like weeds in a wasteland. It is a dark, pessimistic work; almost, one might say, British in its preoccupations (much of the novel is set in England). But against the doom and gloom realism is a strong belief in the process of science; not optimistic in the old, ill-considered forties sense, but certainly affirmative. Benford never denigrates scientific achievement.

Lest we make it seem a formula for dullness, it must be said that there is mystical depth to much of Benford's work. If he takes the close and narrow view of his characters—an all-too-human view, of illness, work and marital problems—his vision of the universe in which such frail beings exist is one of vast perspectives, rather in the tradition of Stapledon and Clarke. Huge spans of space and time form the backdrop of Benford's novels. His aliens and their artifacts are ancient, and we are their creations as often as not. In *The Stars in Shroud* (1978), for instance, we learn that the alien enemy, the Quarn, created intelligence in humankind.

> I lay awake for a while staring into the blank darkness. Outside, Earth waited. Outside was everything, and inside here was my mind. Consciousness was an analogue map, a point-by-point tracing of the world, and it was generated by words. The left side of the brain, painting reality over with a lacquer of language. Yet something inside resisted the steady rain of words. Our time sense, for one. Something stretched and compressed time according to the intensity of experience, following the ticking of its own ancient clock. What part of us did that? The Quarn knew, I was sure. Had there been a time when the right brain ruled? Did the Quarn know us then? . . . The right brain spoke to us now with a thick tongue, muttering below the bright clarity of pressing sentences from the left, raising lids of boxes we could not pry up with language. Was there buried down in there the link between animal shame and human guilt? The swelling hunters' fear that became human anxiety? Perhaps the Quarn knew all that. (Part V)

The interest in anthropological roots, in language and its limitations, and in the curious division of the human brain between thought and feeling, characterizes not merely Benford's work but much of the SF of the seventies. But one other thing should be noted here. *The Stars in Shroud* has an interesting publishing history, indicative of the new attitude towards SF that these writers brought. In the April 1969 edition of *F&SF*, Benford published a novelette, "Deeper than the Darkness". That novelette was expanded and added to and published as a novel, *Deeper than the Darkness*, in 1970. It was Benford's first novel. He rewrote it in the mid seventies as *The Stars in Shroud*. A brief essay on Benford's dissatisfaction with the earlier version was appended to the novel.

Another writer who has expressed dissatisfaction with his earliest novels and who has gone so far as to prevent their republication until he can recast them is Michael Bishop.

Bishop's stories began to appear in the SF magazines some few years after Benford's.[24] His first novel, *A Funeral for the Eyes of Fire*, appeared in 1975. It is an impressive debut. Two human brothers are given the task of moving an alien tribe, the Ouemartsee, to another planet, Glaparca, but find their job complicated by the enigmatic nature of the Ouemartsee.

Peter Baulduin and Gunnar Balduin are the brothers; Peter a coldly analytical and highly rational man, Gunnar an instinctive, empathic being. Their encounter with the Ouemartsee changes them, and makes a god of Gunnar. They are drawn into the mystery of the Ouemartsee, and, in the ritual "reading" of the eyes of a dead alien, Ifragsli, gain a glimpse of something utterly inhuman:

> In the centre of the Crofthouse Quelsern canted the heartseed lantern so that its mouth yawned upward at the two prongs of the *lodzhes* and at the eerie white slope of the wall beyond. An intense light was directed at the wall out of the lantern mouth and the Y-shaped shadow of the *lodzhes* was projected on the wall—an immense, druidic rune, a symbol of how the single branch splits, suffers division, bifurcates.
>
> Squatting to one side, the Pledgeson now had the face of a gargoyle. As he adjusted the clips on the *lodzhes*, his hands and arms made shadow pictures on the wall as if for the amusement of children. Then Quelsern moved the lantern mouth so that the shadow of the dowel disappeared. Even Foutlif now seemed intrigued, caught up against his will. In this disreputable, annoying magic there was the suggestion of inchoate technology. All of us watched.
>
> Suddenly colors swam across the replica of Aerthu's Wall, principally faint blues and assertive emeralds. There was no pattern in their appearance, only fluid motion. The Crofthouse had become a bistro in one of the lower levels of the Urban Nucleus; the mourners of Ifragsli had become stoned spectators of a tawdry light-show.
>
> Except that his show was magnificent; it seemed that some primeval sea roiled in the colours refracted through the dead Ouemartsee's mounted eyes, roiled sinisterly on the cold dead face of the Crofthouse wall. An ocean of undulant, deep-green evil. Magnificent. (Chapter 7)

What they are seeing is, in effect, the soul of a dead alien, captured in his eyes. It is typical of Bishop to take a saying like "the eyes are the window of the soul" and make its metaphysic literal. But the strength of the novel lies in Bishop's ability to convince us of the reality of his alien culture. From the first his aliens made other aliens seem homely, familiar and utterly predictable. They were walking, talking, enigmatically-acting *otherness*, mysterious and potent.

Anthropology and the alien remained an important element in the work that followed from Bishop[25], though not a central concern until the 1979 novel, *Transfigurations*, itself extended from the excellent 1973 novella, "Death and Designation Among the Asadi".

The Asadi, more than the Ouemartsee, provide us with a behavioural enigma to which we respond with an anthropologist's delight. They are huge, ape-like beings with rainbow eyes that spin like pinwheels; a tribe who act out a series of nearly incomprehensible rituals in a clearing of the great forest. We encounter them as mystery and, like the humans of the tale, ache to know more of them. Unfortunately, the novel suffers from a weakness in characterization, particularly in respect of its central character, Thomas Benedict. His theorizing late in the novel undoes much of the marvellous sense of enigma of the beginning. The aliens and not the humans engross us.

Are the Asadi a devolved form of a once highly intelligent species? Or are they a kind of sub-species? Slaves or stock animals? It's an old theme in the genre, but Bishop endows it with new life, a new approach. The first part of the novel—the novella—is presented as an ersatz anthropological report, and gives us an utterly convincing portrait of an alien culture. But though the answers that follow present us with a fully-realized and logical account of the origins of the Asadi, they are never quite as satisfying as the questions.

Perhaps that's why we read science fiction in the first place: for the questions. Answers are invariably dull. A thing known is a thing robbed of its mysterious life.

If *Transfigurations* was a flawed and difficult book, it was also a rewarding one and a clear indication of Bishop's ambition. He was not content to accept a vague notion of *otherness*, but wanted to create a genuine sense of the alien. A working model, so to speak. Bishop produced a variant in 1982, taking more than a leaf or two from Richard Leakey. The aliens were now our distantly-related, unevolved selves. The enigma was now that of our own origins as a species. And Bishop's protagonist was no longer a man of the future, a xeno-anthropologist, but a young, adopted black with the gift of dreaming; a gift used by vague mechanical means to get him back four million years among a tribe of early men. The novel was *No Enemy But Time* and it won Bishop the Nebula award for the best novel of 1982.[26]

No Enemy But Time shares much with Benford's *Timescape*. Both works attempt to integrate their SF ideas into what is, first and foremost, a novel, not an elongated SF story. *Timescape* is more successful in this attempt, a better balanced exercise in counterpointing the SF element and the fictional biography, but Bishop's Joshua Kampa is a more fully realized character than any of Benford's, and those sections of *No Enemy But Time* which deal with his childhood and early adulthood are the best in the book.

Bishop is a less visual writer than most. His landscape of the past is less real than it ought to be. It is not given life in the way that the planet Trope was in *Funeral for the Eyes of Fire*, or the island of Ongladred in *And Strange at Ecbatan the Trees* (1976, also as *Beneath the Shattered Moons*). Nor is the writing as tightly honed as it was in earlier work.[27] The attempted hybridization of Science and Fiction, successful in some instances, reveals its less attractive attributes in *No Enemy But Time*. The dual threads of narrative are ill balanced. Artistic wholeness is sacrificed to a wide, eclectic, but ultimately schizophrenic viewpoint. Carelessness is the key note—an irritant in view of the many excellent passages in the novel and the interest of its subject.

The novel is also, alas, dull in places. The immediate "kick" that most SF thrives on is absent for long stretches of the book, and the time travel element proves to mean very little. A child is produced from Joshua's liaison in the past—a child who can dream of the future and is one of a new breed of Man—but the implications of this are muted. In this regard the novel almost peters out, and one is left with the feeling of having travelled a long way for very little insight.

The novel's ambition is to be commended. The award it won reflects, perhaps, a recognition of intention more than achievement. It is a novel about the inner place of dreams, from which our race and its complex consciousness has evolved, and its central metaphor—the oneiromantic time travel device—reflect this. Its greatest strength, however, has little to do with the science fictional context. Bishop creates a real sense of what it must be like to be the young, half-caste son of a mute Spanish whore, adopted at an early age; a black kid trying to cope with the twin psychological pressures of adoption (of family and culture) and of his gift—his disturbing dreams of ancient days.[28]

Far better were Bishop's shorter fictions of the late seventies and early eighties, amongst them "Saving Face" and "The Quickening".[29]

"Saving Face" is *Dark Passage* given a science fictional inversion. A backwoods American, Tom Rakestraw, discovers his face is identical to that of world famous film star Craig Tiernan. Under the Physiognomical Protection Act he is forced to change his face, because Tiernan has already patented his own. Rakestraw is obliged to do this and returns to his family with a stranger's face. Shades of Kafka and Nathaniel Hawthorne haunt the story as it unfolds from this point, for by changing his face Tom Rakestraw becomes a different man entirely. By slow degrees he becomes a stranger to himself and his family—becomes the perfect mimic of Tiernan in every respect bar facial features. His immaculate mimicry makes him famous and does Tiernan great harm. But this is not a story of revenge. Rakestraw, a common man, has been "opened" to a more colourful life; has stepped out from the shadow of anonymity.

In "The Quickening" another American common man, Lawson, wakes to find himself not in his own bed but in Seville. Nor is he the only one to suffer this strange dislocation. The whole world has been scattered thus, like words from Babel. While some struggle to recreate the old forms, most accept the chance the scattering offers and begin to tear down the old structures and start anew. It is a process of unlearning, of revivification, and Bishop's title suggests that this is some kind of day of judgement. Self-judgement, maybe—a choice of life directions between the dead old ways and the quick, the new. In the final scene we see Lawson and his friends—from all creeds and races—tearing down Seville Cathedral stone by stone.

"The Quickening" is, perhaps, a perfect modern fable. A fable about America and her values. For what is being torn down stone by stone is a world spoiled by the trite commercial values of American culture. A fecund, many-faced world losing its own particularized identities in the face of American *product*. Lawson, like Stewart's Ish in *Earth Abides*, is set free by this quickening. This is not the only reading of the story, but it is the most immediate one.

Both stories blend stark psychological realism (and vivid pictorial realism) with a strong sense of fable. Bishop's prose style is simple, direct and highly effective. There are few rocketships, few planetfalls, and no galaxy-conquering heroes in Bishop's recent short fiction, yet they are clearly science fiction. The inversions and absurd exaggerations of his work are reminiscent of many fifties short stories, yet where Pohl, Tenn or Sheckley would have used such devices for satirical purposes, Bishop treats them with a deadly earnest and seeks the inner meaning, becoming, like Lawson in his story, an interpreter of signs.

George R. R. Martin is the youngest of the writers grouped together here. Not yet in his forties, he began his career in *Galaxy* in 1971, and showed early promise with a beautifully evocative story called "With Morning Comes Mistfall" (1973). Like the majority of Martin's work, "Mistfall" appeared in *Analog*.

From the outset Martin was a romantic whose ideas and imagery spanned a wide and colourful spectrum. Vampires and spacecraft sit cheek by jowl in his stories.[30] Elements of SF, fantasy and horror form a heady, exotic cocktail that some find too rich, others just so. But behind the deceptive surface textures lies a seriousness of intent the equal of Benford's and Bishop's.

Martin uses traditional science fiction elements—one reason for his regular appearances in *Analog*—in unsurprising ways. It is not through inversion or exaggeration that he achieves his ends. Nor has he attempted the kind of counterpoint of contemporary and science fictional concerns that *Timescape* and *No Enemy But Time* exemplify. Martin's revolution, if we can call it such, has been to imbue the expected magazine formulae—romantic, often sentimental and mechanistic—with a degree of realism.

Martin has something of Silverberg's zeal to rework standard themes. His best writing is reminiscent of the more colourful novels of Silverberg's Sombre Period—of *Downward to the Earth* and *Nightwings*. Like Silverberg, he is not content to let his story form his characters. His characters *are* his story.

"A Song for Lya" (1974) is the story of two telepaths, Talents, who are hired by the administration of the planet Shkeen to try to fathom why so many of the human colonists are joining the native religion: a religion which entails a superficially gruesome form of suicide—being eaten alive by a huge, jelly-like parasite. Lyanna has the greater talent, the ability to listen in to thoughts; Robb the lesser, a sense of surface emotions. They are a team, but they are also lovers. Very much in love, it seems. Their talents allow them to share an intimacy most dream of, particularly in their love-making. But in encountering the Greeshka—the parasite—and its converts, the Joined, Lya experiences a love far surpassing anything she could have with Robb.[31]

Ultimately Lya joins with the Greeshka and becomes part of its sharing, passionately loving entity—immortalized by it, *deified*, one might say. But Robb rejects it, recognizing that love is only one of the primal urges that makes us truly human. He chooses a lesser, *human* love before godhead.

"A Song for Lya" can be read as a kind of coda to Silverberg's *Downward to the Earth*: an argument against Silverberg's panacea for human isolation. It's a deeply thoughtful story, which like "Sandkings" and "The Way of Cross and Dragon", won awards, a recognition of Martin's ability to give new vitality to old themes.[32]

As a novelist Martin is less successful, though entertaining enough. In his first novel, *Dying of the Light* (1977), lost love is again the theme, but set within the context of a full-blown space opera. What was successful at shorter length fails here: we tend to lose sight of the reality of the characters amid all those other exotic elements Martin crams into the mix. There's no doubting that he is an evocative and, at moments, emotionally intense writer, but in *Dying of the Light* he attempts too wide a canvas.

Windhaven, a collaboration with the talented Lisa Tuttle, followed in 1980, a novel about a young girl changing an almost feudal society on a world of water and wind. Escapism and mature characterization co-exist quite healthily in *Windhaven*, evidence of a successful partnership.

It is too easy to label Martin a sentimentalist, but occasionally the criticism is apt, as it is for his 1981 novella, "Nightflyers". A tale of suspense in interstellar space, its starcrossed lovers, Royd and Melanctha, irritate more than involve us. Martin's attempts to imbue life into old clichés sometimes failed. This was true also of much of his shorter fiction in the late seventies which simply fulfilled genre expectations, using the same surface elements as in his best work simply to chill or shock.

Martin moved out of the genre for his 1982 novel, *Fevre Dream*, a bizarre cross between Mark Twain and Bram Stoker—a vampire novel set on a Mississippi steam boat! However awful that may sound, Martin produced an excellent *sui generis* horror novel that perhaps indicated where his real strengths lay. Vampires—characters who lived off the life energies of others—were always a major part of his work.

The last of the four writers grouped together here is one of those individualists within the genre who surprise and delight. No banners proclaiming "Hugo and Nebula Award Winner" are emblazoned across his books. The writer is John Crowley and his novel, *The Deep*, slipped into the still, cold waters of publication in 1975. A few people read it, were impressed by it, and spread the word.

The Deep is a remarkable first novel, well written and darkly true to human nature. It portrays a world that rests on a vast pillar rising from the Deep—a world where Man is conducting an experiment with constructed beings. This neo-Mediaeval world, its society focused upon the Hub at the world's centre—a city in the middle of a lake—is somewhat like a chessboard whereupon the Reds and Blacks, two brutal dynasties, battle for power.

Its world is a brutal paradigm of our own; a simpler, primal reality. Its raw desire and greed, its foolishness and schemes, its loves, obsessions and betrayals, are all recognizably human. And though this is a world of Defenders and Protectors, Endwives and scholarly Grays, Just and Neither-Nor, it is still recognizably our own, not just another fantasy world. Its people live and breathe and die horribly in the pages of the novel. What makes *The Deep* a science fiction novel, however, is the presence of the enigmatic, androgynous Visitor. Our slow discovery of his purpose as Recorder of the events of this experimental world, forms a counterpoint to the brutal tale of kings and kingmakers.

The Deep is a complex novel of many layers—too many to unravel here—and its stark landscapes remind one vaguely of Le Guin's Gethen. But there the similarities end. There is nothing Taoist about *The Deep*. It is too raw-edged, too open-eyed to see a balance in man's doings, just a tilt and tilt again of the scales, unending and, one might almost say, uncaring. And yet there is a sense that the novel's author cares that this is how man is.

Crowley's second novel, *Beasts* (1976) is not as immediately potent as *The Deep*, yet it proves far richer and more elaborate on rereading.

Beasts is the story of Painter, whose genetic heritage is part Man, part Lion. He is a kind of second Christ, but a Christ of darkness not of light—of the senses, not the intellect. He is king of the sun, almost a sun god; his "wound of consciousness" allows us—creatures of the light—to penetrate his alien nature, his darkness. In *Beasts* Crowley expresses his mistrust of Man's rationally-contructed civilization and its over-emphasis on things thought rather than things felt.

This mistrust of Man's chosen direction is explicitly stated in the novel by Loren Casaubon, teacher of hawks and tutor of the young "king", Sten Gregorius. It is also enacted by Painter, whose indifference to the small morality of Man and his obedience to Need is so fascinating to us—and in particular to Meric Landseer, the artist-figure of the novel.

This is a post-Collapse novel: it depicts a world divided into small nation-states. The economy of the West has failed. The "Leos", of whom Painter is one, are the end-products of an abandoned genetic experiment. In Man's terms a "failed" experiment. And so the Leos are to be hunted down. The irrational—that powerful source of vitality in Nature—is to be hunted down. One can begin to glimpse Crowley's purpose.

To succeed, Crowley must win our empathy for Painter and the Leos, outlaws from Man's ordered world—stronger and finer creatures than men. He does so by making us share Meric's fascination for these beautiful, golden, wholly alien creatures, and by having us understand why Meric rejects the symbols of Civilization and Christianity, to follow Painter into exile. But what gives it its potency is its strong mythopoeic quality. Not imposed Myth, as in the works of Delany and Zelazny, but a sense of miraculous happenings and wonderful creatures returning to an over-ordered world. With Painter, Vitality itself has returned to the world, a small flame on the horizon of man's circle of social activity.

Beasts is, however, primarily about dark sense and light. About perception itself:

> There are bright senses and dark senses. The bright senses, sight and hearing, make a world patent and ordered, a world of reason, fragile but lucid. The dark senses, smell and taste and touch, create a world of felt wisdom, without a plot, unarticulated but certain. (Chapter 8)

In Painter, and in the half-fox, half-man, Reynard, the light and the dark are mixed. They are a paradigm of ourselves. Of perhaps how we once were: magnificent and proud, intelligent animals, valuing both our intelligence and our animality. There is a passage late in the novel highly reminiscent of Simak's *City*, when we encounter another of these genetically-altered animals, a dog, Sweets, and perceive the world through his senses. Whereas it was Simak's purpose to give a distance to his view of Man by looking at them from the perspective of the intelligent dogs who inherit Man's Earth, Crowley wants to create a close, intimate account of Man. Or, perhaps, of what Man ought to be.

Meric, an artist of words and film—of the bright senses—eventually joins the pride of exiled Leos, but sends back a taped report to the humans.

> In half-darkness, the pride clustered around the embers of a fire and the weird orange glow of a cell heater. Some ate, with deliberate slowness, small pieces of something: dried flesh. In their great coats and plated muscle it was hard to see that any were starving. But there: held close in the arms of one huge female was a pale, desiccated child—no, it wasn't a child; she appeared a child within the leo's arms, but it was a human woman, still, dark-eyed : unfrightened, but seeming immensely vulnerable among these big beasts.
>
> The image changed. A blond, beardless man, looking out at them, his chapped hands slowly rubbing each other. "We will starve with them," he said, his mild, uninflected voice unchanged in this enormous statement. "They are what is called 'hardy', which only means they take a long time to die. They have strength; they may survive. We are humans, and not hardy. There's nothing we can do for them. Soon, I suppose, we'll only be a burden to them. I don't think they'll kill us, though I think it's within their right. When we're dead, we will certainly be eaten."
>
> Again they saw the childlike girl within the leo's great protecting arms.
>
> "We made these beasts", the voice said, "Out of our endless ingenuity and pride we created them. It's only a genetic accident that they are better than we are: stronger, simpler, wiser. Maybe that was so with the blue whale too, which we destroyed, and the gorilla. It doesn't matter; for when these beasts are gone, eliminated, like the whale, they won't be a reproach to our littleness and meanness any more."
>
> The lost king appeared again, with his gun, the same image, the same awesome repose.

"Erase this tape," the voice said gently. "Destroy it. Destroy the evidence, I warn you."

The king remained.[33] (Chapter 6)

Beasts, like *The Deep*, is a modern fable, and a powerful one. In one sense it is a subtle reversal of the experiments on Dr Moreau's island. What if the creatures were beautiful and not monstrous? Would men still hunt them down?

For all the poetry in Crowley's writing, *Beasts* treats its subject matter in a realistic mode that gives the book a resonance and a relevance it might otherwise have lacked. It is much more than an adult fairy tale. Like *The Deep* it is about power and politics and manipulation. About man's abuse of his intelligence.

Crowley's third novel, *Engine Summer* (1980) changed tack yet again. No plot summary could do the book justice, for it unfolds like a mysterious flower. It begins in a post-Catastrophe world, and in a strange commune called Little Belaire, and it is the autobiographical story—told orally—of a character called Rush that Speaks. David Pringle, in his book, *Science Fiction: The 100 Best Novels* (1985), called *Engine Summer* "a beautifully estranged vision of our own world" and "a prose poem". And so it is. Pringle's comments apply to all Crowley's work, but *Engine Summer* marks an escalation of his ambitions as a writer. It is a far more difficult book, though patience delivers rich rewards. In *Engine Summer* there is no straight narrative of events. Even Rush that Speaks's quest for Once A Day, his love, is a quest of a very different kind—not for jewels, or dragons or even the search for a fair maiden it ostensibly is, but a quest for knowledge. Rush that Speaks is as intrigued as Crowley's reader by the enigma of the past—that is, of our present selves and why we are as we are.

Engine Summer unfolds slowly, almost painfully, and cannot be fully understood in a single reading. This alone divorces it from the bulk of science fiction. Yet Crowley's method—mythologization, disguise and fragmentary revelation—is of the purest essence of science fiction. It is the Campbellian puzzle story at its highest level, however, involving not just plot and idea, but character and even the manner of expression. The traditional methods of SF are here used *in extremis*. Crowley's two previous novels seem simplistically structured in comparison.

As if he sensed that he could take the science fictional format no further, Crowley turned to overt fantasy for his fourth (and to date most recent) novel, *Little, Big* (1981). But by that time the word was out. Crowley was a writer to pay attention to. *Little, Big* won the World Fantasy Award for its year and attracted respectful and sometimes awed reviews.

What is of interest is that a writer like Crowley can still emerge from outside the central currents of the SF genre—the magazines—and use the material of SF to forge a unique and startlingly fresh body of work. It argues against the view that SF has used up its materials and can only regurgitate clichés. The attempt to revivify the mode from within could only take this so far: could only add depth of characterization, mainstream counterpoint, artistic balance. It still needs insight, talent and (perhaps most of all) *care* to create something as refreshingly new as *Engine Summer*.

There is no doubting, either, that Crowley possesses a substantial knowledge of the genre and its tropes. All three of his science fiction novels depend on their themes having existed in the genre beforehand. What makes them transcend the formulae of such tales, however, is Crowley's distinctive use of his material. To know and yet not to be too heavily influenced by, that is his particular gift.

Not all writers aim as high as Crowley. One such is a figure much-hailed in the field, John Varley.

Varley, like Martin, rarely strays from tradition. He seems happy to replay old standards, with a garnish of hip sex, New Wave slang, clever gimmickry and state-of-the-art technology.

Varley's short stories began to appear in the magazines in the mid seventies and his first novel, *The Ophiuchi Hotline*, came out in 1977. It was a tightly-crammed post-alien invasion yarn, with clones, data input channels (the Ophiuchi Hotline itself) and the idea that humans can be processed with information and memories rather like cassette tapes. There was richness but no wholeness. It was like a child's box of toys—bits from different games, different puzzles, but nothing complete. Varley showed, from the outset, that he had a clever mind, though little understanding of human nature. His clones, like Asimov's robots, were more interesting than his people.

Titan (1978) was a step backwards. Vast alien artifacts were *in* at the time—Clarke's Rama, Niven's Ringworld, Shaw's Orbitsville. Varley presents us with an insipid variation on this bigness-is-best theme. His alien spaceship is called Gaea, a giant Disneyland orbiting Saturn. Centaurs and angels are woken when a NASA team (a crew of ideologically sound clones, lesbians, neurotic males and engineers who can copulate in free fall) investigates.

Against the syrupy Tolkienesque quest is set a tale of massive, engorged penises the length of one's forearm, abortions that produce four-legged foetuses, rapes, and good old straight gay sex. Its heroine, Cirocco Jones, is a shallow and insensitive young woman, totally incapable of winning an ounce of the reader's empathy: a woman with the sensitivity of an eleven-year-old spoilt child.

The book is purely a product designed for the SF market. It seems contemptuous of its readership. Nothing is ever properly evoked. There's no real sense of Gaea's scale as there is, say, with Niven's super-technological Ringworld.

Some of Varley's work deserves more favourable mention. His novella "The Persistence of Vision" (1978) must be cited for its sensitive portrayal of a utopian commune of deaf and blind people in the New Mexican desert. Its success in overturning our perceptions as to how we use language and our senses proves that Varley has the talent to create good, living SF when he tries. Perhaps he found it too easy not to.

Varley's popularity has much to do with the fact that he—as Edgar Rice Burroughs did long ago—presents his readers with no real challenges. His 1984 story "Press Enter ■", which won both the Hugo and Nebula Awards as best novella of the year, is a case in point.[34]

"Press Enter ■" is a contemporary story; a detective thriller involving computer fraud, Governmental department activities, a love affair between a Korea veteran (epileptic and reclusive) and a Vietnamese girl half his age. These elements are made to cohere rather well, and the story proves highly entertaining.

Is SF a literature of speculation or simple genre entertainment? It's a question that Martin, Benford and Bishop would answer with another—Is there any reason why good, speculative, well-written SF can't also be popular entertainment, and vice versa?

SF ought to and does strive to be more than just a way of passing a wet afternoon or a long train journey. At its best, SF has always been capable of making its audience look at the world anew, from a different perspective. And, as a medium of change, it ought to reflect that change in its strategies and approaches.

All of this seemed suddenly pertinent in the seventies. Literary criticism had discovered the science fiction field with a vengeance, and such questions were being asked openly. Was SF an ever-growing or an already-dead genre? Were its themes, its materials, worn out, despite the claims of such as Silverberg, Martin and Bishop?

One writer who added her substantial critical weight to the argument was Joanna Russ. In a 1971 article, "The Wearing out of Genre Materials"[35], she identified three stages in the development of genre materials: Innocence, Realism and Decadence. In her view the science fiction field was a healthy mixture of the last two. The more traditional writers reflected the Realistic stage, and the *New Worlds* experiment—something approaching a metaphoric approach to SF—was clearly Decadent. But many of the SF writers of the seventies—all, perhaps, but Varley of those mentioned so far—were neither Realists nor Decadents. They were, as Martin has argued, a synthesis of both approaches: a fourth stage Russ missed.

Joanna Russ was herself a Decadent through choice. A university professor of English, she commenced her SF career at the very beginning of the New Wave and adopted its techniques naturally. From the start she used traditional SF materials to radical effect. Russ is a feminist. Perhaps the foremost feminist thinker in the SF field, and a formidable opponent in debate.

Russ's *Alyx* stories[36] were something quite new to the genre. Alyx is a female rebel. A thief and adventuress. A highly competent and aggressive woman. She was a revolutionary fictional character, challenging the competent male/wilting female syndrome that had dominated the magazine genre for forty years. And Russ did it with great style.

It was to be expected that she offended a great many of her male colleagues. She was called bitchy, strident, propagandist. She was also praised. Her two major works of feminist SF, "When It Changed" (1972) and *The Female Man*

(1975) were statements of clarity and considerable power. The former won the
Nebula as best short story of its year. The latter, with its four alternative
women, Joanna, Jeannine, Janet and Jael, and its alternate worlds framework,
spoke eloquently of the frustrations of being a woman now and the potentiality
of being a woman of the future. A woman from the planet Whileaway, to be
precise, where the males all died out some 900 years ago from a plague and
women fill all the social roles. It's a pushy book—an attribute Russ would
probably agree with, arguing necessity—which persuasively juxtaposes crass
chauvinistic reality with a utopian/visionary fervour. In that way it is much like
Marge Piercy's *Woman on the Edge of Time* (1976), though the two novels have
their own distinctive voices. Here's a sample of Russ's voice:

> Women are not used to power; that avalanche of ghastly strain will lock
> your muscles and your teeth in the attitude of an electrocuted rabbit, but
> you are a strong woman, you are God's favourite, and you can endure; if
> you can say "yes, okay, go on"—after all, where else can you go? What
> else can you do?—if you let yourself through yourself and into yourself
> and out of yourself, turn yourself inside out, give yourself the kiss of
> reconciliation, marry yourself, love yourself—
>
> Well, I turned into a man.
>
> We love, says Plato, that in which we are defective; when we see our
> magical Self in the mirror of another, we pursue it with desperate cries—
> *Stop! I must possess you!*—but if it obligingly stops and turns, how on earth
> can one then possess it? Fucking, if you will forgive the pun, is an anti-
> climax. And you are as poor as before. For years I wandered in the desert,
> crying: *Why do you torment me so?* and *Why do you hate me so?* and *Why do you
> put me down so?* and *I will abase myself* and *I will please you* and *Why, oh why
> have you forsaken me?* This is very feminine. What I learned late in life,
> under my rain of lava, under my kill-or-cure, unhappily, slowly,
> stubbornly, barely, and in really dreadful pain, was that there is one and
> only one way to possess that in which we are defective, therefore that
> which we need, therefore that which we want.
>
> Become it. (Part 7, Section II)

Is this SF? Yes, it is. And of a kind which will probably prove more durable
than much of the Gernsback stable's output. There's precious little high-tech
gloss in *The Female Man*, and the Moon walk of 1969 was, for Russ, an
irrelevance in the face of those important social changes she saw happening and
strove to encourage through her writing. There's anger and tenderness in Russ's
work. Too often the latter quality is forgotten. And, as in Shelley's *Frankenstein*
and Orwell's *1984*, there's something prodromic about *The Female Man*. As
Russ herself states in its final pages, when the book itself becomes irrelevant and
loses its sting, its work will be done: "Rejoice, little book!" she writes. "For on
that day, we will be free."

We shall return to the question of feminism in SF in the final chapter. But one interesting and perhaps revealing item should be mentioned here. The case of Alice Sheldon.

Between 1967 and 1977 a new writer named James Tiptree Jr submitted stories to the SF magazines and anthologies, and in that time collected two Hugos and three Nebulas.[37] He was hailed as an equal of Silverberg and Le Guin, stories like "Love is the Plan, the Plan is Death" (1973) formed a vital part of the landscape of new literacy in the genre.

But the *he* proved to be a *she*. A female man. And the guise had been maintained without *anyone* so much as guessing, for ten whole years. James Tiptree Jr was, in fact, Alice Hastings Sheldon. And she was an ex-CIA employee! Charles Platt, in a profile published in *Dream Makers* vol. II (1983) described her thus:

> She turns out to be a strikingly beautiful woman. Only a slight trace of gray at the edges of her curly rufus hair betrays that she might now be over sixty. She has compassionate eyes, and a quick smile; her manner is forthright, with a touch of elegance. She stands with a scrupulously correct military posture, which somehow suggests a refusal to recognize weakness or adversity.

Alice Sheldon's personal history is fascinating, as Platt reveals. The daughter of an explorer and a writer, she travelled the world extensively in her early youth, including a 2700-mile trek across Africa at the age of ten in search of the black gorillas of the Ugandan mountains. Her mother, Mary Wilhelmina Hastings Bradley wrote a book about this and called it *Alice in Jungle Land*. In the late thirties she was a successful painter, and in the forties became the first woman to be put through the US Air Force Intelligence School. In the early fifties she and her husband helped form the CIA. From then on until the mid-sixties she was involved in photo-intelligence work, compiling dossiers on people. Then, when she finally quit that—"I used the techniques the CIA had taught me, and in half a day I had a false name, a false bank account, a false social security card, and had rented an apartment and moved in. I was somebody else".

Her next step was a doctorate in experimental psychology. And a few science fiction stories on the side.

Alice Sheldon had been a science fiction fan since the age of ten. In her early fifties she was suddenly *the* writer on the critics' lips . . . but as James Tiptree Jr.

Alice Sheldon was unmasked in 1977 by an investigative fan, Jeffrey D. Smith. The implications at the time seemed enormous, and feminists leapt on the revelation with delight. Who said women writers couldn't write like men? But from a slightly longer perspective it seems more amusing than telling. There is little that is overtly feminist in Tiptree's writing, even as Raccoona Sheldon, and she never tried to write like a man. Her stories and novels are humanistic, while her deep concern for male-female (even human-alien) harmony ran counter to the developing segregate-the-sexes drive amongst feminist writers. What her work brought to the genre was a blend of lyricism and inventiveness, as if some lyric poet had rewritten a number of clever SF standards and then passed them on to a psychoanalyst for final polish:

> I saw her once more, yes. When dawn came I clambered up a ledge and peered through the mist. It was warm then, the mists were warm. I knew what Mothers looked like; the sudden glimpses of huge horned dark shapes before our own Mother hooted us under . . . Oh yes, and then would come Mother's earth-shaking challenge and the strange Mother's answering roar, and we'd cling tight, feeling her surge of kill-fury, buffeted, deafened, battered while our Mother charged and struck. And once while our Mother fed I peered out and saw a strange baby squealing in the remnants on the ground below. . . .
>
> But now it was my own dear Mother I saw lurching away through the mists, that great rusty-grey hulk so horned and bossed that only her hunting-eyes showed above her armour, swivelling mindlessly, questing for anything that moved. She crashed her way across the mountains and as she went she thrummed a new harsh song. *Cold! Cold! Ice and Lone. Ice! And cold! And end.* I never saw her again.
>
> When the sun rose I saw that the gold fur was peeling from my shiny back. All by itself my hunting-limb flashed out and knocked a hopper right into my jaws.[38]

The seventies saw many more women writers entering the field. Some, like Anne McCaffrey, Kate Wilhelm, the witty Kit Reed, Josephine Saxton and Marion Zimmer Bradley, worked through the decade, adding to their reputations and followings of the sixties. McCaffrey had won a Hugo for "Weyr Search" (1967) and a Nebula for "Dragonrider" (1968), accumulating a whole sequence of novels throughout the seventies, all set on Pern, where the threads fell threateningly from the sky and the dragonriders flew up to meet the menace.[39]

The popularity of the Pern novels is almost matched by that of the Darkover series from the pen of Marion Zimmer Bradley. Fourteen Darkover novels existed by the end of the seventies. Her fiercely individualistic and intense world of Darkover, with its strange psionic powers and hostility towards technology, is reminiscent of Herbert's Dune—but darker in tone.

Kate Wilhelm is married to Damon Knight and co-founded the Milford Science Fiction Writers Conference. Though she began publishing SF in the fifties, it was not until the seventies that the full scope of her talent was in evidence, with novels like *The Clewiston Test* and *Where Late the Sweet Birds Sang* (both 1976). The latter won the Hugo for best novel. Wilhelm is still remembered fondly for her first novel, *The Clone* (written with Ted Thomas) in 1965.

Where Late the Sweet Birds Sang is a post-Apocalypse story about an isolated group of clones in a retreat in the Appalachian Mountains. Its strength lies not in its story-line, which is rather diffuse, but in the manner in which it sets fully-human psychology against cloned-human psychology as if these were two alien species, and in its questioning of the ethics of cloning. Like the novelist Iris Murdoch, Wilhelm's ability to integrate complex philosophical ideas into a narrative gives her work an intellectual frisson much humanistic SF lacks.

Amongst the new generation of women writers were Vonda McIntyre, Suzy McKee Charnas and Joan Vinge. Each produces works of interest, and wins awards.

Vonda McIntyre won a Nebula for her 1973 story, "Of Mist, and Grass, and Sand", later expanded into the Hugo and Nebula winning novel, *Dreamsnake* (1978). "Of Mist . . ." is a sensitive portrayal of a young woman healer and her snakes, to whom she is linked by a strong bond of empathy. She has to cope with hostility and mistrust in a post-Apocalypse world. A similar theme and setting were used for McIntyre's first novel, *The Exile Waiting* (1975). McIntyre is a strong feminist and this is reflected in her writing—particularly at shorter length. She has also hit the bestseller list with *Star Trek* novelizations.

Suzy McKee Charnas was as angry in her first novel, *Walk to the End of the World* (1974) as ever Joanna Russ was. Post-holocaust situations—fresh slates on which to write feminist themes large—were popular with this new group of writers. Their use of genre materials was a legitimate one. In the post-holocaust world of *Walk to the End of the World* Charnas equates masculinity with evil, femininity with slavery. The land of Holdfast and its Boyhouse are brutal, overstated creations. Even so, we cannot dismiss the work as embittered fantasy, for it touches the reality of our own Western society in too many respects. It is not just a howl of anguish; it is a plea for recognition and reason, as is most of Charnas's subsequent work, *Motherlines* (1979) and *The Vampire Tapestry* (1980) included.

Joan Vinge began publishing SF in 1974, at age 26. She used her background in anthropology to create highly detailed social environments for her scientific romances. Working mainly at novella and novel length, she has written a number of fine entertainments. The richness of fairy tales lies behind Vinge's work, as in her Hugo Award-winning novel, *The Snow Queen* (1980). Exotic threads from a dozen space operas (themselves a kind of fairy tale) are woven together in *The Snow Queen*, though to little allegorical effect. "Eyes of Amber", a novelette, won Vinge the Hugo for 1977 and illustrates another aspect of her work—the conflict of the human and the alien.

If Vinge's work lacks one thing, it is the cutting edge of genuine speculation— the elements of her stories are aimed at the heart much more than at the head. Vinge is at the dreaming pole, but she dreams intelligently.

Carolyn Jane Cherry, a classics teacher in her thirties, chose the name C. J. Cherryh to launch her SF career in the mid seventies, producing space operas with a good deal of human insight. Two trilogies emerged before the decade was out, *The Book of Morgaine* and the *Faded Sun* series[40], but it was for her short story, "Cassandra" (1978) that she deservedly won a Hugo. As a writer of hard SF of the *Analog* school, she proved herself in 1981 with *Downbelow Station* (1981), a complexly-plotted political thriller set in the colony worlds, which also won a Hugo. Strong characterization and unflagging narrative are

Cherryh's forte more than original invention; like many of her male contemporaries, she moves between high-tech SF and fantasy with some ease.

It is facile to say that the women write fantasy and the men the hard, technological stuff. There *is* a degree of truth to this, if only statistically, but to lay too great an emphasis on it is to forget that such as Anderson, Vance, Farmer, Heinlein, Simak, and Niven have all written a good deal of fantasy, and writers like Cherryh, Octavia Butler, and Ursula Le Guin have on the other hand written a good deal of SF.

In the seventies there was a great influx of women writers. The revolution they began is still under way and is having an effect on the kind of genre we now enjoy. By the end of the seventies it had become clear that SF was no longer a kind of juvenile men's club. The scent of stale sweat and cigar smoke no longer lingered quite so heavily over the magazines. SF's unexpressed half was beginning to speak out. Angrily, skilfully, persuasively, sometimes—as in all new causes—with ill-considered over-emphasis, but in many instances speaking with a new voice, a new intonation.

This change in emphasis had its effect on many of the male writers entering the genre during those years. There was a growing consciousness that you needn't write for a strictly male, strictly juvenile audience any longer. The sixties had rid the field of many taboos. The seventies rid the field of an inhibition about dealing with genuine, non-sentimentalized emotions.

The upcoming male writer of the seventies was conscious not merely of the years of traditional materials he called upon, but of newer aspects. The *New Worlds* experiment, radical feminism, increasing critical attention—these factors shaped many a young writer, consciously or otherwise. Ed Bryant and Barry Malzberg were two such writers who emerged in this breezier climate.

Bryant owed much to *New Worlds*, in particular to Ballard's use of concentrated images and compacted scenes, as demonstrated in his fragmentary *Cinnabar* (1976). It is decadent in Russ's terms—a technological dream-utopia—and unconventional, yet its materials were familiar.

Malzberg had a much bleaker frame of mind. In his work, Inner Space had reached out and swallowed up the Cosmos. The cherished dream of NASA became, in Malzberg's skilful hands, the stuff of existential nightmare, as novels like *Beyond Apollo* (1972) and *The Men Inside* (1973) demonstrated, the former winning the first John W. Campbell Memorial Award.

The two writers took very different routes through the field. Malzberg, after producing seventeen novels in the four years of 1972–75, grew sour with the genre, his undoubted talent and intelligence never properly harnessed. Bryant, a far less productive writer, worked patiently at his craft and won several awards for his shorter work in the late seventies.[41] But Malzberg's acid portrait of a hack SF writer, *Herovit's World* (1973), is irreplaceable.

Old traditions die hard. Indeed, from traditionalists under threat came a call for a process of retrenchment. The hard SF brigade polished its boots, brushed its epaulettes, put on its helmet, checked the charge in its lasers, and came out fighting. Among the shock troops were hardy veterans like Jack Williamson,

Poul Anderson and Gordon Dickson. Also there were new recruits like Larry Niven, Jerry Pournelle and Spider Robinson. These were SF's hawks, *Analog* writers all, busy drilling while the revolution was raging about them.

Larry Niven, a Californian maths graduate, came up through the ranks of fandom in the sixties and had his first novel, *World of Ptavvs*, published in 1966. Niven's work was heavily influenced by that of Asimov, Anderson, Clarke and Clement, and his earliest stories fell into a future history series Niven called "Tales of Known Space".[42] These were scientific adventures set in a galaxy which Man shared with a few alien species fresh from the cereal packet—Kzin, Pierson's Puppeteers, Grogs, Bandersnatchi, Kdatlyno. The most impressive of these tales was *Ringworld* (1970):

> The Puppeteer Worlds had been moving at nearly lightspeed along galactic north. Speaker had circled in hyperspace to galactic south of the G2 sun, with the result that the *Liar*, as it fell out of the Blind Spot, was already driving straight into the Ringworld system at high velocity.
>
> The G2 star was a blazing white point. Louis, returning from other stars, had seen Sol looking very like this from the edge of the solar system. But this star wore a barely visible halo. Louis would remember this, his first sight of the Ringworld. From the edge of the system, the Ringworld was a naked-eye object.
>
> Speaker ran the big fusion motors up to full power. He tilted the flat thruster discs out of the plane of the wing, lining their axes along ship's aft, and added their thrust to the rockets. The *Liar* backed into the system blazing like twin suns, decelerating at nearly two hundred gravities. (Chapter 8)

Ringworld is a giant alien artifact, 180 million miles in diameter, a thousand miles thick, rotating about a sun. The exploration of this giant technological marvel—an exploration that involves adventurous investigations of the properties of this massive piece of hardware—takes up most of the novel. Unlike much of Niven's work, which suffers from unconvincing plotting and poor characterization, *Ringworld* holds our attention and its central marvel distracts us from Niven's flaws as a writer. The novel won both the Hugo and Nebula awards for its year, and a sequel, *The Ringworld Engineers*, appeared in 1980. By that time even Larry Niven had discovered sex!

In the mid-seventies Niven collaborated with Jerry Pournelle on three novels, all of which proved highly popular: *The Mote in God's Eye* (1974), *Inferno* (1976) and *Lucifer's Hammer* (1977).[43] Pournelle had a doctorate in psychology and had been a professor of political science, but in the SF field he was best known for having written the novelization of *Escape from the Planet of the Apes* (1973).[44]

Pournelle is probably the foremost advocate of technological progress after President Reagan. He was active in the US aerospace industry for more than a decade. His work shows a preoccupation with professional soldiers. Novels like *The Mercenary* (1977), in his John Falkenberg series, and *Janissaries* (1980) depend on fast-paced action and simple adventure elements. Few moral issues are raised, and much of it is standard spacefaring Galactic Empire stuff, for all its political claims. Pournelle's hero, Falkenberg, is a military genius and a believer in firm hierarchies; honourable but firm.

Spider Robinson came to prominence through his stories for *Analog* and his review column for *Galaxy*. A collaboration with his wife, Jeanne, won him the Hugo and Nebula awards for 1977 with the novella "Stardance". It is an unremarkable entertainment.

Unimpressive among this group of writers is Alan Dean Foster, whose name is to be found on the cover of many of the novelizations of big screen SF movies in the last ten years—*Dark Star* (1974), *Alien* (1979), *The Black Hole* (1979) and *Outland* (1981) amongst them.[45] He's also responsible for ten volumes of the *Star Trek* log, ground out between 1974 and '78. More remarkably, under the name George Lucas, Foster wrote the novel version of *Star Wars* (1977). He is the author of novels in his own right, such as *Midworld* (1975).

For many potential readers. Alan Dean Foster's may be the first voice they encounter. Although payment rates have increased dramatically for old-style pulp writing in the modern age, the rules of labour remain essentially unchanged: write fast; do the expected; deliver on time; collect the cheque. As Poul Anderson is quoted as having said: "We're competing for the reader's beer money."

In marketing terms, SF *is* simply another product on the shelves. But in writing a history of SF one must assume that developments in the genre are not directly connected with mass popularity. The field advances *despite* large advances, rather than because of them. Outlaws retain respect.

A rough synopsis of *The Forever War* (1975) by popular Joe Haldeman might make it seem simply another in a line of mass-produced future war books. It is 1997 and Earth is at war with the alien Taurans. The relativistic effects of Faster-than-Light travel between the stars mean that while the troops age subjectively by days and months, decades and centuries pass by at home. When the troops return, things have changed dramatically. They re-enlist. The war lasts 1200 years and Private Mandella, our protagonist, sees it all.

The Forever War is the kind of mixture Heinlein used in *Starship Troopers* (1959), right down to incomprehensible alien gooks, combat spacesuits, and a period of boot-soldier training (set here on Pluto). But Haldeman is a Vietnam veteran[46] and his novel is not about the glory of war but its meaningless stupidity and brutality. It was very much the message of its time. Unfortunately, there is little to stand effectively in the place of human competitiveness and aggression. The cloned societies—both of humans and aliens—which have developed by the end of the War, are curiously under-visualized after the detailed precision of the rest of the novel. The static, passive society of clones, for all its benevolence, seems somehow a worse fate than war: better owned than cloned?

The action sequences in *The Forever War* are gory, but not sickening enough to stop our reading. The technological jargon is persuasive enough to satisfy the hardest-headed *Analog* buff, while the story-line packs the pace of a van Vogtian express. These factors, highly attractive in themselves, act against Haldeman's purpose. The thoughtful twists on relativistic effects—such as the clashes between mis-matched technologies from different eras—make the novel enjoyable. It won both Hugo and Nebula awards for 1975.

Haldeman's second novel, *Mindbridge* (1977) showed that he was a talented writer, if limited in range and originality. He went on to *Star Trek* and TV novelizations before settling to write the *Worlds* trilogy in the late seventies and early eighties.

This school of hard-edged technophilic writing had always found a home in *Analog*, which remained as popular a magazine in the seventies as it had ever been. But in 1978 it found another outlet in a new paperback format magazine, *Destinies*, edited by James Baen. *Destinies*, like *Analog*, had its speculative fact articles.

Baen had been editor of *Galaxy* between 1974 and 1977 and saw the magazine suffer acute distribution problems. Its sister magazine, *If*, had been merged with *Galaxy* in 1974 and in 1980 *Galaxy* itself finally folded after thirty years and 201 issues.

Ben Bova was in charge at *Analog* from 1972 to '78, moving on to become founding editor of a new, huge circulation magazine, *Omni*, launched by the *Penthouse* group. In the early seventies *Analog* had been market leader in the field with a circulation of 110,000. *Omni* was in a different league. Its early issues had a reputed one million circulation, which quickly settled to 800,000 worldwide. *F&SF* still continued, selling 50,000 or so, while *Amazing*, under editor Ted White, carried on, digesting *Fantastic* in 1980 in the face of erratic publication schedules and diminishing readership.

Other magazines led short lives in the States during the seventies. *Cosmos*, under David Hartwell's editorship, appeared all too briefly in 1977. Donald J. Pfeil's *Vertex* lasted for 16 issues between 1973 and 1975; Boston-based *Galileo* fared even less well.

In the Spring of 1977, a new magazine was launched which was quickly to establish itself as a new market leader (*Omni* having a very modest ration of fiction on its monthly menu). This was *Isaac Asimov's Science Fiction Magazine*; by the end of the decade it had become the home of most of the best new writers.

The seventies had also seen the growth of another phenomenon—the theme anthology. A vast number of such original anthologies, most of indifferent quality, glutted the market, to the detriment of writers, editors, magazines and publishers alike. An editor previously unconnected with the SF field was mainly to blame, Roger Elwood. At one stage, estimates suggested that twenty-five percent of the anthologies on the market—numbering hundreds—had been edited wholly or partly by Elwood.

The bubble burst in the late seventies and markets for new writing shrank dramatically and suddenly. Yet it might be argued that the seventies had also seen the short story ousted by the novel as SF's form of expression. In the eighties, as we shall see, the novel seems to have been overtaken by the trilogy. Perhaps, in the nineties, it will become obligatory for writers to sign a fifteen book contract before they can get a single word published.

In Britain *New Worlds* appeared erratically after 1970, changing format to become *New Worlds Quarterly*, an original paperback anthology with issue 202 in September 1971. It kept that form for its next nine issues, which appeared every six months or thereabouts. But its demise as a functioning magazine came with issue 211, published as *New Worlds 10* in 1976. An era was dead. Attempts to provide alternatives, like 1975's two-issue *Other Times* and 1977's five-issue *Vortex* were short-lived. Both carried free material from the generous hand of Michael Moorcock. Moorcock has also featured in the erratic *Something Else*, edited by Charles Partington—three issues to date.

More successful was New English Library's colourful *Science Fiction Monthly*, launched in February 1974. It had none of *New Worlds*'s experimental flair, its layout was poster-sized and it achieved a circulation of 90,000—mainly on account of its artwork—before the plug was pulled on it in May 1976.

By the summer of 1977 Britain found itself without a regular SF magazine for the first time since World War II. British writers became even more dependent on the States for their bread and butter, or strove to become fully-fledged novelists without the apprenticeship of the magazines.

The April 1978 issue of *F&SF* was an all British issue, featuring Brian Aldiss, Christopher Priest, Keith Roberts, Ian Watson, Richard Cowper, Kenneth Bulmer, Robert Aickman and John Brunner. On the face of it, British SF was thriving as never before, with something like two dozen independent, full-time SF writers. Yet this situation was deceptive. Most British writers were living on or just above the breadline. Healthy as it then appeared, British science fiction was in an undiagnosed but seemingly terminal condition.

The seventies had begun strongly for British SF, with a number of the New Wave writers producing their first novels. M. John Harrison was amongst them with *The Committed Men* (1971) and *The Centauri Device* (1974), the latter a New Wave space opera, a highly literate and punk rendition of van Vogt. Harrison also produced non-generic fantasy with his Viriconium stories, beginning with the novel, *The Pastel City* (1974), but really impressed with his shorter fictions, collected in *The Machine in Shaft Ten* (1975), amongst them "Running Down":

> Outside Chapel I took to the shade of the trees and discovered a dead hare, the flies quite silent and enervated as they crawled over its face; a little further on, in the dark well of shadow at the base of the drystone, a motionless adder, eyeless and dried up. The valley had undergone some deterioration in the fifteen years since I had last seen it: shortly after I got my first sight of the Bowfell crags and Mickledon (the Rosset Gill path a trembling vertical scar in the haze), I came upon the rusting corpse of a motor car that had run off the road into the beck.
>
> Here and there, drystone scattered in similar incidents simply lay in the pasture, white clumps infested by nettles, like heaps of skulls; and when I came finally to the address Lyall had given me, I found the fellside below Raw Pike blackened up to the five hundred foot line by fire. I didn't know then what I began to suspect later; I saw it all in terms of the children on the

Ambleside bus, the price of bacon in Wandsworth—symptomatic of another kind of disorder.

Lyall, the enigmatic central character of "Running Down" (not the narrator) is a personification of Entropy itself, a walking disaster area. Harrison's bleak rhythms and desperate poetry are at their best in this story. *A Storm of Wings* saw his return to writing in 1980 after a long break.

Rather more amusing is Josephine Saxton, whose third novel, *Group Feast*, appeared in 1971. A unique mixture of naivety and cunning has militated against a greater popularity, although Saxton is often effective at shorter lengths. This is evident in such sexy stories as "Lover from Beyond the Dawn of Time" in her recent collection *The Power of Time* (1985).

Barrington Bayley is another *New Worlds* regular who began to publish novels in the seventies, starting with *Star Virus* in 1970. Immensely inventive, he turns the materials of science fiction inside out: time travel in *The Fall of Chronopolis* (1974) and robotry in *The Soul of the Robot* (1974).

Keith Roberts won popularity with his *Pavane* series of connected stories in the sixties. They appeared in *Impulse*[47] and, when published together in book form, emerged as one of the finest alternate worlds novels.

It is 1968, but a 1968 none of us ever experienced. Electrical power has been suppressed by the Church Militant—has been declared heretical. Steam locomotives transport heavy freight on the roads of England. Giant sema- phores, like many-armed windmills, send communications across the land. A kind of mediaeval feudalism exists.

The apparent explanation for all this is given at the outset. In July 1588 Queen Elizabeth was assassinated; Philip II of Spain successfully invaded England and became king. The Reformation never happened. The Industrial Revolution never happened. The Catholic Church and its Pope have held sway over the whole of the globe for four hundred years, suppressing all technological development.

We see this changed, somewhat eccentric world through the eyes of various characters: Jesse Strange, a steam locomotive haulier; Rafe Bigland, an apprentice signaller; Becky, a young girl helping smugglers; Brother John of the Adhelmians, a visionary artist and rebel; Margaret Strange, Jesse's niece, who marries into the nobility; and Eleanor, Margaret's daughter and the Lady of Corfe Castle.

Roberts's setting for *Pavane*, as for so much of his work, will be familiar to anyone who has read Thomas Hardy. Rural Dorset at the heart of Wessex is seen with the sharpest of eyes and presented with a haunting visual clarity. Corfe Castle and its surroundings—the Isle of Purbeck—are marvellously and unforgettably evoked. Roberts's alternate world is credible because its land- scape is so lovingly re-created for us.

The story unfolds slowly, like the dance from which the novel takes its title. The story-line itself is one common enough in SF, but its manner of telling is rare. The forces of rebellion—of suppressed technological progress—spark and ignite against a rigidly static society. In simple terms it is the tale of the coming of freedom to the world.

Roberts's gift in *Pavane* is to make us see both the delights and the horrors of this simpler alternative; to see this alternate world as a complex, functioning reality, filled with living, breathing, suffering people. It is a world in which the Old People, sons and daughters of Yggdrasil, the World Ash of the druids, still exist. But it is far from whimsy. These things seem starkly real to us. And it is a world in which unrequited love can blight a life and channel a man's energies elsewhere. Jesse Strange, a shy, awkward man, is rejected by his only love, Margaret. He will go on to build a strong commercial empire, but on the morning after his painful rejection there seems nothing for him. The world has died:

> The fishwives woke him, hawking their wares through the streets. Somewhere there was a clanking of milk churns; voices crisped in the cold air of the yard. He lay still, face down, and there was an empty time before the cold new fall of grief. He remembered he was dead; he got up and dressed, not feeling the icy air on his body. He washed, shaved the blue-chinned face of a stranger, went out to the Burrell. Her livery glowed in weak sunlight, topped by a thin bright icing of snow. He opened her firebox, raked the embers of the fire and fed it. He felt no desire to eat; he went down to the quay instead, haggled absentmindedly for the fish he was going to buy, arranged for its delivery to the George. He saw the boxes stowed in time for late service at the church, stayed on for confession. He didn't go near the *Mermaid*; he wanted nothing now but to leave, get back on the road. (*Pavane*: "The Lady Margaret")

This and the long rejection scene that preceded it and colours it, one of the most poignant in science fiction, compares not unfavourably with Hardy. Roberts is a more lyrical writer, his connection with the old gods and old ways of Wessex more overt than Hardy's.

If there is one complaint to be made about *Pavane* it is that Roberts, in the novel's "Coda", presents this alternative world as a second cycle of Man's civilization. The Church has set up this sequence of events, it appears, to slow the inevitable dance of progress. In this respect *Pavane* gives more than a passing nod to *A Canticle for Leibowitz*. The novel ends with the assumption that Man has learned something, attained a kind of maturity and balance, and the horrors of the Church Militant's campaign of repression are a lesser evil than the horrors of Belsen, Buchenwald and Passchendaele. We aren't wholly convinced.

Pavane is a rare and beautiful novel. Some of that same beauty is to be found in others of Roberts's works—in *The Chalk Giants* (1974) and in some of the stories in *The Grain Kings* (1976), as well as in his recent *Kiteworld* (1985). Roberts often uses a feminine viewpoint—capturing the sensitivities and nuances of his heroines with considerable skill and empathy—as in his *Anita* (1970) sequence, and *Molly Zero* (1980). In all his writings, however, he remains the most English of writers, evoking the sense of rootedness, of how deeply the

English are wedded to their soil, their landscape. What perhaps is surprising is that Roberts chooses to work within SF, though there is no doubting that his use of SF metaphor works marvellously, fulfilling our original definition of SF. It is not post-Gothic, admittedly, calling on traditions far older than Gothic—on the tradition that runs back to *Beowulf.*

Ian Watson is a very different writer from Roberts. For a start there's little definitively English about his work. For him the speculative content of a novel transcends mere character. Highly inventive and plot-oriented, Watson is a cerebral writer with a penchant for exotic locations and alien concepts. Metaphysics rather than physics is his forte.

Some of Watson's earliest stories appeared in *New Worlds* but he really arrived on the SF scene with the publication of *The Embedding* in 1973.

The Embedding is a novel about the limitations of expression of language and its relationship to reality. It's also about governmental and corporate power and first contact with aliens. In style the novel is a hybrid of Arthur C. Clarke's extrapolative fervour and John Brunner's modernism; idea-oriented but fast-paced, charged with an enthusiasm for its own intellectual puzzles. We encounter three experiments in linguistics, two natural and one unnatural: that of the protagonist Chris Sole, who raises children in special contained environments, hoping to nurture the capacity for new concepts into them; that of the Xemahoa, a South American tribe who speak a second, drug-trance language freed of normal syntax; and that of the alien Sp'thra. Language, argues Watson, embeds us in a certain kind of reality, limiting what we can and cannot perceive. Free us from linguistic constraints and . . . ? Well, in *The Embedding* there is a destructive overload effect when these alien ways of perception are brought into contact with more normal (to us) ways of seeing things.[48]

The Embedding was an impressive debut. Two equally interesting works, *The Jonah Kit* (1975) and *The Martian Inca* (1977) added to Watson's reputation. The best of his early novels, though, was *Alien Embassy* (1977). Like all of Watson's previous work it was a novel of the near future, embracing a whole range of state-of-the-art speculations. But what impressed most was its maturation of style. One read Watson for his ideas, not his lyricism: *Alien Embassy* had both.[49]

From *Alien Embassy* onward, Watson's novels began to take a distinctly transcendental turn. Man was something that was to be surpassed, and Watson developed the idea that humankind was a neotenous species— a species in its infancy. This was engaging if not novel.

After *Alien Embassy* Watson moved into overt mysticism, providing a wholly new twist on standard UFO elements in *Miracle Visitors* (1978). Although Watson continued to develop as a writer, his work was never as fresh as in the first few years, despite its energetic and constant movement into new directions. *The Gardens of Delight* (1980), for instance, depicted a spacecraft landing in the midst of the landscape of Hieronymus Bosch's painting. The pleasures of such work were highly esoteric.

In the last few years Watson has produced an SF trilogy, *The Book of the River* (1984), *The Book of the Stars* (1984) and *The Book of Being* (1985) which might almost be viewed as his own metaphysical answer to Farmer's *Riverworld*. Watson has also become a prolific short story writer and the most regular British contributor to several of the American magazines.

A less prolific but no less impressive writer is Christopher Priest. Priest's first story, "The Run", appeared in *Impulse* in 1966, when he was 23. His first novel, *Indoctrinaire*, appeared four years later. It was not until 1972, however, and his second novel, *Fugue for a Darkening Island*, that Priest showed himself to be a capable craftsman with his own unique vision.

Fugue depicted a Britain undergoing social collapse with the sudden pressure of massive immigration from a devastated African continent. We see this process in all its stages, but, unlike most British disaster novels, Priest's is far from being a cosy catastrophe. The novel's first person narrative is so alienated and distanced that it seems third person. Its narrator, Whitman, is a man dissociated from himself as well as from the crumbling, nightmare society through which he stumbles. He is stripped of home and family and ultimately of his own sense of identity. *Fugue* is frighteningly real, and Priest's clear, precise prose—something he has perfected in the years since—gives the novel a paradoxical emotional charge.

Fugue was one of the purest expressions of *New Worlds* realism (and pessimism, one might add), but Priest's next novel proved he could generate a first-rate hard SF idea and present it effectively, convincingly and attractively.

Inverted World (1974) presents us with a concept as impressive as Hal Clement's high-gravity world in *Mission of Gravity*. It is one of the rare, genuinely outré ideas in SF. Our viewpoint character is Helward Mann, a citizen of a moving city which exists in a universe connected to our own. Through his eyes we slowly discover the properties of that strange universe:

> The southwards pressure was now so great upon him that the normal downwards pull of gravity was virtually negated.
>
> The substance of the mountain was changing beneath him. The hard, almost vertical wall was slowly widening to east and west, slowly flattening, so that behind him the summit of the ridge appeared to be creeping down towards him. He saw a cleft in the rock beside him which was slowly closing, so he removed the grapple from under the spur and thrust it into the cleft. Moments later the grapple was securely held.
>
> The summit of the ridge had now distended and was beneath his body. The southward pressure took him, and he was swept over the ridge. The rope held and he was suspended horizontally.
>
> What had been the mountain became a hard protuberance beneath his chest, his stomach lay in what had been the valley beyond, his feet scrambled for a hold against the diminishing ridge of what had once been another mountain.
>
> He was flat along the surface of the world, a giant recumbent across an erstwhile mountain region. . . .
>
> . . . Helward looked ahead of him through the thin, rarefied atmosphere above the clouds. He looked towards the north.

He was at the edge of the world; its major bulk lay before him.

He could see the whole world.

North of him the ground was level; flat as the top of a table. But at the centre, due north of him, the ground rose from that flatness in a perfectly symmetrical, rising and curving concave spire. It narrowed and narrowed, reaching up, growing ever more slender, rising so high that it was impossible to see where it ended.

He saw it in a multitude of colours. There were broad areas of brown and yellow, patched with green. Further north, there was a blueness: a pure, sapphire blue, bright on the eyes. Over it all, the white of clouds in long, tenuous whorls, in brilliant swarms, in flaky patterns.

The sun was setting. Red to the north-east, it glowed against the impossible horizon.

The shape of it was the same. A broad flat disk that might be an equator; at its centre and to north and south, its poles existed as rising, concave spires.

Helward had seen the sun so often that he no longer questioned its appearance. But now he knew: the world too was that shape. (Part Two, Chapter Eight)

Mann's world is, quite literally, the inversion of our own; his world infinite in size, his universe finite. And Priest makes this utterly convincing.

Inverted World is a delightful concealed environment story. The city must keep moving or, like Helward, it will be tugged southward—to its ultimate destruction. But there are those, Terminators, who want to stop the movement; who, in essence, do not understand the physical properties of their universe. On another level, then, the book is about determinism and free will as much as it is about getting the city back to the "window" that links it to our own "normal" universe.

Priest followed *Inverted World* with a homage to H. G. Wells, *The Space Machine* (1976), an enjoyable Victorian romp, set partly on a convincing red planet Mars. It was with his next novel, however, that he was to give an explicit rendering of his favourite theme—the division between reality and dreams. *A Dream of Wessex* (1977) is about the creation and warping of an alternate reality—of an all-too-solid dream which is at first beneficent but later, through the intervention of an ill-balanced man into the corporate dreaming group, begins to disintegrate.

The stories and novels which followed saw Priest moving further away from genre concerns. He began to construct stories set in the "Dream Archipelago", a kind of imaginary, alternative Greek Islands. Some of his stories in *An Infinite Summer* (1979) and the novel *The Affirmation* (1981) fall into this loosely-linked sequence. The prose was more polished than ever, the viewpoint too distanced to win a reader's sympathies. Its subject matter involves us with a writer concerned with writing a novel, reflecting Priest's analytical approach to his craft.

Priest no longer owns to being a science fiction author, though his most recent novel, *The Glamour* (1984), has a patently science fictional device at its core—the invisible man theme. A taut stillness about this novel is immediately distinctive, and is Priest's hallmark.

His sharp intellectual debating manner, in which melancholy is counterbalanced with wit, is prized in SF circles, where he is recognized as a valued rare instance of the dedicated writer.

A elegant writer perennially expressing surprise to find himself in the SF camp is Richard Cowper, best known for his "White Bird of Kinship" sequence, which opened with "Piper at the Gates of Dawn" (1976). Cowper began writing in the late fifties and early sixties, only progressing to SF with his fourth novel, *Breakthrough* (1967), an intensely human parapsychology tale.

Cowper is, in fact, John Murry, son of John Middleton Murry, the literary critic, and can boast of having D. H. Lawrence for a godfather.[50] His style is direct and lyrical. People and their relationships are always paramount in Cowper's works, ideas are secondary. In an age of word processors and floppy-discs he is an anachronism: he hand-writes all of his work in a delicate and attractive style. And, like Keith Roberts, he is an artist, as demonstrated in his turn of phrase, his careful evocation of visual imagery. Like Roberts, he aspires towards that conservative tense, future-historic.

Much of Cowper's work comes straight from the heart of the British tradition of clearing everything away and setting up a simpler, post-catastrophe society. In *The Road to Corlay* (1978) the sea level has risen and, a thousand years hence, we encounter a mediaevalized society, complete with repressive religion. When Cowper chooses to use high-tech SF themes it is usually for the purpose of satire, as in *Clone* (1972) and *Profundis* (1979). All of his work is immensely readable and enjoyable, though little of it is *modern* in a literary sense. In the second half of the seventies Cowper won a following in the States through a series of stories in *F&SF*, such as "The Custodians", "Out There Where the Big Ships Go" and "Incident at Huacaloc". His best novel, however, remains *The Twilight of Briareus* (1974), a post-catastrophe near-future love story.

Cowper was one of a number of writers carrying on the almost ruralized tradition of Wyndham and Christopher in the seventies. Michael Coney turned the West Country into an alien planet on several occasions, in *Hello Summer, Goodbye* (1975, also as *Rax*) for instance. His best work was perhaps the alternate worlds love story, *Charisma* (1975), not Coney's cleverest book but his most lyrical and poignant and nearest to the heart of his very human concerns. D. G. Compton, a writer active in the late sixties, delivered some of his best work in the seventies, with *The Missionaries* (1972), *The Continuous Katherine Mortenhoe* (1974, also as *The Unsleeping Eye*)[51] and *Ascendancies* (1980).

Another writer always popular for his constant creation of fascinating hard SF ideas is Bob Shaw, who with his "slow glass" stories and his two *Orbitsville* novels, has proved to be Britain's most mid-Atlantic writer, fusing very British concerns with a style readily acceptable to the American audience. From *Night Walk* (1967) and *The Two-Timers* (1968) he has presented us with a series of enjoyable novels, of which *A Wreath of Stars* (1976) is perhaps the most original and poetic. *Orbitsville* appeared in 1975 and its sequel, *Orbitsville Departure*, in 1983. *The Ragged Astronauts* (1986) is the first of a trilogy about two worlds set only a few thousand miles apart.

British SF writers generally have few of the advantages of their American colleagues, apart from the mother tongue. The absence of a large home market means that British writers need to sell their work abroad—in particular in the USA—to earn more than a subsistence wage. The lack of a regular magazine and a reluctance among many British publishers to look for new home-grown material exacerbates the problem. Many find it hard to sell their more lyrical, less technological SF in the American marketplace. By the end of the seventies British SF had become a cul de sac. Even the best writers could not guarantee that their novels would be taken up in the States. Few new writers came through.

There was, on the other hand, a continuing slight encouragement for SF from some literary quarters, in contrast to the general atmosphere of disparagement. Kingsley Amis produced two SF novels towards the end of the seventies; his lovely alternate worlds story, *The Alteration* (1976), and the extremely thoughtful and thought-provoking *Russian Hide-and-Seek* (1980), about a Soviet occupation of Britain some fifty or more years hence. There was also a first novel from a writer who was to make a bigger splash in the literary marketplace with *Midnight's Children*: Salman Rushdie's *Grimus* (1975) used many speculative devices and brought him praise from within the SF field.

If it was difficult being a British SF writer at the turn of the decade, the difficulties increased for European writers wishing to jump the hurdle of translations across the Atlantic. One much healthier sign was the emergence in the seventies of a number of East European writers from their obscurity, in particular Stanislaw Lem, Josef Nesvadba, and Arkady and Boris Strugatsky.

Stanislaw Lem has been subjected to the kind of fierce partisanship which can distort the true worth of a writer, while his harsh championing of his own writing has disgusted many. Lem, a Polish intellectual, born in 1921, produced much of his SF in the sixties, but it was only with the translation into English and publication of *Solaris* in 1970 that he came to the attention of a Western audience.

It is claimed that Lem uses science fiction in a way that we in the corrupt and decadent West have forgotten.[52] In fact, such satires on the West as *Memoirs Found in a Bathtub* (1973) appear ponderous and dated. Politics has rarely enlivened imaginative literature. Lem is not read because of ideology, but because he is often genuinely inventive—a skilful writer with his own peculiar vision of how things function. Nor does it serve to claim that Lem's ideas concerning cybernetics and information theory are unique to him. The work of John Sladek, Rudy Rucker and a number of others proves that this just is not so.

Lem's work seems to fall into two distinct categories: intellectual puzzle and moral fable or parable. Where these two categories intersect lie Lem's masterpieces, *Solaris*, and *The Invincible* (1973, written 1964), wittily written and intriguing stories with a strange, unnamable power to them. Lem is rarely dull, often amusing, and his writings have something to commend them; but, to put things in perspective, he is not (as Darko Suvin has repeatedly claimed) "one of the most significant SF writers of our century", despite his adoption by intellectuals beyond the field who approve his anti-science fictional posturing.

As in Dick's novels, there is an overlap of themes and concerns in Lem's work. Whereas in Dick these combine to form a totality which is a powerful, complex work of art (for all its schlock elements), Lem's totality is more the diagram of such a work than the work itself. There is a coldness of intent, a weakness in characterization, and an overall inability to engage the whole of what we are, which makes Lem's writing much less significant than it ought to be. Lem's intellect may be vast. It is also cool and unsympathetic.

Josef Nesvadba, already mentioned, is a Czech writer and psychiatrist. The latter profession is particularly apt, for the stories of *In the Footsteps of the Abominable Snowman* (1970, also as *The Lost Face*) are set in the narrow alleyways of the mind. Black humour is scarcely dispersed by low-wattage electric bulbs: the satire is sharp and downbeat and intensely satisfying. There's a deep-rooted hatred of totalitarianism in Nesvadba's work which comes out in a snarl of liberating laughter. Typical of this is the story "Expedition in the Opposite Direction", with its ill-functioning time machine.

Despite Nesvadba's superior sophistication—he has travelled in the world— his fiction, like much of Lem's, comes out of a long tradition of East European folk tales. There's also the acknowledged influence of fellow Czechs, Karel Čapek and Franz Kafka in Nesvadba's writing. A profound mistrust of science and technology pervades his work, surfacing in "Dr Moreau's Other Island", a tale of ideals and amputations that has much in common with Bunch's *Moderan*.[53]

Last of this small Eastern European bloc are the Soviet brothers Arkady and Boris Strugatsky. The long tradition of Russian SF lies behind the Strugatskys. As with Lem, we had to wait a decade or more before their work saw translation in the West. *Far Rainbow* (1963) was published in 1967 and the intricate and bizarre *Hard to Be a God* (1964) six years later. There was another hiatus until 1976 and *The Final Circle of Paradise* (1965) appeared. After that another ten volumes of the Strugatskys' work were published in five years.

Comparisons with Lem are inevitable, though misleading. Both often use a fabular style, both are intensely, almost obsessively logical (a tortuous, almost Kafkaesque logic in the best of both). Russian film-maker Andrei Tarkovsky has worked with material from both Lem and the Strugatskys, to create two impressive movies, *Solaris* and *Stalker*, the latter from the Strugatskys' novel *Roadside Picnic* (1972, translated 1977). Like Lem, the Strugatskys work from within an inflexible and creatively stultifying political system. The incomprehensible rituals of bureaucracy form a backdrop to much of their fiction. Terry Gilliam's superb film *Brazil* (1985) provides a similar experience in a different medium. *The Snail on the Slope* (1968, translated 1980), is the Strugatskys' best novel, and typifies their approach:

"What's this about an escape?" he asked. "Where are we driving?"

"The usual escape," said Voldemar, lighting up. "We get them every year. One of the engineers' little machines gets away. Order for all, catch it. There they are at it over there."

The habitations fell away. People were wandering around over open country, lit by the moon. It looked as if they were playing blind-man's buff as they went about on bent legs with their arms spread wide. Everybody was blindfolded. One of them went full tilt into a post and probably uttered a cry of pain, for the others at once halted and cautiously began turning their heads.

"Every year the same game," Voldemar was saying. "They've got photoelements and acoustics of all sorts, cybernetics and layabout guards stuck up on every corner—all the same, every year one of their little machines gets away. Then they tell you: drop everything and go and look for it. Who wants to do that? Who wants to get involved? I ask you? If you just catch sight of it out of the corner of your eye—that's it. Either you get drafted into the engineers or they send you off into the forest somewhere, to the advance base to pickle mushrooms, so's you can't talk about what you've seen, for God's sake. That's why the people get around it as best they can. Some of them blindfold themselves so's not to see what's going on. . . . The brighter boys just run around and shout as loud as they can. They ask people for documents, search people or just get up on the roof and howl as if they're taking part, no risk involved. . . ."

"What about us, are we trying to catch anything?" Pepper asked.

"I'll say we are. The public here are out hunting and we're the same as everybody else. Six hours by the clock we'll be on the hunt. There's a directive: if in the course of six hours the runaway mechanism is not detected, it's blown up by remote control. So everything can stay hush-hush. Else it might fall into unauthorized hands. You saw what a mess-up there was in the Directorate? Well, that's heavenly peace—you see what it'll be like in six hours' time. See, nobody knows where the machine's got to. It might be in your pocket. And the charge they use is pretty powerful, just to make sure. Last year, for example, the machine turned up in a bathhouse, and there were plenty of people packed in there—for safety. They think a bathhouse is a damp sort of place, out of the way . . . Well I was there as well. A bathhouse, that's the place, thinks I . . . So I was blown out of the window, nice and smooth like being on a wave. I hadn't time to blink before I was sitting in a snowdrift, burning beams flying by overhead. . . ." (Chapter 9)

It is no surprise to learn that the other protagonist of *The Snail on the Slope* bears the name Kandid, for there is a peculiarly Voltairean taint to the Strugatskys' writing.

We began this chapter ruminating on the Moon landing of 1969. Ten years on, Voyager 1, NASA's outer planet probe, was making a close approach to Jupiter. Back to Earth came those beautiful shots of the gas giant. Another amazingly successful probe, Voyager 2, followed shortly after. Mars, Venus, and later Saturn, were displayed to the wondering eyes of mankind. In 1986, Voyager 2 sent back even more marvellous photographs of Uranus, her moons and rings. Viking 1 had landed on Mars in 1976, and throughout the decade the vacuum round Earth was slowly filled with satellites. Devo, an American new wave band (ah yes, and New Wave now meant music, not SF) wrote a song about a new phenomenon, space junk:

> she was walking all alone
> down the street in the alley
> her name was Sally
> I never touched her
> she never saw it
> when she was hit by space junk[54]

The solar system, setting for so many interplanetary romances, had shrunk, become an outpost of the global village. Package tours weren't far off. This is not to say that the solar system and its planets were dead as a source of imaginative riches, as at least one of the subjects of our next chapter, Arthur C. Clarke, was to prove; but the process that began with the actualization of a dream—the Moon walk—had been completed by the end of the decade. The fast-moving forward edge of science had overtaken the ability of most SF writers to speculate. The scientists themselves had usurped much of what had been traditional SF territory. It was they now who asked "What if?" and "How about . . .?" and "If we substituted this for this . . .?" It made the task of being a hard science SF writer that much harder. New specialist fields were sprouting like the heads of the hydra and it was a wise and tireless man or woman who managed to keep up with it all.

But some did. Or tried to. And some shaped their material in new ways. They are the latest to accept the challenge that SF uniquely offers. But first come seven more hoary figures, honourable dinosaurs of the tribe, already familiar to us: men who, in the late seventies and eighties, were to be sighted on old hunting grounds.

CHAPTER XV

How to be a Dinosaur:
Seven Survivors

> Rooted as they are in the facts of contemporary life, the
> phantasies of even a second-rate writer of modern Science
> Fiction are incomparably richer, bolder and stranger than the
> Utopian or Millennial imaginings of the past.
> —Aldous Huxley: *Literature and Science*

Ask anyone vaguely acquainted with science fiction to name four modern
writers and it's likely that the answer will be Asimov, Clarke, Heinlein and
Herbert. These writers form what we might see as an SF Super League.
Advances for their books are in six, often seven figures. The books themselves
sell in millions and in dozens of translations. They command that ultimate
accolade in a media-oriented world: a "household name". Our aunts have read
Clarke. Our workmates have read Heinlein. Asimov novels clutter the
bookstands of Greek islands—in English, German, French and various Scandinavian editions. The video of *Dune* has visited a million households.

These four writers, these gallant dinosaurs, have seen their faith in a
previously obscure genre rewarded more greatly, in terms of prestige and
money, than even they could have predicted. To rephrase one of the statements
made at the beginning of this work, science fiction is one of the major literary
success stories of the twentieth century; Clarke, Asimov, Heinlein, and
Herbert, among those writers who have emerged from the once despised
magazines, are the brand names most associated with that astonishing success.
They embody the rags-to-riches story.

Some readers have been following Heinlein since his early juveniles, with
their buoyant narrative line, and have no intention of giving up the habit. For
them, Heinlein and the others are beyond criticism. And it is true that Heinlein
and Asimov in particular, with their high profile names and personalities, have a
way of leaping across to the reader, over the heads of critics.

Nevertheless, critics also have their duties. They look beyond the reputations
to the texts themselves. It matters whether the gods and demi-gods write well or
ill, for the future of writers and readers to come. The basic product of Heinlein,
Clarke, Asimov, and Herbert is the SF book, differing very little, at least in
appearance, from all the other short-lived books of any given year.

Add to our four household names three others, L. Ron Hubbard, A. E. van
Vogt and Frederik Pohl, and we have seven writers who represent 309 years of
experience as published science fiction authors. Four of them made their SF

debuts in John W. Campbell's *Astounding*, and even Herbert's most famous work, *Dune*, ran in Campbell's renamed *Analog*.[1]

The work of these seven represents a "tradition" in SF that is, for most casual readers of SF and indeed for many writers yet working in the genre, *the real thing*. When Asimov and others talk of a "Golden Age" of Science Fiction, it is those few years in which five of these writers emerged—1938 to 1946—to which they refer.

Those years in which the Golden Age tradition was being challenged by the literary revolution of the New Wave coincided with years in which relatively little work came from these seven writers. Two—Asimov and Hubbard—had ceased writing SF altogether. Three others—Heinlein, Clarke and Pohl—had produced only a handful of novels between them. By the end of the seventies, all seven writers had returned to writing, producing novels regularly. Significantly, all seven returned to earlier, successful models for part of their output—direct sequels, embellishments and retellings of old stories.

Distinctions must be made between these contrasting writers, their intentions and achievements weighed individually. Yet between them the seven represent a renaissance of Golden Age/Campbellian SF. Is it just coincidence that these writers—all but one products of Campbell's crucible—should become active again at a time when science fiction grew, not simply popular, but all pervasive?

The presence of such giants in the field distorts judgement of what is being done not merely by publishers but by a number of young writers entering the genre.

First a few facts and figures. From 1986.

Both *Foundation's Edge* (1982) and *Robots of Dawn* (1983) by Isaac Asimov sold over a million copies in the USA alone during 1984. Frank Herbert's *Dune* series have all had massive printings. In the USA, *Dune* (1965) is in its 33rd printing with its second publisher with 2,420,892 copies; *Dune Messiah* (1969) in its 47th printing with 2,655,110 copies; *Children of Dune* (1976) in its 23rd printing with 2,445,164 copies; *God Emperor of Dune* (1981) in a 5th printing with 926,000 copies. Arthur C. Clarke's *2010: Odyssey Two* (1982) sold more than 2 million copies in the States in 1984 alone. Robert A. Heinlein's *The Cat Who Walks Through Walls: A Comedy of Manners* (1985) attracted a $1 million advance for the USA alone—an estimated $2 million worldwide. Previous works have had huge printings. *Time Enough for Love* (1973), for instance, is in a 19th printing with 1,254,100 copies. *Friday* (1982) had a first US printing of 708,000 copies. (Figures courtesy of *Locus*.)

These impressive figures should be seen in perspective. An SF novel published in hardback by a new young writer in the UK will probably have a 1500 to 2000 printing and may never see paperback. His equivalent in the States might double this figure and expect a paperback sale. On the other hand, Stephen King's *The Shining* is in a 30th printing with 5,130,000 copies in print. The figures mentioned in the last paragraph represent sales ten to twenty times higher than most "popular" SF writers achieve.

All these figures must be viewed against market trends, over which authors can have little control. In a prosperous USA, the retail price differential between a hard-cover and a paperback book no longer seems as great as it once did. Charles N. Brown, editor of *Locus*, the invaluable newspaper of the SF field, presents a convincing argument concerning the way in which today's audience of readers, geared to immediacy in other fields, will no longer wait for a favourite author to appear in paperback form. This explains some of the large financial deals current, which might otherwise appear to be a form of lunacy. Thus, two books in a new Douglas Adams series, *Dirk Gently's Holistic Detective Agency*, have been signed up for over $3 million. The third in Jean Auel's prehistoric series, *The Mammoth Hunters* (1985), is achieving sales which even Clarke and Asimov might envy: 1.3 million *hard-cover* copies in print before official publication date.

It remains to be seen how this surprising return to strength of the hard-cover book will affect the paperback field. What is interesting is that a comparatively unknown author like Jean Auel could achieve such sales. She is unknown no longer.

Such figures provide a necessary backdrop to this chapter, for when people talk of these writers as science fiction's "greats", it is often a matter of pure sales, plus a little impure hype.

Writers like Asimov, Clarke, Heinlein and Herbert can afford to be self-indulgent in what they write. They can be confident that *whatever* they write will be published. And not merely published, but published in huge numbers, with hundreds of thousands of dollars spent on publicity to launch the work.

I Will Fear No Evil (1970) was the first novel from Robert Heinlein in four years and marked a new direction for him. Heinlein was never a very visual writer, but from *I Will Fear No Evil* onward, external, objective descriptions of things and people are trimmed to a minimum. We begin to sense that everything is subjective, if not solipsistic, in Heinlein's imaginary "multiverse". Everything happens only in the author's head. Internalized colloquies take the place of action and description, creating a feeling of stasis. The novel has become a bull session.

Robert A. Heinlein has become Jubal Harshaw. Or Johann Sebastian Bach Smith, as he named his ageing father-figure in *I Will Fear No Evil*. J. S. B. Smith is dying. But death can be conquered in Heinlein's multiverse. Smith switches his consciousness into the head and body of his secretary—a sexy young woman who shares mental and physical space with him. Their subsequent adventures as a sane schizophrenic form the story. Such a device excuses the use of the colloquy as the principal means of telling the story, but Heinlein found the device comfortable and kept it. In his next novel, *Time Enough for Love* (1973), the dialogues were no less rambling, nor one jot less internalized. Moreover, a further tendency showed itself *in extremis*: Heinlein's penchant for maxims.[2]

Time Enough for Love resurrected an earlier character, Lazarus Long, from Heinlein's 1941 yarn, *Methuselah's Children*, one of the most popular stories ever run in Campbell's *Astounding* (and only the second to score a perfect 1.000 in The Analytical Laboratory). Even old-time fans found Long's new adventure no match for the old.

Long, a product of a genetic experiment to extend life expectancy, gets a twenty-three century run of life in *Time Enough for Love*. Time enough, indeed. Changing names as often as a Ballard character, he trips through space and time, becomes cloned into female twins and eventually travels back to 1916 to make love to his own mother.[3]

It's a long story—Heinlein's longest, and three times the length of *Methuselah's Children*—and despite the various plot elements there's a lot of excess weight. Lazarus Long, like other Heinlein characters, experiences much but is little changed by what happens to him. He ends, as he began, a backwoods philosopher. Heinlein's chief protagonists rarely learn from their experiences. They are the know-alls who tell others.

Time Enough for Love has the saving grace of being readable on a basic, non-innovative level, yet it is also an unsatisfactory book. The intellectual stringency so attractive in the early Heinlein is sadly lacking. The voice, so familiar from better works, carries the tale.

The flaws of the book are those of every Heinlein novel since *I Will Fear No Evil* and several (including *Stranger in a Strange Land*) that prefigured this period. The tone, as Peter Nicholls has rightly diagnosed[4], is not so much juvenile as adolescent, as indeed is the characterization. From a philosophical or political viewpoint the clearest statement that emerges from the novel—and all subsequent Heinlein novels—is "There ain't no such thing as a free lunch", or "TANSTAAFL", as he has taken to abbreviating it.

Heinlein, as so many critics have commented, is a right-wing libertarian of the frontiersman breed. He is a champion of the freedom to *do* things: which is to say that he is champion of the strong and the competent. In his universe the weak and inefficient deserve to go to the wall.[5] This stance has made several critics label him, incorrectly, as a fascist. Like Campbell, Heinlein has a genuine hatred of bureaucracy, whatever its political colouring. His faults are sins of omission rather than commission. His characters are never evil and rarely callous. But they are unsympathetic.

If there are no free lunches, there is, at least, love, loyalty to one's cadre and longevity. In recent novels Heinlein has tried to combine all three: Gwen/Hazel in *The Cat Who Walks Through Walls* (1985) is lover, commandant and grandmother to our protagonist. So it goes. To each his or her own fantasy. This is Heinlein's, it seems.

In *The Number of the Beast* (1980) Heinlein returned to territory he had explored in *Glory Road* (1963), presenting us with a whole series of alternate worlds of varying degrees of reality. For the first time in Heinlein's fiction a veil was torn aside. The fiction had become a game—a Godgame, as John Fowles has termed it[6]—with Heinlein as God the Author. Talk had replaced the Burroughsian sword and sorcery adventure of *Glory Road*—an unending conversation inside the skull of Robert A. Heinlein.

The Number of the Beast, with its use of old Heinlein fictions and its eventual arrival at a science fiction convention, is self-indulgence of the worst kind. A game for the fans. Even so, many of the fans were concerned by what had been lost. The old Heinlein magic was absent from the novel.

Heinlein's next novel, *Friday* (1982), was a pleasant surprise. It deals with a future Earth not so different from our own, and works the seam so tirelessly mined by John Brunner in novels like *Stand on Zanzibar* (1968), *The Sheep Look Up* (1972) and *The Shockwave Rider* (1975). Earth's civilization is going to hell in a bucket: *"You should leave this planet; for you there is nothing here." Friday* is the nadir of Heinlein's feelings for Western civilization. We are beyond hope, he says in *Friday*. We have cocked it all up irredeemably, and not even special organizations can reverse what is happening.

Friday, heroine of the novel, is a competent woman, an "AP" or Artificial Person, who gets gang-raped at the beginning of the novel and spends most of the rest fighting her way out of one hole or another. Eventually she comes across the capable "Boss" figure who dominates most Heinlein novels. Things go uphill from there. She ends up pregnant and happy and off-planet, finally belonging to a family group. Which is the be-all-and-end-all of Heinlein's message to us in this novel. Choose your friends well, and find a safe haven during a storm. As such it's preferable to the solipsist escapism of *The Number of the Beast* and the selfish attitudes of *Time Enough for Love*.

Friday is also the most visual of Heinlein's modern novels and suffers least from his tendency to converse. It is a fast-paced, all-action adventure story in the old mould, a fact which won it favourable comparison from the critics with *The Moon is a Harsh Mistress* (1966). Even so, the world we see in *Friday* is a false world. It does not encompass enough. Once again it is a world of the competent and the also-rans. And the also-rans aren't given a moment's consideration.

This over-simplified viewpoint is a kind of cartoon. Heinlein's world is rough-cast and unfinished. And so the world is, but it is also far subtler and more complex than Heinlein seems able to imagine. He treats his cartoon as the reality and makes his deductions accordingly.

Like so many writers who emerged under John W. Campbell's editorial umbrella, Heinlein found his own distinctive voice early on and has seen no reason to change it in the forty-odd years since. Take the opening to the 1941 *Astounding* story, "Solution Unsatisfactory", as an instance:

> In 1903 the Wright brothers flew at Kitty Hawk.
> In December, 1938, in Berlin, Dr Hahn split the uranium atom.
> In April 1943, Dr Estelle Karst, working under the Federal Emergency Defense Authority, perfected the Karst-Obre technique for producing artificial radioactives.
> So American foreign policy had to change.
> Had to. *Had to.* It is very difficult to tuck a bugle call back into a bugle. Pandora's Box is a one-way proposition. You can turn pig into sausage, but not sausage into pig. Broken eggs stay broken. "All the King's horses and all the King's men can't put Humpty together again."
> I ought to know—I was one of the King's men.

The mixture of hard fact and folk-sayings is characteristic. We glimpse Lazarus Long in the narrator of "Solution Unsatisfactory", which is to say that we glimpse Robert A. Heinlein, the puppet master, there from the start. This use of old adages might be one of the reasons why Heinlein is so popular. Complex matters are presented with a stark simplicity. The reader, confronted by a simple aphorism, familiar from youth, tends to accept Heinlein's viewpoint unquestioningly.

Don't listen to all these experts with their jargons and explanations, Heinlein seems to be saying, it's as simple as this—and we are given a cartoon, an old folk-saying. And that is *the truth*. It is no more complex than that. Whoever says it is is messing with your head, playing a trick on you.

This is not to say that Heinlein is always wrong—very often he is capable of provoking profound agreement—simply that his method of looking at the world is highly suspect. Reading Heinlein's collection of stories and essays from forty years of writing, *Expanded Universe* (1980), one is faced with a hotchpotch of clear insights, muddy over-simplifications and simple addle-brained thinking.[7]

In Heinlein's two most recent novels, contemporary life is a million light-years away. Both are escapist fantasies, one with an apparent purpose, the other a piece of whimsy as empty as *The Number of the Beast*.

Job: A Comedy of Justice (1984) is Heinlein's venture into Philip K. Dick territory. In May 1992 Alexander Hergensheimer, in an act of faith, walks across a burning fire pit, and finds himself in a different universe where he is Alec Graham. This is the beginning of a whole series of switches between universes which are meant to test Hergensheimer/Graham in the same way that God tested Job in the biblical book of that name. It is an excellent idea, and Philip K. Dick attempted something similar in *Eye in the Sky* (1957). Unfortunately, Heinlein's use of the idea betrays an imaginative and creative failing.

In the place of real suffering is material inconvenience. If Alec Graham is being taught anything it is simply that there ain't no such thing as a free lunch. As he and his woman, Margrethe, make their way back to Kansas across several dozen universes—each materially different from the next—they are taught nothing of the real cruelty of the world. The people they meet are homely, honest folks. Any difficulty can be surmounted by the simple expediency of washing up to earn a few coins. Loss of identity seems less important than the fact that the currency keeps changing. And even when Alec comes to experience Heaven and Hell—the latter just as homely as Kansas ever was—there is the sense (indeed, as it proves, the reality) that he's never in fact left the Midwest.

One other element detracts from Heinlein's scheme. As the novel progresses the device of universe-switching grows tedious. We have seen it too often and felt it not at all. Margrethe says precisely what we have been thinking:

> "Alec, a miracle that takes place again and again and again, is no longer a miracle; it's just a nuisance. Too many, too much. I want to scream or break into tears." (Chapter 17)

If *Job* is a poor novel, *The Cat Who Walks Through Walls: A Comedy of Manners* (1985) is perhaps Heinlein's worst.[8] In *The Number of the Beast* Heinlein had toyed with the old idea that fictions were merely alternate realities. In *The Cat Who Walks Through Walls* he goes overboard for this idea[9], culminating in a scene in which all of Heinlein's old favourites—Lazarus Long, Jubal Harshaw, Star Gordon, John Carter of Barsoom and Commander Ted "Doc" Smith amongst them—form a council of heroes struggling to keep the time-lines pure. Central to their plan is the sentient computer of Heinlein's own *The Moon is a Harsh Mistress*, Mike Holmes IV, otherwise known as Adam Selene. For some never-properly-explained reason our protagonist Colonel Colin Campbell (or Richard Ames, or Senator Richard Johnson)[10] has to take part in the operation to remove Adam Selene's memory and bring it back to Supreme Headquarters. Only Selene, it seems, can handle the logistic problems of reality alteration.

Those qualities which shone out in the early Heinlein—his ability to extrapolate, his eye for social quirks—are now achieved so rarely that they jut out from the suet of self-indulgence. *The Cat Who Walks Through Walls* seems the tail-end of this process: a basking in the scenes of old glories. Yet the thing that gave those earlier works resonance is almost wholly lacking. *Job* and *Cat* are lifeless books.

Why should we care? Perhaps because Heinlein once represented a different way of looking at our world. Space cadets wore make-up in his stories—anticipating David Bowie by at least thirty years! In Heinlein's eyes the life of a man could be seen in four dimensions as a long pink worm, the flesh continuous in a fourth dimension. In his work the ballistics of space craft achieved a kind of simple poetry. In these respects and others, Heinlein was genuinely innovative. There is little of this in recent novels.

Since Heinlein is still seen as in some way the senior statesman of modern science fiction, we are entitled to look about us and ask, Why is a new Heinlein so appallingly more dud than the latest John Le Carré, the senior statesman of the spy novel? Is it perhaps less to do with Heinlein than with the corrupting commercial procedures established within SF, which a number of writers in the field have unquestioningly accepted? Why do our older writers not mature, mellow, attain wisdom in their later years, as befits elders of the tribe? Heinlein's is a cruel fate that threatens even our younger creative writers: terminal communication failure.

It is not difficult to market a novel of complexity and artistry. D. M. Thomas's *The White Hotel* (1981) is a case in point. Over a million copies were published in the States alone, with six different covers on the paperback edition. Few complained that the novel was too literary, or that it was too experimental: and this of a novel that begins with forty pages of poetry—poetry which first saw light of day in *New Worlds* at that!

It is, undoubtedly, safer to take a chance on a tried and tested product than a new commodity. Easier to serve up more of the same than trust to your own judgement and tempt the consumer with a new brand.

In SF there is no bigger brand name than that of Isaac Asimov.

Asimov's name on a cover—dwarfing whatever else is printed there—is a talisman, encouraging publisher, bookseller and reader alike to buy, buy, buy!

His books pile up in a veritable mountain chain, three hundred-plus of them to date. Indeed, one of the more playful SF novels of recent years has good-humouredly lampooned this aspect of the "Good Doctor" and his work:

> "Have you ever read any of the early proleptic poems by Asimov? Pre-diaspora, about two thousand years ago?"
>
> "Child, I make it a firm rule never to vid the classics. The only Asimov I've ever heard of is the fellow who directed the compilation of the rather arrogantly titled *Asimov's Encyclopedia Galactica.*"
>
> "That's the chap. I can't see why you think it's arrogant, he wrote the bloody thing."
>
> The gene-sculptor jerked violently, and managed to get his hand up her skirt. "What, all five thousand volumes?"
>
> "Easy with those fingernails. Yes, he's a demon for work, poor old bugger. There's nothing much else for him to do, he was eighty-nine when they perfected the immortality process. If you're interested, he has a retrospective in the DATABANK called *Opus 6000.*"[11]

There is some truth in this extravagant portrait. For most of the sixties and seventies Asimov was known as a prolific science popularizer, and—in SF circles—for his regular science column in *F&SF*.

Asimov had been a writer of the forties and fifties, best remembered for his *Foundation* trilogy.[12] Even he felt that his days as an active SF writer were well in the past.[13] Little SF appeared from Asimov in the sixties. Then, in 1971, he broke a fifteen year "silence" with a new SF novel.

The Gods Themselves is a clever, enjoyable work and demonstrates Asimov's strengths. The inter-faculty rivalry of his scientists is described with an acerbity born of experience. His aliens, whilst somewhat homely, are symbolically effective, and the central idea—that of the Electron Pump between parallel but dissimilar universes—is ingenious and satisfying. It is a good, workmanlike novel, and its clear scientific method—a slow revelation of acquired facts—suits its subject matter, but the fact that it won both Hugo and Nebula Awards for its year (against contenders like Silverberg's *Dying Inside*) was more a reflection of Asimov's standing in the hearts of SF readers and writers alike, than of the novel's quality.

It was a further ten years before Asimov produced another SF novel. This time he returned to work of some forty years before. *Foundation's Edge* (1982) was a continuation of his popular trilogy. It was greeted enthusiastically by the fans and won that year's Hugo. In all but a strictly marketing sense it was a failure.

> "The fact is that for the most part I have been ceaselessly mining the motherlodes I had uncovered by the time I was 22 years old."[14]

This honest admission referred specifically to the three supposedly innovative SF ideas he developed in his earliest years as a writer, but is equally true of his basic style. Determined not to adapt or change the original volumes of the trilogy, Asimov wrote subsequent additions to suit.

Foundation's Edge is a stale reiteration of old themes. In *Second Foundation*, the Second Foundation of psychologists was established on Trantor, at the heart of the old Galactic Empire. Even so, the search for it, an obsession of two of the earlier novels—is resurrected here, together with the search for lost Earth.

At the novel's climax, Gaia, a planetary community of harmonious beings who are also, it seems, robots, have manipulated the characters into having to make a choice between three possible ways of running the Galaxy. The Gaians themselves cannot decide because, as robots, "We do not know whether action or inaction will cost the Galaxy less. . . ." This is the dilemma Asimov first presented to us back in 1942 in "Runaround". There, Speedy the robot circled a selenium pool endlessly, caught between conflicting but balanced impulses (robotic laws two and three). Here the pool proves a bit bigger but the problem is presented as being every bit as simple.

Foundation's Edge, with its passing reference to the three laws of robotics and *The End of Eternity*, begins to weave together elements of Asimov's work. *The Robots of Dawn* (1983) takes up this interweaving in earnest. In an article in June 1985's *Locus*, Asimov spelled out what he was doing: "I now have, then, a single series of novels, combining the robot novels, the Empire novels, and the Foundation novels." Fifteen books were linked in this sequence and Asimov busied himself making linkages, writing interim novels and generally tidying up.

What can one say about this painful obsession? The convolutions of logic necessary to make dissimilar elements fit together—the non-robotic universe of Foundation with the robot-dominated worlds of *The Caves of Steel*—are more ingenious than satisfactory, and more absurd than ingenious.[15]

Asimov has always been most comfortable utilizing the detective format of his Elijah Baley novels. *The Robots of Dawn* re-introduced Elijah Baley for a third adventure, continuing the sequence that began with *The Caves of Steel* (1954) and continued with *The Naked Sun* (1957). However, what is done tautly and economically in the earlier novels is overblown in *The Robots of Dawn*. As with most of Asimov's recent work, it is too long. Its pace suffers badly. A degree of self-indulgence has set in—not, by any means, to the extent of recent Heinlein, but sufficient to tire the reader.

This said, *The Robots of Dawn* is a much better novel than *Foundation's Edge*. With severe editing it might even have been a good novel, provided you could swallow the notion of telepathic robots!

The Robots of Dawn is once more a novel-length embellishment of an earlier robot story, this time of "Liar!" (1941), about a telepathic robot. Asimov adds a few new elements to update the mix—a society that accepts incest and sex with robots.[16] The murder of a humanoid robot is the mystery Baley must solve. And solve it he does, though with far less ingenuity than in the fifties' novels.

As in *Foundation's Edge*, there are signs that Asimov is rethinking his earlier ideas and trying to soften them in the face of criticism. The rigid Three Laws of Robotics are an instance:

"The words of the law are merely an approximate description of the constant variants in positronic force along the robotic brain paths. . . ."

At the same time Asimov is busy trying to find ways of linking in his robot and Foundation novels. To this end we find Asimov's Dr Hans Fastolfe musing about something that, in twenty thousand years or so of fictional time, will become an actuality—

> "Perhaps, though, there may come a day when someone will work out the Laws of Humanics and then be able to predict the broad strokes of the future, and *know* what might be in store for humanity, instead of merely guessing as I do, and *know* what to do to make things better, instead of merely speculating. I dream sometimes of founding a mathematical science which I think of as 'psychohistory', but I know I can't and I fear no one ever will."

We begin to glimpse Asimov's purpose—the reason for the creation of this private universe of inter-related miracles. A Law of Humanics. Telepathic Robots who act to help Mankind. A future world of Gaia with telepathic robots evolving at the same time as psychohistory . . . What does it add up to? Perhaps Giskard, the telepathic robot, gives us our answer at the novel's end when he says this to Baley:

> ". . . but, in the end, human beings will be better off for having worked on their own. And perhaps someday—some long-away day in the future— robots can intervene once more. Who can tell?"

The scheme grows transparent, its machinations long-winded. Tidiness has replaced spontaneity.

The Robots of Dawn fades out unsatisfactorily, with a sense of spoiled expectations. One of Asimov's devices is to present us with enigmas and then delay our satisfaction. Most of the mysteries prove to be either red herrings or matters of little significance. We are only delayed, never surprised.

Asimov's most recent offering is *Robots and Empire* (1985). Set 164 years after Baley's death, it otherwise contains much the same cast as *The Robots of Dawn*. At the end of *Robots and Empire* evil academicians have set a slow-burning radioactive fuse under Earth's crust, R. Daneel Olivaw has learned the tricks of telepathy, and a new robotic law—the Zeroth Law[17]—has been deduced: all necessary steps on the way to Empire and Foundation.

But what, if anything, does *Robots and Empire* add to the speculative wealth of science fiction?

The main purpose of *Robots and Empire* is to create a situation whereby the all-human galaxy of the *Foundation* novels might come about—a Galaxy *without* robots. To this end Asimov has created the circumstances where a first wave of colonization *with* robots has been superseded by a second, larger wave of colonization from earth, without robots. The message to be derived from this is a simple one. Mankind must expand or stagnate. Only through unassisted expansion can Man remain a viable, growing life-form.

In *Robots and Empire* Asimov's message is presented without real force or passion. It is as if Asimov himself senses how stale the idea is. It is, in the end, only a device to link two very different kinds of novel.

But this is the real trouble with putting together a private universe from disparate elements. No matter how ingenious you might be, unless you are willing to rethink and restructure, your work can only be a patchwork of half-convincing explanations. Asimov's Empire never really comes alive for us: it is only a diagram on a blackboard, not a living, developing entity. The spark of lightning never reaches the monster's heart to start it beating.

One might wonder whether Asimov considers this fifteen-novel future history as an alternative *Last and First Men*, sketching out a possible evolutionary course for Mankind. If so, then it is legitimate to ask where the philosophy behind such a venture lies. Why, when the conception is so vast, is the actuality of Asimov's Empire so small?

Part of the reason for this lies in Asimov's inability to provide a proper visual framework for his galaxy. There are so few sensual or visual references, so little evocation of what it would be like to live at such a time and in such a manner. Asimov's is a "No feel" galaxy.

Part lies in the fact that he has made no attempt to envisage what diversity and complexity such an empire might produce. Asimov's galaxy of 22,000 years hence is little different from the America of 1941.[18]

Of course, both Heinlein and Asimov are remarkable for the way in which they continue to produce after such long careers. It is unfortunate that the gap between productivity and creativity remains so wide. Few other writers can lay claim to such spans—though the names of Williamson, Ballard, Moorcock, Dickson, Aldiss, Silverberg and Harrison come readily to mind as aspiring young dinosaurs. Asimov has also been adroit in transferring his name to a magazine; *Isaac Asimov's Science Fiction Magazine* is now a well-established landmark.

Another writer inhabiting a way-back-when future is L. Ron Hubbard. Hubbard was a prolific producer of pulp fiction throughout the thirties and forties, until he published *Dianetics: The Modern Science of Mental Health*. Dianetics was launched in the May 1950 issue of *Astounding* with the wholehearted approval of John W. Campbell. Within a year Campbell had cooled in his enthusiasm and backed off. Dianetics became Scientology, a religion, with Hubbard its cult guru. Hubbard's writing energies were channelled into propagandist work. But in the eighties Hubbard returned to the SF genre, using the resources he had accumulated through Scientology to launch a huge space adventure, *Battlefield Earth* (1982). The media blitz began at the 1982 World Science Fiction Convention, Chicon IV, in September of that year. A giant billboard greeted fans, together with free copies of *Battlefield Earth*. Twelve-foot blow-up models of the book's alien villain, a "Psychlo", made guest appearances at many conventions worldwide. The piles of promotional material mounted, along with the canapés and booze. Hubbard's re-entry into the SF field was aided by all the expertise of modern marketing.

So *Battlefield Earth* achieved lift-off. The novel was boosted into the best-seller lists and stayed there long enough to sell more than 1.5 million copies.

But what of the novel itself? Was *Battlefield Earth*, all half a million words and 819 pages of it, any good?

Back in *Astounding* in 1940 Hubbard had presented a novel called *Final Blackout*, about a future war that devastates Europe. It was heavily militaristic. Although *Battlefield Earth: A Saga of the Year 3000* is not a direct sequel, it takes up where *Final Blackout* left off: heroic fantasy with guns and spaceships replacing swords and horses.

The Psychlos, thousand pound alien monsters with "cruelty" fuses in their solid bone skulls and a penchant for shooting the legs off horses one at a time, have taken over Earth. The Psychlos are materialists, miners and manipulators, but also slaves to an obscene and artificial system. Let the last not worry us— Hubbard spares little sympathy for the Psychlos: they are the baddies, there to be shot and killed in the cause of freedom.

Fighting for humankind is Jonnie Goodboy Tyler, a young, well-muscled hero, supported by a bunch of mad Scots and Russians, brave fighters and dreadful caricatures to the last man. In the course of the story, Jonnie gets the girl (who, naturally, gets left at home while the real excitement is going on) frees the Earth, wreaks vengeance on the Psychlos' home planet, and eventually gets to own the Galaxy.

Just a simple boy-makes-good story. A bit like *Rambo*.

1985 saw the publication of *The Invaders Plan*, the first volume of a "dekalogy"—Hubbardese for a "decalogy", a ten-volume work—by Hubbard. At 559 pages it was less portly than *Battlefield Earth*, but as part of a larger work, corporately titled *Mission: Earth*, a 1.3 million word opus, it is only a matter of perspective. Its lurid red and mauve cover depicts a bronzed hand, its wristband studded with spikes, clutching the Earth. A subtle hint of the novel's contents.

LaFayette Ron Hubbard died on 24th January 1986, aged 74. A full-page advertisement in daily newspapers—placed by the Church of Scientology— provided an extravagant eulogy. Rumours of his death had circulated before, particularly in early 1983. This time, it seemed, it was for certain.

What, then, of the dekalogy? It seems that *Mission: Earth* will be with us for some years to come. Hubbard had written the whole shebang before his death, with a volume due every few months. Like Hari Seldon, Hubbard's dead but he won't lie down.

The Invaders Plan reached the American best-seller lists with ease. We might expect the rest of the volumes to do the same. The tenacity of poor SF is renowned. It has unfortunately formed the hallmark of the genre.

Hubbard was an influential and charismatic figure. In a group dominated by Campbell, he managed to turn the tables and get Campbell under his influence. Another writer who succumbed to Hubbard's dianetic snake-charm was A. E.

van Vogt.[19] Van Vogt got enrolled into the Californian chapter of Scientology; like Campbell his enthusiasm eventually palled and he withdrew.

Obsessed with theories of human behaviour, van Vogt was a natural candidate for Hubbard's pseudo-religion. General Semantics had attracted van Vogt in a similar way, and had spawned the two novels of the forties about Null-A. In 1984 van Vogt published a third volume. It was a disastrous venture.

Null-A Three is nonsense. Gilbert Gosseyn, hero of the earlier volumes, returns here with his double-brain capacity, a superman struggling against aliens who want to conquer the universe. Unfortunately, nobody is up to the task of visualizing what this would mean. Least of all van Vogt.

Van Vogt always relied on the almost surreal shock of non-sequiturs for his effects, and sometimes this worked, even though there was no logical explanation for anything. Here there is not even that pleasant sense we once had from van Vogt's work that it might be failings in *our* comprehension that accounted for our puzzlement. A brief quote from the novel might demonstrate its essential incoherence:

> There they were, then: all of them in that dimly lit duplicate of an Earth restaurant. And his thoughts went back to the fact that they had made an effort to get Earth food. Somehow, the deeds of those millions of chickens back there . . . out there . . . had been observed: still surviving, although most of their eggs had been stolen from them day after day from earliest times. (Chapter 24)

If *Null-A Three* were a movie one would say that it suffered from serious continuity problems. And for a novel supposedly concerned with precise usage of language—with General Semantics—it displays an astonishing ineptness of expression. In *Null-A Three* the secret schlock ingredient has swamped all else in van Vogt's work, like some rampant and contagious virus.

Van Vogt produced a number of novels in the seventies, few of which made any real sense. An instance is *The Anarchistic Colossus* (1977), better written than *Null-A Three*, and at times possessing that hectic sense of inanity which so obviously attracted Dick to van Vogt's work, but ultimately just as disorganized as *Null-A Three*.

It turns out to be a eulogy to the human brain—best in all the galaxy. John W. Campbell would have approved.

Before turning from these four writers, some comment must be made on how the science fiction field views its elder statesmen. These are not merely writers operating in a void, producing discrete literary parcels for the critics to dissect; they are persuasive voices, familiar from long years of association. In the cases of Heinlein and Asimov particularly they are more than SF writers to a great proportion of their readership; they are friends and mentors.

Asimov's voice may seem over-familiar, but one cannot fail to be impressed by the efforts he has made to educate the American people. His polymath activities, which have spawned over 300 volumes, are not merely the outward sign of an obsession with the work ethic; they are genuinely useful and have helped create a better-informed electorate.

In a similar way, Heinlein is more than the idiosyncratic author of the awful *Job* and *Cat*, he is the voice of a certain kind of American pragmatism which has shaped his nation. Of Hubbard little need be said. He leaves us a religion.

In contrast with these four writers, Frank Herbert, Arthur C. Clarke and Frederik Pohl epitomize a more creative aspect of SF. In their work we see growth, change, a continued interest in new things. They have defied the temptation to take it easy, ossify, and let the rewards of fame cushion them from valid criticism.

Frank Herbert died on 11th February 1986 after long treatment for cancer. He was 65. He leaves behind him an impressive list of novels, most of them written since 1965, including the series for which Herbert has received most attention and praise: the six novels of the *Dune* sequence.

The first two novels are dealt with in Chapter XIII. They are, it must be said, the best of the series. Complexity of theme in the later novels does not compensate for an absence of mythic depth. Nonetheless, the later volumes, with one exception, are robust works of science fiction.

Children of Dune was published in 1976, seven years after *Dune Messiah*. Within the time scheme of *Dune* it is nine years on from the events of *Dune Messiah*. The messianic Paul Atreides is believed dead, Paul's sister Alia is Regent to the Empire, and Paul's twin children, Ghanima and Leto, are the centre of plot and counter-plot.

All the complex elements of the first two volumes feed into the power struggle that lies at the heart of *Children of Dune*. This ought to satisfy, and from time to time it does. But there is a genuine absence of vitality at the heart of the novel. Explanations are vaguer than before. Motivations are more diffuse, less immediately comprehensible. Most unfortunate of all, the emasculation of the planet Arrakis—its conversion into an edenic place of greenery and plentiful water—serves to rob the novel of an element vital to our enjoyment. The novel lacks a steady focus.

Plotting has replaced vision in *Children of Dune*. Its canvas is every bit as broad as that of *Dune*—broader, in fact, than *Dune Messiah*'s—but it is not the breadth of epic. *Children of Dune* is a way-station to *God Emperor of Dune* (1981), almost a kind of prologue.

In 1976, *Children of Dune* was presented by Herbert as the culmination of the Dune trilogy. Many felt it had ended on a dying fall.

The three novels which appeared in the eighties make us re-evaluate Frank Herbert's scheme. *God Emperor of Dune* begins this process, widening our perspectives, broadening our sense of time, and providing us with contrasting elements. It paints the portrait of Leto II, one of the twins of the previous volume. 3500 years have passed and Arrakis/Dune has become a lush, water-rich planet. The native Fremen are subsequently soft, almost foppish caricatures of what they once were. And there has been peace in the human galaxy for more than three millennia.

Leto himself has become a god, a seven metre long creature, part-sandworm, part-human. The various factions in the galaxy are planning to kill Leto, wishing to end his "tyranny"; yet Leto himself anticipates each move. He has looked into the future and seen the end of the Golden Path—Mankind's evolutionary development. To prevent this he has begun his own breeding programme, and in the girl Siona he has accomplished what he set out to do: he has created a human whose actions he cannot see within the field of his prescient vision.

God Emperor of Dune is perhaps the least complex of the *Dune* novels in its plotting, yet all the more satisfying for that. Unlike the previous novel it has a strong focus in Leto. His machinations—all for the benefit of the race, if not for individuals—provide a counterpoint to those of Paul in the first two novels. The problems Herbert set himself concerning determinism and the future of Man are partly answered in *God Emperor*. Leto is a predator with a conscience. A racial conscience. His actions in the novel—ostensibly tyrannical—are all designed to create a universe in which surprise and chance might again shape Mankind's destiny. Leto's final overthrow is thus both tragedy and triumph.

God Emperor of Dune added further elements into the already complex mix. The machine-building Ixians have created "No Spaces" where prescience cannot penetrate—discreet little pocket universes. In the next volume Herbert added yet another element, the Honoured Matres, whose key to power is their ability to control men through sexual ecstasy.

Set millennia on from the fourth volume, *Heretics of Dune* is the most complex novel in the sequence and the most difficult to summarize. First, a taste of the novel:

> Her remarkable facial resemblance to Darwi Odrade was no accident, Teg told himself. Back there at the keep, the two women side by side, he had marked the differences dictated by their differing ages. Lucilla's youth showed itself in more subcutaneous fat, a rounding of the facial flesh. But the voices! Timbre, accent, tricks of atonal inflection, the common stamp of Bene Gesserit speech mannerisms. They would be almost impossible to tell apart in the dark.
>
> Knowing the Bene Gesserit as he did, Teg knew this was no accident. Given the Sisterhood's propensity for doubling and redoubling its genetic lines to protect the investment, there had to be a common ancestral source.
>
> *Atreides, all of us,* he thought.
>
> Taraza had not revealed her design for the ghola, but just being within that design gave Teg access to the growing shape of it. No complete pattern, but he could already sense a wholeness there.
>
> Generation after generation, the Sisterhood dealing with the Tleilaxu, buying Idaho gholas, training them here on Gammu, only to have them assassinated. All of that time waiting for the right moment. It was like a

terrible game which had come into frenetic prominence because a girl capable of commanding the worms had appeared on Rakis.

Gammu itself had to be part of the design. Caladian marks all over the place. Danian subtleties piled atop the more brutal ancient ways. Something other than population had come out of the Danian sanctuary where the tyrant's mother, the Lady Jessica, had lived out her days.

Teg had seen the overt and covert marks when he made his first reconnaissance tour of Gammu.

Wealth!

This passage typifies the mode of Herbert's writing in the later *Dune* novels. We are conscious of a far greater authorial control. At the same time, something of the tantalising quality of good storytelling—that powerful attraction of not knowing how things will turn out—is missing. The later novels are less spontaneous, if far more clever. Even so, there is enough here to provide good entertainment. Life is a game of intrigue, played by the very powerful. They desire absolute control, without compromise. The game involves centuries of patience and incredibly complex, slowly-evolved schemes. We have a sense of barely revealed subtleties: nuances of face, body, voice tone and inflection which can be read only by those trained in their intricate language. Most important of all we are given a vast perspective. Human lives are dwarfed by the span of time. Humans become mere gene carriers, messengers of some complex, only partly-glimpsed master plan.

Taking a segment of the novel out of context in this manner reveals another facet of Herbert's writing: its density of internal reference. The later volumes in the sequence require not merely intelligent attention, but some knowledge of the previous volumes. Their webs of subtlety depend greatly on our catching the nuances. Without this knowledge the story functions but lacks depth.

This is perhaps true of most series novels in SF. The first novel derives much of its power from our delight in and discovery of a new environment. The pleasure of future volumes is different in kind. Familiarity and complexity replace the higher satisfaction of revelation. So it is with *Dune*. More so, indeed, for the first volume is one of the finest of its kind in the genre.

Heretics of Dune benefits from the care with which Herbert has constructed his various factions, settings and individual characters. It gives us greater satisfaction than most sequels because it attempts to further an argument while presenting us with an adventure in a familiar setting. In this it differs radically from Asimov's future history which lacks such philosophical depths. However, because Herbert attempts to portray what is a frighteningly complex mode of human behaviour—subtleties most writers in the genre would not contemplate—he sometimes fails to meet his aim and proves either slack or inconsistent. These inconsistencies undoubtedly weaken the later novels, yet Herbert does at least make the attempt most of the time.

Heretics of Dune ends with Arrakis, Dune planet, destroyed, the Honoured Matres—an evil parody of the Bene Gesserit sisterhood—triumphant. The power base shifts again, as it does in every novel in the sequence: a truth we recognize from our own world. *Chapter House Dune* (1985) takes up the reins a few years on. The Bene Gesserit are in retreat, their planets are being destroyed one by one, and their home planet, Chapter House, is being sought by the Honoured Matres. A confrontation seems imminent. Yet there are always other factors scheming, the Bene Tleilax, revealed as Sufi Masters in *Heretics*, amongst them.

Whether *Chapter House Dune* was meant to be the final volume of the *Dune* saga or not is a moot point in view of Herbert's death. We must judge it as such. We do, in fact, have a sense of the wheel coming full circle. Arrakis may have been destroyed, but the Bene Gesserit are turning their own homeworld into a desert planet and breeding worms. Scheme and counter-scheme wind about each other like coiling snakes.

What *Chapter House Dune* brings home most clearly is just how much the focus of Herbert's saga has turned from the chronicling of an individual's life— Paul Atreides'—to the telling of the history of a sect—the Bene Gesserit. The last three novels seek substitutes for Paul—in Leto, in Duncan, in Teg—but in none of these cases have we the sense, as we had with the young Dune Messiah, that these are what the novels are about. These later characters are instruments of fate, not instrumental. Even the all-powerful Leto. It is the fate of the Bene Gesserit which concerns Herbert in the later novels. Individuals can die—after all, new ones can always be grown in the axolotl tanks—but the sect must live on.

In the first two novels we had a very strong sense of the Bene Gesserit sisterhood as a potentially evil force. Were their actions for the good of Man, or were they selfish and misguided? There was a tantalizing ambiguity about it. Within the ruthless matrix of Herbert's future their actions were understandable yet also morally questionable. By the time of *Heretics* such ambiguity is no longer evident. The contrast of the Honoured Matres—so palpably evil in their scheme to rule without responsibility—makes the Bene Gesserit seem gloriously benevolent.

What, in its entirety, does the *Dune* saga represent? Nearly 2300 pages—more than a million words. A saga covering some six thousand or so years. A cast of hundreds. *Dune* is, undoubtedly, an epic. In its own way it achieves what earlier models failed at. It is not merely the present retold as the future. It is much more than power fantasy. Unlike E. E. "Doc" Smith's *Lensman* universe, or Asimov's *Foundation* universe, it has depth as well as breadth. Unlike those earlier models it grasped the concept that the future would have different modes of behaviour, different motivations to our own. For all its seemingly mediaeval setting, *Dune* is a thoroughly futuristic novel. It transcends its *Analog* origins.

The *Dune* sequence is not, in its totality, easy reading. Like the best of anything, it requires and rewards attention. It is not wholly successful, and the later volumes are, perhaps, over-cerebral, yet in its ambitious design the sequence does not fall far short of its target. Its existence has influenced younger writers to attempt more complex schemes than they might otherwise have ventured upon. Bruce Sterling and Greg Bear are writers who can be seen to have benefited from Herbert's trail-blazing efforts, Many others would admit that Herbert's influence has added rigour to their work.

With the arrival of David Lynch's movie version of *Dune*[20], the saga became not so much an epic as a marketing phenomenon. 1984 saw the *Dune* books riding high on the best-seller lists. Guides, film books and an Encyclopedia all surfaced. Whatever might be thought of the movie, it did have the effect of sending a lot of readers back to the original.

What happened to Herbert in 1984 had happened to Arthur C. Clarke back in 1968, when the Clarke-Kubrick collaboration, *2001: A Space Odyssey*, reached the wide screen. The movie revolutionized SF film, and nine years on spawned those other super-technological marvels, *Star Wars* and *Close Encounters*. Clarke returned with a sequel in 1982, *2010: Odyssey Two*. It, too, was made into a film[21], though not by Stanley Kubrick.

In 1971 *Playboy* carried a long story by Clarke, "A Meeting with Medusa". Howard Falcon, an airstrip captain reconstructed after a horrific accident, becomes the first man to pilot a spacecraft in the atmosphere of Jupiter:

> About sixty miles ahead, a disturbance was taking place in the cloud layer. The little red ovals were being jostled around, and were beginning to form a spiral—the familiar cyclonic pattern so common in the meteorology of Earth. The vortex was emerging with astonishing speed; if that was a storm ahead, Falcon told himself, he was in big trouble.
>
> And then his concern turned to wonder—and to fear. What was developing in his line of flight was not a storm at all. Something enormous—something scores of miles across—was rising through the clouds.
>
> The reassuring thought that it, too, might be a cloud—a thunderhead boiling up from the lower levels of the atmosphere—lasted only a few seconds. No; this was *solid*. It shouldered its way through the pink and salmon overcast like an iceberg rising from the deeps. . . .
>
> . . . "What is it?" called Mission Control, "What is it?"
>
> He ignored the frantic pleas from space and concentrated all his mind upon the image in the telescope field. He had to be sure; if he made a mistake, he would be the laughing stock of the solar system.
>
> Then he relaxed, glanced at the clock, and switched off the nagging voice from Jupiter V.
>
> "Hello Mission Control," he said, very formally. "This is Howard Falcon aboard the *Kon Tiki*. Ephemeris Time nineteen hours twenty-one minutes fifteen seconds. Latitude zero degrees five minutes north. Longitude one hundred and five degrees forty-two minutes, System One.
>
> "Tell Dr Brenner that there is life on Jupiter. And it's big. . . ." (Part 4)

"A Meeting with Medusa" is one of the finest pieces of imaginative documentary. Like Falcon, we too feel that we are "not merely on a strange planet, but in some magical realm between myth and reality". The atmosphere of Jupiter comes vividly alive in the pages of Clarke's story. For once characterization is totally irrelevant. The story evokes the sheer wonder of scientific discovery: the mystical power of the real. "A Meeting with Medusa" is a chronicle of wonders: one natural phenomenon after another paraded before us, each marvellous, astonishing. The enormous life forms—Medusae—most marvellous of all.

Another giant, equally astonishing, equally mysterious, was the hero of Clarke's next novel—his first since *2001*—*Rendezvous with Rama* (1973). Rama is a vast alien spacecraft that enters our solar system and uses our sun's gravity field to change course and accelerate away into the depths of space. There are no aliens, scarcely any recognizable humans, yet somehow the proceedings prove quite memorable and at times magical. Once again, it is Clarke's ability to evoke in us a true sense of wonder at unfolding marvels which enlivens the work. Summarized coldly, all that happens is that humans board the ship, explore it and then leave it as it goes its own way, indifferent to Man and to human curiosity. The reading experience is a different matter.

Part of the delight of *Rama* has to do with an intellectual satisfaction we feel at how marvellously the details of this future technology are worked out. More has to do with Clarke's ability to present the whole, vast package as a giant Christmas present, to be unwrapped stage by stage, marvel by marvel. We glimpse our own future in this technological artifact—a future as magical as it is mysterious.

Towards the end of "A Meeting with Medusa" our attention is brought to bear on a sign which reads ASTONISH ME. This seems to be Clarke's credo. At his finest he lives up to it, and has done so for over forty years. His imagination works best when dealing with the abstractly scientific or philosophical. Like certain painters he feels uncomfortable drawing the human form. His brand of mystical realism works best when the conceptual heart of his fiction is of the scale of a Medusa or a Rama.

Clarke's writing has progressed considerably since novels like *A Fall of Moondust* (1961). There the characters were embarrassingly wooden. Engineers dominated the proceedings, and the only problems were engineering problems. By the time of *Imperial Earth* (1975) Clarke had made an effort to rectify this obvious weakness. The characters were still somewhat awkward; in their composition they were still more fibre than flesh. But they had problems. They were recognizably human, not some brand of omnicompetent robot.

Fountains of Paradise (1979) was a far more successful novel than its predecessor. Clarke presented it as his final and finest novel. It was neither, but it was, in its way, rather good. The conceptual giant this time was a Space Elevator, linking Earth and a geostationary space station. *Fountains of Paradise* was a hymn to Man's technological future. At the same time it was a critique of religious bigotry. Bigness—à la *Rama*—was fused with Clarke's belief in the ultimate transcendence of Man; a theme recurrent in his work from *Childhood's End* onward.[22]

Clarke's retirement from SF was short-lived. In 1982 he was back with his sequel to *2001*. It was a far cry from Clarke's work of the forties, fifties and sixties, and if some critics still complained about style and characterisation, they were neglecting to mention the distance Clarke had travelled in both respects. *2010: Odyssey Two* is not high literature, but it is a genuine novel, not simply a vehicle for ideas. Few have recognized this maturation of Clarke's work. In *2001* Dr Heywood Floyd was a mere cypher in a conceptual game. In *2010* he becomes credible.

2010 replaces spectacle with mystery and, eventually, with mysticism. A Russian spacecraft goes out to rendezvous with the *Discovery* orbiting Jupiter, its computer, HAL, being shut down. In a tense, well-told story, Clarke weaves together several elements—the mystery of Jupiter and its moons; the problem of growing East–West hostility on Earth; the technical problems of getting the Russian craft, *Leonov*, back to Earth; the return of the starchild, Dave Bowman; the reactivation of HAL—and then provides us with a startling finale as Jupiter turns into a second sun.

If not as stirring as *Childhood's End*, *2010* is nonetheless filled with the same desire to awaken us to our idiocies as well as to our potentiality as a race. Clarke is an optimist with a giant Oh!

Clarke is, moreover, actively engaged in bringing about that better world of which he writes. From his base in Colombo, Sri Lanka, he has become directly (and financially) involved in a scheme to transfer modern high-technology to the developing countries of the Third World.

The Arthur Clarke Centre for Modern Technologies, sited at the University of Moratuwa, outside Colombo, embraces numerous high-tech disciplines, including computers and alternate energy sources, with plans to expand into the areas of robotics and space technologies. The main emphasis, however, is on developing a cheap communications system tailored to the agricultural needs of the Third World.

Such a project harnesses expensive space technologies in a way which answers those critics who have argued that it is immoral to waste funds on the romantic gesture of spaceflight when problems of poverty, illness and hunger remain in the world. That advanced technology would eventually benefit all of Mankind has always been Clarke's belief—perhaps naïve, but visionaries often function more effectively for a touch of naïvety about them. One has to admire this benevolent, aspiring side of Clarke; it is the other side of the coin to L. Ron Hubbard.

Less optimistic, but every bit as enamoured with science and the accumulation of knowledge is the last of our seven authors, Frederik Pohl. At the time that Campbell was publishing the earliest stories of Heinlein, Asimov, van Vogt and Hubbard, Pohl was editing his own variant magazine, *Astonishing Stories*, and was even, for a brief while, agent to the young Asimov. When the New Wave came along, Pohl, like Asimov, was at first vociferously against it. As time went by Pohl was shrewd enough to recognize its virtues and learn from them. In this respect Frederik Pohl is a rare and valued phenomenon.

Before the seventies, most of Pohl's longer work had been written in collaboration. His four solo novels were interesting but hardly set the Thames or the Hudson on fire. What was impressive was that Pohl somehow found time between editing (*Galaxy, If, Worlds of Tomorrow* and *International SF*) and agenting, to write anything. Then, in the early seventies, he disappeared briefly into those shadows which threaten even the most resilient of authors. A few stories still appeared—"In The Problem Pit" in a special Pohl issue of *F&SF* (1973), for instance.

When Pohl returned to novel writing with *Man Plus* (1976), a difference was immediately apparent. New strength and authority were there. Clarke had finished "A Meeting with Medusa" with a glimpse of the mechanically-adapted Howard Falcon. Pohl, in his novel, is concerned with the question of what it might be like to become a cyborg—part machine, part man. *Man Plus* can be read as a novel about the trauma of becoming.

In response to acute population pressures and the hideous expense of adapting the planets to Man, a decision is made to adapt Man to the planets; specifically, to Mars. Roger Torraway is the young astronaut chosen as pioneer for this project. It is his pain, his trauma we share. As he is stripped of lungs, heart, bowels—all those essentially human organs—we see how he suffers and changes. There is nothing sensational about *Man Plus*, as there is, for example, about *The Six-Million Dollar Man*, that TV over-simplification of this same theme. Pohl was not concerned so much with what such a being could *do*, but with how such a changed being would *feel*. In that lies the distinction between this and Pohl's earlier work: a new perception has dawned.

Man Plus deservedly won Pohl the Nebula award for best novel of 1976. His next novel, *Gateway* (1977), won both Hugo and Nebula.

Like *Rendezvous with Rama*, *Gateway* is concerned with the discovery of a vast, mysterious alien artifact. Any similarity between the two novels ends there. The giant artifact in *Gateway* is a spaceport, Gateway, terminus for a galaxy-spanning transportation system, abandoned by the alien Heechee. This spaceport, an asteroid circling the sun inside the orbit of Venus, comes complete with a thousand small, faster-than-light spacecraft, each with pre-set but unknown destinations. The duration of the voyages is equally unknown.

A kind of interstellar Russian roulette begins. Volunteers must be gamblers—both avaricious and expendable. The death-rate is high. But the possible rewards are phenomenal; an escape-route from over-crowded Earth. Some volunteers return with alien artifacts worth a small fortune. To the lucky go the spoils of the stars. To the unlucky the chance to starve or, maybe, plummet into a black hole. It's a game of hazard not so very far removed from the facts of history.

The focus of the novel is the character Bob Broadhead (full name Robinette), an unsympathetic protagonist. Half of the book is taken up with his psycho-analytic sessions with a robot analyst named Sigfrid. In counterpoint we glimpse the workings of Gateway and the story of how Bob got rich and lost his friends and lover.

Unlike anything Pohl had done before, *Gateway* digested the lessons of the New Wave wholeheartedly. There is no real narrative direction to the novel, which is almost plotless. Broadhead proves a kind of anti-hero, all too human. There's a sad lack of nobility in his make-up. Moreover, the psychoanalytical sections, probing Broadhead's inadequacies, reveal a preoccupation with the human which breaks with the tradition of space opera—the sub-genre *Gateway* would otherwise belong to. In this respect *Gateway* proves a remarkable book, melding the two traditions successfully.

Jem (1979), sub-titled with brutal irony "The Making of a Utopia", is another fine novel: a vision of Man the manipulator; perhaps a story of the American Dream turned American Nightmare, when mankind encounters three alien races on the planet Jem. As with so much of Pohl's work, Earth is never far over the horizon, with its ecological and social problems exaggerated by the passage of time.

Beyond the Blue Event Horizon (1980) continues the story of Bob Broadhead and the Heechee, with an expedition to the Heechee "Food Factory" at the edge of the solar system. The extrapolative content of the novel lives up to its predecessor, although the work is neither so impressive nor so experimental as *Gateway* and obviously designed for a further sequel. Pohl's old strengths as a manipulator of plots carries him through, however.

In both *The Cool War* (1980) and *Syzygy* (1981), Earth is centre-stage once again. Both are near-future scenarios involving social failings and institutionalized idiocy. *The Cool War* proves the more interesting; an energy-crisis novel with CIA conspiracy/thriller elements. It is ambitious but flawed. Both novels lack the innovative insight of the earlier works. As if sensing this, Pohl returns to older models for his next two works, embellishing two earlier stories. The first of these is *Starburst* (1982), a novel-length version of his novella, "The Gold at the Starbow's End" (1972). Concerned with an interstellar journey to Alpha Centauri—and a secret experiment on the crew of the starship—it dissipates rather than enchances the impact of the original work. If anything it is a backward step for Pohl. The same cannot be said for *Midas World* (1983), but that has to do with Pohl's strategy.

Midas World takes as its starting point Pohl's famous 1954 story, "The Midas Plague": a tale about enforced consumption, and one of those beautiful reversals of actuality which throws a clear light on the idiocies of a consumer society. Pohl re-writes the original, adding a sequence of other stories to it, to form a kind of linked novel, a portrait of his dark and delightfully insane future society. The strategy works and the satire is effective.

Pohl stalwartly remains faithful to SF rather than fantasy.

Heechee Rendezvous (1984) continues the *Gateway* sequence. Familiarity always lessens impact. The mystery of the Heechee, enigmatic background presences, is dissipated entirely by encountering them. They help Mankind out against evil alien predators, the Assassins, but somehow it is a dying fall. Again, not so much a bad novel as a disappointment after the promise of *Gateway*. The elements of the old—of space opera—begin to overwhelm the invigorating and enlivening infusions of the new.

The best of Pohl's near future Earthbound scenarios appeared in 1985. *The Years of the City* is another sequence of linked stories forming a kind of novelistic overview of future New York City. As ever in Pohl's work there are crises galore, but there is also a new tendency to depict optimistic outcomes. As at the end of *Jem*, we glimpse a better, almost utopian future born from the ashes of old enmity.

The Merchants' War (1985) is perhaps the most interesting and successful of Pohl's novels since *Jem*. It is a sequel—this time to one of the most famous books in SF, *The Space Merchants*, written by Pohl and Kornbluth back in 1953. It proves as much a reworking of the old themes as a sequel; if it lacks the impact of the earlier volume, that has much to do with the fact that the real world has caught up with the fiction of *The Space Merchants*. Advertising *does* now dominate our lives—does, indeed, create Presidents, sink causes, promote subtle chains of dependencies. This said, the novel—about a conflict between the societies of Earth and Venus—is no disappointment. It offers proof that Pohl is still very much a creative force.

Even within the prodigious SF field, Pohl's record, his continued enthusiasm, is a remarkable one.

A wry humour underlies much of Pohl's writing, as does an acidic sense of satire. This is always an attractive combination. But whereas the pre-seventies Pohl had depended upon slickness and plotting to carry his fiction, his literary renaissance brings new tactics, new emphases into his work.

Pohl is a prolific writer—more now than before his re-birth as a novelist—and old professional habits die hard. He is to be admired for the way he has attempted to accommodate the methods of the New Wave. He is a bridge-builder, a diplomat between the old pulp tradition and the new cult of *auteur*. His benevolent influence within fandom as one of the founders of the internationally-minded World SF indicates the way in which bridge-building is a part of his life as well as his writing.

The seven writers highlighted in this chapter represent more than the ultra-visible side of SF. They represent varied currents and camps within the SF community. All have grown out of the pulp tradition; some have grown and changed, some have stood still, some have moved backwards.

In SF, as in all things, evolution is preferable to stagnation or revolution.

Whatever their degree of success, literary or financial, this older group of writers does not succumb to the rather easy *fin de siècle* mood of Dying Earth to which some of the younger generation like to turn.

Modern SF consists not merely of the new, the fashionable, but represents a vast continuity of effort. We have arrived at a time in the genre's history where it is no longer sufficient to describe only the newcomers: that provides a false picture of the modern genre. Modern SF is like a large, crowded house, filled with generations of relatives. The oldest have lived in that house all their years. The youngest demand changes. New living spaces, new furniture, or snazzy, period decor. The oldest prefer the place as it was when they were young. The family squabbles and feuds, yet remains, curiously, a family, however large it grows. A family and an institution.

Even the younger writers next on our list are shaped by the institution.

CHAPTER XVI

The Future Now

And God lives in underground silos
Hanging on for Judgement Day:
If we don't open our eyes pretty soon, then the
Dark Ages'll be here to stay.
        —Peter Hammill (*Mediaevil*)

The closer we come to the present day the harder it becomes to make a clear judgement on the nature and health of the SF field. The writers of the present seem always taller, fresher in their approach—they cast longer shadows than those who preceded them. It is difficult to relate their present popularity to their ultimate worth. In some cases we can only guess at how good they might become, in others we might too hastily dismiss them. We console ourselves with the thought that history is a process of re-evaluation. This chapter is a first guess; an attempt to come to grips with a genre that has, even in the last five years, grown too big for any individual to grasp in its entirety.

We come to the crest of an ever-breaking wave. What tendencies and trends are recognizable in the SF of the eighties? What new elements and emphases are discernible?

First, and it is something we have already dwelt on in an earlier chapter, the genre no longer exists in vacuum. Films, TV series, computer games, toys, media advertising, music—the science fiction mode is more diverse in its forms than ever before. We live in an SF environment where our children's toys are robots and spacecraft, their cartoon adventures set in the 31st Century or on another planet. We see computer technology proliferating unchecked. We also see our oldest SF dreams being made into believable visual images on the wide screen. All of this feeds back into the written genre. Book sales have increased phenomenally. SF long ago came out of the closet. But is this all to the good or is much of it, in fact, harmful? Has SF become just another product—an exotic-flavoured dog food to cram into an ever-widening maw?

How has this proliferation in other media affected the written form of SF with which this history is primarily concerned?

In this chapter we look closely at the work of some two dozen writers, wide-ranging in their concerns, to attempt a synthesis of the modern genre. While being aware of our own fallibility, we consider such a survey necessary for the completion of our story.

If we were to accept a marketing vision of the SF genre—a view gleaned from glossy ads for latest products—we would be presenting here a genre schismatically divided between hard, technological SF and out-and-out fantasy.

To instance this supposed division, consider a listing of some recent titles in both camps, all published in the mid-eighties.

Lining up for the Galactic Empire we have Orson Scott Card with *Ender's Game*, David Drake with *At Any Price*, Timothy Zahn with *Cobra* and *Spinneret*, Glen Cook with *Passage at Arms* and *Doomstalker* (first in the Darkwar trilogy), Warren Norwood with *Polar Fleet* and *Final Command*, Richard S. McEnroe with *Skinner*, Gordon Kendall with *White Wing*, Merl Baldwin with *The Helmsman*, Vernor Vinge with *The Peace War*, Martin Caidin with *Killer Station*, and W. R. Yates with *Diasporah*. Add to this mountain of hardware a few older names: Larry Niven's *The Integral Trees*, Keith Laumer's *Rogue Bolo*, Ben Bova's *The Astral Mirror* and *Privateer*, Niven and Pournelle's *Footfall* and Poul Anderson's *The Game of Empire* (in which Diana Flandry, daughter of Dominic, makes her debut). This far-from-complete list represents a whole sub-genre, presented with a sameness of cover illustrations which deliberately irons out any diversity of writing within to suggest (and perhaps promote) a commonality of purpose. Glossy spacecraft hang in the star-strewn velvet void. Harsh, militarized shapes: like unpainted models, masculine and brutal. Brand image: American Empire.

In the Wands and Wizardry team we have John Lee's *Unicorn Quest*, Manuel Mujica Lainez's *The Wandering Unicorn*, Barbara Hambly's *Dragonsbane*, Meredith Ann Pierce's *A Gathering of Gargoyles*, Cherry Wilder's *A Princess of the Chameln*, Patricia C. Wrede's *The Harp of Imach Thyssel*, Sheri S. Tepper's *Marianne, The Magus and the Manticore*, Jo Clayton's *Changer's Moon*, Asa Drake's *Warrior Witch of Hel*, Chelsea Quinn Yarbro's *To the High Redoubt*, and Michael Jan Friedman's *The Hammer and the Horn*. Add to this flood of faeryland ephemera the following series novels; *The Silver Crown* by Joel Rosenberg, Book Three of the Guardians of the Flame trilogy; *The Book of Kantela* by Roland Green and Frieda Murray, first volume in the Throne of Sherran trilogy; *The Dark Tide* by Dennis L. McKiernan, Book One of the Iron Tower trilogy, and *Magician: Apprentice* by Raymond E. Feist, Volume One of the Rift War saga. Dragons, unicorns, wizards and half-naked warriors (often women) adorn these covers in rich autumnal colours. Once again we sense a commonality of packaging if not purpose. Brand image: Tolkien's children.

This impression of uniformity and product marketing is by no means the whole story. There is a diversity in the SF field at present which bodes well for the genre's future. Nor is that diversity limited to one particular part of an ever-widening field: good writing is flourishing throughout the spectrum.

We begin with one writer whose influence upon the eighties is unmistakable: a writer whose death in 1982 was recognized as a grave loss. Philip K. Dick.

After the hectic production of the sixties, Philip K. Dick slowed his pace in the seventies. It was understandable. The late sixties had been dark years for Dick. He had experienced the ugly side of the drug scene—an experience vividly retold in *A Scanner Darkly* (1977). In those years he produced one masterpiece, the eloquent and truly frightening *Flow My Tears, the Policeman Said* (1974) in which a TV personality, Jason Taverner, crosses into another drug-induced reality where he does not exist.

One common factor in both books was Dick's obsession with streetwise, dark-eyed girls—products of an amoral, punk society he might enter by means of drugs and self-abasement. Both novels were, in some respects, novels about possession, and had echoes of Dostoevsky, treading the same back-alleys of human degradation. Dick had become the SF poet of the streets.

For a time it seemed as though Dick would not return to writing. Then, in the last year of the seventies and the first two years of the eighties, he produced what might be seen as a thematically-connected trilogy of novels in which the subdued theological element in his writing came to the fore. *Valis* was the first of these, a fictionalization of something Dick claimed had actually happened to him—no less than some kind of contact with a God-like intelligence, a divine madness. But if it seemed to some that Dick had finally fallen through the floor of his own wild imaginings, there was no one more aware of this than Dick himself:

> It is amazing that when someone else spouts the nonsense you yourself believe you can readily perceive it as nonsense. In the VW Rabbit as I had listened to Linda and Eric rattle on about being three-eyed people from another planet I had known they were nuts. This made me nuts, too. The realization had frightened me: the realization about them and about myself. (Chapter 13)

In *The Divine Invasion* (1981) Dick took a step off the edge and wrote about the final contest of Good and Evil and the Second Coming. The theme that had been fictionally clothed in *The Three Stigmata of Palmer Eldritch* now emerged naked. But before it is thought that Dick had lost his sense of humour, we ought to quote a passage that is inimitably, classically Dickian:

> "Everything you have said since I grappled onto you has been recorded," the cop said. "It will be analysed. So you're God's father."
>
> "Legal father."
>
> "And that's why you're wanted. I wonder what the statute violation is, technically. I've never seen it listed. Posing as God's father."
>
> "Legal father."
>
> "Who's his real father?"
>
> "He is," Herb Asher said. "He impregnated his mother."
>
> "This is disgusting."
>
> "It's the truth. He impregnated her with himself, and thereby replicated himself in microform by which method he was able to—"
>
> "Should you be telling me this?"
>
> "The battle is over. God has won. The power of Belial has been destroyed."
>
> "Then why are you sitting here with the cuffs on and why am I pointing a laser gun at you?"

"I'm not sure. I'm having trouble figuring that out. That and *South Pacific*. There are a few bits and pieces I can't seem to get to go in place. But I'm working on it. What I am positive about is Yah's victory." . . .

The cop said, "I don't mean to compound your troubles, but you are the most fucked-up human being I have ever met. And I see a lot of different kinds of people. They must have slushed your brain when they put you in cryonic suspension. They must not have gotten to you in time. I'd say that about a sixth of your brain is working and that sixth isn't working right, not at all." (Chapter 18)

Dick's last novel was *The Transmigration of Timothy Archer* (1982), which he did not live to see published. It was scarcely SF, yet it was unmistakably linked to the rest of his work in its concerns and its compassion. For some it represents a more balanced Dick than that displayed in *Valis* and *The Divine Invasion*.

It is one of those profound and often repeated tragedies of life that genuine artists are rarely recognized until they have conveniently died. So it was for Dick in terms of wider acceptance. Since his death unpublished mainstream work has been picked up by publishers and is slowly appearing, together with new uncut versions of novels like *Lies, Inc.* (1984), known in its much-butchered earlier version as *The Unteleported Man* (1964). One new SF novel has also emerged, *Radio Free Albemuth* (1985).

A mini-industry has sprouted about the corpse. Books by, on, and about Dick push their way to the surface with the regularity of daisies. Let us not carp here; the publication of Dick's mainstream work and of biographical material is important. More vital for the living genre was the influence Dick's work began to exert on new writers.

That fusion of wild SF ideas, near-future scenarios and streetwise, drug-culture characters evident in late sixties, early seventies Dick, proved attractive. It accorded with what was happening in youth culture itself. Films like *Videodrome* (1983) and *Repo Man* (1984) and musicians like Gary Numan seemed to borrow directly from Dick's imagination. A new "punk" SF seemed to spring up in the early eighties, with writers like Rudy Rucker, K. W. Jeter, Russell M. Griffin and William Gibson as its chief proponents.

A professor of mathematics, Rudy Rucker called his first novel *Spacetime Donuts* (serialized first in *Unearth* in 1978, and published second in 1981); it established him as a wild talent, grafted direct from Dick's ribs. Rock music, drugs, sex, good and evil and infinity were Rucker's chosen looking-glasses, and in his second novel, *White Light* (printed first in 1980), Rucker proved himself adept at popping down rabbit holes in space and time. A one-time cartoonist, Rucker mixes those qualities of outrageousness and earnestness so necessary for successful and exciting SF. Those early works were by no means masterpieces and some found them all too cerebral, but Rucker has progressed and has now written a clutch of novels, including a highly enjoyable robot novel, *Software* (1982), which almost out-Dicks Dick and unsurprisingly won the first Philip K. Dick Award. *The Fourth Dimension* (1984), a popularizing book on mathematics, sub-titled, "Toward a Geometry of Higher Reality", showed another side to Rucker's inventive mind.

K. W. Jeter had two novels out in the Laser Books series in the seventies, but only came to prominence in the eighties when a twelve year old novel, *Dr Adder* (1984) appeared with an afterword by Philip K. Dick. Set in the heart of Dick country, Southern California, it is a novel about drug-induced telepathy, written in a disturbing but up-tempo manner. *The Glass Hammer* (1985) is more immediate, more modern, with its video clips, computers and pulse-phase particle beams. Jeter provides a bleak but potent vision of our near-future world, somewhat less palatable than Dick's, unrelieved by humour.

Russell M. Griffin's first novel, *The Makeshift God*, was published in 1979. It is a well-wrought space adventure concerned with linguistics, genetics, anthropology, theology and an alien race, the Albar. It was highly intelligent but did not suggest—except in its subtle style—what was to come in Griffin's next two novels.

Century's End (1981) is a delightful satire of all things cranky, wrapped up in a story about the turn of the century, and *The Blind Man and the Elephant* (1982) dispenses with all but one SF element in its tale of a freak and his origins. *The Blind Man and the Elephant* is an engaging book, reminiscent of Dick not merely in its chosen subject matter—the absurdity of small town America and its distractions—but in its humour, its poignancy and its slightly askew way of viewing things. As in Dick's work we spare little sympathy for the cruel, the authoritarian and the evil, though we see them with a clarity that is almost hallucinatory: our sympathies are engaged by the oppressed, the disadvantaged and the incapable. Griffin's Elephant Man is immaculately conceived and the subject of some strange diseases linked to his birth. He is brilliantly drawn:

> But while he was anything but stupid, it was also true that Elephant Man believed in the world of Romance which television brought him, a world where virtue always triumphed and vice could ultimately be defeated or at least contained in cycles based on multiples of thirty minutes. (Chapter 7)

William Gibson first came to the attention of SF fans with a series of well executed stories in *Omni*, among them "Burning Chrome", nominated for a Nebula Award in 1982. "Burning Chrome" was set in a near future world dominated by computer technology, massive cartels and cyberspace, an artificial universe created through the link-up of tens of millions of machines. This same world was to be the setting for his first two novels, *Neuromancer* (1984) and *Count Zero* (1986).

Neuromancer is the story of a computer cowboy named Case. In synopsis his is a slender tale of computer theft, corporate manipulation and machine intelligence. A very slender tale indeed, with few levels beyond that of slick, fast-paced thriller. It's a garishly violent book with a wholly unsympathetic protagonist. Case is a cold fish with more in common with his console than with the equally degraded humans around him. Such coldness between people is somewhat reminiscent of William Burroughs's *The Wild Boys* (1971).

Even so, *Neuromancer* won the Philip K. Dick award, the Nebula and the Hugo for its year. What makes it a remarkable debut, rather than a remarkable novel, is Gibson's style:

> Cold steel odor. Ice caressed his spine.
>   Lost, so small amid that dark, hands grown cold, body image fading down corridors of television sky.
>   Voices.
>   Then black fire found the branching tributaries of the nerves, pain beyond anything to which the name of pain is given. . . .
>
>   Hold still. Don't move.
>   And Ratz was there, and Linda Lee, Wage and Lonny Zone, a hundred faces from the neon forest, sailors and hustlers and whores, where the sky is poisoned silver, beyond the chainlink and the prison of the skull.
>   Goddamn don't you move.
>   Where the sky faded from hissing static to the noncolor of the matrix, and he glimpsed the shuriken, his stars.
>   "Stop it, Case, I gotta find your vein."
>   She was straddling his chest, a blue plastic syrette in one hand. "You don't lie still, I'll slit your fucking throat. You're still full of endorphin inhibitors." (Chapter 2)

This emphasis on surface style, which continually manifests itself in Gibson's work through sparkling visual one-liners, is reminiscent of Bester and Delany, as is the portrait of a society glimpsed from its heights and its stygian depths. Gibson's is a high-gloss world and one cannot imagine anyone normal living there and bringing up their kids: only the punks and the powerful, degrees of perversion separating them. It's an attractive yet curiously unhealthy mixture— again like Delany, like Burroughs. Where it differs from Delany is in its cold realism. Cyberspace is a credible reality in both novels; a frightening place where defensive systems, black ice, can cause brain-death for an unwary cowboy. If Gibson is like Delany, it is the Delany of *Dhalgren* and *The Tides of Lust* (1973), not of the early Ace novels.

Count Zero sketched out more of this future world. In essence, it is *Neuromancer* II, with a hit-man, Turner—a specialist in removing important men from one giant corporation and establishing them in another—as our focus. Count Zero himself is another young computer jockey, Bobby, whose ambition is to get out of the slum he's in and into the Sprawl, where the wealth is. The opening four pages of the book are superb, breathtaking stuff. But the pace quickly relents. As a novel *Count Zero* lacks tension, nor do its characters engage one—a serious flaw to set against the surface brilliance that manifests itself time and again. There is also a trace of best-sellerdom in the mix: that modern tendency to label everything which one expects from Shirley Conran but not from one of SF's young bucks:

"I suppose you understand this sort of thing, "the Spaniard said glumly. He wore an expensive-looking blue shirt cut in Parisian business style, a white broadcloth shirt, and a very English-looking tie, probably from Charvet. He didn't look at all like a waiter now. There was an Italian bag of black, ribbed rubber slung over his shoulder. (Chapter 14)

There are pages more of such superficial descriptions, often, as here, of minor characters. *Count Zero* lacks real depth. Its three plot threads mean very little in themselves and little more when they're joined. Turner, like Case, lacks those qualities of character we need to engage us wholly in his fate, and surface colourings, however beautifully achieved, can only titillate, not satisfy.

It is clear that Gibson is a talented young writer who could develop into one of the genre's best. It is hoped that too early praise will not stifle that development. There is also a doubt as yet concerning Gibson's range: he has still to write much that falls outside his near future scenario, or to provide a moral or philosophical dimension even to that. In the unfolding of time Gibson's true worth will become apparent. For now he is all potential—an exciting commodity in an ever-changing field.

Gibson's *Neuromancer* has been picked up by a film company and—if reports are to be believed—has been given a healthy $25 million budget. In the late seventies and early eighties two bestselling writers from the horror genre crossed the great divide into science fiction and presented SF novels which were subsequently filmed, Ira Levin and Stephen King.

Levin's dystopian novel *This Perfect Day* appeared in 1970, followed two years later by *The Stepford Wives* (1972), as much a comment on small town conformity and male chauvinist piggery as a tale of female robot replicas. His most interesting work was *The Boys from Brazil* (1976) which blended two then very popular themes, Nazi hunting and cloning, to produce a satisfying thriller (if not quite so satisfying a novel of ideas).

Far more interesting in terms of their science fictional content are Stephen King's two novels, *The Dead Zone* (1979) and *Firestarter* (1980). King leapt into the bestseller lists with *Carrie* (1973), subsequently filmed, and demonstrated there a fascination with the paranormal. *Firestarter* can be seen as a psychologically richer and more profound reworking of that early novel, for both are concerned with young female protagonists trying to come to terms with their psychokinetic powers. The horror framework of the former owed much to Levin's *Rosemary's Baby* (1967), which had spawned a cinematic horror boom. But the later "version" demonstrates not merely King's literary maturity but his mastery of several pure SF themes. In *Firestarter* religious mania has been traded for conspiracy theory, and a vague satanic power for a specific by-product of a scientific experiment, to create paranormal powers.

This shift from a horror format to a pure science fictional approach seems to have had nothing to do with the genre's increased popularity at horror's expense. In both *Firestarter* and *The Dead Zone*, King seems genuinely fascinated with the implications of his ideas. What would it be like to have these powers?

Are they blessing or curse? What are the moral consequences? Moreover, King attempts to create a plausible, if highly improbable, explanation for the existence of these powers.

In *The Dead Zone*, King presents us with what is one of the most intelligent studies of the psychic ever to have hit the bestseller lists. Plain Johnny Smith has an accident as a child and damages part of his brain. Long years later he has a bad car crash and goes into coma for four and a half years. When he wakes, it is to find that he has developed a form of psychic power, at first very specific and highly limited, but later to develop into a form of precognition. In a moment of pure SF explication, his doctor, Sam Weizak, gives the technical details to the press corps:

> "You may also quote me as saying I believe this man is now in possession of a very new human ability, or a very old one. Why? If I and my colleagues do not understand the brain of an ant, can I tell you why? I can suggest some interesting things to you, however, things which may or may not have bearing. A part of John Smith's brain may be vital. He calls this his 'dead zone', and there, apparently, a number of trace memories were stored. All of these wiped-out memories seem to be part of a 'set'— that of street, road, and highway designations. A subset of a larger overall set, that of where is it. This is a small but total aphasia which seems to include both language and visualization skills.
>
> "Balancing this off, another part of John Smith's brain appears to have *awakened*. A section of the cerebrum within the parietal lobe. This is one of the deeply grooved sections of the 'forward' or 'thinking' brain. The electrical responses from this section of Smith's brain are way out of line from what they should be, nuh? Here is one more thing. The parietal lobe has something to do with the sense of touch—how much or how little we are not completely sure—and it is very near to that area of the brain that sorts and identifies various shapes and textures. And it has been my own observation that John's 'flashes' are always preceded by some sort of touching." (Chapter 11)

For Johnny Smith, his ability or "talent" is a curse. With it he helps save property and lives, tracks down a murderer and, with his final act, ends the career of a fascist politician whom he has "seen" pushing the button for World War Three. Even so, in personal terms this power cripples him, ostracizes him, makes him a freak in normal company. He loses his girl, faces huge hospital bills, flees the unpitying eye of the media. Like Jonah he is both God-blessed and God-cursed. Atheist though he is, King realistically shuns the temptation to make a superman figure of his protagonist.

King is a very American writer. You can taste and smell America in his evocative but direct prose, heavily salted as it is with cultural referents. But his message is universal, as is his mixture of the personal and the political. Both *Firestarter* and *The Dead Zone* are novels about good and evil—about psychotics seeking power and those with special powers seeking only peace, or at the very least, surcease from society's pressures on them. King is Bradbury with a little less poetry and a bit more documentary in the mix; an interesting and intelligent addition to the list of SF's practitioners.

Bruce Sterling is a Texan, born in 1954. In person, he gives the doubtless calculated impression of being in a state of genial and energizing despair over practically everything, including Texas.

Sterling's first novel, *Involution Ocean*, appeared in 1977 when he was just twenty-three. A flawed but fascinating first novel, it created the dreadful planet of Nullaqua with considerable skill, surviving an introduction by Harlan Ellison designed to kill off a dozen lesser writers from bashfulness.

It was clear from the outset that Sterling wanted to assimilate a whole range of literary influences into his work. In *Involution Ocean* he didn't quite succeed, but his second novel, *The Artificial Kid* (1980) proved he had learned an awful lot in the interim. This brash, punkish novel with its slick, fast-moving plot prefigures the later work in its concern with artificial environments, longevity and power politics.

The mid-eighties saw Sterling appearing with greater regularity in the magazines. "Swarm" (1982) presented a near-future solar system shared by two factions, the Mechanists and the Shapers, representatives of life directions. The Shapers, with their Ring Council, are geneticists, set on changing Mankind to suit the environments encountered in space, and on improving the racial stock. The Mechanists are more interested in prosthetics and rejuvenation techniques. They represent the New and the Old.

"Swarm", although it lost out to Connie Willis's over-rated "Fire Watch" for the Nebula, was an exceptional story with its vast perspectives of time, its sense of frighteningly rapid progress and its marvellous creation of the alien Swarm. The moment when the Swarm speaks through the dead mouth of Mirny, one of the protagonists, is apocalyptic.

Schismatrix (1985) is set in the same solar system of Mechanists and Shapers and covers 170 years in the personal history of Abelard Malcolm Tyler Lindsay, a young aristocrat trained to Shaper ways. The social and political background to the novel is reminiscent of the Italian City states of the Renaissance, yet *only* reminiscent. Man has taken the first steps into space and built huge artificial environments. These are the City States of the future. This artificial, high-tech society is incredibly diverse in its sects, cults, philosophies and even *kinds* of people. Lindsay is a social chameleon, making his way through this society, learning and changing and maturing constantly as the novel progresses. And as his life shifts, so we see society shifting and changing, as rapidly as he. Bacteriological engineering, microsurgery techniques and genetic experimentation race ahead, creating what Sterling calls "clades"; new, daughter species to Mankind—a form of posthumanity, growing steadily more diverse.

Lindsay finds and loses love; aliens arrive—the Investors—and the pace of the novel accelerates as the years peel past. Sterling presents us with "Superbrights"—genetically-enhanced geniuses—a consciousness-shattering drug, PDKL-95 (note the initials!), biofeedback machines, alien tape-mimics and all manner of ingenious extrapolations and inventions. Yet through all of this Sterling never loses sight of his protagonist, Lindsay, nor of how everything affects him as a person. In this lies the strength of *Schismatrix*. For all its marvellous inventiveness, it is above all a novel, not a logical conundrum. The worlds of *Schismatrix* have a vivid reality that few such complex extrapolations have ever possessed.

Ultimately *Schismatrix* is about the birth of a new, Posthuman consciousness with what Sterling calls "the four Prigogenic Levels of Complexity". The phraseology is daunting, but it is a very human portrait—perhaps the first ever offered in science fiction—of a time when "the march of science had become a headlong stampede". This is not Future Shock, but Future Blitzkrieg. Changes of technology bring changes of philosophy and perception. Lindsay faces a world where basic assumptions change as fast as fashions, an age where time itself has changed its properties:

> To the truly old, time was as thin as air, a keening and destructive wind that erased their pasts and attacked their memories. Time was accelerating. Nothing could slow it down for him but death. (Part Two, Chapter 6)

Schismatrix avoids all temptations to lecture or obfuscate with technical jargon. It is readable, comprehensible, even, perhaps, poetic in its expression. It presents its complexity with the vividness of a mainstream author describing a 1970s bedsit. It is a novel that takes the most difficult concept of all in science fiction—the social complexity resulting from technical and biotechnical progress—and presents it as naturally as if it had been experienced and were merely being described afterwards. No higher praise can be given.

Greg Bear had his first story published in 1967, but it was not until the late seventies that his stories began to appear with regularity in the magazines, mainly in *Analog*. Despite his interest in SF poetry—he edited the *Speculative Poetry Review*—Bear's fiction was high-tech orientated in the tradition of Clarke and Clement. In the eighties these two influences were married, producing an eloquent form of hard SF.

The novelette "Blood Music" (1983) won Bear a Nebula and was expanded to novel length in 1985. Bear's canvas was, in this instance, narrower than Sterling's but impressive nonetheless for its vivid realism. *Blood Music* has been called "a *Childhood's End* for the 1980s" and there is a certain justification for this label. But the element of transcendence involved in *Blood Music* is not of the individual but of the species: Man becomes not Superman but something wholly other, something alien, incomprehensible.

Vergil Ulam, a brilliant researcher, working to develop the "biochip"—an organic, cellular means of storing information—instead creates (or accidentally stumbles upon) intelligent cells, noocytes. Like many a researcher on the payroll of someone else's company, Vergil plans to keep his research to himself, set up his own concern, and reap the rewards. He is caught and fired from his job, but injects himself with his experimental samples before he leaves.

The rest is inexorable if by no means predictable. The noocytes thrive in Vergil's bloodstream and spread through his body like a virus, restructuring his bones, his organs and eventually his mental processes.

Vergil is only the first victim of this transformation. The noocytes spread through the population of North America like a plague, changing almost everything they encounter. The continent is sealed off, the plague apparently contained, but there is one further change—another quantum leap of evolution—to come. The trillions of intelligent noocytes—their number greater, it is stressed, than all the grains of sand on Earth and all the stars in the sky—form an entity or, more accurately, a community with aims wholly removed from those of mankind. They look not outward to the stars, but inward to the galaxies of the infinitesimally small.

Blood Music presents the experience of sudden, unanticipated change in a way quite different from most science fiction. Bear's vision of an evolutionary leap so vast that it changes the rules of the universe is Stapledonian in its conception, though with more than a touch of *New Worlds* in its execution. Stapledon's cold, clear view from the mountain's peak is replaced by the equally clear view through the electron microscope. Inner space is our evolutionary future, Bear seems to be saying; a terrifying but also beautiful prospect, as he depicts it in *Blood Music*.

The parallels with Clarke were strengthened with the publication late in 1985 of Bear's *Eon*. The arrival of the Stone, a mysterious asteroid, in Earth orbit, seems to be a page out of Clarke—like the sentinel in *2001* or, more particularly, like the arrival of the giant alien spacecraft Rama in *Rendezvous with Rama*. That said, Bear's imagination takes him off in directions Clarke has yet to explore.

The Stone proves to be the planetoid Juno, third largest of the minor planets. But it is not *our* Juno. It is from a parallel universe which has intersected with our own. What's more, it has been hollowed out into seven chambers by humans some 1200 years more advanced than ourselves. And the seventh chamber is infinite in length. . . .

Eon is every bit as complex and audacious as *Schismatrix* and almost as satisfying. It is one of those novels we read with the feeling that we *almost* understand what is being shown to us of higher maths and physics—an enjoyable *frisson* that modern-day SF all too rarely provides. Gates in space and time, bow waves of relativistic forces, alien philosophies, incomprehensible technologies—Bear presents these to us with just the right amount of explanation, awe and bluster to convince us that he knows what he's up to even as we flounder in culture shock, relishing every moment.

What also strikes us as important about *Eon* is its genuine concern for the fate of mankind in the next twenty years. Within the novel's pages we see the inevitable outcome of power politics and arms build-ups. The Earth is destroyed. Nuclear winter sets in. Eventually the future humans and the survivors team up—to prevent a recurrence. One applauds the priorities of Bear's novel.

Much of Bear's work has an apocalyptic tone to it. Earth is constantly under threat of destruction, as it was in his early story, "The Wind from a Burning Woman" (1977). But Bear is not so much concerned with the disaster scenario as with the potentiality for change and re-Birth. Although not always the most lyrical of writers, he uses a prose which is effective and often far superior to that we've come to expect from the hard SF camp—evidence of great care and craft on his part.

David Brin has a lighter, much more colloquial tone to his writing than Bear or Sterling. He is more charming, more human, if less adventurous in his speculations. Nonetheless, he is an author of ideas and cannot be placed alongside writers like Pangborn from earlier times. In his three Progenitor novels, *Sundiver* (1980), *Startide Rising* (1983) and *The Uplift War* (1985), he presents a wide scenario space opera which is a variant on all those crowded galaxies that preceded it.

Startide Rising won Brin the Hugo and Nebula awards against such contenders as Varley's *Millennium* and Asimov's *The Robots of Dawn*, both highly popular works. Brin shows every sign of becoming a best-seller in the late eighties.[1] Part of *Startide Rising*, "The Tides of Kithrup", appeared first in *Analog* (May 1981), and Brin's movement between his humane portrayal of the human and sentient-dolphin space crew, stranded on an alien planet, and the diverse multitude of powerful aliens trying to get at what they have, is an enjoyable mixture of old and new traditions. There are flaws in the novel—the sing-song haiku of the dolphins, similar to a device used in Somtow Sucharitkul's *Light on the Sound* (1982), proves irritating—but it is one of those books which gives enjoyment enough to calm such minor irritations.

Brin is immensely readable, without the pejorative that usually implies. His most recent novel, *The Postman* (1985), is set much closer to home; seventeen years after the collapse of modern-day America, and in the post-Catastrophe wilderness of Oregon. Gordon K., taking on the role of Pony Express rider, sells hope to the small, struggling communities and gradually links them up into a mail network. What was a confidence trick becomes a reality.

The Postman is a variation on the post-holocaust theme, simply but effectively told, although the morality of depicting a post-disaster world where life still goes on and a nice girl is readily available is always open to question. Brin sidesteps the issue.

Brin's popularity will grow and grow. His latest venture is a novel with Greg Benford, called *Heart of the Comet* (1986). Gardner Dozois, on the other hand, seems fated to be more influential than popular, especially now that he has taken over the editing of *Isaac Asimov's Science Fiction Magazine*.

Dozois's first novel was the interesting *Nightmare Blue* (1975), co-authored with Geo. Alec Effinger. His solo debut came three years later with *Strangers*, an evocative tale of alien ways and star-crossed lovers. Dozois's strength, however, seems to be as a short story writer, and the eighties have seen him join the award winners for two excellent short stories, "The Peacemaker" and "Morning Child". Dozois is a big man with an ever-growing talent who writes far too little. Anything new by him is worth seeking out.

Donald Kingsbury attracted attention for his first novel, *Courtship Rite* (1982), though his novella "The Moon Goddess and the Son" (1979 in *Analog*) had demonstrated Kingsbury's modern approach to old materials. *Courtship Rite* (UK title, *Geta*) is a big, sprawling novel, advertised as "in the mighty *Dune* tradition". One can see why. Epigrams from non-existent tomes adorn each chapter head. Geta itself is a harsh, famine world containing exotic cultures. It is traditional *Astounding/Analog* fare in many respects. But it would be mistaken to push the analogy too far, for the novel is about the powerful emotions surrounding love and not the love of power we see displayed in *Dune*.

Like Kingsbury, Dr Robert L. Forward is an occasional science fact contributor to *Analog*. His first novel, *Dragon's Egg* (1980), capitalized upon his knowledge of gravitational physics to describe an alien race, the Cheela, who live on the edge of a neutron star's event horizon. It was a fascinating but deeply flawed novel—flawed in many of the old ways; a piece of Campbellian fiction stranded out of its time. *The Flight of the Dragonfly* (1984) was a huge leap forward from the earlier novel, a work no less audacious in its speculative content but far more human and approachable.

So, from hard to soft, to three of the more lyrical writers who have chosen to work within the SF field in the eighties: Kim Stanley Robinson, Hilbert Schenck and Paul O. Williams.

Kim Stanley Robinson is a critic of the genre and his doctoral dissertation, a study of the writings of Philip K. Dick, has been published.[2] He emerged as a writer to watch in 1983 with an impressive novelette, "Black Air". Ace published his first novel, *The Wild Shore* (1984), in their new Specials series, alongside *Neuromancer* and Lucius Shepard's *Green Eyes*.

The Wild Shore is patently a journeyman work. Too long, too dull in parts, it needs severe editing. It is leisurely in its characterization, slow-paced in its adventure sections, and ultimately means very little indeed—its parts not adding up to any kind of whole. Its post-holocaust scenario is straight from Stewart's *Earth Abides* via Pangborn, and says nothing new about the subject.

It is a sterile, rather lifeless book.

Why mention *The Wild Shore* if this is so? Simply that Robinson's novel has been hailed in some quarters as the new SF; a new, more literary SF, subtler in its expression. It is nothing of the kind. It is thin-boned, and its images—sharply captured as they are—are over-familiar.

Robinson's future California is a dull place, too much a backwater of the imagination, to engage us; its people too ordinary, its events too mundane. It's a fatal combination:

> The hours passed ever so slowly—cramped, stiff, hungry, boring, miserable hours—another of those stretches that are skipped over when adventure tales are told, although if mine is any example, a good part of every adventure is spent in such a way, waiting in great discomfort to be able to do something else. (Part two, Chapter 10)

Well, yes, so it is in life.

Subsequent works, *Icehenge* (1984) and *The Memory of Whiteness* (1985), if not wholly free of such faults, are proof that Robinson is a capable writer, while there are several passages in *The Wild Shore*—like the scene in the bathhouse after the torrential storm[3]—which excel. Our point here is that, in the quest for a more mature form of SF, the appearance of literature should not be mistaken for the actuality. SF has its own distinctive qualities: shed them and the result is often an unsatisfactory product of no real interest to anyone.

Hilbert Schenck is a writer of some quality, a fine, committed novelist and—to cement his connection with SF—a professor of mechanical engineering and director of the ocean engineering program at the University of Rhode Island. So, at least, reads the introductory preface in *F&SF* to Schenck's "Three Days at the End of the World" (1977).

Schenck writes whereof he knows. The ocean and its ways are magically conveyed to us in his work, and, in his first novel, *At the Eye of the Ocean* (1981), it becomes a character of varying moods and shifting faces. The novel is just barely SF and its setting, the years 1828 to 1888, give it the feel of a historical romance, yet its evocation of the ocean as a mysterious alien entity is the book's imaginative heart. Closer to the pure thing was his second novel, *A Rose for Armageddon* (1982), an outstanding tale of scientific enquiry, love, time, and the ultimate decline of the West. There is a real poetry and intensity to the novel that raises the book above its simple plot elements. That and an intelligence underlying the passionate concerns of the book:

> Elsa cleared her throat again and suddenly looked at me with a very intense glance. "Jake, is a simple *thought* really so *tiny* a thing? A man watches a woman's breasts moving, the black hairs standing on her arm, her mouth suddenly slack and uncaring in her release. The visions, real then and maybe imagined later, come as photon patterns, displayed on a nervous optical matrix and coded as mostly digitized neural potentials entering the brain and discharging memory, pleasure, and related centres. Surely these are the tiniest of signals, the most ephemeral of triggers, yet the instant result is a total convulsion of the man's body and sometimes a spreading nodal structure that may eventually include the death of many persons, even of Troy itself, the ruin of great companies and nations, and the destruction of every sort of treasure. If our simple knowledge of that place on Hawkins is the only key that unlocks its gate, I don't find that so remarkable or unexpected." (Section 2: Dr Jake Stinson)

Elsa Adams and Jake Stinson are university professors running a "morphological study" of Hawkins Island on the north east coast of the USA. It is a super computer programme, incorporating many disciplines— archaeology, zoology, economics, sociology, anthropology and mathematics amongst them—and called Archmorph. As their study comes to its strange and unexpected conclusion, the collapse of Western Civilization begins. They flee to Hawkins, not merely as refuge, but to try to understand the nature of the "anomaly"—a blank space where no such space ought to be—on the computer-produced map of land-use on the island. One further element adds a sharp immediacy to this "scientific" quest. In their youth, Elsa and Jake made love there, at the anomaly on Hawkins Island.

The idea of morphology is strongly presented in *A Rose for Armageddon*, yet the strengths of the novel, and its success as a piece of science fiction, lie elsewhere. We are too often encouraged to *think* about SF, but too rarely to *feel* what an idea means in human terms. Schenck's is one of the most human of SF novels and makes us feel what time and memory and the process of ageing in the body really mean. This is as much a genuine science fictional concern as any speculation on the moons of Uranus.

Paul O. Williams won the John W. Campbell award for best young writer a few years back. That recognition aside, few have realized that his ever-evolving Pelbar Cycle has produced much good writing. Seven novels have so far been published in the sequence[4] and it seems likely that further novels will continue to appear as Williams sketches out his far-future, post-Industrial America, with its various tribes and cultures. Perhaps the neglect has to do with a critical consciousness that series novels rarely do more than serve up cold formula fiction as new.

All the Pelbar novels have emerged direct in paperback, packaged like classy fantasy novels. This is a strategy which may reach a number of fans. It unfortunately by-passes the process by which a writer reaches a far wider audience.

Let's get the record straight. Williams is a fine writer and his Pelbar Cycle novels, beginning with *The Breaking of Northwall* (1980), contain little that is formulaic. What they are is a re-imagining of America and its vast and complex currents of cultural diversity. Enclaves of civilization have survived the fall of the West and have built great citadels along the upper reaches of the Heart River, once the Mississippi. These form the Pelbar Heartland. About them the eastern lands of Urstadge have been divided amongst tribes which, like the old Amerind tribes, live close to the Earth, primitives in a land of hidden wonders. This much is not remarkable. What impresses is the degree of realism with which Williams invests his characters and settings. While being interrelated, each novel in the sequence is a separate entity. One's knowledge of the future land of Urstadge grows, book by book, with a sense of unfolding history, yet each novel stands by itself.

The central book in the sequence will serve as an instance: *The Fall of the Shell* (1982). At the novel's beginning there is a literal fall and breakage of a conch shell: an incident that results in punishment and exile for a young boy, Gamwyn. The shell is important because it is the model for the giant citadel at Threerivers, whose fall—again caused, but this time deliberately, by Gamwyn—closes the novel. Between the two events is a thoughtful adventure on the river, counterpointed by the story of rebellion against matriarchal tyranny within the citadel.

The Fall of the Shell is deep-rooted in American literature and owes much to

Thoreau's *Walden*. "God but patented a leaf," Thoreau said, and this forms
Williams's model for the book, his shell:

> As they continued downriver, Gamwyn was troubled by a recurring
> dream in which the whirling tornado smashed through the Tusio tower
> again and again, sending people and pieces of the structure flying.
> Sometimes the tornado became the shell in his mind, then a river eddy, a
> twist of rope, a spiral of climbing vine, the curl of a fern fiddlehead, the
> three-tiered loops of the protector's hair, the curve of the main staircase at
> Threerivers, all whirling, shifting, and mixing, all smashing through the
> tower, spraying it out on the gale-wild air. (Chapter 14)

Williams was once president of the Thoreau Society, and the influence shows.
A strong vein of storytelling, more Twain than Thoreau, makes these works
not merely literary but highly readable.

This said, it remains to be asked what is lacking from works like the Pelbar
Cycle? They are entertainments, but hardly escapist. Moral questions are posed,
genuine life choices must be made. Without resources people starve or are
enslaved. Weakness is punished. But where is that element of speculation which
makes such an exercise more than a return to old patterns?

The lesson, if there is one, of such works as Pelbar and *A Rose for Armageddon*
seems to be this: that our civilization is a fragile, ill-balanced thing. The
holocaust is only a step or two away. Both novelists value those qualities of
civilization and technology which have eased man's suffering. They are not
primitivists or luddites, but deplore the misuse that has created our present
circumstances in the West. *The Fall of the Shell* ends with the destruction of the
old rigid patterns and the beginnings of a new settlement, a new pattern to
things. Williams recognizes that our problems are not out there in the stars but
here on Earth.

Williams is not alone in such a recognition, but his Pelbar Cycle serves as one
of the most extensive explorations of the moral problem involved. Writers with
a moral sensibility are relatively thick on the ground at present—a healthy sign
to counter the increasing tendency to *market* SF. Despite rampant consumerism,
writers obstinately refuse to be categorized, and speak with a humane and
intelligent voice. Among them are Gene Wolfe, Tim Powers, Lucius Shepard,
Octavia Butler, John Calvin Batchelor and James Morrow.

Gene Wolfe is perhaps the new giant of the eighties, his *Book of the New Sun*
establishing him amongst the top rank of writers. But those in the know had
prior warning of his excellence. In 1972 Wolfe produced a book containing three
connected novellas about the worlds of Sainte Croix and Sainte Anne, *The Fifth
Head of Cerberus*. Our definition of SF—that it is characteristically cast in the
Gothic or post-Gothic mode—was never truer than of Wolfe. *The Fifth Head of
Cerberus* is a superbly told Gothic mystery with a slowly unfolding revelation of
its central enigma. In Wolfe's hands the future becomes the past. Technological
marvels are rather commonplace and old-fashioned. His is a far-future
viewpoint which inverts all our normal expectations. Like Wilkie Collins's *The*

Moonstone, Wolfe's story approaches its mysteries—the cloned brother, the exterminated alien race—obliquely and through differing voices.

Wolfe's reputation grew throughout the seventies. His 1973 novella, "The Death of Dr Island"[5] won a Nebula. A special island provides an environment where a mentally-disturbed boy is being treated. The computer-generated "moods" of the island reflect those of the boy, providing a kind of therapy. Or so, at first, it seems. Nothing is certain in Wolfe's fiction. There is always a hidden purpose, a concealed meaning. Wolfe is a Catholic, and a magician.

The Shadow of the Torturer (1980) began the sequence of novels which comprise *The Book of the New Sun*. It is an extremely mannered novel that reads like a fantasy. Its tone is reminiscent of some sword and sorcery novels—as, indeed, are its constituent elements. The sun has grown old and mankind is in decline. The golden age of technology has long passed. What was once comprehended technology has become a kind of magic, all explanations lost or concealed.

In the largest city of the southern continent of this future Urth, Nessus, lives Severian, an apprentice to the Guild of Torturers. The first volume in the sequence follows his adventures as far as the city's gate. On the way he is confronted with the necessity of torturing the woman he loves. He avoids personal involvement but cannot save her from death.

Realism was never Wolfe's purpose, it must be said, but *The Book of the New Sun* owes much of its popularity to the sense one has that this is intelligent, meaningful sword and sorcery—appealing thus to our wondering as well as our more thoughtful selves. Archaic language clutters the prose—mystes, steles, dholes, exultants, amschaspand, archtolker, asimi, Vodalarii, armigers, optimates, cacogens, wildgrave, nenuphars, diatrymae, and so forth—which conjures a strong sense of this far future time. This fantastic creation is enjoyable even if not quite believable.

If there was one major flaw to *The Shadow of the Torturer*, it was that it did not so much end as fade out, awaiting the second volume. The same could be said of Proust's vast work, *A la recherche du temps perdu*. Here it is a failing, despite the fact that we know—through the "autobiographical" context—that Severian is to become Autarch. The book was not a novel in its own right, only a fragment. Even so, within the eventual context of the four-volume work[6] it serves to introduce us to this queer, outlandish future.

The Claw of the Conciliator (1981) followed swiftly on from the first volume. Wolfe had written all four segments of his long tale before publishing the first: perhaps the sanest way of approaching such a venture. Again it was a work which did not stand in isolation. Nor did it do much more than repeat the formula of the first book—pushing Severian through a picaresque that gave us insights into his world and into his own developing character. Such comments fail to describe the richness of the prose and the complexity of the insights. In this novel and its two successors, *The Sword of the Lictor* (1981) and *The Citadel of the Autarch* (1983), we begin to glimpse Wolfe's hidden purpose.

The Book of the New Sun, read in its entirety, proves to be a highly religious work—a work about the Parousia, the second coming of a Conciliator, a kind of Christ-figure, who will revitalize the sun itself and bring a new age to the dying, decadent Urth. It is a grandiose vision indeed. Some have complained that Wolfe explains too much in his final volume, others that to release so complex a story in sections over a relatively long period lessened its effectiveness. Whatever, *The Book of the New Sun* is not quite the masterpiece that some claim it is, though it is magnificent in its flawed and lengthy state, and a delightful addition to the ranks of Dying Earth novels; a work that repays re-reading. An excerpt from *The Sword of the Lictor* may capture the flavour of Wolfe's writing:

> There have been many times when I have felt I have gone mad, for I have had many great adventures, and the greatest adventures are those that act most strongly upon our minds. So it was then. A man, larger than I and far broader of shoulder, stepped from between the feet of a cataphract, and it was as though one of the monstrous constellations of the night sky had fallen to Urth and clothed itself in the flesh of humankind. For the man had two heads, like an ogre in some forgotten tale in *The Wonders of Urth and Sky*.
>
> Instinctively, I put my hand on the sword hilt at my shoulder. One of the heads laughed; I think it was the only laughter I was ever to hear at the baring of that great blade.
>
> "Why are you alarmed?" he called. "I see you are as well equipped as I am. What is your friend's name?"
>
> Even in my surprise, I admired his boldness. "She is *Terminus Est*," I said, and I turned the sword so he could see the writing on the steel.
>
> "'This is the place of parting'. Very good. Very good indeed, and particularly good that it should be read here and now, because this time will truly be a line between old and new such as the world has not seen."
> (Chapter 25)

One notes the similarities to fantasy, yet also the other levels of the work poke through, bones through the flesh of narrative: "the greatest adventures are those that act most strongly upon our minds." *The Book of the New Sun* certainly stays in the mind.

The theme of Dying Earth, used elegantly by Gene Wolfe, is one of the preoccupations of the present day. The mood prevails whether the Earth has died by the folly of mankind or from what we may term natural causes. This is the swing of the pendulum, away from the bright harsh colours of the Gernsback era, with its rivets and its twenty-five cent optimism. However much American science fiction may think of itself as—in the rather ridiculous phrase—"maintaining faith in the future", the prevailing tint of *fin de siècle* is unmistakable. In that way it echoes the literary mood of the 1890s, the colours of Whistler rather than Frank Paul.

We can only anticipate a deepening of this mood as the century draws to what we hope will be merely an ambiguous close.

Other writers can be old-fashioned in modern ways. Another writer working on that nebulous frontier between SF and fantasy is Tim Powers, whose novel, *The Anubis Gates* (1983), won the Philip K. Dick award.

The Anubis Gates is a delightfully plotted, highly atmospheric time travel novel, with much of the action set in the London of 1810. Its elements are traditional enough, even old-fashioned, one might say—a Dickensian under-world, an evil clown in spring-heeled boots, scheming Egyptians: like something from a 1930s serial, in fact, visually fantastic, literally incredible. And yet Powers controls these elements and weaves them into a convincing and entrancing story. As in the best of Dick's novels, the combat between good and evil underlies this tale of attempted reality alteration. There is also something of the fantastical quality of George MacDonald's work, particularly of *Lilith* (1895). Streaks of visual realism reveal not the expected but aspects of the supernatural—a flashlight picking out sharp details in the darkness on the far side of the mirror.[7]

At times the novel is stagey—particularly when it goes farther back, into Tudor times, though even there it's vivid and fun. At other times the subtlety of reasoning delights: the oldest joys of SF are captured in such moments, when the mind is twisted out of its mundane course of thought:

> Suddenly a thought struck him. My God, he thought, then if I stay and live out my life as Ashbless—which the universe pretty clearly means me to do—then *nobody wrote Ashbless' poems.* I'll copy out his poems from memory, having read them in the 1932 *Collected Poems,* and my copies will be set in type for the magazines, and they'll use tear sheets from the magazines to assemble the *Collected Poems!* They're a closed loop, uncreated! I'm just the . . . messenger and caretaker. (Chapter 10)

Doyle, a specialist in the Romantic poets, takes a group of "tourists" back to see a lecture by Samuel Taylor Coleridge, and gets stranded in 1810 with Coleridge and a duplicate of Lord Byron. In the course of the plot he *becomes* the poet he studied for his dissertation, William Ashbless. But he is not the only person from our present back in that year. One of the most delightful and understated moments of the book is when Doyle, walking down a rough-cast road in the London of 1810, hears someone nearby whistling Lennon and McCartney's "Yesterday". Body-changers, golems (*ka*), devils and dark gods tramp the pages of this novel, making it seem some kind of garish fantasy—Coleridge's drug dream (a humorous moment near the end of the novel makes this connection overt)—but its form, its intellectual structure, is purest science fiction.

The Anubis Gates is a deeply considered work. Powers has taken the trouble time and again to consider the implications of the things he is describing. This is why the book lives on more than the one level of simple adventure. He invests each scene, each character, with vivid life: complex, oft confused, but concentrated life. He neatly resolves the time paradoxes and convincingly conjures up the London of 1810. Powers began publishing SF back in 1976, with two novels in Roger Elwood's Laser Books series, *The Skies Discrowned* (rewritten as *Forsake the Sky* (1986)) and *Epitaph in Rust*, neither of them exceptional in any respect. A fantasy, *The Drawing of the Dark* (1979) showed greater promise, but it was only with *The Anubis Gates* that Powers won critical attention.

Dinner at Deviant's Palace (1985) is Powers's most recent work, set in a post-holocaust LA. Once again it's something of a phantasmagoria, though far more recognizably SF than *The Anubis Gates*. The novel was eight years in the writing, it appears, and gives no real indication of where Powers's work might be heading, but its richness, and the richness of *The Anubis Gates*, suggest that Tim Powers is a writer to treasure.

Lucius Shepard has appeared in the magazines with an almost Silverbergian regularity since "Solitario's Eyes" (1983), and a number of his stories have been nominated for awards. His stories move between SF, horror and fantasy, never clearly one or the other, and most of his work is set in the more "colourful" parts of this world—Central and South America, the Caribbean, Spain. Much of it is contemporary or very near future. Little hardware is involved. What machines there are peripheral—gates for other powers. There seems little chance, then, that Shepard will ever become an *Analog* writer. Sometimes he'll even break the cardinal rules, as in "A Spanish Lesson" (1985), where he provides a moral after the story: and for once it works.

One of Shepard's finest stories to date is "Salvador" (1984), with its vivid writing. Dantzler, a soldier fighting in El Salvador, takes special drugs which harden his resolve and sharpen his senses, but he grows addicted and begins to abuse them. The story sinks into a realm of primal forces—into darkness, evil and the world of spirits, reminiscent of Greene and Conrad. And when Dantzler is returned to the civilized world he behaves much like the 'Nam veterans of a generation before. We realize that this is not a story about drug-assisted warfare—the usual SF slant—but about "the organized pretence", as Shepard calls it, of being a man.

Shepard, like the *Galaxy* writers of the fifties, is very critical of the more blindly consumerist aspects of American society. America for him is "the land of silk and money, of mindfuck video games and topless tennis matches and fast-food solutions to the nutritional problem". This attribute runs counter to the wave of patriotic sentimentality affecting new writers like Connie Willis.

Shepard's only novel so far is *Green Eyes* (1984). Its southern states and swampland settings, its successful experiments to raise the dead, and its CIA conspiracy background, might make it seem anything but promising material. Shepard links and illuminates these mundane, almost clichéd elements in impressive fashion. Donnell Harrison and Jocundra Verret, experimental subject and attendant, run away from the Shadows, the sinister study centre, while Harrison tries to find what his true purpose is as a resurrectee. His unusual gifts—particularly his peculiar vision and his superb intelligence—have been activated by a special virus in his brain. He is dying even as his life flares brightly once again. In this sense *Green Eyes* is a work in the tradition of "Flowers For Algernon" and *Camp Concentration*. In other regards it is a novel with a distinctive voice. Shepard's subtleties sometimes blossom into scenes of vividness and power. One such is when the escaping Harrison usurps the role of a faith-healer and, in the middle of his crowded tent, turns to face the crowd of faithful, his virus-ridden luminous green eyes revealed:

> He looked up. The tent had been magicked into a cavernous black drape ornamented with silver arabesques and folds, furnished with silver-limned chairs, and congregated by ebony demons. Prisms whirled inside the bodies of most, masked the faces of others with glittering analogues of human features; and in the case of two, no, three, one standing where Papa Salvatino had been, the prisms flowed through an intricate circuitry, seeming to illuminate the patterns of their nerves and muscles, forming into molten droplets at their fingertips and detonating in needle-thin beams of iridescent light, which spat through the crowd. Yet for all their fearsome appearance, the majority of them edged away from the stage, huddling together. Curious, Donnell held up his hand to his face, but saw nothing, not even the outline of his fingers.
>
> Jocundra, a gemmy mask overlaying her features, knelt beside him and pressed the cane into his hand. The instant she touched him, his vision normalized and his head began to throb. . . .
>
> They were more alien to him now than their previous appearance of ebony flesh and jewelled expressions had been. Lumpy and malformed; protruding bellies, gaping mouths, drooping breasts; clad in all manner of dull cloth; they might have been a faded mural commemorating the mediocrity and impermanence of their lives. Wizened faces topped by frumpy hats; dewy, pubescent faces waxed to a hard gloss with makeup; plump, choleric faces. And each of these faces was puckered or puffed up around a black seed of fear. As he looked them over one by one, bits of intelligence lodged in his thoughts, and he knew them for bad-tempered old men, vapid old women, thankless children, shrewish wives, brutal husbands. But the complications of their lives were only a facade erected to conceal the black ground which bubbled them up. (Chapter 10)

This doubled way of seeing things—both mystical and real—is the very tone of Shepard's writing. *Green Eyes* opens us to this way of perception. Like so many of the stories—perhaps most like "A Traveller's Tale" (1984)—it achieves a lucidity which is in itself a form of magic. One senses in him, as in Crowley, the power to revivify, perhaps even to transform utterly, the genre materials to which we have become accustomed.

Less revolutionary in her approach, but impressive nonetheless, is Octavia Butler. Recently she has been receiving awards for her shorter fiction[8], but she has been a writer to watch since her first novel, *Patternmaster*, was published in 1976.

Most of Butler's work has been at novel length, in a series she has called "Patternists". A protegé of Samuel R. Delany, Butler shares Delany's preference for the more fantastic themes of SF, presenting them within a realistic framework. The Patternists are an elite strain of human beings who have developed psionic powers. *Patternmaster* presents us with a far future Earth structured to accommodate these new powers. In subsequent novels Butler chose a more difficult task than most—not content to set further adventures in the same environment, she began to trace the origins and development of her envisaged society. *Mind of my Mind* (1977), a more impressive novel than her first, began this process.

Survivor (1978) uses the Patternist culture as a backdrop for a separate story and—as is often the case with such series—proved a more enjoyable and comprehensible novel if you had read the first two. Butler's elitist Patternists and mutant Clayarks, her chameleon-like aliens and other exotic elements cluttered a simple storyline and weakened the novel. She may have sensed this, for her next novel, *Kindred* (1979), moved out of the sequence. *Kindred* is the story of a young contemporary black woman who is jolted back in time and space to the old pre-Civil War Southern States. This direct confrontation with the issues of racism and sexism (Octavia Butler is young and black) proved far more satisfactory, and revealed many of Butler's strengths as a writer. .

About the question of disguised themes. SF metaphor can prove a most effective way of dramatizing a contemporary issue. Yet if a writer chooses not merely to dramatize the issue in this way, but to create a fully-functional and realistic environment—a workable social system—this somewhat changes the situation. The matter becomes less metaphorical, more a logical extension of a fantasy. SF has always thrived on such extensions but rarely questioned them. Private worlds, meticulously-detailed, abound in the genre.

Psi powers relate to nothing *real* in human experience, unless it be a means of reflecting on human limitations—Silverberg's main use of telepathy, for instance, is to this end, to emphasize human isolation and alienation. In *More Than Human*, Theodore Sturgeon uses telepathy as means of illuminating for us the fate of social freaks and outcasts, to make us empathize with them. Telepathy is not all the book is about, though it is a convincing and exciting subject in Sturgeon's hands. It is when the metaphor is set centre stage, itself the subject of the story, that difficulties arise.

What then of Octavia Butler's Patternist culture, as fully envisaged as it is? There is a degree of reflection and illumination in these novels, particularly in the finest of them, *Wild Seed* (1980), but one experiences a certain reluctance in accepting a realistic, fully-realized society based on such a phantasm. In too many places Butler's scheme relates to nothing in the human condition. Only where it touches us with the force of metaphor does it convince.

Wild Seed we take as an exception to the above. David Pringle has called it "some unholy cross between *Roots* and *Wuthering Heights*"[9]. It is hard to better that description.

In the later *Clay's Ark* (1984), Butler attempted to fill in further background to the development of the Patternist Culture. The novel deals with the return of the starship *Clay's Ark* and the plague it carries which mutates humans. Here is the genesis of the Clayarks of the "later" novels. But *Clay's Ark* is somehow less convincing than its predecessors; perhaps because it takes the disguise—the science fictional metaphor—as a reality in its own right. The story means little outside of the "Patternist" sequence. It becomes a slice of private world, simple genre SF, meaning nothing beyond itself. It might be argued that there is nothing wrong with that, but it does seem a misdirection of Butler's obvious talents. *Kindred* and *Wild Seed* are revelatory, *Clay's Ark* is a confection by comparison.

It is important to note this distinction. As Dick realized in writing *Valis*, to begin to believe in the disguise and not in what the disguise means is to embrace a delusory system—pure fantasy. *Clay's Ark*, for all its "realism", is only fantasy. It is a lesser work than *Wild Seed*, lacking a dimension.

Back in the fifties psi powers and mutations in the human stock were often related to post-holocaust scenarios; and even before then, psionics, acceptable to John W. Campbell, was a popular theme. In the modern genre psi powers and post-holocaust Earths have gone their separate ways. For most modern writers psi powers seem un-scientific and unreal. They prefer the wasteland—smouldering or otherwise—to be peopled with humans, not radioactive ghouls and beasties. Yet how many critics or writers have challenged the validity of a post-holocaust scenario? Back in the forties and fifties—even as late as the seventies, perhaps—it was possible to believe that the human race could survive a nuclear war. From what we have learned since then of the effects of even a limited war—using only a tenth of the Superpowers' capacity—we realize that the bleakest science fiction scenario of the outcome is extremely optimistic. Perhaps the most realistic post-holocaust novel would be a massive tome containing nothing but blank pages, frost-hardened and charred at the edges. Even so, SF writers persist in presenting us with ruralized versions of the USA after the Bomb.

If, as it seems, there is no realistic possibility of a post-Bomb civilization, what does the recent spate of post-nuclear scenarios represent? The Bomb has become a popular subject once again, after years of public indifference, and TV films like *The Day After*, *Testament* and *Special Report* have increased popular consciousness of the nuclear threat. These films vividly personalize the issues; yet while that is often an effective way of conveying a potential situation, nuclear war cannot be personalized. If it ever happens it will not be about small groups struggling to survive in the wild. The reality is billions of tons of muck in the upper atmosphere, cutting off the sun's rays for years: nuclear winter and the death of countless species of fauna and flora, mankind probably among them. The effective sterilization of Earth, if the worst of the scenarios offered are to be believed.

Two novelists currently earning praise are John Calvin Batchelor and James Morrow. Batchelor's second novel, *The Birth of the People's Republic of Antarctica* (1983) is set in 1995 with the Western World finally coming apart at the seams. It is the story of Grim Fiddle, a young Swede who becomes part of a vast sea-borne Odyssey south, a "Fleet of the Damned". The book is a vivid account of

necessity confronting the realities of social collapse. The death of the West
proves a painful, ugly process. Not for Batchelor the escapism of easy adventure
and wish-fulfilment. Like Conrad he seeks the darker side of Man and stares it
squarely in the face.

James Morrow's *The Wine of Violence* (1982) was presented to the reading
public as "a science fiction fable". Its fantastic, divided world of Quetzalia
certainly bears no relationship to our own, yet we recognize the powerful
metaphor at its heart and see the truth of our own divided selves mirrored back
at us: its Jekyll and Hyde societies, separated by the river of liquefied hate,
represent aspects of us. It's an amusing novel, too. As is *The Continent of Lies*
(1984), an intricate excursion between reality and fiction rather like John
McGahern's *The Pornographer* (1979). Morrow takes risks, particularly with his
readers' credulity.

Morrow's third novel, *This is the Way the World Ends* (1986) is a savagely
tender fable, its subject matter clearly spelt out in its title. The worst happens,
the bombs fall and the Earth dies. But before the curtain falls, six survivors are
taken to Antarctica and put to trial by the Unadmitted—the inhabitants of a
future which never happened because of mankind's collective insanity.

There are elements of Swiftian satire and Carrollian logic inversion in
Morrow's writing, yet what is primarily at work in *This is the Way* . . . is a
concerned American middle-class sensibility. George Paxton, our Everyman
figure in the novel, is forced to confront the whole question of nuclear
brinkmanship and find himself guilty by reason of neglect. Yet what ought to
have been sharp-teethed satirical condemnation is somehow watered down in
the lengthy trial scene. Morrow tries hard to be neither hawk nor dove and in
empathizing with those who have actively created the atmosphere of hostility
and suspicion he blunts the edge of his satire. This said, the novel is intelligent,
humorous and at times deeply moving, steering just a fraction clear of
sentimentality in its depiction of George's 4-year-old child, Holly, lost in the
Holocaust.

Morrow is a lyrical, inventive writer who shows signs of becoming a major
talent. It is easy to imagine that with the right theme he will produce something
not merely significant—*This is the Way*. . . is undoubtedly a significant addition
to the debate on the arms race and its layers of doublethink—but genuinely
great. Time will tell.

Significant. What do we mean by that in the context of a science fiction novel?
Significant in what respect? That it makes us think of something in a new light?
Partly that. That it makes us feel something about a situation where previously
we expressed indifference? That also. Both are true of Suzette Haden Elgin's
Native Tongue (1984).

> That was very good, they thought. It showed that she did understand. She
> had a scrap of knowledge here, a scrap there . . . enough to know that
> Encodings were precious. The little girls heard the stories at their mothers'
> knees, when their mothers had time to tell them, and from the women of

the Barren Houses otherwise. How women, in the long ago time when women could vote and be doctors and fly spaceships—a fantasy world for those girlchildren, as fabulous and glittering as any tale of castles and dragons—how women, even then, had begun the first slow gropings toward a language of their own.

The tales were told again and again, and embroidered lovingly with detail; and prominent in their ornament were the jewels of the Encodings. *A word for a perception that had never had a word of its own before.* Major Encodings, the most precious because they were truly newborn to the universe of discourse. Minor Encodings, which always came in the wake of a Major one, because it would bring to mind related concepts that could be lexicalized on the same pattern, still valuable. "A woman who gives an Encoding to other women is a woman of valor, and all women are in her debt forevermore." (Chapter 13)

Native Tongue is the story of Nazareth Joanna Chornyak Adiness, an alien linguist who gives a whole series of Major Encodings to her fellow women, and in effect single-handedly creates the basis of a native tongue, *Láadan*, for the women of her time. Set two hundred years or so from now, *Native Tongue* depicts a world in which all of the advances made by women in respect of civil rights have been reversed. For all that it is a world of starships and aliens, it is a curiously nineteenth-century world. Elgin loads the dice heavily against the males in this novel, yet one senses a fairness even in that. Her purpose is to draw an extreme situation—an exaggeration of our own. The males we encounter are smug, arrogant, self-satisfied and convinced that their females are good only for breeding, housework and translation duties (the last grudgingly admitted from necessity—there prove to be too many alien groups requiring translators).

Why should women *need* a language of their own? Why is the language we have insufficient for their needs? In posing and answering these questions Elgin's novel is significant, for, in its deliberately exaggerated fashion, it makes us feel how cruel the masculinity of language is.

One major dissatisfaction with *Native Tongue* concerns its ending. What is foreseen is a fragmentation of society into separate male and female enclaves, each serving its own purposes alone. As with so many feminist SF novels of its ilk, we may applaud its diagnosis but find its solution unacceptable. We cannot isolate the sexes. Or rather, we can, but we must look at the *likely* results, not at some theoretical ideal.

A novel like *Native Tongue*, through its exaggerations, examines the problem of cultural stereotyping. That done, we do not wish to establish new stereotypes in their place. We say this recognizing that much feminist SF differs in kind from other SF in that it has a directly political purpose beyond SF's occasional proselytizing zeal. We might set Le Guin's *The Dispossessed* against *Native Tongue* as an instance of a novel which does look at both the pros and cons of its utopian theory by placing living human beings into that blueprint and seeing how they fare—not merely as political cyphers but as people.

The separatist movement in SF—that part of feminist SF that seeks, in its fictions, to separate off the sexes—is a form of over-reaction founded in suspicion and hostility—in the fear that unless we segregate we might return to the bad old power balance detrimental to the female. It is understandable, but it must be countered. And in fact was countered in Kit Reed's elegant 1974 story, "Songs of War".

Would an all-woman society be less oppressive, less aggressively competitive, more peaceful and cooperative? And in arguing this are we also then arguing that aggression and oppression are purely masculine traits? The one seems to follow from the other, yet sets up another cultural stereotype. It attempts to blame males for all the ill and praise females for all the good. Simple experience and observation of the human animal says this isn't so. Both sexes have a share in virtues and vices, and in the same genetic material shaped by an unrelenting environment. To argue otherwise is to set up a cartoon in place of the complex reality.

But feminist SF is not only about separatism, it raises many issues: the demand for individual autonomy; the problem of child indoctrination and child-rearing; the riddle of linguistic expression of special areas of experience. Many of these issues, presently in the feminist domain, will eventually be seen as purely humanistic problems. The demand for individual autonomy within society is a problem for the majority of humankind, regardless of gender. The questions of child-bearing, child-rearing and child-indoctrination are more fundamental to the sexual issue, yet there are solutions other than the communalism proposed by so many feminist SF novels.[10] For instance, the hideous solution offered in *Brave New World*. But do we want that either?

Returning specifically to Elgin's *Native Tongue*, we use this as an instance because it seems to contain both the best and worst traits of feminist SF as it now exists. Scenes like the disposal of Michaela's child and her subsequent (and emotionally justifiable) murder of her husband, and the pitiless treatment of Nazareth when she has to have her breasts removed, make us feel strongly. Yet it must be said that we feel *as humans* for another suffering person, not because Michaela and Nazareth are on our gender "team". The strength of feeling in both scenes comes from a justifiable anger at patriarchal stupidity, however, and we must recognize that such stupidity still exists, despite the slow erosion of "sexist" patterns in our lifetimes. In this sense feminist SF does a good job in reminding us of what we might otherwise overlook.

Speculative fiction has, in general, benefited from the introduction of feminist themes and concerns, yet, like many forms of radical socialism, feminism itself often demands a simplistic choice—you are either with them wholly, or against them.

Gender oppression—oppression in social, economic, psychological, sexual, political and linguistic terms—has been a concern of novelist Doris Lessing for more than two decades. Her novel, *The Golden Notebook* (1962), became a bible for sectors of the Women's Liberation movement. It is not for her trail-breaking work as a feminist that we come to her now, but as one of the most interesting SF writers of the eighties.

Lessing is a major novelist and works infrequently in SF, but it is wholly unfair to say of her, as Octavia Butler is reported to have done at the 1984 LACon, that she takes "a clichéd SF plot and write(s) a bestseller". Such resentment from within the field is misguided and misinformed. Lessing has a far better understanding of the uses of SF metaphor than Butler; and has, incidentally, published seven novels which are recognizably SF, beginning with *Briefing for a Descent into Hell* (1971). *Memoirs of a Survivor* followed in 1974, depicting the collapse of the West from what might, in retrospect, be seen to be a magical realist perspective. Lessing's attraction to Sufism surfaces in both novels.

Of greater significance is the sequence of five novels produced between 1979 and 1983. *Canopus in Argos: Archives*.

Lessing is a writer in the tradition of Wells, Huxley and Stapledon. There is the same sense in her work of the future as a reflection of the present—as *metaphor* for some present state of mankind. Yet Lessing's life experience—as a young woman growing up in Africa—makes her work distinct from those writers. She is less cerebral, more visionary. Visionary, that is, not simply in providing us with vast perspectives of time and space, but in creating in us a sense of a multi-dimensional cosmos, of worlds alien to our senses. She is a mystic.

Two mighty Galactic Empires, one—Canopus—spiritual, one—Sirius—technological, are interested in the degenerate planet Shikasta, once a paradise world called Rohanda. Shikasta is Earth, a spiritual wasteland in the final throes of its civilized existence. Agents from Canopus and Sirius walk its surface and witness stages in its development and decay.

This description makes the Canopus sequence seem not so very different from Asimov's *Foundation* series, where two different forces—psychological and technological—struggle to control the galaxy for its own good. Both sequences chart a kind of fall into barbarism, but all such comparisons are superficial. For all its talk of Gaia, Asimov's galaxy lacks all levels but the material, whereas the very essence of Lessing's cosmos is that it operates on several levels—in six zones of experience, in fact—only one of which is accessible to humankind in an unawakened state. Indeed, one might see the purpose of *Canopus* as a metaphysical consciousness-raising exercise. Lessing is drawing spiritual ley-lines for us to follow.[11]

The history of Shikasta parallels the Biblical story of the Fall of Man and the expulsion from Eden, but Lessing's is no simple Adam and Eve story dwelling on guilt and free will. Hers is a very modern, almost existentialist version and depicts not disobedience but a loss of harmony and balance; a pantheist's vision of the Fall, but with a very Von Daniken-like twist. Man, it seems, was an experiment in accelerated evolution which went wrong.

If Lessing's use of familiar materials is eccentric (one might also say inspired) it works because of its realistic context, presenting the metaphysical states as solid actualities and not as mere dreams. Johor and Ambien II, the agents of the two great Empires, are not indifferent spirits commenting from afar on Man, but are actors in Man's drama. They are also connected to the other Zones. Lessing allows us a very real sense of those other zones, crowding close, like the alternate worlds in a Keith Laumer novel but somehow more tangible. A shadowland of otherness with a concrete existence of its own. In the first novel, *Shikasta* (1979), these zones are only glimpsed or briefly passed through, but in the second, *The Marriages Between Zones Three, Four and Five* (1980), Lessing creates these realms of otherness in some detail, dramatizing their relationship through the marriage of Al*Ith, the Queen of Zone Three, to Ben Ata, the soldier-King of Zone Four. Their marriage is at one and the same time a fable and a very human reality.

What do the Zones represent? States of spiritual refinement perhaps, for our passage down the Zones towards Zone Six, Shikasta, is a journey into coarseness and barbarism, whereas our movement up the Zones towards Zone Two is a journey into the empyrean:

> "And what is Zone Two like?" he enquired.
>
> "You know more about our Zone than I can tell you about *there*. All I can say is that you stand and gaze and look, and never have enough of it. It is as if you looked at blue mists—or waters or—but it is blue, blue, you've never seen such a blue. . . ."

Our sense of a living cosmos grows stronger with each novel in the sequence, as does our understanding of Lessing's purpose. The third novel, *The Sirian Experiments* (1981) reveals something of the plans of Canopus to raise the backward Sirian Empire to its own high spiritual level. And, of course, we would be slow not to recognize that it is our own arrogance as a species—our own erroneous belief in the advanced, sophisticated and civilized nature of contemporary humanity—in progress—that is the real target for Lessing's space fiction.

The five novels of the *Canopus* sequence[12] represent something unique in SF, and not merely because they are the work of one of the world's finest writers. They formulate an extensive and complex portrait of a philosophy (perhaps a theosophy); a concrete rendering of the intangible familiar to SF readers, yet here of an impossible actuality rather than a possible unreality. *Canopus* is, to be more succinct, more than a game of conceptual breakthrough, it is a statement of spiritual potential.

Another modern literary figure who has been influenced by and has in turn influenced SF is the Argentinian writer, Jorge Luis Borges.

Born in Buenos Aires in 1899, Borges was bilingual from childhood and assimilated a great deal of English literature. Brought up in a bookish household (his father was a novelist), he began writing at six. Chief amongst his influences were Wells, Chesterton, Valéry (in turn influenced by Poe) and, later, Kafka.

Borges's first volume of poetry was published when he was only 24, but the work for which he will primarily be remembered is his *Ficciones* (1944, translated as *Fictions*, 1962).

From 1927 onwards Borges struggled against encroaching blindness. As a result a tendency in his work towards brevity was reinforced. His stories and essays are concise, cut almost to the bone, and yet resonant in the manner of poetry. Their richness make them seem like diagrams for novels. The accent in Borges's work is upon the idea, not character, though sometimes, as in "Funes, the Memorious", the two are indistinguishable.

"Funes" is a perfect example of Borges's craft—of what makes his work so appealing to the SF reader even as it transcends genre cliché. Funes is a boy with total recall—a device frequently used in SF. But where Borges's tale differs is in its intellectual stringency. Borges is not content to toy with the idea but pushes it to the limits. What does total recall imply? What are the practical and philosophical implications of such a condition?

Perfect, total recall—it sounds an amazing, wonderful gift. The kind of thing one of van Vogt's supermen might have just for starters. But for Funes it is an intolerable burden:

> He was, let us not forget, almost incapable of ideas of a general platonic sort. Not only was it difficult for him to comprehend that the generic symbol 'dog' embraces so many unlike individuals of diverse size and form. . . .

Funes's life is the cumulative and unbearable weight of re-lived experience (of taste, touch, sound, sight and smell, all in the smallest detail). It cripples him. It prevents him from living.

Such a way of taking an idea and pushing it to its ultimate is distinctly science fictional, but rarely has it been done with such rigour. In "The Library of Babel" he gives us a library which is the philosophical reflection of our physical universe, infinite in size. And within the library are an infinite number of books, combining twenty-five symbols in an infinity of random ways. Most books contain nothing but nonsense. Some contain an odd word, a sentence. Very few are whole, complete. In its infinite rooms, amongst its infinite shelves, Inquisitors work patiently, looking for the single volume that will make sense of it all. A better metaphorical description of the scientific quest has not been penned.

In "Tlön, Uqbar, Orbis Tertius" Borges describes how scholars create an alternate world on paper and release details of it to a credulous world by means of an encyclopedia. What Borges posited as fiction we see, in smaller form, happening daily in the SF field!

One might go on itemizing the riches of Borges's work, but let these instances suffice. Borges is the master of the intellectual puzzle, playfully breaking down the barriers between the real and the fictional. His death, on June 14th 1986, as this volume was in final preparation, leaves the world poorer. His blindness forced him to look inward and dream, but his intellect questioned the nature of his dreams. What resulted was a perfect fusion of the Wellsian and Burroughsian poles expounded earlier in this volume. Writers like Robert Silverberg have openly stated the influence Borges had on them, in making them look again at commonplace genre materials.

Many other writers, some popular, some obscure, are currently working the SF seam. Somtow Sucharitkul we've already mentioned in passing. His flair for invention and delightful humour are in evidence in several novels about the Inquestors. Julian May, a name from the fifties, has returned with a four volume epic of the near future and the distant past, her *Saga of the Exiles*, which began with *The Many-Coloured Land* in 1981. William John Watkins (not to be confused with the Walter Jon Williams of *Ambassador of Progress* (1984)) has produced an interesting, quirky novel with *The Centrifugal Rickshaw Dancer* (1985), while that old giant of TV astronomy, Carl Sagan, has given us the bulky *Contact* (1985) for our edification. *First* contact is its theme.

Sharon Baker's *Quarreling, They Met the Dragon* (1984) was badly presented, with a misleading title and rotten cover art. In consequence, it has received less than its deserved attention. There are no dragons. The planet Naphar is a sleazy particle in a galactic empire. People come in various sizes and the central figure is a young male prostitute, Senruh. It is hardly a traditional theme. Baker says—it's a good polemical point—that she has invented as little as possible; the result is a considered originality.

Emprise (1985) is the first novel from another new writer, Michael P. Kube-McDowell, and the first volume in the "Trigon Disunity". Set early in the next century it depicts the collapse of the West and the coming of the aliens. *Enigma*, the second volume, followed in 1986. Other American writers, too, have independent thoughts, or pursue a career which runs against the commercial current. Ed Bryant is an elusive writer, much concerned with the effects of civilization on the human psyche. His collection of related short stories, *Cinnabar* (1976), has already been mentioned. A graduate of the University of Wyoming, Bryant later produced a collection of science-fantasies entitled *Wyoming Sun* (1980), set in that state, of which the most haunting is "Strata", where the landscape carries a memory of the ancient sea which once covered it.

Born in the same year as Bryant, George Zebrowski has acquired a name as an editor and anthologist. His first novel, *The Omega Point* (1972), was well-received, but the later, more ambitious, *Macrolife* (1980) passed largely unnoticed. No higher praise could be offered than to say that *Macrolife* is almost Stapledonian in its approach to the subject of man in the galaxy. The bullish mood engendered by the success of *Star Wars* perhaps told against more thoughtful work.

Kit Reed has always had a thoughtful and humorous approach to the medium. Her first novel, *Armed Camps* (1969) uses a spiky prose to describe the collapse of the USA, but Reed is much more successful in a more domestic vein, and at short story length. Most of her fictions have appeared in *F&SF*. Her shrewd humour and a kind of deflationary common sense, which run side-by-side with a dragon-free sense of fantasy, have won her not a wide audience but a small devoted following. Each decade sees a good Reed collection: *Mister da V and Other Stories* (1967), *The Killer Mice* (1976), and *The Revenge of the Senior Citizens* ⋆⋆ *Plus* (1986) are all worth seeking out. Her non-SF novels are also enjoyable.

Charles Grant has presented the genre with many well-crafted stories over the past decade and several attractive novels, *The Ravens of the Moon* (1978) amongst them. His horror orientation has won him a strong personal following. Michael Shea is another writer working the borderlands of SF and horror, with novels like *Nifft the Lean* (1982). Other names appearing with some regularity in the magazines are Timothy Zahn, Charles Sheffield, Connie Willis, Michael Swanwick and George Alec Effinger.

From West Germany comes publisher and writer Wolfgang Jeschke, whose novel *The Last Days of Creation* ventures 5.3 million years into the past for a war between the superpowers over oil. Other nations have their own thriving internal scene—Japan and France especially—but have had little influence as yet on the mainstream of science fiction.

Of recent years, Australia has made some attempt to spread the renown of its native SF writers abroad. Of course, such attempts have not come from any official literary body but rather from within the body of SF fandom itself, as usual; although the University of Queensland Press, which has been active in this respect, has received assistance from the Literature Board of the Australia Council.

This Press has issued a good introduction to the scene down under in *Australian Science Fiction* (1982), edited and introduced by Van Ikin. As well as an historical section, which reminds us that utopian dreams struggled to exist everywhere last century, and not least in Joseph Fraser's *Melbourne and Mars: My Mysterious Life on Two Planets* (1889), the anthology includes several well-known modern writers.

Lee Harding's anthology, *Beyond Tomorrow* (1967) was a successful attempt to publish Australian authors alongside English and American ones. Harding's fiction is often concerned with another ambiguous world, gradually perceived; these concerns lend distinction to both *Displaced Person* (1979) and the haunting *Waiting for the End of the World* (1983).

More modernist in his approach is Damien Broderick. His *The Dreaming Dragons* (1980) is playful in tone, as is the more complex *Transmitters* (1984). *Transmitters* takes as its text a statement of Robert Scholes, "Now we know that fiction is about other fiction, is criticism in fact, or meta-fiction." Its sub-title, *An Imaginary Documentary 1969–1984*, conceals the fact that it relates, in a sort of a way, the tortured life of a fanzine editor. Stuffed with fannish references, *Transmitters* is something of a tour de force, as if Sheckley had decided to rewrite Ballard in the manner of Italo Calvino. Or vice versa. Perhaps the book was inspired by one of its dedicatees, Bruce Gillespie, whose fanzine, *SF Commentary*, began publication in 1969, and contained chunks of Gillespie's (and his readers') private lives cheek-by-jowl with the criticism.

George Turner is more iconoclastic, and a critic as well as a novelist. His novel, *Beloved Son* (1978) is an ambitious future-world novel, heavily built and argumentative in tone. Its sequels, *Vaneglory* (1981) and *Yesterday's Men* (1983), while distinguished by some interesting passages on war, were less of a success.

Van Ikin discerns a drift towards fantasy in Australian SF, which shows the Australians following a world trend. Peter Carey, author of *The Fat Man in History* (1974), and *Illywhacker* (1985) may be regarded as a fantasist. It can scarcely be denied that Australia's most distinguished author, Nobel Prize-winning Patrick White, came close to a science-fictional vein in *A Fringe of Leaves* (1976), the story of an encounter between two alien races, English and Aborigine, in the Australia of the 1840s. It is one of the most sensuous and memorable of modern novels.

Margaret Atwood, a Canadian author, is enjoying wide success with *The Handmaid's Tale* (1986). Our world has sunk below the horizon and a totalitarian state prevails, in which women are breeders and slaves. Offred, the handmaid, tells a sombre story, shot with wit, which is the more impressive for being offered in a prosaic style, without sensationalism.

Back in the British literary scene, another prominent figure using SF metaphor in her own distinct manner is Angela Carter, to whom the magical realism label has been attached. It's an uncomfortable label to append to works like *Heroes and Villains* (1969), whose post-nuclear war scenario is so grotesquely distorted and presented that it is nearer hallucination than any form of realism. Angela Carter writes on the edge, a gothic with a huge G. Little of her work is as overtly science fictional as *Heroes and Villains*. The greater part is borderline fantasy; a surrealistic looking-glass of images and characters vividly portrayed. In the eighties she is presenting her best work, like the accomplished and entertaining *Nights at the Circus* (1984).

Two remarkable pillars of the English scene help to support a fairly ruinous situation.

Although J. G. Ballard may appear superficially in danger of repeating himself, his desiccated urban technologies, in which soiled human lives are no more than transitory landmarks, gain in power by compulsive cross-referencing.

The sado-masochism of *Crash* was not to everyone's taste, even to those who relish a general *Schadenfreude* in most of Ballard's work; but the overall precision of that work, the sybilline quality of the imagery, have rendered his position among contemporary writers unique and unassailable. His influence on younger writers may have been damaging: but no man is responsible for his imitators. Since publication of *The Drowned World* and *The Terminal Beach*, now over a quarter of a century ago, the mere existence of J. G. Ballard—rather like the existence of Jorge Luis Borges, who died in June, 1986—has been an inspiration to other writers to write sense and write it well—and, of course, to defy what "the market" says it is politic to write.

A Russian critic, V. Gopman, in a remarkable survey of current English literature (which, owing to the British class structure, could have no exact English equivalent), sums up a consideration of Ballard's achievement in these words: "The evolution in Ballard's writing is not simply the seekings of an artist, not simply an advance from traditional science fiction to science fiction of a new type, but is a process of his social and civic maturity, for in his work he raises one of the main ethical problems of our epoch."[13]

Ballard's old *eminence grise* from *New Worlds* days, Michael Moorcock, has greatly enlarged his scope during the last decade, in the face of only grudging recognition. Putting the over-worked Jerry Cornelius behind him, he established in *Gloriana* (1978) an amazing Jacobean alternative world, a great zyme of a novel, well described by Peter Nicholls as a masque, and part of Moorcock's mask.[14] A great deal of Moorcock's various work may be briefly designated as chaos barely contained within a framework of irony. This reductive formulation applies less to *Gloriana*—which aims at a squalid gorgeousness—than to what was to follow: a magnum opus with few parallels.

Prodigal as ever, Moorcock has embarked on a massive chronicle of the twentieth century, which, commencing when the century does, represents an endeavour before which even Edward Gibbon might have quailed. This imposing major variation on a theme of decline and fall so far encompasses *Byzantium Endures* (1981) and *The Laughter of Carthage* (1984). The ironies of history are enfolded within the turbulent memories of Colonel Pyat. Pyat, Moorcock's crazed narrator, now living in Westbourne Grove in London, is a rebarbative creature whose egotism alerts us to mistrust what we read. Various set-pieces, such as the portrait of Odessa in pre-revolutionary times, the dissolution of Petrograd, and the bustle of a youthful America, are detailed and remarkable. The ever-amazing Moorcock is creating one of the most amazing novels of the eighties.

Like Ballard, Moorcock must be admired for his independence of mind. Where he triumphs—and has done for many years—is in his ability always to produce good new work. It can be said of him, as of few other writers connected with SF, that his latest writing is both his most surprising and his best.

Otherwise, it must be admitted, British SF was in retreat in the eighties. Many publishers who previously supported SF lists—Faber, Hutchinson, Dobson, Hale—dropped them. No new anthology series took up from where *New Worlds* and *New Writings in SF* had left off. Only *Interzone*, a pallid successor of *New Worlds*, biased towards the metafictional aspect of SF, played host to new writing.

In such a climate it is hardly surprising that few new writers appeared in the eighties. Among them are Mary Gentle, Gwyneth Jones, Phillip Mann, Christopher Evans and David Langford. British publishers were looking to the USA for new material and new writers. Established authors like D. G. Compton, Garry Kilworth and Christopher Priest were unable to find wider popular acclaim. British SF was dying of cold. Many writers—including some of the above—took to writing fantasy and horror as much out of discouragement as out of temperament.

An untypical and admirable attempt to look into the future and over the next thousand years is *The Third Millennium: A History of the World: AD 2000–3000* (1985). The authors, Brian Stableford and David Langford, are both well-known in their own fields, Stableford being an active critic and historian of the SF field, Langford a nuclear physicist, and both with previous novels to their credit. Their book is presented as an album, coming complete with photographs, diagrams, and figures, in an optimistic coverage of future world affairs. The critic W. Warren Wagar has compared it with H. G. Wells's *The Shape of Things to Come.*

Alasdair Gray could hardly be called a newcomer—or indeed even a SF writer—but his *Lanark* (1981), which homes in on the dark heart of Glasgow, is certainly one of the great rumbustious fantasies of the eighties. *1982 Janine* continues the good black Scottish humour. Somewhat similarly, Russell Hoban is neither a newcomer nor a SF writer, but *Riddley Walker* (1980), telling of a broken-down post-nuclear future in a broken-down language, captured many imaginations. It was performed as a play in 1986.

Among the newcomers, Mary Gentle showed herself an acolyte of Ursula Le Guin with her *Golden Witchbreed* (1983), a minor best-seller about an envoy encountering a complex, apparently devolved alien race. Her depiction of the world of Orthe is vividly imagined and subtly observed. The textures of *Golden Witchbreed* are fantastic but its substance is acutely realistic. Gwyneth Jones's first adult novel, *Divine Endurance* (1984) was a complex near future tale set in the far east. A difficult, flawed book, it suggests we might see good work from this writer in future; unfortunately, *Escape Plans* (1986), her second novel, proves indigestibly jargon-bound.

Chris Evans produced a fine second novel with *The Insider* (1981), a delightfully ambiguous novel about alien possession and alienation. Phillip Mann's *The Eye of the Queen* (1982) was the most forceful of the new crop, however, with its marvellous portrait of the alien Pe-Ellians and their metaphysical metamorphoses.

In his first two novels Mann has shown himself to be fascinated by the alien. The Pe-Ellians of *The Eye of the Queen* are as they are because of their telepathic powers. Thought, in their world, can shape environment and self, and that ability changes both the use and nature of Thought. It becomes a thing to be nurtured, not abused. With power comes discipline.

In Mann's second novel, *Master of Paxwax* (1986), we encounter a far more orthodox scenario, with man having brutally conquered the galaxy. But Mann both avoids and transcends the formulaic. His aliens possess a philosophic strangeness that makes them much more than extras in a *Star Wars* adventure.

Odin worked his way through the ranks of aliens until he reached the rich loam at the base of the shining silver tree. The damp soil gave him ease. The presence of the Tree was a balm which dulled his chafing sense of worry. For a long time Odin had felt dull premonitions in his fibres. At times the stone which he carried deep inside his body felt hot, as though it was burning. Ever since the time of his hatching he had been aware that there was a strangeness in his future. He both feared the strangeness and was thrilled by it, and at the same time did not understand it. Odin felt the future in the same way that a mouse feels the beating wings of the diving owl.

He settled close to the Tree and let himself be swept up by the gentle assured systalsis of its thought.

Other Gerbes were already there, each in its black gown and hunkered down. They were sifting the rich thought patterns in the cavern. Gerbes were very important to the workings of the Inner Circle for they belonged to that minority of species which are mobile, intelligent and magnificently telepathic.

Settled, Odin cast about with his mind to discover a creature with eyes. Though blind in himself, Odin loved the spectrum of visible light. He encountered a Hooded Parasol which floated tall and graceful on the upper tiers of the chamber. He slipped gently into the Parasol's mind, being careful not to disturb the creature's repose. He adjusted to its eyes and was amused to discover that at the moment of possession, the Hooded Parasol was staring down over the backs of the aliens to where Odin himself sat. (Chapter 8)

Sanctum, "one of the last holds of alien life", presents us with a variety of otherness that is imaginatively rich. But the strangeness does not end with Mann's aliens. His dynastic, all-powerful Families are far removed from the commonplace.

Inter-familial war, alien revenge and a young man's accession are the overt plot elements of *Master of Paxwax* but the novel's fascination lies in Mann's ability to conjure up a galaxy as strange as any dream and yet as consistent as any likely reality. One might, if only in terms of complexity, compare the novel to Sterling's *Schismatrix*; both works envisage the future not as a gimmick-ridden version of our own time but as an alien state of being, only tentatively linked to what we now know. Both writers have a creative energy that bodes well for science fiction's continued health.

Garry Kilworth made his debut in 1977 with *In Solitary*, a pleasant but standard alien take-over story. His best novel is perhaps *The Night of Kadar* (1978), though the stories in his 1984 collection, *The Songbirds of Pain*, show him to be strongest as a short story writer.

Robert Holdstock wrote two ambitious but flawed SF novels in his late twenties with *Eye Among the Blind* (1976) and *Earthwind* (1977). They brought him praise from such as Ursula Le Guin, but it was not until 1984 and the publication of *Mythago Wood*, a fantasy told in a science fictional mode, that he gained widespread recognition for his work, winning the British SF Award and the World Fantasy Award.

Mythago Wood is a powerful, engaging novel which successfully evokes those old mythic patterns which lie deep-rooted in English culture. It is a pagan work written with sensitivity and intelligence, as divorced from the sword and sorcery ethos of most fantasy (some of it written by Holdstock under pseudonyms!) as could be. Subtitled "A fantasy", its subject matter is the fantastic, yet its preoccupations are those of Holdstock's earlier SF novels. In its early stages its method shares much with fifties British SF of the *Quatermass* school:

> The mythogenetic process is not only complex, it is reluctant. I am too old! The equipment helps, but a younger mind could accomplish the task unaided, I'm sure. I dread the thought! Also, my mind is not at rest and as Wynne-Jones has explained, it is likely that my human consideration, my worries, form an effective barrier between the mythopoetic energy flows in my cortex—the *form* from the right brain, the *reality* from the left. The pre-mythago zone is not sufficiently enriched by my own life for it to interact in the oak vortex. (Part One, Chapter 4)

The wood, one of the last few stands of old primal forest, seems to equate with those primal levels of human consciousness, perhaps with Jung's racial memory. From that level—from the centre of the wood—come *mythagos*, all-too-solid creatures conjured up by the human mind. And the deeper one ventures into the wood, the farther one comes adrift from the mundane measurement of time. One seems to travel relativistically at the heart of the psyche. Consequently, *Mythago Wood* is as much a novel of inner space as it is a fantasy, comparable to Ballard's early disaster novels in its symbolic potency yet richer in its emotional content. The love of Steven Huxley for the conjured dryad, Guiwenneth, is vividly and realistically conveyed; a love affair set against a haunting strangeness:

> "How old were you when this happened?" I asked.
>   She shrugged. "Very young. I can't remember, it was several summers ago."
>   Several summers ago. I smiled as she said the words, thinking that only two summers ago she had not yet existed. How *did* the generic process work, I wondered, watching this beautiful, solid, soft and warm human creature. Did she form out of the leaf litter? Did wild creatures carry sticks together and shape them into bones, and then, over the autumn, dying leaves fall and coat the bones in wildwood flesh? Was there a moment, in the wood, when something approximating to a human creature rose from the underbrush, and was shaped to perfection by the intensity of the human will, operating outside the woodland?
>   Or was she just suddenly . . . there. One moment a wraith, the next a reality, the uncertain, dreamlike vision that suddenly clears and can be seen to be real. (Part Two, Chapter 10)

That scientific curiosity regarding the origins of the *mythagos* is revealing. As a fantasy the novel attains much of its power from its science fictional mode. There is a degree of realism to *Mythago Wood* rarely encountered in fantasy.

Nor is the novel escapist in any way. The heartland of the wood is not a refuge but a confrontation with the most primitive images of self. In this, as in other ways, *Mythago Wood* transcends its fantasy labelling and merits a mention in this history. Its subject matter—those primal folk images of the human psyche—is no less science fictional than telepathy or much of the magic masquerading as science in space opera. Indeed, its rigorous logical exposition of its theme makes it one of the most intelligent examinations of the human myth-making faculty ever published, returning us full circle to Shelley's *Frankenstein*, that dark dream made real through the power of the human imagination.

Whither, then, the trillion year spree? Whither that long journey on the wings of progress into darkness and ice?

One thing is certain, Science fiction is now an industry, not a genre. Nor will it ever return to what it was—a family affair with its hideout in a gaudy 25-cent pulp.

SF has grown huge and, in some respects, bloated. It has grown self-conscious as well as self-indulgent. But it has survived as a form, and diversified. Despite the vast amount of derivative work being done in the field, there remains a healthy proportion of interesting and sometimes exciting new work, as we have demonstrated.

Even so, there is no sign at all that science fiction can ever become more than a department of literature. Little sign of it growing into the natural form of expression for young writers, as some hoped in the sixties.

A stratification of the field into high-brow and low-brow, spoken of in *Billion Year Spree*, has, to a great extent, come about. It may be expected to grow into a schism by the end of the century—not so far away now that we cannot talk of it familiarly.

Such a schism will be accompanied by a process of self-labelling, acrimony and hectic internecine fighting. All camps will claim they represent *the real thing*, the genuine form of SF. Each will have its champions, its critics, its individual magazines. The day of the SF *salon* will arrive.[15] There will be bridge-builders, of course, but they will have a hard time of it. The academic critics must in consequence choose to be less cautious.

A new generation of giants will rise up—the Silverbergs and Wolfes of tomorrow—and earn ever more phenomenal advances. At the same time a new generation of feminists will bring an increasing complexity and maturity to their themes[16]: the most vociferous of a number of splinter groups we expect to see using SF as a mode of expression.

Human nature being what it is, we confidently expect that a few individualists will always stand against the popular tide. That the notion of science as quest rather than conquest may still animate a few Benfords. That iconoclastic Harrisons and Sheckleys will still maintain guerilla warfare on behalf of the readers. That Vonneguts and Lessings will continue to slip across frontiers. That there will be critics as well cheerleaders for the idea of progress—in the name of which forests go down for every rocket going up. That the mass market will occasionally—if by accident—turn up something not designed merely for mass taste. That storytelling will go on.

Of course, all of this depends on the continued economic stability of the West and its ability to walk the nuclear tightrope. The old SF stories have come true to an extent. The doomsday weapon is here, scattered about our globe in silos, rocket launchers and submarines. This is the Future Now. The few years before century's end will prove a long time in world history; we live, as they say, in interesting times.

In the coming years we expect to see continued growth and proliferation of mass media technology. Will books themselves remain unaffected by this radical shift in our entertainment habits? Of one thing you can be certain—there's an SF story about it somewhere in the magazines.

Finally, we predict a growing predilection in the non-literary artistic media for using SF metaphor as an art form; something that will, in time, feed back into the literary form. We see the beginnings of this in the pop video, with its abrupt, telescoped imagery. Art often revitalizes itself by refashioning the popular.

This volume has told an amazing story, of a virtually secret movement that has, by appealing to the imagination, become a vivid popular success. Such success makes modern-day SF a challenging place in which to work. A beginner writer's voice must contest against a thousand clamouring tongues—many of them equipped with loud-hailers. But writing is something always done against the odds.

We have also told another story. The story of how science fiction began largely outside the United States, and of how it is becoming mainly an American activity. Contributions from other countries—England in particular—have grown increasingly marginal as the nineteen-eighties progress. In emphasis or in fact, it concerns itself with the renaissance power-centred world which the United States inherits from Europe. From the time of *Frankenstein* onwards, SF's main preoccupation has been with power in one form or another. It is no coincidence that the widest span of its popularity comes at a period of rapid technological evolution, which is linked with the rise of the USA to solo super-power status. Themes of empire and conquest naturally predominate.

SF often exhibits a brazen whorish face to the world at large. It is more important than ever that it should continue its old role of evaluating the pluses and minuses of progress, and that hubris should continue to be clobbered by nemesis. For SF is in crisis.

Where it belongs.

This is our prayer for the future: "Oh Lord, make SF perfect—but not quite yet. . . ."

Notes

INTRODUCTION

1. Although SF is better described as a mode rather than a genre, the term genre has stuck, and so is often used in these pages where the term mode might have been more accurate but more obtrusive. For an excellent investigation of popular genres other than science fiction, see John G. Cawelti, *Adventure, Mystery, and Romance: Formula Stories as Art and Popular Culture*, Chicago, 1976.

    Although Cawelti does not discuss SF, his comments often throw light on its virtues and problems, as for instance here:

    > When I began my study of popular genres, I assumed that popular literature was simply an inferior form of high art; that is, I viewed it as art for lowbrows or middlebrows, or as Abraham Kaplan puts it, as an immature form of art. As my thinking on this subject has developed, I have come increasingly to feel that it is important to stress that there are different kinds of artistry rather than a single standard in terms of which all fictional creations should be judged. Our age places a particularly high value on innovation and originality, to the extent that we tend to judge our most strikingly inventive writers and artists as the most significant creators of the age. But an examination of formulaic art also suggests that there is an artistry based on convention and standardization whose significance is not simply a reflection of the inferior training and lower imaginative capacity of a mass audience. Each conventional formula has a wide range of artistic potential, and it has come to seem mistaken to automatically relegate a work to an inferior artistic status on the ground that it is a detective story or a western. (Final chapter)

2. A recent volume on the Gothic in fiction is William Patrick Day, *In the Circles of Fear and Desire: A Study of Gothic Fantasy*, Chicago, 1985. Day makes clear the relationship between imagination and reality of which other commentators often seem unaware:

    > At the heart of the novels intended to provide escape and entertainment, nineteenth-century readers came face to face with the very thing from which they were trying to escape. The great power of the Gothic stems from its capacity to transform these fears into pleasure. (Introduction)

    Cannot as much be said for the latest manifestation of the Gothic, the science fiction mode?

3. This question of virtue versus popularity has bedevilled many writers, in all kinds of writing, over which intense snobberies are generated. Bram Stoker, author of *Dracula* and other supernatural novels, is one example. An anonymous critic reviewing new editions of several of Stoker's novels in *The Times Literary Supplement* (December 8th 1966) has this to say on the vexed question of sales versus sainthood:

    > The trouble, it is usually said, is that whatever his gifts as an inventor of spine-chilling situations, he does not "write well". The phrase is used, generally, as though its meaning were self-evident. But any such assumption would be optimistic. It is a sign, perhaps, as much as anything, that we remain slaves of the intentional fallacy in literature, pathetically ready to accept writers according to their ambitions rather than their achievements. We will suppose, for instance, that George Moore must in some mysterious way be a better writer than Bram Stoker, even if Stoker is still read and Moore on the whole is not, because Moore spent a lot of time and energy carrying on about his dedication to high art while Stoker churned out best-sellers in the spare moments of an

otherwise busy life. Moore, in his later books, writes with extreme care and self-conscious artistry, but the result is unreadable; Stoker, whatever else may be said of him, is still intensely readable. So which, in the final analysis, writes better?

CHAPTER I

1. H. G. Wells, Preface to *The Scientific Romances*, 1933.
2. Eric S. Rabkin, *Fantastic Worlds: Myths, Tales, and Stories*, 1979. Rabkin attempts to establish a continuum of the Fantastic, from realistic narratives which are minimally fantastic to thorough-going fantasies which are minimally realistic. Where this laudable scheme comes to grief, it seems, is in the elusiveness of the labels, rather than in the rigidity of Rabkin's structure.
3. Alex Eisenstein puts forward the story of Daedalus and Icarus, who flew too near the sun on homemade wings and perished, as an early SF story. The sense in which Eisenstein is correct is immediately obvious. Here is hubris clobbered by nemesis. Nevertheless, the story of Icarus is a legend and SF is not legend, however much it may aspire to that condition. SF consists of texts, those totems of a literate age. Icarus has no written text. Even today, his story is handed on semi-verbally, or through artistic interpretation. It is this, more than the impossibility of a man flying with artificial wings, I believe, which distinguishes the two cases.
4. Sequestered parts of the globe evidently include New York. There in December 1979, some years after the first publication of *Billion Year Spree*, Lester del Rey published *The World of Science Fiction 1926–1976*. Del Rey believes that SF is "precisely as old as the first recorded fiction. This is the *Epic of Gilgamesh*".
5. Darko Suvin, *Od Lukijana do Lunika*, Zagreb, 1965.
6. For instance, Roger Lancelyn Green, *Into Other Worlds*, 1957, and del Rey, *op. cit.*
7. Marjorie Hope Nicolson, *Voyages to the Moon*, New York, 1949.
8. *The Essential Writings of Erasmus Darwin*, chosen and edited with linking commentary by Desmond King-Hele, 1968. References to Darwin in relation to the exploration of the South Seas are contained in Bernard Smith, *European Vision and the South Pacific 1768–1850*, 1960.
9. Benedict Nicolson, *Joseph Wright of Derby: Painter of Light*, 1968. The Derby Art Gallery also produces an illustrated booklet, *Joseph Wright of Derby*, 1979.
10. See Desmond King-Hele, *Erasmus Darwin*, 1963; Donald M. Hassler, *Erasmus Darwin*, 1973; and Desmond King-Hele, *Doctor of Revolution*, 1977.
11. *Doctor of Revolution, op. cit.*, p. 215.
12. Alethea Hayter, *Opium and the Romantic Imagination*, 1968. "The whole Gothic Revival in English literature was in fact launched by a dream." Hayter goes on to illustrate a "general preoccupation with dreams in early nineteenth-century literature".
13. Horace Walpole, letter to the Reverend William Cole, Strawberry Hill, March 9th, 1765. Explaining to Cole how he came to write *The Castle of Otranto*, he says, "Shall I even confess to you, what was the origin of this romance! I waked one morning, in the beginning of last June, from a dream, of which, all I could recover was, that I had thought myself in an ancient castle (a very natural dream for a head filled like mine with Gothic story), and that on the uppermost banister of a great staircase I saw a gigantic hand in armour. In the evening I sat down, and began to write, without knowing in the least what I intended to say or relate . . ."
14. Piranesi engraved his *Carceri* in Rome in 1745, heralding the whole Romantic movement or certainly its gloomier side. For the lighter side, one would have to turn to the etchings of another Italian, the Venetian G. B. Tiepolo, whose *Capricci* appeared at almost the same time as Piranesi's *Carceri*. In these pictures, mysterious figures talk or wait among mysterious ruins; in a later series, the *Scherzi di Fantasia*, the beautiful people are surrounded by magic and death, although they are still bathed in Tiepolo's glorious light.
15. For further details, consult, for instance, Margaret Dalziel, *Popular Fiction 100 Years Ago*, 1957.
16. Peacock's best novels remain very readable. *Gryll Grange*, published when the

author was seventy-five, is a satire on progress in Victorian days, with the Reverend Dr Opimian representing a churlish anti-scientific viewpoint sounding less strange in our time than it must have done in the 1860s: "The day would fail, if I should attempt to enumerate the evils which science has inflicted on mankind. I almost think it is the ultimate destiny of science to exterminate the human race." (Chapter 19)

17. A fine example is Ursula Le Guin, *The Left Hand of Darkness*, 1969. The town of Suzlik, in David Brin, *The Practice Effect*, 1984, is a more recent example.

18. H. Beam Piper, "Temple Trouble", 1951.

19. H. B. Fyfe, "Protected Species", 1951.

20. A. E. van Vogt, "Asylum", 1942.

21. F. L. Wallace, "Big Ancestor", 1954.

22. Some while before Ward Moore's novel appeared, a volume was published called *If It Had Happened Otherwise*, edited by J. C. Squire, 1931 (published in the USA as *If: or History Rewritten*), which is full of alternative universes dreamed up by scholars and historians. One of the most interesting is Winston Churchill's "If Lee Had Not Won the Battle of Gettysburg".

23. Shelley, *Hymn to Intellectual Beauty*, Stanza 5.

24. A question of nomenclature arises with Mary Shelley, as with Erasmus Darwin. Since Charles Darwin has pre-empted the cognomen Darwin, his grandfather is here Erasmus. Similarly, as P. B. Shelley has pre-empted Shelley, his second wife is here Mary.

25. Edward John Trelawny, *Recollections of the Last Days of Shelley and Byron*, 1858.

26. Samuel H. Vasbinder, *Scientific Attitudes in Mary Shelley's Frankenstein*, Ann Arbor, 1984.

27. The best biography is Jane Dunn, *Moon in Eclipse: A Life of Mary Shelley*, 1978. Other biographies include R. Glynn Grylls, *Mary Shelley: A Biography*, 1938; Eileen Bigland, *Mary Shelley*, 1959; and William A. Walling, *Mary Shelley*, New York, 1972.

28. Mary Shelley also contributed Lives of "Eminent Literary and Scientific Men of Italy, Spain, and Portugal" and of "Eminent Literary and Scientific Men in France" to *The Cabinet Cyclopaedia* for 1835 and 1838 respectively.

29. Edited by Elizabeth Nitchie in *Studies in Philology*, Extra Series, no. 3, Chapel Hill, N.C., 1959.

30. Jane Dunn, *op. cit.*

31. "The Transformation" was published in one of the Keepsakes beloved by the early Victorians. It is collected with other pieces in *Tales and Stories by Mary Wollstonecraft Shelley*, edited by Richard Garnett, 1891.

32. Letter to Leigh Hunt, September 9th 1823, in Betty T. Bennett (ed.), *The Letters of Mary Wollstonecraft Shelley*, Vol. I, Baltimore, 1980. The play was entitled *Presumption*, and opened on July 28th. On August 18th, another adaptation, entitled *Frankenstein: or, The Demon of Switzerland*, opened at another theatre.

33. How was it that Mary Shelley was astute enough to set her story on the Continent, and to have Victor go to the University of Ingolstadt, rather than setting it in the England she knew, and having Victor go to the University of Oxford (visited in Chapter XIX of the novel)? Could it be that there was a political attraction as well as a scenic one? Switzerland was newly formed and named only the year before the Shelleys visited it, following the Congress of Vienna. One historian (C. D. M. Ketelbey: *A History of Modern Times from 1789*) speaks of a possible leader for the new entity, formed from the old Helvetic Republic, who "might be capable of welding into a whole the discordant parts". Here is a territorial and political analogy for the monster— sexually neutral, as Switzerland was designed to be constitutionally neutral.

34. Samuel Holmes Vasbinder, *op. cit.* The volume is also valuable for a summary of the conclusions of previous critics.

35. Description taken from Sir David Brewster, *Letters on Natural Magic, Addressed to Sir Walter Scott*, 1832.

36. *The Letters of Mary Wollstonecraft Shelley*, Vol. I, *op. cit.*

37. It would be interesting to discover if Polidori supplied a copy of de Sade's Gothic fantasy *Justine*, published in 1791. There is a Justine in *Frankenstein*, wrongfully imprisoned, and "gazed on and execrated by thousands"—a very de Sade-like situation; though innocent, she perishes on the scaffold. Mario Praz indicates this parallel in *The Romantic*

Agony, 1933. Curiously enough, de Sade's Justine perishes by lightning, the force that brings life to Frankenstein's creation in the James Whale film.

38. There is some discussion of this point by M. K. Joseph, in his edition of *Frankenstein*, published in the Oxford English Novels series, 1969. See also Maurice Hinde's long Introduction to his edition of *Frankenstein*, 1985.

39. Christopher Small, *Ariel Like a Harpy: Shelley, Mary and "Frankenstein"*, 1972.

40. Ellen Moers, "Female Gothic: The Monster's Mother", *The New York Review*, 21st March 1974, reprinted in *Literary Women*, 1976, and as "Female Gothic" in the excellent collection of essays, *The Endurance of Frankenstein*, edited by George Levine and V. C. Knoepflmacher, Los Angeles, 1979.

41. While in *Juliette*, Saint-Fond cries, "Quelle jouissance! J'étais couvert de malédictions, d'imprécations, je parricidais, j'incestais, j'assassinais, je prostituais, je sodomisais!"

42. The link between the "lost" summer of 1816 and Byron's poem is discussed in Antony Rudolf's pamphlet *Byron's Darkness: Lost Summer and Nuclear Winter*, Menard Press, 1984.

43. See Percy G. Adams, *Travel Literature and the Evolution of the Novel*, Lexington, Kentucky, 1983.

44. "The book from which Felix instructed Safie was Volney's *Ruins of Empires* . . . Through this work I obtained a cursory knowledge of history, and a view of the several empires at present existing in the world; it gave me an insight into the manners, governments, and religions of the different nations of the earth . . . I heard of the discovery of the American hemisphere, and wept with Safie over the hapless fate of its original inhabitants." The creature speaks. *Frankenstein*, Chapter XIII.

45. See for instance A. M. D. Hughes, *The Nascent Mind of Shelley*, Oxford, 1947.

46. This prodromic nightmare—presenting familiar objects out of context—is surrealist. Verney has found the beloved Lord Raymond dead in the ruins of plague-stricken Constantinople, and falls asleep: "I awoke from disturbed dreams. Methought I had been invited to Timon's last feast: I came with keen appetite, the covers were removed, the hot water sent up its satisfying streams, while I fled before the anger of the host, who assumed the form of Raymond; while to my diseased fancy, the vessels hurled by him after me were surcharged with a fetid vapour, and my friend's shape, altered by a thousand distortions, expanded into a gigantic phantom, bearing on its brow the sign of pestilence. The growing shadow rose and rose, filling and then seeming to endeavour to burst beyond the adamantine vault that bent over, sustaining and enclosing the world. The nightmare became torture; with a strong effort I threw off sleep, and recalled reason to her wonted functions." (*The Last Man*, Volume 2, Chapter 3)

Mary Shelley uses the same device just before Victor Frankenstein wakes to find his "miserable monster" has come to life. There again, the dream is of someone loved (in this case his fiancée) transformed into a symbol of horror and disgust: "I slept, indeed, but I was disturbed by the wildest dreams. I thought I saw Elizabeth, in the bloom of health, walking in the streets of Ingolstadt. Delighted and surprised, I embraced her; but as I imprinted the first kiss on her lips, they became livid with the hue of death; her features appeared to change, and I thought that I held the corpse of my dead mother in my arms; a shroud enveloped her form, and I saw the graveworms crawling in the folds of the flannel. I started from my sleep with horror; a cold dew covered my forehead, my teeth chattered, and every limb became convulsed. . . ." (*Frankenstein*, Chapter V) David Ketterer uses this passage to emphasize necrophile and incest themes in the novel.

47. Rosemary Jackson, *Fantasy: The Literature of Subversion*, New York, 1981.

48. Muriel Spark, *Child of Light*, 1951.

49. Examples are Byron's poem, *Darkness*, already mentioned; Thomas Campbell's poem, *The Last Man*; Jean-Baptiste Cousin de Grainville's *Le Dernier Homme* (1805); and John Martin's paintings *The Last Man* (watercolour, c. 1832; oil, 1849). The popularity of these works was international. For details of Byron's poem being translated into Russian, see Antony Rudolf, *op. cit.*

50. Introduction to *The Last Man*, by Brian Aldiss, 1985.

51. Norman Longmate, *King Cholera*, 1966.
52. David Ketterer, *Frankenstein's Creation: The Book, The Monster and Human Reality*, Victoria, Canada, 1979.

CHAPTER II

1. *Pages from the Goncourt Journal*, edited and translated by Robert Baldick, 1962. The entry is for July 16th, 1856.
2. As has at least one critic, David Galloway, editor of *Selected Writings of Edgar Allan Poe*, 1967.
3. A dependable life is Edward Wagenknecht's *Edgar Allan Poe: The Man Behind the Legend*, New York, 1963. An illustrious psychoanalytical view is Marie Bonaparte's *Edgar Poe, Étude Psychoanalytique*, Paris, 1933, which contains a Foreword by Sigmund Freud.
4. Preface to Poe's *Tales of the Grotesque and Arabesque*, 1840.
5. Cf. T. S. Eliot's remark that Poe possessed "the intellect of a highly gifted young person before puberty" (*From Poe to Valéry*).
6. D. H. Lawrence, "Edgar Allan Poe", *Studies in Classic American Literature*, 1924. Though in the same book, Lawrence says in his essay on Hawthorne, "You *must* look through the surface of American art, and see the inner diabolism of the symbolic meaning. Otherwise it is all mere childishness."
7. Aldous Huxley, "Vulgarity in Literature", *Music at Night*, 1930.
8. H. Bruce Franklin, *Future Perfect: American Science Fiction of the Nineteenth Century*, 1966.
9. *The Science Fiction of Edgar Allan Poe*, collected and edited by Harold Beaver, 1976.
10. Oliver Wendell Holmes (1809–1894), most famous for *The Autocrat of the Breakfast-Table*, 1857. He was Professor of Anatomy at Dartmouth and later Harvard; he wrote three novels with psychiatric themes, of which *Elsie Venner*, 1861, is best known. He also coined the term "anaesthesia".
11. For a discussion of this point, consult Joseph Patrick Roppolo's "Meaning and 'The Masque of the Red Death'", *Tulane Studies in English XII*, 1963.
12. "The Gold Bug" provides the most eminent example. See also "The Purloined Letter", "X-ing the Paragreb", and *The Narrative of Arthur Gordon Pym*.
13. Particularly interesting in this connection, because of its linking of recurrent clock symbols in many stories with Poe's sexual motivation, and the possibility that the infant Poe observed his parents in the throes of love, is Jean-Paul Weber's article "Edgar Poe and the Theme of the Clock", *La Nouvelle Revue Française*, nos. 68 and 69, 1958.
14. For example, the orang-outang in "Murders in the Rue Morgue", the birds in *Arthur Gordon Pym*, the raven crying "Nevermore", and the black cat crying murder.
15. He played a part in the Great Moon Hoax of 1836, when a series of articles appeared in the *New York Sun* purporting to describe the lunar world as viewed through Herschel's telescope. There is also "The Balloon-Hoax", while in "Maelzel's Chess-Player" he unmasks a real-life hoaxer.
16. Examples are "Von Kempelen and His Discovery", "The Facts in the Case of M. Valdemar", and "The Premature Burial".
17. In "The Spectacles", a man is tricked into virtually marrying his great-great-grandmother. "The Imp of the Perverse" is a man's conscience, which tricks him into confessing a murder.
18. There is a man who is hanged because his powers of utterance are impeded, in "Loss of Breath", the hiccupping in "Bon-Bon", and—to name an actual physical obstruction—a length of whalebone down the throat of a corpse in "The Purloined Letter".
19. Paul Valéry: "Poe is the only impeccable writer. He was never mistaken." In a letter to André Gide, 1891.
20. "That an enthusiasm for Poe should have been shared by the three most influential poets in modern French literature, that this American writer should have become the pivot on which for the past century French literature has turned, this by itself is sufficiently extraordinary. But even this statement of the case does no more than suggest the force of Poe's impact. There is scarcely one French writer from the time of Baudelaire to the present who has not in one way or another paid his respects to Poe. Villiers de l'Isle Adam, Verlaine, and Rimbaud,

Huysmans, Claudel, Gide, Edmund Jalour—these are names at random, but they will serve to indicate the scope of the interest Poe has had for France." Patrick F. Quinn, "The French Response to Poe". Mr Quinn omits the name of Verne from his list. This essay, together with those mentioned in Notes 11 and 13 are reprinted in *Poe: A Collection of Critical Essays*, edited by Robert Regan, (*Twentieth Century Views*), Englewood Cliffs, New Jersey, 1967.

21. Leslie A. Fiedler, *Love and Death in the American Novel*, 1967.

22. A thorough examination of the various icons of the science fictional mode is the subject of Gary K. Wolfe: *The Known and the Unknown: The Iconography of Science Fiction*, Kent, Ohio, 1979. Wolfe deals mainly with the spaceship, the city, the wasteland, the robot, and the monster. His book gives the lie to the idea that genre materials, imaginatively used, wear out. Rather, they are enriched by complexity of reference. If we accept the spaceship as a quantal development of the mysterious machine, then all of Wolfe's icons are inheritances from Gothic originals—and the richer for it. If we discard what is old merely because it is old, we are left with the merely superficial.

23. Robert A Heinlein, "Science Fiction: Its Nature, Faults and Virtues" in *The Science Fiction Novel: Imagination and Social Criticism*, Chicago, 1964.

CHAPTER III

1. The widespread influences of Newton's ideas on the writers of his day is traced in Chapter VI of A. J. Meadows's *The High Firmament*, Leicester, 1969, a study of astronomy in literature. A good example of Newton and Newton's laws clothed in blank verse is contained in Edward Young's *The Complaint: or, Night Thoughts* (1742). For instance, this passage about the stars:

> As these spheres
> Measure duration, they no less inspire
> The godlike hope of ages without end.
> The boundless space, through which these rovers take

> Their restless roam, suggests the
>   sister thought
> Of boundless time. (*Night, ix*)

2. J. M. Roberts, *The Triumph of the West*, Chapter VIII, 1985.

3. Translation by Dr Thomas Franklin.

4. Kenneth Clark, *Civilisation: A Personal View*, 1969.

5. The translation is Rosen's. The *Somnium* is very short. After it was written, Kepler added notes, almost one per sentence, which run to many more pages than the *Dream* itself. Kepler's *Somnium: The Dream, or Posthumous Work on Lunar Astronomy*, translated with a commentary by Edward Rosen, Madison, 1967.

6. The best English translation of the two books is *Other Worlds*, translated and with an introduction by Geoffrey Strachan, 1965.

7. John Carey, *John Donne: Life, Mind and Art*, chapter 8, 1981.

8. Marjorie Hope Nicolson, *Voyages to the Moon*, New York, 1949.

9. Philip B. Gove, *The Imaginary Voyage in Prose Fiction*, 1941.

10. I. F. Clarke, *The Pattern of Expectation 1644–2001*, Prologue, 1979. For predictions made seriously and otherwise, a useful guide is Chris Morgan: *The Shape of Futures Past: The Story of Prediction*, Exeter, 1980. It is particularly thorough on the period 1800–1945.

11. At one time, it was fashionable to class Defoe as one of the Pilgrim Fathers of the English novel, whose pioneering work included studies of character, such as *Roxana, Colonel Jack*, and so forth. Recently, Ian A. Bell, in *Defoe's Fiction* (1986), argues that Defoe should not be conscripted into this continuity; rather, his narratives are not intended as criticism of life but were designed as escapist fantasies, salted with realist detail to make them acceptable to a popular audience. Both versions of Defoe's achievements come loaded with class judgements. The parallel with the acceptance or otherwise of SF, and its relationship with the moral-artistic tradition of the English novel, is instructive.

12. George Sampson, *The Concise Cambridge History of English Literature*, 1941.

13. Percy G. Adams. *Travel Literature and the Evolution of the Novel*, op. cit.

14. George Orwell, "Politics vs. Literature", *Collected Essays*, 1961.

15. See the Preface to *Erewhon*, Enlarged Edition, 1901.
16. Translation by Norman Cameron (1947).

CHAPTER IV

1. George Saintsbury, in *The English Novel*, speaks of a "half-ebb" in the novel.
2. *Pelham, or The Adventures of a Gentleman* (1828) provides an example of how novels influence life. The dandy Pelham's mother remarks to him that he looks best in black, "which is a great compliment, for people must be very distinguished in appearance to do so". The wearing of coloured evening coats, based on the costume of the hunting field, went out of style forthwith, and black has remained the only acceptable formal style for evening-wear ever since. In our century, the revelation that Clark Gable wore no undervest ruined the undergarment trade. Writers, hacks, beware of your powers.
3. Mary Shelley, *Journal*, January 11th, 1831.
4. John Martin (1789–1854), painter of awful spectacles, was the Cecil B. de Mille of the Romantic movement. His grand gloomy canvases and engravings had tremendous influence on other artists (Turner imitated him in such paintings as *The Destruction of Sodom*) and writers. The little Brontës slept with Martin's engravings hanging over their beds. In France, his vogue was such that an adjective "Martinien" (an early example of Franglais) was coined for mighty extravaganzas. Martin's canvas *The Last Man*, of which more than one version exists, was based on the poet Thomas Campbell's poem of the same name: "I saw a vision in my sleep. . . ." Another imitator was Francis Danby, whose *Opening of the Sixth Seal* was bought by Beckford in 1828; but Beckford was friendly with many artists, and had Martin sketch Fonthill for him.
   Martin, like Erasmus Darwin, was a forward-looking man; he proposed grandiose schemes for the modernisation of London, including farsighted plans for sewage disposal. It may be wondered how such men as Martin and Erasmus Darwin were so easily forgotten by their fellow-countrymen; the answer lies in a conservative streak in the English, which sets itself against innovation.
5. Or perhaps not. Disraeli's *Sybil: or The Two Nations* was published in 1845. Later novels had taken up the "two nations" theme. The propagandist novelist Charles Kingsley deals with the rural poor in *Yeast* (1848—a good year for such a topic). In *Yeast*, the labourers are portrayed as hopelessly degenerate beings; young Lancelot wonders if they are "even animals of the same species". Works such as Steven Marcus's *The Other Victorians* have shown how the exploitation of the "nation" in the darkness was not only financial but sexual. This moral division lay at the basis of Victorian hypocrisy. Lytton was well aware of the Victorian underworld, and the concluding passage of *The Coming Race* may contain an echo of it.
   Later, this great Victorian theme of the submerged nation, the hidden life awaiting the hour of its revenge, expressed so often in novels (Dickens's among others) and paintings, finds science fictional embodiment in Wells's *Time Machine*, with its subterranean Morlocks.
6. What Frankenstein's monster hoped for, SF writers later accomplished. The funniest application of the idea of machines reproducing themselves is to be found in John Sladek's *The Reproductive System* (1968, US title *Mechasm*), that most Butlerian of novels. The inventors explain the system to a general who has been called in:

> During the week, they explained, the boxes had devoured over a ton of scrap metal, as well as a dozen oscilloscopes with attached signal generators, thirty-odd test sets, desk calculators both mechanical and electronic, a pair of scissors, an uncountable number of bottle caps, paper clips, coffee spoons and staples (for the lab and office staff liked feeding their new pet), dozens of surplus walky-talky storage batteries and a small gasoline-driven generator.
>
> The cells had multiplied—better than double their original number—and had grown to various sizes, ranging from shoeboxes and attaché cases to steamer trunk proportions. They now reproduced constantly but slowly, in

various fashions. One steamer trunk emitted, every five or ten minutes, a pair of tiny boxes the size of 3 × 5 card files. Another box, of extraordinary length, seemed to be slowly sawing itself in half.

General Grawk remained unimpressed. "What does it do for an encore?" he growled.
(Chapter 4)

7. The theme of men becoming slaves of the machines runs through much of twentieth century literature, from Italian futurism, French Impressionism, and German Expressionism onwards. An example. "It was like a vision. Perhaps gnomes and subterranean workers, enslaved in the era of light, see with such eyes. Perhaps that is why they are absolutely blind to conventional ugliness." From "The Lost Girl", by D. H. Lawrence. This theme occurs throughout Lawrence's work. The end of *Women in Love*, for instance, leaves a sense of existence as an eternal process in which humanity might be merely a dead end, leading nowhere.

8. Eric S. Rabkin, *The Fantastic in Literature*, Princeton, N.J., 1976. Chapter 1.

9. C. S. Lewis, *Selected Literary Essays*, ed. Walter Hooper, Cambridge, 1969.

10. *Life and Habit*, 1877, *Evolution, Old and New*, 1879, *Unconscious Memory*, 1880, *Luck or Cunning?* 1886.

11. Remark by Proust recorded in Harold Nicolson's diary for June 21st, 1933, and quoted by J. I. M. Stewart in his *Thomas Hardy: A Critical Biography*, 1971. One may speculate pleasurably that the entire germ of *A la récherche du temps perdu* might be contained in a sentence of Hardy's closely following the passage quoted: "Time closed up like a fan before him."

12. F. R. Southerington, *Hardy's Vision of Man*, 1971. "Perhaps the most powerful influence of all, however, was that of Darwin. . . ." (Chapter 14) Darwin's somewhat valetudinarian life and his enormous patience in unravelling gigantic riddles as well as the habits of earthworms are in tune with Hardy's whole tenor of being; Darwin, in Hardy's phrase, "was a man who used to notice such things". In Florence Emily Hardy's *Life of Thomas Hardy*, an entry records Hardy's presence at Darwin's funeral, adding, "As a young man he had been among the earliest acclaimers of *The Origin of Species*." (Chapter 12)

13. Perhaps the best-known passage in this long and difficult work—it occurs near the beginning—is a stage direction:

The nether sky opens, and Europe is disclosed as a prone and emaciated figure, the Alps shaping like a backbone, and the branching mountain-chains like ribs, the peninsular plateau of Spain forming a head. Broad and lengthy lowlands stretch from the north of France across Russia like a grey-green garment hemmed by the Ural mountains and the glistening Arctic Ocean.

The point of view then sinks downwards through space, and draws near to the surface of the perturbed countries, where the peoples, distressed by events which they did not cause, are seen writhing, crawling, heaving and vibrating in their various cities and nationalities.

The methods of D. W. Griffith, Eisenstein, and de Mille are here presaged.

14. Equally absurd to regard John Cowper Powys, who greatly admired Thomas Hardy, as an SF writer. It is not sufficient for a writer's oeuvre to contain some form of speculative event; SF is as much a matter of form and tone as of content. Powys's best-known novel is *A Glastonbury Romance*, 1932. Among his other novels is *Up and Out*, 1957, in which a hydrogen bomb blows a big chunk of Earth into space; four people survive on it, a husband and wife created by vivisection called Org and Asm, and an ordinary man and woman. The chunk of matter meets Time, which is a slug, and kills it; it also encounters Eternity ("pitifully unimpressive"), Aldebaran, the devil, and God.

15. Marc Chadourne, *Restif de la Bretonne ou le siècle prophétique*, Paris, 1958.

16. Robert Baldick, in the Introduction to his translation of *Monsieur Nicolas: or The Human Heart Laid Bare*, 1966.

17. See the exposition in Mark Poster's *The Utopian Thought of Restif de la Bretonne*, New York, 1971.

18. Robert Baldick, *op. cit.*

19. Gérard de Nerval, *Selected Writings*, translated by Geoffrey Wagner, 1958.

20. The remark is quoted in Richard Holmes's *Footsteps: Adventures of a Romantic Biographer*, 1985. Holmes has this to say of Nerval's descent into madness. "I also felt, obscurely, that this passage from outer to inner travelling marked some vital transformation or watershed in the history of Romanticism. The imagination of the Hero had finally doubled back on itself, and the rivers and mountains, the visions and revolutions had become in this last phase those of a purely internal landscape, or moonscape, the world of dreams." (Chapter 4, *Dreams*)

21. For derivations of automata before de l'Isle-Adam and Hoffman, see the curious interdisciplinary book by John Cohen, *Human Robots in Myth and Science*, 1966.

22. Villiers de l'Isle-Adam, *Cruel Tales*, translated by Robert Baldick, 1963.

23. Even *The Times* called his "wonderful books . . . terribly thrilling and absolutely harmless". It is quoted as doing so in a cheap edition (one shilling) of *Around the Moon*, issued by the authorized publishers, Sampson Low, Marston, Searle, and Rivington, 1876.

24. Marcel More, *Le très curieux Jules Verne*, Paris, 1960.

25. I. O. Evans, *Jules Verne, Master of Science Fiction*.

26. Michel Butor, *Repertoire*, Paris, 1953.

27. The best and most thorough examination of this grand theme is contained in Jean Chesneaux, *The Political and Social Ideas of Jules Verne*, translated by Thomas Wikeley, 1972.

28. An exception to this sweeping remark may be made for *Les cinq cents millions de la bégum*, 1879, known more briefly in English as *The Begum's Fortune*. This is Verne's only utopia.

    The fortune of the title is divided between Sarrasin, a French authority on hygiene, and Schultz, a German professor of chemistry. The two men use the money to build rival towns in Oregon. Frankville is established as a model city, Stahlstadt is a small police state. Verne was clearly feeling a touch of *revanchisme* when he wrote, although the Franco-Prussian War had been over for several years. Stahlstadt tries to destroy Frankville, but Schultz happily blows himself up.

    Some commentators see this story as a prophecy of German militarism to come. The utopian aspects concern the use or misuse of modern machinery and capabilities. But the unlikeliness of the events and the somewhat ludicrously diagrammatic plot make it unlikely that readers will take the social reformer as seriously as the patriot.

29. *Hector Servadac*, in *Novels by Jules Verne*, selected and edited by H. C. Harwood (Chapter 22). This is the authorized translation also used in the Ace Books edition—"abridged and modernized"—retitled *Off on a Comet*, 1957.

30. The dates in England: W. H. Smith secured the rights to sell books and newspapers on railway stalls in 1848. "Railway libraries", "Yellow Backs", and other numerous series, featuring novelists such as Lytton, were published to stock the stalls. The Education Act was passed in 1870. Circulating libraries had been operative in various forms since the eighteenth century; Mudie's, the most well known, was opened in London in 1842. The official tax on paper was abolished in 1861.

31. Illustrations of a set of French postcards dating from about 1900 and depicting such advances as dictaphones, underwater hunting, automated learning, and mechanized beauty parlours (if indeed these are advances) are to be found in the last chapter of *The Nineteenth Century: The Contradictions of Progress*, edited by Asa Briggs, 1970. Some examples of Robida's work are also included.

32. I. F. Clarke's preliminary skirmish with the subject is contained in *The Tale of the Future: From the Beginning to the Present Day*, 1961, which is a check list. His brilliant full-scale operation is *Voices Prophesying War 1763–1984*, 1966.

33. The Bodleian Library lists 142 titles by Le Queux (1864–1927). He seems to have been afflicted by a lust for war and was as right-wing in his opinions as were most of the writers of future war stories—Wells being a notable exception to this rule. Among Le Queux's titles are *German Atrocities*, published in 1914, and presumably intended to whip up war lust. In 1915, he published a science fiction title, *The Mystery of the Green Ray*.

34. As one literary critic puts it, when speaking of the eighteen-sixties, "*Lorna Doone* and *Harry Richmond* are isolated outcrop-

pings of romance in a decade when realism was entrenching itself in the English novel. It must also be observed, however, that the same decade witnessed a remarkable output of fantasy. Indeed, not until then is fantasy (when not used merely as a device for satire) identifiable as a distinct mode in English fiction." Lionel Stevenson, *The English Novel: A Panorama*, 1960.

35. There is an interesting discussion of the meaning of *Dr Jekyll and Mr Hyde* in Chapter 4 of *Into the Unknown* by Robert M. Philmus (Berkeley and Los Angeles, 1970), which considers various interpretations. It also touches on Stevenson's reference to "Mr Darwin's theory" in 1874. Philmus adds a great deal to our appreciation of Stevenson's story by his perceptive look at the other characters involved in Dr Jekyll's downfall, showing how, for instance, Utterson, acting as detective, embodies an approach to the mystery of human nature which is antithetical to Jekyll's, thus underlining the point that more than one approach to inner truth is possible.

36. "On Science Fiction" is collected in C. S. Lewis, *Of Other Worlds: Essays and Stories*, edited by Walter Hooper, 1966.

37. Darko Suvin: *Metamorphoses of Science Fiction*, New Haven, 1979.

CHAPTER V

1. James to Wells, letter dated Rye, Sussex, November 19th, 1905. The two books to which James refers are *A Modern Utopia* and *Kipps*. Printed in full in *Henry James and H. G. Wells: A Record of their Friendship*, edited by Leon Edel and Gordon N. Ray, 1959. The letter, brimming with rare enthusiasm, is quoted in a biography by Vincent Brome, *H. G. Wells*, 1952. Earlier, in a letter dated September 23rd, 1902, James suggested to Wells that they collaborate on a Mars novel.

2. A fair example is Bert Smallways, hero of *The War in the Air*. "Bert Smallways was a vulgar little creature, the sort of pert, limited soul that the old civilization of the early twentieth century produced by the million in every country of the world. He had lived all his life in narrow streets, and between mean houses he could not look over, and in a narrow

circle of ideas from which there was no escape. He thought the whole duty of man was to be smarter than his fellows, get his hands, as he put it, 'on the dibs', and have a good time. He was, in fact, the sort of man who had made England and America what they were." (Chapter 3)

3. For a thoroughgoing account of the reception of Wells's books as they were published, see Ingvald Raknem, *H. G. Wells and His Critics*, Oslo, 1962.

4. Bernard Bergonzi, *The Early H. G. Wells: A Study of the Scientific Romances*, Manchester, 1961.

5. *Experiment in Autobiography*, Chapter 6.

6. John Huntington, *The Logic of Fantasy: H. G. Wells and Science Fiction*, New York, 1982. "'Directed thought' is an accomplishment of a high order, to be sure, yet it is only within the inconclusive ironic universe of undirected thought that Wells can do justice to one of the great puzzles of the late Victorian era, the conflict between evolution and ethics." (Preface)

7. Mention should be made also of the good psychological timing of *The War of the Worlds*. The new journalism was bringing word of the solar system to Wells's public, while Mars in particular was in the general consciousness. It had been in close opposition in 1877, 1879, and 1881, and Percival Lowell's first book on Mars, containing speculations about the "canals" and possibilities of life there, had been published in 1895.

8. Wells does not mention himself as a second Camille Flammarion. The parallels between the great French astronomer's novel *La fin du monde* (published in 1893 and translated into eleven European languages) and Wells's "The Star" are striking. There is a discussion of this derivation and others in Raknem, *op. cit*, Chapter 22.

9. *Experiment in Autobiography*, Chapter 8.

10. See the end of Wells's *Outline of History*. Also printed as a separate extract under the title "The Federation of Man" in *H. G. Wells: Journalism and Prophecy 1893–1946*, edited by W. Warren Wagar, New York, 1964.

11. Frank McConnell, *The Science Fiction of H. G. Wells*, 1981.

12. For an amplification of my argument, see the edition of the book published by

Chatto & Windus, 1985, with my Introduction.

13. David Lodge, *The Language of Fiction*, new edition, 1984.

14. A new edition with an interesting Introduction by Christopher Priest, published 1985.

15. Wells's shrewd and uncomplaining view of this curious matter should be given, if only in a footnote. He speaks of "this supreme importance of individualities, in other words of 'character' in the fiction of the nineteenth century and early twentieth century. Throughout that period character-interest did its best to take the place of adjustment-interest in fiction . . . It was a consequence of the prevalent sense of social stability . . . Throughout the broad smooth flow of nineteenth-century life in Great Britain, the art of fiction floated on this same assumption of social fixity. The Novel in English was produced in an atmosphere of security for the entertainment of secure people who liked to feel established and safe for good. Its standards were established within that apparently permanent frame and the criticism of it began to be irritated and perplexed when, through a new instability, the splintering frame began to get in the picture.

"I suppose for a time I was the outstanding instance among writers of fiction in English of the frame getting into the picture." (*Experiment in Autobiography*, Chapter 7 §5)

16. This assumption lies behind the otherwise sympathetic biography by Lovat Dickson, *H. G. Wells: His Turbulent Life and Times*, 1969.

17. George Orwell, "Wells, Hitler, and the World State", *Critical Essays*, 1946.

CHAPTER VI

1. A just and sympathetic essay on Senarens by E. F. Bleiler appears in the latter's *Science Fiction Writers*, New York, 1982.

2. Thomas D. Clareson has described an interesting development in the contents of the Frank Reade tales, in that the settings turn increasingly from the West to the international scene, while motive power shifts from steam to electricity.

These and other developments are thoroughly charted in Thomas D. Clareson, *Some Kind of Paradise: The Emergence of American Science Fiction*, Westport, Conn., 1985.

3. Susan Sontag, *Against Interpretation*. The essay in which the quoted passage occurs, "The Imagination of Disaster", is included in *Science Fiction: The Future*, edited by Dick Allen, New York, 1971.

4. See cover of Ballantine's "Adult Fantasy" edition, New York, 1969.

5. See entries for Rider Haggard in Neil Barron (editor), *Anatomy of Wonder: A Critical Guide to Science Fiction*, 2nd edition, 1981. A reliable and pleasantly nondoctrinaire key to the labyrinth.

6. Interest in this sub-genre was strong enough for a remarkable publishing venture. In the late seventies, Arno Press, under its advisory editors, R. Reginald and Douglas Menville, launched a library of 69 reprints of "Lost Race and Adult Fantasy Fiction". These included such authors as Edwin Arnold, Algernon Blackwood, Robert W. Chambers, Stanton A. Coblentz, E. R. Eddison, George Griffith, E. C. Large, Upton Sinclair, Ruthven Todd, and others.

7. Richard Kyle, "Out of Time's Abyss: The Martian Stories of Edgar Rice Burroughs, A Speculation", *Riverside Quarterly*, vol. 4, no. 2.

8. *Ibid.*

9. Roger Lancelyn Green, *Tellers of Tales*, 1965, Chapter 14.

10. Lupoff's argument is presented in the Introduction to *Gulliver of Mars*, Ace, New York [1964], and more fully in his *Edgar Rice Burroughs: Master of Adventure*, New York, 1965, Chapter 3. In the latter volume Lupoff argues that Burroughs derived Barsoom from *Gulliver of Mars* and the character of John Carter from *Phra*. Since neither Phra nor Carter has much in the way of character beyond muscle, this argument must remain open. Whatever Burroughs's sins, they were his own!

11. H. G. Wells, *Experiment in Autobiography*, Chapter 8.

12. Quoted in William B. Fischer's "German Theories of Science Fiction" in *Science-Fiction Studies*, vol. 3, pt. 3, November 1976.

13. Bram Stoker, *Dracula*, The World's

Classics. Introduction and Notes by A. N. Wilson, Oxford, 1983.

14. See my essay, "Dracula", in *Survey of Modern Fantasy Literature*, ed. Frank N. Magill, La Canada, Conn., 1983.

15. Harry Ludlam, *Biography of Dracula: The Life Story of Bram Stoker*, 1962.

16. Daniel Farson, *The Man who Wrote Dracula: A Biography of Bram Stoker*, 1975.

17. Maurice Richardson, *Psychoanalysis of Ghost Stories*, 1959.

18. Bram Stoker's mother was quick off the mark. She wrote enthusiastically to her son, "No book since Mrs Shelley's *Frankenstein* or indeed any other at all has come near yours in originality, or terror—Poe is nowhere."

19. David G. Hartwell, Introduction to the Gregg Press *The Purple Cloud*, 1977, and Colin Wilson, "Why is Shiel Neglected?" Both are collected in the marvellous compendium, *Shiel in Diverse Hands*, a collection of essays by "Twenty-Nine Students of M. P. Shiel, Lord of Language", Cleveland, Ohio, 1983.

20. E. F. Bleiler, "M. P. Shiel", in *Science Fiction Writers*, ed. Everett F. Bleiler, *op. cit.*

21. Speaking of Shiel's "rhythmical word-play", Bleiler also says, "it is at times reminiscent of a one-man band at a carnival". E. F. Bleiler, "M. P. Shiel", E. F. Bleiler (ed.), *Supernatural Fiction Writers: Fantasy and Horror*, N.Y., 1985, 2 vols.

22. Sam Moskowitz, "The Dark Plots of One Shiel", in *Shiel in Divers Hands*, *op. cit.*

23. For some discussion of the yellow peril theme in SF and fantasy, see Thomas B. Clareson's essay on "The Emergence of Science Fiction", in *Anatomy of Wonder*, *op. cit.* Also worth consulting is William F. Wu, *The Yellow Peril: Chinese Americans in American Fiction*, Hamden, Conn., 1982, and Chris Morgan, *The Shape of Futures Past: The Story of Prediction*, 1980.

24. The name of Robert Sidney Bowen, always somewhat obscure, has lapsed further into twilight. Bowen wrote a number of air-war stories for the pulps. He switched over to future air warfare with a pulp magazine entitled *Dusty Ayres and his Battle Birds!* which lasted for

twelve issues between 1934 and 1935. Bowen wrote each issue in its entirety. Dusty was America's ace pilot, fighting the dreaded Asiatic hordes, who were led by Fire-Eyes. The Asiatics had conquered the rest of the world and tried constantly to invade the USA. Remarkably, the last issue of the magazine presented a conclusion. Fire-Eyes was killed and the world set free, thanks to Dusty. Thus the British tradition of such scientific romances as Griffith's *Olga Romanoff* and Shiel's *The Yellow Danger* was continued in America.

25. *The Invasion of 1910* was filmed in summer of 1913 as *If England Were Invaded*. When war came in 1914, the film was released as *The Raid of 1915*, and helped to stoke war fever.

26. "William Le Queux (who was born in 1864 and died in 1927) must have been one of the most prolific writers of all time. Edgar Wallace was hardly in the same class. I have sixty books of his on my shelves (with the imprints of fifteen different publishers) and I doubt whether I have one book in four of his total output. All, he claimed, were written in his own hand: he never dictated or used a typewriter." Hugh Greene, *The Rivals of Sherlock Holmes*, 1970.

27. Such fears have been expressed over every armament escalation up to and including the Cruise missiles and the SDI. They occurred to Erskine Childers. A note by M. A. Childers in a late edition of *The Riddle of the Sands* reads as follows: "Erskine Childers advocated preparedness for war as being the best preventative for war. During the years that followed, he fundamentally altered his opinion. His profound study of military history, of politics, and, later, of the causes of the Great War convinced him that preparedness induced war. It was not only that to the vast numbers of people engaged in fostered war services and armament industries, war meant the exercise of their professions and trades and the advancements of their interests; preparedness also led to international armament rivalries, and bred in the minds of the nations concerned fears, antagonisms, and ambitions, that were destructive to peace."

28. "Jack London by Himself", used as Autobiographical Introduction to the

1963 edition of *The Star Rover*, Macmillan, New York.

29. Margaret Lane, *Edgar Wallace: The Biography of a Phenomenon*, 1938. Wallace is one of the few best-selling writers, or writers outside the world of established letters, whose life has been written in such literate terms.

30. Information kindly supplied and verified by Edgar Wallace's daughter, Mrs Penny Halcrow.

CHAPTER VII

1. Burroughs's response is quoted fully in Q. D. Leavis, *Fiction and the Reading Public*, 1932.

2. E. F. Bleiler, "Edgar Rice Burroughs", in E. F. Bleiler (ed.), *Science Fiction Writers, op. cit.*

3. Robert E. Howard borrowed Burroughs's way of transposing Carter to Mars in most of his novels: the cave, the sleep, the sudden awakening elsewhere, occur in *Almuric*, for example.

4. "I was not writing because of any urge to write nor for any particular love of writing. I was writing because I had a wife and two babies . . . I loathed poverty. . . ." Autobiographical article in *Open Road* magazine, September 1949, quoted in Chapter 12 of Richard Lupoff's biography of Burroughs, *Barsoom: Edgar Rice Burroughs and the Martian Vision*, Baltimore, 1976.

5. *Edgar Rice Burroughs: The Man Who Created Tarzan*, by Irwin Porges, 2 volumes, New York, 1975.

6. For an investigation of imaginative treatments of Venus through the years, see my *Farewell, Fantastic Venus! A History of the Planet Venus in Fact and Fiction*, 1968.

7. And worse and drugged. "The Story of Kirk" in Robert Lindner's *The Fifty Minute Hour, and Other True Psychoanalytic Tales*, New York, 1954, relates the case of a young man, Kirk, who identified with an interplanetary hero much like John Carter, whose adventures spread over a long series of fantasies; though the evidence presented by Lindner suggests the series might be, not Burroughs's, but the Lensman series by E. E. Smith (see Chapter 9). By coincidence, the hero has the same name as Kirk's (an assumed name). Soon, Kirk is away with his fictional namesake, "far off on another planet, courting beautiful princesses, governing provinces, warring with strange enemies". The identification becomes part of a self-sustaining psychosis, which Lindner ameliorates only with great difficulty. (This "Story of Kirk" is included in *Best Fantasy Stories*, 1962, edited by the present writer.)

8. For the full list, consult Richard D. Mullen, the Elder, "Edgar Rice Burroughs and the Fate Worse Than Death", in *Riverside Quarterly*, vol. 4, no. 3.

9. The dream is related in "Psychiatric Activities", *Memories, Dreams, Reflections*, Chapter 4, 1963.

10. Richard D. Mullen, "The Undisciplined Imagination: Edgar Rice Burroughs and Lowellian Mars", *SF: The Other Side of Realism*, ed. Thomas D. Clareson, 1971.

11. North Hollywood, California, Leisure Books, 1970.

12. Kingsley Amis, *New Maps of Hell*, 1961, Chapter 1.

13. Leslie A. Fiedler, *The Return of the Vanishing American*. The chapter on "The Basic Myths, III: Two Mothers of Us All". To be guided entirely by Fiedler's theories would probably cause one to see the alienation surrounding the births of ERB's characters as explicable in terms of the latter's rejection of his European (or European cultural) ancestry. "What a lovely American dream—to be born as a fatherless Indian boy from a husbandless Indian mother, to have no father at all, except for the Forest itself: all fear of miscegenation washed away in the same cleaning metaphor that washes away our European ancestry," says Fiedler.

14. For a discussion of mysticism in one SF magazine of the thirties see Leland Sapiro's "The Mystic Renaissance: A Survey of F. Orlin Tremaine's *Astounding Stories*", *Riverside Quarterly*, vol. 2, nos. 2–4.

15. Once one has read Damon Knight's description of Merritt's appearance, one never forgets it: "Merritt was chinless, bald and shaped like a schmoo." *In Search of Wonder*, Chapter 2, 1967.

16. Colin Wilson, *The Strength to Dream*, 1962. Chapter 1. Since publishing this book, Wilson has increasingly fallen under the spell of Lovecraft, whom he likens to W. B. Yeats and Peter Kurten,

the Düsseldorf murderer. He has written two novels which utilize the Lovecraftian cult of Cthulhu, one of which, *The Space Vampires*, was filmed as *Lifeforce*.

17. H. P. Lovecraft & Willis Conover, *Lovecraft at Last*, Arlington, Va., 1975, is a charming, eccentric, expensively produced tribute by Conover to HPL—"the first adult who treated me as if I too were an adult."

18. L. Sprague de Camp, *Lovecraft: A Biography*, New York, 1975.

19. For further details concerning Lovecraft, Howard, Smith, and other fantasy writers, consult Lin Carter's *Imaginary Worlds*, New York, 1973, and L. Sprague de Camp's *Literary Swordsmen and Sorcerers*, Sark City WI, 1976.

CHAPTER VIII

1. *Modern Boy* was the British equivalent of *The American Boy*. Both ceased publication in the early nineteen-forties. Whereas the latter magazine carried Carl H. Claudy's serials about the exploits of Dr Alan Kane and his sturdy chum, Ted Dolliver—*The Doom Tocsin* (1937–38) being representative—*Modern Boy* carried Captain Justice stories throughout the thirties. Justice handled problems like run-away planets which were too big for the united governments of Britain and America. Captain Justice was written by Murray Roberts, the pen name of Robert Murray Graydon. The Justice serials were later brought out in a primitive paperback form in The Boys' Friend Library. Perhaps the most memorable of the bunch is *The World in Darkness* (1935), but all are now unbearable to read, like most ephemeral writing.

   There is an article on Claudy in *Riverside Quarterly* no. 25, March 1980: James Wade, "On Being Scared Out of One's Knickers: Carl Claudy's Kane-Dolliver Juveniles".

2. Figures taken from John Terraine's *First World War*, 1983.

3. Tony Goodstone, *The Pulps*, New York, 1970.

4. And perhaps there is room in a note to be reminded of how often opera uses a great fantasy theme. Wagner's *Ring of the Nibelung* immediately comes to mind, with its climax of flood and fire; also his use of the legend of *The Flying Dutchman*. Weber's *Der Freischütz* forges diabolically magic bullets; Offenbach's *Tales of Hoffmann* comes full of Hoffmann fantasy, a dancing mechanical doll, the theft of a reflection, and a singing portrait. Berlioz, Gounod and other composers have used the legend of Faust selling his soul to the devil to win Marguerite. Stravinsky's *Oedipus Rex* depicts the dangers inherent in seeking out the truth. Bartok's one-act opera *Bluebeard's Castle* shows the disaster that can attend a woman who seeks to know everything about her lover's past. And so on. There is probably a case to be made for arguing that opera, with all its colour, music, and ritual, is the most powerful way of conveying fantasy.

5. An entirely new translation, the first since World War II, made by Ewald Osers, was published in England in 1986.

6. Darko Suvin, *Metamorphoses of Science Fiction*, op. cit. See Chapter XII on Čapek.

7. "*Nacht und Nebel Erlass*—Night and Fog Decree. This grotesque order was issued by Hitler himself on December 7th, 1941. Its purpose, as the weird title indicates, was to seize persons 'endangering German security' who were not to be immediately executed, and make them vanish without a trace into the night and fog of the unknown in Germany." William L. Shirer, *The Rise and Fall of the Third Reich*, Book 5, The New Order.

8. Erich Heller, "The World of Franz Kafka", in *The Disinherited Mind*. Cambridge 1952.

9. *Tagebucher 1910–1923*, translated into English as *The Diary of Franz Kafka*, edited by Max Brod, 2 vols., 1948–49. "Unnoticeable life. Noticeable failure," reads one entry.

10. For the influence of psychoanalysis on Kafka, see Charles Neider's *The Frozen Sea*, 1948. An extract from this book, under the title "The Castle: A Psychoanalytical Interpretation", is included in a useful collection of critical essays, *Twentieth Century Interpretations of The Castle*, edited by Peter F. Neumeyer, Englewood Cliffs, New Jersey, 1969.

11. Marthe Robert, *Franz Kafka's Loneliness*, 1982.
12. Johann Bauer, *Kafka and Prague*, New York, 1971.
13. *Ibid.*
14. For further details of golem films, see Phil Hardy's *The Aurum Film Encylopaedia: Science Fiction*, 1984.
15. For my knowledge of this book and the next, I am indebted to Mr Peter Kuczka, the well-known Hungarian authority on science fiction. The original title of *The Nightmare* is *A Golya Kalifa.* An English translation was published by Corvina Press, Budapest, in 1966.
16. Original Hungarian titles: *Utazás Faremidóba* and *Capillaria.* An English translation by Paul Tabori was published by Corvina Press, Budapest, in 1965.
17. Robots are not always so chaste. It may be that the future holds eventual union between humanity and its machines. Robots show an increasing tendency towards close encounters of a sexual kind. Even Asimov is at it in *The Robots of Dawn*, where the female lead has a shame-free relationship with her humanoid robot. In an inspired paper, "Loving that Machine: or, The Mechanical Egg, Sexual Mechanisms and Metaphors in Science Fiction Films", Donald Palumbo examines the movie *Star Trek: The Motion Picture*, and says, "Thus the idea, at least, of sex between man and machine is here presented explicitly, as it is also explicit in films from Fritz Lang's venerable *Metropolis* to the more recent *Stepford Wives, Westworld, Futureworld, Demon Seed, Saturn 3*, and even *Barbarella* and Woody Allen's *Sleeper*." Palumbo's is one of many papers in Thomas P. Dunn and Richard D. Erlich (eds.), *The Mechanical God, Machines in Science Fiction*, Westport Conn., 1982.
18. Other large claims can be made for *Brave New World*. Peter Edgerly Firchow has this to say in his study, *The End of Utopia* (Lewisburg, 1984): "It is one of the most remarkable pieces of writing in the modern British novel." In *Writer at Work: The Paris Review Interviews*, Aldous Huxley claimed that *Brave New World* "started out as a parody of H. G. Wells's *Men Like Gods*, but gradually it got out of hand. . . ."
19. In his travel book, *Jesting Pilate*, Huxley refers to Los Angeles as The City of Dreadful Joy. "The joy, in a word, of having what is technically known as a good time."
20. Lawrence sometimes sounded like a man who knew Aldous Huxley personally. He also had his synoptic visions. This passage, for instance, comes towards the end of *Women in Love* (1920):

> God could do without the ichthyosauri and the mastodon. These monsters failed creatively to develop, so God, the creative mystery, dispensed with them. In the same way the mystery could dispense with man, should he too fail creatively to change and develop. The eternal creative mystery could dispose of man, and replace him with a finer created being. Just as the horse has taken the place of the mastodon.
> It was very consoling to Birkin to think this. If humanity ran into a cul-de-sac, and expended itself, the timeless creative mystery would bring forth some other being, finer, more wonderful, some new, more lovely race, to carry on the embodiment of creation. The game was never up. The mystery of creation was fathomless, infallible, inexhaustible, for ever. Races came and went, species passed away, but ever new species arose, more lovely, or equally lovely, always surpassing wonder. The fountainhead was incorruptible and unsearchable. It had no limits. It could bring forth miracles, create utterly new races and new species in its own hour, new forms of consciousness, new forms of body, new units of being. To be a man was as nothing compared to the possibilities of the creative mystery. To have one's pulse beating direct from the mystery, this was perfection, unutterable satisfaction. Human or inhuman mattered nothing. The perfect pulse throbbed with indescribable being, miraculous unborn species.

Earlier, Lawrence writes: "Whatever the mystery which has brought forth man and the universe, it is a non-human mystery, it has its own great ends, man is not the criterion. Best leave it all to the vast, creative, non-human mystery. But strive with oneself only, not with the universe." (Which is why he never chose explicitly science fictional subject matter). Perhaps Lawrence and Huxley were cross-pollinating influences.

21. As one critic observes, neither *Time Must Have a Stop* nor *After Many a Summer* is as depressing as the underlying pessimism would suggest. "Huxley's pessimism tends to backfire so that the very intensity of his gloom provides a springboard for a return to cheerfulness based on the reflection that we can't possibly all be as bad as that." Philip Thody, *Aldous Huxley: A Biographical Introduction*, 1973.

22. Part of Mr Scrogan's speech (in Chapter XII) runs as follows: "In the Rational State, human beings will be separated out into distinct species, not according to the colour of their eyes or the shape of their skulls, but according to the qualities of their mind and temperament . . . Duly labelled and docketted, the child will be set, in adult life, to perform those functions which human beings of his variety are capable of performing." Here lies the germ of the idea behind *Brave New World*, with its hatcheries.

23. In Julian Huxley (ed.), *Aldous Huxley: A Memorial Volume*. 1965.

24. For a further comparison between Wells and Huxley see Brian Aldiss, "The Hand in the Jar: Metaphor in Wells and Huxley", *Foundation* 17, September 1979.

25. One commentator adds, "Finally, it is an ironic farewell to Huxley's past; there are many deliberate and playful echoes from the earlier novels, and personal ghosts are laid at last." George Woodcock, *Dawn and the Darkest Hour: A Study of Aldous Huxley*, 1972.

26. From Philip Toynbee's review of *Island*, *Observer*, Sunday, April 1st, 1962.

27. Laura Archera Huxley, *This Timeless Moment: A Personal View of Aldous Huxley*, 1969.

28. The standard life is the two-volume *Aldous Huxley: A Biography*, by Sybille Bedford, 1973.

29. A passage that will remind admirers of A. W. Kinglake's *Eothen* of the traveller's conversation with a pasha, from which it is concluded that "the intervention of the dragoman is fatal to the spirit of the conversation".

30. Aldiss: "I would have thought that you constructed *Perelandra* for the didactic purpose." Lewis: "Yes, everyone thinks that. They are quite wrong . . . The story of this averted Fall came in very conveniently. Of course it wouldn't have been that particular story if I wasn't interested in those particular ideas on other grounds. But that isn't what I started from." (From C. S. Lewis's "Discussion of Science Fiction", recorded by Brian Aldiss, *SF Horizons 1*, 1964; reprinted in *Of Other Worlds*.)

31. Perhaps the difficulty one has with *Perelandra* is suggested by Lois and Stephen Rose, authors of *The Shattered Ring: Science Fiction and the Quest for Meaning*, 1970, when they say "The evil antagonist, Weston, is often compared to a nasty little boy. His 'naughtiness' is epitomized by his cruel teasing and senseless torture of animals. . . ." Lewis gives us nastiness and a dose of horror. But he confronts us with no real evil.

32. Those who find *A Voyage to Arcturus* readable but baffling are advised to seek out the 1963 Gollancz edition, which includes a Note examining the novel in the light of Milton's epic. This note is by E. H. Visiak, who died in 1972, aged ninety-four. Like Lewis, Visiak was a Milton scholar. His esoteric novel *Medusa* (1929) also bears Miltonic traces.

33. Roger Lancelyn Green, *C. S. Lewis*, a Bodley Head Monograph, 1963, p. 26.

34. Very ambivalent. Lewis apologizes to Wells in a special note in *Out of the Silent Planet*; but Jules in *That Hideous Strength* is a spiteful and personal caricature. It was hardly Wells's fault that he was a Cockney, or that his legs were short.

35. Humphrey Carpenter, *The Inklings: C. S. Lewis, J. R. R. Tolkien, Charles Williams, and their Friends*, 1978. The Eagle and Child still stands in Oxford's St Giles.

36. For a discussion of this theme, see Mark R. Hillegas, *The Future as Nightmare: H. G. Wells and the Anti-Utopians*, New York, 1967. Hillegas deals fully with Lewis, Forster, Zamyatin, and Orwell, and looks rather tentatively at the world of standard science fiction. Hillegas's study was reviewed at some length by C. C. Shackleton in a two-part criticism in *New Worlds*, nos. 182–183.

37. The passage awakens memories of Lilith's speech at the end of George Bernard Shaw's ambitious play on creative evolution, *Back to Methuselah* (1921): "Of Life only is there no end; and though

of its million starry mansions many are empty and many still unbuilt, and though its vast domain is as yet unbearably desert, my seed shall one day fill it and master its matter to its uttermost confines." (Readers who discover their own favourite author too briefly dealt with in these pages should note that probably the greatest dramatist of our century is passed over in this footnote.)

38. This point is made by Leslie Fiedler in his study, *Olaf Stapledon: A Man Divided*, 1983. For a discussion of Fiedler's approach to Stapledon, see the chapter "The Immanent Will Returns", in Brian Aldiss, *The Pale Shadow of Science*, Seattle, 1985.

39. Patrick A. McCarthy, *Olaf Stapledon*, Boston, 1983.

40. Leslie Fiedler, *op. cit.*

41. For an analysis of the novel, see Anthony Storr's Introduction to the 1978 reprint.

42. For a study of Fowler Wright and other British authors, consult the comprehensive Brian Stableford, *Scientific Romance in Britain, 1890–1950*, 1985. Stableford deals with the major writers of the period as well as lesser known names, such as J. D. Beresford, Neil Bell, John Gloag, and Guy Dent.

43. Facts which seem to be cautiously confirmed by Tymn and Ashley (Eds), *Science Fiction, Fantasy, and Weird Fiction Magazines*, Westport, Conn., 1985.

44. Lundwall is also author of *Science Fiction: An Illustrated History*, 1978. This is an exuberant polemical volume which advances proof that science fiction had a strong tradition in Europe before the First World War. Lundwall's interpretation of what constitutes SF is somewhat broad and lax. His work met with a hostile reception.

45. Sam J. Lundwall, "Adventures in the Pulp Jungle", *Foundation* 34, Autumn 1985. Lundwall also produced an early book of SF criticism, *Science Fiction: What It's All About*, New York, 1971.

46. When an SF fan approached Stapledon in 1936, the latter was treated to his first glimpse of science fiction magazines. "My impression was that the stories varied greatly in quality," Stapledon politely said. The anecdote is told at greater length in Sam Moskowitz's *Explorers of the Infinite*, Cleveland [1963]. Chapter 16.

47. The date of the first use of the term "science fiction" has been established as 1851, until earlier claimants appear. I examined in the Bodleian Library in Oxford a copy of William Wilson's *A Little Earnest Book upon a Great Old Subject* which had remained unread and unopened there for one hundred and twenty-four years. It was published by Darton & Co. in 1851, the year Mary Shelley died, the year of the Great Exhibition. In Chapter X, Wilson wrote, "Campbell says that 'Fiction in Poetry is not the reverse of truth, but her soft and enchanting resemblance'. Now this applies especially to Science-Fiction, in which the revealed truths of Science may be given, interwoven with a pleasing story which itself may be poetical and true. . . ." It is a reasonable prescription for SF at any time. Note that the Campbell referred to is not the editor John W. Campbell, but the poet Thomas Campbell.

48. "The real 'Father of Science Fiction' is Hugo Gernsback and no one can take the title away from him." Sam Moskowitz: *Explorers of the Infinite, op. cit.* Chapter 14.

49. A late competitor to enter this fat-headed paternity hunt is Isaac Asimov, in his Introduction to *Astounding: John W. Campbell Memorial Anthology*, edited by Harry Harrison, 1973. Asimov's tribute to Campbell is headed "The Father of Science Fiction".

50. Robert A. W. Lowndes in a letter to *Foundation* 35.

51. A story suspiciously similar to this apocryphal one appears in the April 1929 issue of *Amazing Stories*.

CHAPTER IX

1. The famous SF fan, Forrest J. Ackerman, "Mr Science Fiction", has complete mint runs of *all* SF magazines, housed in his fabulous home in Hollywood, the Ackermansion.

2. Writing in an Italian magazine in 1919, De Chirico makes these remarks on Verne: "Joyful but involuntary movements of the metaphysical can be observed both in painters and writers, and speaking of writers I would like to

remember here an old French provincial who we will call, for clarity's sake, the armchair explorer. I refer to Jules Verne, who wrote travel and adventure novels, and who is considered to be a writer for children.

"But who was more gifted than he in capturing the metaphysical element of a city like London, with its houses, streets, clubs, squares and open spaces; the ghostliness of a Sunday afternoon in London, the melancholy of a man, a real walking phantom, as Phineas Fogg appears in *Around the World in Eighty Days*?

"The work of Jules Verne is full of these joyous and most consoling moments; I still remember the description of the departure of a steamship from Liverpool in his novel *The Floating City*."

The essay "On Metaphysical Art", from which this extract is taken, is included in Massimo Carra's *Metaphysical Art*, 1971.

3. The art editor of the series was the Italian Germano Facetti. The covers mentioned were, in chronological order: *Penguin Science Fiction*, edited by Brian Aldiss—Oscar Dominguez's *Memory of the Future* (1961); *The Day it Rained Forever*, by Ray Bradbury—Max Ernst's *Jardin Globe-Avions* (1963); *A Case of Conscience*, by James Blish—Ernst's *The Eye of Silence* (1963); *The Evolution Man*, by Roy Lewis—Picasso's first cover for *Minotaure* (1963); *Mission of Gravity*, by Hal Clement—Yves Tanguy's *The Doubter* (1963); *The Dragon in the Sea*, by Frank Herbert—Paul Klee's *Underwater Garden* (1963); *More Penguin Science Fiction*, edited by Brian Aldiss—Kandinsky's *Small Worlds* (1963); *Deathworld*, by Harry Harrison—Pavel Tchelitchev's *Citron* (1963).

4. A move towards coherence was made in the lavishly illustrated Brian Aldiss (ed.), *Science Fiction Art* (1975), in which covers from all SF magazines were illustrated for the first time. A valuable essay is Vincent di Fate, "Science Fiction Art: Some Contemporary Illustrators", in Marshall B. Tymn (ed.), *The Science Fiction Reference Book*, Washington, 1981. Di Fate is both an artist and a scholar.

5. In sequence the series runs, *Triplanetary*, *First Lensman*, *Galactic Patrol*, *Gray Lens-man*, *Second Stage Lensman*, *Children of the Lens*.

6. There is even a concordance to the works of "Doc" Smith, an honour he shares with Shakespeare, Charles Dickens, and other greats. It is Ron Ellik and Bill Evans, *The Universe of E. E. Smith*, Chicago, 1966—another publication from the dedicated House of Advent.

7. Fearn's devoted biographer, Philip Harbottle, claims that the Liverpudlian Fearn used more pseudonyms than any other fantasy writer, and tells me of thirty-three; there were perhaps more. There were certainly other pseudonyms used for other fields. All the details are given in *The Multi-Man: A Biographic and Bibliographic Study of John Russell Fearn*, by Philip Harbottle, privately printed by the author, 1968.

8. See the long article "Judgement at Jonbar", by Brian Aldiss in *SF Horizons* I, 1964.

9. Campbell's unremitting attempts to build telepathy, ESP, and other odd psychic phenomena into a science called psionics were based on unscientific premises. These premises are revealed in something Campbell says in an article "The Story Behind the Story", about his novelette "The Double Minds", published in the August 1937 issue of *Thrilling Wonder Stories*. What Campbell mildly calls a "pet idea" was in fact to become an obsession.

In most instances, I think, authors have some "pet" ideas, that gradually work themselves into the shape of a story, given time. The present yarn, "The Double Minds", is based on the interesting fact that no man ever used, or began to use so much as a quarter of the capacity of his brain. The total capacity of the mind, even at present, is to all intents and purposes, infinite. Could the full equipment be hooked into a functioning unit, the resulting intelligence should be able to conquer a world without much difficulty.

Leaving aside the question of whether greater intelligence might not reject the idea of conquest, this view of the brain is erroneous. The functionalism of nature does not allow any organ to operate at twenty-five per cent capacity for many generations; that we still do not understand all the workings of the brain is entirely another matter. Campbell may have caught his "pet idea" from John Russell Fearn, whose very first story, *The Intelligence Gigantic* (*Amazing*, 1933), uses the same theme. "We only think and receive impressions in snatches, imperfectly understood, but—and this is the vital point—with a nerve connection to make the entire brain of use, we can operate our brain power to the full! It means a power of thought five times greater than we now have." What a gift to power-fantasy the idea was!

10. An analysis of Campbell is to be found in Chapter 17 of Donald Wollheim's dogmatic *The Universe Makers*, New York, 1971. He points out the frustrations of Campbell's long editorial job on *ASF* (a job so devotedly done, so wretchedly paid), and the way in which his policies later isolated him from the sympathies of fandom.

11. *Ibid.*

12. The quote is taken from a 1960 editorial, "Unimaginable Reasons", and incidentally gives a demonstration of the way in which Campbell loved to lecture his authors. As Harry Harrison has said, "When John Campbell was talking, a lot of solemn nodding went on all round!"

13. Alva Rogers, *A Requiem for 'Astounding'*, Chicago, 1964. Chapter 5, "The Dawn of the Golden Age, 1939–1940".

14. The point is well brought out by Joseph F. Patrouch, in *The Science Fiction of Isaac Asimov*, New York, 1974. Patrouch is good on the weaknesses of the *Foundation* stories—and their strengths.

15. Though several novels from *Astounding*'s fantasy companion *Unknown* preceded it: L. Sprague de Camp's *Lest Darkness Fall* (1941), de Camp and Fletcher Pratt's *The Land of Unreason* (1941) and *The Incomplete Enchanter* (1942), and Eric Frank Russell's *Sinister Barrier* (1943). *Lest Darkness Fall* and *Sinister Barrier* are both SF.

16. Introduction to revised Berkley Medallion edition of *The World of Null-A*, 1970.

17. I owe this observation to Dr Leon Stover of I.I.T., Chicago.

18. John W. Campbell, *Collected Editorials from Analog*, selected by Harry Harrison, New York, 1966. In his Introduction to the volume, Harrison points out the impact of Campbell on his writers and

adds, "None of these writers has been so small as to deny the influence of John Campbell, and the number of books that have been dedicated to him gives evidence of this. At a guess I would say there are at least thirty, a record that I am sure is unique in literature."

19. For use of the submarine as phallic symbol, see Arnold Kohn's cover painting on *Fantastic Adventures* for March 1949; mention of this cover is also made in note 24 below.

20. Examples: Van Vogt's "Far Centaurus", *Astounding Science Fiction*, January 1944, uses the spaceship as symbolizing the spirit of dedication—in this case ironically defeated. L. Ron Hubbard's *To the Stars*, *ASF*, February–March 1950, uses it as a symbol of manly togetherness—most noticeable when the crew of the *Hound of Heaven*, travelling at near light speed, bursts into its favourite chorus, "Viva la *Hound*, viva la *Hound*, viva la company". As for romanticized industrial processes, this is so all-pervasive it is hard to exemplify; but one might stipulate most of the Venus Equilateral stories by George O. Smith, or the same author's "The Impossible Pirate", *ASF*, December 1946. For the spaceship as a symbol of the imprisonment of life that technological advancement can bring about, one must turn to a later generation of writers—for example, the present writer's *Non-Stop*, 1958, published as *Starship* in the United States.

21. Observations similar to these first saw the light of day in Dr Leon Stover's study of the processes behind literature, *American Science Fiction: An Anthropological Exegesis*, Chapter 5. This thesis has been published only in France, as *La Science Fiction Americaine*, Paris, 1972.

22. For instance in "The Time Trap", in *Marvel Science Stories*, Vol. 1, No. 2, November 1938. There are at least three naked ladies in this fantasia of Kuttner's. The voluntary stripper is Nirvor, priestess with silver hair, eternally accompanied by two leopards. She declares her love for the hero and strips. He rejects her on the grounds that she was once a leopardess. Vivisection has done a brilliant conversion job. How Dr Moreau would have laughed!

23. For example, in *The Issue at Hand*, pp. 78–79, where it is pleasant to note

that Blish also seizes on that same passage about the candle-flame thoughts of goldfish. Blish has vigorously refuted Moskowitz's view of Kuttner as a derivative hack, in "Moskowitz on Kuttner", an article in *Riverside Quarterly*, Vol. 5, No. 2; he concludes by saying that Moskowitz's "sole critical principle is one of infinite regress"—a remark not made any kinder by its high accuracy quota.

24. A comment that applies even more to the other magazines in the field. If the present authors ever compile a companion volume to this, they will concentrate on magazines other than *Astounding*. Meanwhile, to take a lucky dip and pick up one issue of one magazine: *Fantastic Adventures* for March 1949. Here are some of the story blurbs: "Beneath the ocean floor lay a great secret—guarded by the giant mer-race. . . ."; "The people of Loran looked into the sky and saw the great spaceship approach. Was it possible that God had returned?"; "Is existence as we know it but a series of locked doors in time? And is the mind the key that will open them?"; "Dave had to win the chess game—for if he lost, the Earth would be destroyed. . . .". They give an idea, which pictures and stories powerfully reinforce, of the way the genre dealt with matters and images which have legendary power over us. The none-too-concealed erotic meaning of that particular issue's cover, with the immense mermaid clutching a submarine in one hand, reinforces the feeling that mere likelihood was not and should not have been given first consideration.

25. Here is how one commentator saw the sensational Dianetics affair and its launching in the pages of Campbell's magazine. In *The Creation of Tomorrow: Fifty Years of Magazine Science Fiction*, New York, 1977, Paul A. Carter says:

The May 1950 *Astounding* featured a forty-page article by one of its regular (and most popular) writers, L. Ron Hubbard, "Dianetics: A New Science of the Mind". Simultaneously, Hubbard's hard-cover book, *Dianetics: the Modern Science of Mental Health*, came off the press, and by August it had sold

55,000 copies. Never had a writer more spectacularly broken out of science fiction's magazine ghetto, and seldom had science fiction so confidently put its worst foot forward.

Campbell, on the other hand, changed feet, as Carter reports. In an editorial accompanying the Hubbard article ("Concerning Dianetics", *ASF*, May 1950), Campbell proclaimed: "I want to assure every reader, most positively and unequivocally, that this article is *not* a hoax, joke, or anything but a direct, clear statement of a totally new scientific thesis." It is ironic indeed that what John Campbell proposed to treat as a hypothesis should so speedily have evolved into a religion, and after about a year's flirtation with Hubbard's new faith, Campbell backed off. Haywiring electronic circuitry, he admitted, was a good deal simpler than tinkering with the mind.

26. Mike Ashley, *The History of the Science Fiction Magazines*, 4 vols., 1974–76 & 1978.

27. Marshall B. Tymn and Mike Ashley (eds), *Science Fiction, Fantasy, and Weird Fiction Magazines*, Westport, Conn., 1985. This massive compilation of almost 1,000 pages contains details with commentaries of all relevant magazines. Albert I. Berger contributes a magisterial survey of *Astounding/Analog* from its first number to the present. All English language magazines are listed and intelligently discussed.

28. See for instance, Tony Goodstone, (ed.), *The Pulps: Fifty Years of American Pop Culture*, New York (n.d.)

29. *Ibid*, Chapter 7.

30. Evidence of Campbell's response to his times is contained in *The John W. Campbell Letters, Volume I*, editors Perry A. Chapdelaine, Sr., Tony Chapdelaine, George Hay, 1985. (All so far published.)

This interesting volume shows Campbell in full spate, arguing and expatiating with his authors and colleagues. One example will demonstrate the style. In a letter to Theodore Sturgeon, written in November 1954, Campbell dismisses fantasy as "nice, safe, comfortable reading", and speaks of the kind of story he wants: "I'm still looking for the stories that get in and really twist things in the reader—and that does *not* mean a few endocrine glands. You can scare a guy for ten seconds with a rubber dummy in a dimly lighted room; that gives his glands a work-out.

"But you can shock him out of a lifetime pattern, and change him for the rest of his natural existence, if you can find and break one of his false cultural orientations. You'll scare hell out of him too—for weeks, not seconds, incidentally—because, when he gets through, he discovers that a barrier he thought was a great stone wall . . . has become painted cellophane. . . .

"Yeah—I know this isn't as popular a type of story . . . yet! But give us some time! We're developing an art form that hasn't been more than started—as a *conscious* effort.

"I suspect it'll never be really a mass-audience type either. You can kill people with a really good story of that type—and I am *not* kidding. It's a fine exercise for strong minds—and our readers wouldn't be the speculative philosophical people they are if they didn't have tough resilient minds—but it's not good for the weak ones."

31. For further comments on *Astounding*'s effect on readers—and for a full selection of the best-remembered stories mainly from its Golden Years, see *The Astounding-Analog Reader*, edited by Harry Harrison and Brian Aldiss, 2 vols. New York, 1972–73.

CHAPTER X

1. Characteristically, on neutral ground! This was the First International SF Symposium, held in Tokyo in 1970, to coincide with Expo '70; organized by Sakyo Komatsu, Chairman, and first suggested by the present writer. Those present included Frederik Pohl, Judith Merril, Vasily Zakharchenko, E. I. Parnov, Julius Kagarlitski, Arthur C. Clarke and Brian Aldiss.

2. *Tiger! Tiger!*, Chapter 15.

3. "Trap", first published in *Galaxy*, February 1956, as by Finn O'Donnevan. Collected in *Pilgrimage to Earth*, New York, 1957.

4. Damon Knight refers to *More Than Human* and *The Demolished Man* as "the two most famous SF books of the fifties", in his introduction to *A Science Fiction Argosy*, ed. Damon Knight, New York, 1972.

5. Gardner Dozois, "Damon Knight" in E. F. Bleiler, ed., *Science Fiction Writers*, *op. cit.*

6. Malcolm Edwards, "William Tenn" in Bleiler, *ibid.*

7. Interview with Brad Linaweaver in *Riverside Quarterly*, Dec. 1985.

8. See *In Memory Yet Green: The Autobiography of Isaac Asimov, 1920–1954*, New York, 1979, Chapter 53, Section 10, page 650.

9. Under the name of William Atheling, Jr, Blish wrote two books of SF criticism, both published by Advent: *The Issue at Hand* (1964), and *More Issues at Hand* (1970). His critical work in the field of James Joyce studies is also well known.

10. The four volumes in the *Cities in Flight* sequence are as follows: *They Shall Have Stars* (1956), *A Life for the Stars* (1962), *Earthman, Come Home* (1955), and *A Clash of Cymbals* (1958—*The Triumph of Time* in the USA). The books cover a time scale of 1992 years.

11. For a fuller discussion of Blish's work see Brian W. Aldiss, "James Blish and the Mathematics of Knowledge" in *This World and Nearer Ones* (1979). Brian W. Aldiss's *The Pale Shadow of Science*, *op. cit.*, includes an examination of Blish's novel about instantaneous galactic communication, *The Quincunx of Time*.

12. The point has been made many times. One statement of it, from the viewpoint of a "human biologist" may be found in Alex Comfort's *Nature and Human Nature*, 1966.

13. Orwell commented on *We*: "It is in effect a study of the Machine, the genie that man has thoughtlessly let out of its bottle and cannot put back again." Written in 1920, Zamyatin's dystopia prefigures Stalin's "One State" in its concern with obsessive, mathematical conformity. The narrator, D-503, is a mathematician, and his language and imagery are purely mathematical. As with Orwell's Winston Smith, D-503 is tempted off the straight and narrow by a dark-haired anarchistic female—E-330, the Julia of Zamyatin's tale. But Zamyatin's story is less overtly political than Orwell's. He

intended to talk not of politics but of life-directions: and these life directions are vividly illustrated in his text, forming polarities. Primitivism and anarchy are opposed against Mechanism and Order, Liberty against Control.

We has, at its finality, a similar triumph of the State to Orwell's: E-330 is suffocated in a bell-jar-like execution chamber, and D-503 suffers a kind of lobotomy—the fantasiectomy. The escape into a creative and vital life is only transient: perfect order returns to the city beneath the dome, where the horror of the irrational—expressed by D-503 as the corresponding curve or solid to the square root of minus one (an impossibility), "an entire immense universe . . . there, below the surface"—is forever held at bay. Brian Aldiss's dystopian novel *Enemies of the System* (1978) is more directly in the tradition of *We* than of *1984*.

14. While examining boys' magazines in his article, "Boys' Weeklies", written in 1939, Orwell comments, "The one theme that really is new is the scientific one. Death rays, Martians, invisible men, robots, helicopters, and interplanetary rockets figure largely; here and there are even far-off rumours of psychotherapy and ductless glands." He had *Modern Boy* and *Champion* mainly in mind, though a glance at the *Chums* annual for 1921 shows that Orwell's comments held good for most British magazines between the wars. In one "amazing and thrilling" adventure, "The Lost Planet" by Eric Wood, our heroic chums are seen waving from the window of a submarine-like rocket as its propellor-tail thrusts it along and up a Jules Vernian ramp, heading for Mars. The rocket is, of course, a Marsobus, and when it reaches Mars a Rider Haggard-like adventure follows, with pigmy tribes, thinly-disguised blacks and an assortment of stereotyped situations. Along with pirate and Arabian adventures, tales of schooldays, football sagas and cowboys and indians, a crude science fiction supplemented the standard fictional diet of most middle class British schoolboys in the twenties and thirties.

Orwell's article also mentions "threepenny Yank Mags"—the Woolworth's counter which was the tra-ditional spot at which future British addicts were infected with the SF virus. In terms of quality there is little to choose between the likes of Eric Wood and, in *Amazing* say, Ralph Milne Farley. The racism and sexism is more overt in Wood.

15. Orwell was one of the Angry Young Men of his day, in a line stretching back through Shelley and Wells and forward to Amis and Osborne—men whose sympathies, at least during the flush of youth, lay with the submerged classes. Like calls to like over the years; as Desmond King-Hele notes in *Shelley: His Thought and Work*, Chapter 8, the song "Beasts of England" in *Animal Farm* is a parody of Shelley's challenge to the ruling classes, "Song of the Men of England":

> Men of England, wherefore plough
>   For the lords who lay ye low?
> Wherefore weave with toil and care
>   The rich robes your tyrants wear?

Again like Shelley, Orwell wrote a parody of the national anthem. It appears in *Animal Farm*, as "Comrade Napoleon". This was the book banned, not in England, but in the USSR.

16. The point is made, with different emphasis, by Chad Walsh in his *From Utopia to Nightmare*, 1962. Chapter 8.

17. Something of the same viewpoint appears more diffusely in H. F. (Gerald) Heard's *Doppelgangers*, New York, 1947. Heard postulates two worlds, an upper and a lower, both ruled by tyrants, one rather like *Brave New World* and one similar to *1984*. The central character has his personality wiped out as Winston Smith does (Zamyatin's D-503 also), but by means of very elaborate and futuristic behaviourist devices.

18. In the months before June 1983 the Conservatives used Orwell's message against the Labour party, warning the electorate by means of huge billboards that socialism equated with strict State control.

19. Sir Richard Rees, *George Orwell: Fugitive from the Camp of Victory*, 1961. Chapter 8.

20. Another way in which to portray the corrosive effects of technological civilization is to depict man as dehumanized, as robot or android—the message of *R.U.R.* and most significant robot stor-

ies since. Stories of robots becoming "humanized" have always seemed perverse, a confusion of symbols.

21. In this respect, it is interesting to compare the translation of the two books into other media. Orwell's *1984* was one of the early successes of post-war British television—the programme everyone watched—its gritty subject matter well matched by the gritty techniques of the flickering small screen. Later, it was made into a less successful film, with Michael Redgrave as O'Brien and Patrick O'Brien as Smith. *Animal Farm* became an animated cartoon. The 1984 film of *1984*, with John Hurt as Winston and Richard Burton as O'Brien, returned to the grittiness of 1948 for its inspiration.

22. Before *2001*, Kubrick made *Dr Strangelove* (1963) from Peter George's *Red Alert* and, after *2001*, *A Clockwork Orange* (1971) from Anthony Burgess's novel of the same name. The latter is one of the masterpieces of the SF cinema. On the strength of this, Kubrick should perhaps be acknowledged as a great SF writer of our time.

23. Filmed twice by Hollywood, first by Howard Hawks in 1951 as *The Thing From Another World*; there Campbell's original idea of shape-mutation and imitation was abandoned. The special effects didn't run to it. The second version, John Carpenter's 1982 film, *The Thing*, is much more faithful. There, for the first time on celluloid, we can see with our own eyes what those writers of the early fifties fearfully expressed. But Hawks was better on character.

24. Richard Lupoff was later to use Tenn's idea in his 1979 fix-up novel, *Space War Blues*.

25. But how often SF reads like religion-for-unbelievers. Dehumanization is an atheist's version of demonic possession. The two disciplines are fused in the Bent One's seizure of Weston in *Perelandra*.

26. Three slightly later British versions may be noted, Brian Aldiss's "Outside" (1955), Eric Frank Russell's *Three to Conquer* (a 1955 *ASF* serial as *Call Him Dead*; book form 1956) and Kingsley Amis's "Something Strange", (1960).

27. More accurately, a theme will not die while there is a socio-economic reason for its survival. The British theme of "submerged nations"—derived from Disraeli's two nations—finally petered out at the end of World War II, interred between Party and prole in *1984*. From which we may deduce that aliens-among-us will continue for some while to be a feature of American SF.

28. The Russian director, Andrei Tarkovsky, in his two SF films: *Solaris* (1971) and *Stalker* (1979), has shunned the spectacular special effects with which Hollywood decks its SF films. Along with Kubrick he might be said to be a genuine SF talent working in a different medium. Concerning the film of *Solaris*, see "The Film Tarkovsky Made", in *This World and Nearer Ones* by Brian Aldiss, *op. cit.* Tarkovsky's *Sculpting in Time* (1986) is a discussion of his film-making methods and philosophy.

29. Four films have been made from John Wyndham's writings. *The Day of the Triffids* was filmed by director Steve Sekeley in 1963, and starred Howard Keel in a role that was nothing to sing about. A short story, "Random Quest", was filmed as *Quest for Love* in 1971. *The Midwich Cuckoos* was filmed twice, as *Village of the Damned* (1960) and *Children of the Damned* (1963). Each of these versions has its champions and detractors, but *Village*, for all its unsophisticated techniques, still has considerable impact more than twenty years on. The blond-haired, golden-eyed children, of alien origin, became an element—like triffids—in popular folklore.

30. In *Earth Abides* a strain of super-influenza is the culprit—leaving the protagonist, Isherwood Williams (modelled on an Amerind legend, Ish) to stalk through a decimated but structurally undamaged world in search of other survivors. As such, the story owes much to earlier Last Men tales—Mary Shelley's *The Last Man*, for instance—and has a muted Adam and Eve theme to it. Eventually a form of savage civilization (again, based on an Amerind model) is re-established, and the old days become Myth. One of Stewart's strengths is in the way he depicts Ish as the "Last American" in the finale of the novel—one of the old men, surviving into a new culture: a culture wholly alien to him. His great grandson, Jack, becomes tribal leader in a world where America and technology have

become myths. Like all good themes in SF it has been refurbished and re-told many times since Stewart wrote in 1949.

31. De Camp's most impressive work of scholarship is his biography of H. P. Lovecraft, a 500-page study, published in 1975.

32. As *Charly*, it was filmed in 1968 by Ralph Nelson, with Cliff Robertson as Charly Gordon. Robertson won that year's Oscar for his role.

33. Leigh Brackett shared co-screenplay credits for George Lucas's 1980 box office SF hit, *The Empire Strikes Back*, the second film in the *Star Wars* sequence. Brackett's style of colourful space opera was well suited to the film.

34. The question, presumably, which interested Michael Moorcock. See his introduction to the Roberts & Vinter edition of *The Rose*, 1966. This short novel had previously been published only in the British *Authentic* SF magazine, edited by H. J. Campbell.

35. British edition published by Faber & Faber in 1964. Introduction by Brian Aldiss. Paperback edition, 1967. Later, another edition was published in the SF Master series, edited by Brian Aldiss and Harry Harrison (1976). This edition carried a new Introduction by Brian Aldiss.

36. "Tolkien worked on it with a fair degree of consistency for 12 years before he completed the initial manuscript in 1950. Length of time in the making is not necessarily a reflection of the quality of a work, but in the case of *Lord of the Rings*, it is. Simply expressed, *LOTR* has become the norm according to which all other fantasy works must now be judged." Marshall B. Tymn, Kenneth J. Zahorski, and Robert H. Boyer, *Fantasy Literature: A Core Collection and Reference Guide*, New York, 1979. Two useful books on Tolkien are Humphrey Carpenter, *J. R. R. Tolkien: A Biography* (1977) and T. A. Shippey, *The Road to Middle Earth* (1982).

37. Sam Lundwall, *Science Fiction: What It's All About*, 1971, Chapter 5.

38. Joseph F. Patrouch, Jr: *The Science Fiction of Isaac Asimov*. N.Y., 1974.

39. This segment was renamed "The Encyclopedists" by Asimov for book publication. The large introductory section, "The Psychohistorians", was the last part of the original trilogy to be written—in March 1951, introducing the psychohistorian, Hari Seldon, "in life". From the start, however, Asimov usually managed to breathe more life into his robots than his humans, and in view of recent developments in the future history series, it might be speculated upon that Hari Seldon is, in fact, a robot—maybe even R. Daneel Olivaw himself!

40. Others have expressed serious reservations regarding the *Foundation* series without in any way denting its popularity. "From just about any formal perspective, the *Foundation* trilogy is seriously flawed," Charles Elkins, "Asimov's *Foundation* Novels: Historical Materialism Distorted into Cyclical Psychohistory", in *Isaac Asimov*, ed. Joseph D. Olander and Martin Harry Greenberg, New York, 1977.

   Asimov's innate conservatism led him to follow the decline and fall of the Roman Empire as a model. This was Damon's Knight's complaint in *In Search of Wonder*. Asimov himself said on this score, "I always felt it wisest to be guided by past-history." (In Isaac Asimov, *The Early Asimov*, New York, 1972.) This innate conservatism has probably contributed to the durability of the three novels, despite the fallacy of the assumption that history is merely cyclic.

41. In the most recent novel in the sequence, *Robots and Empire*, 1985, we are left with one final enigma to solve; to "find where the missing Solarians" have gone. One might posit some kind of obsessive trait in Asimov from this constant pattern in his work. The closing words of "Foundation" hinge upon another such dilemma, and the whole *Foundation* sequence is based on a series of searches—first for the whereabouts of the Second Foundation, then for lost Earth (perhaps one of the oldest clichés in magazine SF, and the *idée fixe* of E. C. Tubb's even lengthier Dumarest saga). In Asimov it might be a sign, also, of an obsession with the scientific method.

42. Despite which, one critic claims this novel is "not melodramatic, but sure and real". The remark occurs in Chapter 3 of Alexei Panshin's *Heinlein in Dimension: A Critical Analysis*, Chicago, 1968. This is a long, honourable, and painstaking study of Heinlein's work, recommended

simply as a popular guide. But Panshin has no grasp of critical method, or of what makes literature. His own prose style is blind to grace and meaning; "By 2075 one assumes that everybody will talk enough differently from the present to need translation into our terms."

43. And at the same time occasionally humorous—take two essays from the 1980 collection, *Expanded Universe*, as instances: "How to be a Survivor" and "Pie from the Sky", both about the negative aspects of Nuclear War. However, essays like "1950 Where To?" (updated in 1965 and 1980 and printed in the same collection) tumble from rational argument into gung-ho power fantasy, often within the same paragraph: "For Man is rarely logical. But I have great confidence in Man, based on his past record. He is mean, ornery, cantankerous, illogical, emotional—and amazingly hard to kill." This is pure rhetoric. One might set against Heinlein's sentiments a reminder that Hitler, Stalin and, more recently, Pol Pot, found Man amazingly easy to kill—and in large numbers.

44. Panshin, *op. cit.*, Chapter 7.

45. *A Canticle for Leibowitz* was originally published as three novellas: "A Canticle For Leibowitz" (*F&SF*, April 1955); "And The Light Is Risen" (*F&SF*, August 1956); "The Last Canticle" (*F&SF*, February 1957).

46. Judith Merril, "What Do You Mean—Science Fiction?", Pt. 2, *Extrapolation*, Vol. 8, No. 1. One of Miss Merril's great gifts as anthologist and catalyst—not to mention female incendiary—has been her enthusiasm. Here it runs away with her slightly, but in the main what she says is incontrovertible. She goes on to add of Boucher that "he would not buy a story just for the idea; he had to like the writing. And unlike most earlier editors, he was not style-deaf".

47. Strictly as codified in the immortal couplet by Robert Conquest:

"SF's no good," they bellow till we're deaf.
"But this looks good."—"Well, then, it's not SF."

48. A word must be said for Pat Frank's novel, *Alas, Babylon* (1959), in which World War III breaks out and the States is bombed back to the Stone Age. A little community survives, cut off in Florida. At last, a helicopter arrives, and the community can get some news of the outside world. One of the survivors asks, "Who won the war?" The helicopter pilot is amazed: "You mean you really don't know? . . . We won it. We really clobbered 'em!"

49. "Common Sense" was first published in *Astounding* in 1941, following on from "Universe". The two novellas form the short novel, *Orphans of the Sky*, published in book form in 1963.

CHAPTER XI

1. *Publishers Weekly* for January 10th, 1986 shows fewer than usual in the hard-cover bestseller list—only four in the top fifteen: *Contact* by Carl Sagan (4), *Galápagos* by Kurt Vonnegut (6), *The Cat Who Walks Through Walls* by Robert Heinlein (8), and *The Invaders Plan* by L. Ron Hubbard (11). Clarke, Asimov, McCaffrey, Donaldson, Piers Anthony, David Eddings, Harrison and Herbert appear regularly these days in both the hard-cover and paperback bestseller lists.

2. *LACon*, the 42nd World Science Fiction Convention, held in Anaheim, California, in September 1984, had a paid membership of 9282 with 8365 in actual attendance. Door prices ranged from $35 for one day to $75 for the full convention. The Art Show auction alone took $97,000. (Figures courtesy of *Locus*, October 1984.) The first convention, in Philadelphia in 1936, had nine attendees, Frederik Pohl and Don Wollheim of DAW Books among them.

3. *The Science Fiction Source Book*, 1984, (ed.) David Wingrove, lists 364 titles in this respect, but this is only scratching the surface of an ever-widening field of study. Regular critical magazines, *Science-Fiction Studies*, *Riverside Quarterly*, *Extrapolation*, *Foundation* and *Vector* add to this plethora of learned commentary.

4. Herewith a brief list of some which did contain fresh ideas or fresh approaches. *Phase IV* (1973), a film ostensibly about intelligent ants, but with a non-anthropocentric viewpoint. *Dark Star*

(1974), which took the standard materials of modern SF as natural elements in its laid-back storyline. *Quintet* (1979), for trying to create a complex and original post-Ice Age scenario, can be forgiven its obscurity. *Android* (1982), which, with a nod to *Metropolis*, created the most charming and likeable robot in the film genre. *Videodrome* (1982), another Cronenberg film, frighteningly realistic in its pursuit of fake realities and melting flesh. *Spacehunter: Adventures in the Forbidden Zone* (1983), the first intelligent and superbly visual B-feature. *The Terminator* (1984), a tremendously effective combination of time travel, future war and woman hunt. *Repo Man* (1984), which creates a punk era UFO movie from typically Dickian ingredients. *Brazil* (1985), a remarkable visual feast and a damning indictment of bureaucracy.

5. Special effects have become an industry in their own right. The huge budgets for most SF films are generally soaked up in special effects work, and teams working on modern films can be anything up to a hundred strong. Several independent companies have formed. Lucas's Industrial Light and Magic, Douglas Trumbull's Entertainment Effects Group, and John Dykstra's Apogee Effects are three such. This heavy emphasis on special effects tends to overwhelm the needs of normal literacy. Action takes precedent over dialogue. Scripts cost very little in comparison with the filming of Deathstars and aliens; nonetheless, scripts seem to be a last consideration in the budget stakes. If an inversion of this state of affairs were to happen and more care and emphasis put into getting the script right, we might see a few real classics appearing on our screens. The potential is now there. There seems to be nothing that the film-makers cannot show us on the screen. All we need now is to harness that ability.

6. *The Last Starfighter* (1984) went one stage further. The publicity handout stated, "For the first time in motion picture history, the marvels of deep space have been created, not with miniature props and motion control photography, but by computer graphics simulation." This has made SF film critic John Brosnan write, "Then again the idea that everything in a feature film, including actors, might be

one day generated entirely within a computer sounds like pure science fiction." ("Special Effects In Science Fiction Cinema" in *The Science Fiction Film Source Book*, ed. David Wingrove, 1985).

7. Gary Alan Fine's *Shared Fantasy: Role-Playing Games as Social Worlds*, Chicago, 1983, investigates this sub-culture. He concludes that such games sublimate sex and power drives for teenagers; the median age for gamers was fifteen.

8. We see the same in the latest spate of role-playing fantasy books, which are proving more popular than real novels. Like their computer kin, there is no characterization, no plot, just a choice of paths—a progression from event to event. Such experience is without meaning. Even so, some would claim that with present high levels of indifference to the reading experience, any means of getting teenagers hooked on books—whatever it is they first sample—is a good thing. The long-term effect of role-playing books has yet to be gauged.

9. A good, partisan—what else?—history of fandom is Joe Siclari, "Science Fiction Fandom: A History of an Unusual Hobby", in Marshall B. Tymn (ed.), *The Science Fiction Reference Book* (1981).

10. Some anthologies—a trickle—are beginning to appear again. Kingsley Amis's *The Golden Age of Science Fiction* (1981), and Isaac Asimov and Martin H. Greenberg's series of *The Great SF Stories* (fourteen volumes covering 1939 to 1952 published so far) are instances.

11. Terry Carr's *Universe* continues in its place, however, printing some of the best of the new writing by writers like Bishop, Sterling and Shepard.

12. Heinlein seems to agree on this specific. When the written word was the only medium of communication, the rationality of literacy was valued. Now that there are less demanding media the need for rationality seems to have slipped away. Television as a medium requires no scholarly background, no training in the disciplines of thought. Indeed, the medium is designed these days to cater for shorter and ever-shorter attention spans. This might be a contributory factor in spreading fantasy.

13. One might speculate whether the afore-

mentioned role-playing books form some kind of bridge between the home computer and the book. In an age where the home computer dominates the domestic household (and the domestic TV set) this seems an important link with literacy.

CHAPTER XII

1. As Philip K. Dick wrote in his 1981 novel, *Valis*, "the symbols of the divine show up in our world initially at the trash stratum . . . The divine intrudes where you least expect it." (Chapter 14) It was never more true than about Dick's own work, but as a thesis about science fiction in the fifties and sixties it has much to commend it—much that was truly inspired emerged from an unconscious transformation of pulp materials.
2. Originally published in *Of Worlds Beyond*, ed. Lloyd Arthur Eshbach, Reading, PA, 1947. Heinlein was one of seven practising science fiction writers who contributed to the volume, among them being Jack Williamson, A. E. van Vogt, E. E. Smith and John W. Campbell, Jr. The "symposium" is unabashedly concerned with markets and money, though van Vogt's recipe for the 800-word scene, "Complication in the Science Fiction Story" must be read to understand his own brand of maniacal story-telling.
3. *Expanded Universe*, New York, 1980, page 403.
4. A lively discussion of the wish-fulfilment aspects of the novel is contained in Dr Robert Plank's article, "Omnipotent Cannibals: Thoughts on Reading Robert Heinlein's *Stranger in a Strange Land*", *Riverside Quarterly*, Vol. 5, no. 1.
5. James Blish, writing as William Athel-ing, "Cathedrals in Space", in *The Issue at Hand*.
6. It is interesting to compare Heinlein's novel, written before the hippie thing, with Brian Aldiss's *Barefoot in the Head* (1969). In the latter, the entire culture is freaked out after the Acid Head War, and the central character, Charteris, is elevated to the role of Messiah. But such power as he has comes from abnegation

and, when he finds himself on the brink of believing in his ability to work miracles, he deliberately throws away the Christ role.
7. Heinlein's own reaction can be best summarized with a passage from "The Happy Days Ahead" (*Expanded Universe, op. cit.*, p. 546): "The mindless yahoos, people who think linearly like a savage instead of inductively or deductively, and people who used to be respectful to learned opinion or at least kept quiet, now are aggressively on the attack. Facts and logic don't count; their intuition is the source of 'truth'."
8. Panshin, *Heinlein in Dimension: A Critical Analysis*, Chicago, 1968; Chapter 4, portions of which appeared in *Riverside Quarterly* in 1965. Which demonstrates that Panshin has some of the qualities needed to criticize SF.
9. From Chapter 1, Section 1 of Ed Sanders's *The Family: The Story of Charles Manson's Dune Buggy Attack Battalion*, New York, 1971. Manson was also turned on by Dr Eric Berne's *Transactional Analysis* and the Beatles' totally innocuous "I Wanna Hold Your Hand". To complete the circle of influences, rock singer Neil Young wrote a song, "Revolution Blues", about the Manson family's Dune buggy exploits, for his 1974 album, *On the Beach*.
10. This coinage is first used in Brian Aldiss's Afterword, "A Day in the Life-Style of. . . ." in *Best SF: 1971*, edited by Harry Harrison and Brian Aldiss, where it is applied to such novels as Luke Rhinehart's *The Dice Man*.
11. In Delany's essay, "Faust and Archimedes", in *The Jewel-Hinged Jaw*, New York, 1977.
12. A good critical introduction to Delany's work is Douglas Barbour's *Worlds out of Words: The SF Novels of Samuel R. Delany*, Bran's Head Books, Somerset, 1979. But see also Delany's own essays in "Section III: Writing SF", in *The Jewel-Hinged Jaw, op. cit.*
13. Of particular note in this respect is Delany's 1976 novel, *Triton: An Ambiguous Heterotopia*, where macho protagonist Bron Helstrom, misunderstanding his own sexual motivations in a society where sexuality is the primary motivating force, eventually becomes a woman in an attempt to understand him-herself.

This is "Life-Style SF" in its most extreme form!

14. *The Jewels of Aptor*, revised edition, London, 1968, pp. 71/2. This passage is little changed from the 1962 Ace edition.

15. *The Fall of the Towers* was first published in a single volume (with the revisions Delany made in 1968) in 1971. The three original Ace novels that comprise the trilogy were, *Captives of the Flame* (1963), *The Towers of Toron* (1964), and *City of a Thousand Suns* (1966).

16. Judith Merril, as ever, had the sanest things to say about the book at the time. In her Books column in *F&SF* for November 1967, she wrote: "If the book has a serious flaw, it is in the over-tight weaving, the too-careful pruning and packing of meaning into deceptively simple and rhythmic language: that is, that it is in large part closer to poetry than prose, without any of the typographical, linguistic, or structural formalities which usually serve as clues to the reader to proceed more attentively than he expects to do with an adventure novel (let alone an adventure novel in cheap paperback format with a lurid red demon-thing on the cover)." What she neglected to say is that the comic book SF elements tend to outweigh the serious literary attempt and make this an unsuccessful rather than simply flawed hybrid.

17. "Time Considered as a Helix of Semi-Precious Stones" was a product of the annual Milford Science Fiction Writers' Conference, organized by Damon Knight and Kate Wilhelm, and to which most of the influential "New Wave" (and a number of the old guard) writers of the sixties went. Delany, Joanna Russ, Fritz Leiber, Harlan Ellison, Gordon Dickson, Gene Wolfe, Avram Davidson, Robert Silverberg, James Blish and Terry Carr were regular attendees. It is also interesting to note that a great number of the Nebula Award-winning stories of the mid sixties (those chosen by the SFWA, a writers' body formed by Knight) were Milford products, adding fuel to the argument that there was a "Milford Mafia". Against this argument lies the fact that these were also some of the best writers in the genre.

18. William Gibson's 1984 Nebula and Hugo Award winning novel *Neuromancer* is a direct literary descendant of this kind of writing, so often imitated in the genre since Delany reintroduced it in the sixties.

19. Delany's work as a structuralist critic can be traced through to *The American Shore: Meditations on a Tale of Science Fiction by Thomas M. Disch—"Angoulême"*, a lengthy critical volume about one of Disch's 5000-word stories (later to become part of the novel, *334*). Delany's recent fiction has straddled the fantasy and SF fields more overtly, with three volumes set in Neverÿon/Neveryöna.

20. Two early examples of the use of myth to underpin science fiction are C. S. Lewis's *Perelandra* (1943) and Robert Graves's *Seven Days in New Crete* (1949). Douglas Barbour, in his book *Worlds out of Words* (op. cit.) points out the debt Delany owed Graves, whose *The White Goddess* (1948; enlarged 1952) lies behind much of Delany's early myth-based novels. It might also be noted that Philip José Farmer's *Flesh* (1960) also owes much to Graves's *The White Goddess*, perhaps strengthening the influence upon Delany.

21. In the Introduction to *Four for Tomorrow*, New York, 1967, Sturgeon had this to say of Zelazny: "I do not know him personally, but if I did, if I ever do, I would want more than anything else to convey to him the fact that he can and has evoked this awe—that the curve he has drawn with his early work can be extended into true greatness, and that if he follows his star as a writer all other things will come to him . . . He gives no evidence to date that he has stopped growing or that he ever will." Alas for the field, Zelazny had stopped growing almost as Sturgeon was putting pen to paper. But to his credit, Sturgeon could see the flaws that were to become an overwhelming blight in the later Zelazny. Another interesting view of this phenomenon—echoing Sturgeon's praise for the early Zelazny—can be found in Richard Cowper's "A Rose is a Rose is a Rose . . . in search of Roger Zelazny", in *Foundation* 11/12, March 1977.

22. Carl B. Yoke for one. In his Starmont Reader's Guide to Zelazny, Yoke says: "*Lord of Light* is fated to be a science fiction classic. It is well-conceived and well-implemented. It is organic, and it is

well-paced. It is humorous and sublime. Its characters are believable and sympathetic. More than any of Zelazny's other novels, it is always under tight control. Considering the morass of background material from which it was hewn, it is in the last analysis quite remarkable." If the reduction of a complex and powerful myth to a comic book formula with technological trimmings can be deemed "remarkable", then so the book is. Joanna Russ, writing in *F&SF* (January 1968) gave a more realistic view of the book: "The beginning of *Lord of Light* promises much more than the book ever delivers", and adds, "The mechanics of the plot are satisfied; that's all." As Russ points out, the shell of story lacks an "inside"—lacks any real depths.

23. Notable exceptions are his novella, "Home is the Hangman", (*Analog*, November 1975) which justifiably won the Hugo and Nebula Awards for that year, and, for less literary reasons, the entertaining Amber books, in which sequence six novels have thus far appeared.

24. 1965 was Zelazny's year as far as winning awards was concerned. ". . . And Call Me Conrad" shared the Hugo award for best novel, "He Who Shapes" won the Nebula for best novella, and "The Doors of his Face, the Lamps of his Mouth" won the Nebula for best novelette.

25. The first three albums by the Mothers of Invention were part of the social revolution of the sixties. Frank Zappa was as critical of the stylistic revolution— "Every town must have a place where phoney hippies meet/Psychedelic dungeons popping up on every street"—as he was of the social matrix then prevalent in the USA—"Plastic people, Oh baby, now you're such a drag." *Freak Out* (1966), *Absolutely Free* (1967) and *We're Only in it for the Money* (1967, and a direct, sharply-satirical parody of the Beatles' *Sergeant Pepper*) present, in a rock format, many of those images Ellison and others drew upon—America as a plastic, vegetable, materialist culture, ridiculously conformist ("Brown shoes don't make it"), afraid of sex and love with cars, booze and violence. Zappa tended to use the same kind of hyperbolic and fantastic mode as Ellison, particu-

larly in songs like "Let's Make The Water Turn Black". It might also be noted that the chief inspiration for *We're Only in it for the Money* was Franz Kafka's "In the Penal Colony". The sixties saw the beginning of a process of cross-pollination between popular music and the written genre of science fiction which was to escalate in the seventies. Jimi Hendrix ("1983 . . . A Merman I Should Turn To Be"), Jefferson Airplane ("Have You Seen the Saucers"), Crosby, Stills and Nash ("Wooden Ships"), Pink Floyd ("Set the Controls for the Heart of the Sun") and others made science fiction ideas and imagery available in another medium.

26. From Ellison's introduction to *Dangerous Visions*, "Thirty-Two Soothsayers".

27. However, Harlan Ellison was not always the most conscientious editor. Brian Aldiss's story in *Dangerous Visions*, "The Night That All Time Broke Out", was purchased from agent Scott Meredith and inserted in the anthology without consultation with the author.

28. One might look at James Gunn's letter of 11th July 1977 to *Foundation* 13 as an instance; a letter presented under the heading "On the aesthetic fallacy". Gunn defends science fiction as a special case, not to be judged by normal literary criteria.

29. American writers appeared in Carnell's *New Worlds* during the fifties, among them Poul Anderson, Alfred Bester, Lester del Rey, Philip K. Dick, Harlan Ellison, Harry Harrison, Robert Heinlein, Damon Knight, C. M. Kornbluth, Judith Merril, Robert Sheckley, Robert Silverberg, Theodore Sturgeon, Wilson Tucker and Richard Wilson. A glimpse at this list should convince that *New Worlds* was far from being a simple parochial magazine before Moorcock took it over, though the appearance of American writers in *New Worlds* in the early sixties was rare.

30. Editorial, "A New Literature for the Space Age", *New Worlds* 142, May–June 1964.

31. Charles Platt has, in recent years, produced two volumes of incisive and indispensable interviews with science fiction authors, *The Dream Makers* vols. I and II (1980, 1983).

32. This list gives some idea of the way in

which popular science fiction always had good intellectual and cultural support in Britain, possibly because the pulps were not a native phenomenon. In the States, support in the main came from scientists rather than literary people—from John R. Pierce rather than J. B. Priestley. America's answer to C. S. Lewis and Marghanita Laski was Clifton Fadiman and Spring Byington. When popular science fiction began to be published in hard-cover during the early fifties, critics such as Amis and Conquest and Philip Toynbee did a great deal to see that it received a favourable reception. Edmund Crispin's *Best SF* anthologies from Faber & Faber, starting publication in 1955, were crucial in establishing valid critical standards.

33. Indeed, in recent years the literary establishment in the United Kingdom has taken Ballard to its bosom. His 1984 novel, *Empire of the Sun*, may not have won the coveted Booker Prize, but it received more attention than the eventual winner and has been a best-seller both in hardback and paperback. A case of Ballard writing in pure, semi-autobiographical terms what he had presented as modern metaphor in so many science fiction novels!

34. Colin Greenland, *The Entropy Exhibition*, London, 1983, Chapter 8, "The Works of Michael Moorcock".

35. The five Cornelius books by Moorcock are *The Final Programme* (1968), *A Cure for Cancer* (1971), *The English Assassin* (1972), *The Lives and Times of Jerry Cornelius* (1976) and *The Condition of Muzak* (1977). Jerry and his friend, Miss Brunner, became Underground favourites when Mal Dean's Cornelius strip appeared in *International Times*. His adventures were chronicled by several other writers, among them Langdon Jones, James Sallis, Maxim Jakubowski, M. John Harrison, Norman Spinrad, and Brian Aldiss. These adventures were collected in *The Nature of the Catastrophe*, edited by Michael Moorcock and Langdon Jones, 1971.

36. Moorcock acknowledges this debt often, most recently in the introduction to a special *New Worlds* anthology, selected and edited by Moorcock in 1983: "Only in the SF magazines did one occasionally come across some imaginative work.

Bester's remarkable *The Demolished Man* and *The Stars My Destination* appeared in *Galaxy* in 1952 and 1956."

37. Zelazny published four short stories in *New Worlds* under Moorcock's editorship, including "The Keys to December". Delany's "Time Considered . . ." appeared in issue 185 (December 1968) and Ellison's "A Boy and his Dog" in issue 189 (April 1969).

38. A possible influence might be traced through to Canadian film director David Cronenberg, whose film *Shivers* (1974) again uses the central idea of a venereal "plague"—though this brings thoughtless hedonism, not intellectual ecstasy.

39. *Roderick: or, The Education of a Young Machine* (1980) and *Roderick At Random: or, Further Education of a Young Machine* (1983).

CHAPTER XIII

1. "The Jungle Rot Kid on the Nod", *New Worlds* 200, April 1970.

2. *The Big Time*, New York, 1961. Chapter 11. A magazine version first appeared in 1958.

3. *Changewar*, New York, 1983, brings together the rest of the Change War stories—seven in all—in a single volume for the first time. Leiber produced these stories for the magazines between 1958 and 1965.

4. See Leiber's autobiographical essay, "Mysterious Islands", in *Foundation* 11/12, March 1977.

5. Leiber was first published in Campbell's *Unknown* in 1939, appeared there and in *Astounding* and *Weird Tales* in the forties, and in *Galaxy* and *F&SF* in the fifties, finally finding a home writing stories (often to match the garish covers) of *Fantastic* under Cele Goldsmith's editorship.

6. "A Pail of Air" (1951), in *The Best of Fritz Leiber*, London, 1974.

7. A snippet to give the flavour of Sally Harris's exploits:

Sally Harris saw the stars squiggle just as she and Jake, momentarily shedding thirty pounds of weight apiece, started to come atop the sixth summit of the

Ten-Stage Rocket at Coney Island. In the blind, egoistic world of sexual fulfilment that lies exactly on the boundary between the conscious and unconscious regions of the mind, she knew that the stars were a provincial district of herself—the Marches of Sally Harris—and so she merely chortled throatily: "I did it, Christ! I said I'd do it and I did it!" *The Wanderer,* Chapter 7.

8. *The Image of the Beast* (1968), *A Feast Unknown* (1969) and *Blown* (1969). These tongue-in-cheek (*whose* cheek and *which*?) books are best seen as playful parody. *Blown,* for instance, has SF fan Forrest J. Ackerman as a character.

9. Leiber produced *Tarzan and the Valley of Gold* in 1966, while Farmer wrote *Tarzan Alive: A Definitive Biography of Lord Greystoke* in 1972. But anyone doubting the influence on these two writers might consult Chapter Eleven of *The Wanderer* (where Don Merriam flies straight through a gap in the moon, emulating one of John Carter's exploits) or Farmer's *Hadon of Ancient Opar* (1974) and its sequel.

10. The "World of Tiers" sequence runs as follows: *The Maker of Universes* (1965), *The Gates of Creation* (1966), *A Private Cosmos* (1968), *Behind the Walls of Terra* (1970) and *The Lavalite World* (1977).

11. In the same way that we might marvel at Burroughs's 15-foot tall red Martians and their mounts, or at their guns which can fire accurately over 200 miles!

12. In both the Tiers sequence and the Riverworld novels, Farmer shies away from final answers. Both *The Lavalite World* and *Gods of Riverworld* are, consequently, something of a disappointment—the perpetual problem in SF of promising the glittering Earth and delivering only a few benighted sods. The Riverworld novels are: *To Your Scattered Bodies Go* (1971), *The Fabulous Riverboat* (1971), *The Dark Design* (1977), *The Magic Labyrinth* (1979) and *Gods of Riverworld* (1983). Two other books complete the sequence of tales: *Riverworld and other Stories* (1979) and *Riverworld War* (1980). The novelette "Riverworld" first appeared in *Worlds of Tomorrow* in January 1966 and demonstrates how action-oriented Farmer's original conception of the Riverworld was.

13. "Riders . . ." appeared in Ellison's *Dangerous Visions* and went on to win the 1968 Hugo award for best SF novella. It might be noted that Leiber's "Gonna Roll the Bones", also in *Dangerous Visions,* won the same award for best novelette.

14. From the Introduction to *The Earth Book of Stormgate,* New York, 1978, a collection of twelve stories in Anderson's Polesotechnic League series, a future history of the "Technic Civilization" from the 21st century to 7100 AD.

15. It pipped Zelazny's "A Rose for Ecclesiastes" and Edgar Rice Burroughs's posthumous "Savage Pellucidar" to win the Hugo for best short story of 1963.

16. E. E. "Doc" Smith's *Lensman* series and Robert A. Heinlein's Future History stories might be seen as forerunners to this fad. In both, a whole number of separate stories and tales (in Smith's case novels) were placed within the same future historical template. Poul Anderson's Technic Civilization—mentioned above—is also in this mould, but writers like Isaac Asimov and C. J. Cherryh are actively interlocking their novels and stories into a more rigid historical framework by writing bridging stories and novels. The popularity of this activity has spawned the series-novel, as much a marketing phenomenon as anything, where a new writer will break into the genre not through publishing short stories in the magazines—as was once the case—but by presenting a publisher with six to eight novels, with common characters, settings and historical/fictional backgrounds. For a genuine philosophical use of the future history concept one might return to Stapledon's vast timescales in *Last and First Men.* Or forward—to Ursula Le Guin's looser use of a coherent future as setting for novels like *The Left Hand of Darkness* and *The Dispossessed.*

17. Dorsai's popularity has been reflected in the awards the series has won—the first in 1965 for "Soldier Ask Not", the latest in 1980 for "Lost Dorsai". The books in the sequence are as follows: *Necromancer* (1962, also as *No Room for Man*), *The Tactics of Mistake* (1971), *Dorsai!* (1959, also as *The Genetic General*), *Soldier Ask Not* (1967), *The Spirit of Dorsai* (1979; a collection of associated pieces), *Lost*

Dorsai (1980), *The Final Encyclopedia* (1984). The historical novels will range from the fourteenth century, and once the whole is completed Dickson plans to revise all twelve volumes to form a single statement about Man's development. Such scope of vision must be admired, whatever one feels about the actual writing.

18. See Timothy O'Reilly's excellent article on The Childe Cycle in Frank Magill. ed., *Survey of Science Fiction Literature*, Englewood Cliffs, NJ, 1980.

19. Reprinted variously in book form under much less apposite titles, *The Dragon in the Sea* and *21st Century Sub*. The introductory blurb to *Dune World* in *Analog*, December 1963, shows that *Under Pressure* was still very much in the minds of *Analog*'s readers: "Herbert's last great novel was a tale of men Under Pressure of war and deep water. This is a story of men under pressure of politics and the dehydration of a waterless world. . . ."

20. *Dune World* was serialized in three parts, December 1963–February 1964, and comprises the first Book of the novel *Dune*. *The Prophet of Dune* was serialized in five parts, January–May 1965 in *Analog* (again with illustrations by Schoenherr, who remained Herbert's illustrator for the *Galaxy* serialization of *Dune Messiah*, July to September 1969). This second instalment formed Books 2 and 3 of the novel. The serialized version of Book 1 was heavily amended between magazine and novel versions, with much that was melodramatic removed and several incidents that damaged the work's dramatic tension—Herbert had the usual *Analog* habit of showing too much, too soon—were taken from early in the story and inserted later on, giving them greater dramatic impact. The rewriting, however, is a very close and subtle one that gave the novel a greater sense of mystery and implied more: it made the readers do much more work than they were used to, and that too was unusual in an *Analog*-type story. More was added than deleted in the revision.

21. A prime instance is the 1972 novel, *The God Makers*, which, like much of Herbert's work, shares a future-history context with the Dune novels—a loose-knit Galactic Empire. The Nattrians

seem to be remnants of the Bene Gesserit sisterhood, sharing their traits. If this was Herbert's intention, then *The God Makers* is a codicil to the six *Dune* novels.

22. For anyone interested in an author's anguish at Hollywood's treatment of original material, Danny Peary's excellent *Omni's Screen Flights/Screen Fantasies* (1984) gives several instances, amongst them Harry Harrison's essay on *Soylent Green*: "A Cannibalized Novel Becomes *Soylent Green*".

23. *Time is the Simplest Thing* has strong affinities with Zenna Henderson's "People" series—and, indeed, with Philip K. Dick's 1954 story, "The Golden Man". In each a paranormal minority are witch-hunted by the normal majority. It was a common, effective theme, reflecting, perhaps, a response to what had been happening in real life America in the fifties, particularly under Senator Joseph McCarthy.

24. Beating Vonnegut's *Cat's Cradle*, the magazine version of Herbert's *Dune World*, and Heinlein's *Glory Road*.

25. Edgar Pangborn died February 1st 1976. One SF novel, *The Atlantean Nights Entertainment*, was published posthumously in 1980, and a collection of stories, *Still I Persist in Wondering*, in 1978.

26. Zenna Henderson died May 11th 1983, of cancer. She began publishing SF in *F&SF* in 1951.

27. A third Fuzzy novel, *Fuzzies and Other People* was discovered in 1982 amongst Piper's papers. *Golden Dream: A Fuzzy Odyssey*, by Ardath Mayhar, also exists, but has little to do with the ethical concerns of Piper's books, preferring to wallow in the more sentimental aspects of the originals. To confuse further, William Tuning has also produced a "Fuzzy" novel.

28. See introduction by John F. Carr to H. Beam Piper, *Federation*, New York, 1981.

29. For a lucid market evaluation of how things stood at the end of the sixties and beginning of the seventies, the reader is referred to Isaac Asimov's article introducing *Nebula Award Stories 8* (1973), "So Why Aren't We Rich?". Asimov, of course, *was*.

30. An even more negative side of Panshin's

creative work can be seen in the Anthony Villiers adventures, such as *The Thurb Revolution* (1968), which could—with characters like Torve the Trog and his speedy red tricycle—be said to have regressed rather than enhanced the genre stylistically and in terms of granting the medium serious critical attention.

31. And are still highly popular. The latest novel in the series, *The Return of Retief* (1984), comes eighteen years after the first, *Retief's War* (1966). In the interim were *Retief and the Warlords* (1968) and *Retief's Ransom* (1971). There are also a large number of collections of Retief tales, with *Envoy to New Worlds* (1963), *Galactic Diplomat* (1965), *Retief: Ambassador to Space* (1969), *Retief of the CDT* (1971), *Retief, Emissary to the Stars* (1975) and *Retief at Large* (1979). Anyone sick to the teeth of Retief might seek out the three Imperium novels: *Worlds of the Imperium* (1962), *The Other Side of Time* (1965) and *Assignment in Nowhere* (1968).

32. Norman Spinrad's *The Iron Dream* (1972) can be said to serve a similar purpose, but more explicitly. In Spinrad's work Adolf Hitler, an American immigrant in an alternate world to ours, has become a science fiction writer and produced the 1954 Hugo-winning novel, *Lord of the Swastika!* It might also be noted that in George Hill's film of *Slaughterhouse Five* Howard Campbell Jr makes an appearance as an American Nazi, recruiting patriotic Americans to help the Nazis fight the Communist Russians.

33. Philip José Farmer, fond of such games, delivered a novel by Kilgore Trout to *F&SF*, where it was serialized in the December 1974 and January 1975 issues, as *Venus on the Half-Shell*. As a parody of science fiction clichés it is remarkable and very funny. As a commentary on Vonnegut's own use of science fictional ideas, it is rather telling. It was subsequently published in book form.

34. Despite director George Roy Hill's faithfulness to the original, the film version of *Slaughterhouse Five*, made in 1971, is less coherent than the novel, and the richness of the film is only really evident after several viewings. Michael Sacks and Valerie Perrine starred.

35. *Slapstick* was finally released in 1984, some years after it was made—its star,

Marty Feldman, had been dead several years by then. Apart from filming only half the novel and giving it a spoof *Close Encounters* ending, it remains—along with Jerry Lee Lewis's inane performance—poor even by 1950s sci-fi B-movie standards.

36. A distinctive feature of Dick's novels is the use of anything from six to a dozen characters, between whom the viewpoint constantly switches. This creates a rounded sense of the strange worlds into which Dick throws us, but it can also be both disconcerting and confusing at times.

37. For an interesting explication of the novel and the role of the *I Ching* in it, see Willis E. McNelly's essay in Frank Magill, *op. cit.* Also Patricia S. Warrick's "The Encounter of Taoism and Fascism in *The Man in the High Castle*", in *Philip K. Dick*, ed. Martin Harry Greenberg and Joseph D. Olander, New York, 1983.

38. *Martian Time-Slip* originally appeared as *All We Marsmen* in the August 1963 issue of *Worlds of Tomorrow*. It was vastly expanded for its novel appearance. The earlier version focused on the experiences of Jack Bohlen and underplayed the importance of Manfred Steiner. Bohlen's hallucination, however, exists in both versions.

39. Interesting in this respect is an article Philip K. Dick wrote called "The Android and the Human", which appeared in the British *Vector* and the Australian *SF Commentary*, in March 1972, and was reprinted in *Philip K. Dick: Electric Shepherd*, ed. Bruce Gillespie, Melbourne, 1975. There Dick spells out his views on the dehumanization process and the relationship of psychotic to android. Also relevant is Dick's "Man, Android and Machine", in the collection *Science Fiction at Large*, ed. Peter Nicholls (also as *Explorations of the Marvellous*), 1976. In the latter, Dick talks of "sly and cruel entities which smile as they reach out to shake hands. But their handshake is the grip of death, and their smile has the coldness of the grave.

"These creatures are among us, although morphologically they do not differ from us; we must not posit a difference of essence, but a difference of behaviour. In my science fiction I write about them constantly. Sometimes they themselves do not know they are androids."

40. To emphasize this point the reader is referred to the conclusion of *Martian Time-Slip* where Manfred, prematurely aged from his experiences, bcomes a thing of metal and wires and is presented as such to Jack Bohlen, thus making his hallucination something real and concrete.

41. See Brian W. Aldiss. "Robots: Low-Voltage Ontological Currents", Preface to *The Mechanical God*, ed. Thomas P. Dunn and Richard D. Erlich, Westport, Conn., 1982.

42. See particularly Dick's interview with Daniel De Prez, dated September 10th 1976, in *Science Fiction Review* 19.

43. See "The Lucky Dog Pet Store", introduction to *The Golden Man* (1980), reprinted in Greenberg & Clander, *op. cit.*, where Dick discusses his poverty as a freelance writer. He and one of his wives regularly had to eat horse meat. With regard to the matter of Philip K. Dick's novels, it is worth noting that amongst the manuscripts unpublished at Dick's death in 1982 was *Voices from the Street*, a 652-page mainstream novel.

44. Recently published letters of Dick's suggest that this was as much financial necessity as choice. Publishers would take his SF novels but would not touch his mainstream work. The Philip K. Dick Society published a letter dated February 1st 1960 (PKDS Pamphlet No. 1) which discusses Dick's own response to his mainstream work in answer to rejections from a major US publisher.

45. See *Clans of the Alphane Moon* (1964).

46. In Brian Aldiss's introduction to the American and British paperback editions of *Ice*. "Her catastrophe victims do not leap up and embrace their catastrophe; nor do they flee from it; they accept it as part of life."

CHAPTER XIV

1. Interview with Robert Silverberg by Christopher Fowler in *Vector* 76/77

(August/September 1976). Silverberg had been out of writing for a year when he gave this interview in April 1976, and *Shadrach in the Furnace* (1976) seemed to be his final statement in the genre.

2. The three novellas which comprise *Nightwings* appeared in *Galaxy* magazine between September 1968 and February 1969. Their original titles were "Nightwings", "Perris Way" (retitled "Among the Rememberers") and "To Jorslem" (retitled "The Road to Jorslem").

3. See in particular Chapters 64 to 67 of *A Time of Changes*.

4. "I discovered that much of what I was writing in 1971 was either barely SF at all or was a kind of parody of science fiction or borrowed a genuine science fiction theme for use in an otherwise 'straight' mainstream novel." Robert Silverberg in *Hell's Cartographers, op. cit.*

5. "Tissue" (part 1: "at the fitting shop") in *Again, Dangerous Visions*, ed. Harlan Ellison, New York, 1972.

6. Silverberg toyed with time travel in three other novels of the late sixties: *Hawksbill Station* (1968, also as *The Anvil of Time*), *The Masks of Time* (1968, also as *Vornan-19*), and *The Time Hoppers* (1967).

7. After *Shadrach in the Furnace*, Silverberg wrote no more SF for three full years. It will thus be seen that his most meaningful work falls between *Thorns* in 1967 and *Shadrach* in 1976. As is customary with writers who do not conform, readers and critics have yet to appreciate the Sombre Period Silverberg. But see Thomas D. Clareson's excellent essay on *Downward to the Earth* in Magill's *Survey of SF Literature, op. cit.*

8. Subsequently collected with two unconnected novellas as *Born with the Dead*, 1975.

9. "The pursuit of art, by artist or audience, is the pursuit of liberty." Le Guin in her introduction to the US edition of *The Word for World is Forest*, collected in *The Language of the Night*, New York, 1979.

10. The philosophy of the novel is distinctly Taoist. Le Guin's Gethen is a world not merely of pragmatism but of profound mysticism. The religion of Gethen/Winter is that of the Handdarata and their creed of ignorance and unlearning—"Ignorant, in the Handdara

sense: to ignore the abstraction, to hold fast to the thing. There was in this attitude something feminine, a refusal of the abstract, the ideal, a submissiveness to the given, which rather displeased me." (Chapter 15) The novel derives its title from a piece of Handdara taoism:

"Light is the left hand of darkness
and darkness the right hand of light.
Two are one, life and death, lying
together like lovers in kemmer,
like hands joined together,
like the end and the way."
(Chapter 16)

On the trek across the glacier, Genly Ai makes a direct link between the Yin/Yang symbol of the Taoist Way and this Handdarata poem ("Tormer's Lay"): "It's found on Earth, and on Hain-Davenant, and on Chiffewar. It is yin and yang. *Light is the left hand of darkness* . . . how did it go? Light, dark. Fear, courage. Cold, warmth. Female, male. It is yourself, Therem. Both and one. A shadow on snow." (Chapter 19) In this diction lies the heart of Le Guin's novel.

11. In Chapter 16 Genly Ai defines this shaping factor precisely: "I suppose the most important thing, the heaviest single factor in one's life, is whether one's born male or female. In most societies, it determines one's expectations, activities, outlook, ethics, manners—almost everything. Vocabulary. Semiotic usages. Clothing. Even food. Women . . . women tend to eat less. . . ." In this regard, *The Left Hand of Darkness*, by depicting a society outside of the expected male/female dualist mould, is a feminist novel. Even so, feminists criticized Le Guin for her use of "he" throughout the novel when discussing her androgynes.

12. *Planet of Exile* was actually written in 1963–64, and prefigures *The Left Hand of Darkness* in several ways. The stark qualities of its external settings—especially its use of "snowlands" as a landscape of the psyche—its Taoism, its contrast of alien cultures, and its use of mindspeech, are all elements developed in the later novel.

13. This said, an attempt could be made to place the Hain Cycle into a rough chronological order, as follows: "The Day Before the Revolution"; *The Dispossessed*; "Vaster Than Empires and More Slow"; *The Word for World is Forest*; *Roccanon's World*; *Planet of Exile*; "Winter's King"; *The Left Hand of Darkness*; and *City of Illusions*.

14. *The Left Hand of Darkness* won Le Guin both the Hugo and Nebula awards for the best novel of 1969. In the seventies she won Hugo Awards for *The Word For World is Forest* (1972) and "The Ones Who Walk Away from Omelas" (1973), and a Nebula for "The Day Before the Revolution" (1974), as well as Hugo and Nebula Awards for the 1974 novel, *The Dispossessed*. The best of her short fiction from this period is collected in *The Wind's Twelve Quarters* (1978).

15. The three *Earthsea* novels are *A Wizard of Earthsea* (1968), *The Tombs of Atuan* (1971) and *The Farthest Shore* (1972). The last volume won Le Guin an American National Book Award for 1972. For one opinion on this trilogy see "Juvenilia? A Child's View of Earthsea", by David Wingrove in *Vector* 81 (May/June 1977). There is also a sound chapter on *Earthsea* in Barbara J. Bucknall's book *Ursula Le Guin*, New York, 1981.

16. There is a rhetorical basis to much of Le Guin's writing that some critics have found *literary* in a pejorative sense, an emotional coloration to the prose that can alienate the reader unsympathetic with Le Guin's Taoism or idealism. Such a tone can, in works like *The Word for World is Forest*, provoke a cynical response, particularly in view of the complex realities of the Vietnam war then being fought: the almost fairy tale nature of that novella undermines rather than strengthens her didactic purpose.

17. Another critic to draw attention to this image is Douglas Barbour: "One major local image—a brilliantly ambiguous one—is the wall, introduced on the first page of the novel. It is connected to the image/idea of the prison throughout; time after time the question of who is being locked out or in, which side of the wall one is on, is the focus of the narrative." See "Wholeness And Balance" in the Le Guin issue of *Science-Fiction Studies*, Vol 2, Pt 3, Nov 1975.

18. A diagram of the cycle of return in *The Dispossessed*.

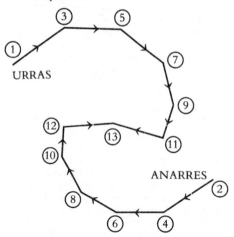

Chapter One has Shevek going from Anarres to Urras, Chapter Thirteen Shevek making the return journey. Odd chapters are concerned with Shevek's visit to Urras, even chapters with the events that led him to make that "return" visit. One can see a taoist symbolism in such a structure.

19. "In *The Dispossessed* the author is writing explicit social commentary; it is, she states in a 1975 interview with Jonathan Ward, utopian fiction, and in a specific tradition—that of anarchist utopianism from Thoreau to Paul Goodman, the 'anti-centralized state'. Obviously, Le Guin's Taoism and Goodman's Gestaltist concept of the 'whole' form a common current." George Edgar Slusser, *The Farthest Shores of Ursula K. Le Guin*, (Milford Series), San Bernadino CA, 1976.

20. "Science Fiction and Mrs Brown" first appeared in *Science Fiction at Large*, ed. Peter Nicholls, 1976 (also as *Explorations of the Marvellous*) and was reprinted in Le Guin's own collection of essays, *The Language of the Night*, op. cit. One might comment that this particular remark of Le Guin's lacks the intellectual rigour one might have expected from the author of *The Dispossessed*. To place this much emphasis on subject, on character, seems to undermine Le Guin's own Taoist thought.

21. One interesting codicil to *The Dispossessed* is its "prequel", "The Day Before the Revolution", set some 200 years before the action in the novel. It tells of Odo and her creation of the anarchistic society we meet in *The Dispossessed*—a society she does not live to see. *Orsinian Tales* (1977) is a collection of stories, some of which are science fiction, but many of which are set in a vaguely Eastern European context reminiscent of *The Dispossessed*, and given fullest form in the 1979 novel, *Malafrena*; another novel concerned with social change and the prison experience.

22. Such as the slender home-produced volume of poetry, "Walking in Cornwall", privately produced by Le Guin in 1977. Something of her mood was reflected in the poem:

> "We don't need very much:
> water and warmth and walls, the
> flickering ring of faces."

23. From "Why is There so Little Science in Literature?" in *Nebula Award Winners* 16, ed. Jerry Pournelle, New York, 1982. Benford is kindly critical of the old traditional SF in this essay: "[Science Fiction] has had a long era now existing as a well-tended private garden in which the fans loyally mistook domestic cabbages for literary roses. The confusion was usually benign. It allowed authors to say what they saw, without feeling the press of the past on their backs." It is assumed that Benford and his colleagues were feeling that press of the past.

24. Bishop's first story, "Darktree, Darktide" appeared in the April 1971 issue of *F&SF*. Benford had been published as early as 1965 but was appearing regularly in the magazines at the turn of the decade.

25. *Funeral for the Eyes of Fire* shares a common background with Bishop's two novels about the Hive Cities of Earth, *A Little Knowledge* (1977) and *Catacomb Years* (1979), but their theme was alienation and not the alien.

26. This and a Nebula for "The Quickening" (1981) are his only awards.

27. Let this quote from Chapter 28 of *No Enemy But Time* serve as illustration of Bishop's occasional stylistic hiccups: "Like a boiler full of clabbered tapioca Mount Tharaka was churning inside, its sticky contents threatening to burst, brim, and overflow. The thunderstorm, along with the confusion attending the

birth of the Grub, had disguised from us the mountain's premonitory rumblings. . . ."

28. Bishop's most recent novel pushes this theme to its ultimate. *Ancient of Days* (1985) is a novel-length version of an excellent novella, "Her Habiline Husband", where a proto-human encounters the complexity of modern day America.

29. In the 1985 collection, *One Winter in Eden*.

30. See for instance "Bitterblooms" (1974), collected in *Sandkings* (1981).

31. Robb's response to Lya's actions is of interest here: "Did I see? I don't know. I was confused. Would I love Lya if she was 'herself'? But what was 'herself'? How was it different from the Lya I knew? I thought I loved Lya and would always love Lya—but what if the real Lya wasn't like my Lya? *What* did I love? The strange abstract concept of a human being, or the flesh and voice and personality that I thought of as Lya? I didn't know. I didn't know who Lya was, or who I was, or what the hell it all meant. And I was scared. Maybe I couldn't feel what she had felt that afternoon. But I knew what she was feeling then. I was alone, and I needed someone." It might also be noted that the original magazine publication possessed an epigraph from Byron which the anthologized version lacked:

For the sword outwears its sheath,
And the soul wears out the breast,
And the heart must pause to breathe,
And Love itself have rest.

These lines have a real resonance in the context of Martin's sensitive story.

32. "Sandkings" won both Hugo and Nebula awards for best novelette of 1979, "The Way of Cross and Dragon" the Hugo for best short story in the same year. Both are collected in *Sandkings, op. cit.*

33. The image referred to is encountered several times in the book: Painter standing in the doorway of the tent with a rifle over his arm, looking every bit the king of the beasts. One must also mention at this juncture the importance of Darwin to *Beasts*: an overt influence—often mentioned—in the later part of the novel.

34. Varley won both Hugo and Nebula awards for his 1978 novella, "The Persistence of Vision", Hugo for his 1982 story, "The Pusher", and Hugo and Nebula for his 1984 novella, "Press Enter ■".

35. Russ's article appeared in the October 1971 issue of *College English* (USA) and was reprinted in *Vector* 62 (November–December 1972).

36. The Alyx stories, including the novel *Picnic on Paradise* (1968) have been collected in *The Adventures of Alyx* (1983). "Bluestocking", the first in the sequence, was first published in 1967.

37. She won awards in the seventies for the following: "The Girl who was Plugged In" (1973, Hugo), "Love is the Plan, the Plan is Death" (1973, Nebula), "Houston, Houston, Do You Read?" (1976, Hugo and Nebula) and, as Raccoona Sheldon, "The Screwfly Solution" (1977, Nebula). This is not to overlook stories like "And I Awoke and Found Me on the Cold Hill's Side", "Painwise" and "Faithful to Thee, Terra, in our Fashion", which were of no lesser quality. Most of her stories of the seventies are collected in three books, *Ten Thousand Light Years from Home* (1973), *Warm Worlds and Otherwise* (1975) and *Star Songs of an Old Primate* (1978). She published one novel in the late seventies, *Up the Walls of the World* (1978).

38. From "Love is the Plan, the Plan is Death" in *Ten Thousand Light Years from Home, op. cit.*

39. McCaffrey's Dragonriders take to the skies in the following books: *Dragonflight* (1968), *Dragonquest* (1971), *Dragonsong* (1976, juvenile), *Dragonsinger* (1977, juvenile), *The White Dragon* (1978), *Dragondrums* (1979, juvenile), *Moreta, Dragonlady of Pern* (1983) and *Nerilka's Story* (1986, juvenile).

40. *The Chronicles of Morgaine* consist of *Gate of Ivrel* (1976), *Well of Shiuan* (1978) and *Fires of Azeroth* (1979) and deal with a number of alien worlds linked by malfunctioning "gates". They are very close to fantasy in their materials. *The Faded Sun* consists of *Kesrith* (1978), *Shon'ir* (1978) and *Kutath* (1979) and follows the adventures of an ex-military Earthman, Sten Duncan, who fights for the alien *mri*. One might see the second series almost as a homage to the forties space opera.

41. Bryant won Nebulas for two short stories; "Stone" in 1978, and "giANTS" in 1979. Earlier, *Analog*-style stories like "Particle Theory" (in *Analog*, February 1977) showed that Bryant, like Martin, was keen to refashion old materials as well as seek new.

42. The stories in the Known Space series are to be found in *Neutron Star* (1968), *Tales of Known Space* (1975, which has a chronology of Niven's future history), and in the novels *World of Ptavvs* (1966), *A Gift from Earth* (1968), *Ringworld* (1970), *Protector* (1973) and *The Ringworld Engineers* (1980). The collections *The Shape of Space* (1969) and *The Long ARM of Gil Hamilton* (1976) contain some Known Space Tales. Niven's sequence covers the next thousand years, slightly longer than Heinlein's and rather less (by 6000 years) than Anderson's. All three future histories depict Mankind as genetically and psychologically much as he is now. One might query such an assumption in view of the rapidity of developments in the field of genetics. See Bruce Sterling's recent *Schismatrix* (1984) for a more searching extrapolation.

43. *The Mote in God's Eye*, a lengthy alien contact tale, is probably the best of these collaborations, though in terms of style and characterization it emphasizes the weaknesses of both Niven and Pournelle. The aliens, however, are fascinating creations. In 1985 Niven and Pournelle joined the bestseller ranks with an alien invasion blockbuster, *Footfall*.

44. Pournelle won the John W. Campbell award for Most Promising New Writer in 1973.

45. Foster has a Masters Degree in Fine Arts, specifically in Cinema. His entry into the SF field was encouraged by August Derleth, that champion of all things Lovecraftian.

46. Haldeman published a mainstream novel, *War Year* (New York, 1972) based on his experiences between 1967 and '69 in Vietnam.

47. *Science Fantasy*, a long-running companion to *New Worlds*, became *Impulse* with the March 1966 issue. Roberts's Pavane stories were run in the first five issues in the order "The Signaller", "The Lady Anne" (later renamed "The Lady Margaret"), "Brother John", "Lords and Ladies" and "Corfe Gate". A sixth story,

"The White Boat", was omitted from the novel in the UK until Gollancz brought out a complete edition in April 1984. Roberts was both illustrator and editor of *Science Fantasy* and *Impulse* at different times.

48. Interestingly, Suzette Haden Elgin develops a similar clash of alien and human linguistic perceptions in her 1985 novel, *Native Tongue*. There the clash of inimical perception systems results in the horrific deaths of the interfacing baby humans used in the experiments. This novel is discussed further in Chapter 16.

49. For a consideration of Watson's first four novels, see "Amazed and Afterwards/ Avoiding Neoteny: The SF of Ian Watson" by David Wingrove in *Vector* 86, March–April 1978.

50. John Murry/Richard Cowper has published two works of autobiography, *One Hand Clapping* (1975) and *Shadows in the Grass* (1977) both as by Colin Middleton Murry.

51. *The Continuous Katherine Mortenhoe* was filmed by Bernard Tavernier in 1979 as *Deathwatch*, with Harry Dean Stanton, Romy Schneider, Max Von Sydow and Harvey Keitel.

52. John Scarborough, in his article on Lem in E. F. Bleiler's *Science Fiction Writers*, *op. cit.*, begins: "Readers accustomed to the numbingly repetitive themes and plots of American and British science fiction are quite often surprised to learn of the rich variety and occasionally superb writing produced in Eastern Europe." This sweeping statement grossly oversimplifies matters. One swallow does not mean a summer, nor one Lem a glut of great Polish writers. As for English language SF being numbingly repetitive, it is bewilderingly diverse, as this volume shows.

    Controversy raged about Lem during the mid-seventies. Ursula Le Guin, reviewing two of Lem's books in *Vector* 73, March 1976, spoke of this: "Lately, when Lem is mentioned at all in American SF circles, it is with sour mouths and sometimes hateful sneers. A little of this is due to sheer envy; some to natural resentment, for Lem is a heavy-handed, polemicizing critic; and a good deal is due to Franz Rottensteiner [Lem's Viennese agent], who, in his zeal to praise Lem, has too often insisted that, next to the Master, all SF writers are incompetent hacks—neither true, nor endearing. But envy, resentment, and Mr Rottensteiner all accounted for, still there is a mysterious insistence upon bad-mouthing Lem (whom nobody has met) personally. His books are ignored; he is vilified."

53. For more on Nesvadba see "Nesvadba: In the Footsteps of the Admirable Čapek" in *This World and Nearer Ones*, Brian Aldiss, *op. cit.* It is also of interest to note Nesvadba's own comments in "Reason and Rationalism", his Guest of Honour Speech given to the European Science Fiction Convention in 1984 and reprinted in *Vector* 122, Summer 1984.

54. "Space Junk" by Devo, from *Are We Not Men? We Are Devo!* (1978).

Chapter XV

1. Pohl's most recent novel, *The Coming of the Quantum Cats*, is serialized in the January–April 1986 issues of *Analog*.

2. In *Time Enough for Love* Heinlein collected many of these backwoods "saws" in two "Intermissions", which he subtitled, "Excerpts from the Notebooks of Lazarus Long", twenty-three pages of homespun philosophy. Here's one example: "Anyone who cannot cope with mathematics is not fully human. At best he is a tolerable subhuman who has learned to wear shoes, bathe, and not make messes in the house." These nuggets of "wisdom", supposedly mined from over two thousand years of human experience read like a Disney version of Nietzsche.

3. In his early short stories, "By His Bootstraps" (*Astounding*, October 1941) and "All You Zombies—" (*F&SF*, March 1959), Heinlein dealt with time paradoxes—the closed loop of self-creation and duplication—with an admirable economy.

4. See Nicholls's review of *Time Enough for Love* in *Foundation* 7/8, March 1975. Heinlein's tone manifests itself in a coy, almost smutty attitude towards sex—particularly towards female breasts—which presents itself as liberated but is, in fact, no more than a *Penthouse* cartoon of sexuality. No one is ever confused, hurt or disturbed by sex in a Heinlein novel. Wives and partners are always understanding when the aged hero beds a fourteen-year-old relative. In fact, they generally encourage it. Sex, in a Heinlein novel, has become a mixture of calisthenics and fantasy. The ability to avoid death by various means represents another reality evasion. More disturbing, however, is the general indifference towards human suffering.

5. Nicholls (*op. cit.*) diagnoses this as "Social Darwinism". Heinlein is consistently for the strong against the weak. Just occasionally we glimpse how callous such a philosophy actually is. In *The Cat Who Walks Through Walls*, two of his characters are discussing hunting dinosaur for sport—an expensive hobby, it seems. The conversation then turns to uses of time travel:

"A dinosaur more than a year old is tough and tasteless. I did try them, years back, when some thought was being given to using dinosaur meat to quench a famine on time line seven. But the logistics were dreadful and, when you come right down to it, there is little justice in killing stupid lizards to feed stupid people; they had earned their famine." (Book Three: Chapter XXIX)

At a time of African famine, we may view this aside with distaste and ask *how* they had earned their famine. Heinlein doesn't elucidate. Here, as in so many instances in Heinlein's work, an oversimplification is symptomatic of an inability to consider more than a single viewpoint.

6. For an intelligent investigation of the "Godgame", see John Fowles' article, "Notes on an Unfinished Novel" in *The Novel Today*, ed. Malcolm Bradbury, 1977.

7. Generally, when Heinlein is most stridently rhetorical he is least to be trusted. See Chapter X, Note 43 for an instance.

8. Most of the reviewers in the SF magazines were kinder in their assessments, and it is worth looking at what they said, if only to gauge the esteem with which Heinlein is held for his past work. In *Asimov's*, Baird Searles suggested we look at the novel as if it were by an unknown writer, Robert A. Nonymous—a slight but enjoyable

chase adventure that falls apart at the end. Robert Coulson, in *Amazing*, had a similar response to the book: "The story is interesting enough to keep one reading, but not enough to avoid disappointment at the finish." In *F&SF*, Algis Budrys looked not merely at the novel, but at what it suggested about the later Heinlein's attitude towards writing: "Taken cold—assuming a naïve reader who never heard of any other Heinlein work—*Cat* is okay. Parts of it are more than that. . . . But *Number of the Beast* began the same way, then crashed, and so does *Cat*, though not as badly." He adds, "This thing makes O.K. reading until you try to make it a story, and the more you bring to it the measurements that define a story, the more it becomes evident that Heinlein is simply putting down whatever pleases him that particular day. He is expressing himself, and, if you are fond of him, that's probably charming. I am fond of him. But a certain thread has been lost, and we are off the map." Tom Easton in *Analog* reacted to the hype that launched the book, and expresses in his comments a timid sadness that *Cat* wasn't as good as earlier work: "I enjoyed the book. Yes, I did. But, dammit, it ain't the greatest thing since sliced bread! It is ultimately a trivial tale, extending the story begun in *Time Enough for Love* for no purpose other than to continue the unification of the Master's body of work into a Future History that makes some kind of sense. If I were to take an iconoclastic turn, I might even suggest, hesitantly and respectfully, that the Masters of our favourite literature are taking the worship offered them by their readers too seriously."

9. Especially in Chapter XXVIII of *The Cat Who Walks Through Walls*:

"I tell you three times. Oz. Oz. Oz. They did indeed visit the fairyland dreamed up by L. Frank Baum. And the Wonderland invented by the Reverend Mr Dodgson to please Alice. And other places known only to fiction. Hilda discovered what none of us had noticed before because we were inside it: the World *is* Myth. We create it ourselves—and we change it ourselves. A truly strong myth maker,

such as Homer, such as Baum, such as the creator of Tarzan, creates substantial and lasting worlds . . . whereas the fiddlin', unimaginative liars and fabulists shape nothing new and their tedious dreams are forgotten."

Heinlein's strong connection to the irrational, dreaming pole is clear in this passage, as is his philistine, bully-boy opinion of anything not to his taste. Homer to Baum!—what a culmination!

10. One might view this uncertainty of names—only minor characters in Heinlein's recent fiction have a single name—as another aspect of Heinlein's increasing solipsism.

11. *Valencies*, Australia, 1985, by Rory Barnes and Damien Broderick. This workaholic aspect of Asimov, so alien to the British psyche it seems, connects Asimov with that most American of figures, Benjamin Franklin, the father of the self-help philosophy.

12. The series won a Hugo for "Best All-Time Novel Series" at the 24th World SF Convention in Cleveland, in 1966.

13. In *In Joy Still Felt* Asimov is fairly blunt about this:

"Over and over [Harlan Ellison] asked me to contribute something [to *Dangerous Visions*] and each time I refused. My excuse was that I lacked the time, and that was true enough. My *real* reason, however, was that I couldn't face trying to write a story that would pass muster in the 1960s, when such talent as I had suited only the 1950s.

"I felt that I didn't measure up any longer and I didn't want to prove it."

14. Isaac Asimov, "The Little Tin God of Characterization", *Asimov's*, May 1985: "At about the same time [as "Nightfall"] I had three more ideas of first-class importance, each one of which I exploited to the full. They were 1) the all-human galaxy, 2) psychohistory, and (most important) 3) the Three Laws of Robotics." Much has been made of these, but their status as ideas "of first-class importance" is questionable. Neither psychohistory nor the Three Laws has stood up to rigorous critical examination.

15. Particularly so when one considers that in the 32 years between the last story in

the trilogy and *Foundation's Edge*, there have been vast scientific leaps: nuclear power, spaceflight, robots, the contraceptive pill, spare-part surgery, the double-helix of DNA, home computers and mass media technology amongst them. Asimov's future history ignores most of these aspects because it must, Asimov having decided that he would not re-write the earlier volumes. The sequence subsequently consigns itself to the outmoded and pre-Technological viewpoint of the forties. It is, paradoxically, a long-past future history.

16. *The Robots of Dawn*, 10, "Again Vasilia", 41:

> Baley stirred uneasily and said in a mumble, "He didn't want to make love to his daughter?"
> "Oh, don't be a fool. What difference does that make? Considering that hardly any man on Aurora knows who his daughter is, any man making love to any woman a few decades younger might be—but never mind, it's self-evident."

17. R. Daneel defines this clearly at the book's end:

> Daneel said, "You see, Dr Mandamus, some time ago, on Solaria, we encountered robots who narrowly defined human beings as Solarians only. We recognize the fact that if different robots are subject to narrow definitions of one sort or another, there can only be measureless destruction. It is useless to try to have us define human beings as Aurorans only. We define human beings as all members of the species, *Homo Sapiens*, which includes Earthpeople and Settlers, and we feel that the prevention of harm to human beings in groups and to humanity as a whole comes before the prevention of harm to any specific individual."

We might unthinkingly applaud this were it not for the fact that in so allowing his robots to create a "Zeroth Law" for themselves, Asimov unwittingly opens up one of the biggest cans of worms in moral philosophy. Who decides what is for the best? How are the relative needs of different groups weighed against each other? What Asimov presents here as

Man's possible salvation, others might regard as the recipe for a Frankenstein creation—telepathic robots with an utilitarian urge.

18. Stoutly defending Asimov is James Gunn in *Isaac Asimov: The Foundations of Science Fiction*, New York/Oxford, 1982. Gunn argues that Asimov "is one of those writers upon whom the case for science fiction as a field with a different set of values must rest" (Robert Scholes, Editor's Foreword). To do so one has to abandon all normal literary criteria, and this Gunn advocates, calling his approach "criticism in context". Such an approach places emphasis on the conditions in which the work was written, but does not come to terms with whatever was significant or good about Asimov's fiction. Asimov's stories, like Heinlein's, *did* stand out from those of their contemporaries producing work under similar pressures.

19. Van Vogt relished Hubbard's return to writing, making the following comment about *Battlefield Earth*: "Pure science fiction. 430,000 words written by a super-writer of the Golden Age . . . the great pulp music in every line . . . will be talked about for a decade . . . wonderful adventure . . . great characters . . . a masterpiece." (Quoted in the Church of Scientology advertisement following Hubbard's death.)

20. Herbert was apparently heavily involved as consultant throughout the filming of *Dune*. He was quoted widely as being satisfied at the end result, remaining silent on the necessary ambiguity surrounding Paul Atreides's motives and morality disappearing from the film. A sensitive study of power and responsibility was thus reduced to a power fantasy of goodies and baddies. The film is best viewed (with the sound turned off) as a succession of animated *Astounding* covers from way-back-when. This aspect of the film—its glorious pictorial quality—is to be applauded despite all else.

21. *2010* (1984) perhaps heralds a new generation of SF movies, much as its prequel did. Movie technology and story-line are for once harmoniously blended.

22. *The Fountains of Paradise* won Clarke the Hugo and Nebula awards for best novel of 1979. Earlier, "A Meeting with Medusa" had won Clarke a Nebula, and

Rendezvous with Rama won both Hugo and Nebula.

CHAPTER XVI

1. One might cite here publishing figures on three of Brin's novels. As of late 1985, *Startide Rising* was in a fifth US printing with 225,000 copies in print; *Sundiver* was in a seventh printing with 205,000 copies, and *The Practice Effect* (1984) in a fourth printing of 165,000 copies. Whilst these are only something like a tenth of the figures Heinlein and co might expect, they equate with the best second-level authors in terms of sales.
2. *The Novels of Philip K. Dick*, UMI Research Press, 1985.
3. The scene is at the beginning of chapter four, and provides evidence of an artist's eye at work: "I sat in my usual corner listening to Kathryn and looking around contentedly: we were a room of fire-skinned animals, wet and steaming, crazy-maned, beautiful as horses."
4. The Pelbar Cycle, at the time of writing, consists of the following novels: *The Breaking of Northwall* (1980), *The Ends of the Circle* (1981), *The Dome in the Forest* (1981), *The Fall of the Shell* (1982), *An Ambush of Shadows* (1983), *The Song of the Axe* (1984), and *The Sword of Forbearance* (1985).
5. Not to be confused with "The Island of Dr Death and Other Stories" and "The Doctor of Death Island", also by Wolfe. All three similarly-titled stories can be found in the collection, *The Island of Doctor Death and Other Stories and Other Stories*, New York, 1980. Connections between the three stories might be discerned, though not ones of a superficial nature.
6. A coda to the four volumes of *The Book of the New Sun* is *The Castle of the Otter*, Willimantic, Ct., 1983, a whimsical, temptingly obscure volume throwing a very dim light on the meaning of the tetralogy.
7. Instances of this are the moments in the vast cavern where the underworld chief and his beggar hordes meet, and in the final encounter with the boat of the dead. But Powers also excels at conjuring up the simplest details of the past:

The flickering lamplight seemed to fall with reluctance across the overhanging housefronts of Buckeridge Street, laying only the faintest of dry brush touches on the black fabric of the night—here an open window high in one wall was underlit, though the room beyond was in darkness; there the mouth of an alley with another lamp somewhere along it was discernible only by a line of yellowly glistening wet cobblestones, like a procession of toads only momentarily motionless in their slow crossing of the street; and ragged roofs and patches of scaling walls were occasionally visible when the vagrant breeze blew the lamp flame high. (Chapter 4)

8. "Speech Sounds" (1983) and "Bloodchild" (1984) both won Hugo Awards. Both are worthy of applause.
9. In *Science Fiction: The 100 Best Novels*, London, 1985. Pringle's 92nd selection is *Wild Seed*, one of seven novels chosen from the 1980 crop.
10. Lest it be argued that the authors of this volume know not whereof they speak, let us—as feminists often insist we do—talk of a personal instance: specifically, that of the junior author of this volume, David Wingrove.

I am, for half the week, a househusband, looking after a 21-month baby girl, Jessica, who has her mother's surname, not mine. My common law wife, Susan, is a magazine editor earning three times my income—a factor usually stressed in feminist propaganda (to make the point that males are obsessed with status and in being chief provider: I am not: what we achieve is achieved jointly). We share household tasks (unequally, I admit—my upbringing was very much under the old dispensation. I expect the next generation to get it right), and most of our financial arrangements are—deliberately—in my wife's name. That "biological tyranny" (the "slavery" of child-rearing) which feminists talk of has no place in our household simply because we do not allow it. The burden is shared and more than halved. Both partners are enriched by this. We are both "mother" to our daughter and shall be to all our children. It seems a healthy arrangement and we seem to be producing a joyful, lusty little girl who we hope will have no sex-related misconceptions. But, like most genuine revolutions, it must be done in practice, not on paper. Though—as SF constantly proves—the paper models can help formulate the practical effort.

As a point of interest, it appears that Frank Herbert did a similar job of househusbanding some thirty years ago. His first wife, Bev, worked, while he brought up the kids and wrote.

11. An excellent assessment of the first three novels in the sequence, and of the themes and background of *Canopus*, is Andrew Sawyer's "An Interim Report from the Archives" in *Vector* 103 (August 1981).

12. The full titles of the five novels are as follows: *Re: Colonised Planet 5 Shikasta: Personal, Psychological, Historical Documents Relating to Visit by Johor (George Sherban): Emissary (Grade 9) 87th of the Period of the Last Days*, (1979), *The Marriages Between Zones Three, Four, and Five (As Narrated by the Chroniclers of Zone Three)* (1980), *The Sirian Experiments: The Report by Ambien II, of the Five* (1981), *The Making of the Representative for Planet 8* (1982), *Documents Relating to the Sentimental Agents in the Volyen Empire* (1983). The sequence is still incomplete.

13. *20th Century English Literature: A Soviet View*, Moscow, 1982. (No editor given.)

14. Peter Nicholls, "Michael Moorcock", in E. F. Bleiler ed., *Science Fiction Writers, op. cit.*

15. The inevitability of such a schism is a result of the proliferation of SF in the last fifteen years. Because it is no longer possible to read even half of what is being published, people will tend to specialize in their reading and seek out those publishers, magazines and recommended texts that fall within their sphere of interest. Such is already happening in the high-tech "Hard" SF camp, with its magazine *Far Frontiers*, the successor to the 1970s *Destinies*. Baen Books and Tor in the States already cater for this specific market.

The February 1986 issue of *Locus* provides statistics for 1985—apparently a record year for SF both in the number of books published and in the number of copies sold. 1332 books were published in the States alone—715 new, 617 reprints. Included in this figure are 74 reference books, sign that critical interest in SF is increasing.

16. Mention must be made in this respect of London's Women's Press, who are encouraging and publishing much of the new feminist SF as well as doing the sterling work of rediscovering the unheralded roots of this sub genre.

Select Critical Bibliography

This bibliography cites those books and monographs most frequently consulted, and includes only writings which refer to authors within the SF field. Many further citations are to be found in the chapter notes.

Aldiss, Brian W., *This World and Nearer Ones*. 1979.
——, *The Pale Shadow of Science*. Seattle, WA, 1985.
——, *. . . And the Lurid Glare of the Comet*. Seattle, WA, 1986.
—— and Harrison, Harry (eds.), *Hell's Cartographers*. 1975.
Amis, Kingsley, *New Maps of Hell*. 1961.
Atheling, William, Jr, *The Issue at Hand*. Chicago, 1964.
——, *More Issues at Hand*. Chicago, 1970.
Bailey, J. O., *Pilgrims Through Space and Time*. New York, 1947.
Barron, Neil (ed.), *Anatomy of Wonder*, 2nd edition. New York, 1981.
Bergonzi, Bernard, *The Early H. G. Wells*. Manchester, 1961.
Bleiler, Everett F. (ed.), *Science Fiction Writers*. New York, 1982.
—— (ed.), *Supernatural Fiction Writers: Fantasy and Horror*, 2 vols. New York, 1985.
Clareson, Thomas D., *Some Kind of Paradise: The Emergence of American Science Fiction*. Westport, Conn., 1985.
—— (ed.), *SF: The Other Side of Realism*. Bowling Green, Ohio, 1971.
Clarke, I. F., *The Tale of the Future*, 2nd edition. 1972.
——, *Voices Prophesying War, 1763–1984*. 1966.
——, *The Pattern of Expectation, 1644–2001*. 1982.
Dunn, Jane, *Moon in Eclipse: A Life of Mary Shelley*. 1978.
Franklin, H. Bruce, *Future Perfect: American Science Fiction of the Nineteenth Century*. New York, 1966.
Gunn, James, *Alternate Worlds: The Illustrated History of Science Fiction*. Englewood Cliffs, NJ, 1975.
Hardy, Phil, *The Aurum Film Encyclopedia: Science Fiction*. 1984.
Hillegas, Mark R., *The Future as Nightmare: H. G. Wells and the Anti-Utopians*. New York, 1967.
Huntington, John, *The Logic of Fantasy: H. G. Wells and Science Fiction*. New York, 1982.
Kagarlitski, Julius, *The Life and Thought of H. G. Wells*. 1966.
Knight, Damon, *In Search of Wonder*, revised edition. Chicago, 1967.
Lewis, C. S., *Of Other Worlds: Essays and Stories*. 1966.
——, *Selected Literary Essays*, ed., Walter Hooper. Cambridge, England, 1969.
Lundwall, Sam J., *Science Fiction: What It's All About*. New York, 1971.
——, *Science Fiction: An Illustrated History*. 1978.

Lupoff, Richard A., *Edgar Rice Burroughs: Master of Adventure*. New York, 1965.

Magill, Frank N. (ed.), *Survey of Science Fiction Literature*, 5 volumes. Englewood Cliffs, NJ, 1980.

McConnell, Frank, *The Science Fiction of H. G. Wells*. 1981.

Moskowitz, Sam, *Explorers of the Infinite: Shapers of Science Fiction*. Cleveland and New York [1963].

—— , *Seekers of Tomorrow: Masters of Modern Science Fiction*. New York, 1967.

—— (ed.), *Under the Moons of Mars: A History and Anthology of "The Scientific Romance" in the Munsey Magazines, 1912–1920*. New York, 1970.

Nicholls, Peter (ed.), *The Encyclopedia of Science Fiction*. 1979.

Nicolson, Marjorie Hope, *Voyages to the Moon*. New York, 1949.

Philmus, Robert, *Into the Unknown: The Evolution of Science Fiction from Francis Godwin to H. G. Wells*. Berkeley and Los Angeles, 1970.

Porges, Irwin, *Edgar Rice Burroughs: The Man Who Created Tarzan*. New York, 1970.

Smith, Curtis C. (ed.), *Twentieth Century Science Fiction Writers*, 2nd edition. Chicago, 1986.

Stableford, Brian, *Scientific Romance in Britain, 1890–1950*. 1985.

Suvin, Darko, *Metamorphoses of Science Fiction*. New Haven, Conn., 1979.

Tuck, Donald (compiler), *The Encyclopedia of Science Fiction and Fantasy*, 3 vols. Chicago, 1974–1982.

Tymn, Marshall (ed.), *The Science Fiction Reference Book*. Mercer Island, WA, 1981.

Tymn, Marshall and Ashley, Mike (eds.), *Science Fiction, Fantasy, and Weird Fiction Magazines*. Westport, Conn., 1985.

Wagar, W. Warren, *Terminal Versions: The Literature of Last Things*. Bloomington, IL, 1982.

Walsh, Chad, *From Utopia to Nightmare*, 1962.

Wingrove, David (ed.), *The Science Fiction Source Book*, 1984.

—— , *The Science Fiction Film Source Book*. 1985.

Wolfe, Gary K., *The Known and the Unknown: The Iconography of Science Fiction*. Kent, Ohio, 1979.

The invaluable indexes:

Index to the Science Fiction Magazines, 1926–1950, compiled by Donald B. Day, revised edition. Boston, 1982.

Index to the SF Magazines, 1951–1965, compiled by Erwin S. Strauss, Cambridge, Mass. (the MIT Science Fiction Society), 1966.

Index to the Science Fiction Magazines, 1966–1970. West Hanover, Mass. (New England Science Fiction Association), 1971.

And the equally invaluable periodicals. In particular we have relied on long runs of *Extrapolation, Fantasy Review, Foundation, Locus, Riverside Quarterly, Science Fiction Studies, Vector*.

Index

Abbey, Lynn, 283
Abbott, Edwin A., 112
"Abominations of Yondo, The", see Clark Ashton Smith
Absolute At Large, The, see Karel Čapek
Ace Books, 260, 291, 318, 334, 339
Ackerman, Forrest J., 461, 475
Across the Zodiac see Percy Greg
Adams, Douglas, 326–7, 385
Adams, Richard, 246
Adams, Robert, 279–80
Adventures in Time and Space, see R. J. Healy and J. McComas
Aerodrome, The, see Rex Warner
Affirmation, The, see Christopher Priest
After Doomsday, see Poul Anderson
After London, see Richard Jefferies
After Many a Summer, see Aldous Huxley
Agrippa, Cornelius, 40
Aickman, Robert, 60, 372
Ainsworth, Harrison, 90
Alas, Babylon, see Pat Frank
Albertus Magnus, 40
Aldiss, Brian W., 18, 273, 298, 299, 372, 393, 462, 473; *Barefoot in the Head*, 471; *Enemies of the System*, 466; *Science Fiction Art*, 462
Alexandria Quartet, The, see Lawrence Durrell
Alice in Wonderland, see Lewis Carroll
Alien (1979), 274, 370
Alien Embassy, see Ian Watson
Allan and the Ice-Gods, see H. Rider Haggard
Allan Quatermain, see H. Rider Haggard
Allen, Grant, 142
All-Story, 156, 158, 176, 177
All We Marsmen, see Philip K. Dick
"All You Zombies –", see Robert A. Heinlein
Almuric, see Robert E. Howard
Alteration, The, see Kingsley Amis
Alternate Worlds, see James Gunn
Always Coming Home, see Ursula K. Le Guin
Alyx, see Joanna Russ
Amazing Stories, 19, 27, 39, 104, 177, 202, 204–5, 209, 211, 215, 371, 466
Amazing Stories Annual, 204
Amazing Stories Quarterly, 204
Amber novels, see Roger Zelazny
American Boy, 458
American Graffiti, (1973), 273
Amerika, see Franz Kafka
Amis, Kingsley, 164, 246, 379, 467, 470, 474; *The Alteration*, 36, 379; *New Maps of Hell*, 240, 327

Amis, Martin, 274
Analog see *Astounding*
Anarchistic Colossus, The, see A. E. van Vogt
Anatomy of Wonder, see Neil Barron
". . . And Call Me Conrad", see Roger Zelazny
Anderson, Poul, 247, 255, 314, 339, 369, 408, 475, 482; *Tau Zero*, 314
L'an deux mille quatre cent quarante, see Louis-Sébastien Mercier
Andrea, Johann Valentin, 77
Android (1982), 470
"Android and the Human, The", see Philip K. Dick
". . . And Searching Mind", see Jack Williamson
And Strange at Ecbatan the Trees, see Michael Bishop
Angel of the Revolution, The, see George Griffith
Animal Farm, see George Orwell
Anita, see Keith Roberts
Ann Veronica, see H. G. Wells
"Answer", see Fredric Brown
Antarctic Mystery, An, see Jules Verne
Anticipations, see H. G. Wells
"Antonius", 53–4
Anubis Gates, The, see Tim Powers
Anvil, Christopher, 316
Ape and Essence, see Aldous Huxley
Appleton, Victor, 136
Apuleius, 70
Arabian Nights, 33, 312
Argosy, 160
Argosy All-Story, 170
Ariosto, 28
Aristophanes, 68
Arkham House, 172
Armed Camps, see Kit Reed
Arno Press, 455
Arnold, Edwin Lester, 139–141, 455
Arrhenius, Svante, 159, 160
Artificial Kid, The, see Bruce Sterling
"Artist of the Beautiful, The", see Nathaniel Hawthorne
Art, 207–9
"As Easy As ABC", see Rudyard Kipling
Ashley, Mike, 228
Asimov, Isaac, 218–19, 226, 239, 264–267, 282, 308, 339, 383–5, 389–396 *passim*, 461, 468, 470, 475, 476, 485; *The End of Eternity*, 266–7; *Foundation* series, 218–9, 224, 235, 265–6, 318, 386, 390–393, 433, 468, 485; . *Robot* series, 218, 226, 266, 362, 391–3; *Robots*

Asimov, Isaac—continued
  and Empire, 392–3, 468; The Robots of Dawn,
  386, 391–2, 459
Asleep in the Afternoon, see E. C. Large
Asprin, Robert Lynn, 283
Astonishing Stories, 216, 402
Astor, John Jacob, 141
Astounding Science Fiction (Analog), 205, 207,
  211, 214, 216–229, passim, 234–235, 239,
  240, 251, 265, 268, 277, 286, 315, 316, 320,
  371, 387, 463, 464, 465, 476
"Asylum", see A. E. Van Vogt
Atheling, William, Jr. see James Blish
Atomic Phantasy, An, see Krakatit
Atrocity Exhibition, The, see J. G. Ballard
At the Back of the North Wind, see George
  MacDonald
At the Earth's Core, see Edgar Rice Burroughs
At the Eye of the Ocean, see Hilbert Schenck
Atwood, Margaret, 438
Auden, W. H., 180
Auel, Jean M., 385
Auf Zwei Planeten, see Kurd Lasswitz
Aurelia (Aurelie), see Gérard de Nerval
Austen, Jane, 34, 86
Australian SF, 437
L'Autre Monde, see Cyrano de Bergerac
Axel, see Villiers de l'Isle Adam

Babel-17, see Samuel R. Delany
Babits, Mihaly, 183
"Baby is Three", see Theodore Sturgeon
Back to Methuselah, see George Bernard Shaw
Back to the Future, (1985), 272
Bacon, Francis, 77
Baen, James, 371
Bailey, Hilary, 300
Baker, Sharon, 436
Balchin, Nigel, 246
Balcombe, Florence, 144
Baldwin, Merl, 408
Ballard, J. G., 182, 235, 254, 277, 299–303
  passim, 308, 337, 339, 393, 437, 438, 439, 442,
  474; The Atrocity Exhibition, 300–301, 304;
  "The Terminal Beach", 301–2
Balmer, Edwin, 201
Banks, Iain, 246
Barefoot in the Head, see Brian W. Aldiss
Barnes, Rory, 392
Barron, Neil, 139
Barsoom, see Edgar Rice Burroughs
Barth, John, 246
Barthelme, Donald, 246
Bataille de Berlin en 1875, La, 109
Batchelor, John Calvin, 429–30
Battlefield Earth, see L. Ron Hubbard
Battle of Dorking, see Colonel George Chesney
Battlestar Galactica, (1977), 273, 274
Baudelaire, Charles, 56
Bayley, Barrington, 299, 305, 373

Bear, Greg, 278,˙400, 416–18
Beasts, see John Crowley
"Beast That Shouted Love at the Heart of the
  World, The", see Harlan Ellison
Beatles, The, 308
Beaumont, Charles, 255, 269
Beckett, Samuel, 27, 246
Beckford, William, 33
"Beep", see James Blish
Before Adam, see Jack London
Before the Dawn, see John Taine
Begum's Fortune, The, see Jules Verne
Behold the Man, see Michael Moorcock
Belgariad, The, see David Eddings
Bellamy, Edward, 77, 94–5
Bellow, Saul, 343
Beloved Son, see George Turner
Beneath the Shattered Moons, see Michael Bishop
Benford, Gregory, 278, 352–354, 443, 480
Beowulf, 27, 375
Bergonzi, Bernard, 127
Bester, Alfred, 235–6, 242, 260, 278, 291,
  303, 311, 412; The Stars My Destination
  (Tiger! Tiger!) 235, 242; "Time is the
  Traitor" 236
Best of Science Fiction, The, see Groff Conklin
Bettyann, see Kris Neville
Beynon, John, see John Wyndham
Beyond Apollo, see Barry N. Malzberg
Beyond the Blue Event Horizon, see Frederik Pohl
Beyond Tomorrow, see Lee Harding
Bid Time Return, see Richard Matheson
Bierce, Ambrose, 64
"Big Ancestor", see F. L. Wallace
Big Time, The, see Fritz Leiber
Bill, The Galactic Hero, see Harry Harrison
Birds, The, see Aristophanes
Birds of Prey, see David Drake
Birth of the People's Republic of Antarctica, The,
  see John Calvin Batchelor
Bishop, Michael, 354–357, 363, 480, 481; A
  Funeral for the Eyes of Fire, 354; No Enemy
  But Time, 355–6, 357; "The Quickening",
  356–7; "Saving Face", 356
"Black Air", see Kim Stanley Robinson
Black August, see Dennis Wheatley
Blackburn, John, 254
"Black Destroyer", see A. E. Van Vogt
Black Easter, see James Blish
Black Hole, The (1979), 274, 370
Blade Runner, (1982), 271, 274, 335
Blade Runner (novel) , see Philip K. Dick
Blake, William, 34, 61
Bleiler, E. F., 146, 156
Blind Man and the Elephant, The, see Russell M.
  Griffin
Blind Spot, The, see Austin Hall and Homer Eon
  Flint
Blish, James, 196, 226, 240–242, 243, 289, 465,
  472; Cities in Flight, 240, 465; The Frozen

Blish, James—*continued*
Year, 241, 242
Blithedale Romance, The, see Nathaniel Hawthorne
Bloch, Robert, 60, 172
Blood Music, see Greg Bear
Blown, see Philip José Farmer
Boisgilbert, Edmund, see Ignatius Donnelly
Boland, John, 254
Book of Morgaine, The, see C. J. Cherryh
Book of the New Sun, The, see Gene Wolfe
Borges, Jorge Luis, 130, 246, 327, 434–5, 438
"Born of Man and Woman", see Richard Matheson
"Born With the Dead", see Robert Silverberg
Boswell, James, 30
Boucher, Anthony, 227–8, 237, 268–9
Boulle, Pierre, 259
Bova, Ben, 227, 371, 408
Bowen, John, 246
Bowen, Robert Sidney, 147
Bowie, David, 389
"Boy and His Dog, A", Harlan Ellison
Boys From Brazil, The, see Ira Levin
Brackett, Leigh, 258
Bradbury, Ray, 26, 60, 112, 163, 172, 237, 247–8, 275, 339, 415; *The Martian Chronicles* (*The Silver Locusts*), 247–48, 275
Bradley, Marion Zimmer, 158, 259, 277, 281, 366
Brain Wave, see Poul Anderson
Brass Butterfly, The, see William Golding
Brave New World, see Aldous Huxley
Brazil, (1985), 380
Breaking of Northwall, The, see Paul O. Williams
"Breaking Point", see James Gunn
Breakthrough, see Richard Cowper
Brin, David, 418, 447
Bring the Jubilee, see Ward Moore
British Barbarians, The, see Grant Allen
Brod, Max, 180, 181
Broderick, Damien, 392, 437
Brooke-Rose, Christine, 246
Brown, Charles Brockden, 57, 60, 64
Brown, Charles N., 22, 385
Brown, Fredric, 225, 251
Brown, Rosel George, 259
Browne, Sir Thomas, 198
Brunner, John, 227, 247, 252, 298, 316–318, 339, 372, 375, 387; *Stand on Zanzibar*, 292, 299, 316–318
Bryant, Edward, 368, 436, 482
Buchan, John, 138, 147
Buck Rogers, see Philip Francis Nowlan
Budrys, Algis, 255, 269, 484
Bug Jack Barron, see Norman Spinrad
Bulmer, Kenneth, 255–6, 298, 340, 372
Bulwer-Lytton, Edward, 90–92, 93–94, 122; *The Coming Race*, 84, 91–92, 94, 97, 111, 199, 451

Bunch, David R., 323–5, 331, 380
Bunyan, John, 80, 82
Burdick, Eugene, 246
Burgel, Bruno H., 204
Burgess, Anthony, 243, 246, 300
Burke, Edmund, 33, 36, 64, 91, 106
Burne-Jones, Sir Edward, 138, 144
Burning, The, see James Gunn
"Burning Chrome", see William Gibson
Burns, Jim, 208
Burn, Witch, Burn!, see Abraham Merritt
Burroughs, Edgar Rice, 139, 152, 153, 155–166, 167, 170, 176, 177, 205, 217, 293, 303, 311, 312; *At the Earth's Core*, 158–160; *The Land That Time Forgot*, 161; *Pellucidar*, 159, 163–5; *A Princess of Mars*, 156–7; *Tarzan of the Apes*, 158
Burroughs, William, 246, 297, 298, 299, 300, 310, 411, 412
Butler, Octavia, 368, 422, 427–29, 433, 486
Butler, Samuel, 92–3, 97; *Erewhon* 77, 92–3
Butor, Michel, 14, 104, 107
Butterworth, Michael, 299, 305
"By His Bootstraps", see Robert A. Heinlein
Byron, Lord, 33–47 *passim*, 102, 425
Byzantium Endures, see Michael Moorcock

Cabell, James Branch, 262
Caesar's Column, see Ignatius Donnelly
Caidin, Martin, 408
Caleb Williams, see William Godwin
Caltraps of Time, The, see David I. Masson
Calvino, Italo, 437
Campanella, Tommaso, 77, 80
Campbell, John W., 14, 207–229 *passim*, 250, 265, 269, 271, 276, 286, 289, 290, 315, 316, 327, 384, 386, 393, 394, 395, 429, 461–5 *passim*, 477; "The Cloak of Aesir", 215–6
Campbell, Ramsey, 60
Camp Concentration, see Thomas M. Disch
Candide, see Voltaire
Canning, George, 31
Canopus in Argos series, see Doris Lessing
Canticle for Leibowitz, A, see Walter M. Miller Jr
Čapek, Josef, 179, 180
Čapek, Karel, 176–180, 183, 186, 201, 214, 380; *R.U.R.*, 178–9, 183, 218, 250, 466; *War With the Newts*, 179
Capillaria, see Frigyes Karinthy
Captain Future, see Edmond Hamilton
Captain Justice, 176, 458
Card, Orson Scott, 408
Carey, Peter, 438
Caricature, Le, see Albert Robida
Carlyle, Thomas, 94, 123
Carnell, E. J. ("Ted"), 298
Carpenter, John, 467
Carr, Terry, 470, 472
Carrie, see Stephen King
Carroll, Lewis, 90, 111–2, 119, 217, 246, 430

Carter, Angela, 438
Cartier, Edd, 208
Cartmill, Cleve, 224
Case of Conscience, A, see James Blish
"Cask of Amontillado, A", see Edgar Allan Poe
"Cassandra", see C. J. Cherryh
Castle, The, see Franz Kafka
Castle of Otranto, The, see Horace Walpole
Cat's Cradle, see Kurt Vonnegut, Jr.
Cat Who Walks Through Walls: A Comedy of Justice, The, see Robert A. Heinlein
Cave Girl, The, see Edgar Rice Burroughs
Cavendish, Margaret, Duchess of Newcastle, 18, 72–3
Caves of Steel, The, see Isaac Asimov
Cawelti, John G., 445
"Celestial Publicity", see Villiers de l'Isle Adam
Centauri Device, The, see M. John Harrison
Centrifugal Rickshaw Dancer, The, see William John Watkins
Century's End, see Russell M. Griffin
Chalk Giants, The, see Keith Roberts
Challenger, Professor, see Arthur Conan Doyle
Chandler, A. Bertram, 234
Changewar, see Fritz Leiber
Chapter House Dune, see Frank Herbert
Charisma, see Michael Coney
Charly (1968), 468
Charnas, Suzy McKee, 367
Chaucer, Geoffrey, 70
Cheon of Weltenland, see Stone, Charlotte
Cherryh, C. J., 367–8, 475
Chesney, Colonel George, 108–9, 120
Chesterton, G. K., 148
Childers, Erskine, 147, 456
Childhood's End, see Arthur C. Clarke
Children of Dune, see Frank Herbert
Children of the Damned (1963), 467
Christianapolis, see Johann Valentin Andrea
Christopher, John, 255, 378
Chrysalids, The, see John Wyndham
Churchill, Winston, 447
Cinnabar, see Ed Bryant
Cinq cents millions de la Bégum, Les, see Jules Verne
Cinq semaines en ballon, see Jules Verne
Citadel of the Autarch, The, see Gene Wolfe
Cities in Flight, see James Blish
City series, see Clifford D. Simak
City of Illusions, see Ursula K. Le Guin
"City of the Singing Flame, The", see Clark Ashton Smith
City of the Sun, see Tommaso Campanella
Clans of the Alphane Moon, see Philip K. Dick
Clareson, Thomas D., 345, 455, 478
Clark, Sir Kenneth, 70
Clarke, Arthur C., 215, 227, 247, 248–9, 353, 382, 384, 396, 400–402, 416, 417, 469; *Childhood's End,* 249, 401, 416; "A Meeting with Medusa", 400–401, 403; *Rendezvous with*

Rama, 362, 401, 403, 417; *2001: A Space Odyssey,* 249, 271, 298; *2010: Odyssey Two,* 15, 384, 400, 402
Clarke, I. F., 77, 107, 108
"Clash by Night", see Henry Kuttner
Claudy, Carl H., 458
Claw of the Conciliator, The, see Gene Wolfe
Clay's Ark, see Octavia Butler
Clayton, Jo, 408
Clement, Hal, 219, 224, 226, 369, 376, 416
Cleopatra, see H. Rider Haggard
Clifton, Mark, 225
Clingerman, Mildred, 269
Clipper of the Clouds, see Jules Verne
"Cloak of Aesir", see John W. Campbell
Clockwork Orange A, see Anthony Burgess
Clone, see Richard Cowper
Close Encounters of the Third Kind (1977), 272, 400
"Cloudcuckooland", see Aristophanes
Coblentz, Stanton A., 204
Coetzee, J. M., 246
Cogswell, Theodore, 256, 269
Coleridge, Samuel Taylor, 30, 32, 34, 81, 337, 425
Collier, Marie, 178
Collins, Wilkie, 17, 110, 422
"Colloquy of Monos and Una, The", see Edgar Allan Poe
Colonial Survey, see Murray Leinster
"Colony", see Philip K. Dick
Comet Stories, 216
Comfort, Alex, 465
Coming Race, The, see Edward Bulwer-Lytton
"Command Performance", see Walter M. Miller Jr.
"Common Sense", see Robert A. Heinlein
Commonwealth of Oceania, The, see James Harrington
Company of Glory, The, see Edgar Pangborn
Compton, D. G., 378, 439
Computer Connection, The, see Alfred Bester
Conan, see Robert E. Howard
Condillac, Etienne Bonnot de, 37
Condition of Muzak, The, see Michael Moorcock
Coney, Michael, 378
Conklin, Groff, 233
Connolly, Cyril, 130
Conquest, Robert, 469, 474
Conquest of the Earth, The (1980), 273
Conrad, Joseph, 126, 426, 430
Contact, see Carl Sagan
Contes Cruels, see Villiers de l'Isle Adam
Continent of Lies, The, see James Morrow
Continuous Katherine Mortenhoe, The, see D. G. Compton
"Conversation of Eiros and Charmion, The", see Edgar Allan Poe
Cook, Captain James, 34
Cook, Glen, 408

Cool War, The, see Frederik Pohl
Cooper, Fenimore, 64
Cooper, Merian C., 152
Coover, Robert, 246, 328
Copernicus, 67
Coppel, Alfred, 257
Corman, Roger, 257
Cornelius, Jerry, see Michael Moorcock
Cosmic Stories, 216
Cosmos, 371
Cosy Catastrophes, 252–255
Coulson, Robert, 484
"Counterfeit", see Alan Nourse
Counterfeit World, see Daniel Galouye
"Country of the Blind, The", see H. G. Wells
Count Zero, see William Gibson
Courtship Rite, see Donald Kingsbury
Cowper, Richard (John Murry), 372, 378
Crabbe, Buster, 158
Crane, Robert, 256
Crispin, Edmund, 300, 474
Cronenberg, David, 274, 470, 474
Crosby, Stills and Nash, 473
Crowley, John, 352, 358–362, 427; *Beasts*, 359–361; *The Deep*, 358–359
Crystal Age, A, see W. H. Hudson
"Crystal Egg, The", see H. G. Wells
Crystal World, The, see J. G. Ballard
Cummings, Ray, 94, 166
Currents of Space, The, see Isaac Asimov
Cyrano de Bergerac, 28, 70, 73–5

"Dagon", see H. P. Lovecraft
"Danger!", see Arthur Conan Doyle
Dangerous Visions, see Harlan Ellison
Dante Alighieri, 27, 28, 65, 180, 201
Dark Dominion, see David Duncan
Darker Than You Think, see Jack Williamson
Darkover series, see Marion Zimmer Bradley
Dark Star (1974), 469–70
Dark Universe, see Daniel Galouye
Darwin, Charles, 17, 42, 452, 481
Darwin, Erasmus, 29–34, 44, 100, 451; *Zoonomia*, 30, 32
Davidson, Avram, 269, 326, 472
Da Vinci, Leonardo, 28
Davy, see Edgar Pangborn
Dawn in Andromeda, see E. C. Large
Day After, The, 429
Day After Judgement, The, see James Blish
"Day Before the Revolution, The", see Ursula K. Le Guin
Day of the Triffids, The, see John Wyndham
Day of Timestop, The, see Philip José Farmer
Day of Uniting, The, see Edgar Wallace
"Deadline", see Cleve Cartmill
Dead Zone, The, see Stephen King
Dean, Mal, 300, 474
Dean Drive, 227

"Death and Designation Among the Asadi", see Michael Bishop
"Death Module, The", see J. G. Ballard
"Death of Dr Island, The", see Gene Wolfe
Death of Grass, The, see John Christopher
Deathwatch, 482
Deathworld, see Harry Harrison
de Bergerac, Cyrano, see Cyrano de Bergerac
De Camp, L. Sprague, 172, 173, 235, 259
de Chirico, Giorgio, 208, 337, 461–462
Découverte Australe, La, see Restif de la Bretonne
Deep, The, see John Crowley
"Deeper Than the Darkness", see Gregory Benford
Definition of SF, 18–19, 20, 25–27
Defoe, Daniel, 26, 79, 80, 81; *Robinson Crusoe*, 79, 80, 81, 86, 87
DeFord, Miriam Allen, 26, 259
de Grainville, Jean-Baptiste Cousin, 448
de la Bretonne, Restif, 100–101
Delany, Samuel R., 128, 260, 291–293, 294, 305, 307, 311, 359, 412, 427, 471–2, 474
de l'Isle Adam, Villiers, 102–103, 119–120, 202
del Rey, Lester, 215, 251, 446, 473
de Maupassant, Guy, 120, 202
Demolished Man, The, see Alfred Bester
de Nerval, Gérard, 101–2, 103
Derleth, August, 172, 482
de Sade, Marquis, 45, 447–8
Description of a New World, called The Blazing World, The, see Margaret Cavendish, Duchess of Newcastle
Destination Moon (1950), 95
Destinies, 371
de Tocqueville, Alexis, 89, 90, 100
Devo, 382
Dhalgren, see Samuel R. Delany
Diamondking of Sahara, The, see Sigurd Wettenhovi-Aspa
"Diamond Lens, The", see Fitz-James O'Brien
Dianetics, see L. Ron Hubbard
Dick, Philip K., 53, 56, 65, 184, 196, 220, 233, 247, 251, 269, 287, 326, 327, 328–335, 339, 348, 380, 388, 408–410, 411, 419, 470, 473, 477, 478; *The Divine Invasion*, 333, 409–10; *Do Androids Dream of Electric Sheep?*, 274, 292, 334–5; *Flow My Tears, the Policeman Said*, 331, 408–9; *The Man in the High Castle*, 36, 275, 329–30; *Martian Time-Slip*, 330–31, 332, 477, 478; *The Three Stigmata of Palmer Eldritch*, 332–3, 409
Dickens, Charles, 109, 110, 113, 119, 133, 135, 150, 181, 334
Dickson, Gordon R., 314, 369, 393, 472, 475–6
Diderot, Denis, 29, 53, 123
Di Fate, Vincent, 208, 462
Dimension of Miracles, see Robert Sheckley
Dinner at Deviant's Palace, see Tim Powers
Dirk Gently's Holistic Detective Agency, see Douglas Adams

Disch, Thomas M., 235, 305–6, 472; *Camp Concentration*, 299, 306, 426
Discovery of a New World, see John Wilkins
Disney, Walt, 106, 272, 274, 275, 362
Dispossessed, The, see Ursula K. Le Guin
Disraeli, Benjamin, 90–92 *passim*, 451
Divine Endurance, see Gwyneth Jones
Divine Invasion, The, see Philip K. Dick
Do Androids Dream of Electric Sheep?, see Philip K. Dick
Doc Savage, 228
Dr Adder, see K. W. Jeter
Dr Cyclops (1939), 271
Dr Jekyll and Mr Hyde, see Robert Louis Stevenson
"Dr Moreau's Other Island", see Josef Nesvadba
Dr Strangelove (1963), 467
Dr Who, 277
Dold, Elliott, 207, 208
Dominik, Hans, 143, 203
Donaldson, Stephen, 277
Donne, John, 74, 78, 226
Donnelly, Ignatius, 97
"Door in the Wall, The", see H. G. Wells
Doppelgangers, see H. F. Heard
Dorsai series, see Gordon R. Dickson
Dostoevsky, Fyodor, 86, 171, 334, 409
Double Star, see Robert A. Heinlein
Doughty, C. M., 198
"Down Among the Dead Men", see William Tenn
Downbelow Station, see C. J. Cherryh
Downward to the Earth, see Robert Silverberg
Doyle, Sir Arthur Conan, 17, 138, 147, 148–9, 153, 161; *The Lost World*, 137, 148–9
Dozois, Gardner M., 238, 418
Dracula, see Bram Stoker
Dragon in the Sea, The, see Frank Herbert
Dragon's Egg, see Dr Robert L. Forward
Drake, Asa, 408
Drake, David, 281, 408
Dream Millennium, The, see James White
Drawing of the Dark, The, see Tim Powers
Dray Prescot, see Kenneth Bulmer
Dream, The, see H. G. Wells
Dreaming Dragons, The, see Damien Broderick
Dream Master, The, see Roger Zelazny
Dream of Wessex, A, see Christopher Priest
Dreamsnake, see Vonda N. McIntyre
Driftglass, see Samuel R. Delany
Drought, The, see J. G. Ballard
"Drowned Giant, The", see J. G. Ballard
Drowned World, The, see J. G. Ballard
Druillet, Philippe, 209
Duel (1971), 257, 272
Dumarest series, see E. C. Tubb
"Dumb Waiter", see Walter M. Miller Jr
Duncan, David, 256
Dune series, see Frank Herbert

Dune (1984), 271, 274, 383, 400, 485
Dune Messiah, see Frank Herbert
Dungeons and Dragons, 275–6
Dunne, J. W., 201
Dunsany, Lord, 171
Durdane, see Jack Vance
Durrell, Lawrence, 59, 235–6, 246
Dusty Ayres and his Battle Birds, 147, 456
Dwellers in the Mirage, see Abraham Merritt
Dying of the Light, see George R. R. Martin
Dying Inside, see Robert Silverberg
Dynamic Science Stories, 216

Earth Abides, see George R. Stewart
Earth Book of Stormgate, The, see Poul Anderson
Earthsea, see Ursula K. Le Guin
Easton, Tom, 484
"Eastward Ho!", see William Tenn
Eddings, David, 283
Edwards, Malcolm, 238
Effinger, Geo. Alec, 418, 437
Eisenstein, Alex, 446
Einstein, Albert, 195
Einstein Intersection, The, see Samuel R. Delany
"Eleanora", see Edgar Allan Poe
Elgin, Suzette Haden, 430–32, 482
Eliot, T. S., 171, 245, 449
Ellis, Edward S., 135–6
Ellison, Harlan, 60, 296–99, 304–5, 339, 415, 472; *Dangerous Visions*, 297–8, 304, 324, 475, 484
Elwood, Roger, 371, 425
Embedding, The, see Ian Watson
Emerson, Ralph Waldo, 94
Empire of the Atom, see A. E. van Vogt
Empire of the Sun, see J. G. Ballard
Empire Strikes Back, The, 271, 468
Emprise, see Michael P. Kube-McDowell
Emshwiller, Ed, 208, 222
End of Eternity, The, see Isaac Asimov
Enemies of the System, see Brian W. Aldiss
Engine Summer, see John Crowley
Enigma, see Michael P. Kube-McDowell
"Envoy Extraordinary", see William Golding
Eon, see Greg Bear
"Equalizer, The", see Jack Williamson
Erasmus Magister, see Charles Sheffield
Erewhon, see Samuel Butler
Erewhon Revisited, see Samuel Butler
Ernst, Max, 141
Escape from the Planet of the Apes, see Jerry Pournelle
Escape Plans, see Gwyneth Jones
E.T. (1982), 272, 274, 321
Eureka, see Edgar Allan Poe
Evans, Christopher, 439, 440
Eve Future, L', see Villiers de l'Isle Adam
Evolution and Darwinism, 29–31
"Exiles on Asperus", see John Wyndham
Exile Waiting, The, see Vonda N. McIntyre

Expanded Universe, see Robert A. Heinlein
"Expedition in the Opposite Direction", see Josef Nesvadba
Experiment in Autobiography, see H. G. Wells
Experiment on a Bird in the Air Pump, An, see Joseph Wright
Extrapolation, 308, 469
Extro, see Alfred Bester
Eye in the Sky, see Philip K. Dick
Eye of the Heron, The, see Ursula K. Le Guin
Eye of the Queen, The, see Phillip Mann
"Eyes of Amber", see Joan Vinge

F&SF, see *Magazine of Fantasy and Science Fiction, The*
"Facts in the Case of M. Valdemar, The", see Edgar Allan Poe
Faded Sun, The, see C. J. Cherryh
Fahrenheit 451, see Ray Bradbury
Fail Safe, see Eugene Burdick & J. H. Wheeler
Fallen Star, see James Blish
Fall of Chronopolis, The, see Barrington Bayley
Fall of Moondust, A, see Arthur C. Clarke
"Fall of the House of Usher, The", see Edgar Allan Poe
Fall of the Shell, The, see Paul O. Williams
Fall of the Towers, The, see Samuel R. Delany
Famous Fantastic Mysteries, 140
Fandom, 207–8, 276, 469, 470
Fantastic Adventures, 216, 463, 464
Fantastic Voyage, see Isaac Asimov
Fantasy Review, 21
Far Frontiers, 487
Farley, Ralph Milne, 166, 466
Farmer, Philip José, 297, 309, 312–3, 368, 472, 477; "The Jungle Rot Kid on the Nod", 309–10; "Riders of the Purple Wage", 297, 313; *Riverworld* series 312–3, 376
Far Rainbow, see Boris and Arkady Strugatsky
Farson, Daniel, 144–5
Faulkner, William, 64
"Fear", see L. Ron Hubbard
Fearn, John Russell, 139, 211, 463
Feist, Raymond E., 408
Female Man, The, see Joanna Russ
Feminist SF, 340, 363–6, 367–8, 430–2, 479
Ferman, Edward L., 269
Fevre Dream, see George R. R. Martin
Fiedler, Leslie, 63, 165–6, 461
Fifth Head of Cerberus, The, see Gene Wolfe
57th Franz Kafka, The, see Rudy Rucker
Films, 45–6, 131–2, 271–275, 469–70
Final Blackout, see L. Ron Hubbard
Final Countdown, The, (1980), 274
Final Programme, The, Michael Moorcock
Finland, 113, 201
Finlay, Virgil, 207, 208
Finney, Jack, 256
"Fireman, The", see Ray Bradbury
"Fireproof", see Hal Clement

Firestarter, see Stephen King
"Fire Watch", see Connie Willis
"First Contact", see Murray Leinster
First Men in the Moon, The, see H. G. Wells
Fitzgibbon, Constantine, 246
Five Weeks in a Balloon, see Jules Verne
Flammarion, Camille, 454
Flash Gordon, 158
Flatland, see Edwin Abbott
Fleming, Ian, 153, 234, 275
Flesh, see Farmer, Philip José
Flight of the Dragonfly, The, see Dr Robert L. Forward
Flint, Homer Eon, 166
Flint, Kenneth C., 281
Floating City, A, see Jules Verne
"Flowers for Algernon", see Daniel Keyes
Flow My Tears, the Policeman Said, see Philip K. Dick
Food of the Gods, The, see H. G. Wells
Footfall, see Larry Niven and Jerry Pournelle
Forbidden Planet, (1956), 271
Forever War, The, see Joe Haldeman
Forster, E. M., 86, 184–5, 193
Fort, Charles, 213
Forward, Dr Robert L., 419
Foss, Chris, 208
Foster, Alan Dean, 370, 482
Foster, Hal, 158
Foundation, 469, 473, 474, 483
Foundation series, see Isaac Asimov
Foundation's Edge, see Isaac Asimov
Fountains of Paradise, The, see Arthur C. Clarke
"Four in One", see Damon Knight
Fowles, John, 386, 483
Frank, Pat, 469
Frankenstein: or, The Modern Prometheus, see Mary Shelley
Frankenstein Unbound, see Brian W. Aldiss
Franklin, Dr H. Bruce, 58
Fraser, Joseph, 437
Frayn, Michael, 246
Freas, Kelly, 208
Freeland, see Theodore Hertzka
French SF, 100–101
Freud, Sigmund, 117, 182, 219, 449
Friday, see Robert A. Heinlein
Friedman, Michael Jan, 408
Fringe of Leaves, A, see Patrick White
Frogs, The, see Aristophanes
Frozen Year, The, see James Blish
Fugue for a Darkening Island, see Christopher Priest
Fu Manchu, see Sax Rohmer
"Funes, the Memorious", see Jorge Luis Borges
Fury, see Henry Kuttner
Fuseli, Henry, 32, 33, 35
Future Fiction, 216
Future Science Fiction, 238
Future Shock, see Alvin Toffler

Future War Stories, 146–7
Fuzzy novels, see H. Beam Piper
Fyfe, H. B., 447

Galactic Empires, see Brian W. Aldiss
"Galactic Gadgeteers", see Harry Stine
Galápagos, see Kurt Vonnegut, Jr
Galaxy Science Fiction, 224, 228, 235–40 *passim*,
   251, 259, 269, 277, 320, 326, 370, 371
Galileo, 67, 80
Galileo, 371
Galouye, Daniel, 256
Game of Empire, The, see Poul Anderson
Gardens of Delight, The, see Ian Watson
Garis, H. R., see Victor Appleton
Garrett, Randall, 316
Gaskell, Elizabeth, 90, 109
Gateway, see Frederik Pohl
Gaughan, Jack, 208
General Semantics, 221, 244, 395
Genesis, 28, 29, 64
Genet, Jean, 292
Gentle, Mary, 439, 440
Genus Homo, see L. Sprague de Camp and P.
   Schuyler Miller
George, Henry, 95, 96
George, Peter, 467
Gernsback, Hugo, 19, 100, 113, 176, 177, 202–
   205, 209, 217, 242, 278, 424, 461; *Ralph 124C
   41+*, 136, 203, 222
Geta, see Donald Kingsbury
"Giant Mole, The", see Franz Kafka
Gibbon, Edward, 439; *Decline and Fall of the
   Roman Empire*, 224, 265
Gibson, William, 329, 410, 411–413, 472
Gide, André, 43
Giesy, J. U., 166–7
Gilgamesh (Epic of), 27, 446
Gillespie, Bruce, 437
Gilliam, Terry, 380
Gilman, Charlotte Perkins, 95–6
Gilman, Robert Cham, see Alfred Coppel
Gladiator-at-Law, see Frederik Pohl and C. M.
   Kornbluth
Glamour, The, see Christopher Priest
Glass Hammer, The, see K. W. Jeter
Gloriana, see Michael Moorcock
God Bless You, Mr Rosewater, see Kurt Vonne-
   gut, Jr
God Emperor of Dune, see Frank Herbert
God Makers, The, see Isaac Asimov
Godwin, Bishop Francis, 71–2
Godwin, William 32, 37, 41, 142
Goethe, Johann Wolfgang von, 143, 180
Gold, Horace L., 235, 237, 240, 268, 269
"Gold at the Starbow's End, The", see Frederik
   Pohl
"Gold Bug, The", see Edgar Allen Poe
Golden Age SF, 19, 217–8, 304, 384
Golden Amazon, The, see John Russell Fearn

Golden Dream: A Fuzzy Odyssey, see Ardath
   Mayhar
"Golden Man, The", see Philip K. Dick
Golden Witchbreed, see Mary Gentle
Golding, William, 80, 100, 120, 124, 246, 259,
   262
Goldsmith, Cele, 324, 474
Goldsmith, Oliver, 285
Golem, The, see Gustav Meyrink
Goncourt Brothers, 54, 56
"Gonna Roll the Bones", see Fritz Leiber
Goodman, Paul, 480
Goodstone, Tony, 228
Gopman, V., 438
Gor, see John Norman
Gordon, Giles, 299, 305
Gordon, Rex, 26, 80
Gorki, Maxim, 129
Gothic, 16, 18, 19, 25, 32–36, 44, 64–5, 87, 247,
   422, 437, 445, 446
Grain Kings, The, see Keith Roberts
"Grandpa", see James H. Schmitz
Grant, Charles, 437
Graves, Robert, 224, 472
Gravy Planet, see Frederik Pohl and C. M.
   Kornbluth
Gray, Alasdair, 440
Great Stone of Sardis, The, see Frank Stockton
Great War in England in 1897, The, see William
   Le Queux
Great War Syndicate, The, see Frank Stockton
Green, Roger Lancelyn, 140, 156, 193
Green, Roland, 408
Greene, Graham, 426
Greene, Hugh, 456
Greener Than You Think, see Ward Moore
Green Eyes, see Lucius Shepard
Greenland, Colin, 303
Green Man, The, see Kingsley Amis
Greg, Percy, 141
Griffin, Russell M., 235, 410, 411
Griffith, George, 141–2, 175, 456
Grimus, see Salman Rushdie
"Grisly Folk, The", see H. G. Wells
Griswold, Reverend Rufus W., 56
"Grotto of the Dancing Deer, The", see Clif-
   ford D. Simak
Group Feast, see Josephine Saxton
Guardi, Francesco, 107
Guerre au vingtième siècle, La, see Albert Robida
Gulliver of Mars, see Edwin Lester Arnold
Gulliver's Travels, see Jonathan Swift
Gunn, James, 207, 251, 256, 473, 485
Gygax, Gary, 275–6

Hackett, General Sir John, 109
Haggard, H. Rider, 137, 138–9, 149, 153, 166,
   168, 201, 246, 455
Hagman, Tyko, 113
Haldane, J. B. S., 193

Haldeman, Joe, 370–1, 482; *The Forever War*, 278, 370–71

Hall, Austin, 166

Hambly, Barbara, 408

Hamilton, Edmond, 211, 256

Hammer's Slammers, see David Drake

Handmaid's Tale, The, see Margaret Atwood

Harbottle, Philip, 462

Harding, Lee, 437

Hard to be a God, see Boris and Arkady Strugatsky

Hardy, Thomas, 20, 27, 86, 97–100, 114, 118, 126, 194, 373–4

Harness, Charles, 259–60

Harrington, James, 77

Harris, John Beynon, see John Wyndham

Harrison, Harry, 19, 227, 235, 242, 273, 276, 316, 318–320, 339, 393, 443, 463, 469, 473

Harrison, M. John, 300, 305, 372–3, 474

Harryhausen, Ray, 132

Hartley, L. P., 246

Hartwell, David G. 146, 279, 371

Hašek, Jaroslav, 178

Haskin, Byron, 258

Hasse, Henry, 94

Hawks, Howard, 467

Hawthorne, Nathaniel, 57, 58, 60, 64, 109, 120, 202, 356, 449

Hazlitt, William, 32, 36

Healy, R. J., 233

Heard, H. F. (Gerald), 466

Heart of the Comet, see Gregory Benford and David Brin

Hebdomeros, see Giorgio de Chirico

Hector Servadac, see Jules Verne

Heechee Rendezvous, see Frederik Pohl

Heinlein, Robert Anson, 15, 65, 218–9, 247, 254, 267–70, 282, 287–291, 293, 324, 344, 368, 383–389, 395–6, 469, 470, 475, 476, 483–4; *The Cat Who Walks Through Walls*, 384, 386, 388–9; *Double Star*, 267–8, 288; *Job: A Comedy of Justice*, 388, 389, 396; *The Moon is a Harsh Mistress*, 291, 387, 389; "Solution Unsatisfactory", 387; *Starship Troopers*, 104, 218, 267, 288, 318, 370; *Stranger in a Strange Land*, 26, 288–90, 318, 343, 386, 387, 389; *Time Enough for Love*, 288, 344, 384, 385–6, 387, 389

Hello Summer, Goodbye, see Michael Coney

Helprin, Mark, 283–4

Henderson, Zenna, 259, 269, 320, 322–3, 476

Hendrix, Jimi, 473

Herbert, Frank, 227, 247, 314–6, 383–5 *passim*, 396–400, 476; *Dune* series 20, 273, 314–6, 366, 384, 396–400, 419

"Herbert West, Re-animator" see H. P. Lovecraft

"Here Gather the Stars", see Clifford D. Simak

Heretic, The, see Robert A. Heinlein

Heretics of Dune, see Frank Herbert

"Her Habiline Husband", see Michael Bishop

Herland, see Charlotte Perkins Gilman

Heroes and Villains, see Angela Carter

Herovit's World, see Barry N. Malzberg

Hertzka, Theodore, 97

Hesse, Herman, 214, 289–90, 347

"He Who Shapes", see Roger Zelazny

High, Philip E., 298

Hill, Douglas, 300

Hill, George Roy, 477

Hilton, James, 201, 246

Histoire des états et empires du soleil, L', see Cyrano de Bergerac

Historian's History of the World, The, 266

History of Mr Polly, The, see H. G. Wells

History of Rasselas: Prince of Abissinia, The, see Samuel Johnson

History of the Science Fiction Magazine, see Mike Ashley

Hitch-Hiker's Guide to the Galaxy, see Douglas Adams

Hitler, Adolf, 146, 179, 244, 469, 477

Hoban, Russell, 440

Hobbit, The, see J. R. R. Tolkien

Hodgson, W. H., 167–9, 171; *The House on the Borderland*, 167–8, 171, 195

Hoffmann, E. T. A., 102

Hogarth, Burne, 158

Holberg, Baron Ludvig, 78; *Niels Klim*, 78–79, 159

Holdstock, Robert, 441–2

Holmes, Oliver Wendell, 60, 64, 120, 449

"Home is the Hangman", see Roger Zelazny

Homer, 68, 256

Honeymoon in Space, A, see George Griffith

Hope, Anthony, 138, 268

"Hop Frog", see Edgar Allan Poe

Hopkins Manuscript, The, see R. C. Sherriff

Horseclans series, see Robert Adams

Horwood, William, 246

House of Usher, The, (1960), 257

House on the Borderland, see William Hope Hodgson

Howard, Robert E., 172–3, 457; *Conan*, 158, 173, 259, 279, 283, 303

Hubbard, Lafayette Ron, 218, 219, 227, 234, 290, 384, 393–5, 396, 402, 463, 464; *Battlefield Earth*, 393–4, 485

Hudson, W. H., 77, 113

Huge Hunter, The, see Edward S. Ellis

Hugin, 202

Hugo Awards, 208, 278, 279, 294, 295, 310–314 *passim*, 320, 330, 358, 365–371 *passim*, 390, 403, 412, 418, 473, 475, 479, 481, 484, 486

Hugo, Victor, 102

Humanoids, The, see Jack Williamson

"Humpty Dumpty", see Henry Kuttner

Huntington, John, 121

Hutton, James, 30–31

Huxley, Aldous, 15, 34, 55, 56, 82, 84, 103, 176–77, 184–89, 193, 201, 222, 244–5, 288–9, 334; *After Many a Summer*, 185–7, 288, 317–8; *Ape and Essence*, 186–7; *Brave New World*, 184–6, 188, 244, 299, 320, 432; *Island*, 77, 187–9, 289
Huxley, Julian, 177
Huxley, Thomas H., 115, 118, 130, 188

I Am Legend, see Richard Matheson
Icaro-Menippus, see Lucian of Samosata
Ice, see Anna Kavan
Icehenge, see Kim Stanley Robinson
I Ching, 329, 330
If, see *Worlds of If*
If England Were Invaded, see William Le Queux
If It Had Happened Otherwise, see J. C. Squire
"If Lee Had Not Won the Battle of Gettysburg", see Winston Churchill
"If This Goes On. . ." see Robert A. Heinlein
I Have Been Here Before, see J. B. Priestley
"I Have No Mouth and I Must Scream", see Harlan Ellison
Ikin, Van, 438
Immortality Inc., see Robert Sheckley
Imperial Earth, see Arthur C. Clarke
"Imp of the Perverse, The", see Edgar Allan Poe
"Impostor", see Philip K. Dick
Impulse, 373, 482
Incredible Hulk, The, (1977), 274
Incredible Shrinking Man, The, (1957), 257
Incredible Shrinking Woman, The, (1981), 274
Indoctrinaire, see Christopher Priest
Infinite Summer, An, see Christopher Priest
Inheritors, The, see William Golding
In Joy Still Felt, see Isaac Asimov
Inklings, The, 193
In Memory Yet Green, see Isaac Asimov
In Search of Wonder, see Damon Knight
Insect Play, The, see Josef and Karel Čapek
Insider, The, see Christopher Evans
In Solitary, see Garry Kilworth
Intelligence Gigantic, The, see John Russell Fearn
International Association for the Fantastic in the Arts (IAFA), 21, 282
International Fantasy Award, 322
International SF, 405
International Times, 474
Interzone, 438
In the Days of the Comet, see H. G. Wells
In the Footsteps of the Abominable Snowman, see Josef Nesvabda
"In the Penal Colony", see Franz Kafka
"In the Problem Pit", see Frederik Pohl
Invaders Plan, The, see L. Ron Hubbard
Invasion of 1910, The, see William Le Queux
Invasion of the Body Snatchers, (1955), 251, 256, 271
Invasion of the Body Snatchers, (1978), 274
Inverted World, see Christopher Priest

Invincible, The, see Stanislaw Lem
"Invisible Girl, The", see Mary Shelley
Invisible Man, The, see H. G. Wells
Invisible Man Returns, The, (1939), 131
Invisible Woman, The, (1940), 131
Involution Ocean, see Bruce Sterling
Ionesco, Eugene, 182
Iron Dream, The, see Norman Spinrad
Iron Heel, The, see Jack London
Irving, Washington, 64, 150
Isaac Asimov's Science Fiction Magazine, 278, 371, 393, 418
Isherwood, Christopher, 248
Island, see Aldous Huxley
Island of Dr Moreau, The, see H. G. Wells
Island of Lost Souls, 131
Issue at Hand, The, see James Blish
"It", see Theodore Sturgeon
Itinerarium Exstaticum, see Athanasius Kircher
I Will Fear No Evil, see Robert A. Heinlein

Jacobs, Harvey, 325
Jakubowski, Maxim, 474
James, Henry, 63, 64, 86, 118, 128, 130, 346
Janáček, 178
Janissaries, see Jerry Pournelle
Jan of the Jungle, see Otis Adelbert Kline
Japanese SF, 100
Jefferies, Richard, 100, 113–4, 115
Jefferson Airplane, 473
Jem, see Frederik Pohl
Jeschke, Wolfgang, 437
Jeter, K. W., 410, 411
Jewels of Aptor, see Samuel R. Delany
Job: A Comedy of Justice, see Robert A. Heinlein
John W. Campbell Memorial Award, 279, 368
Johnson, B. S., 297
Johnson, Denis, 246
Johnson, Samuel, 30; *Rasselas*, 33, 84–5, 86
Jones, Gwyneth, 439, 440
Jones, Langdon, 300, 305, 474
Journey Beyond Tomorrow, see Robert Sheckley
Journey into Other Worlds, A, see John Jacob Astor
Journey to the Centre of the Earth, see Jules Verne
Journey to the World Underground, A, see Holberg, Baron Ludwig
Joyce, James, 297, 311, 352
Jung, Carl, 139, 162–3, 169, 187, 309, 441
"Jungle Rot Kid on the Nod, The", see Philip José Farmer
Jungle Tales of Tarzan, see Edgar Rice Burroughs

Kafka, Franz, 114, 171, 177–183 *passim*, 192, 201, 222, 260, 337, 356, 380; *The Castle*, 180–183
Kahn, Herman, 233
Kampus, see James Gunn

Karinthy, Frigyes, 183–4
Karloff, Boris, 45
Karp, David, 243
Kavan, Anna, 336–7
Keats, John, 36, 58, 73
Keller, David H., 204
Kendall, Gordon, 408
Kepler, Johannes, 28, 67, 70–71 , 143
Ketterer, David, 51–2
Keyes, Daniel, 256–7, 426
"Killdozer!", see Theodore Sturgeon
Kilworth, Garry, 439, 441
Kindred, see Octavia Butler
King, Stephen, 35, 60, 64, 384, 413–5
King-Hele, Desmond, 30, 32
King Kong (1933), 152
King Kong (1976), 274
Kinglake, A. W., 460
Kingsbury, Donald, 419
Kingsley, Charles, 90, 109
King Solomon's Mines, see Rider Haggard
Kipling, Rudyard, 123, 125, 138, 139, 148, 152,
    202, 268
Kircher, Athanasius, 71, 78
Kiteworld, see Keith Roberts
Kline, Otis Adelbert, 148, 158, 165–66
Knight, Damon, 166, 214, 237–8, 251, 260,
    276, 366
Knight, Harry Adam, 254
Knight, Norman L., 243
Komatsu, Sakyo, 465
Korda, Alexander, 132
Korda, Vincent, 222
Kornbluth, Cyril M., 239–40, 473; *The Space
    Merchants*, 239, 243, 275, 405; *Wolfbane*, 239–
    40
Korzybski, Alfred, 221
Krakatit, see Karel Čapek
Kraken Wakes, The, see John Wyndham
Krenkel, Roy, 208
Kube-McDowell, Michael P., 436
Kubrick, Stanley, 249, 271, 400, 467
Kuttner, Henry, 112, 225–6, 234, 346, 463
Kyle, Richard, 139, 141

Lafayette, Rene, see L. Ron Hubbard
Lafferty, R. A., 326
Lambert, Diane, 300
Lanark, see Alasdair Gray
"Land Ironclads, The", see H. G. Wells
Land That Time Forgot, The, see Edgar Rice
    Burroughs
Land Under England, see Joseph O'Neill
Lane, Ann J., 96
Lang, Fritz, 143
Langford, David, 439
Language of the Night, The, see Ursula K. Le
    Guin
Laniez, Manuel Mujica, 408
Large, E. C., 201

Larson, Glen A., 273
Laski, Marghanita, 300, 474
Lasswitz, Kurd, 142–3, 155, 202
Last and First Men, see Olaf Stapledon
Last Days of Creation, The, see Wolfgang Jeschke
"Last Lonely Man, The", see John Brunner
Last Man, The, see Mary Shelley
Last Men in London, see Olaf Stapledon
Last Starfighter, The (1984), 470
Lathe of Heaven, The, see Ursula K. Le Guin
Laughter of Carthage, The, see Michael Moor-
    cock
Laumer, Keith, 325–6, 408, 434
Lawrence, D. H., 56, 97, 100, 185, 245, 290,
    297, 347, 378, 452, 459
Leary, Timothy, 285, 290
Leavis, F. R., 83
Leavis, Q. D., 156, 161
Leben des Quintus Fizlein, see J. P. F. Richter
Le Carré, John, 389
Lee, John, 408
Le Fanu, Sheridan, 109–110
Left Hand of Darkness, The, see Ursula K. Le
    Guin
Legend of Time, The, see Jack Williamson
Le Guin, Ursula K., 200, 282, 346–352, 365,
    368, 431, 439, 440, 475, 478–80, 482; *The
    Dispossessed*, 348–351, 479, 480; *The Left
    Hand of Darkness*, 275, 346–50 *passim*, 447,
    478–9
Leiber, Fritz, 172, 269, 283, 309–12, 314, 472,
    The Big Time, 310–11, 321; *The Wanderer*,
    311–12
Leinster, Murray, 204, 225, 257, 316
Lem, Stanislaw, 252, 379–80, 482–3
Lensman series, see E. E. Smith
Le Queux, William, 109, 129, 147
Lessing, Doris, 432–434, 443
Lest Darkness Fall, see L. Sprague de Camp
Levin, Ira, 413
Lewis, Brian, 208
Lewis, Clive Staples, 15, 67, 96, 112, 122, 189–
    193, 194, 196–7, 204, 339, 474; *Out of the
    Silent Planet* 190–92; *Perelandra* 67, 190–92;
    That Hideous Strength 190–193
Lewis, Matthew, 34
Lewis, Roy, 208
Ley, Willy, 259
"Liar!", see Isaac Asimov
"Liberation of Earth, The", see William Tenn
"Library of Babel, The" see Jorge Luis Borges
Lies, Inc., see Philip K. Dick
Lieut. Gulliver Jones: His Vacation, see Edwin
    Lester Arnold
Life and Adventures of Peter Wilkins, see Robert
    Paltock
Life and Astonishing Adventures of John Daniel, see
    Ralph Morris
"Lifeline", see Robert A. Heinlein
Life-Style SF, 250, 285–6, 290–1

"Ligeia", see Edgar Allan Poe
Light on the Sound, see Somtow Sucharitkul
Limbo 90, see Bernard Wolfe
Lindner, Robert, 457
Lindsay, David, 192
Linnaeus, 33
Little, Big, see John Crowley
Little Earnest Book Upon a Great Old Subject, A,
  see William Wilson
Llewellyn, Alun, 199–201
Locke, John, 37
Locus, 384, 385, 391, 487
Lodge, David, 128
"Logic of Empire", see Robert A. Heinlein
London, Jack, 120, 150–152; *The Iron Heel*,
  150–151
Looking Backward, see Edward Bellamy
Lord of Light, see Roger Zelazny
Lord of the Flies, see William Golding
Lord of the Rings, see J. R. R. Tolkien
Lord of the Sea, see M. P. Shiel
Lord Valentine's Castle, see Robert Silverberg
Lorenz, Konrad, 148
"Loss of Breath", see Edgar Allan Poe
Lost Face, The, see Josef Nesvadba
Lost Horizon, see James Hilton
"Lost Planet, The", see Eric Wood
Lost World, The, see Arthur Conan Doyle
Love and Napalm: Export USA, see J. G. Ballard
Lovecraft, H. P., 53, 58, 60, 77, 148, 155, 165,
  167, 171–2
Loved One, The, see Evelyn Waugh
"Love is the Plan, the Plan is Death", see James
  Tiptree, Jr.
"Lover From Beyond the Dawn of Time", see
  Josephine Saxton
Lovers, The, see Philip José Farmer
Lowell, Percival, 141, 143, 159, 163
Lowndes, Robert A. W., 204
Lucas, George, 271, 273–4, 282, 370
Lucian of Samosata, 15, 28, 29, 68–70, 81, 113
Lukacs, Georg, 87
Lundwall, Sam J., 202–3, 261
Lupoff, Richard, 140, 141, 467
Lynch, David, 400

Macbeth, George, 305
MacDonald, George, 109, 321, 425; *Lilith*, 321,
  425
MacDonald, John D., 269
Machen, Arthur, 58
Machine in Shaft Ten, The, see M. John Harrison
"Machine Stops, The", see E. M. Forster
MacLean, Katherine, 258
Macpherson, James, 33
Macrolife, see George Zebrowski
Mad Max, films, 274
Magazine of Fantasy and Science Fiction, The
  (*F&SF*), 224, 227–8, 235, 237, 255, 259, 268–
  9, 345, 372, 390, 436

Maine, Charles Eric, 254, 257
Maître du Monde, see Jules Verne
Make Room, Make Room, see Harry Harrison
Makeshift God, The, see Russell M. Griffin
Makropoulos Case, The, see Karel Čapek
Malafrena, see Ursula K. Le Guin
Mallarmé, 58, 60
Malzberg, Barry N., 345, 368
Mammoth Hunters, The, see Jean M. Auel
Manabe, Hiroshi, 209
Man Divided, A, see Olaf Stapledon
Man in the High Castle, The, see Philip K. Dick
Man in the Moone, see Bishop Francis Godwin
Mann, Phillip, 439, 440–1
Mann, Thomas, 175, 306
Man Plus, see Frederik Pohl
Manson, Charles, 290
"Ms. Found in a Bottle", see Edgar Allan Poe
"Man Who Could Work Miracles, The", see
  H. G. Wells
Man Who Was Thursday, The, see G. K. Chester-
  ton
Marcus, Steven, 451
*Marriages Between Zones Three, Four and Five,
  The*, see Doris Lessing
Mars, 141, 159
Martian Chronicles, The, see Ray Bradbury
Martian Time-Slip, see Philip K. Dick
"Martian Way, The", see Isaac Asimov
Martin, George R. R., 352, 357–8, 363; "A
  Song For Lya", 357–8, 481
Martin, John, 91, 448, 451
Marvel Science Fiction, 216, 226, 463
Marx, Karl, 95, 200
Masaryk, Thomas, 179
"The Masque of the Red Death", see Edgar
  Allan Poe
Masson, David I., 305, 325
Master of Paxwax, see Phillip Mann
Master of the World, see Jules Verne
Matania, Fortunino, 252
Matheson, Richard, 60, 257, 269
"Matilda", see Mary Shelley
Matkustus Kuuhun, see Tyko Hagman
Matthey, Hubert, 58
Maturin, Charles, 177
May, Julian, 436
Mayhar, Ardath, 476
McCaffrey, Anne, 227, 366, 469
McCarthy, Senator Joseph, 239, 476
McCarthy, Shawna, 278
McComas, J. F., 233, 269
McConnell, Frank, 127
McEnroe, Richard S., 408
McGahern, John, 430
McIntosh, J. T., 254, 257
McIntyre, Vonda N., 367
McKiernan, Dennis L, 408
McLuhan, Marshall, 246, 285
Mechasm, see John Sladek

"Meeting with Medusa, A", see Arthur C. Clarke
"Mellonta Tauta", see Edgar Allan Poe
Melly, George, 308
Melmoth the Wanderer, see Charles Maturin
Melville, Herman, 27, 63, 64, 86, 90, 109, 145, 297
Memoirs Found in a Bathtub, see Stanislaw Lem
Memoirs of a Survivor, see Doris Lessing
Memory of Whiteness, The, see Kim Stanley Robinson
Men Inside, The, see Barry N. Malzberg
Men Like Gods, see H. G. Wells
Men on the Moon, see Donald A. Wollheim
Mercenary, The, see Jerry Pournelle
Merchants' War, The, see Frederik Pohl
Mercier, Louis-Sébastien, 53
Meredith, George, 109
Meredith, Scott, 473
Merril, Judith, 260, 269, 298, 307, 465, 472, 473
Merritt, Abraham, 148, 167, 170–71, 209, 211; *Dwellers in the Mirage*, 170–71
Messiah, see Gore Vidal
"Metamorphosis", see Franz Kafka
"Metamorphosite", see Eric Frank Russell
Methuselah's Children, see Robert A. Heinlein
Metropolis, 271, 459, 470
"Metzengerstein", see Edgar Allan Poe
Meyrink, Gustav, 183
Micromégas, see Voltaire
"Microcosmic God", see Theodore Sturgeon
"Midas Plague, The", see Frederik Pohl
Midas World, see Frederik Pohl
Midwich Cuckoos, The, see John Wyndham
Midworld, see Alan Dean Foster
Milford Science Fiction Writers' Conference, 238, 472
Miller, Henry, 297
Miller, P. Schuyler, 259
Miller, Walter M., Jr, 255, 268–70; *A Canticle for Leibowitz*, 238, 268–70, 275, 374
Mills, Robert P., 269
Milton, John, 46, 73; *Paradise Lost*, 27, 46, 50, 52, 77, 192, 198, 330, 333
Mindbridge, see Joe Haldeman
Mind of Mr Soames, The, see Charles Eric Maine
Mind of My Mind, see Octavia Butler
Mindswap, see Robert Sheckley
Miracle Visitors, see Ian Watson
Mirror for Observers, A, see Edgar Pangborn
Miss Golem, see Josef Nesvadba
Mission Earth, see L. Ron Hubbard
Mission Galactica: The Cylon Attack (1979), 273
Mission of Gravity, see Hal Clement
Mr Britling Sees It Through, see H. G. Wells
Mists of Avalon, The, see Marion Zimmer Bradley
Mitchell, Silas Weir, 64
Moderan, see David R. Bunch
Modern Boy, 176, 458, 466

Modern Electrics, 203
Modern Utopia, A, see H. G. Wells
Moers, Ellen, 44
Molly Zero, see Keith Roberts
Monk, The, see Matthew Lewis
Monsieur Nicholas, see Restif de la Bretonne
Montgolfier Brothers, 107
Moon is a Harsh Mistress, The, see Robert A. Heinlein
"Moon Goddess and the Son, The", see Donald Kingsbury
Moon Maid, The, see Edgar Rice Burroughs
Moon Pool, The, see Abraham Merritt
Moorcock, Michael, 222, 260, 298–305 *passim*, 308, 310, 316, 318, 339, 372, 393, 438–9; *Behold the Man*, 303–4; *Jerry Cornelius Stories*, 242, 303, 305, 318, 474
Moore, Catherine L., 225–6, 258–9, 269
Moore, George, 445–6
Moore, Ward, 36, 257
More, Marcel, 104
More, Thomas, 28, 113, 245; *Utopia*, 15, 76–7
More Issues at Hand, see James Blish
Morel, Dighton, 254
More Than Human, see Theodore Sturgeon
Morgan, Chris, 450, 456
Morris, Ralph, 73
Morris, William, 89, 94, 96–7, 138, 170; *News From Nowhere*, 96–97
Morrow, James, 235, 422, 429–30
Moskowitz, Sam, 146, 171, 461, 463–4
Mote in God's Eye, The, see Larry Niven and Jerry Pournelle
Mother Night, see Kurt Vonnegut, Jr.
Mothers of Invention, 297, 473
"Mouth of Hell" see David I. Masson
Mullen, Richard D., 162, 240
Müller-Fokker Effect, The, see John Sladek
Mundus Subterraneus, see Athanasius Kircher
Munro, H. H. ("Saki"), 147, 167
"Murders in the Rue Morgue, The", see Edgar Allan Poe
Murdoch, Iris, 86, 367
Murray, Frieda, 408
Murry, John ("Colin"), see Richard Cowper
Murry, John Middleton, 378
Mutant, see Henry Kuttner
Mysteries of Udolpho, The, see Ann Radcliffe
"Mystery of Marie Roget, The", see Edgar Allan Poe
Mythago Wood, see Robert Holdstock

Nabokov, Vladimir, 130, 246, 290
Naked Lunch, The, see William Burroughs
Naked Sun, The, see Isaac Asimov
Narrative of Arthur Gordon Pym, The, see Edgar Allan Poe
NASA, 26, 275, 362, 368
Native Tongue, see Suzette Haden Elgin

Nature of the Catastrophe, The, see Michael Moorcock
Nazism, 146, 175, 179, 180, 329–30
Nebula Awards, 279, 292, 294, 297, 314, 321, 325, 343, 355, 358, 364–371 *passim*, 390, 403, 411, 412, 415, 416, 418, 423, 473, 479, 480, 481, 482, 486
Nesvadba, Josef, 183, 379, 380
Neuromancer. see William Gibson
Neville, Kris, 257
New Atlantis, The, see Francis Bacon
New Battle of Dorking, The, 109
New Journey to the World in the Moon, A, 166–7
New Maps of Hell, see Kingsley Amis
News From Nowhere, see William Morris
Newton, Sir Isaac, 26, 40, 67, 80, 450
New Worlds, 222, 291, 298–308, 310, 316, 320, 368, 372, 373, 389, 437, 439
New Writings in SF, 255–6, 439
"*Nice* Girl with Five Husbands", see Fritz Leiber
Nicholls, Peter, 386, 438
Nicolson, Marjorie Hope, 28, 75
Niels Klim, see Baron Ludwig Holberg
Nietzsche, Friedrich, 105, 145, 324
Nifft the Lean, see Michael Shea
"Nightflyers", see George R. R. Martin
Night Land, The, see William Hope Hodgson
Nightmare, The, see Mihaly Babits
Nightmare Blue, see Gardner M. Dozois and Geo. Alec Effinger
"Nightmare Brother", see Alan E. Nourse
Night of Kadar, The, see Garry Kilworth
Nights At the Circus, see Angela Carter
Nightwings, see Robert Silverberg
"Nine Billion Names of God, The", see Arthur C. Clarke
1984, see George Orwell
1982 Janine, see Alasdair Gray
Niven, Larry, 324, 362, 368, 369, 408
No Enemy But Time, see Michael Bishop
No Man Friday, see Rex Gordon
"None But Lucifer", see Horace Gold and L. Sprague de Camp
Non-Stop, see Brian W. Aldiss
Norman, John, *Gor*, 281
Norton, Andre, 259
Norwood, Warren, 408
"No Truce with Kings", see Poul Anderson
Nourse, Alan E., 250–1, 258, 269, 335, 339
Nova, see Samuel R. Delany
Nowlan, Philip Francis, 204
Null-A Three, see A. E. van Vogt
Numan, Gary, 410
Number of the Beast, The, see Robert A. Heinlein
Nunquam, see Lawrence Durrell

O'Brien, Fitz-James, 94
Occam's Razor, see David Duncan
Odd John, see Olaf Stapledon

O'Donnell, Lawrence, see Henry Kuttner and Catherine L. Moore
O'Donnevan, Finn, see Robert Sheckley
Odyssey, The, 27
Offenbach, Jacques, 102
Off On a Comet, see Jules Verne
"Of Mist, and Grass, and Sand", see Vonda N. McIntyre
Olga Romanoff, see George Griffith
Ole Doc Methuselah, see L. Ron Hubbard
Oliver, Chad, 256
Olsen, Bob, 204
Omega Point, The, see George Zebrowski
Omni, 227, 371, 411
O'Neill, Joseph, 17, 175, 199
One Thousand Eight Hundred and Twenty-Nine, 46
"On Science Fiction", see C. S. Lewis
On Two Planets, see Kurt Lasswitz
Ophiuchi Hotline, The, see John Varley
Orban, Paul, 208
Orbit, 238, 276
Orbitsville, see Bob Shaw
Orchideengarten, Der, 202
Orsinian Tales, see Ursula K. Le Guin
Orwell, George, 15, 83, 123, 126, 132–3, 244–246, 348, 460, 465–6; *Animal Farm*, 126, 243, 245–6; *1984*, 77, 83, 111–2, 243–6, 326, 340
Other Times, 372
Other Worlds, see Cyrano de Bergerac
Ouida, 150, 151
Out of the Deeps, see John Wyndham
"Outside", see Brian W. Aldiss
Outward Urge, The, see John Wyndham
"Overload, An", see Barrington Bayley
Ovington, John, 82

Padgett, Lewis, see Henry Kuttner and Catherine L. Moore
"Pail of Air, A", see Fritz Leiber
Pal, George, 131, 258
Palos of the Dog Star Pack, see J. U. Giesy
Paltock, Robert, 73, 78, 101
Pangborn, Edgar, 269, 320–23, 419, 476
Panshin, Alexei, 268, 290, 292, 325, 468–9
Paracelsus, 40
Paradox Men, The, see Charles Harness
Partington, Charles, 372
Passing Show, The, 252, 253
Pastel City, The, see M. John Harrison
Pasteur, Louis, 101
Patrouch, Joseph F., 264, 463
Patternmaster, see Octavia Butler
Paul, Frank R., 207, 208, 424
Pavane, see Keith Roberts
Pawns of Null-A, The, see A. E. van Vogt
Peacock, Thomas Love, 34–36, 90, 93, 185, 288
Peake, Mervyn, 255, *Gormenghast Trilogy*, 262–4
"Pedestrian, The", see Ray Bradbury

Pellucidar, see Edgar Rice Burroughs
Pendulum, see John Christopher
Pennington, Bruce, 208
People, The (1971), 323
"People, The", see Zenna Henderson
Perelandra, see C. S. Lewis
"Persistence of Vision, The", see John Varley
Pfeil, Donald F., 371
Phase IV (1973), 469
Philip K. Dick Award, 279, 410, 412, 425
Philmus, Robert M., 454
Phra the Phoenician, see Edwin Lester Arnold
Picture of Dorian Gray, see Oscar Wilde
Pierce, Meredith Ann, 408
Piercy, Marge, 128, 364
Pilgrimage to Earth, see Robert Sheckley
Pink Floyd, 473
Piper, H. Beam, 323, 447, 476
"Piper at the Gates of Dawn", see Richard Cowper
Pirandello, Luigi, 329
Piranesi, 33
Pirates of Venus, see Edgar Rice Burroughs
"Pit and the Pendulum, The", see Edgar Allan Poe
Planet Explorer, see Murray Leinster
"Planetfall", see John Brunner
Planet of Exile, see Ursula K. Le Guin
Planet of Peril, see Otis Adelbert Kline
Planet of the Apes, see Pierre Boulle
Planet of the Damned, see Harry Harrison
Planetoid 127, see Edgar Wallace
Planet Plane, see John Wyndham
Planet Stories, 216, 228, 248
Plato, *Republic*, 68, 75–6, 89, 113, 121, 127, 245
Platt, Charles, 299, 365
Player Piano, see Kurt Vonnegut, Jr.
Poe, Edgar Allan, 17, 53–64, 68, 80, 85, 94, 100, 102, 103, 120, 124, 146, 161, 167, 171, 181, 202, 204, 248, 257; "Colloquy of Monos and Una", 59, 61–2; "The Facts in the Case of M. Valdemar", 56, 59; "The Masque of the Red Death", 56, 60, 63; *The Narrative of Arthur Gordon Pym*, 59, 61, 62–3, 103
Pohl, Frederik, 215, 216, 222, 227, 233, 237, 239–40, 242, 269, 383, 402–5; *Gateway*, 403–4; *Jem*, 404, 405; *Man Plus*, 26, 403; "The Midas Plague", 237, 404; *The Space Merchants* (with C. M. Kornbluth), 239, 243, 275, 405; *Wolfbane* (with C. M. Kornbluth), 239–40
Poison Belt, The, see Arthur Conan Doyle
Polidori, John, 42
Pol Pot, 469
Pope, Alexander, 34, 36, 80, 82
Popular Mechanics, 209
Possessors, The, see John Christopher
Possible Worlds, see J. B. S. Haldane
Postman, The, see David Brin
Potter, Beatrix, 112
Pournelle, Jerry, 104, 282, 324, 369–70, 408

Power, The, (1967), 258
Power of Time, The, see Josephine Saxton
Powers, Richard, 208
Powers, Tim, 422, 424–6, 486
Powys, John Cowper, 27, 100, 452
Practice Effect, The, see David Brin
Pratt, Fletcher, 258, 259
"Press Enter ■", see John Varley
Priest, Christopher, 65, 372, 376–8, 439; *Inverted World*, 376–7
Priestley, J. B., 201, 246, 300
Priestley, Joseph, 37
Princess of Mars, A, see Edgar Rice Burroughs
Pringle, David, 361, 428
Profundis, see Richard Cowper
"Protected Species", see H. B. Fyfe
Proust, Marcel, 65, 98
Psycho, see Robert Bloch
"Purloined Letter, The", see Edgar Allan Poe
Purple Cloud, The, see M. P. Shiel
Pynchon, Thomas, 27

Quarreling, They Met the Dragon, see Sharon Baker
Quatermass Xperiment, The, (1955), 271, 441
"Quickening, The", see Michael Bishop
Quincunx of Time, The, see James Blish
Quintet, (1979), 470

Rabelais, François, 28, 70, 85
Rabkin, Eric S., 96
Rackham, John, 298
Radcliffe, Mrs Ann, 17, 32, 34–5, 68
Radford, Michael, 244
Radio Free Albemuth, see Philip K. Dick
Radio Man, The, see Ralph Milne Farley
Ragged Astronauts, The, see Bob Shaw
Raid of 1915, The, see William Le Queux
Ralph 124C 41+, see Hugo Gernsback
"Rappaccini's Daughter", see Nathaniel Hawthorne
Rasselas, see Samuel Johnson
Rat Race, The, see Alfred Bester
Ravens of the Moon, The, see Charles Grant
Raymond, Alex, 158
Reade, Charles, 109
Reade, Frank, 100, 136, 455
Reade, Winwood, 198
Reagan, Ronald, 305, 369
Réage, Pauline, 337
"Rebel of Valkyr, The", see Alfred Coppel
Re-birth see John Wyndham
Red Planet, see Robert A. Heinlein
Reed, Kit, 366, 432, 436–7
Rees, Richard, 245
Rendezvous With Rama, see Arthur C. Clarke
Rennie, Michael, 149
Repo Man, (1984), 410, 470
Report on Probability A, see Brian W. Aldiss

"Report on the Nature of the Lunar Surface", see John Brunner
Reproductive System, The, see John Sladek
Retief series, see Keith Laumer
Return of Tarzan, The, see Edgar Rice Burroughs
Return of the Jedi, (1983), 271
"Reynard the Fox", 70, 360
Reynolds, Mack, 227, 316
Rhinehart, Luke, 471
Richardson, Maurice, 145
Richter, Jean Paul Friedrich, 143
Riddley Walker, see Russell Hoban
"Riders of the Purple Wage", see Philip José Farmer
Riders of the Sidhe, The, see Kenneth C. Flint
Rimbaud, Arthur, 449
Ring Around the Sun, see Clifford D. Simak
Ringworld, see Larry Niven
Ringworld Engineers, The, see Larry Niven
Rite of Passage, see Alexei Panshin
Riverside Quarterly, 465, 469
Riverworld, series, see Philip José Farmer
Roadside Picnic, see Boris and Arkady Strugatsky
Road to Corlay, The, see Richard Cowper
Road to Science Fiction, The, see James Gunn
Roberts, J. M., 67
Roberts, Keith, 372, 373–5, 378; *Pavane*, 36, 275, 373–4
Roberts, Murray, 458
Robida, Albert, 107
Robinson, Frank, 258
Robinson, Jeanne, 370
Robinson, Kim Stanley, 322, 419–20
Robinson, Spider, 369, 370
Robinson Crusoe, see Daniel Defoe
Robots and Empire, see Isaac Asimov
Robots of Dawn, The, see Isaac Asimov
Robur le Conquerant, see Jules Verne
Rocannon's World, see Ursula K. Le Guin
Roderick, see John Sladek
Rogers, Alva, 217
Rogers, Hubert, 208, 222
Rohmer, Sax, 166
Roosevelt, Franklin D., 129
Rose, The, see Charles Harness
Rose for Armageddon, A, see Hilbert Schenck
Rosemary's Baby, see Ira Levin
Rosenberg, Joel, 408
Rostand, Edmond, 74
Rottensteiner, Franz, 482–3
Rousseau, Jean-Jacques, 51, 123
Rousseau, Victor, 166
Rucker, Rudy, 112, 379, 410–11
Rudolf, Anthony, 448
"Run, The", see Christopher Priest
"Runaround", see Isaac Asimov
"Runaway Skyscraper, The", see Murray Leinster

"Running Down", see M. John Harrison
Rushdie, Salman, 379
Ruskin, John, 94, 96
Russ, Joanna, 277, 363–4, 367, 368, 472, 473; *The Female Man*, 363–5
Russell, Bertrand, 200
Russell, Eric Frank, 112, 213–4, 225, 226, 250, 467
Russian Hide-and-Seek, see Kingsley Amis

Sadoul, Jacques, 221
Sagan, Carl, 436, 469
Saga of the Exiles, see Julian May
St. Clair, Margaret (Idris Seabright), 259
"Saki", see H. H. Munro
Sallis, James, 344, 474
"Salvador", see Lucius Shepard
Sanders, Ed., 290, 471
"Sandman, The", see E. T. A. Hoffman
Saturn 3 (1980), 274
Savage Pellucidar, see Edgar Rice Burroughs
"Saving Face", see Michael Bishop
Saxton, Josephine, 366, 373
Scanner Darkly, A, see Philip K. Dick
Scanners (1981), 274
Schenck, Hilbert, 419–422
Schiaparelli, G. V., 141
Schismatrix, see Bruce Sterling
Schmidt, Stanley, 227
Schmitz, James H., 258, 316
Schmoo, see Abraham Merritt
Schneeman, Charles, 208
Schoenherr, John, 208, 315
Scholes, Robert, 437
Schomburg, Alex, 208
Schopenhauer, Arthur, 194
Science Fantasy, see *Impulse*
Science Fiction, 216
Science Fiction Art, see Brian W. Aldiss
Science Fiction Handbook, The, see L. Sprague de Camp
Science Fiction Monthly, 372
Science Fiction Research Association (SFRA), 21, 282
Science Fiction Studies, 469
Science Fiction Writers of America (SFWA), 238, 279, 472
Science Wonder Stories, 204
Scientology, see L. Ron Hubbard
Scott, Ridley, 335
Scott, Sir Walter, 35, 36, 90, 145, 161
Seabright, Idris, see Margaret St. Clair
Search the Sky, see Frederik Pohl and C. M. Kornbluth
Searles, Baird, 483–4
Second Foundation, see Isaac Asimov
"Second Variety", see Philip K. Dick
Secret People, The, see John Wyndham
"Sector General" stories, see James White
Sellings, Arthur, 298

Senarens, Luis Philip, 136, 176
Sense of Obligation, see Harry Harrison
Seven Days in New Crete, see Robert Graves
Seven Footprints to Satan, see Abraham Merritt
SF Commentary, 437
Shadow, The, 228
Shadow of the Torturer, The, see Gene Wolfe
Shadows in the Sun, see Chad Oliver
Shadrach in the Furnace, see Robert Silverberg
Shakespeare, William, 28, 41, 77, 80, 124, 133
"Shambleau", see Catherine L. Moore
Shape of Things to Come, The, see H. G. Wells
"Shattered Like a Glass Goblin", see Harlan Ellison
Shaver, Richard, 177
Shaw, George Bernard, 75, 129, 460–61
Shaw, Bob, 339, 362, 378–9
She, see H. Rider Haggard
Shea, Michael, 437
Sheckley, Robert, 86, 112, 235, 236–7, 242, 251, 269, 307, 326–7, 331 357, 437, 443; "Trap", 236–7
Sheep Look Up, The, see John Brunner
Sheffield, Charles, 32, 437
Sheldon, Alice, see James Tiptree, Jr.
Shelley, Mary Wollstonecraft, 25, 29, 32, 34, 36–52, 53, 57, 91, 120, 145, 165, 222, 243, 340; *Frankenstein: or, The Modern Prometheus*, 16, 18, 25, 26, 30, 32, 34–52 *passim*, 54, 59, 67–68, 87, 90, 111, 125, 143, 145, 179, 192, 198, 218, 243, 270, 275, 323, 334, 336, 337, 364, 443, 444; *The Last Man*, 37, 44, 46–50, 57, 91, 146
Shelley, Percy Bysshe, 25, 32, 34, 36–48 *passim*, 50–51, 100, 142, 179, 187
Shepard, Lucius, 419, 422, 426–7
Sherriff, R. C., 253, 254
Shiel, Matthew Phipps, 53, 145–6, 175
Shikasta, see Doris Lessing
Shining, The, see Stephen King
Ship of Ishtar, The, see Abraham Merritt
Shivers (1974), 474
Shockwave Rider, The, see John Brunner
Shores of Another Sea, The, see Chad Oliver
Shute, Nevil, 246, 268
Siegel, Don, 256
Silverberg, Robert, 227, 247, 280–2, 340–346, 347, 351, 357, 363, 365, 393, 428, 443, 472, 473; "Born With the Dead", 345–6; *Downward to the Earth*, 342–3, 357–8; *Dying Inside*, 343–4, 347, 390; *Nightwings*, 341–2, 357; *Up the Line*, 344–5; *Valentine Pontifex*, 280–1
Silver Locusts, The, see Ray Bradbury
Simak, Clifford, 225, 239, 256, 320–323, 326, 368; *City* series, 225, 234–5, 320, 360; *Way Station*, 320–1
Simulacron-3, see Daniel Galouye
Sinclair, Upton, 455
Sinister Barrier, see Eric Frank Russell
Sirens of Titan, The, see Kurt Vonnegut, Jr.

Sirian Experiments, The, see Doris Lessing
Sirius, see Olaf Stapledon
Six-Million Dollar Man, The, 405
Skinner, B. F., 243
Skylark Series, see E. E. Smith
Sladek, John, 305, 306–7, 328, 379, 451–2; *The Müller-Fokker Effect*, 307, 331
Slan, see A. E. van Vogt
Slapstick (1984), 477
Slapstick, or Lonesome No More, see Kurt Vonnegut Jr
Slaughterhouse Five (1971), 477
Slaughterhouse Five, see Kurt Vonnegut Jr
Sleeper Wakes, The, see H. G. Wells
Smith, Clark Ashton, 139, 172, 173
Smith, Cordwainer, 292
Smith, Edward E. "Doc", 15, 78, 177, 209–11, 212, 214, 215, 219, 260, 389; *Lensman* series, 112, 209–11, 273, 399, 457, 475
Smith, George O., 226, 463
Smith, Jeffrey D., 365
Snow, C. P., 192, 246
"Snowball Effect, The", see Katherine MacLean
Snail on the Slope, The, see Boris and Arkady Strugatsky
Snow Queen, The, see Joan Vinge
Software, see Rudy Rucker
Solaris, see Stanislaw Lem
Solaris (1971), 252, 380, 467
"Solution Unsatisfactory", see Robert A. Heinlein
Something Else, 372
Somnium, see Johannes Kepler
Songbirds of Pain, The, see Garry Kilworth
"Song For Lya, A", see George R. R. Martin
"Songs of War", see Kit Reed
Sontag, Susan, 137
Soul of a Robot, The, see Barrington Bayley
Southerington, F. R., 98
Soylent Green, *(Make Room! Make Room!)* 242, 319, 476
Spacehunter: Adventures in the Forbidden Zone (1983), 470
Space Machine, The, see Christopher Priest
Space Merchants, The, see Frederik Pohl and C. M. Kornbluth
Space Science Fiction, 251
Spacetime Donuts, see Rudy Rucker
Space Vampires, The, see Colin Wilson
Space War Blues, see Richard A. Lupoff
"Spanish Lesson, A", see Lucius Shepard
Speculative Poetry Review, 416
Spengler, Oswald, 194, 240
Sphinx of the Ice Fields, The, see Jules Verne
Spielberg, Steven, 257, 272, 274, 321
Spinrad, Norman, 235, 297, 300, 474, 477
Spock Must Die!, see James Blish
Squire, J. C., 447
Stableford, Brian, 439, 461

Stainless Steel Rat, The, see Harry Harrison
Stalin, Joseph, 129, 200, 243, 469
Stalker (1979), 380, 467
Stand on Zanzibar, John Brunner
Stapledon, Olaf, 99, 120, 176, 190, 193, 194–99, 201, 204, 222, 249, 334, 341, 353, 417, 433, 435, 475; *Last and First Men*, 20, 193, 194–5, 196, 197–8, 395; *Star Maker*, 195–8, 199
Star SF, 240
Starburst, see Frederik Pohl
"Stardance", see Jeanne and Spider Robinson
Star Maker, see Olaf Stapledon
Starman Jones, see Robert A. Heinlein
Star Rover, The, see Jack London
Starship Troopers, see Robert A. Heinlein
Stars in Shroud, The, see Gregory Benford
Stars My Destination, The, see Alfred Bester
Startide Rising, see David Brin
Startling Stories, 216
Star Trek, 219, 240, 277, 367, 370, 371
Star Trek – The Motion Picture (1979), 273, 274, 459
Star Virus, The, see Barrington Bayley
Star Wars (1977), 234, 271–2, 273, 274, 275, 279, 282, 340, 370, 400, 436, 439
Steam Man of the Plains, The, see Frank Reade
Steam Man of the Prairies, The, see Edward S. Ellis
Steinbeck, John, 64, 256
Stella, 202
Stepford Wives, The, see Ira Levin
Sterling, Bruce, 86, 278, 329, 400, 415–6, 417, 441, 482
Stevenson, Robert Louis, 110–11, 120, 138, 139, 153; *The Strange Case of Dr Jekyll and Mr Hyde*, 50–1, 110, 121, 138, 213, 430
Stewart, George R., *Earth Abides* 243, 254, 275, 357, 421, 467–8
Stilson, Charles B., 166
Stine, Harry, 224
Stirring Science Stories, 216
Stochastic Man, The, see Robert Silverberg
Stockton, Frank, 142
Stoker, Bram, 144–5, 358, 445–6; *Dracula*, 16, 43, 60, 143–5, 445
Stone, Charlotte, 283
"Storm, The", see A. E. van Vogt
Stormbringer, see Michael Moorcock
Storm of Wings, A, see M. John Harrison
Storr, Anthony, 461
Story of Ab, The, see Stanley Waterloo
"Story of the Stone Age, A", see H. G. Wells
Stover, Dr Leon, 463
Stowaway to Mars, see John Wyndham
Strachan, Geoffrey, 75
Strand, The, 135, 147, 177
Stranger in a Strange Land, see Robert A. Heinlein
Strangers, see Gardner M. Dozois

"Strata", see Ed Bryant
Stravinsky, Igor, 458
Strobl, Karl Hans, 202
Strugatsky, Arkady and Boris, 379, 380–1
Stuart, Don A., see John W. Campbell
Stubbs, George, 33
Sturgeon, Theodore, 218, 219, 226, 234, 291, 293, 472, 473; *More Than Human*, 237, 275
Sucharitkul, Somtow, 420, 436
Sugar in the Air, see E. C. Large
Superman, 156, 228
Superman—The Movie (1978), 273, 274
Super Science Stories, 216
Survivor, see Octavia Butler
Suvin, Darko, 113, 179, 380
Swanwick, Michael, 437
"Swarm", see Bruce Sterling
Swift, Jonathan, 15, 28, 75, 80–84, 99, 165, 334; *Gulliver's Travels*, 70, 78, 79, 80–84, 86, 87, 112, 124, 126, 183–4, 246
Sword of Rhiannon, The, see Leigh Brackett
Sword of the Lictor, The, see Gene Wolfe
Swordsman of Mars, The, see Otis Adelbert Kline
"Symbiotica", see Eric Frank Russell
Symmes, John, 158–9
"System of Dr Tarr and Prof Fether, The", see Edgar Allan Poe
Syzygy, see Frederik Pohl

Taine, John, 201
"Tale of Ragged Mountains, A", see Edgar Allan Poe
"Tales of Known Space", see Larry Niven
Tales of Space and Time, see H. G. Wells
Tam, Son of the Tiger, see Otis Adelbert Kline
Tanguy, Yves, 141
Tarkovsky, Andrei, 252, 380, 467
Tarzan Series, see Edgar Rice Burroughs
Tau Zero, see Poul Anderson
Tavčar, Ivan, 113
Tavernier, Bernard, 482
"Tell-Tale Heart, The", see Edgar Allan Poe
"Temple Trouble", see H. Beam Piper
Tenn, William, 238–9, 251, 269
Tennyson, Lord Alfred, 31, 93, 98
Tepper, Sheri S., 408
"Terminal Beach, The", see J. G. Ballard
Terminator, The (1984), 470
Thackeray, William Makepeace, 82, 84, 90, 101
Them! (1953), 271
They Found Atlantis, see Dennis Wheatley
Thieves' World, see Robert Lynn Asprin
Thing, The, (1982), 274, 467
Thing From Another World, The (1951), 467
Things to Come (1936), 132, 222, 271
Third Millennium, see Brian Stableford and David Langford
Third World War, The, see General Sir John Hackett
This Immortal, see Roger Zelazny

This is the Way the World Ends, see James Morrow
This Perfect Day, see Ira Levin
Thole, Karel, 209
Thomas, D. M., 305, 389
Thomas, Ted, 366
Thoreau, Henry David, 94, 422, 480
Thorns, see Robert Silverberg
"Thrawn Janet", see Robert Louis Stevenson
Three Stigmata of Palmer Eldritch, The, see Philip K. Dick
Thrilling Wonder Stories, 248, 250, 462
"Thunder and Roses", see Theodore Sturgeon
Thurb Revolution, The, see Alexei Panshin
Tides of Lust, The, see Samuel R. Delany
Tiepolo, G. B., 107
Tiger! Tiger!, see Alfred Bester
Time After Time (1979), 132
Time and the Conways, see J. B. Priestley
Time Bandits (1984), 274
"Time Considered as a Helix of Semi-Precious Stones", see Samuel R. Delany
Time is the Simplest Thing, see Clifford D. Simak
"Time is the Traitor", see Alfred Bester
Time Machine, The, see H. G. Wells
Time Must Have a Stop, see Aldous Huxley
Time of Changes, A, see Robert Silverberg
Time Out of Joint, see Philip K. Dick
Timescape, see Gregory Benford
Time Stream, The, see John Taine
"Time Trap, The", see Henry Kuttner
Timmins, William, 208
Tiptree, James , Jr (Alice Sheldon), 227, 365–6
"Tissue-Culture King, The", see Julian Huxley
Titan, see John Varley
"Tlön, Uqbar, Orbis Tertius", see Jorge Luis Borges
Toffler, Alvin *Future Shock*, 286, 351, 416
Tolkien, J. R. R., 193, 255, 260–64, 276, 279, 325, 348, 362, 408; *Lord of the Rings*, 193, 260–64, 289, 325
Tolstoy, Leo, 145, 347
"Tom Swift", see Victor Appleton
Tono-Bungay, see H. G. Wells
"To Serve Man", see Damon Knight
Tower of Glass, see Robert Silverberg
Toynbee, Arnold, 266
Toynbee, Philip, 188, 474
To Your Scattered Bodies Go, see Philip José Farmer
Transatlantic Tunnel, Hurrah!, A, see Harry Harrison
Transfigurations, see Michael Bishop
"Transformation, The", see Mary Shelley
Transmigration of Timothy Archer, The, see Philip K. Dick
Transmitters, see Damien Broderick
"Trap", see Robert Sheckley
"Traveller's Rest", see David I. Masson
"Traveller's Tale, A", see Lucius Shepard

Trelawny, Edward John, 37
Tremaine, F. Orlin, 216
Triplanetary, see E. E. Smith
Tripods, The, see John Christopher
Triton, see Samuel R. Delany
"Trog", see Murray Leinster
Trollope, Anthony, 90, 91, 109, 160
Tron (1982), 275
Trumbull, Douglas, 470
"Truth About Pyecraft, The", see H. G. Wells
Tsiolkovsky, Konstantin, 30
Tubb, E. C., 298, 339
Tuck, Donald, 345
Tucker, Wilson, 258, 473
Tuning, William, 476
Tunnel, The (1935), 271
Tunnel Through the Deeps, see Harry Harrison
"Tunnel Under the World, The", see Frederik Pohl
Turner, George, 437
Tuttle, Lisa, 358
Twain, Mark, 64, 352, 358, 422
Twentieth Century War, The, see Albert Robida
21st Century Sub, see Frank Herbert
Twenty Thousand Leagues Under the Sea, see Jules Verne
"Twilight", see John W. Campbell
Twilight of Briareus, The, see Richard Cowper
2001: A Space Odyssey (1968), 271, 400
2001: A Space Odyssey, see Arthur C. Clarke
2010: Odyssey Two (1985), 275, 400
2010: Odyssey Two, see Arthur C. Clarke
Tymn, Marshall B., 228
"Typewriter in the Sky", see L. Ron Hubbard

Ubik, see Philip K. Dick
Uncharted Seas, see Dennis Wheatley
Uncle Silas, see Sheridan Le Fanu
"Under the Moons of Mars", see Edgar Rice Burroughs
Under Pressure, see Frank Herbert
Unearth, 410
"Universe", see Robert A. Heinlein
Universe, see Terry Carr
Unknown, 214, 216, 219, 235, 259, 268, 463
Unsleeping Eye, The, see D. G. Compton
Unteleported Man, The, see Philip K. Dick
Up the Line, see Robert Silverberg
Utopia, see Thomas More

Valencies, see Rory Barnes and Damien Broderick
Valentine Pontifex, see Robert Silverberg
Valéry, Paul, 58, 60
Valis, see Philip K. Dick
Vallejo, Boris, 283
Valperga, see Mary Shelley
Vance, Jack, 269, 313–4
van Vogt, A. E., 15, 196, 217–222 *passim*, 226, 244, 250, 260, 327, 370, 372, 383, 394–5, 402,

van Vogt, A. E.—*continued*
    447, 463, 471; *Null-A* series, 221, 244, 395
Varley, John, 362–3, 420
Vasbinder, Samuel Holmes, 40
Vathek, see William Beckford
Vaughan Williams, Ralph, 261
Vector, 469
Venus, 160–1
Venus Equilateral, stories, see George O. Smith
Venus on the Half Shell, see Philip José Farmer
Verne, Jules, 17, 58, 71, 90, 100, 103–7, 113,
    122, 136, 141; *Hector Servadac*, 105–6
Vertex, 371
Viagens Interplanetarias series, see L. Sprague de
    Camp
Vian, Boris, 221
Vidal, Gore, 20, 246
Videodrome (1982), 410, 470
Vie Electrique, La, see Albert Robida
Village of the Damned (1960), 467
Vincent, Harl, 204
Vinge, Joan, 367
Vinge, Vernor, 408
Visiak, E. H., 460
Volney (Constantin François de Chasseboeuf),
    48
Voltaire, 84–86, 185, 188, 326, 381; *Candide*,
    84, 85–86, 87, 329
Von Hanstein, Otfrid, 204
Vonnegut, Kurt, Jr, 243, 247, 268, 269, 307,
    326, 327–9, 443; *God Bless You, Mr Rosewater*,
    327–8; *The Sirens of Titan*, 85, 327, 328
Vortex, 372
Voyage au centre de la Terre, see Jules Verne
Voyage dans la Lune, see Cyrano de Bergerac
Voyages extraordinaires, Les, see Jules Verne
Voyage of the Space Beagle, The, see A. E. van
    Vogt
Voyages of Pantagruel, see François Rabelais
Voyage to Arcturus, A, see David Lindsay
Voyage to Faremido, see Frigyes Karinthy
Vulcan's Hammer, see Philip K. Dick

Wagar, W. Warren, 440
Wagner, Richard, 458
Waiting for the End of the World, see Lee Harding
Walden, see Henry David Thoreau
Walk to the End of the World, see Suzy McKee
    Charnas
Wallace, Edgar, 152–3
Wallace, F. L., 447
"Wall Around the World, The", see Theodore
    Cogswell
Walpole, Horace, 18, 33, 36
Wanderer, The, see Fritz Leiber
Wandrei, Donald, 172
War in the Air, The, see H. G. Wells
Warner, Rex, 192
War of the Worlds, The, see H. G. Wells
War with the Newts, see Karel Čapek

Waterloo, Stanley, 152
Watkins, William John, 436
Watson, Ian, 372, 375–6
Waugh, Evelyn, 186, 243
Way Station, see Clifford D. Simak
Way the Future Was, The, see Frederik Pohl
We, see Yevgeny Zamyatin
Weapon Shops of Isher, The, see A. E. van Vogt
"Wearing Out of Genre Materials, The", see
    Joanna Russ
Weber, Carl M., 458
Weird Tales, 172, 177, 205, 258
Well at the World's End, The, see William Morris
Welles, Orson, 131
Wells, G. P., 130
Wells, Herbert George, 26, 40, 46, 57, 71, 82,
    90, 93, 97, 104, 105, 111, 115, 117–133, 135,
    137–143 *passim*, 163–5, 181, 183–190 *passim*,
    193, 194, 195, 200, 222, 233, 272, 321, 377,
    440, 454–5, 460; *The First Men in the Moon*,
    71, 119, 122, 127, 132, 133, 186, 193; *The
    Island of Dr Moreau*, 111, 119, 120, 121, 122,
    123–26, 131, 133, 246, 361; *Men Like Gods*,
    119, 163–5; *The Time Machine*, 93, 118–9,
    121, 122, 127, 130, 131, 133, 140, 144, 215,
    303; *The War of the Worlds*, 109, 119, 120–21,
    122–3, 124, 126, 131, 133, 142, 143, 194
Wesso, (H. Wessolowski), 207, 208
West, Anthony, 130
West, Rebecca, 130
Wettenhovi-Aspa, Sigurd, 201
Weyman, Stanley, 138
"Weyr Search", see Anne McCaffrey
Whale, James, 45, 131
"What Have I Done?", see Mark Clifton
Wheatley, Dennis, 201
Wheeler, H. *Fail Safe*, 246
"When It Changed", see Joanna Russ
When the Sleeper Wakes, see H. G. Wells
"When the World Screamed", see Arthur Con-
    an Doyle
When the World Shook, see H. Rider Haggard
When William Came, see H. H. Munro
When Worlds Collide, see Edwin Balmer and
    Philip Wylie
Where Late the Sweet Birds Sang, see Kate
    Wilhelm
White, James, 258, 298
White, Patrick, 438
White, Ted, 371
White, William Anthony Parker, see Anthony
    Boucher
White Light, see Rudy Rucker
Whitman, Walt, 324
Who?, see Algis Budrys
"Who Goes There?", see John W. Campbell
Wieland, see Charles Brockden Brown
"Weird of Avoose Wuthoqquam, The", see
    Clark Ashton Smith
Wild Boys, The, see William Burroughs

Wilde, Oscar, 33, 119, 144
Wilder, Cherry, 408
Wild Seed, see Octavia Butler
Wild Shore, The, see Kim Stanley Robinson
Wilhelm, Kate, 238, 278, 366–7, 472
Wilkins, John, 72
Williams, Charles, 192, 193
Williams, Paul O., 322, 419, 421–3
Williams, Tennessee, 64
Williams, Walter Jon, 436
Williamson, Jack, 204, 209, 211–5, 368, 393; *Darker Than You Think*, 212–3, 216; *The Legion of Time*, 211–2, 462
"William Wilson", see Edgar Allan Poe
Willis, Connie, 415, 426, 437
Wilson, A. N., 144, 456
Wilson, Angus, 246, 300
Wilson, Colin, 171, 456
Wilson, Richard, 473
Wilson, William, 461
"Wind From a Burning Woman, The", see Greg Bear
Wind from Nowhere, The, see J. G. Ballard
Windhaven, see George R. R. Martin and Lisa Tuttle
Wine of Violence, The, see James Morrow
Wingrove, David, 21, 469, 482, 486–7
Winter's Tale, see Mark Helprin
"With Folded Hands—", see Jack Williamson
"With Morning Comes Mistfall", see George R. R. Martin
"With the Night Mail", see Rudyard Kipling
Witt, Otto, 202
Wodehouse, P. G., 262, 327
Wolfbane, see Frederik Pohl and C. M. Kornbluth
Wolfe, Bernard, 258
Wolfe, Gene, 422–4, 443, 472
Wollheim, Donald A., 216, 225, 339, 463, 469
Wollstonecraft, Mary, 32, 37, 43
Woman a Day, A, see Philip José Farmer
Woman on the Edge of Time, see Marge Piercy
Women's Press, The, 96, 487
Wonder Stories, 19, 201, 211
Wood, Eric, 466
Wood Beyond the World, The, see William Morris
Woodroffe, Patrick, 208
Word for World is Forest, The, see Ursula K. Le Guin
Wordsworth, William, 32
World Below, The, see S. Fowler Wright
World Fantasy Awards, 361, 441

World in Darkness, The, see Murray Roberts
World Inside, The, see Robert Silverberg
World in Winter, The, see John Christopher
World of Null-A, The, see A. E. van Vogt
World of Ptavvs, The, see Larry Niven
"World of the Red Sun, The", see Clifford D. Simak
World of Tiers, see Philip José Farmer
Worlds trilogy, see Joe Haldeman
World Set Free, The, see H. G. Wells
World SF, 405
Worlds of IF, 228, 240, 371, 403
Worlds of the Imperium, see Keith Laumer
Worlds of Tomorrow, 403
Wreath of Stars, A, see Bob Shaw
Wrede, Patricia C., 408
Wright, Farnsworth, 205
Wright, Joseph, 30, 33, 40
Wright, S. Fowler, 119, 201
Wylie, Philip, 201
Wyndham, John (John Wyndham Parkes Lucas Beynon Harris), 119, 252–5, 269, 301, 337, 378, 467; *The Day of the Triffids*, 149, 253–4
Wyoming Sun, see Ed Bryant

Xenogenesis, see Miriam Allen DeFord
Xiyouji, 138

Yarbro, Chelsea Quinn, 408
Yates, W. R., 408
Year of the Comet, The, see John Christopher
Year's Best SF, see Harry Harrison and Brian W. Aldiss
Years of the City, The, see Frederik Pohl
Year 2440, see Louis-Sébastien Mercier
Yellow Danger, The, see M. P. Shiel
Yesterday's Men, see George Turner
Youd, Sam, see John Christopher
Young, Neil, 471

Zahn, Timothy, 408, 437
Zamyatin, Yevgeny, 179, 460; *We*, 77, 244, 465–6
Zappa, Frank, 297, 332
Zebrowski, George, 436
Zelazny, Roger, 260, 291, 293–6, 305, 307, 311, 359, 472–3; *Lord of Light*, 294–5; "A Rose For Ecclesiastes", 260, 293, 295–6; *This Immortal*, 293–4, 473
Zoline, Pamela, 299, 305
Zoonomia, see Erasmus Darwin
Zukunftroman, 143

BRIAN W. ALDISS has won most of the prizes in the international science fiction field. These include a Hugo and a Nebula from the USA, a Kurd Lasswitz Award from West Germany, a Jules Verne Award from Sweden, and a BSFA Award from England. The Australians voted him "World's Best Contemporary Writer of Science Fiction." His novels and short stories have been translated into many languages. His most recent success is with the three Helliconia novels, *Helliconia Spring, Helliconia Summer,* and *Helliconia Winter.* He is also unique among novelists in holding three major prizes for criticism, the SFRA Pilgrim Award, the James Blish Award, and the new IAFA Distinguished Scholarship Award.

DAVID WINGROVE'S best known books are *The Immortals of Science Fiction, The Science Fiction Source Book,* and *The Science Fiction Film Source Book.*